Schubert's Metamorphoses

Leonor Dill

Schubert's Metamorphoses

C. G. Jung's Archetypal Theory as a Foundation for Musical Analysis—a Research on the Creative Process

J.B. METZLER

Leonor Dill
Musicology / Science & Art
Mozarteum University Salzburg
and Paris-Lodron University Salzburg
Salzburg, Austria

ISBN 978-3-662-73475-9 ISBN 978-3-662-73476-6 (eBook)
https://doi.org/10.1007/978-3-662-73476-6

This work was supported by Author.

This J.B. Metzler imprint is published by the registered company Springer-Verlag GmbH, DE, part of Springer Nature.
The registered company address is: Heidelberger Platz 3, 14197 Berlin, Germany

Dedicated to my parents and in memory of my grandparents and great-grandparents.

Abstract

C.G. Jung consistently emphasized how the self-driven autonomous archetypes are highly influential for and even directly involved in the creative process itself. Consequently, archetypes and archetypal processes can be found reflected in the musical language of a composer, which can be identified by means of an integrative approach applying music analytical tools and concepts of Jungian psychology. In this way, the symbolic meaning of the individual yet simultaneously existing musical motifs is revealed – the ambivalent and ineffable aspects of music can be approached and interpreted in the overall context of a transformational process, i.e., the individuation process. Such an interdisciplinary method proposes a new way of understanding music and allows a deeper approximation to the "soul" of a composition than could be realized from a purely musicological perspective. The findings of this project, which represents fundamental research on the works of Franz Schubert, are relevant to artistic interpretation. In addition, this study provides the basis for further lines of research and encourages increased collaboration between the fields of musicology and Analytical Psychology.

Keywords: Creative Process · Archetypes · Musical Language · Franz Schubert · Individuation Process.

Zusammenfassung

C.G. Jung hat im Zusammenhang mit dem kreativen Schaffen immer wieder betont, wie die eigenwilligen, autonom-wirkenden Archetypen einen großen Einfluss haben, ja sogar direkt am schöpferischen Prozess selbst beteiligt sind. Dem folgend spiegeln sich in der musikalischen Sprache eines Komponisten Archetypen und archetypische Prozesse wider, die durch einen integrativen Ansatz, eine Anwendung musikanalytischer Mittel und Konzepte der Jungschen Psychologie, identifiziert werden können. Auf diese Weise wird die symbolische Bedeutung der einzelnen, gleichzeitig existierenden musikalischen Motive enthüllt, wodurch das Ambivalente und Unaussprechliche der Musik angenähert und im Gesamtkontext eines Transformations- bzw. Individuationsprozesses interpretiert werden können. Diese interdisziplinäre Methode plädiert für eine neue Art des Musikverständnisses und ermöglicht eine tiefere Annäherung an die „Seele" einer Komposition, als dies aus einer rein musikwissenschaftlichen Perspektive realisierbar wäre. Die Ergebnisse dieser Arbeit, die eine Grundlagenforschung zum Werk Franz Schuberts darstellt, sind für die künstlerische Interpretation relevant. Zudem dient diese Studie als Fundament für weitere Forschungsfelder und regt eine verstärkte Zusammenarbeit zwischen Musikwissenschaft und Analytischer Psychologie an.

Schlüsselworte: Schöpferischer Prozess · Archetypen · Musikalische Sprache · Franz Schubert · Individuationsprozess.

Preamble

> The soul is the mother and the vessel of all sciences, as it is of any work of art[1].

The theme of this dissertation emerged from a series of questions related to musical interpretation. As a musician, I was intrigued by the simultaneity of ambivalent and polyvalent musical elements, and by what seized me on a deep emotional level. In particular, I wondered about the immediate emotions that arise and are primarily expressed through an abstract or metaphorical language. The expressive movement that lies between or beyond the notes, and is in constant semantic transformation, interested me. I was eager to understand the origins of that aspect of music that is not easily describable in words, and which ultimately remains a direct experience of all the senses. Equally fascinating was the thought of how the inner world of composers takes musical shape, how their unique and distinctive vocabulary is developed through (inner) experiences and expressed in their compositions. Lastly, my quest as a pianist had to do with the important mission of the interpreter to do justice to the true nature of creativity and the musical statement.

My research was motivated by an interdisciplinary and keen interest in the themes of music as expression or music as a language and Jungian psychology.

---

[1] Jung, Carl Gustav. (2011). *Über das Phänomen des Geistes in Kunst und Wissenschaft.* P. 99. (Trans. by the author). German expression: "Die Seele ist ja die Mutter und das Gefäss aller Wissenschaften sowohl wie jeglichen Kunstwerkes".

Initially, I was moved by an unconscious drive to bridge the chasm or to search for the similarities between science and art – a thematic concern that has taken shape in this project. The application of tools of music analysis was essential to explain what was objectively observable in the music and to understand the musical language of the composer. In addition, the integration of concepts from C.G. Jung's archetypal theory enabled an exploration of the archetypal content and the ineffable phenomenon of music, thereby enriching the analytical component of musicology. Creativity is directed, according to C.G. Jung, by autonomous unconscious structures that affect and shape the outcome of creative work[2]. Thus, operating with concepts related to the soul, such as archetypes, which are characterized by their polarity and veiled nature, allowed such an endeavor.

It has been a true honor to learn from both of my academic supervisors, whose guidance and encouragement have been vital at every step of the way. A special thank-you goes to Prof. Dr. Barbara Dobretsberger who warm-heartedly always provided me with perspicacious comments that allowed me to develop a critical view of my writings, and for the extreme care and meticulous attention to detail with which she accompanied my work. I would like to express my heartfelt thank-you to Prof. Dr. Christian Roesler who has been a pillar of support, always ready with a kind word and thoughtful advice, for pointing the way to the essential through his constructive feedback and important impulses that allowed me to develop my work. Both supervisors offered me numerous opportunities to present at seminars and conferences, which were essential to my professional development. There are no words to express my profound gratefulness for their dedication, their esteemed technical advice, and stimulating conversations. This dissertation would not have been possible without them.

I am truly indebted to my dear friend and cellist colleague, MA GradD Paul-Edouard Senentz, for the fruitful discussions about Schubert's music, my cousin Dr. Mallika Snyder, who was a precious help in proofreading my dissertation in record time, and my uncle Prof. Dr. José Eduardo dos Reis for his insightful comments and suggestions regarding the translations of the poems into English. My acknowledgements are to be extended to Prof. Dr. Sonu Shamdasani for sharing passages of Jung's writings that elucidate Jung's relationship to music and his inner musical experiences, Dr. med. Jörg Rasche for his thought-provoking exchange of ideas on the topic of music as a language, and for sharing his lecture-recital essays, Mag. Angelica Löwe for sending me her articles on the symbolism in Jung's study room, and to M.A. Antje Barber for inspiring conversations about Neumann's ideas exposed in *Der schöpferische Mensch.*

[2] Cf. Ibid.

Given that archetypes manifest themselves symbolically, images constitute a significant element of this dissertation. I would therefore like to convey my sincere appreciation to the Foundation of the Works of C.G. Jung and in particular to Dr. Carl C. Jung who kindly provided a digitized copy of C.G. Jung's "Phanes I", and to M.A. Elisabeth Leuenberger from the Picture Archive of the C.G. Jung Institut Zurich for the digitized copy of the anonymous picture "008 AHAF" of a C.G. Jung's patient. Additional thanks to the librarians at the Mozarteum University Salzburg, Paris-Lodron University Salzburg, C.G. Jung Institut Zurich, and Schweizer Bibliotheksverbund, who helped me with their technical expertise. Mr. Philipp Rothe, from the study and examination management of the Mozarteum University, is to be thanked for his assistance with administrative questions.

I cannot forget to mention maestro Paul Coker, my former piano professor, who deeply molded my musicianship and intellectual involvement with the musical scores, and "maître d'enseignement" HES Victor Cordero, who imparted his knowledge and enthusiasm for music analysis in such a profound way that sharpened my early interest in the musical language and the use of music analysis for interpretative purposes.

My entire family and close friends played an important role by their example and moral support. I especially think of my dearest sister Bárbara, my aunts Rinati and Margarida, my uncles Luís and Paulo, as well as my "fada madrinha" Eduarda, and my godfather Paulo Machado de Jesus, who offered crucial support for this project.

Above all, I would like to express my wholehearted gratitude to my parents, Eduard and Amélia. They have been a source of support and encouragement throughout this journey, and provided me with my first encounter with the works of C.G. Jung. Our discussions about the creative process have been a great inspiration to me. This study is dedicated to them with love.

Introduction

> There are two kinds of composers, one who, like Schubert, is born in a state of clairvoyance or somnambulism, without any arbitrariness on the part of the composer, but, as he must, by force majeure and inspiration. The second way of composing is through arbitrariness, deliberation, endeavor, science.[1].

Schubert's extraordinary way of working was well known and was described by several of his friends. The spontaneity that characterizes Schubert's creative process is strongly indicative of an archetypal musical language. According to C.G. Jung, archetypes emerge in specific life stages and are thus part of the life path of the human being, which is ultimately called the individuation process. As autonomous structures, archetypes not only impact the creative "I", but are also capable of shaping the musical language and even directing the will of the composer. The creative work is hence understood as a reflection of psychic processes of an archetypal nature. The title of this dissertation, *Schubert's metamorphoses*, refers precisely to the processes of transformation in Schubert's works. These

[1] Vogl, Johann Michael. Citated after: Stadler, Albert: "Biographisches Material". (Begun on January 17th 1858). In: Deutsch, Otto Erich. (1983). *Schubert. Die Erinnerungen seiner Freunde*. P. 170. (Trans. by the author). German expression: „Es gibt zwei Arten von Komponisten, eine, die wie bei Schubert in einem Zustande von Clairvoyance oder Somnambulismus zur Welt kommt, ohne alle Willkür des Tonsetzers, sondern wie er muß, durch höhere Gewalt und Eingebung. Die zweite Art zu komponieren ist die durch Willkür, Überlegung, Anstrengung, Wissenschaft.".

transformations are marked by archetypal stations that will be unveiled, or at least approximated, by means of an integrative approach. Operating with several music analytical tools and C.G. Jung's theory of the archetypes, this method features a new approach in the understanding of music, ultimately an attempt to get closer to the heart of Schubert's music.

In order to best guide the reader through this analytical process, the dissertation was structured into four main parts: The first three sections provide the foundation or building blocks for the central final section, which comprises the music analysis. For this reason, Part I, II and III are together less extensive than Part IV. They have not been combined into one main section as they were conceived as independent areas, each of these three sections covering a specific topic. By doing so, the author gives the reader the opportunity to engage first with these topics, which are then dealt with and assembled in the final section.

Part I gives a concise historical overview on the emergence of the depth psychology current (1), followed by an extensive perspective on some biographical facts of C.G. Jung's life (2). The inclusion of this part was carefully considered and finally seen as essential, since Jung's concepts arose mainly from an empirical attitude, i.e., they were the result of his own inner lived experiences – as Jung himself emphasized[2]. Hence, these aspects have been dealt with first in order to explain his archetypal concepts and the developments of his theories (3). To conclude this main section, the attention was drawn to the intrinsic relationship between nature, the human psyche and creativity (4), which introduces Part II.

While Part I serves to introduce the reader to the basic psychological concepts and their origins, Part II contributes with reflections on the concept of music as a language. The main intention is to highlight the similarities and dissimilarities between music and language from a depth psychological point of view, facilitating the understanding of the analysis method proposed in this thesis. Although the chapters of Part II may seem like a digression at first glance, they provide a consciously pondered purpose: They actually follow the approach and procedure that Jung himself had chosen for the development of his concepts. This comprises a concise longitudinal study on the topic of music as expression, which involves an investigation that reaches back into the past, i.e., to the cave dwellers and the *ethos* doctrine of the ancient Greeks (5), extending until the theory of the affects and the doctrine of the musical rhetoric figures of the Baroque (6). The latter had

[2] Cf. Jung, Carl Gustav. (1961). Ma vie.

an enormous influence on composers, including those of Romanticism – an influence that continues to this day[3]. On the one hand, going back to the roots and origins of such concepts establishes a bridge to the archetypal content of music in general (7); on the other hand, it allows a better understanding of some aspects of Schubert's musical language that will follow. In this way, both Part I and Part II aim to cover the essential fundamentals of the theories that are applied later.

Part III precedes the analysis section by providing background information on Schubert's life and career as well as an understanding of his relationship to the historical-political and cultural context (8–10). This is important, because the environment in which a composer finds himself undoubtedly has an effect on the psyche and thus on the creative act, shaping the musical language. Dynamic aspects of Schubert's creativity will also be addressed (11). The subchapters are organized in such a way as to create an outline of some major archetypal motifs in Schubert's life and work. Simultaneously, the main debates currently taking place in the Schubert research community are addressed, and several hypotheses are put forward, which are subsequently verified and discussed in the analysis section. Such topics include questions concerning Schubert's religiosity (11.2), the discussion of the "years of crisis" (12), and the categorisation of early and late works (12), which are related to one of the key concerns of this research – the development of Schubert's musical language.

Part IV represents the core of this dissertation. This section opens with a concise review of some of the current and relevant academic literature on music analytical approaches, specifically regarding Schubert's works, and the presentation of the method proposed and applied in this dissertation (13). Although it deviates from the usual procedure of presenting the state of the art and methodology at the beginning of the dissertation, this placement was deliberate. It was important, on the one hand, to provide a content-specifically divided literature review in the respective chapters given that Part I-III function as the individual building blocks. On the other hand, it was critical to focus solely on the analytical literature for Part IV since this is the section in which the author proposes the applied method of a music analysis based on C.G. Jung's archetypal theory.

This last section contains an in-depth analysis of five main works: *Forellenquintett* D 667 (14), the song cycle *Die Schöne Müllerin* D 795 (15), the string quartet in D minor D 810 *Der Tod und das Mädchen* (16), and the second movements of the piano sonatas A major D 959 (17) and B-flat major D 960 (18), as well as analytical observations on the *Wandererfantasie* D 760 and the Piano

[3] Cf. Krones, Hartmut. "Musik und Rhetorik". (2016). In: Laurenz Lütteken (Ed.). *MGG Online.*

Trio in E-flat major D 920 (19). Related compositions, which include e.g., songs, are introductorily examined in the respective subchapters, providing an overview across the years. Throughout, a major concern has been to contextualize the symbolic musical motifs in the works and in the historical-biographical background. In addition, the author opted occasionally to favour straight metaphoric formulations over technical terms due to the nature of archetypal language that is lastly a figurative, emotional and direct language. The titles of the analytical chapters and subchapters have been deliberately designed to reveal the inherent psychological processes that will be focused on and are therefore longer than usual.

To conclude this analytical section, all information is overlapped and correlated in order to provide the promised analytical overview of the creative process in all the works analysed (20). To achieve this aim, it was essential to highlight the main analytical findings of each work in the form of a synopsis. It was crucial to include some of the musical observations that were presented in Part III. The addressed works are considered in chronological order, relating the findings to the archetypal manifestations and psychological processes as well as on the creative process and the development of Schubert's musical language. The following enumerated questions, which constitute the Ariadne's thread of each synopsis, will serve to highlight the concluding results: (i) what are the emerging archetypes and how do they change in their semantics from one work to the other (metamorphoses), (ii) what are the inherent psychological processes and (iii) idiosyncrasies of Schubert's musical language; finally, (iv) how do these archetypal manifestations and psychological processes coincide with specific and important biographical events. This procedure will permit answering the hypotheses put forward in Part III and in the analysis chapters, and ultimately, gaining an overview of what may have constituted the individuation process of Franz Schubert. Finally, the author hopes to stimulate interest in further research by suggesting some potential lines of investigation. These reflections will be included in the last chapter.

Contents

List of Figures

Part I
Jung, the unconscious mind and creativity

The zeitgeist of the respective era has, in any case, an impact on the philosophy of every thinker. Equally, every thinker's thought process is undeniably shaped by biographical facts and (inner) experiences. This was the case with the Swiss psychiatrist Carl Gustav Jung. C.G. Jung lived during a period marked by a scientific urge to understand the unknown and was thus directly involved in the emergence of the depth psychology current.

The first chapter will deal with the historical frame around the 20th century zeitgeist and the emergence of depth psychology. This is followed by a second chapter, which covers some of the key biographical aspects of C.G. Jung's life. The emergence of Jung's psychological concepts is understood as being deeply anchored within his personality, his childhood, upbringing, his readings and foremost his inner experiences. Therefore, the origins of his concepts are considered in relation to the historical context, life events and some of the major philosophic influences that shaped his thinking[1]. This will be done mainly in the light of the existent autobiography *Erinnerungen, Träume, Gedanken* which constitutes the primary source of information of these facts. However, as of any kind of (auto)biographical narrative, there is a major subjective component, which makes this source not entirely substantial as scientific and factual literature.

There are many sources which document differing opinions of Jung's personal nature, stating how paradoxical and contradictory Jung's attitude can be, which extends to his concepts and scientific methods as well. For this reason, the author will try to come to a more objective plane of debate, by including other sources of biographical information and the current critical scientific literature, namely by outlining some points of the present state of research within Analytical Psychology. However, as this dissertation aims for the study of the creative process, all

[1] The influence of Jung's readings on the emergence of his own concept of the human psyche and the unconscious will not necessarily be presented in a chronological order but rather along a thematic line, either in relation to biographical events or where a particular concept is put in focus.

utterances of private nature that might be understood as controversial, paradoxical, and polemic will not be matter for discussion here.[2] For the same reason, it is occasionally necessary to directly draw from the reflections, parallels with the creative process. This permits establishing a better orientation line for the reader in posterior chapters. Since this dissertation uses Jung's archetypal theory as the foundation for a music analytical approach, it is important to define the concepts that will be applied later. While the third chapter provides the theoretical foundation of Jungian concepts and definitions, the last one establishes the bridge between the psyche, nature and the source of creativity.

[2] These exclusions entail for instance, more personal facts of how Jung engaged with politics, women, and patients.

The Quest for the Unknown—The Emergence of Depth Psychology

1

"There begins the journey 'into the void', into which Mephisto sends Faust and 'in the nothingness of which he hopes to find the universe'."[1]

It is with this Faustian idea that Jean Gebser introduces the history of the beginnings of psychology as a science[2], and with which he substantiates the collective motivation of all sciences at the turn of the century to fulfill the "purpose to'dig in depth'."[3]. In those days the human being had begun to undertake a "quest for the unknown: the unconscious […]"[4] or, as Gebser later describes, for "the impersonal"[5] quality.

These matters, which had already been mentioned in the earlier centuries, notably by Leibniz, Kant, Schelling, C.G. Carus[6] and Edward von Hartmann[7]

---

[1] Gebser, Jean. (1986). *Ursprung und Gegenwart.* P.527. (Trans. by the author). German expression: „Es beginnt jene Wanderung ‚ins Leere', in die Mephisto den Faust sendet und in ‚deren Nichts er das All zu finden hofft'."

[2] Although nowadays psychology is considered among the subjects of the humanities or at least standing in between the humanities and natural sciences, at that time, psychology was seen as a science, a new science that was emerging.

[3] Gebser, Jean. (1986). *Ursprung und Gegenwart.* P.527. (Trans. by the author). German expression: „[…] die Aufgabe, ‚ins Tiefe zu schürfen'."

[4] Ibid. (Trans. by the author). German expression: „Nun sucht man das Unbekannte: das Unbewusste".

[5] Ibid. (Trans. by the author). German expression: „[…] selbst nicht mehr Individuum und Person, sucht er das Unpersönliche […]".

[6] Carus can be seen in a way as a predecessor of Jung's thinking, specifically of the idea of the collective unconscious. Cf. Casement, Ann. (2001). *Carl Gustav Jung.* P. 46.

[7] Cf. Jung, Carl Gustav. (2020). *Archetypen. Urbilder und Wirkkräfte des Kollektiven Unbewussten.* P.136.

L. Dill, *Schubert's Metamorphoses*,
https://doi.org/10.1007/978-3-662-73476-6_1

and explored at the extent by the artists, composers, and poets of Romanticism (4.3), became subject of a new research object in the 20th century. With the emergence of many important innovations and advancements in the scientific world, psychology was considered, at the start of the 20th century, a young science influenced by a line of scientific methods applied in the 19th century, which still prevails—positivism and empiricism shaped scientific thought[8]. By means of the method of "observation and by carrying out experiments"[9] biology, chemistry, physics and medicine were able to make great discoveries. This formed the basis for the origin of the so-called "materialistic"[10] currents in the field of psychology, e.g., Hermann von Helmholtz's sensory neurosciences. Further lines of psychological research that were influenced by the natural sciences were e.g., Franz Brentano's genetics psychology, Gustav Theodor Fechner's psychophysics[11], and Hermann Ebbinghaus' associations-psychology (engaged in memory research)[12]. One of the schools that emerged out of the scientific understanding was the experimental psychology (psychology of consciousness), also known as the "Leipziger Schule", founded by Wilhelm Wundt[13], and which constituted, by C.G. Jung's

[8] Cf. Lück, Helmut E. (2009). *Geschichte der Psychologie.* P.38.

[9] Ibid. (Trans. by the author). German expression: „[…] der Forscher könne ‚wahre' Erkenntnisse über die Natur gewinnen, indem er über Beobachtung und Experiment Gesetzmäßigkeit erkennt, die im Idealfall Naturgesetze sind.".

[10] Ibid. P.47.

[11] Helmut Lücke elucidates that "Already the term 'psychophysics' chosen by Gustav Theodor Fechner indicates the intention to study psychological processes according to the model of physics as a natural science.". (Trans. by the author). German expression: "Schon der von Gustav Theodor Fechner gewählte Begriff der ‚Psychophysik' lässt die Absicht erkennen, psychologische Vorgänge nach dem Vorbild der Physik als Naturwissenschaft zu studieren". Ibid. P. 48. His thinking was furthermore characterized by rationalism and mysticism. Cf. Ibid. P.49. Fechner is credited as being a "pioneer in establishing psychology as a scientific discipline". Casement, Ann. (2001). *Carl Gustav Jung.* P. 45.

[12] Cf. Schlüter, Christiane. (2014). *Die wichtigsten Psychologen im Porträt.* At the beginning of his career as a Doctor at the Burghölzli, Jung had undertaken experiments as well, e.g., the so-called associations experiments from which originated his theories of the feeling-toned complexes.

[13] Cf. Lück, Helmut E. (2009). *Geschichte der Psychologie.* P.57–66. Wundt believed on psychology as an empirical science—"For Wundt,'psychology from the natural sciences perspective' means to explain mental processes on the basis of physiological changes". Ibid. P.58. (Trans. by the author). German expression: „Eine ‚Psychologie vom naturwissenschaftlichen Standpunkt' bedeutet für Wundt, seelische Vorgänge auf der Grundlage physiologischer Veränderungen erklären zu wollen.".

time, the subject of academic psychology[14]. Wundt and his universalist perspective, his word-association test, and his publication of 1888 *Völkerpsychologie* had therefore a significant impact on how certain of C.G. Jung's ideas evolved[15].

It was the Charcot School in France (Jean-Martin Charcot, Hippolyte Bernheim and Pierre Janet), which came from a line of "heritage" that goes back to Franz Anton Mesmer in the 18th century in Vienna[16], that played a role in the development of depth psychology[17] and of "psychotherapy of neuroses"[18]. Hypnosis and suggestion (and later the "talking cure", i.e., "Redekur") were used as therapeutic tools, having a great cathartic effect[19] and allowing great advances in the field of neurosis and so-called hysteria[20]. Sigmund Freud, who had studied with Charcot and Bernheim, and worked at the Salpêtrière Hospital in Paris, was greatly influenced by the "intellectual assumptions of his time"[21]. Supported by Josef Breuer, both contributed significantly to further findings—discoveries which, subsequently, interested Jung. From the research made in that context, it was realized that the origins of hysteria lay in trauma, associated with

---

[14] Cf. Jung, Carl Gustav. (2014). "Two Essays in Analytical Psychology". In: *The Collected Works, Vol.7*. Translation: R.F.C. Hull. Chapter: "Psychoanalysis". Paragraph 2.

[15] Cf. Roesler, Christian. (2024). *Deconstructing Archetype Theory.* P.119.

[16] Cf. Walach, Harald. (2013). *Psychologie.* P.223.

[17] The term of depth psychology was introduced by Eugen Bleuler and it marked the difference to the psychology of consciousness that prevailed before. Its founders were Sigmund Freud (psychoanalysis), C.G. Jung (analytical psychology) and Alfred Adler (individual psychology). Jacques Lacan has also followed the depth psychology and "linked Freuds concept with the linguistics". Schlüter, Christiane. (2014). *Die wichtigsten Psychologen im Porträt.* P.87. (Trans. by the author). German expression: "Jacques Lacan verknüpfte Freuds Lehre mit sprachwissenschaftlichen Theorien.".

[18] Jung, Carl Gustav. (2014). "Two Essays in Analytical Psychology". In: *The Collected Works. Vol.7*. (Trans. by R.F.C. Hull). Chapter: "Psychoanalysis", Paragraph 2.

[19] Catharsis (gr. Κάθαρσις) meaning purification is a concept that goes back to the ancient Greeks. Aristotle is considered the "first ancient author who attempted to write a psychology in the true sense of the word" and used this concept in relation to the Greek tragedy. Walach, Harald. (2013). *Psychologie.* P.117. (Trans. by the author). German expression: "Aristoteles war der erste antike Autor, der wirklich eine Psychologie im eigenen Sinne zu verfassen versucht hat".

[20] Hysteria—a kind of neurosis with a traumatic background, in which patients showed physical and neurological symptoms, yet the cause remains purely psychological—represented in those days an important research field, which was thoroughly investigated in the Charcot School, specifically by Charcot himself, Freud, Breuer, among others. The 1909 studies of Breuer and Freund on hysteria are considered as "the birth of psychoanalysis". Ibid. P.224.

[21] Wehr, Gerhard. (1969). *C.G. Jung*. P. 27. (Trans. by the author). German expression: "[…] Freud ist zu sehr von den Denkvoraussetzungen seines Jahrhunderts bestimmt.".

repressed affects (repression theory). From here, and through the development of the method of the "cathartic talking cure", the first steps of psychoanalytical procedures were outlined[22] and Freud's own path in depth psychology was paved when he wrote *Die Traumdeutung* (1900)—considered to be "the first substantial representation of psychoanalysis in theory and method"[23] and which was attentively read by Jung.

By writing *Die Traumdeutung*, Freud not only marks an epoch in history[24] but also delivers important proof of the existence of unconscious processes: *Die Traumdeutung* was considered at the time the "most important source of information of processes in the unconscious"[25]. Freud dedicated himself to the underlying driving forces, interconnected with his concept of sublimation, and developed his libido theory, being Eros (gr. *Ἔρως* god of love) and Thanatos (gr. *Θάνατος* personification of death) two driving forces: desire and destruction. Freud's structural model of the psyche is constituted by the three agencies of the Id, the Ego and the Superego[26], with which he came to the division of the psyche into consciousness, subconscious and unconscious[27]. Although Freud's work aroused Jung's interest, Jung had an utterly different perception of the psyche, the unconscious, dreams, the libido, and the overall ideology was different, which will be explained later. Furthermore, as the Jung historian Sonu Shamdasani highlights, and as Jung himself declared, the relationship between Freud and Jung was in fact "mythologized" giving the erroneous idea that Jung "stemmed" from Freud[28]. In contrary, Jung refers in particular to Bleuler, Pierre Janet and Théodore Flournoy as his major mentors that influenced his thinking[29].

---

[22] Cf. Schlüter, Christiane. (2014). *Die wichtigsten Psychologen im Porträt.* P.40.

[23] Lück, Helmut E. (2009). *Geschichte der Psychologie.* P. 94. (Trans. by the author). German expression: "Die erste große Darstellung der Psychoanalyse in Theorie und Methode.".

[24] C.G. Jung described "Freud's *'Traumdeutung'* (1900) [as] an epoch-making work". Jung, Carl Gustav. (2011). *Über das Phänomen des Geistes in Kunst und Wissenschaft.* P. 56. (Trans. by the author). German expression: "Freuds '*Traumdeutung*' (1900) ist ein epochemachendes Werk […]".

[25] Cf. Ibid.P. 57. (Trans. by the author). German expression: „[…] als wichtigste Informationsquelle über die Vorgänge im Unbewußten […]".

[26] In the Id the driving forces are contained as well as the emotions, the Ego is the conscious perception with its functions and the Superego is governed by a control system which is a moral instance. Cf. Schlüter, Christiane. (2014). *Die wichtigsten Psychologen im Porträt.* P.45–46.

[27] Cf. Ibid. P.42.

[28] Cf. Shamdasani, Sonu. (2012). *C.G. Jung. A Biography in Books.* P.44.

[29] Cf. Ibid.

These theories of the unconscious represented crucial advancements in psychology and were reflected in the collective artistic movements of the time. For instance, in surrealism there was the intrinsic will of the artists to reconstruct the "absurdity" of the realm of dreams[30], in cubism to include the fourth dimension of time[31]. Writers and poets of 20th-century Europe, like Baudelaire and Mallarmé in France were submerged in the symbolist movement, where the reality of the dreamworld and correspondingly mythological figures formed the content of their poetry.

Jean Gebser, as a lecturer of the "Institut für angewandte Psychologie" in Zurich, considered the aspects of time through the dimension of dreams[32], and that of "overcoming the duality"[33] by taking the path of individuation[34] (3.1), i.e., "a process of inner transformation"[35], to be crucial concepts of the depth psychology, particularly of C.G. Jung. In relation to this statement, it seems noteworthy to recall that the development of psychology as a science was shaped by the exact sciences and the application of their methods, perceiving the human psyche as a structure model, and in philosophical terms, rather following the rationality of Cartesian thought process. In other words, C.G. Jung lived in a century that was characterized by "reason"[36] to a high degree, when scientists and intellectuals had the tendency to believe that everything was measurable, when "[…] history and

[30] Cf. Sproccati, Sandro. (2014). *Guia de História da Arte.* P.212.

[31] Cf. Ibid. P.159.

[32] Cf. Gebser, Jean. (1986). *Ursprung und Gegenwart.* P.527–542. In dreams there is no perception of time. In collective dreams, after Jung's reports of his patients' dreams, even the future could be foretold. Cf. Jung, Carl Gustav. (1957). *Great Minds of the 20th Century: Dr. Carl Jung. Evans, Richard.* [Interview]. Minutes: 11:44/3:02:34.

[33] Gebser, Jean. (1986). *Ursprung und Gegenwart.* P.530. (Trans. by the author). German expression: "[…] überwindet sie [Tiefenpsychologie] den Dualismus".

[34] This occurs, on the one hand, by accepting and confronting the shadow side of the psyche, which is often neglected or repressed (in the unconscious realm), and on the other hand, by the integration of the inner soul images. This will allow the encounter with the mana-personalities and, if these are also integrated, eventually the Self is experienced.

[35] Jung, Carl Gustav. (1961). *Ma vie.* P.324. (Trans. by the author). French expression: "Or, au centre de mes découvertes psychologiques se trouve à nouveau un processus de transformation intérieur: l'individuation".

[36] Cf. Wehr, Gerhard. (1969). *C.G. Jung.* P. 7.

future were understood in terms of mere cause and effect"[37]. In depth psychology the (collective) unconscious could have come with the role of compensating and fulfilling the gap which emerged out of those facts, bringing in one facet of "the fourth dimension"[38].

[37] Van der Post, Laurens. (1972). *The Story of Carl Gustav Jung*. [Documentary]. Minute: 57:38/1:33:23.

[38] Gebser, Jean. (1986). *Ursprung und Gegenwart.* P. 530. (Trans. by the author). German expression: „[…] so ist psychologisch betrachtet das ‚Unbewußte' ein anderer Aspekt der vierten Dimension.".

2 Mosaics of C.G. Jung's Life and Thinking

C.G. Jung was born in Kesswil, Switzerland in 1875, into a family with a traditional Swiss Reformed Church background, of German descent, mainly constituted of scientists, doctors and theologians. He was brought up as an only child until his ninth birthday, when his sister Trudi was born[1]. From a young age on, Jung demonstrated a strong connection to his inner world, filled with a vast array of inner experiences, dreams, fantasies, and visions that accompanied him until his death. Those inner memories were called by Jung himself to be "simple islands of memories […] which float on an uncertain sea."[2] and it was "only through these inner adventures that [he] was able to understand [himself]"[3]. Gerhard Wehr, a Jung biographer, points out the importance of the etymological value of the German word "Erinnerung" (memories) and mentions how essential it is to take it by its literal meaning, i.e., "Er-Innerungen"[4], which could be translated as inner-turned memories. These inner-turned memories are hand in hand with the inner experiences and dreams Jung had already from an early age. All of these can be seen as being the roots of his theories. On the other hand, philosophic and theological readings also played a significant role for the development of his thinking. To "satiate" his thirst for knowledge and in particular to seek the

[1] Cf. Casement, Ann. (2001). *Carl Gustav Jung.* P.4.

[2] Jung, Carl Gustav. (1961). *Ma vie.* P.29. (Trans. by the author). French expression: "Ce sont de simples îlots de souvenirs, […] qui flottent sur une mer indécise.".

[3] Ibid. P.28. French expression: "Je ne puis me comprendre que par les aventure intérieures.".

[4] Wehr, Gerhard. (1969). *C.G. Jung.* P.9.

L. Dill, *Schubert's Metamorphoses*,
https://doi.org/10.1007/978-3-662-73476-6_2

answers to all of his religious questions Jung turned to the library of his father[5]. Some of these influences will be briefly outlined in this chapter[6].

2.1 The Early Search for the Ultimate Truth

From the father, a clergyman, he mainly adopted his philological skills[7], which he later used in his efforts to prove the existence of the collective unconscious. Jung's aversion to doctrines and dogmas were, among other aspects, the fruit of early observation of his father's private religious classes as well as the conversations between his father and his theologian colleagues, who were frequent guests in their house. As early as that period, Jung had the innermost conviction that it was through personal experience only that genuine discourse is possible[8]. He seemed to have been highly influenced by the connotation of the term *Imago Dei* used by the church fathers and by the means of which, they understood that "the image of God was imprinted in the soul of the human being"[9]. Later, Jung stated that the image of God could be considered as a "reflection of the Self or, in contrary, to see the Self as '*Imago Dei in Homine*'"[10]. Likewise, Rudolf Otto made a decisive impression on him and influenced his archetypal conception in some way—this refers, more precisely to what Otto termed as *tremendum, fascinosum* or *numinosum.* Jung spoke of the numinous feeling or the numinous experience. This theological influence led Jung's concept of the archetypes to be intrinsically linked to an experience of spiritual nature, connecting archetypes to "religious feelings and beliefs"[11].

---

[5] Cf. Shamdasani, Sonu. (2012). *C.G. Jung. A Biography in Books.* P.11.

[6] Only the most important points or concepts of the respective philosophers that were particularly relevant for Jung, are to be laid here.

[7] Cf. Wehr, Gerhard. (1969). *C.G. Jung*. P.14.

[8] Van der Post explained: "It was an essential part of his philosophy ever since he had been a boy that man was not only to think things, but must also live them". Van der Post, Laurens. (1972). *The Story of Carl Gustav Jung.* [Documentary]. Minute: 25:53/1:33:23.

[9] Jung, Carl Gustav. (1961). *Ma vie.* "Glossaire". P.628. (Trans. by the author). French expression: "Terme emprunté aux Pères de l'Église. Selon eux l'*Imago Dei* est imprimée dans l'âme humaine".

[10] Jung, Carl Gustav: "Symbolik des Geistes". In: Ibid. French expression: "On peut considérer l'image de Dieu…comme un reflet du Soi, ou, inversement, voir dans le Soi une *Imago Dei in Homine*".

[11] Cf. Roesler, Christian. (2024). *Deconstructing Archetype Theory.* P. 27.

Undoubtedly, Jung's profound relationship towards God and his own faith, which manifested in several personal events throughout his life, has marked his own psychology; specifically, in his understanding of the human soul, in the concept of the Self and the process of individuation (3). For Jung, "the human soul has an inherent natural religious function"[12] by which the human psyche is archetypically moved[13] and instinctively seeks wholeness. This thought is based on Tertullian's conception that the soul is Christian in nature (*Anima naturaliter christiana*)[14]. His conviction in the importance of speaking from personal experience and the words he pronounced in response to the question of whether he believed in God are equally explanatory of his profound religiosity: "I know!—I don't need to believe—I know!"[15]. The same applies to the Latin inscription over the entrance of Jung's house, namely *"Vocatus atque non vocatus Deus aderit"* meaning "Called or not called God will be there".

However, Jung's understanding of God and religion differs from the traditional Christian thought. Jung stated that his Christian faith was shaped by his "[…] encounters with Eastern religions and Greek philosophy"[16]. The crucial point is that Jung was mainly influenced by intimate events which he later reencountered in his readings of Master Eckhart's ideas. Jung considered that the grace of God is to be experienced from within, rather than by seeking God outside oneself[17] or by following the dogmas of the Church. Consequently, in terms of communion, the unification with God is to happen through the inner experience only and by allowing the counterparts to join[18]. Continuing this line of thought, in God Jung saw not only light but darkness as well, i.e., God would not only symbolize the heavenly but the submergence in the underground at the same time:

---

[12] Wehr, Gerhard. (1969). *C.G. Jung*. P.62. (Trans. by the author). German expression: "[…] daß der menschlichen Seele eine natürliche religiöse Funktion innewohnt.".

[13] Cf. Kast, Verena. (2014). *Die Tiefenpsychologie nach C.G. Jung*. Chapter: "Das religiöse Bedürfnis".

[14] Cf. Wehr, Gerhard. (1969). *C.G. Jung*. P.62.

[15] Jung, Carl Gustav. (1959). *Face to Face, Carl Jung*. Freeman, John (Presenter). [Interview]. Minutes: 07:46 /38:05.

[16] Jung, C.G. (1977). "The Symbolic Life". In: Casement, Ann. (2001). *Carl Gustav Jung*. P. 40.

[17] Cf. Wehr, Gerhard. (1969). *C.G. Jung*. P.65.

[18] Cf. Jung, Carl Gustav. (1961). *Ma vie*. P.98–103.

> "To the 'world of God' belonged all that was 'superhuman', the blinding light, the darkness of the abyss, the cold apathy of infinity of time and space, and the frightening, grotesque character of the irrational world of chance"[19].

According to Verena Kast, from this epiphany Jung developed his concept of the shadow[20].

2.2 Philosophical and Theological Influences[21]

Jung's early interest in matters of philosophy and religion was provoked by the religious teachings that he received, and conversations he followed notably at home. Although he disliked being seen as a philosopher, he used to delve into reading the theology and philosophy books of his father. Therein he searched for his unanswered questions about the mysteries of the soul, of God's grace, God's will, fate, and destiny. In his philosophical readings he found the confirmation of his own early convictions and through them Jung understood that "on the bottom of everything there is the reality of psyche. Without soul there is no knowledge, nor profound understanding"[22]. According to Jung himself[23], he was rather drawn towards the philosophy of Pythagoras, Heraclites[24], Empedocles,

---

[19] Ibid. P.126. (Trans. by the author). French expression: "Appartenait au 'monde de Dieu' tout ce qui était 'surhumain', la lumière aveuglante, les ténèbres des abîmes, la froide apathie de l'infini du temps et de l'espace et le caractère grotesque effrayant du monde irrationnel du hasard.". This thought is to be found in many of Jung's writings, *inter alia* in "Answer to Job". Cf. Jung, Carl Gustav. (2014). " Psychology and Religion: West and East". In: *CW. Vol. 11*. (Trans. by Gerhard Adler and R.F.C. Hull). Further examples feature *Aion*. Cf. Jung, Carl Gustav. (1970). *Aion.*

[20] Cf. Kast, Verena. (2009). *Das sagenumwobene 'Rote Buch' von C.G. Jung—Die Psychologin Verena Kast im Gespräch mit Norbert Bischofberger*. [Interview]. Minutes: 53:03/ 1:01:45.

[21] The main literary influences on Jung's thinking are narrated in his own autobiography *Erinnerungen, Träume, Gedanken.* Furthermore, the Jung historian Sonu Shamdasani offers an overview, exposing how Jung's concepts evolved through his literary encounters. Cf. Shamdasani, Sonu. (2012). *C.G. Jung. A Biography in Books.*

[22] Jung, Carl Gustav. (1961). *Ma vie.* P.169. (Trans. by the author). French expression: "Mes lectures philosophiques m'avaient appris qu'il y avait, au fond de tout, la réalité de la psyche. Sans l'âme il n'y avait ni savoir, ni connaissance approfondie.".

[23] Cf. Ibid. P.121.

[24] Ann Casement refers especially to Heraclites' concept of "enantiodromia" and the state of flux, which is to be related to Jung's idea of the opposites, respectively of the process of turnover into the opposite (3). Cf. Casement, Ann. (2001). *Carl Gustav Jung*. P. 40.

and Plato than towards the Christian scholastics or Aristotle's thinking[25]. He was not particularly inclined to "intellectualism"[26] and pure rationalism. According to Jung, the human being is bound to the collectivity of humankind but is at the same time highly individual. Here lies the singularity of his approach to psychology and to the human being. The origin of these thoughts might lie within the concept of the monad.

According to Leibniz, the monad is "like a minimal atom [...] the smallest building block of the world as material-spiritual unity"[27] and implies the unification of individuality and the whole cosmos at once[28]. Leibniz considered the central monad, which contained all other monads, to be God. Reading it through Jung's eyes this means that within the whole psyche there is the distinctive individual. Jung brings into attention that the number one is not only a unity but "the unity" and thus relates directly to an archetype and more specifically to the "attribute of God"[29]. These thoughts are at the base of Jung's concept of the Self, the "purpose of psychic development"[30]—it is the center of the psyche and yet it represents the whole psyche (3.1).

Jung experienced new creative expressions of his dynamic Self on a daily basis: "My mandala drawings were cryptograms about the state of my Self, which were delivered to me daily"[31]. This occurred for the first time in 1916 (although only later, Jung claimed to have begun to understand its real meaning)[32] and through the images of mandalas, i.e., a representation of his own monad, which

---

[25] In relation to the Scholastics, Jung specifically referred his "indifference" to Thomas Aquinas. Cf. Jung, Carl Gustav. (1961). *Ma vie.* P. 121. In addition, Ann Casement finds evidence that the category of "teleology", namely the doctrine of final causes from Aristotle, is to be found in Jung's individuation process. Cf. Casement, Ann. (2001). *Carl Gustav Jung.* P.41.

[26] Jung, Carl Gustav. (1961). *Ma vie.* P.121.

[27] Walach, Harald. (2013). *Psychologie.* P.167–168. (Trans. by the author). German expression: "[...] so etwas wie ein Minimalatom. [...] Die Monade war jedoch gleichzeitig nicht rein materiell, sondern kleinster Baustein der Welt als materiell-geistige Einheit.".

[28] Cf. Ibid. P. 168.

[29] Jung, Carl Gustav. (1961). *Ma vie.* P.487. (Trans. by the author). French expression: "Le UN, premier nom des nombres, est une unité. Mais il est aussi 'l'unité', l'Un, le Tout-Un, L'Unique, le Non-Deux, non plus un nom de nombre mais une idée philosophique ou un archétype et un attribut de Dieux, la monade.".

[30] Ibid. P. 315. French expression: "but du développement psychique".

[31] Ibid. P. 314. French expression: "Mes dessins de mandalas étaient des cryptogrammes sur l'état de mon Soi, qui m'étaient livres journellement".

[32] Cf. Ibid. P. 313.

"corresponds to the microscopical nature of the soul"[33]. As one of the symbols of the Self, Jung attributes the mandala, which often takes the form of a circle, a square and is strongly linked with the quaternity, the number four:

> "It is the expression of all paths; it is the road that leads towards the middle, towards individuation"[34].

Contrary to the general popular presumptions, the mandalas are not only present in the orient but are imprinted in the occidental culture as well, more precisely since the Middle Ages and are to be seen within the Christian tradition[35], e.g., rose windows of cathedrals and churches or stained glasses. As Jung explains, the figure of Christ and that of the four evangelists are frequently present in such representations[36], being Christ in the middle and "the evangelists in the four cardinal points"[37].

Jung claimed to have certain reservations about Hegel's philosophy[38]. The main reasons therefore are explained by Casement as being Hegel's "idealistic rationality", dogmatic in character: "[...] Jung rejected Hegel for being too collective and focused too much on the outer world in his thinking"[39] instead of grounding himself on the inner experiences. Yet, Jung's understanding of the duality nature of the human psyche and more precisely his concept of the individuation process, i.e., the union of opposites and the transcendental function, can be analogously found within the Hegelian dialectics as well, where the absolute truth emerges from the tension created by the juxtaposition of contrary ideas[40]. Lastly, Jung's archetypal idea consists in understanding the archetypes bearing a polarity, structured in a positive and a negative pole (3). Nevertheless, Jung

---

[33] Ibid. P. 314. French expression: "Il m'apparaissait comme la monade que je suis et qui est mon monde. Le mandala représente cette monade et correspond à la nature microscopique de l'âme".

[34] Ibid. P. 315. French expression: "Il est l'expression de tous les cheminements; il est sente qui mène vers le milieu, vers l'individuation".

[35] Cf. Ibid. P.631.

[36] Cf. Ibid.

[37] Ibid. French expression: "[...]beaucoup entre eux, ont le Christ au centre et les quatre évangélistes, ou leurs symboles, aux quatre points cardinaux".

[38] Cf. Ibid. P.121–122.

[39] Casement, Ann. (2001). *Carl Gustav Jung.* P. 42.

[40] Cf. Collins, Alfred. (1994). "The Dialectics of Individuation Sean M. Kelly. Individuation and the Absolute: Hegel, Jung and the Path toward Wholeness". In: *The San Francisco Jung Institute Library Journal.* P. 31–42.

himself rather stated that his concept of archetypes should be understood as a synonym for Plato's understanding of *eidos,* namely the Platonian concept of the idea[41]. As a basis for each idea Jung assigned a primal image[42]. Jung would consequently understand that archetypes belong to a "transcendental sphere"[43]. Christian Roesler, as expert of the Jungian archetypal concept states that "in his theories around the archetype concept, Jung is an outspoken Platonian."[44].

Impressed by Schopenhauer's pessimistic perception of the world, yet less by the solutions he proposed, Jung found his answers rather within the Enlightenment ideas of the Kantian philosophy[45]. Kant's transcendental idealism impacted the development of Jung's thinking, in so far the "thing-in-itself" and the categories of understanding affected the development of his concepts of the "archetype as such" (3), his understanding of phenomena and the "a-priori" requirements of the human psyche. These requirements, according to Jung, are firstly understood as the instincts[46], which would lastly correspond to a predisposed, inherited matrix that is said to be the collective unconscious[47]:

> "There is an a-priori of all human activities, and that is the innate and thus preconscious and unconscious individual psychic structure. The preconscious psyche [...] is [...] an enormously complicated and individually most sharply determined prerequisite [...]"[48].

[41] Cf. Jung, Carl Gustav. (2020). *Archetypen. Urbilder und Wirkkräfte des Kollektiven Unbewussten.* P.95.

[42] Cf. Ibid. P.43.

[43] Roesler, Christian. (2024). *Deconstructing Archetype Theory.* P.30.

[44] Roesler, Christian. (2022). *Development of a Reconceptualization of Archetype Theory.* Report to the IAAP. P.45.

[45] Cf. Jung, Carl Gustav. (1961). *Ma vie.* P.123.

[46] Jung's line of argumentation, which is based on biological theories, is seen nowadays as highly questionable. Cf. Roesler, Christian. (2024). *Deconstructing Archetype Theory.*

[47] Cf. Jung, Carl Gustav. (2020). *Archetypen. Urbilder und Wirkkräfte des Kollektiven Unbewussten.* P.86.

[48] Ibid. P.98. (Trans. by the author). German expression: "Es gibt ein Apriori aller menschlichen Tätigkeiten, und das ist die angeborene und damit vorbewusste und unbewusste individuelle Struktur der Psyche. Die vorbewusste Psyche […] ist […] eine enorm komplizierte und individuell aufs schärfste determinierte Voraussetzung […]".

Moreover, Jung was an enthusiast of Master Eckhart, C.G. Carus, Edward von Hartmann[49] but also found inspiration in Paracelsus, Tertullian and Augustine. The latter, according to Christiane Schlüter, had "founded a psychological method"[50] of introspection. It was Augustine who was convinced by the importance of the observation of the inner experiences. This opinion, shared by Jung, was based on the term *Imago Dei*: "The soul [could] only [come] to insight and divine awareness by contemplating itself, since [God] has left his signature in the depths of the soul"[51], explains Harald Walach. Consequently, within the "idea" would inhabit the divine knowledge[52].

Jung felt close to Nietzsche. Although Jung studied Nietzsche in depth in 1914, his first encounter with the Nietzschean literature was in 1897, during a time in which he particularly felt a duality within himself[53]. In *Erinnerungen, Träume und Gedanken* Jung confessed that he feared his resemblance to Nietzsche, based on their "inner adventures"[54] that were incomprehensible to most people. As a philologist, Nietzsche returned to the Hellenic world. He reflected on how the ancient Greeks created a numinous world of Gods—the "shining dream-birth of the Olympian world"[55]—in order to support the tragedies of life. Nietzsche addressed the inner-outer world problematics and referred to the important role of myth: "Without myth, however, every culture loses its healthy, creative natural power"[56]. This view is shared by Jung[57]. Nietzsche's

---

[49] As Shamdasani delineates C.G. Carus and Edward von Hartmann were particularly important to Jung and his conception of the unconscious. To mention is Hartmann's principal work of *The Philosophy of the Unconscious.* Cf. Shamdasani, Sonu. (2012). *C.G. Jung. A Biography in Books.* P.27–28.

[50] Schlüter, Christiane. (2014). *Die wichtigsten Psychologen im Porträt.* P. 14. (Trans. by the author). German expression: „Damit begründet er [Augustinus] eine psychologische Methode, die später sehr wichtig wird: die Selbstbeobachtung, die Schau nach innen (Introspektion).".

[51] Walach, Harald. (2013). *Psychologie.* P. 128. (Trans. by the author). German expression: "Die Seele [könne] nur durch Einkehr in sich selbst zu einer Schau und Erkenntnis Gottes [kommen], da dieser ja im Seelengrund selbst seine Signatur hinterlassen hat".

[52] Cf. Jung, Carl Gustav. (2020). *Archetypen. Urbilder und Wirkkräfte des Kollektiven Unbewussten.* P.8.

[53] Cf. Shamdasani, Sonu. (2012). *C.G. Jung. A Biography in Books.* P.29.

[54] Jung, Carl Gustav. (1961). *Ma vie.* P.174.

[55] Nietzsche, Friedrich. (2020). *The birth of tragedy.* (Translated by WM.A. Haussmann). Chapter 3.

[56] Ibid. Chapter 23.

[57] Cf. Van der Post, Laurens. (1972). *The Story of Carl Gustav Jung.* [Documentary]. Minute: 51:54/1:33:23.

Also sprach Zarathustra: Ein Buch für Alle und Keinen represented to him one major discovery, and he dedicated a seminar lecture to it in 1934. Written in a poetic-hieratic language, to which Jung assigns the attributes of archetypal manifestation[58], he understands Zarathustra as the expression of the wise old man. This archetype would have appeared to Nietzsche as a compensation or as an "involuntary confession"[59], embodying a "personified immediate experience"[60], in the moment where he "strayed away from God"[61]. Similarly, Nietzsche's concept of the "Übermensch"—which could be linked to Jung's individuation process[62] (3.1)—and the enunciation about God's death resonated within him. It is important to understand this consideration as being related to the God outside[63] and not the (image of the) inner, "living, immediate God"[64] that, due to Jung, would exist within every human being. According to Shamdasani, the influence of Nietzsche's *Zarathustra* is to be noted later in the structure of Jung's own *Liber Novus* (*Red Book*):

> "It [*Thus Spoke Zarathustra*] strongly shaped the structure and style of *Liber Novus*. Like Nietzsche in *Zarathustra,* Jung divided the material up into a series of books comprised of short chapters. But whereas Zarathustra proclaimed the death of God, *Liber Novus* depicts the rebirth of God in the soul."[65].

Regarding Jung's contemporaries, it appears that Henri Bergson had a major function in Jung's life and on the development of his own Analytical Psychology. Pete

58 Cf. Jung, Carl Gustav. (2020). *Archetypen. Urbilder und Wirkkräfte des Kollektiven Unbewussten.* P.48.

59 Cf. Ibid.

60 Ibid. P. 49. (Trans. by the author). German expression: „Die drei bisher besprochenen Archetypen, der Schatten, die Anima und der alte Weise, sind solche, die in der unmittelbaren Erfahrung personifiziert auftreten.". Prior to this statement, Jung addressed Nietzsche's Zarathustra as an archetype. Cf. Ibid. P.48.

61 Ibid. P.48. German expression: "Zarathustra ist für Nietzsche mehr als poetische Figur, er ist ein unwillkürliches Bekenntnis. Auch er hatte sich in den Dunkelheiten eines gottabgewandten, entchristlichten Leben verirrt, und darum trat zu ihm der Offenbarende und Erleuchtende, als redender Quell seiner Seele.".

62 Cf. Casement, Ann. (2001). *Carl Gustav Jung.* P. 47–48.

63 Cf. Kast, Verena. (2009). *Das sagenumwobene 'Rote Buch' von C.G. Jung—Die Psychologin Verena Kast im Gespräch mit Norbert Bischofberger.* [Interview]. Minutes: 21:15/ 1:01:45.

64 Jung, Carl Gustav. (1961). *Ma vie.* P.78–79. (Trans. by the author). French expression: "[…] le Dieu vivant, immédiat, […]".

65 Shamdasani, Sonu. (2012). *C.G. Jung. A Biography in Books.* P.77.

A. Y. Gunter, an expert in Bergsonian Philosophy, explores the parallels between them both, incorporating particularities to which Jung himself pointed out in several of his writings. He notes, for instance, the correlation between Jung's acquaintance with Bergson's work and his rupture with Freud being synchronous, emphasizing Bergson's "catalytic"[66] effect on him. In this context Gunter highlights the parallelism between Bergson's concept of "Élan Vital" (life force) and Jung's perception of psychic energy: Libido is for Jung a "life energy in general"[67], consequently he differed from Freud's solely sexual understanding of the term. The work of *L'évolution créatrice*, in which the concept of "Élan Vital" is exposed, relates how the "human unconscious becomes suprapersonal"[68] by addressing the so called "'memories' of a common past"[69] and of a shared nature. Bergson's perception of memory derives from his original concept of "la durée", a distinction in the perception of time as a "qualitative duration"[70]. "Pure duration" includes the understanding that "past and present originates an organic whole"[71] and "inner duration" implies a pattern of creativity[72]. Jung uses this term to "describe creation through time"[73] and therefore alludes to the "dynamis" of the creative psyche. Gunter explains:

> "The purely formal concept of time is, Jung concludes, expressed in mythology by transformations of the creative libido."[74].

---

[66] Cf. Gunter, Pete A. Y. (1982). "Bergson and Jung". In: *Journal of the History of Ideas. Vol.43, Nr.4.* P. 635–652.

[67] Ibid. P.642. English expression: "Only two years later Jung equated the concept with Bergson's élan vital, with life energy in general, and thus robbed it of its [Freud's] distinctive sexual connotation". It is to be noted that Jung has pointed to these parallels himself in several of his writings, e.g., "From a broader standpoint libido can be understood as vital energy in general, or as Bergson's *élan vital.*". Jung, Carl Gustav. (2014). „Freud and Psychoanalysis". In: *CW. Vol. 4.* Part III: "Psychoanalysis and Neurosis".

[68] Gunter, Pete A. Y. (1982). "Bergson and Jung". In: *Journal of the History of Ideas. Vol.43, Nr.4.* P.637. English expression: "For our purposes the important thing to note in all this is that with *Creative Evolution* the human unconscious becomes suprapersonal.".

[69] Ibid. P.644. Bergson speaks of "memories of a biological past". Ibid. P.637.

[70] Ibid. P.635.

[71] Ibid.

[72] Cf. Ibid. P.636.

[73] Ibid. P.641. English expression: "In *Wandlungen II,* written in 1912, Jung uses Bergson's *durée* to describe creation through time. His description appears in the context of a mythological investigation".

[74] Ibid.

For Bergson Self-realization is a synonym for differentiation[75]. In a similar manner for Jung, the individuation process consists of the differentiation between the ego, respectively the persona, and the Self, respectively the archetypal structures[76]. This differentiation culminates in the expression of the highly individual nature of every human being. Further parallels are mentioned to be Bergson's vision of instincts and of intuition and Jung's archetypal theory, respectively the dynamis of the psyche[77].

2.3 "Two Souls, Alas! Inhabit my Chest!"[78]

From his mother, Jung inherited his sensitive and intuitive side. Early on, Jung recognized in himself two distinct personalities[79], which he was able to distinguish in the course of time and eventually named as Nr.1 and Nr.2. In this regard, Jung felt close to his mother[80], whom by day was the personification of the kind mother and by night transformed herself into an unpredictable, "terrifying and mysterious" person[81], recurrently possessed by an "archaic nature"[82]. Each of Jung's "personalities" had interests of their own. The second seemed to be an "autonomous personality"[83] with an independent will[84]. This reflection postulates a sort of a preamble to his later core concept of the archetypes and their self-driven nature. E.A. Bennet, a psychiatrist and Jungian analyst, alleged that

[75] Cf. Ibid. P.648.

[76] Cf. Jung, Carl Gustav. (2023). *Die Beziehung zwischen dem Ich und dem Unbewussten.*

[77] Cf. Gunter, Pete A. Y. (1982). "Bergson and Jung". In: *Journal of the History of Ideas. Vol.43, Nr.4. P.635–652.*

[78] Goethe, Wolfgang. "Faust". Cited after: Jung, Carl Gustav. (1961). *Ma vie.* P.373. French expression: "Deux Âmes, hélas! Habitant en ma poitrine!".

[79] As Gerhard Wehr explains, these two personalities are not to be taken as a "medical pathology condition of split personality [Schizophrenia]". Wehr, Gerhard. (1969). *C.G. Jung.* P. 12. (Trans. by the author). German expression: "Jung weist darauf hin, daß dies Spiel und Gegenspiel der beiden ‚Personen' nichts mit einer Spaltung im medizinisch-pathologischen Sinne zu tun habe.".

[80] Cf. Jung, Carl Gustav. (1961). *Ma vie.* P.93–94.

[81] Cf. Ibid. P.47. (Trans. by the author). French expression: "terrifiante et mystérieuse.".

[82] Ibid. P.94.

[83] Ibid. P.152–153.

[84] Cf. Ibid. P. 75. French expression: "D'où vient cette terrible volonté?". P.85: "Qui donc parle ainsi?". P.102: "C'était une volonté plus forte que la mienne qui me les avaient imposés tous deux.".

this was the genesis of Jung's concept of the collective unconscious[85]. In Jung's thinking, the idea of autonomy extends to other aspects of existence.

Van der Post explained that even time was considered by Jung to have a "nature and character of its own"[86], which can be attributed to the influence of his inner experiences and his personal world perception. Nr.1 was the "schoolboy"[87] with all its "outer" characteristics and Nr.2 was "the inner man"[88], who seemed to live within another epoch[89], thus "intemporal"[90], conveying a transcendental wisdom[91] and living in an intimate, pantheistic relationship with God and nature[92]. Jung himself described his second side as "the one who knows God as a secret mystery, personal and at the same time suprapersonal"[93]. This metaphysical interpretation of timelessness is an underlying quality of his concept of the collective unconscious, to which Gebser referred, when speaking of the fourth dimension. Related to this idea is also the understanding that the unconscious is the source of knowledge[94], in the same sense as Augustine perceived the "idea".

For Jung, archetypes possess their own kind of intelligence, an absolute knowledge which is independent of consciousness[95]. Jung intuitively witnessed the existence of the duality nature and the two contradictory wills within the human

[85] Cf. Casement, Ann. (2001). *Carl Gustav Jung.* P.4.

[86] Van der Post, Laurens. (1972). *The Story of Carl Gustav Jung.* [Documentary]. Minute: 59:21/1:33:23.

[87] Wehr, Gerhard. (1969). *C.G. Jung.* P.12.

[88] Jung, Carl Gustav. (1961). *Ma vie.* P.87. French expression: "L'homme intérieur".

[89] Cf. Ibid. P.69, p.71, p.85.

[90] Ibid. P.153.

[91] Cf. Ibid. P.96. French expression: "Il m'est arrivé assez souvent dans ma vie de savoir soudain certains événements qu'il m'était pourtant impossible de connaître. Ce savoir m'assaillait à la façon d'une idée subite. Il était de même pour ma mère".

[92] Cf. Ibid. P.85–86.

[93] Ibid. P.86. (Trans. by the author). French expression: "Ici vivait l''autre', celui qui connaissait Dieu comme un mystère secret, personnel, en même temps que suprapersonnel.".

[94] Cf. Ibid. P.496. French expression: "Par suite de sa relativité spatio-temporelle, l'inconscient a de meilleures sources d'information que la conscience, qui ne dispose que des perceptions sensorielles.".

[95] Cf. Kast, Verena. (1974). *Kreativität in der Psychologie von C.G. Jung.* P.95. German expression: "Jung postuliert im Aufsatz 'Der Geist der Psychologie', dass die Archetypen eine Art von 'Eigenintelligenz' hätten, abgelöst von unserm Bewusstsein, die dieses absolute Wissen ausmacht.".

being since an early age and therefore similarly, the triggers related to those discrepancies[96]:

> "My number 2 aspect was not a simple character, but a 'vita peracta', a completed life; he was born, alive, dead, all in one, a total vision of the human nature, of a ruthless clarity [...]"[97].

According to Jung, the discovery of Goethe's *Faust* was owed to his mother's second voice, who instinctively and spontaneously encouraged him to start its readings[98]. *Faust* had profoundly affected him, and foremost in the sense that Jung's Nr.2 identified himself with the protagonist, Faust was seen by him as the "living equivalent"[99] of his Nr.2. In the same manner, he associated himself with *Zarathustra*, who was "the *Faust* of Nietzsche, [...therefore his] nr. 2 side was [his own] *Zarathustra*"[100]. In the character of Faust lies a dissociation, the nature of which resides in the great contrasts. Jung himself brings to attention the following verse of *Faust*: "'Two souls, alas! Inhabit my chest!'"[101]. Mephisto resides within Faust, and it was in this dichotomy towards which Jung felt strongly and fatefully related to: "the Faust-Mephisto dichotomy merged into a single man, and that man, was me!"[102].

Years later, Jung held a lecture "Über die Beziehung der analytischen Psychologie zum dichterischen Kunstwerk"[103], where he approaches the interconnections between the creative psyche, science, art and literature and develops

---

[96] Cf. Jung, Carl Gustav. (1961). *Ma vie.* P. 312. French expression: "J'éprouvais de la façon la plus aiguë l'opposition entre le monde extérieur et le monde intérieur".

[97] Ibid. P.148. (Trans. by the author). French expression: "Mon aspect numéro 2 n'était pas en somme un caractère, mais une 'vita peracta', une vie parachevée; il était né, vivant, mort, le tout en un, vision totale de la nature humaine, d'une claret impitoyable pour lui-même [...]".

[98] Ibid. P.108.

[99] Ibid. P.149.

[100] Ibid. P.175. French expression: "Zarathoustra était le Faust de Nietzsche, et mon côté numéro 2 était mon Zarathoustra [...]".

[101] Ibid. P.373. French expression: "Deux Âmes, hélas! Habitant en ma poitrine!".

[102] Ibid. P.375. French expression: "La dichotomie Faust-Méphisto se confondait pour moi en un seul homme et cet homme, c'était moi!".

[103] This lecture was originally published in 1922 in *Wissen und Leben* and reprinted as: Jung, Carl Gustav. (1931). "Über die Beziehung der analytischen Psychologie zum dichterischen Kunstwerk". In: *Seelenprobleme der Gegenwart.* Zurich: Rascher. The English version is to be found translated by H.G. Baynes under the title "On the Relation of Analytical Psychology to Poetry" originally in the *British Journal of Psychology* (1923) and reprinted in *Contributions to Analytical Psychology.* London and New York (1928).

the idea of the visionary work of art[104], i.e., the work that instinctively emerges out of the depth of the psyche, a place where the creative force has an autonomous will and takes over the artist's. Thus, Jung said: "It is not Goethe who creates Faust, but the spiritual component of 'Faust' which creates Goethe"[105]. Similarly, in his Zarathustra Seminar, Jung states:

> "You don't create, you are created; in creation you are created. Something makes you do it, something is working through you, you are most tremendously instrumental."[106].

This view of the unconscious creative psyche is particular to Jung and represents an additional factor of differentiation from his contemporary colleagues.

2.4 The Transformation of the Soul

Jung was always particularly avid for knowledge and, due to this characteristic, became an extraordinarily cultivated person with a wide range of interests: In particular, he was drawn to Archeology (especially from the Greco-Roman, Egyptian and prehistoric period), but his interests also included the natural sciences, anthropology, history of philosophy and religion[107] and ethnology. His Nr.1 sought the

---

[104] In Jung's publication he supports himself upon Friedrich von Schiller's writings on the *Naïve and Sentimental Poetry and on the sublime*, where a distinction is made on the subject of the different creation processes, the sentimental and the naïve. Jung argues with his own words calling the sentimental introverted art and the naïve extraverted. Cf. Jung, Carl Gustav. (2011). *Über das Phänomen des Geistes in Kunst und Wissenschaft*. Paragraph 11. P.84.

[105] Ibid. Paragraph 159. P.118. (Trans. by the author). German expression: "Nicht Goethe macht den Faust, sondern die seelische Komponente 'Faust' macht Goethe". Having Faust an archetypal quality, Jung explained: „That is why Faust touches something in the soul of every German". (Trans. by the author). Ibid. Paragraph 153. P.112. German expression: "Deshalb berührt der 'Faust' etwas in der Seele jedes Deutschen […]".

[106] Jung, Carl Gustav. (2014). *Nietzsche's Zarathustra*. Vol. II, Part I, Lecture III, 30 October 1935. P.1554. Similarly, the composer Hans Zender expressed the following experience: "[…] he [the musician] experiences his artistic activities as being carried by certain laws. […] even in the seemingly free activity of composing, he [the musician] encounters a spiritual power that inexorably controls him.". Zender, Hans. In: Moritz. Reiner, E. (2020). *Hans Zender—Mit den Sinnen denken*. [DVD]. (Trans by the author). Minutes: 30:37. German expression: "[…] er [der Musiker] erfährt sein künstlerisches Tun als von bestimmten Gesetzmäßigkeiten getragen. […] auch in der scheinbar so freien Tätigkeit des Komponierens begegnet ihm eine geistige Macht, die ihn unerbittlich steuert.".

[107] Cf. Wehr, Gerhard. (1969). *C.G. Jung*. P. 16.

spiritual, his Nr.2 the historic premises[108], and accordingly in science he "missed the fact of meaning; that of empiricism [in religion]"[109]. Historically, there was a collective fascination for the orient, which coincides also with Jung's lifetime and his own later discoveries. He found many explanations for his concepts within the oriental culture. Besides, he developed an interest in Gnosticism[110], which he studied in depth between 1918 and 1926[111]. Such influence on Jung's thinking is to be heard in Jung's perception of the divine, repleted with contradictions[112]. Eventually, these were the subject of his thoughts unveiled in the *Black Books.*

In addition, Jung developed a strong interest in alchemy, particularly stimulated when he began working closely with the sinologist Richard Wilhelm on ancient Chinese alchemy in 1928[113]. He felt the hand of Fate behind it, guiding him towards researching these subjects. His dedication to alchemy, accompanied him on several of his excursions, including the journey to India in 1938[114]. Alchemy represented to Jung the historic basis he had long been searching for[115]. In alchemy, he saw above all the important reconciling factor, which historically would connect the loss of continuity that Jung acknowledged between past and present, between "primitive" folks and the modern human being. In contrast to the modern human being, who according to Nietzsche and later Jung had fallen into

---

[108] Cf. Ibid. P. 17. German expression: "Die Naturwissenschaft entsprach in hohem Masse den geistigen Bedürfnissen von Nr.1, die geisteswissenschaftlichen, beziehungsweise historischen Disziplinen hingegen bedeuteten einen wohltätigen Anschauungsunterricht für Nr.2".

[109] Jung, Carl Gustav. (1961). *Ma vie.* P. 127.

[110] Jung has been accused of being a Gnostic, as Hegel, Blake, Goethe, Byron, Nietzsche, Hesse, Heidegger, among others were, due to their apparent gnostic attitude. Ann Casement brings into attention that they were the earliest people who had, in a certain manner, explored the collective unconscious and solely herein would Jung's interest lie. Accordingly, Jung expressed that his inquisitiveness upon these matters came from an empiricist attitude with the main interest in anthropomorphic ideas and "[...] the autonomous aspects of the objective psyche [which] act as the counter-pole to the subjective ego". Casement, Ann. (2001). *Carl Gustav Jung.* P. 120.

[111] Cf. Jung, Carl Gustav. (1961). *Ma vie.* P.322.

[112] Cf. Kast, Verena. (2009). *Das sagenumwobene 'Rote Buch' von C.G. Jung—Die Psychologin Verena Kast im Gespräch mit Norbert Bischofberger.* [Interview]. Minutes: 21:56/ 1:01:45.

[113] Cf. Wilhelm, Richard., Jung, Carl Gustav. (1929). *Das Geheimnis der Goldenen Blüte.*

[114] Cf. Wehr, Gerhard. (1969). *C.G. Jung.* P.83.

[115] Cf. Jung, Carl Gustav. (1961). *Ma vie.* P.321–322.

the tragic fate of losing myth and the capability to perceive the world symbolically, "primitive" peoples were considered to be "myth-making men"[116], who had the living symbols within themselves and who were still strongly rooted within their "instinctive selves"[117]. In Europe, this break of continuity was explained by Jung as being linked to, for instance, Christianity[118], which banned the works of the Gnostics and implemented dogma, and thus the "despised alchemists"[119] were to Jung those who had created the bridge between the gnosis and the present[120]. The alchemist's quest was, for Jung, "[…] to search 'the secret of God' in the unknown matter […]"[121].

The aspect that was of particular interest to Jung during the study of alchemical texts and images was the observation of the inner processes that alchemists lived during the act of metal transmutation:

> "[The alchemist] experienced his projection as a property of the substance. What he actually experienced was his unconscious"[122].

The metamorphosis of the soul, a process occurring in parallel to the transmutation of metal, would culminate in the becoming one with oneself, analogously with the generation of the "supreme" alchemic gold. This is one of the facets that underlies his concept of individuation, i.e., the act of becoming one with oneself through the conjunction of the opposites (3.1). This process includes a deep descent in the unconscious realm within the own psyche, where archetypes

---

[116] Van der Post, Laurens. (1972). *The Story of Carl Gustav Jung*. [Documentary]. Minute: 51:54/1:33:23.

[117] Ibid. It should be brought into attention that this view is nowadays understood as problematic, as Christian Roesler explains in: Roesler, Christian. (2024). *Deconstructing Archetype Theory*.

[118] Van der Post, Laurens. (1972). *The Story of Carl Gustav Jung*. [Documentary]. Minutes: 53:44.

[119] Ibid.

[120] Cf. Jung, Carl Gustav. (1961). *Ma vie*. P.322.

[121] Cf. Ibid. "Glossaire": Alchemie. French expression: "L'alchimiste cherchait 'le secret de Dieu' dans la matière inconnue et s'engagea par cela dans des préocupations et des cheminements qui ressmeblent à ceux de la psychologie modern de l'inconscient.".

[122] Wehr, Gerhard. (1969). *C.G. Jung*. P.81. (Trans. by the author). German expression: "Er erlebte seine Projektion als Eigenschaft des Stoffes. Was er in Wirklichkeit erlebte, war sein Unbewusstes".

lie, and consists of the differentiation between the ego and the archetypal structures[123]. The alchemical model contains the following four stages: *nigredo* (as regression, death), *albedo* (a development of consciousness, i.e., the differentiation between the 'I' and the unconscious structures), *citrinitas* (as a transition phase), *rubedo* (as wholeness)[124]. It was with the study of alchemy that Jung achieved to designate the different stages that the human being experiences in the individuation process. Each of these stages would then correspond to the emergence of a particular archetype[125].

As demonstrated later, the creative process is equally characterized by such archetypal stages. The artist likely encounters himself in a constant process of individuation during the creative act which tends to unfold unconsciously and directly. These stages often coincide with turning points of the artistic language. Such occurrences might best be described with what Jung called synchronicity. His concept of synchronicity emerged alongside the study of the I-Ging, his own interests in metaphysics and the collaboration with the physicist Wolfgang Pauli. As synchronicity, Jung understood the occurrence of an outer event, which materializes itself at the same time as the incident of an inner experience[126], i.e., "a principle of a-causal succession"[127]. Such concepts represented primarily provocative thoughts on scientifically unexplainable phenomena.

Embedded in an historic time where the matters of the occult were of great interest, Jung researched and dedicated himself to occult phenomena, especially for his thesis "Psychologie und Pathologie sogenannter occulter Phänomene" ("On the psychology and pathology of the so-called occult phenomena") and undertook several experiments, which made up his dissertation for his medical degree. The source for his growing interest in this matter possibly came from within his own family circle and might be attributed to his cousin Hélène Preiswerk, who possessed psychic abilities[128]. In addition, important sources

[123] Cf. Jung, Carl Gustav. (2023). *Die Beziehung zwischen dem Ich und dem Unbewussten.* Chapter "Die Individuation".

[124] Vogel, Ralf T. (2017). *Individuation und Wandlung.* P.59.

[125] Cf. Roesler, Christian. (2024). *Deconstructing Archetype Theory.* P.34.

[126] Cf. Jung, Carl Gustav. (1957). *Great Minds of the 20th Century: Dr. Carl Jung. Evans, Richard.* [Interview]. Minutes: 53:20/ 3:02:34.

[127] Jung, Carl Gustav. (1961). *Ma vie.* P.473. (Trans. by the author). French expression: "La synchronicité comme principe d'enchaînement a-causal".

[128] Cf. Casement, Ann. (2001). *Carl Gustav Jung.* P. 38.

of inspiration were, as already stated, the works of Théodore Flournoy[129], but also of William Crookes and William James' holistic principle[130]. While dealing with spiritualistic phenomena, Jung was seized by Karl du Prel's view on dreams[131]. To mention is Karl du Prel's *Die Philosophie der Mystik.* Here, as Shamdasani explains, du Prel advocates for "the atemporal and spatial existence of the soul"[132] and the idea of "dreams as symbolic self-representations of the psyche"[133]. Later, he continued to be fascinated by the unexplainable occurrences and phenomena which lay within the realm of the veiled and had never been taken as evidence. Thus, all his concepts were born out of the complementarity of his multiple sources of interests.

2.5 The Fateful Inner Encounters

The path leading towards the final completion of Jung's conception of the unconscious started just after his break with Freud and accompanied him for the rest of his life. He searched within himself for further evidence of the collective unconscious, namely by the confrontation with the "impulses of the unconscious"[134]. Jung wanted to understand in what manner his inner vivid experiences were interconnected with those of the collectivity[135]. It was then, when he encountered his contrasting inner archaic characters, who came to him in form of fantasies, day or night dreams, and with whom he made conversation. Philemon, for instance, was a pagan with a "winged spirit"[136] and an innate, transcendental intelligence[137].

[129] Of major inspiration for Jung was Flournoy's "[…] psychological approach to mediumship, one that stressed the importance of the subconscious creative imagination.". Shamdasani, Sonu. (2012). *C.G. Jung. A Biography in Books.* P.38.

[130] Cf. Casement, Ann. (2001). *Carl Gustav Jung.* P. 46. Shamdasani additionally lists the works of Eschenmayer, Passavant, Gorres, Alfred Wallace, Friedrich Zöllner, and Emanuel Swedenborg. Cf. Shamdasani, Sonu. (2012). *C.G. Jung. A Biography in Books.* P.29.

[131] Cf. Ibid.

[132] Ibid. P.30.

[133] Ibid. P.30. Moreover, he believed on the healing capacity of dreams. Cf. Ibid.

[134] Jung, Carl Gustav. (1961). *Ma vie.* P. 278. (Trans. by the author). French expression: "J'abandonnai de la sorte consciemment aux impulsions de l'inconscient".

[135] Cf. Ibid. P.283.

[136] Ibid. P.296.

[137] Cf. Ibid. P.294.

This archetype helped him to understand "the reality of the soul"[138], to differentiate "between [himself] and the object of his thoughts"[139] and thus to unravel "the involuntary creations of his imagination"[140]. According to Shamdasani, Jung's Philemon character finds corresponding traits to Nietzsche's Zarathustra and to Dante's Virgil[141]. Similarly, Jung's *Liber Novus* features parallels with Dante's *Divina commedia*, narrating a descent to Hell[142].

Later, Jung had another apparition, which he called Ka, and which seemed to embody the counterpart of Philemon. Contrary to Philemon, Ka was rather earth bounded and presented traits of Mephistopheles[143]. In addition to Philemon and Ka, Jung also experienced a female voice, which he identified as being a voice of a former patient of his, who had become a living character within himself[144]. This inner voice had the function of establishing the connection with the unconscious, the "mythical realm of the dead, of the ancestors"[145]. From this encounter emerged his concept of the soul image Anima. It is also from this period, where he experienced the inner urge to "give a creative form to his inner life"[146], narrated and illustrated in the *Red Book*. This experience undoubtedly led Jung to understand the integration of the Anima figure as being associated with great creative inspiration.

From the readings of *Erinnerungen, Träume, Gedanken* it becomes apparent how the notion of fate was important to Jung: He used to speak of the "book of his own destiny"[147]. From the way in which *Erinnerungen, Träume, Gedanken* unfolds, it seems as if he understood his vocation as a "doctor of the soul" in this connection. The feeling of being pursued by the purpose of "access[ing] the secret of personality"[148] comes to light through his words. This driving factor

---

[138] Ibid.

[139] Ibid.

[140] Ibid.

[141] Cf. Shamdasani, Sonu. (2012). *C.G. Jung. A Biography in Books.* P.79.

[142] Cf. Ibid.

[143] Cf. Jung, Carl Gustav. (1961). *Ma vie.* P.296.

[144] Cf. Ibid. P.297.

[145] Ibid. P.307.

[146] Ibid. P.304.

[147] Ibid. P.26. French expression: "C'est ainsi que les êtres, eux aussi, ne sont devenus pour moi d'impérissables souvenirs que dans la mesure où leur nom était depuis toujours inscrit dans le livre de mon destin: faire connaissance avec eux équivalait à un ressouvenir".

[148] Ibid. P.330. (Trans. by the author). French expression: "Ma vie est imprégnée, tissée, unifiée par une œuvre, et axée sur un but, celui de pénétrer le secret de la personnalité".

took form as an inner force that presented itself as missions[149] throughout his life, that propelled him to dedicate himself to the inner world[150], and to which he ought to respond[151]:

> "From the beginning I felt within myself a strong feeling of an implacable, unique destiny, as if I had been placed in a life that had to be accomplished"[152].

Equally, he considered the task of writing a book as a "confrontation with fate"[153]. Later, Jung asked himself if his destiny was linked to his ancestors. This would make fate to be not only of personal essence but also possessing an impersonal quality[154], akin to his concept of the archetypes[155]:

> "If the pre-established destiny with which the human being enters life is the result of the actions and accomplishments of past lives, there is a personal continuity"[156].

This thought came from the profound conviction that fate propelled him to follow the unanswered tasks left behind by his past relatives[157] and to which he later linked the Indian notion of *Karma*. This can be a further indicator of Jung's thinking that the term of archetype is extended to life situations, such as birth, death, fate, etc.

---

[149] Ibid. P.355. (Trans. by the author). French expression: "Tous mes écrits sont pour ainsi dire des taches qui me furent imposes de l'intérieur. Ils naquirent sous la pression du destin.".

[150] "Then fate wants – as it always wanted – that in my life everything that is external is accidental and only what is provided from the inside has a substantial and determining value". Cf. Ibid. P.16. French expression: " Or le destin veut – comme il l'a toujours voulu – que dans ma vie tout ce qui est extérieur soit accidentel et que seul ce qui est intérieur ait une Valeur substantielle et déterminante".

[151] Cf. Ibid. P. 308.

[152] Ibid. P 90. French expression: "Dès le début j'avais en moi le sentiment d'une destinée implacable, unique, comme si j'avais été place dans une vie qu'il fallait accomplir."

[153] Ibid. P.13. French expression: "Écrire un livre est toujours, pour moi, une confrontation avec le destin. Il y a toujours, dans l'acte de création, quelque chose d'imprévisible et je ne peux rien fixer ni prévoir à l'avance.".

[154] Cf. Ibid. P.372.

[155] Cf. Ibid. P.412.

[156] Ibid. P. 498. French expression: "Si la destinée préétablie avec laquelle un être humain entre dans la vie est le résultat des actions et des accomplissements des vies antérieures, il existe une continuité personnelle".

[157] Cf. Ibid. P.372.

Late in his life, he confessed to have understood the importance of accepting one's own fate[158]. In a similar way, Schiller's verse "In your chest are the stars of destiny"[159] might have been, eventually, of additional influence[160]. In Jung's understanding every human being is predestined to undertake a deep descent into the own soul and to be confronted with the shadow realm of the unconscious, a procedure leading to individuation. This Jungian idea transpires the notion of an archetypal fate within every human being.

It is known, notably from *Das Rote Buch* (*Red Book*), that this time of his life was particularly rich in what regards his own creativity. Moreover, he found enjoyment in wood carving and stone construction. In many of his interviews and writings, Jung spoke of the inner world as bearing a vast sea of "moving images"[161], which can be expressed through dreams, fantasies and through the creative act. Within the unconscious lies the creative force (libido), namely archetypal images, narrative patterns, which urge to take form and propel to create. During the creative impulse, psychic energy comes into movement and an exchange of energy between the unconscious and consciousness happens, through the ego-Self axis. This exchange of energies generates transformations which reflect an individuation process. This means that underlying each creative act there is an individuation process taking place. During this individuation process, several archetypes arise, standing for several stages of this process. The extent of conscious constructions inflowing in a given creative work is subject to variation. According to Jungian thought, when the connection of the antagonistic forces within happens, it is possible to access knowledge that transcends the conscious condition of the ego.

In relation to this, Sonu Shamdasani brings particularly to attention Jung's interest on Flournoy's thesis of "[...] the existence of non-pathological and creative components of the subconscious [...]"[162], which includes the idea of automatic activity. This idea in turn derives from the theory of the subliminal

---

[158] Cf. Ibid. P.468. Only punctually, during his youth, Jung confessed his belief that by answering to the challenges of fate, he was responsible for his life and consequently had the faculty to rule his own destiny. Cf. Ibid. P.90. This conviction however, changed in his later years, especially after his illness in 1944.

[159] Jung, Carl Gustav. (2020). *Archetypen. Urbilder und Wirkkräfte des Kollektiven Unbewussten.* P.11.German expression: "In deiner Brust sind deines Schicksals Sterne".

[160] Cf. Ibid.

[161] Jung, Carl Gustav. (1957). *Great Minds of the 20th Century: Dr. Carl Jung. Evans, Richard.* [Interview]. Last accessed 08:01:23 at 15:00.

[162] Shamdasani, Sonu. (1998). "From Geneva to Zurich: Jung and French Switzerland". Cited after: Casement, Ann. (2001). *Carl Gustav Jung.* P.8.

self of the British poet and philologist Frederic W.H. Myers. Shamdasani further explains that "the medium of automatic writing becomes a 'psychoscope' that reveals the unseen movements of the psyche"[163]. This was then applied as a therapeutic method notably by Pierre Janet, who also influenced Jung a lot, and consists of "[…] a means of exploring the subconscious […]"[164]. Jung was one of the pioneers of introducing artistic activities for therapeutic purposes, enabling patients to give shape and expression to their inner experiences.

2.6 A Different Perception of the Human Psyche

C.G. Jung carried his own vision of the world, of the human psyche and the inner driving forces, which finally differed greatly from the conception of Freud or other contemporary colleagues—"the soul does not end there, where the physiological or any other condition ends […]"[165], he alleged. In his perception, the unconscious is the bearer of the creative energy. All psychical events (including dreams and fantasies) are facts and reality[166]: "Psyche is the ultimate real entity[167], because it represents the sole directness"[168]. Jung had the inner urge to understand the unintelligible, and his pledge was to take his vocation of a psychiatrist as a "doctor of the soul"[169], as a "soul researcher"[170] by its meaning: "Without soul there is no knowledge nor profound awareness"[171], so Jung. According to Jung's view, to believe and to follow a dogma could not lead

[163] Ibid. P. 47.

[164] Casement, Ann. (2001). *Carl Gustav Jung*. P. 47.

[165] Jung, Carl Gustav. (2020). *Archetypen. Urbilder und Wirkkräfte des Kollektiven Unbewussten*. P.73. (Trans. by the author). German expression: "Die Seele kommt nicht da zum Ende, wo die Reichweite einer physiologischen oder sonstigen Voraussetzung aufhört […]".

[166] Cf. Wehr, Gerhard. (1969). *C.G. Jung*. P. 35.

In the German language there is the distinction between "Realität" and "Wirklichkeit". The last one encompasses not only what is perceptible as a fact and appearance of what is outside but includes the inner experience as well. It is in this sense that the word reality is applied here.

[167] The ultimate real entity or the most real being. In lat. "Ens Realissimum" is a concept originally from scholastic Philosophy.

[168] Wehr, Gerhard. (1969). *C.G. Jung*. P. 35. (Trans. by the author). German expression: "Psyche ist das allerrealste Wesen, weil es das einzig Unmittelbare ist.".

[169] Ibid. P.34. German expression: "Seelenarzt".

[170] Ibid. German expression: "Seelenforscher".

[171] Jung, Carl Gustav. (1961). *Ma vie*. P.169. (Trans. by the author). French expression: "Sans l'âme il n'y avait ni savoir, ni connaissance approfondie.".

to the ultimate knowledge, only the proper inner experience could provide it. Equally, Jung emphasized the fact that his archetypal notions are not concepts of an "abstract nature but generated by proper experience"[172]. Undoubtedly, personal experience of psychological phenomena and its individual nature was for Jung of utmost importance.

Jung considered himself an empiricist[173]. He had a vast source of interest and was influenced by many currents of thought, which naturally reflected in his statements. Therefore, he is also acknowledged of having a phenomenological mind[174], a hermeneutical[175], epistemological[176] approach or of being transcendental[177]. Ann Casement draws additional attention to Jung's "existential thinking"[178], where philosophy and his religious nature meet. Jung's kind of crisscrossing arguments, notably from other scientific fields, can be regarded as problematic, in that it brings on an "epistemological confusion"[179].

Jung realized that establishing fixed models, or the mere treatment of symptoms, through the methods applied then, like suggestion and hypnotism, would not be sufficient to unravel the mysteries underlying psychic experiences[180]:

> "The space of the soul is immensely large and full of living reality. On its borders lies the mystery of matter and that of spirit; or that of meaning."[181].

---

[172] Jung, Carl Gustav. (2020). *Archetypen. Urbilder und Wirkkräfte des Kollektiven Unbewussten.* P.77. (Trans. by the author). German expression: "Es handelt sich eben nicht um einen abstrakten, sondern um einen Erfahrungsbegriff, dem die Gestalt, in der er erscheint, notwendigerweise anhaftet, und den man auch gar nicht anders beschreiben könnte als eben durch dessen spezifische Phänomenologie.".

[173] Cf. Jung, Carl Gustav. (1961). *Ma vie.* P.585.

[174] Hillman, James. (2010, June 19th). In: *Carl Gustav Jung and the Red Book.* [Symposium]. Minutes: 1:30:00/2:29:34.

[175] Cf. Roesler, Christian. (2024). *Deconstructing Archetype Theory.* P.58.

[176] Cf. Ibid. P.64.

[177] Cf. Ibid. P.47.

[178] Cf. Casement, Ann. (2001). *Carl Gustav Jung.* P. 38.

[179] Cf. Roesler, Christian. Personal communication between Christian Roesler and the author. Küsnacht: February 3, 2023.

[180] It should be mentioned that Jung himself engaged in the practice of hypnotism during the early stages of his career as a psychiatrist, subsequently discontinuing it. Cf. Jung, Carl Gustav. (1961). *Ma vie.*

[181] Ibid. P.587. (Trans. by the author). French expression: "L'espace de l'âme est immensément grand et plein de réalité vivante. Sur ses frontières est le mystère de la matière et celui de l'esprit; ou encore, celui du sens.".

This statement could indicate the perception that psyche at the end remains an enigma[182], then "[...] any amount of unconscious things occur in [parallel to] the conscious condition [...]"[183]. In dreams Jung saw the gateway to the impersonal aspect within the human psyche: "the dream was the personal possession of everybody who dreamed it [...]"[184]. Jung differentiated personal dreams from great, collective dreams and observed that medicine men in African tribes did the same distinction as well[185]. His analysis of dreams included a unique approach, called the amplification method. It does not consist of a reduction of the dream content (as in Freud's interpretation of dreams), nor necessarily of free associations, but, on the contrary, of an expansion and enrichment of its content, done through the historic comparison of symbolic material and analogies with motifs from myths, legends, etc.[186]. This approach reveals Jung's thinking about the nature of unconscious content: For Jung the psyche is ambivalent or polyvalent and as such needs a corresponding broader approach.

Van der Post explains that for Jung the tension between two opposite poles characterized the nature of the psyche and that the one-sidedness represents the principal danger:

> "[...] anything that comes from the unconscious is ambiguous, a paradox, it is the one and the other. The great danger of consciousness is to be one-sided. Thus, the greatest concern for Jung was to look for both sides. The one is always compensating the other [...]"[187].

Due to the paradoxical and ambiguous nature of the human psyche, Jung intentionally opted to choose a double-meaning language when referring to it and to all interrelated processes, then, in his understanding, only by regarding all the contradictory aspects, its meaning comes nearer to reality:

---

[182] Cf. Jaffé, Aniéla. In: Van der Post, Laurens. (1972). *The Story of Carl Gustav Jung.* [Documentary]. Minutes: 1:12:55 /1:33:23.

[183] Jung, Carl Gustav. (1957). *Great Minds of the 20th Century: Dr. Carl Jung. Evans, Richard.* [Interview]. Minutes: 11:05 / 3:02:34.

[184] Van der Post, Laurens. (1972). *The Story of Carl Gustav Jung.* [Documentary]. Minutes: 48:25/1:33:23.

[185] Ibid. Minutes: 50:47/1:33:23.

[186] Cf. Jacobi, Jolande. (2006). *Die Psychologie von C.G. Jung.* P. 87–89.

[187] Van der Post, Laurens. (1972). *The Story of Carl Gustav Jung.* [Documentary]. Minutes: 1:14:00/1:33:23.

> "When it comes to experience, nothing escapes the ambiguity of the psyche. The biggest experience is at the same time the smallest and the most limited one and that is why we are afraid to speak of it too loudly or even to philosophize about it. It is certain that we are far too small and incapable to allow ourselves such audacity. I therefore prefer two-way language because it takes into account, in a fair proportion, the subjectivity of archetypal representations and the autonomy of the archetype"[188].

The paradoxical attitudes towards definitions of concepts, his methodology and thoughts present in various of his statements, can be subject for criticism and can raise certain problematics. Jung attempted to address "[the] mystery, as [the] matter [is] for the physicists"[189], which can be subjective and objectionable, from the scientific community's point of view. His attitude, in addition to Jung's aforementioned justification, might have various reasons. For psycho-analytical purposes, the lack of proper definitions and clear statements might lead to confusion, misuse or misunderstanding of his concepts[190], which can cause a serious problem, namely, to be the basis for the emergence of unscientific, even esoteric kind of interpretations or approaches[191]. This exerts a damaging effect on the reception of Jungian analytical psychology[192]. For this reason, the problem is nowadays critically addressed, so that new terms and approaches are researched and suggested, notably by Christian Roesler[193].

[188] Jung, Carl Gustav. (1961). *Ma vie*. P. 587. French expression: "Dés qu'il s'agit d'expérience, rien n'échappe à l'ambiguïté de la psyché. La plus grande expérience est aussi la plus petite et la plus limitée et c'est pourquoi l'on craint d'en parler á trop haute voix ou même de philosopher à son sujet. Il est certain que nous sommes bien trop petits et incapables pour nous permettre une telle audace. Je préfère donc le langage à double sens car il tient compte, dans une juste proportion, de la subjectivité des représentations archétypiques et de l'autonomie de l'archétype.".

[189] Van der Post, Laurens. (1972). *The Story of Carl Gustav Jung*. [Documentary]. Minutes: 1:12:55 /1:33:23.

[190] Cf. Roesler, Christian. (2024). *Deconstructing Archetype Theory*.

[191] Cf. Mills, Jon. (2018). "The Essence of Archetypes". In: *International Journal of Jungian Studies. Vol.10, Nr.3*. P. 1–22.

[192] Cf. Roesler, Christian. (2024, October 4th). "Introduction to the conference theme 'The process of transformation'. In: *The Process of Transformation*. [Conference Lecture].

[193] Roesler, Christian. (2024). *Deconstructing Archetype Theory*.

2.7 Summa Summarum

The biographical background shows the importance of reading Jung's concepts, that are to be laid out in the next chapter, bearing in mind his historical context and his personality: Jung was a person whose intuitive and thinking functions were particularly pronounced, who perceived the world in a rather introverted way[194]. The unfolding and development of his concepts are a reflection of his zeitgeist, i.e., the cultural unconscious of the epoch he lived in, "towards which he had access to"[195] and which, after Jung, fatefully spoke through him.

It became apparent that Jung's main concern in the cross-cultural and cross-religious studies he undertook during the development of his theories was the idea of a process of transformation that underlies the various traditions and that can be linked to the idea of a spiritual quest[196]. This led to his theory of the individuation process, that is nowadays seen as the core concept of Analytical Psychology[197].

In turn, the question of Jung's religious convention is highly complex[198]. Ann Casement, a Jungian analyst, affirms that "Jung was a life-long Protestant who tried to reintroduce dogmatic symbolism"[199]. He did grow up in a Protestant pastor's house, as it has already been explained before. However, in his theological studies, Jung also showed a significant curiosity towards Catholicism, which is particularly visible through his interest towards the mass, specifically rites of passages in the mass that point to transformational processes, etc.[200]. The same concern is to be noted in Jung's interest towards the alchemists (the metamorphoses of the metals described by alchemists being analogically understood

[194] Cf. Jung, Carl Gustav. (1959). *Face to Face, Carl Jung*. Freeman, John (Presenter). [Interview]. Minutes: 27:06 /38:05.

[195] Kast, Verena. (2009). *Das sagenumwobene 'Rote Buch' von C.G. Jung—Die Psychologin Verena Kast im Gespräch mit Norbert Bischofberger*. [Interview]. Minutes: 22:43/1:01:45. (Trans. by the author). German expression: "Das ganze kulturelle Unbewußte von seiner Zeit ist eigentlich…auf das hat er Zugriff, […]".

[196] This topic has been brought to discussion by Christian Roesler in the form of a joint conference for the IAAP/ Catholic University of Applied Sciences Freiburg, in cooperation with DGAP and INFAP3 dedicated to this theme. Cf. *The Process of Transformation*. [Conference]. (2024, October 4–6).

[197] Cf. Roesler, Christian. (2024). *Deconstructing Archetype Theory*.

[198] Due to this reason, this topic will not be further developed in this endeavor, as it would require a separate study of its own.

[199] Casement, Ann. (2001). *Carl Gustav Jung*. P.2.

[200] Roesler, Christian. Telephonic communication between Christian Roesler and the author. Freiburg im Breisgau/Noiraigue: October 16, 2024.

as transformations of the soul). Jung highlighted two critical points towards the Christian tradition: (i) the dogmatic thinking, evident in *Erinnerungen, Träumen, Gendaken*, and (ii) the exclusion of evil in the image of God, which he conveyed in "Antwort auf Hiob"[201]. Lastly, referring to Van der Post's statement mentioned above, he saw the latter facet included in the alchemists and in the Gnostics.

He differentiated himself from Freud and his contemporaries, mainly by regarding the spiritual quest as an essential need[202] to become whole, i.e., an individuation process, where the unconscious with its images, patterns and creative force has a crucial implication. One of the divergent points between Jung and Freud was Jung's thoughts about psychic energy and the nature of the unconscious, namely its creativity and its potential for being dynamic and self-regulating. In contrast to Freud's perspective, the unconscious was not a "storeroom"[203] where solely repressed feelings of personal nature lay, and the libido was not understood as a mere sexual instinct. Foremost, it is a creative force within the human being, which floods consciousness and therefore it generates the "I"[204]—a rather revolutionary approach to the unconscious taking into consideration his historical context.

For the artists, these dynamic processes and the access to the symbolic language of the unconscious are understood by Jungians as being particularly accentuated, as Jung himself explained, when stating that Faust had created Goethe. By allowing the opposites to meet and by undertaking a journey into the deep unconscious Self, the ultimate destiny of the human being unfolds—it becomes whole, i.e., the human being returns to the "nothingness of which he hopes to find the universe"[205].

---

[201] Ibid.

[202] Cf. Kast, Verena. (2014). *Die Tiefenpsychologie nach C.G. Jung*. Chapter "Das religiöse Bedürfnis". P.59.

[203] Ibid.

[204] Cf. Wehr, Gerhard. (1969). *C.G. Jung*. P.39.

[205] Gebser, Jean. (1986). *Ursprung und Gegenwart*. P.527. (Trans. by the author). German expression: „Es beginnt jene Wanderung ‚ins Leere', in die Mephisto den Faust sendet und in ‚deren Nichts er das All zu finden hofft'."

3 The Emergence of the Concept of the Collective Unconscious and the Theory of the Archetypes

Jung's research for the unconscious is said to have started at the Burghölzli Hospital, where he first developed his theory of the feeling-toned complexes[1], through the association experiments, which constituted a common method in his time. However, C.G. Jung had an idiosyncratic approach to psychotherapy. Sonu Shamdasani explains that the main point in which Jung distinguished himself from other concurrent psychotherapeutic approaches was by turning to the method of philology[2]. His keen interest in the study of mythology, folklore and religion was intensified with the readings of Friedrich Creuzer's *Symbolik und Mythologie der alten Völker*, Albrecht Dietrich's *Eine Mithrasliturgie* and the anthropological writings of Lévy-Bruhl[3], from whom Jung made reference to the idea of the "représentations collectives"[4]. Additionally, Shamdasani notes Jung's inclusion of Jacob Burckhardt's term of "urtümliches Bild" and "Urbild" in his own lexicon[5]. With the aim to understand the history and the significance of myths to psychology, Jung turned not only to the study of his own dreams and fantasies but also to the origins and the study of the evolution of the human being, with the specific focus of "the myth-creating function of the mind"[6].

---

[1] It has to be noted that the discoveries of the feeling-toned complexes is attributed to Theodor Ziehen in 1898 and that Jung's interest upon them grew from Pierre Janet's seminars in Salpêtrière. Cf. Casement, Ann. (2001). *Carl Gustav Jung.* P. 9.

[2] Cf. Shamdasani, Sonu. (2012). *C.G. Jung. A Biography in Books.* P. 134.

[3] Cf. Ibid. P. 50–55.

[4] Jung, Carl Gustav. (2020). *Archetypen. Urbilder und Wirkkräfte des Kollektiven Unbewussten.* P. 9.

[5] Cf. Shamdasani, Sonu. (2012). *C.G. Jung. A Biography in Books.* P. 57.

[6] Ibid. P. 65.

L. Dill, *Schubert's Metamorphoses*,
https://doi.org/10.1007/978-3-662-73476-6_3

Jung was deeply convinced that "it exists an archaic component of the soul, which cannot penetrate the individual soul out of any tradition"[7]. He goes even further when he says:

> "[…] Archetypes are by no means spread universally merely by tradition, by language nor by migration, but can spontaneously re-emerge at any time, and in a way that is not influenced by any outside transmission[8]".

Jung sought to prove his early intuitive convictions about the existence of a collective unconscious, and therefore he travelled the world to collect material from different cultures and primitive tribes[9]. He felt the need to research the "history of man", to undertake an inquiry of religion and mythologies by engaging in a longitudinal study. Based on personal experience in his youth, Jung stated that the human being is "[…] not of yesterday, [but] of an immense age!"[10] and that he is shaped not only by personal conditions but by impersonal, primordial ones as well[11]. According to him, the human being is not born "tabula rasa"[12], but comes to the world with an innate psychic structure[13], which reaches far beyond the bounds of their own cultural traditions. According to Jung, the term

[7] Jung, Carl Gustav. (1961). *Ma vie*. P. 54. (Trans. by the author). French expression: "[…] j'acquis pour la première fois la conviction qu'il existe des composantes de l'âme qui ne peuvent avoir pénétré dans l'âme individuelle à partir d'aucune tradition".

[8] Jung, Carl Gustav. (2020). *Archetypen. Urbilder und Wirkkräfte des Kollektiven Unbewussten*. P. 100. (Trans. by the author). German expression: "[…], dass die Archetypen keineswegs bloß durch Tradition, durch die Sprache und durch die Migration sich allgemein verbreiten, sondern jederzeit und überall spontan wiederentstehen können, und zwar in einer Art und Weise, welche durch keine Übermittlung von außen beeinflusst ist.".

[9] Cf. Van der Post, Laurens. (1972). *The Story of Carl Gustav Jung*. [Documentary]. Minute: 57:38/1:33:23.

[10] Jung, Carl Gustav. (1959). *Face to Face, Carl Jung*. Freeman, John (Presenter). [Interview]. Minute: 22:10 /38:05.

[11] Cf. Jung, Carl Gustav. (1961). *Ma vie*. P. 312.

[12] Jung, Carl Gustav. (1957). *Great Minds of the 20th Century: Dr. Carl Jung. Evans, Richard*. [Interview]. Minutes: 1:34:20/ 3:02:34.

[13] This idea is nowadays disputed. Cf. Roesler, Christian. (2024). *Deconstructing Archetype Theory*.

of the collective unconscious means "cum grano salis"[14] the same in every human being—a concept which transcends time and space.

In divergence to Freud's view, for whom the unconscious was a product of consciousness, where repressed feelings were stored, Jung's concept encompassed a deeper understanding of it, as the following citation demonstrates:

> "[…] to me the unconscious then was already a matrix, a sort of basis of consciousness of a creative nature, namely capable of autonomous acts, autonomous intrusions into consciousness. In other words, I took the existence of the unconscious for a real fact; or for a real autonomous factor capable of independent actions."[15].

The genesis of the archetypal theory is to be found within the year of 1912 and signals not only the divergences and the definite split between Freud and Jung that same year, but also marks the "[…] beginning of Jung's independent stream of depth psychology […]"[16]. This materialized itself especially with the publication of Jung's book *Wandlungen und Symbole der Libido.* Significant for the genesis of Jung's archetypal theory were Adolf Bastian's "elementary ideas"[17] and Lévy-Bruhl's "representations collectives"[18].

An archetype is most often synonymously termed as "Urbild", i.e., as primordial image. Etymologically, its roots come from the Greek *arkhē* meaning primal, original source and *typos* signifying imprint or model. For C.G. Jung and for Jungian analysts, this etymological definition hints, among other aspects, to the "position of a leader"[19], to a conducting force, which underlines their

---

[14] Jung, Carl Gustav. (2020). *Archetypen. Urbilder und Wirkkräfte des Kollektiven Unbewussten.* P. 8. (Trans. by the author). German expression: "[…] Inhalte und Verhaltensweisen, welche überall und in allen Individuen cum grano salis die Gleichen sind. […] in allen Menschen sich selbst identisch und bildet damit eine in jedermann vorhandene, allgemeine seelische Grundlage überpersönlicher Natur".

[15] Jung, Carl Gustav. (1957). *Great Minds of the 20th Century: Dr. Carl Jung. Evans, Richard.* [Interview]. Minutes: 2:19:13/3:02:34.

[16] Cf. Roesler, Christian. (2022). *Development of a Reconceptualization of Archetype Theory.* Report to the IAAP. P. 6.

[17] Cf. Jung, C.G. (2014). "The Structure and the Dynamics of the Psyche". In: *CW. Vol. 8.* Part III. Chapter: "On the nature of the Psyche"—"1. The unconscious in Historical perspective".

[18] Cf. Jung, Carl Gustav. (2020). *Archetypen. Urbilder und Wirkkräfte des Kollektiven Unbewussten.* P. 9.

[19] Daniel, Renate. Personal communication (online lecture). Küsnacht/Lisbon: February 11, 2022.

dynamis and autonomous nature[20]. Archetypes are frequently defined as "structural elements of the collective psyche and give psychic energy a defined form, which alone is formless and imperceptible"[21]. The first description of archetypes is to be noted in 1919, although Jung had already spoken of primal images ("Urbilder") earlier on. They are described as a-priori, preformed psychic elements of perception and a form of intuition, owning an independent will, being capable of self-driven acts and therefore exerting great influence on the life of a human being. They carry a meaning and are highly affectively and emotionally charged, i.e., they have a numinous effect on the person who experiences them. Consequently, they act as a mediator and have a self-regulating effect on the psyche. When archetypes arise to consciousness, or at least when they are made available to conscious observation, they manifest themselves in the form of images and symbols.

The symbol corresponds thus to the form or shape that an archetype can take, which can already be perceived by consciousness[22]. Descending from the Greek word *symbállein*, meaning "to put together"[23], the word *sýmbolon* is to be understood as "the visible something of an also invisible, ideal reality"[24]. This means, to put it in Verena Kast's words, that "the symbol gives form to [an] emotion"[25]. In the Jungian literature, symbols are synonymously understood as "psychic images"[26]. As such, the symbolic manifestations of archetypes can be perceived in dreams, fantasies, myths, fairy tales, but also in art works, musical compositions and through human actions. Examples of the classic archetypes include: the Anima/Animus, the shadow, the mother, the father, the son/the maiden, the divine child, the trickster, the Great Mother, the wise old man, etc.

[20] Jung mentioned in several of his utterances the autonomous nature of archetypes, including the interview with Richard Evans: Jung, Carl Gustav. (1957). *Great Minds of the 20th Century: Dr. Carl Jung. Evans, Richard.* [Interview]. Minutes: 02:19:13/3:02:34.

[21] Roesler, Christian. (2022). *The Archetype Concept of C.G. Jung.* (Trans. by Alexander Ulyet and Christian Roesler). Chapter: 2. The classic definition and theory of Jung's concept of archetypes. 2.1. Definition.". P. 6.

[22] Cf. Neumann, Erich. (2021). *Die Große Mutter.* P. 19.

[23] Kast, Verena. (2014). *Die Tiefenpsychologie nach C.G. Jung.* Chapter: "Das Symbol".

[24] Ibid. German expression: "das sichtbare Etwas einer auch unsichtbaren, ideellen Wirklichkeit.".

[25] Ibid. German expression: "Symbole [...] geben unseren Emotionen aber auch eine Form, fassen sie.".

[26] Neumann, Erich. (2021). *Die Große Mutter*. P. 19.

A new specification of archetypes, namely the differentiated concept of the "archetype as such" was defined by Jung in 1947[27] and is described as the "[…] real nature of the archetype […]"[28], a "structure without content"[29], metaphorically explained by Jung as being alike the structure of a crystal[30]. This implies a more abstract notion of archetypes, namely that the "archetype as such" can never be fully perceived by consciousness and therefore it represents possibilities.

> "We must, however, constantly bear in mind that what we mean by archetype is in itself irrepresentable, but has effects which make visualizations of it possible, namely, the archetypal images and ideas."[31].

According to Ralf T. Vogel, this aspect of C.G. Jung's concepts is what distinguishes Jungian Psychology from other depth-psychological currents. He elucidates the importance of the prefix "un" from the word unconscious, as a key feature of the "archetype as such" and as the "place" out of where archetypes originally emerge from (the soul). The importance of this prefix would essentially reflect the core of Jung's worldview, and this characteristic of the archetypes would reveal "the secret of the soul"[32]. It explicitly indicates the polyvalent and ambivalent character of the archetypes and their paradoxical nature[33]. Consequently, their veiled character makes a clear definition challenging at times.

Ralf Vogel pledges for the importance of preserving the abstract character of the "archetype as such", and suggests, for instance, to operate with the term of "opacity", i.e., to imagine the "archetype as such" as a sort of a blurred image, charged with meaning. Methodologically, this means that its research is inseparably connected with the ancient Greek's term "aporetic", i.e., the study of the unknowable, nowadays also termed as "the research on the negative"[34]. As Vogel

---

[27] Cf. Roesler, Christian. (2024). *Deconstructing Archetype Theory.* P. 29.

[28] C.G. Jung in: Roesler, Christian. (2022). *Development of a Reconceptualization of Archetype Theory.* Report to the IAAP. P. 43.

[29] This terminology used by Jung can be seen as unspecific, to which Roesler proposes an "information theory approach". Roesler, Christian. (2024). *Deconstructing Archetype Theory.* P. 37–38.

[30] C.G. Jung. "CW Vol.9/1". Cited after: Roesler, Christian. (2022). *Development of a Reconceptualization of Archetype Theory.* Report to the IAAP. P. 43.

[31] C.G. Jung. "CW Vol. 8". Cited after: Ibid.

[32] Cf. Vogel, Ralf T. (2024). *Das Geheimnis der Seele.*

[33] Cf. Vogel, Ralf T. Personal communication (online lecture). Küsnacht/Noiraigue: April 23, 2022.

[34] Ibid. German expression: "negative Forschung".

explained, this term ought to be understood under the umbrella term of "opacity", as an epistemological research of the veiled aspect, of the "un"[35]. In turn, Christian Roesler identified a "definition chaos"[36]. Roesler has notably drawn attention to this problematic and the ethical need within the practice of psychotherapy, proposing to narrow down the concept of the archetype, *inter alia*, to understand the classical archetypes as part of a narrative process of psychological transformation[37].

Nowadays, some of C.G. Jung's lines of argument are debated, thought further, or even questioned. An extensive study in this regard and for the purpose to come to a clearer definition of archetypes was notably done by Christian Roesler[38], who suggests for instance (i) not to use the term archetypes for the inborn psychological capacities and behavioral patterns and (ii) to base upon the theory of diffusion, i.e., migration and to switch to the concept of cultural unconscious or cultural complexes, initially presented by Joseph Henderson and further proposed by Singer & Kimbles[39], rather than to continue the usage of the original term of the collective unconscious. In fact, Christian Roesler[40] has shown that within Jungian archetypal theory there are four distinct theories inherent to be acknowledged, each one based in theories of different fields (Fig. 3.1). The final conclusion drawn by Roesler is that all argumentation lines that have as a foundation biological theories or the notion of universals from cultural theories are to be regarded as highly problematic or even refuted[41]; in turn, what is defended and highly encouraged is Jung's idea of a transformational process, in which the classic archetypes are seen as the central stations of such a process[42] (Fig. 3.1). Thus,

---

[35] Cf. Ibid.

[36] Roesler, Christian. Personal communication between Christian Roesler and the author. Küsnacht: February 3, 2023.

[37] Cf. Roesler, Christian. (2024). *Deconstructing Archetype Theory.*

[38] Cf. Ibid.

[39] Cf. Ibid. P. 151. The term of cultural unconscious has been meanwhile adopted and used by different analysts, e.g., by Verena Kast. Cf. Kast, Verena. (2009). *Das sagenumwobene 'Rote Buch' von C.G. Jung—Die Psychologin Verena Kast im Gespräch mit Norbert Bischofberger.* [Interview]. Minutes: 56:18/1:01:45.

[40] Cf. Roesler, Christian. (2024). *Deconstructing Archetype Theory.*

[41] Cf. Ibid. The legitimacy of Jung's initial idea of archetypes being biologically rooted or cross-culturally existent, in the sense of human universals, will not be further discussed in this work since it would go beyond the scope of this dissertation. Important for this dissertation is the ground concept of a transformation process characterized by archetypal stages—with which the author operates—and that is well accepted.

[42] Cf. Ibid.

taking the actual state of art in Analytical Psychology, to all intents and purposes, Jung's archetypal theory remains scientifically accepted when in connection to the process of transformation (individuation)[43].

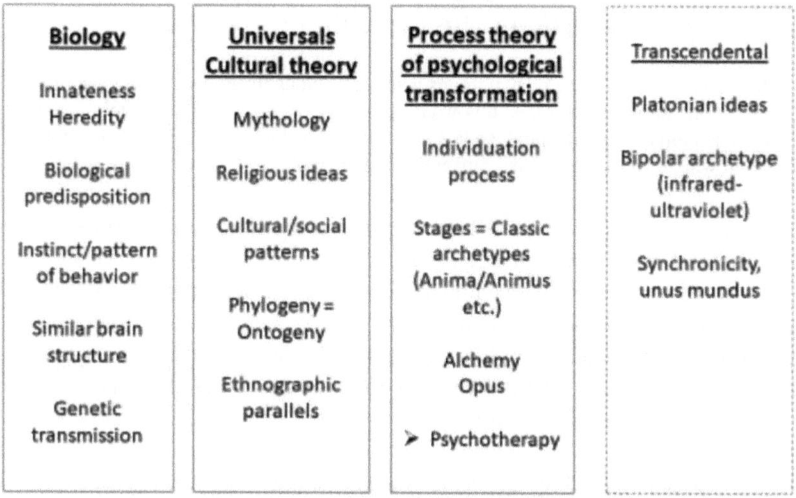

Fig. 3.1 Christian Roesler on the "four different theories inherent to archetype theory", of which the third from the left is the valid approach. (Figure and cited legend taken from: Roesler, Christian. (2022). *Development of a Reconceptualization of Archetype Theory*. P. 80)

Thus, it should be clarified, that what is relevant for the scope of this dissertation is to see how Jung's initial concept developed and generated his core concept of an inner transformation process, narrative in character, characterized by different stages with their respective archetypes—a concept which, as just seen, is accepted nowadays. This process of transformation, known as the individuation process, is indeed considered to be the main point of Jung's theory, and what makes his Analytical Psychology so distinctive and singular[44]. The idea that creativity is at the basis of the formation of personality[45] is also regarded as being particular to Jung. These ideas, that will be developed in the next chapters, are

[43] Ibid. Chapter: "Conclusions". P. 225–249.

[44] Cf. Ibid.

[45] Cf. Kast, Verena. (2009). *Das sagenumwobene 'Rote Buch' von C.G. Jung—Die Psychologin Verena Kast im Gespräch mit Norbert Bischofberger*. [Interview]. Minutes: 56:18/1:01:45., minutes: 55:55/1:01:45.

not only regarded as a substantial theory of great value in Analytical Psychology but also recommended for purposes of hermeneutical approaches[46].

3.1 The Classical Archetypes and the Narrative Characteristic in the Individuation Process

> "If the descent into one's own night leads to a conscious integration of shadow parts and a unification of opposites, this would probably be what Jung ultimately understood as individuation, a spiral, so to speak, that leads down and up at the same time and in which circular and linear movement are united."[47].

The classical Jungian theory of the archetypes is firstly to be understood within the context of, what Jung called, a "centering process"[48]. This centering process, known finally as the individuation process, is a transformational process and the ultimate goal of the unconscious, which is to move towards wholeness by integrating all parts of the psyche, including the shadow, then archetypes are organized in opposing, dualistic tensions (often addressed as the polarity of the archetypes)[49]. In Jung's own words:

> "Individuation means: becoming an individual and, insofar as we understand individuality as our innermost, ultimate and incomparable uniqueness, to become one's own Self. One could therefore also translate 'individuation' as 'self-creation' or 'self-realization'."[50].

[46] Cf. Roesler, Christian. (2024). *Deconstructing Archetype Theory.* P. 242–244.

[47] Rasche, Jörg. (2014). *Das Lied des Grünen Löwen.* P. 293. (Trans. by the author). German expression: "Wenn der Abstieg in die eigene Nacht zu einer bewussten Integration von Schattenanteilen und einer Vereinigung von Gegensätzlichem führt [...], wäre es wohl das, was Jung letztlich als Individuation verstanden hat, sozusagen eine Spirale, die gleichzeitig hinab- und hinaufführt und in der zirkuläre und lineare Bewegung vereint sind.".

[48] Roesler, Christian. (2024). *Deconstructing Archetype Theory.* P. 234.

[49] Cf. Roesler, Christian. Personal communication between Christian Roesler and the author. Basel: January 12, 2023.

[50] Jung, Carl Gustav. (2023). *Die Beziehung zwischen dem Ich und dem Unbewussten.* P. 67. (Trans. by the author) German expression: "Individuation bedeutet: zum Einzelwesen werden, und, insofern wir unter Individualität unsere innerste, letzte und unvergleichbare

This implies a model containing specific stages, to which several archetypes are attributed[51]. Jung saw this process unfolding over a lifetime (Fig. 3.2), where two distinct phases are described: (i) the first half, where the focus mainly lies in the social-realization, "detachment from parental complexes"[52], where the personas are developed and the ego is strengthened, and (ii) the second being, characterized by facing the unconscious figures within, i.e., the shadow, freeing the Anima/Animus and discovering the mana-personalities. Eugen Drewermann explains:

> "While in the first half of life the symbols of the soul have to be opened to the outer reality, in the second half of life it is the other way around, to open the entire outer reality for the symbolism of the soul"[53].

As a result, so to say, the realized Self is achieved, which often remains a utopia.

Einzigartigkeit verstehen, zum eigenen Selbst werden. Man könnte 'Individuation' darum auch als 'Verselbstung' oder als 'Selbstverwirklichung' übersetzten.".

[51] Cf. Roesler, Christian. (2022). *Development of a Reconceptualization of Archetype Theory.* Report to the IAAP. P. 49.

[52] Kast, Verena. (2014). *Die Tiefenpsychologie nach C.G. Jung*. Chapter: "Wie Individuation vor sich geht".

[53] Drewermann, Eugen. (1993). *Lieb Schwesterlein, lass mich herein.* "Vorwort". (Trans. by the author). German expression: "Während in der ersten Lebenshälfte die Symbole der Seele zur äußeren Wirklichkeit hin geöffnet werden müssen, gilt es in der zweiten Lebenshälfte umgekehrt, die gesamte äußere Wirklichkeit für den Symbolismus der Seele zu öffnen".

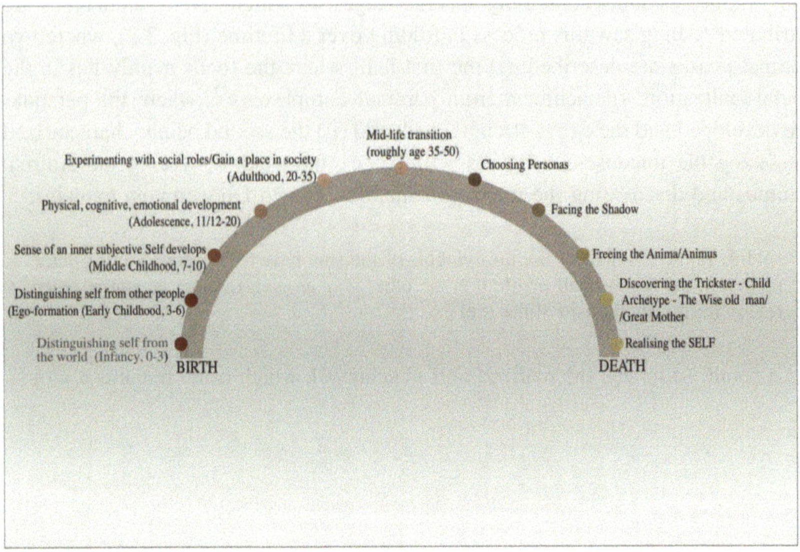

Fig. 3.2 Individuation as a lifelong process, a model of archetypal stages. (Figure taken and adapted from the Handout given at the Seminar: "Introduction to Jungian Psychology. Individuation" by Claudine Koch Morgenegg. Jung Institut Küsnacht (online broadcasted): February 12, 2022)

Complementing this idea, Verena Kast brings into attention how the individuation process is similar to the creative process[54]. This brings the insight that each creative work contains a stream of internal transformations, which carry the resonating symbolic and archetypal elements, expressed through a poetic, artistic or musical language. However: "[...] these universal factors are variable, and it is this variability which makes individual uniqueness possible"[55]. This highlights the need to consider various influential factors, particularly biographical ones, and to exercise caution when assigning fixed semantics to archetypes. The meaning can differ from person to person, and from work to work in the case of

[54] Cf. Kast, Verena. (2014). *Die Tiefenpsychologie nach C.G. Jung.* Chapter: "Wie Individuation vor sich geht".

[55] Jung, Carl Gustav. (2023). *Die Beziehung zwischen dem Ich und dem Unbewussten.* P. 68. (Trans. by the author). German expression: "[...] diese universalen Faktoren sind variable, und es ist diese Variabilität, welche individuelle Eigenart ermöglicht.".

compositions: they are constantly in motion. Consequently, the semantical interpretation of the archetypes expressed in compositions might differ from one work to the other. Only as a last step within a comparative analysis of several works of a composer, is it possible to delineate, in greater line, the development of the expression of these structures (20).

Not being a straightforward process as theoretically described in Fig. 3.2, this unfolding life-process occurs in a cyclical, spiral-like manner[56], meaning the constant return to similar situations which need to be overcome and integrated, regenerating itself again and again[57]. As mentioned in the previous chapters, this transformation process is characterized by a ground structure of collective nature, i.e., of general valid motifs of the psyche, which can be observed in narrative forms in myths, fairy tales, respectively, in programmatic compositions as well as in absolute music. There is a distinction between myths and fairy tales, namely that myths are culturally based and fairy tales non-geographically specific[58], which makes the latter the description of deeper anchored processes in the unconscious of a collective nature. From the ethnological studies, there is the evidence that fairy tales arose out of dreams, exposing in that way the evolution of the human psyche and its transformations throughout centuries[59]. Dreams as well as fairy tales are experienced and told in a psychological language through metaphors. An important observation of Jung is that these narrative forms of expression resonate within every human being (i.e., have a strong affective charge), mainly out of a subject level understanding and through the description of certain constellations, psychical situations, and their proposed solutions: "[…]

[56] Additionally to the above-mentioned quotation of Jörg Rasche, Verena Kast also makes this description. Cf. Kast, Verena. (2014). *Die Tiefenpsychologie nach C.G. Jung*. Chapter: "Wie Individuation vor sich geht". Christian Roesler also points to this characteristic. Cf. Roesler, Christian. (2016). *Das Archetypenkonzept C.G. Jungs*. Section 2.5.8. "Abschließendes zum Individuationsprozess in seiner Gesamtheit". For Jung's reference see Jung, Carl Gustav. (2014). "Psychology and Alchemy". In: *CW. Vol. 12*. (Trans. by Gerhard Adler and R.F.C. Hull). Chapter 3: "IV. The Symbols of the Self.". The same thought is described in *Traumsymbole des Individuationsprozesses*. See also: Jung, Carl Gustav. (2019). *Dream symbols of the Individuation process*. Gieser, Suzanne. (Ed.).

[57] Cf. Rasche, Jörg. (2014). *Das Lied des Grünen Löwen*. P. 293. German expression: "Es geht um einen Zyklus, in dem sich die Psyche immer wieder regeneriert, auch wenn er unbewusst durchlaufen wird.".

[58] Cf. Buser, Steven. Personal communication (online lecture). Küsnacht/Noiraigue: April 24, 2022.

[59] Cf. Roesler, Christian. Personal communication between Christian Roesler and the author. Basel: January 12, 2023.

unconscious processes stand in a compensatory relationship to consciousness"[60], which means that in a fairy tale "[…] each character is part of the personality, [namely] a component of a greater personality […]"[61].

As above mentioned, the development of the Persona (Fig. 3.3) represents an important first step in the individuation process. Etymologically persona comes from the Latin word *personare*: to speak through and is derived from the ancient Greek *prosopon*—πρόσωπον, meaning mask. It denotes how the person would like to be, which is strongly bounded to external values, e.g., society, moral values[62], etc. There is an important turning point, usually in mid-life, in which the person will have to deal with the repressed aspects of the own psyche. This generates inner movement and activates a flow of psychic energies in the ego-Self axis.

The personal shadow (Fig. 3.3), said in general terms, is understood as the antithesis of the persona and represents all aspects that are understood by the ego as "negative"—what one does not want to be, which subsequently is also strongly bounded with social and moral values of a culture, upbringing, etc[63]. These are the repressed aspects, which can split up and consequently develop a dynamic of its own[64]. The shadow is often firstly perceived as a means of projection. In addition to the personal shadow Jung speaks of a collective shadow as well, which is to be understood as the antithesis of the Self, i.e., the general malevolent tendency which seeks annihilation[65], the "[…] duality in every image of god […]"[66] and which reveals itself in the same projection-based mechanism, only in a collective dimension.

---

60 Jung, Carl Gustav. (2023). *Die Beziehung zwischen dem Ich und dem Unbewussten.* P. 72. (Trans. by the author). German expression: "[…] dass die unbewussten Vorgänge in einer kompensatorischen Beziehung zum Bewusstsein stehen".

61 Cf. Roesler, Christian. Handout "Regeln und Vorgehen bei der Märcheninterpretation—Interpretationsregeln—Deutung auf der Subjektstufe" from the seminar at the Psychologische Fakultät der Universität Basel (12.01.23): "Praxis der analytischen Psychotherapie C.G. Jungs—Methoden, Anwendung, Selbsterfahrung"—"Regeln und Vorgehen bei der Märcheninterpretation". (Trans. by the author). German expression: "Alle Figuren des Märchens sind Teilpersönlichkeiten/Anteile einer Gesamtpersönlichkeit […]".

62 Cf. Roesler, Christian. (2016). *Das Archetypenkonzept C.G. Jungs.* Section 2.5.2. "Die Persona". The Persona stands in opposition to the nature of the archetypes, which are described of being amoral.

63 Cf. Ibid. Section 2.5.3. "Der Schatten".

64 Cf. Ibid.

65 Cf. Ibid.

66 Roesler, Christian. (2022). *The Archetype Concept of C.G. Jung.* (Trans. by Alexander Ulyet and Christian Roesler). "Section 2.5.3. The Shadow". P. 26.

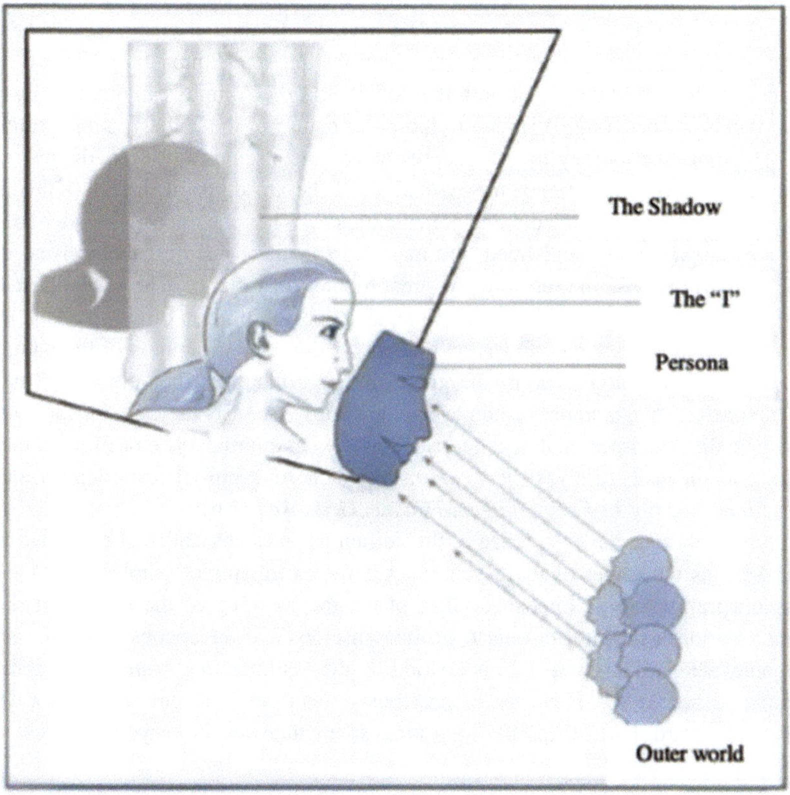

Fig. 3.3 "The 'I', the Persona and the shadow". (Picture and legend taken and adapted by the author to English from: Adam, Klaus-Uwe. (2000). *Therapeutisches Arbeiten mit Träumen.* P. 31. © 2000 Springer Verlag, Berlin Heidelberg)

After the confrontation with the shadow, there is the encounter with the so-called inner soul images, the Anima and Animus[67]. These are the opposite-gender parts of the psyche within every human being, respectively related with the feminine and masculine qualities. The Anima/Animus will "[...] act as a gateway to the deepest levels of the unconscious"[68], with the main function to be "[...] a

[67] Cf. Ibid. "Section 2.5.4. "The image of the soul: Anima and Animus". P. 26.
[68] Ibid. P. 27.

mediator between the ego and the inner world, so that the person can be conveyed between the ego and the outside world."[69]. Each soul image has its own stages of development, which are described by Jung and Emma Jung (his wife). Important to underline is that both the Anima and the Animus can embody light and darker aspects (e.g., 16), due to the polar nature of the archetypal structure.

The more the journey into the depths of the unconscious advances, the nearer the person gets to experience the expression of the archetype of the Self—this is the purpose of the so-called mana-personalities[70]. When the opposite-gender soul images are integrated and freed, the mana-personalities manifest themselves, in the form of the wise old man and the great mother for instance. The wise old man is said to represent the spiritual principle, as a "personification of the intellect, as boundless knowledge and understanding, as wisdom and awareness of the nature of being"[71]. The archetype of the great mother symbolizes the "objective truth of nature"[72], the "material principle"[73], the earthly. As it is the case for the soul images, the mana-personalities, described as the "extraordinary impactful"[74], can also contain in themselves their contrasts, which Jung himself experienced and described notably in *Erinnerungen, Träume, Gedanken* (2.6).

Lastly, there is the experience of the numinous and transcendental character of the Self, as the center of the psyche[75]. It is the expression of wholeness, where the integration of the opposites takes place, the merging of the outer and the inner world, of the subject-object, of the conscious and the unconscious, into an organic whole. This is to be understood as the "culminating point of the individuation process"[76]. However, as previously stated, these stages are not always straightforward. Part of this life-long process, include specific psychic processes

---

[69] Ibid.

[70] Mana-personalities are archetypes such as the great mother or the wise old man, that are located in close proximity to the Self. Consequently, they exert an immense power and fascination ("mana") on the "I". To integrate the mana-personalities is crucial to achieve the purpose of individuation. Cf. Ibid. Jung describes it as an "extraordinarily active power", which can be of supernatural nature. Cf. Jung, Carl Gustav. (1961). *Ma vie*. "Glossaire". P. 631.

[71] Roesler, Christian. (2022). *The Archetype Concept of C.G. Jung*. (Trans. by Alexander Ulyet and Christian Roesler). "Section: 2.5.6. The old sage and the great mother (the mana personalities)". P. 30.

[72] Ibid.

[73] Ibid. P. 31.

[74] Ibid.

[75] Cf. Ibid. Section: 2.5.7. "The Self".

[76] Cf. Ibid. "Section 2.5.8. The Individuation process". P. 36.

that may occur, e.g., inflations, regressions (Fig. 3.4, left image), *abaissement du niveau mentale* (Fig. 3.4, right image), enlargement of the personality (Fig. 3.4, left image), psychological turning points ("Enantiodromia", Fig. 3.5) symbolic deaths and symbolic rebirths, etc., all of which are considered to be part of processes of transformation[77].

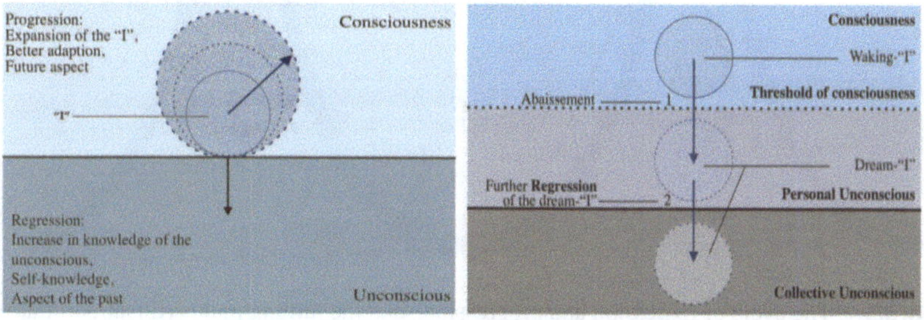

Fig. 3.4 Left image: Representation of the two energetic movements "progression" and "regression". (Picture taken and adapted by the author to English from: Adam, Klaus-Uwe. (2000). *Therapeutisches Arbeiten mit Träumen.* P. 72. © 2000 Springer Verlag, Berlin Heidelberg. Right image: Representation of the "abaissement du niveau mentale". Picture taken and adapted by the author to English from: Ibid. P. 271)

A characteristic thought of Jungian psychologists is that the "I", as the center of consciousness, emerges out of the Self[78]:

> "The Ego then, as the center of consciousness, always draws from the Self as the center of the overall psyche and is oriented and renewed from this."[79].

This point of view was further developed by Jung's disciple, Erich Neumann, who assumed that there is a fruitful connection between the center of consciousness, i.e., the ego, and the center of the whole psyche, i.e., the Self, and coined the term "Ego-Self axis". The Ego-Self axis has thus an important function, then

[77] Cf. Jung, Carl Gustav. (2011). *Four Archetypes.* These processes will be addressed directly in the analysis chapters (IV).

[78] Cf. Daniel, Renate: "Das Selbst—ein zentraler Begriff der Analytischen Psychologie". [Lecture]. Broadcasted on the 21.02.2019. Minutes: 07:12/58:28.

[79] Roesler, Christian. (2022). *The Archetype Concept of C.G. Jung.* (Trans. by Alexander Ulyet and Christian Roesler). "Section 2.5.7. The Self". P. 34.

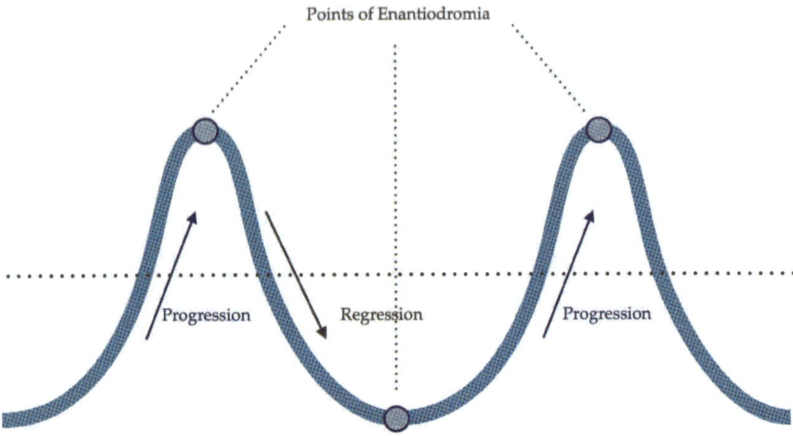

Fig. 3.5 "The cycle of regression and progression" and the turning points (Enantiodromia). (Picture and cited legend taken and adapted by the author to English from: Adam, Klaus-Uwe. (2000). *Therapeutisches Arbeiten mit Träumen*. P. 71. © 2000 Springer Verlag, Berlin Heidelberg)

it permits to establish and to maintain the contact and the exchange of psychic energies between these two worlds (Fig. 3.6).

Fig. 3.6 Relationship between the ego and the Self, where the ego-Self axis represents the unifying vector, permitting the constant exchange of psychical energies. (Figure taken and adapted from: Edinger, Edward. (1972). *Ego and Archetype*. P. 5. © 1972 C. G. Jung Foundation for Analytical Psychology, New York)

There are central archetypes, to which Jung dedicated special attention, in addition to his own experiences of the Anima and the wise old man, which among others constitute of the great mother[80], the divine child[81], the trickster[82], the Self[83] and rebirth[84], as an archetypal process. C.G. Jung's *Die Beziehung zwischen dem Ich und dem Unbewußten*[85] features Jung's main reflections on the relationship between the consciousness and the unconscious, where he discusses several psychic processes along the individuation process. These include the Persona-Shadow confrontation, the integration, respectively, appropriation of the mana-force of the soul images, and finally, the meeting with the great mana-personalities, such as the Great Mother or the wise old man.

Many of Jung's direct disciples not only applied his concepts but also developed them, contributing to new findings in archetypal manifestations; such disciples include Jolande Jacobi, Marie-Louise von Franz, Erich Neumann, *inter alia.* In addition, his wife, Emma Jung-Rauschenbach conducted research and significant contributions, particularly to the concepts of Animus in *Animus und Anima*[86] and the Grail's legend in *Die Graalslegende in psychologischer Sicht*[87]. Jolande Jacobi's reference work *Die Psychologie von C.G. Jung* presented a clear systematization of C.G. Jung's theories[88]. Marie-Louise von Franz has mainly dealt with the interpretations of fairy tales[89], dreams[90] and alchemical studies. With regard to the application of the archetypal theory from a developmental psychological perspective, Erich Neumann sees the unfolding of the human being's life subdivided into three phases, shaped by mythological motifs[91]. Phase 1 corresponds to the "creation myth" ("Schöpfungsmythos"), consisting of a threefold differentiation: "the uroboros, the great mother, the separation with the world

---

[80] Cf. Jung, Carl Gustav. (2011). *Four Archetypes.*

[81] Ibid.

[82] Ibid.

[83] Cf. Jung, Carl Gustav. (1970). *Aion.*

[84] Cf. Jung, Carl Gustav. (2011). *Four Archetypes.*

[85] Cf. Jung, Carl Gustav. (2023). *Die Beziehung zwischen dem Ich und dem Unbewussten.*

[86] Jung-Rauschenbach, Emma. (1988). *Animus und Anima.*

[87] Jung-Rauschenbach, Emma., von Franz, Marie-Louise. (1980). *Die Graalslegende in psychologischer Sicht.*

[88] Cf. Jacobi, Jolande. (2006). *Die Psychologie von C.G. Jung.*

[89] Cf. von Franz, Marie-Louise. (1995). *L'interprétation des contes de fées.*

[90] Cf. von Franz, Marie-Louise. (2014). *Dreams.*

[91] Cf. Vogel, Ralf T. (2017). *Individuation und Wandlung.* P. 65.

parents or the principle of opposition"[92]; phase 2 relates to the myth of the hero ("Heldenmythos"), composed of the birth of the hero, the mother-killing ("Muttertötung") and the father-killing ("Vatertötung") as dragon battles; Phase 3 being "the myth of the transformation" ("Wandlungsmythos"), comprising a two-fold subphase: "the prisoner and the treasure, [and] the Osiris transformation"[93]. The second phase is considered as one of the powerful archetypal processes, which is of great importance nowadays, and which narrates the hero's journey.

The work of C.G. Jung and of his close disciples have influenced further scholars. Particularly, Joseph Campbell intensively dealt with the Hero myth (Fig. 3.7). The path of the hero metaphorically narrates the inner processes taking place during the journey through the unconscious, the difficulties that need to be overcome, the split aspects of one's own personality that need to be integrated, etc.

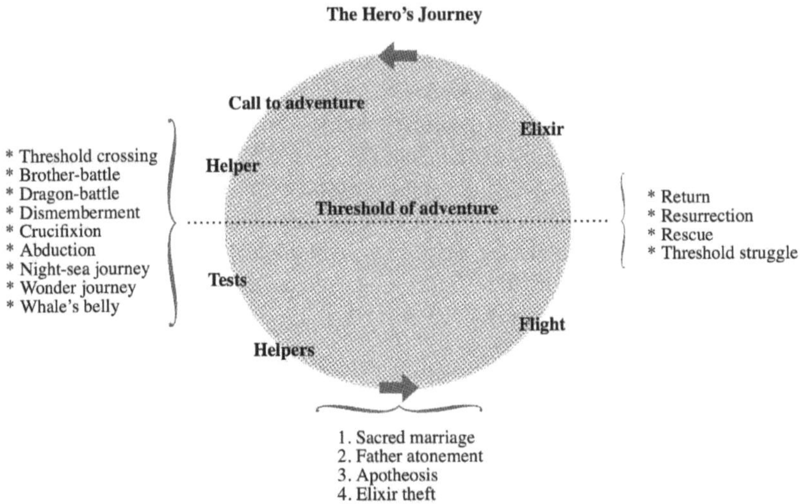

Fig. 3.7 The hero's journey and its archetypal stages. (Picture taken and adapted from: Campbell, Joseph. (2004). *The Hero with a thousand faces*. P. 227. © 2004 Princeton University Press, New Jersey)

[92] Neumann, Erich. Cited after: Ibid. "1. Der Uroboros, 2. die große Mutter, 3. die Trennung der Welteltern oder das Gegensatzprinzip".

[93] Neumann, Erich. Cited after: Ibid. German expression: "1. Die Gefangene und der Schatz, 2. Die Wandlung der Osiris".

In summary, these statements show how archetypes are to be understood as linked to the individuation process, i.e., along the unfolding and evolution of the human being's life, characterizing the different stations and the different psychological processes. This centering process is to be found narrated in a multiplicity source of what underlines a culture.

In addition to the concisely mentioned primary and secondary literature, more contemporary sources will be used as a guideline to identify archetypal stations and psychological processes later on (IV), such as Verena Kast's *Die Tiefenpsychologie nach C.G. Jung*[94], Christian Roesler's *Das Archetypenkonzept C.G. Jungs*[95] and Ralf Vogel's *Individuation und Wandlung*[96].

3.2 On Neumann's *The Great Mother*[97]: The Inner Structure of the Archetype, its Phenomenology and Impact Explained

As just seen, archetypes are considered to be structural elements from the collective unconscious psyche[98], which have a great impact on the life of every human being. By studying the inner structure of an archetype, it is possible to give more insight into their phenomenology and impact, while still preserving their concealed nature, as it was notably done by Erich Neumann[99].

---

94 Kast, Verena. (2014). *Die Tiefenpsychologie nach C.G. Jung.*

95 Roesler, Christian. (2016). *Das Archetypenkonzept C.G. Jungs.*

96 Vogel, Ralf T. (2017). *Individuation und Wandlung.*

97 This excursion seems to be valuable since Neumann's conception contributes to clarity as for the structure, phenomenology and dynamics of an archetype. Furthermore, the Great Mother archetype specifically plays an important role in Schubert's life and work. The author has used the German version of Neumann's book for the main the references. Cf. Neumann, Erich. (2021). *Die Große Mutter*. In addition, it was punctually necessary to consult the English version in order to provide the exact equivalent of the translation of technical terms. Cf. Neumann, Erich. (2015). *The Great Mother.* (Trans. by Ralph Manheim). Where applicable, the author will add in brackets the authorship of the used translation, i.e., Ralph Manheim, providing the corresponding page of the English version as well.

98 Roesler, Christian. (2016). *Das Archetypenkonzept C.G. Jungs.* Chapter 2 "Die klassische Definition und Theorie des Archetypenkonzepts bei Jung—2.1. Definition".

99 Cf. Neumann, Erich. (2021). *Die Große Mutter.*

According to Neumann, the analysis of an archetypal structure consists of the observation of its dynamics, symbolism and "material component"[100]. The dynamics of an archetype is strongly tied with an emotional component[101] and an inner autonomous will[102]; the keyword being "das Ergriffensein", i.e., being seized, awestruck or deeply moved. This feeling can be positive and/or negative. Proceeding with Neumann's expositions, there is often a group of symbols, a "symbol canon"[103] or a circle or "wreath of symbolic images"[104] around one archetype that comes forth. These, being in a "state of contamination"[105], are mutually permeable and can fuse together; therefore, this quality could explain the veiled character of an archetype. The "material component" of an archetype refers to the inner meaning of an archetype and the processing and assimilation of the same by consciousness[106]. Symbols also have in themselves an own dynamic and an own "material component", being an "energy transformer"[107], respectively, having the power "to set consciousness in motion"[108].

In the process of becoming consciously perceived, an archetype goes through several stages, going from its inconceivable core nature to their manifold symbolic manifestations, perceived by consciousness. It goes from (i) a chaos condition, wherein the four[109] polyvalent elements such as male and female

[100] Ibid. P. 20. German expression: "Inhaltliche Komponente". (Trans. by Ralph Manheim, P. 3).

[101] Cf. Ibid. P. 19.

[102] Cf. Ibid. P. 20.

[103] Ibid. P. 22. (Trans. by Ralph Manheim, P. 6).

[104] Ibid. P. 26. (Trans. by Ralph Manheim, P. 12).

[105] Ibid. P. 22. German expression: "[...] sie befinden sich im Zustande der Kontamination, der völligen wechselseitigen Durchdringung und Verschmelzung.". (Trans. by Ralph Manheim, P. 7.).

[106] Cf. Ibid. P. 20.

[107] Ibid. P. 23. (Trans. by Ralph Manheim, P. 8).

[108] Ibid. P. 23. (Trans. by Ralph Manheim, P. 17).

[109] In Jung's conception the archetype is two-poled, while in Neumann's understanding, it is four-poled. This detail represents a current discussion line in Analytical Psychology, which however, is irrelevant for this dissertation. The central aspect remains the antagonistic principle, i.e., the fact that there is a tension between opposite poles that characterizes the ambivalence or polyvalence of the archetype.

energy, positive and negative are blended together and all experienced at once (uroboric stage), (ii) to a structured inner order, where these singular elements slowly split up and come forth individually in an archetype, forming an archetypal group, to (iii) take symbolic form and forming further symbolic groups. This unfolding process corresponds to the differentiations of an archetype in distinct stages, what Neumann also termed as "Aufspaltung"[110], i.e., the splitting up of an archetype (e.g., 14). This means that out of an inconceivable archetype, different archetypes can emerge, forming a group of interrelated archetypes[111]. Parallelly and simultaneously to this process, the forthcoming of a symbol takes place. Finally, an archetypal phenomenon can be perceived as a spontaneous manifestation, or as standing in a compensatory relationship to consciousness. For the former the experience is felt independently and autonomously; for the latter, the personal complexes and the individual's typology structures play a role[112].

The psychological concept of projection is an essential part of the whole process. Two levels of projections are to be mentioned, the outer projection and the inner one[113]. With the former it is meant that the inner unconscious elements are projected to the outer world, which are perceived as such (the Hellenic Olympian world can be taken as an example); in contrast, the latter takes place in the inner world, in dreams. Dreams, in addition, contain in themselves a projection level. Due to that reason, the dreamworld is sensed as external to the dreamer[114]. Projections communicate an important fact since they narrate the inner-outer world relationship and how archetypes are perceived. Thus, the developmental process described above refers to the inner rising up to consciousness, a movement from an archetypal stage to the symbolic language: how a person initially perceives the world mythologically within the primordial unity, i.e., without the separation subject-object, respectively, inner-outer world, and moves towards consciousness, where these inner elements are seen, from the subject's perspectives, as objects, and are put externally, as elements belonging to the outer world[115]. A further important aspect to note during this process is the tension that exists between the unconscious, i.e., between the archetypal structures with their own

[110] Ibid.

[111] Cf. Neumann, Erich. (2021). *Die Große Mutter*.

[112] Cf. Ibid. P. 25.

[113] Also Jacobi elucidates the difference of the two types of projections. Cf. Jacobi, Jolande. (2006). *Die Psychologie von C.G. Jung*.

[114] Cf. Neumann, Erich. (2021). *Die Große Mutter*. P. 34.

[115] Cf. Ibid. P. 30, respectively, P. 34 and P. 36.

poly-ambivalent microcosmos (whereby each archetype fulfills a particular function) and consciousness with its corresponding projections[116]. These archetypal structures have a significant impact on the human being who is experiencing them.

One of the primordial experiences of the human being is the archetype of the great mother, as C.G. Jung discovered. Neumann dealt with this archetype in depth and particularly, explained its origins and development, in the sense described above, and as the image below illustrates (Fig. 3.8).

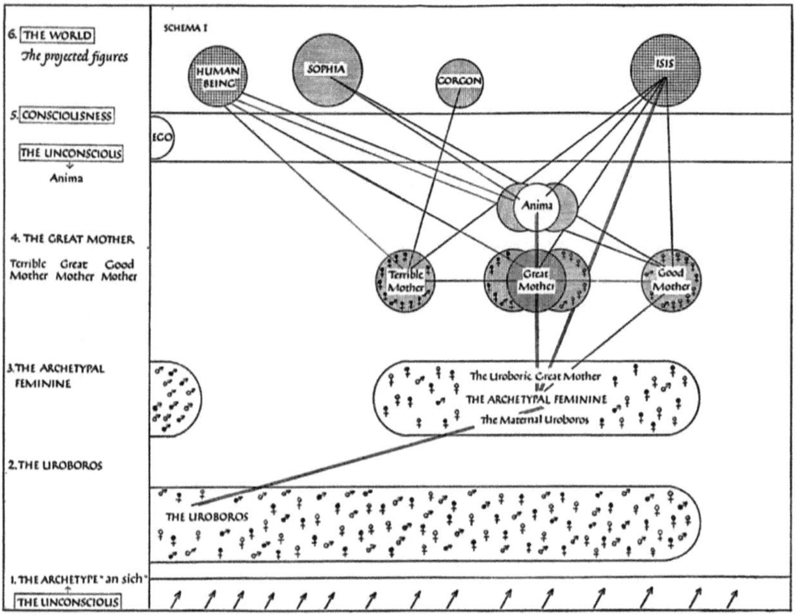

Fig. 3.8 The archetypal Feminine and its stages of development. Figure retrieved from: Neumann, Erich. (2015). *The Great Mother.* [Illustration between P. 18–19]. © 2015 Princeton University Press, New Jersey

[116] Cf. Ibid. P. 41.

As Neumann explains with this illustration, it becomes clear that prior to the formation of the great mother archetype there is the undifferentiated stage of the great female, also known as "the motherly uroboros" and the "uroboric mother", which in turn emerges from the original uroboros state and the inconceivable "archetype as such". From this stage it is deduced that the inner structure of the psyche is, psychologically speaking, primordially hermaphroditic, whereupon Neumann clarifies that this fact "enables an own experience of the opposite gender"[117]. In this case, its further development consists of the splitting up and the emerging of the inner soul image Anima, which is then projected. For the purpose of this dissertation and for the time being, it suffices to note that: (i) The essence of the female is considered to contain two "ordering principles"[118], the so-called "elementary character"[119] and "transformative character"[120], (ii) these are omnipresent, although one character might dominate over the other, respectively, be recessive, depending on the situation; (iii) this subdivision explains the double nature of the mother archetype and how the mother archetype and the Anima figure are interwoven in each other. The transformative potential, conceded to the Anima, can be understood in Jungian terms as the origins of creativity[121]. The following scheme of Neumann illustrates this statement (Fig. 3.9).

[117] Ibid. P. 39. German expression: "Das Vorhandensein gegengeschlechtlicher innerer Instanzen, die jede menschliche Struktur psychologisch als hermaphroditisch erscheinen lässt, ermöglicht aber auch gerade eine innere ‚Eigenerfahrung' des Gegengeschlechts.".

[118] Ibid. P. 50. German expression: "Ordnungsprinzipien". (Trans. by Ralph Manheim, P. 38).

[119] Ibid. P. 40. German expression: "Elementarcharakter". (Trans. by Ralph Manheim, P. 25).

[120] Ibid. P. 43. German expression: "Wandlungscharakter". (Trans. by Ralph Manheim, P. 24).

[121] This is especially the case when the Anima aspects are integrated in the personality (e.g., 16).

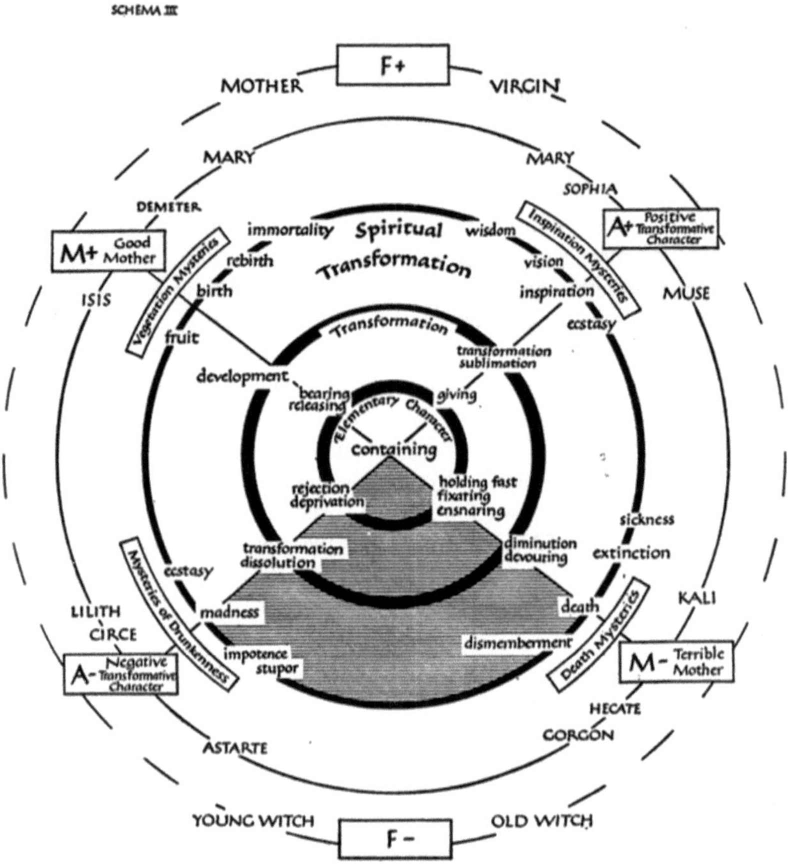

Fig. 3.9 The poles of the archetypal Feminine. Figure retrieved from: Neumann, Erich. (2015). *The Great Mother.* [Illustration between P. 82–83]. © 2015 Princeton University Press, New Jersey

Neumann's scheme shows four main poles, each of them with their respective representative archetype, and several circular stages in the development, being the spiritual change (the third circle) the highest developmental phase[122]. It shows how the dynamics of this archetype and its inherent potential undergoes the

[122] Neumann, Erich. (2021). *Die Große Mutter*. P. 85.

so-called "phenomenon of reversal"[123], i.e., a turnover phenomenon. In C.G. Jung, this phenomenon is described under the term of Enantiodromia[124]. Each archetype exerts a power over the conscious "I", which is therefore also in danger. When approaching one of the poles, the "I" might have no capabilities of differentiation[125] and the turnover can happen: "the pole is not only an endpoint but a 'turning point'"[126]. As an example, the abyss or the void as a symbolic expression can generate a new creative beginning[127].

In short, based on what has been outlined about Neumann's writings on the structure of archetypes, their phenomenology, and their impact it can be said that archetypes are initially primordial psychological elements and experiences of abstract nature, that during the evolution from the unconscious state to consciousness, i.e., from the chaos state to order, become structured. This means that they gain form and/or shape, while still preserving in themselves their opposites and poly-ambivalent essence. Their manifestations go from an undifferentiated state of emotions to differentiated archetypal and symbolic elements, which due to their uroboric primordial nature are split into an archetypal group and symbolic canon[128]. They can be experienced in a spontaneous (creative) act, or be a matter of projections, due to their self-regulatory mechanism. The latter reflects a compensatory relationship between the unconscious and consciousness. An archetypal experience can be perceived by the person involved in them as a ("numinous")

---

[123] Ibid. P. 83. German expression: "Umschlagsphänomen". (Trans. by Ralph Manheim, P. 75).

[124] Roesler, Christian. Personal communication between Christian Roesler and the author. Freiburg im Breisgau: June 18, 2024. The definition of Enantiodromia is to be found in: Cf. Jung, Carl Gustav. (2013). *Kleines Lexikon der Analytischen Psychologie.*

[125] Cf. Neumann, Erich. (2021). *Die Große Mutter*. P. 83.

[126] Ibid. P. 84. German expression: "Der Pol ist nicht nur ein Endpunkt, sondern auch ein 'Wendepunkt'". (Trans. by Ralph Manheim, P. 76).

[127] As it will be examined later, this phenomenon is to be observed in many of Schubert's works. The void is often expressed as a result of the musical rhetoric figure *aposiopesis.* Often, after such a musical phenomenon, the "I" sets out into another realm (IV), what in Jungian terms is translated as Enantiodromia.

[128] With that distinction it should be emphasized that an archetypal group still belongs to the unconscious sphere, whereas a symbolic canon includes a group of images that have already risen from the unconscious state into consciousness. In an analytical procedure, the symbolic canons are subject of examination through the amplification method, mentioned before (2.6).

transformation. This can lead to living, in a quite unexpected and unforeseen way, the state of wholeness. These primordial images are described to especially emerge in specific life phases, shaping the own individuation process. Therefore, they reflect a narrative character, which can be found expressed in what grounds a specific culture, namely in fairy tales, legends and myths, literary and art works, in science, films and music.

4 Nature and the Creative Psyche: Nature as Bearer of all Archetypes that Propels to Create

One significant philosophical source of inspiration to the development of Jung's concept of the psyche, which was consciously spared to address only in this chapter due to its thematic content, is to be attributed to Schelling's *Naturphilosophie.* Verena Kast refers that Schelling's thoughts impacted him significantly, especially the idea of "nature and spirit as an entity"[1], which would be found reflected in Jung's concept of the Self[2] and which will be a matter of closer observation in this chapter.

This chapter will be about the relation between the artist, respectively the composer, and nature, being nature a primary source of inspiration, which has an impact on the creative process. For this purpose, this chapter will comprise a short excursion through the historic periods and its philosophic and aesthetic components that shaped that relationship. A special emphasis will be put on the romantic period, as this dissertation relates to Schubert. As nature and the creative human psyche stand in a direct relationship, the creative process will be analyzed through the Jungian perspective, taking into consideration the intrinsic relationship of nature and the archetypes in the creative process.

Nature, the human being and creativity stand in a direct relationship to each other, which has always been a matter of constant philosophical, aesthetic and artistic involvement. It can be seen as a primary source of inspiration for the human being and as a poetic stimulus for artists and composers: nature animates the spirit, the fantasy, and excites the imagination. It acts in the psyche as the connecting element of a primordial, poetic and enlivening essence between the

[1] Kast, Verena. (2009). *Das sagenumwobene 'Rote Buch' von C.G. Jung—Die Psychologin Verena Kast im Gespräch mit Norbert Bischofberger*. [Interview]. Minutes: 22:20/1:01:45.
[2] Cf. Ibid.

L. Dill, *Schubert's Metamorphoses*,
https://doi.org/10.1007/978-3-662-73476-6_4

antagonistic forces, the inner and outer world, the light and shadow, the conscious and the unconscious.

Long before the development of civilizations, prehistoric humans had a particular relationship to nature. Not only was the path leading to the caves of great symbolic value, as described by Erich Neumann[3], but so was the changing of environments: the going from the inside of a cave to the outside world, into nature. This transition "might have functioned as a passage from one [under]world to another [the surface]"[4]. The inside of a cave was possibly a place that enabled a special connection with the unconscious forces, a place for the practice of rites, but conceivably also for creative expression. This relationship between prehistoric individuals and nature is thus accompanied by a self-reliant creativity, which is particularly to be acknowledged with the appearance of *Homo Sapiens* in the European continent: "An exceptional artistic development"[5] is noted specifically during the Aurignacian period (ca. 43 000–29 000 bp), due to the first rock painting vestiges found in caves, notably on French soil[6]. However, not only rock paintings, mammoth ivory sculptures (as the one of the Venus figure) are part of their forms of creative expression, but it is believed that the origins of music could be traced back to the so-called "cave dwellers" as well (5). Thereby, their relationship to nature and creativity is remarkable. Not only the discovered painted rock images could be a means of establishing a mystical connection with the soul of animals[7], but music, as well as dance, might have been all part of certain rituals, revealing the artistic facet of the prehistoric tribes.

> "They [were] hunter-gatherers, and are thought to have been animists, i.e., people who were in constant dialogue with nature, with animals, plants and even with stones—this means that everything has a spirit and [they] dialoged with it. For these groups, everything is intertwined, the sacred with the profane [...]. Music could accompany the rites, so why not totemic, shamanic rites, the relationship with the spirits, etc. And

[3] The path in itself with all its different shadows in meaning (the ritual path, the suffering path, the fateful path, etc.) are considered to be an archetype. Cf. Neumann, Erich. (2021). *Die Große Mutter*. P. 23.

[4] Goblot, Pascal. (2020). *Sapiens, et la musique fut*. Pérès, Guillaume (Producer). [Documentary]. (Trans. by the author). French expression: "Au sortir de la grotte les sons de la nature reprennent vie. Aux oreilles de *Sapiens* ce brusque changement sonore a peut-être fonctionné comme un passage d'un monde à un autre.". Minutes: 13:54/52:13.

[5] Ibid. (Trans. by the author). French expression: "C'est un moment d'un développement artistique exceptionnel". Minutes: 05:29/52:13.

[6] Cf. Ibid.

[7] Cf. Ibid.

so there is a dialogue with the walls [of the caves] because the walls are inhabited by spirits, by animals, by spirits of the ancients, and so on."[8].

Another example can be found in ancient Greece: Aristotle in his philosophical conception believed that the human being carries inside a goal and a purpose[9] and that through interaction with the perception of senses, the human being is propelled to create. For the ancient Greeks, the origins of music came from the gods—notably Apollo and Athene, followed by Hermes—who created the first instruments, cithara, aulos, zither, shawm and later the syrinx[10]. Gods, who in fact were projections of the population's unconscious, incorporated the force of nature outside and the creative nature inside. For the Romans, music was the result of the echo phenomena in the mountains, a place inhabited by satyrs, nymphs and fauns, who played their string and flute instruments at night[11]. In this way, the "sound experiences [were lived as] mysterious reverberations in the lonely nature, [and] led to fantasies about mystical beings [...]"[12]. Further reports between the relation of nature and a form of creative expression are to be found in other ancient mythologies[13].

---

[8] Serge Maury. In: Ibid. (Trans. by the author). French expression: "Ce sont des chasseurs-cueilleurs, dont on pense que ce sont des animistes, c'est-à-dire des gens qui était en dialogue permanent avec la nature, avec aussi bien les animaux, les plantes, mais même les pierres—c'est-à dire: tout a un esprit et on dialogue avec. Pour ces groupes là tout est imbriqué l'un dans l'autre, le sacré avec le profane [...]. Si bien, que la musique pouvait accompagner les rites, alors pourquoi pas des rites totémisme, chamaniques, la relation avec les esprits, etc., et donc, il y a un dialogue avec la paroi, parce que les parois sont habitées par les esprits, les animaux, par les esprits des anciens, etc.". Minutes: 32:45/52:13.

[9] Cf. Weischedel, Wilhelm. (1988). *Die philosophische Hintertreppe.*

[10] Cf. Schlesinger, Max. (1967). *Symbolik in der Tonkunst.* P. 20.

[11] This description is to be found in the 4th book of *De rerum natura* by the Roman philosopher Lucretius. Cf. Sorgner, Stefan Lorenz., Schramm, Michael. (2010). *Musik in der antiken Philosophie.* P. 222.

[12] Ibid. P. 222–223. (Trans. By the author). German expression: "Klangerlebnisse, ein geheimnisvoller Hall in der einsamen Natur, führten demnach zu Phantasien über mystische Wesen [...]".

[13] For a further short exemplification, the epic stories of *Kalevala* from Scandinavian mythology, relates how the hero and musician Vaïnämöinen makes a "Kantele" (a national Finnish string folk instrument) out of a jaw of a big mythical creature and enchants with his playing and singing all nature and living creatures around him.

Evolving in time—in the Renaissance period, Paracelsus believed that "[Nature] is within the human being as well as it is outside"[14]. Jung, who dealt with Paracelsus' texts, explained:

> "It is like a mirror, and this consists of four elements, for in the elements the microcosmos is reflected"[15].

Two of these elements are from the upper sphere (heaven) and the other two from the under sphere (earth). Each of these four main elements are associated with so-called creatures without spirit. Thus, the mountains created the gnomes, the water the undines, the fire the salamanders and the air the elves.

According to Jung's own studies, the unconscious of the "primitive men" carries an "[...] insurmountable urge to assimilate all external sensory experiences as psychical events [...]"[16], and thus, they take "[...] objective experiences [as] symbolic expressions of the inner and unconscious drama of the soul [...]"[17]. These processes, which are perceived by the senses of the human being, i.e., by its conscious mind, are symbolically expressed projections of their unconscious psyche, which Jung called the "mythicized processes of nature"[18]. Herein lies one of Jung's statements as of the importance of a symbolic life for the human being, namely the meaning of symbols:

---

[14] Paracelsus. Cited after: Jung, Carl Gustav. (2011). *Über das Phänomen des Geistes in Kunst und Wissenschaft*. P. 37. (Trans. by the author). German expression: "[Natur] ist im Menschen und außerhalb. Sie ist wie ein Spiegel, und dieser besteht aus den vier Elementen, denn in den Elementen spiegelt sich der Mikrokosmos.".

[15] Ibid. German expression: "Sie ist wie ein Spiegel, und dieser besteht aus den vier Elementen, den in den Elementen spiegelt sich der Mikrokosmos.".

[16] Jung, Carl Gustav. (2020). *Archetypen. Urbilder und Wirkkräfte des Kollektiven Unbewussten*. P. 10. (Trans. by the author). German expression: "An einer objektiven Erklärung der offenkundigen Dinge liegt dem Primitiven zunächst wenig, dagegen hat er ein unabweisbares Bedürfnis, oder besser gesagt, hat seine unbewusste Seele einen unüberwindlichen Drang, alle äußere Sinneserfahrung an seelisches Geschehen zu assimilieren.".

[17] Ibid. (Trans. by the author). German expression: "Alle mythisierten Naturvorgänge, [...] sind nichts weniger als Allegorien eben dieser objektiven Erfahrungen, sondern vielmehr symbolische Ausdrücke für das innere und unbewusste Drama der Seele, welches auf dem Wege der Projektion, das heißt gespiegelt in den Naturereignissen, dem menschlichen Bewusstsein fassbar wird.".

[18] Ibid.

> "Their function is to play a psychological mediatory and transitional role through which they can add to the personality of an individual and point attention to another position which may help to resolve an individual's conflict"[19].

In this line of thought, the outside natural processes only carry true meaning if they are found to be mirrored in the inner reality ("Wirklichkeit") of the soul[20].

For Jung, the unconscious is to be found symbolically expressed through the archetypes, which in turn, he links to the inner urge, a force of nature[21]. Kast explains: "creativity [is] an instinct, the most essential instinct of the human being"[22]. Jung stated how the human psyche, more precisely "[…] the unconscious […] is like Nature itself—prodigiously conservative, and yet transcending her own historical conditions in her acts of creation."[23]. Accordingly, the influence of nature on the artists lies in an intrinsic relationship with the depths of the human soul, the unconscious mind, which searches and propels the whole expression of the spirit in the creative work. In other words, nature can be understood as the bearer and creator of all archetypes, the fundamental carrier of the creative energy.

Nature is more than just what is immediately apparent through a sensing experience of the outer world; it also includes the soul's inner images, as the Norwegian expressionist painter Edvard Munch thought[24]. In a similar sense Jung stated: "[…] when you observe yourself within; you see moving images, a world of images; generally known as fantasies. […]"[25]. These fantasies were considered by Jung to be facts and manifestations of nature and its creative energy, which in turn, resides within the human being, i.e., the archetypes: "[…] when you observe the streams of images within, you observe an aspect of the world;

[19] Casement, Ann. (2001). *Carl Gustav Jung*. P. 1.

[20] Similarly, in the Hellenic period, the Greeks placed the inner gods "outside" in order to cope with the discrepancies between the nature inside and the tragedies of the real, "outer" world.

[21] Cf. Gieser, Suzanne. (2005). *The Innermost Kernel*.

[22] Kast, Verena. (1974). *Kreativität in der Psychologie von C.G. Jung*. P. 126. (Trans. by the author). German expression: "[…] das Schöpferische [ist] ein Instinkt, der wesentlichste Instinkt im Menschen.".

[23] Jung, Carl Gustav. "CW. Vol. 8". Cited after: Gieser, Suzanne. (2005). *The Innermost Kernel*. P. 215.

[24] Cf. Munch, Edvard., Langaard, J.H., Revol, R. (1963). *Edvard Munch: malerier og grafik*.

[25] Jung, Carl Gustav. (1957). *Great Minds of the 20th Century: Dr. Carl Jung. Evans, Richard.* [Interview]. Minutes: 19:11/3:02:34.

of the world within."[26]. Verena Kast, in *Kreativität in der Psychologie von C.G. Jung*, brings into attention Jung's thought that nature processes are metaphors of the inner processes of the psyche and within this context, that the "creative process is a process of nature"[27]. Thereafter, nature can be seen as the unifying element between the individual's inner world, his interaction with the outer world and its expression in artistic works, respectively in musical compositions: it is a conciliatory and self-regulatory component of the psyche.

Intuitively and in a direct manner, the artist can grasp the essence of nature, its deepest secrets[28] and all that surrounds him. Through the inner interchange of antagonistic forces, this direct experience relates to the primordial absolute or to the "world soul" ("Weltseele")[29], i.e., read in Jungian terms, to the primordial wholeness, subsequently and spontaneously expressed in the artistic work and musical compositions.

4.1 Relationship Between Music and Nature

When the influence of nature on the composer, along the history of music, is taken into consideration, it is noticeable that its way of expression had undergone a natural transformation through the cultural unconscious, which is interrelated with the historical, philosophical and aesthetic demands of each historic period. Nature is capable to enliven and evoke feelings, and in this sense, nature also inhabits the inside of the human being and is part of the psyche.

Early in music history the composer sought to convey musically the descriptive aspect of nature[30] and its influence on the affects of the human being. The tradition of the doctrine of the affects (6) is already to be noted in medieval and renaissance scholars and artists, notably "through the art of the madrigal,

---

26 Ibid. Minutes: 20:35/3:02:34.

27 Kast, Verena. (1974). *Kreativität in der Psychologie von C.G. Jung*. P. 126. (Trans. by the author). German expression: „[Für Jung ist] der schöpferische Prozess ein Naturprozess, […]".

28 Cf. The several quotations of Gustav Mahler in Floros, Constantin. (2016). *Gustav Mahler I: Die geistige Welt Gustav Mahlers in systematischer Darstellung*. P. 142–143.

29 These terms refer to Schelling's treatise "Von der Weltseele" (1798), which not only characterized his ideas of the "Naturphilosophie" but significantly impacted Romanticism, as Kremer explains. Cf. Kremer, Detlev. (2007). *Romantik*. Chapter: "Philosophische und wissenschaftliche Aspekte der Romantik". P. 61.

30 Prehistoric humans are believed to have imitated the sound of nature and animals. Cf. Goblot, Pascal. (2020). *Sapiens, et la musique fut*. Pérès, Guillaume (Producer). [Documentary].

both in literature (Petrarca) and in music"[31]—and can be traced back to the ancient Greek's concept of *Ethos*[32] (5.1). For this purpose, stylization, mimesis and madrigalism had a central role as a compositional tool. Through these musical elements, composers sought to reproduce nature musically, to tone-paint the movement which is to be found in nature. In other words, they sought to put in music the phenomena of nature[33], e.g., the singing of the bird, the rustling of water or leaves, the whispering of the wind, the sunrise, etc. and consequently through these elements to transmit the related affect such as for example the act of quivering from the cold in Vivaldi's winter concerto from *The four Seasons.* All these natural processes are metaphors for the affects and state of spirit[34]. Johann Mattheson believed that music was rooted in the orderly laws of nature[35]: "[…] of the sun, moon and stars: God orders them so, that they do not have to go in any other way."[36]; "[…] that the art of music draws its water from the well of nature, and not from the puddles of arithmetic."[37]. For Mattheson the rhetoric musical figures were a means to transmit the state of mind in instrumental music[38]. These rhetoric figures, as well as key characteristics, etc., had become elements part of the cultural unconscious, having subsequently an immense influence on future composers (6.2).

31 Correspondence between Barbara Dobretsberger and the author. Salzburg/Noiraigue: August 26, 2023.

32 For the purpose of this chapter, the emphasis will be put on the element of nature and its influence on artistic expression, especially in music. Therefore, a more detailed exposition of the concept of music as expression and as a language with the correspondent historic background will be presented in Part II.

33 Heinrich Ignaz Franz Biber's (1690–1644) sonata for violin solo, the so-called *Representatio avium* in A major can be taken as an example.

34 This tone painting technique prevailed and influenced future composers. As one example Schubert's song "Der stürmische Morgen" from *Winterreise* shall be cited. Cf. Correspondence between Barbara Dobretsberger and the author. Salzburg/Noiraigue: August 26, 2023. Here, the feelings of the subject, who appropriates the properties or qualities of nature, are painted in the sky as he sings: "My heart beholds heaven/painted its own imagery—/ It is nothing but the winter / the winter cold and wild.". (Trans. by the author). German expression: "Mein Herz sieht an dem Himmel, /Gemalt sein eignes Bild—/ Es ist nichts als der Winter, /Der Winter kalt und wild.".

35 Cf. Mattheson, Johann. (2020). *Der vollkommene Capellmeister*.

36 Ibid. P. 17. "Vorrede". (Trans. by the author). German expression: "[…] von Sonn, Mond und Sternen: Gott ordnet sie, dass sie nicht anders gehen müssen […]".

37 Ibid. P. 26. German expression: "[…] dass die Tonkunst aus dem Brunnen der Natur ihr Wasser schöpfet; und nicht aus den Pfützen der Arithmetik.".

38 Cf. Ibid. P. 211–126/127 §45.

In classicism the beauty of the rural resided in its innocence, in the simplicity and sublimity, bounded with an airiness and lightness, cheerfulness and irony, which, for instance, is illustrative of Haydn's heroic pastoral style[39]. The following subchapters will explain how this relationship developed in Romanticism, starting with the "Sturm und Drang" movement in literature, which preceded the romantic epoch.

4.2 Nature in the "Sturm und Drang" and the Concept Of Genius in Relation to the Collective Unconscious

> "Were the eye not of the sun, how could we behold light? If God's might and ours were not one, how could His work enchant our sight?"[40].

The above cited poem of Goethe, written in the "Sturm und Drang" period, speaks not only of an "outer" nature, but of the connection with the one "within". It is to be noted that the "Sturm und Drang" epoch, which preceded and shaped the romantic period and ideals, is particularly characterized by the concept of genius. According to Grimm, the genius is "the inner divine voice of the heart, which can reveal secrets"[41]. In this context, Verena Kast speaks of the force of nature being the creative force, which the genius carries within him[42]. Relating the divine with Jung's concept of the Self, the genius within the artist and composer can be understood as the manifestation of a transcendent force and wisdom. There are other authors who associate the nature of the genius with the world within. According to Helmut Schanze, the genius is considered to be the one "[...] who walks the way inwards, [and] has past, present and future within him; [...]"[43].

---

[39] Cf. Rosen, Charles. (1997). *The Classical style: Haydn, Mozart, Beethoven.* Part III: "Haydn from 1770 to the death of Mozart"—. Chapter 2 "Symphony".

[40] Goethe, Wolfgang. (1988). *Gedichte und Epen I.* P. 367. German expression: "Wär' nicht das Auge sonnenhaft, Die Sonne könnt' es nie erblicken; Läg' nicht in uns des Gottes eigne Kraft, Wie könn' uns Göttliches entzücken!".

[41] Kast, Verena. (1974). *Kreativität in der Psychologie von C.G. Jung.* P. 28. Kast refers to Grimm's definition of genius being "the inner divine voice of the heart, which can reveal secrets". (Trans. by the author). German expression: "Der Genius ist nach dem Grimm'schen Wörterbuch 'eine göttliche Stimme im Herzen, die uns Geheimes offenbaren kann'".

[42] Cf. Ibid.

[43] Schanze, Helmut. (2018). *Erfindung der Romantik.* P. 135. (Trans. by the author). German expression: "[Das Genie], das den Weg nach Innen beschreitet, hat in sich Vergangenheit, Gegenwart und Zukunft; [...]".

Thus, the artist enters in, what nowadays is called, the state of flow, namely the artist becomes one with nature, one with him-Self and with the artistic work. Psychologically said, the artist transcends, so to speak, his own ego, even his own time, by touching the realm of the unknown which carries a transcendental knowledge, connected with the collective unconscious and ultimately with the Self. When this happens, the "[…] two realms […are] united by what Jung termed the transcendent function […]"[44] and consequently wholeness is reached, i.e., the expression of the Self. In this way, the artist (re)creates the primordial feeling of wholeness and undergoes with each work a path of individuation. In sum, a new dimension is urged: the composer's inner world[45].

4.3 Romanticism: Nature and Psyche as an Entity

> "Music is nothing else than the archetypal rhythm of nature and of the universe itself, that, by the means of this art, breaks through into the represented world"[46].

Historically speaking, the exact time frame of the so-called Romantic period is a delicate matter still today. The main reason might lie in the considerable divergences in definitions in the fields of literature, art history and music, all of which mutually influenced each other. It is apparent that this difficulty lies not only in the time fixation but extents to the terminology "romanticism" itself, for instance, the understanding of the term as (i) "historic time-bounded" or, in contrary, as a "timeless-typological" phenomenon, (ii) with philosophic-aesthetical relation to the literary early Romantics (as defended by Dahlhaus or Rummenhöller) or in contrary without any relation to them and as "the immediate emotional impact of a music (the factor 'mood') or/and the means used by its creator for

[44] Casement, Ann. (2001). *Carl Gustav Jung*. P. 2.

[45] Michael Tilson Thomas mentions this fact in close relation to Beethoven. Cf. Tilson Thomas, Michael. (2004). *Keeping score. Ludwig van Beethoven: Eroica.* [Documentary]. Halvorson, Gary (Director). Minutes: 1:51:39. Last accessed 12.08.22 at 15:19.

[46] Schelling, Friedrich Wilhelm Joseph. Cited after: Wehnert, Martin. (2016). "Romantik und romantisch". In: Laurenz Lütteken (Ed.). *MGG Online*. Section III: "Problemfelder". 2. "Musik aus romantischer—Romantik aus musikalischer Sicht.". (Trans. by the author). German expression: "Die Musik [ist] nichts anderes als der urbildliche Rhythmus der Natur und des Universums selbst, der mittelst dieser Kunst in der abgebildeten Welt durchbricht.".

this psychologization (e.g., E. Kurth 'romantic harmony')"[47]. As Charles Rosen states:

> "The history of Romanticism is—to a far greater extent than the history of any other artistic or philosophical movement—a history of redefinitions."[48].

These redefinitions are mainly based in "progressively changing [ideals]"[49], as he later explains. Additionally, this fact can be seen as a result of the stylistic pluralism that existed, as already debated among art historians. The *conditio sine qua non* of every so-called romantic artist, as Klebe elucidates, consisted of developing a style characterized by individual, personal attributes[50], which made a generalist attribution to the artistic movement in question difficult. In literature the term Romanticism in the sense of an intellectual movement and a spiritual basic attitude can be found quite often, with its fundamentals lying initially in Schlegel, specifically in a fragment out of the *Athenaeum*[51].

Undoubtedly, the historic, political events, as the philosophic ideals and aesthetic premises of a specific time in history had their impact in the emergence of the respective artistic movements:

> "Like every other movement, Romanticism started as an opposition to what had existed just before it."[52].

Therefore, it can be understood as a reaction to the Enlightenment ideals. The directness of emotion takes up a central expression in Romanticism, and the psychic unconscious phenomena flew directly into the work of art.

---

[47] Wehnert, Martin. (2016). "Romantik und romantisch". In: Laurenz Lütteken (Ed.). *MGG Online*. Martin Wehnert in his *MGG Online Article* delineates the main problems related to this debate. (Trans. by the author). German expression: "Romantisch meint hier zum einen die unmittelbare emotionale Wirkungsstärke einer Musik (den Faktor 'Stimmung') oder/und die von ihrem Schöpfer zu dieser Psychologisierung verwendeten Mittel (z.B. bei E. Kurth ‚romantische Harmonik'; s.u.).".

[48] Rosen, Charles., Zerner, Henri. (1984). *Romanticism and Realism*. P. 16.

[49] Ibid. P. 22. Original expression: " […] it is not a definable ideal but a progressively changing one that can never be completely realized.".

[50] Cf. Klebe, Giselher: "Die Traumata der Neuen Musik". In: Wehnert, Martin. (2016). "Romantik und romantisch". In: Laurenz Lütteken (Ed.). *MGG Online.*

[51] Cf. Wehnert, Martin. (2016). "Romantik und romantisch". In: Laurenz Lütteken (Ed.). *MGG Online.*

[52] Rosen, Charles., Zerner, Henri. (1984). *Romanticism and Realism*. P. 23.

The end of the 18th century and the beginning of the 19th century was a time of great turmoil in Europe, which brought along "[...] a change in the intellectual life of revolutionary character"[53]. In this context, the wars, e.g., the Napoleonic wars, and other state political events are to be mentioned. It was the period when industrial and mechanical production and locomotion were developing and consequently nature offered the artist a refuge, a gateway to freedom and to eternity[54]. There was a growing interest in the Middle Ages, the ruins, obscurity and darkness that characterizes it, as well as the adventurous spirit[55], and it includes the fascination by alchemy and wizardry[56]. This fascination, which was probably driven by a collective archetypal instinct, would be acting as a compensation of the zeitgeist[57]. Psychologically speaking, and also taking the historical events into account, this period strongly advocated listening to the "inner dialogue[s]"[58], as Jörg Rasche states. Furthermore, he says that "the human being discovers himself, with his shadow, as an 'I'"[59].

The term Romantic implies the expression of the emotions, the fantastic, the veiled[60], but etymologically from the French *romant* or *roman* also the popular

---

53 Wehnert, Martin. (2016). "Romantik und romantisch". In: Laurenz Lütteken (Ed.). *MGG Online*. German expression: "[...] kam es im späteren 18. Jahrhundert zu einem Wandel des Geisteslebens mit revolutionärem Charakter.".

54 Cf. Ackroyd, Peter. (2011). The romantics—Nature. Sam Hobkinson (Director, Producer). [Documentary]. Minutes: 01:50/58:06.

55 Cf. Werner-Jensen, Arnold., Ratte, Franz-Joseph., Ernst, Manfred. (2001). *Das Reclambuch der Musik*. P. 202.

56 Cf. Kremer, Detlev. (2007). *Romantik*. Chapter: "Philosophische und wissenschaftliche Aspekte der Romantik".

57 Cf. Jung, Carl Gustav. (2011). *Über das Phänomen des Geistes in Kunst und Wissenschaft*. "Vorwort der Herausgeber".

58 Rasche, Jörg. (2014). *Das Lied des grünen Löwen*. P. 297. (Trans. by the author). German expression: "[...] Ausdruck der sublimsten seelischen Regungen und inneren Dialogue [...]".

59 Ibid. P. 296. (Trans. by the author). German expression: "Der Mensch entdeckte sich selbst, mit seinem Schatten, als 'ein Ich'".

60 Cf. Boetticher, Wolfgang. (1983). *Einführung in die musikalische Romantik*. P. 15. German expression: "[...] unter Romantik [wird] ein Ausdruck des Gefühlsbetonten, Phantastischen, auch des Sonderbaren (ja Abgründigen, Verschleierten) verstanden, und zwar nicht nur in Bezug auf ein Kunstwerk, sondern auch als allgemeine Weltauffassung.".

and the folklore[61]. The term was then adopted to describe the literary movement and style in Germany, to which Novalis, Schlegel, Tieck, Arnim, Brentano, Eichendorff, Möricke, E.T.A. Hoffmann, and others belonged. Nature, literature, and music were a unity, from which later a new sound conception emerged: for Novalis "A fairy tale is the musical fantasy, the harmonic implications of an aeolian harp, nature itself"[62]. After Eichendorff, "the human voice, that speaks and sings poetically, merges with the nature sounds of the woods or with other voices of nature"[63]. Schiller believed in the "correspondence between the sensuous experience of nature and the spiritual and intellectual workings of the mind."[64]. Jung complements Schiller's statement: "the sentimental poet seeks nature [...]"[65]. In the Arts, with the main representatives being Caspar David Friedrich and Philipp Otto Runge, the painter had become independent and unbounded himself from painting themes of traditional and biblical nature grounded in ancient history[66]. Instead, the artist sought to paint what had an impact on him, e.g., his relation to myth and nature, the real and the imaginary[67]. This included landscapes and the "expression of the religious and the metaphysical"[68] world.

From the standpoint of music history, inflowing into the romantic period[69], the focus was increasingly turning towards the inexpressible, to the direct spiritual

[61] Wehnert explains the etymological origins of the word Romanticism, from the French word "romant"/"roman", as lying in the Romansh language, i.e., a vernacular language of the folk. Cf. Wehnert, Martin. (2016). "Romantik und romantisch". In: Laurenz Lütteken (Ed.). *MGG Online.*

[62] Novalis in: Boetticher, Wolfgang. (1983). *Einführung in die musikalische Romantik.* P. 26. (Trans. by the author). German expression: "Ein Märchen ist die musikalische Phantasie, die harmonischen Folgen einer Äolsharfe, die Natur selbst".

[63] Floros, Constantin. (2016). *Gustav Mahler I: Die geistige Welt Gustav Mahlers in systematischer Darstellung.* P. 147. (Trans. by the author). German expression: "Die menschliche Stimme, die poetisch spricht und singt, verschmilzt mit den Naturlauten des Waldes.".

[64] Rosen, Charles. (1998). *The romantic generation.* P. 129.

[65] Jung, Carl Gustav. (2014). "Psychological Types". In: *CW. Vol. 6.* Chapter II: "Schiller's ideas on the Type problem—2. A discussion on Naïve and Sentimental poetry".

[66] Cf. Sproccati, Sandro. (2014). *Guia de História da Arte.* P. 107.

[67] Cf. Ibid.

[68] Werner-Jensen, Arnold., Ratte, Franz-Joseph., Ernst, Manfred. (2001). *Das Reclambuch der Musik.* P. 202. (Trans. by the author). German expression: "[...] zum Ausdruck religiöser und metaphysischer Gehalte überhöht wurde; [...]".

[69] It has to be noted, that the romantic period in history of music includes a vast period of time, which should be an aspect to take into consideration when speaking of a certain composer or analyzing a composition. In music the period is usually divided into early romanticism, high romanticism, late romanticism, and post-romanticism, all of which have specific traits and characteristics. Werner-Jensen drives the attention to this issue, especially

experiences and to ambiguity[70]. In this regard, Beethoven, as the predecessor of Romanticism, represented an important turning point. Composers of Romanticism sought not only to express the apollonian, as generally in classicism, but to include the barest aspect of the dionysian, i.e., to incorporate the opposites in order to unify the split. This rupture will continually be incorporated within the romantics, as the darker and transparent aspect of nature[71]. It is also during this period, where the so called "Natursprache"[72] and "Naturmusik" is found interrelated to the language of dreams[73].

As mentioned above, the romantic aesthetics is not only to be seen as an artistic and literary movement, but consists in a basic attitude of mind[74], which generally went against the ideas of the Enlightenment thoughts[75]. The inner experiences shaped the Romantic artist and composer[76]. "Empfindung" and "Sehnsucht" were important characteristic keywords. There was an entire new worldview[77] arising, mainly through Schelling's *Naturphilosophie:* nature is not barely an outer appearance, manifestation or a phenomenon which inspires, but it comprises also the creative energy within[78]. Natural and spiritual processes are therefore seen as complementary to each other and stand in a direct and constant dualistic relationship between the objective and the subjective, the outer and the inner, subsequently also the conscious and the unconscious, which in turn creates

---

regarding music and the "romantic" terminology, referring to Dieter Borchmeyer. Cf. Ibid. P. 202–203.

[70] Cf. Bernstein, Leonard. (1973). *The 'Unanswered Question'.* [Lectures]. Smith, Douglas (Producer). Lecture 4: "The delights and dangers of ambiguity". Minutes: 02:23:25.

[71] In literature for instance, the aspect of "Zerrissenheit" (i.e., to be torn asunder) can be found through the element of irony in Heine's poems. Ingo Müller has done an interdisciplinary study comprising literary studies and musicology and in which he also addresses this particular subject. Cf. Müller, Ingo. (2020). *Maskenspiel und Seelensprache.*

[72] This term refers to the *Natursprachenlehre* of Jakob Böhme. The next term of "Naturmusik" on the other hand is in reference to E.T.A. Hoffmann and Eichendorff, although the first references were found already in Johann Gottfried Herder. Cf. Floros, Constantin. (2016). *Gustav Mahler I: Die geistige Welt Gustav Mahlers in systematischer Darstellung.* Chapter: "Die Idee der Naturmusik bei E.T.A. Hoffmann und bei Eichendorff". P. 145–148.

[73] Cf. Ibid.

[74] Werner-Jensen, Arnold., Ratte, Franz-Joseph., Ernst, Manfred. (2001). *Das Reclambuch der Musik.* P. 202.

[75] Cf. Rasche, Jörg. (2014). *Das Lied des grünen Löwen.* P. 295.

[76] Cf. Ibid. P. 296.

[77] Cf. Boetticher, Wolfgang. (1983). *Einführung in die musikalische Romantik.* P. 15.

[78] Cf. Kremer, Detlev. (2007). *Romantik.* P. 61.

a constant tension[79]. This dissonance can be solved by the creative Self, namely through the means of art, being music the ultimate art capable of the most direct expression of "the invisible core of nature"[80]. Thus, the primordial feeling of wholeness, to which Schelling attributed the concept of the "Weltseele", is re-created through the means of art, poetry and music. In other words, the artist sought to become one with nature—what is on "the outside reflects and realizes [itself] in the inside"[81]. However, the reverse is also appropriate: the artist looks into nature through his or her own unconscious, as it is perceptible, for instance, through Caspar David Friedrich's paintings where the protagonist has his back turned to the observer and peers into the landscape. This experience will then shape and develop the artist's individual language. Schelling's ideology of nature and spirit as an entity strongly shaped and characterized the romantic aesthetics, in the same way that it influenced and shaped Jung's psychology, more specifically his concept of the Self[82].

For Schelling, as for C.G. Jung, nature contains the creative energy, and within the constant tension that is created by the discrepancies of the dualistic process of the psyche lies what Jung called the dynamis of the soul. Following Jung's thought, through creativity, the autonomous and self-driven archetypal structures spontaneously push out of the collective unconscious to consciousness.

4.3.1 Landscape, Time and Space

In Schiller's understanding, the landscape should have become a "symbol of the human [through] the representation of feelings or as representation of ideas."[83]. For the so-called romantics, the landscape and the aspects of space and time

---

[79] Cf. Ibid. Chapter 4: „Philosophische und Wissenschaftliche Aspekte der Romantik—4.1. Naturphilosophie". P. 59–63.

[80] Ibid. P. 66. German expression: "Der unsichtbare Kern der Natur offenbart sich in der Musik direkt, indem er als Bewegung hörbar wird.". This elevated notion of music as an artistic form of expression was already described by Schopenhauer. Cf. Schopenhauer, Arthur. (2024). *Die Welt als Wille und Vorstellung.*

[81] Rasche, Jörg. (2014). *Das Lied des grünen Löwen.* P. 295. (Trans. by the author). German expression: "das Draußen spiegelt und realisiert sich innen".

[82] Cf. Kast, Verena. (2009). *Das sagenumwobene 'Rote Buch' von C.G. Jung—Die Psychologin Verena Kast im Gespräch mit Norbert Bischofberger.* [Interview]. Minutes: 22:14/ 1:01:45.

[83] Rosen, Charles. (1998). *The romantic generation.* P. 127.

associated with it, are central[84], as are the aspects of light and shadow. This includes the sensory perception of distance, which is to be understood as a "[…] natural metaphor for absence […]"[85]. In music, the rhythm is considered to be the "Natur-Urelement", i.e., primal element of nature, which is common to music and stands symbolically for the aspect of time and of the inner life[86]. Space, on the other hand, is symbolized by the movement of sound, i.e., the melody[87]. The sound movement, can, similarly as the voice inflections, be viewed as an expressive movement of the unconscious, which "[says] more than […] words at first"[88]. In this sense, they can be interpreted as carriers of specific symbolic semantics, moved by archetypal forces (7).

After Rosen, the landscape got its prominent role in Romanticism, especially with the appearance of the lied and the song cycles in music. In the Romantic lied for instance, it is the task of music to express what is not pronounced within the poetry, what lies in between the lines, what in fact, is not expressible in words, but only music can transmit—this is referring to the archetypal level. This means that in the romantic aesthetics of music, the ultimate aspiration lies in "[…] making perceptible the inner movements of the spirit analogously through outer ones."[89]. This idea should be complemented with the Jungian thought that archetypal structures and symbols are linked to these inner movements. Pursuing with the statements of Rosen he counts *An die ferne Geliebte* of Beethoven (probably the first song cycle in music history), *Winterreise* of Schubert, Liszt's *Album d'un voyageur* and Schumann's *Liederkreis* as examples. These are compositions, in which "[…] the landscape in music reaches its transcendental level"[90]. Furthermore, he remarks that while the painter and poet use elements of nature such as "rocks, foliage, mountains, and […] the unifying power of light"[91] the composer recurs to the harmonies and motifs to musically portray the [inner] landscape[92].

---

84 Cf. Ibid. Chapter 3: "Mountains and Song Cycles". P. 116–236.

85 Ibid. P. 135. English expression: "[…] and the sense of distance stands as a natural metaphor for absence.".

86 Cf. Schlesinger, Max. (1912). *Symbolik in der Tonkunst.* Kapitel: "Neuzeit—Rhythmus". P. 38–40.

87 Cf. Ibid. Chapter: "Neuzeit—Tonbewegung". P. 40–41.

88 Rasche, Jörg. (2014). *Das Lied des grünen Löwen.* P. 389. (Trans. by the author). German expression: „zunächst mehr als […] Worte [sagen]".

89 Rosen, Charles. (1998). *The romantic generation.* P. 127.

90 Ibid. P. 132.

91 Ibid. P. 135.

92 Cf. Ibid.

These harmonies and motifs carry deep meaning and can thus express specific archetypal patterns (7). Resuming Gebser's idea of depth psychology (2. 4), archetypes in music can be the manifestations of the fourth dimension, i.e., the timelessness of the deeply moving and universally unifying elements (7).

4.3.2 The Wanderer and the Individuation Process

Characteristic motives and subjects of Romanticism are profoundly related to the unconscious: the inner turmoil of the soul, folk music and fairy tales, the unseen and the veiled, the enchanting and the fantastic, the dreamworld, the eerie and witchcraft, the aeolian harp as the unifying element with nature, the mysticism of the forests and the gloominess of the night[93], where shadow figures such as the "Doppelgänger" are to be seen[94]. Constantin Floros speaks of the "[…] so characteristic romantic phenomenon of the split personality […]"[95], to which the new form of a compilation of short compositions was proper, namely often composed in ABA form. The "Doppelgänger" figure is, in literature, often perceived as a sublimation element of the poet or writer. In psychological terms, the "Doppelgänger" is understood as an Alter-Ego, i.e., another ego, which can comprise elements of light but also of the darker aspects of one's own personality. In this context, it is the split aspect of the subject that will enable the "I" to get in touch with elements of the own unconscious. The "Doppelgänger", which is tied to a shadow figure, can be understood as the symbolic manifestation of the shadow archetype, but which is subject to change as it can bear light elements within itself as well (e.g., 16).

Another major representative archetype of the Romantic period, especially in the early Romanticism, is the wanderer archetype. This archetype lives in the soul of every Romantic artist and is tied to the term "Sehnsucht". It is one with nature, and still the painful discrepancies between the outer reality and the inner world are perceptible, like the contrast of the transparent romantic darkness and the juxtaposition with the bright painful light. Existential questions echo in the

93 Cf. Boetticher, Wolfgang. (1983). *Einführung in die musikalische Romantik.*

94 Cf. Schubert, Franz. (1828). *Der Schwanengesang:* "Der Doppelgänger" D 957. Poem by: Heine, Heinrich. (1827). *Buch der Lieder:* "Der Doppelgänger".

95 Floros, Constantin. (1989). *Musik als Botschaft.* P. 40. (Trans. by the author). German expression: "Sehr lehrreich sind manche Klavierzyklen von Schumann (etwa die "Davidsbündlertänze op. 6) und von Brahms (etwa die "Variationen op. 9), in denen teilweise äußerst erregte Stücke mit sehr ruhigen abwechseln, als gelte es, das für die Romantik so charakteristische Phänomen der Persönlichkeitsspaltung musikalisch zu demonstrieren.".

wanderer's soul: "What do I want? What am I? What to ask nature? […]"[96]. He is trapped in the inner reality of his own self, like a stranger, he dwells within the melancholy of his own being: "and my sigh ever asks: where?"[97] inhabits incessantly the wanderer's soul. And so, the wanderer roams through valleys and mountains, as psychologically he explores the deep unconscious Self, to thereafter rise anew, transformed, towards the peak of the mountain, i.e., to the light of consciousness. Jung himself made this analogy between the valley and the peak of the mountain, which symbolize the unconscious and the consciousness, respectively[98]. In other words, by wandering he "undertakes", so to say, a process of individuation and goes through the different archetypal stages. While admiring the outer landscape he in fact looks "within". In this sense the wanderer archetype might be understood as a connecting element with nature. Whereupon it can be concluded that, the individuation process can analogously correspond to a certain pattern of nature, namely the cyclical laws of nature: descent, death and rebirth; an "eternal return" in the Nietzschean sense[99]. Similarly to Shiva, the dancing god of creation and destruction, of life and death, who dances to awaken the volcanos and permit total destruction, with the purpose of rebirth. Psychologically this would mean a metamorphosis, so that the Self is incorporated in the "I"[100] allowing it to become whole.

96 Senancour, Etienne Pivert. *Obermann.* (1804). In: Liszt, Franz. (1976). *Les années de pèlerinages*: "Vallée d'Obermann". French expression: Que veux-je? Que suis-je? Quoi demander à la nature? […]".

97 Schubert, Franz. (1816). "Der Wanderer" D.489. Poem by Lübeck, Georg. (1808). "Des Fremdlings Abendlied". German expression: "Und immer fragt der Seufzer: wo?".

98 Cf. Van der Post said that "the mountains of Switzerland were always profoundly symbolic to Jung.". Cf. Van der Post, Laurens. (1972). *The Story of Carl Gustav Jung.* [Documentary]. Minute: 00:31:16 /1:33:23.

99 Cf. Nietzsche, Friedrich. (2010). *Also sprach Zarathustra.*

100 Cf. Rasche, Jörg. (2014). *Das Lied des grünen Löwen.*

4.4 Jung on the Creative Process

For Jung, "Music is the art of feeling par excellence"[101]. According to Margaret Tilly, Jung would have also said: "[...] music is dealing with such deep archetypal material"[102]. The subject of the creative process was the focus of several essays by Jung. He understands the arts in their practice as a psychological activity, worthy of being analyzed for their emotional and symbolic contents or phenomena[103]. Following Jung's thoughts, Marie-Louise von Franz, a disciple of Jung, claimed that "creativity has its roots in the unconscious, from the same material than dreams"[104]. In such an analysis, it is important to focus mainly on the inner creative processes and to maintain a vigilant and respectful attitude, whenever being confronted with pathologies and complexes. According to Jung, artists, poets, and composers are seen as collective individuals, transcending the own zeitgeist by creating works of art rooted within the collective unconscious and transmitting a message directed to all "mankind"[105].

The Self with the inherent natural forces imposes itself over the artist's ego, and in this sense, he is not the artist, but he is the creative form itself. Archetypes move, touch, and have an immense power over the artist, i.e., a will of their own. They can act out of themselves and in this manner, they influence and shape the work of art and the life of the artist. This is reflected in Jung's statement: "It is not Goethe that creates 'Faust', but the soul component 'Faust' that creates Goethe."[106]. This means that the force of the archetypal structures works through

[101] Almén, Byron: "Jung's function-attitudes in music composition and discourse.". (2008). In: Rowland, Susan. (Ed.). *Psyche and the Arts.* P. 118. Here, Byron Almén refers to a statement by Jung himself, in turn to be found in: Jung, Carl Gustav. (1938/1984). *Dream Analysis.* McGuire, William (Ed.). P. 11.

[102] Tilly, Margaret. (1956). "The Therapy of Music". (1956). In: McGuire, William., Hull, R.F.C. (Ed)., *C.G. Jung Speaking* (1977). P. 274.

[103] Cf. Jung, Carl Gustav. (2011). *Über das Phänomen des Geistes in Kunst und Wissenschaft.* P. 75.

[104] Von Franz, Marie Louise. (1982). Selhofer, Françoise (Director). De Rahm, Diana (Interviewer). [Interview Bollingen September 1982]. Minutes: 36:00/42:17. (Trans. by the author). German expression: "Das Kreative kommt aus dem Unbewussten, aus demselben Stoff aus dem die Träume kommen.".

[105] Cf. Jung, Carl Gustav. (2011). *Über das Phänomen des Geistes in Kunst und Wissenschaft.*

[106] Ibid. P. 118. (Trans. by the author). German expression: „Nicht Goethe macht den ‚Faust', sondern die seelische Komponente ‚Faust' macht Goethe. Und was ist ‚Faust'? ‚Faust' ist ein Symbol, nicht ein bloßer semiotischer Hinweis auf oder eine Allegorie für ein längst Bekanntes, sondern der Ausdruck eines urlebendig Wirkenden in der deutschen Seele, dem Goethe zur Geburt verhelfen musste.".

the artist, through the composer, so that "his inner nature can reveal itself"[107]. It manifests as an impulse coming from the unconscious, spontaneously and directly into consciousness.

As Verena Kast mentions, creativity is a dynamic self-regulating process of the own psyche: "[...] a dialogue of consciousness with the unconscious [...]"[108]. During this process time is transcended, the artist has access to the deepest archaic level of the collective psyche, through key archetypes, which in turn enclose all times. Here resides the arising "visionary work of art", as Jung referred to it:

> "The creative process [...] consist in an unconscious revival of the archetype and in a development and formation of the same, up to the finished work. The shaping of the primordial image is, so to speak, a translation into the language of the present, which makes it possible for everyone to find access to the deepest sources of life that would otherwise be buried"[109].

[107] Ibid. P. 84. German expression: "Selbst widerwillig, muss er doch erkennen, dass in all dem sein Selbst aus ihm spricht, dass seine innerste Natur sich selbst offenbart und laut verkündet, was er seiner Zunge nie anvertraut hätte. Er kann nur gehorchen und dem anscheinend fremden Impulse folgen, fühlend, dass sein Werk größer ist als er und darum eine Gewalt über ihn hat, der er nichts vorschreiben kann.".

[108] Kast, Verena. (2014). *Die Tiefenpsychologie nach C.G. Jung*. P. 49. (Trans. by the author). German expression: "Dieser schöpferische Prozess ereignet sich zwischen dem Unbewussten, den archetypischen Strukturen und den Komplexen, und dem Bewusstsein—im Dialog des Bewusstseins mit dem Unbewussten. [...] Kreativität ist ein dialogischer Prozess.".

[109] Jung, Carl Gustav. (2011). *Über das Phänomen des Geistes in Kunst und Wissenschaft*. Chapter VI: "Über die Beziehung der analytischen Psychologie zum dichterischen Kunstwerk". Paragraph 139. P. 95. (Trans. by the author). German expression: "Der schöpferische Prozess [...] besteht in einer unbewussten Belebung des Archetypus und in einer Entwicklung und Ausgestaltung desselben bis zum vollendenten Werk. Die Gestaltung des urtümlichen Bildes ist gewissermaßen eine Übersetzung in die Sprache der Gegenwart, wodurch es sozusagen jedem ermöglicht wird, wieder Zugang zu den tiefsten Quellen des Lebens zu finden, die ihm sonst verschüttet wären.".

4.5 Summa Summarum

Nature and the unconscious psyche stand in a direct and symbolic relationship to each other, i.e., in the same sense that archetypes emerge out of the unconscious, nature can be seen as the bearer of all archetypes, in which the transcendent function of the human psyche, the creative urge are central to connect the two realms of the human psyche.

There is a transformation of this relationship to be noted through the different historic periods: musical-rhetorical figures run through history as a more or less present constant. Starting from the *ethos* doctrine, further decisive steps of development up to the elaborated musical rhetorics of the Baroque period can be mentioned, for example, Quintilian, Tinctoris and Burmeister (6). In addition to the practical musical application of musical rhetorics, the madrigal also plays a decisive role as the starting point for the emergence of the recitative as a newly developed form in the Baroque. These musical rhetoric figures and madrigalism thus became the basis of a cultural unconscious (II). A similar phenomenon occurs regarding the importance of the landscape in music and the urge for wholeness. The focus in the Romantic music increasingly shifts towards the directness of the inner experiences, the inner landscapes, the dionysian, the "Zerrissenheit" (i.e., the state of being torn), the "Sehnsucht". In this chapter, several symbolic motives were briefly touched on, which are particularly significant for Schubert (III) and will (among others) be a matter for the main analysis in Schubert's music (IV).

The return to nature (within), or to the ouroboric state—to use Neumann's language—seems to be a primordial necessity that seeks artistic expression. Therefore, the origin of creativity has something primordial about it. As seen from Schelling's viewpoint, which Jung shared, the dualistic tension with nature is of great importance. Through this antagonistic relationship, psychic energies are set in motion, and thus wholeness—i.e., the expression of the Self—can be attained. In this context, nature is understood as a metaphor for the inner reality ("Wirklichkeit"), and is seen as the creative energy within the composer, as the bearer of archetypal manifestation.

Part II
The topic of music as a language

The theories around the topic of music as a language were considered to have reached their apogee in the baroque era[1], when they were developed and systematically formulated – (*Musica poetica*) (6). These doctrines, which included the musical rhetoric figures, had a great impact on composers of subsequent historic periods, have lasted until today[2], and have their heritage in the notion of "music as expression" (5).

The understanding that music has a communication function is a notion in music history that dates back to prehistoric times and has remained so to this day. This presupposes the semantic content of music as the bearer of a message with great potential to impact human beings and society. Similarly, another topic that has been discussed and aspired time and again is the discussion of the direct musical affinity to speech, related to both external parameters and metaphorical ones[3]. The close relationship between music and language has evolved throughout the centuries and should ideally be regarded as being highly related to the respective historical, social and aesthetic contexts[4].

Both music and language are grounded on a specific idea, thought, theme or subject, which feature a meaningful content and emotional reference[5]. Akin to

---

[1] Cf. Krones, Hartmut. "Musik und Rhetorik". (2016). In: Laurenz Lütteken (Ed.). *MGG Online.*
"Geschichtlicher Überblick—2. Die Hochblüte (1599–1754)".

[2] Cf. Ibid."Geschichtlicher Überblick—3. Weiterwirken" and "Geschichtlicher Überblick—4. Spätes Nachwirken (1821 bis heute)".

[3] Cf. Ibid. "I. Kategorien der musikalischen Rhetorik—1. Gesamtsicht".

[4] It is not the focus of this dissertation to relate everything in detail. Only the main lines will be here delineated. For more insight, Zoltai's *Ethos und Affekt* covers the developments that this notion has undergone through the historic and aesthetical premises along a great period of music history. Cf. Zoltai, Dénes. (1970). *Ethos und Affekt*.

[5] Cf. Krones, Hartmut. "Musik und Rhetorik". (2016). In: Laurenz Lütteken (Ed.). *MGG Online.* "I. Musik als 'Sprache' im Sinne der Rhetorik.".

language, music has its own grammar, logic, syntax and vocabulary[6] and also its own rhetorics and semantics. The semantic value has equally been a constant aim for composers[7]. Nonetheless, Constantin Floros, for instance, emphasizes that musical semantics, in opposition to speech related semantics, tends to be "vaguer" or of abstract character[8] – a perspective shared by other scholars from other fields[9]. This key aspect makes the rational formulation about music more challenging and conveys its archetypal nature (7): as a language emerging from the unconscious, directly from the archetypes, it naturally contains their features of abstractedness, ambivalences and of the ineffable. Music reflects an immense interconnection and superpositions of contradictory emotional-musical elements, which as a whole can have a transformative and balancing function for the psyche of everyone involved (composer, interpreter and listener). This other aspect can be translated as: music as a language narrating the inner psychic processes (7).

[6] Cf. Liszt, Franz. Cited after: Floros, Constantin. (2008). *Hören und verstehen.* P. 31.

[7] Cf. Floros, Constantin. (2008). *Hören und verstehen.* P. 32.

[8] Cf. Ibid.

[9] Jörg Rasche might be cited as an example. Cf. Rasche, Jörg. (2014). *Das Lied des grünen Löwen.*

5 The Origins of Music as Expression

The origin of the concept of music as expression is often traced back to the ancient Greek notions of the *ethos* doctrine. For the Greeks the effects of music on the human being were given a particular importance. This perspective is the core on which their music aesthetic concept is based, and it has influenced the history of music. Going further back in the history of humankind, it is possible to conclude that there was already the necessity for artistic expression, both visually and musically, in prehistoric times. Vestiges of frescos and sculptures have already been found and studied for centuries. However, the question of their relationship to music remained veiled for a long-time, even though remnants of bone-made flutes were found, which have been considered as a proof for the existence of musical activity for prehistoric people.

The use of natural artefacts found in nature, such as stones, leaves, etc., and the use of their own vocalizations to produce or imitate the sounds of animals and even as a means of communication, seems an expected inference. However, recent studies have brought more intriguing insights. One of them is the fact that Neandertals (~ 190 000—30 000 bp) possessed and developed the ability to sing, as the research results of the anthropologist Ann Mac Larnon have shown[1]. This discovery opens a new hypothesis among prehistorians, anthropologists and musicologists. These findings mean that their own bodies were already used as a source for artistic expression (as for instance the voice) and it is to assume that they did so with a specific intention, probably even knowing intuitively of its impact. Effectively, anthropologists, musicologists and prehistorians, now believe that singing was part of their rituals, which included dancing and rock-painting inside the caves: rituals and gatherings in a "sacred place", where there was

[1] Goblot, Pascal. (2020). *Sapiens, et la musique fut*. Pérès, Guillaume (Producer). [Documentary]. Minutes 45:22/52:13.

L. Dill, *Schubert's Metamorphoses*,
https://doi.org/10.1007/978-3-662-73476-6_5

a "dialogue" between music, animal spirits and natural elements[2]—and possibly also: a dialogue with their unconscious. The idea that music can reflect a dialogue is a notion that has always been present, as it will be shown later.

Substantial insights for these hypotheses are the findings of Iégor Reznikoff. He has concluded that there is a link between the rock-paintings and the acoustics inside a cave, and that more images are to be found in particular places with more resonance[3] (places with church or cathedral-like acoustics). He notes examples where this relationship is directly proportional[4]. Moreover, he has recognized the red markings in the Paleolithic caves perceivable in the stalactites as acoustical markers or cartographical markings[5]. This means that the prehistoric individuals had a "fine listening capability"[6] and that they searched for good acoustical resonance inside a cave to hold the above-mentioned rituals and give form to their creativity.

The deductions of the prehistorian Serge Maury regarding the discovered flutes are of equal interest. He concluded that prehistoric people, 36 000 years ago, were sensitive to the different sonorities and had already their own musical scale system[7]. Additionally, the findings of Erik Gonthier concerning the so-called "stalagmitic organs"[8] underlines, once more, the creative aptitude and musicality of prehistoric persons. These stalagmitic organs correspond to natural lithophones, i.e., are natural instruments that they had at their disposal and which they probably used as such.

> "By dreaming a little, we could imagine these caves as the scene of a 'prehistoric opera', [...] where the voice, the dance, the flutes and natural sounds would have been associated, in what Serge Maury describes as a 'strong dialogue, in the mother earth that nourishes what is on the surface'"[9].

---

[2] Cf. Ibid. French expression: "[...] lors de rassemblements rituels [...] ce site était sans doute un lieu sacré, dans lequel il s'établissait le dialogue par les sons des flutes, avec les esprits des animaux, des pierres et des éléments.". Minutes:33:30/52:13.

[3] Iégor Reznikoff. In: Ibid. Minutes: 11:20/52:13.

[4] Ibid. Minutes: 11:20/52:13.

[5] Ibid. Minutes: 12:40/52:13.

[6] Ibid. Minutes: 12:57/52:13. French expression: "[...] les tribus du temps préhistorique avaient une écoute extrêmement fine [...] une écoute très attentive et développé, ils devraient avoir une finesse musicale aussi fine, si extraordinaire, que celles des peintures.".

[7] Goblot, Pascal. (2020). *Sapiens, et la musique fut*. Pérès, Guillaume (Producer). [Documentary]. Minutes: 32:00/52:13.

[8] Ibid. Minutes: 25:07/52:13.

[9] Machart, Renaud. (2021). „Sapiens, et la musique fut', sur Arte: des orgues stalagmitiques pour symphonie préhistorique.". French expression: "En rêvant un peu, on pourrait imaginer

These statements demonstrate that music has been important as a means of expression for the human being since prehistoric times and that it was purposefully used: the ground conception remains the same, whether the intention (i) is directed towards a mystical aim in the context of shamanic rituals as in prehistory, (ii) are of pedagogical purposes as in the ancient Greek civilizations or (iii) focused on the religious devotion in the context of masses, motets or profane songs, as in the Renaissance for instance.

The willingness to systematize the musical components into a distinct vocabulary network with specific semantic and symbolic meaning, notably in the Renaissance, led to significant further development of this concept. How this concept evolved from the first formalized notions of music as expression in the Hellenic era to the later formation of *Musica poetica* in the Renaissance until the Baroque will now be briefly outlined.

5.1 The Greek Concept of *Ethos*

Ethos: "the doctrine of the divine origin of music and its influence on human education"[10] refers to the ancient Greek's belief that "music had a great impact on the soul"[11]. Depending on the mode[12] used it could evoke certain emotions,

ces caverns comme la scene d'un 'opéra préhistorique', […] où la voix, la danse, les flutes et les sons naturels se seraient associés, dans ce que Serge Maury décrit comme un 'dialogue fort, dans la terre mère qui nourrit ce qui est à la surface'".

[10] Nestler, Gerhard. (1997). *Geschichte der Musik.* P. 14 (Trans. by the author). German expression: "[…] und die Ethoslehre, die Lehre vom göttlichen Ursprung der Musik und von ihrem Einfluss auf die Menschenbildung, die uns, von Herodot und Platon überliefert, noch bei der Musik der Griechen beschäftigen wird.".

[11] Amon, Reinhard. (2005). *Lexikon der Harmonielehre.* P. 288. (Trans. by the author). German expression: "Schon die Griechen schrieben der Musik eine große Wirkung auf die Seele des Menschen zu […]".

[12] The Pythagorean subdivision of the string and its resulting numeric relations are of primary importance for the arising of the *ethos* doctrine. The reason mainly lies in the placement of the semitones within each modal scale, which were responsible for giving each mode a different character and sound quality. This accomplishment arose from the aim to "create a scale through a system of fifths". Nestler, Gerhard. (1997). *Geschichte der Musik.* P. 28. (Trans. by the author). German expression: "Pythagoras versuchte, eine Tonleiter durch das Quintensystem zu bilden.". His theories were, moreover, of great influence for Plato and Aristotle.

which were then purposefully used[13]. Etymologically, *ethos* means "character, nature, custom"[14]. In music, the first formulations of this doctrine in relation to the different modes are to be found by Damon of Athens, who in turn had a great impact, not only on Plato[15] and his contemporaries, but also on the following generations, as for instance on Aristotle. Scholars speak of two important system branches in the *ethos* doctrine: the Platonian and the Aristotelian[16].

Damon recognized the political, social and pedagogical impact of music[17], which was widely used in education and subsequently adopted by Plato in his *Politeia* scriptures (*The republic*). Additionally, Stefan Sorgner explains Plato's theories on the conception of the world soul (*anima mundi*) and human soul as being fundamental for Plato's conception of *ethos*[18]. These, in contrast to Damon[19], are related with the Pythagorean numeric and symbolic relations[20]: the human soul is created in a similar manner as the world soul[21]; consequently, the microcosm is perceived as an imprint of the macrocosm; out of which it is

---

[13] A summary of the emotional qualities that music can evoke, and the respective characteristics of each mode can be read in: Amon, Reinhard. (2005). *Lexikon der Harmonielehre.* P. 288 and P. 303.

[14] DWDS—Digitales Wörterbuch der deutschen Sprache.

[15] Cf. Arlettaz, Vincent: „L'expression dans la musique ancienne (I)". In: *Revue musicale de Suisse Romande. Vol. 65/3.* Septembre 2012. P. 4–24.

[16] Cf. Zoltai, Dénes. (1970). *Ethos und Affekt.* P. 30.

[17] Damon was convinced that rhythm and melody have an effect on the human soul. Moreover, Zoltai emphasizes that Damon's understanding of *Musiké*, was related to poetry texts; thus, diverged from the "Pythagorean manner of analyzing abstract tone systems". Ibid. P. 26. German expression: "[…] dass er die Musiké nicht auf pythagoreische Art, in der Gestalt abstrakter Tonsysteme analysierte, sondern als ursprüngliche griechische Gesamtkunst, in der die eigenartigen musikalischen Elemente stets mit dem Text der Dichtung in Verbindung stehen.".

[18] Cf. Sorgner, Stefan Lorenz., Schramm, Michael. (2010). *Musik in der antiken Philosophie.* Chapter: „Die Seelenkonzeption als Grundlage der Ethoslehre und der Dreiteilung der Musik.".

[19] Cf. Zoltai, Dénes. (1970). *Ethos und Affekt.* P. 26.

[20] Cf. Sorgner, Stefan Lorenz., Schramm, Michael. (2010). *Musik in der antiken Philosophie.* Chapter: „Die Seelenkonzeption als Grundlage der Ethoslehre und der Dreiteilung der Musik.". P. 324–325.

[21] Here simplified: the creator Demiurge takes three ground principles—these being the selflessness, the diversity and the being—and by shuffling them he creates the world soul, whereby the three principles stand in a certain ratio to each other, these representing an important numeric symbolism. A similar procedure is then applied for the conception of the human soul. Cf. Ibid. P. 323. It should be noted that the concept of the world soul (*anima mundi*) influenced other scholars and moreover, later on, Gnosticism.

deduced that, the individual's hearing and capacity for perception stand in a direct relationship with how an individual's soul is constituted[22]. Thus, the numeric ratio and the corresponding symbolism play an important role.

In his theories, Plato advocates that music has the power to change society and was, among others, especially used for educational purposes: "[…] it is not possible to change these musical structures without changing society itself."[23]. For him, the dorian and phrygian modes are of particular significance, being able to evoke courage and peace[24], respectively. This means, that not only a certain kind of music or mode could give rise to specific types of feelings but could also have an impact on the will of the listener[25]. According to Cleonides, music had the ability, to influence and mold the will of the listener in a threefold way[26]: diastaltic, systaltic and hesychastic, i.e., (i) "exalting the spirit and infringe heroic deeds" ("expanding"), (ii) "inflicting passion, lamentations or supplications" ("contracting"), or (iii) "outbalancing the spirit and set a peaceful attitude" ("soothing")[27]. For Aristotle, the effect of music was understood in regard to the affects and emotions it could induce, but foremost, in its capacity for purification (*Katharsis*) which was then deliberately applied in the theater[28]. Furthermore, Aristotle understood the metric as a musical category independent from the word[29].

[22] Cf. Ibid. P. 325.

[23] Arlettaz, Vincent: „L'expression dans la musique ancienne (I)". In: *Revue musicale de Suisse Romande. Vol. 65/3.* Septembre 2012. P. 7. (Trans. by the author). French expression: „[…] il n'est pas possible de modifier ces structures musicales sans modifier la société elle-même.".

[24] Cf. Plato. "Republic". Cited after: Ibid. P. 4–24.

[25] Cf. Floros, Constantin. (2008). *Hören und verstehen.* P. 38.

[26] Cf. Ibid.

[27] These descriptions are to be found in: Ibid. German expression: „Nach Kleonides vermochte das diastaltische Ethos die Energie des Willens zur Größe, zu männlichem Mut und heroischen Taten aufzureizen. Das systaltische Ethos versetzte die Psyche in seinen Augen hingegen in eine unmännliche Stimmung und eignete eher erotischen Leidenschaften, Klagegesängen und flehentlichen Bitten. Das hesychastische Ethos schließlich stelle das innere Gleichgewicht und den Frieden der Seele her.".

[28] Cf. Sorgner, Stefan Lorenz., Schramm, Michael. (2010). *Musik in der antiken Philosophie.* Chapter: „Katharsis". P. 178.

[29] Cf. Krones, Hartmut. "Musik und Rhetorik". (2016). In: Laurenz Lütteken (Ed.). *MGG Online.* „Die Entstehung der musikalischen Rhetorik—a. Frühgeschichte.".

Vincent Arlettaz draws particular attention to divergences among the theorists that can be acknowledged in regard to "the concrete attribution of the qualities for each mode"[30]; a fact, which "tends to relativize the real value of this principle"[31]. Therein might lie one of the reasons for its decay: Zoltai sees the decline of the *Ethos* doctrine already in the so called "musical scepsis" of the Hellenic age[32]. However, it remained a common fact that, for the ancient Greek and Roman civilizations, music and speech were considered to be related arts[33]—the term "poet-singers" was universally used and is, furthermore, to be found in ancient mythologies. For the Roman rhetoricians Cicero and Quintilian, for example, speech remained a "hidden chant"[34] and one with content and affectively charged ("*composition et sonus*")[35], respectively. Hereby, for Quintilian, the ethical function—alike the ancient Greeks—remained present[36].

30 Arlettaz, Vincent: „L'expression dans la musique ancienne (I)". In: *Revue musicale de Suisse Romande. Vol. 65/3.* Septembre 2012. P. 7. (Trans. by the author). French expression: "Cela étant, il est intéressant d'observer que les théoriciens grecs ne sont pas d'accord entre eux quant aux qualités à attribuer concrètement aux différents modes—ce qui tend à relativiser la valeur réelle de ce principe théorique.".

31 Ibid. (Trans. by the author). French expression: "Cela étant, il est intéressant d'observer que les théoriciens grecs ne sont pas d'accord entre eux quant aux qualités à attribuer concrètement aux différents modes—ce qui tend à relativiser la valeur réelle de ce principe théorique.". Curiously, the same phenomenon has happened later in history, not only with the key characteristics, but to a certain degree also with the musical rhetoric figures. Cf. Krones, Hartmut. "Musik und Rhetorik". (2016). In: Laurenz Lütteken (Ed.). *MGG Online.*

32 Cf. Zoltai, Dénes. (1970). *Ethos und Affekt.* P. 25.

33 Cf. Krones, Hartmut. "Musik und Rhetorik". (2016). In: Laurenz Lütteken (Ed.). *MGG Online.* „Die Entstehung der musikalischen Rhetorik—a. Frühgeschichte.".

34 Cf. Ibid. German expression: „[…] dass das Sprechen einen gewissen verborgenen Gesang beinhalte, […]".

35 In other words: music and speech were related in what concerned their form, sonority, gesture and rhythmic. Cf. Ibid.

36 Cf. Ibid.

5.2 Towards the "Moralized *Ethos*" in the Middle Ages. Towards the Music of the Renaissance

Even though the Greek concept of *ethos* had its apparent final decline, it found its continuity in history after all. Similarities with the Greek doctrine are to be found long before the growing interest of the Renaissance towards the ancient civilizations. The bridge of this tradition into Middle Ages is partially due to Calcidius' and Boethius' Latin reception and translations of works by ancient philosophers such as Plato (among other the *Timaios* scriptures) and Aristotle[37]. Additionally, the church songs reflected similar beliefs[38] during the Christian worldview of the Middle Ages. However, the reference to the *ethos* is not perceived equally. Zoltai states that while the early Christian music was a "product of the Hellenistic age"[39] it featured certain aesthetic divergences; these were mainly: (i) the rhythm, especially dance rhythms, which receded into the background, while the so-called "pneumatic *melos*" was in the foreground[40] and (ii) the hierarchical system that was developed by the church fathers and feudal lordships of a "subordination of the individual in the system", which led to a concept of "moralized *ethos*"[41]. From this latter perspective resulted an "impersonal" musical practice, where "the ideal way of reciting Psalms [was] to evoke religious devotion; hence, the chant [was] impersonal and renounce[d] any worldly, theatrical effect [...]"[42]. In this conception, contrarily to the Greeks unified view of mind and body, any allusions to carnal matters or to beauty was considered to be a product of the devil and

[37] Cf. Ibid. „Die Entstehung der musikalischen Rhetorik—b. Textausdeutung, Affekt und Effekt seit dem Mittelalter.".

[38] Cf. Ibid.

[39] Zoltai, Dénes. (1970). *Ethos und Affekt.* P. 67. (Trans. by the author). German expression: „Die Musikgeschichte sowie die vergleichende Musikwissenschaft unserer Zeit erbrachten den vielfachen Beweis dafür, dass die frühe christliche Musik, von der Psalmodie bis zur Hymnodik, in ihrem Melodienmaterial ebenso wie in ihren Formprinzipien das Produkt des hellenistischen Zeitalters, die auf hoher Stufe integrierte Einheit der verschiedensten antiken hellenischen, jüdischen, syrischen, etc. Elemente darstellt.".

[40] Ibid.

[41] Ibid. P. 71.

[42] Cf. Ibid. P. 79. (Trans. by the author). German expression: "[...] dass die ideale Vortragsweise der Psalmen darauf gerichtet ist, religiöse Andacht hervorzurufen; daher ist der Gesangsvortrag unpersönlich und verzichtet auf jede weltliche, theatralische Wirkung; [...]". Furthermore, Zoltai elucidates that the chant, even though it should be an expression from the heart, ought not to be sensual or beautiful, but the expression of a lament or a sigh.

were thus to be banished[43]. These statements translate that a deviation resulted from the original Greek *ethos* conception in the medieval age.

Music in the Middle Ages still belonged to the *septem artes liberales* as a component of the *Quadrivium.* With the growing interest in the relation between music and language, due to the Humanism movement, music was approaching an important turning point in its development: from the late 15th century on, music eventually fell into the *ars dicendi* and became a component of the *Trivium* (the literary, speech related subjects)[44]. This change translates the growing affinity between music and speech, implicating its communication (as a message), expression and effect function[45]. This concurs with advancements in the systematization of the doctrine of the affects and the music rhetoric figures. Yet, as Vincent Arlettaz points out in his several articles on "L'expression dans la musique ancienne", vestiges of the musical concern regarding a text-affect relationship can be traced back within the context of the Gregorian chant to Johannes Cotto, also known as Johannes Afflighemensis (~1100), who, seemingly for the first time, had theorized on the function of music: "music ought to express the sense implicated by the words"[46]. It appears that Cotto's treatise was possibly inspired by certain passages of Guido d'Arezzo's (~1030) *Musica enchiriadis* and *Micrologus*[47], which means that the lineage of this specific aim in the Middle Ages goes back further to ~ 1030.

The concept of the "modal *ethos*" of the medieval age is based on the eight, melodic, so-called ecclesiastic modes (Fig. 5.1): dorian, hypodorian, phrygian, hypophrygian, lydian, hypolydian, mixolydian and hypomixolydian.

[43] Cf. Ibid.

[44] Cf. Krones, Hartmut. "Musik und Rhetorik". (2016). In: Laurenz Lütteken (Ed.). *MGG Online*. „Die Entstehung der musikalischen Rhetorik—e. Musik und Rhetorik im Bildungskanon.".

[45] Cf. Müller, Jan. (2002). *Der Komponist als Prediger*. P. 83.

[46] Cf. Arlettaz, Vincent: „L'expression dans la musique ancienne (I)". In: *Revue musicale de Suisse Romande. Vol. 66/1.* Mars 2013. P. 38.

[47] The exact passages upon which Cotto based himself are to be found in: Ibid. *Vol. 67/1.* March 2014. P. 45.

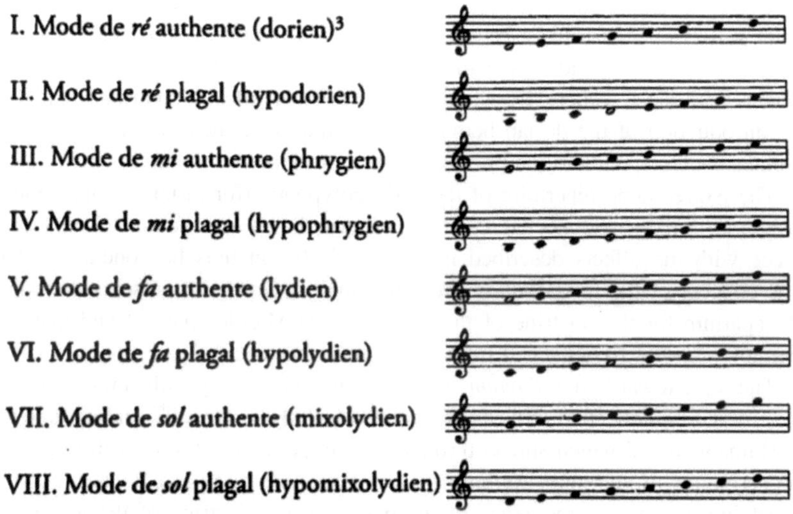

Fig. 5.1 The eight ecclesiastic medieval modes. Figure taken from: Arlettaz, Vincent: „L'expression dans la musique ancienne (I)". (In: *Revue musicale de Suisse Romande. Vol. 65/3.* September 2012. P. 6)

Each mode has its own character and is applied in accordance with the specific character expressed by each text. Yet, one major distinction between the antiquity modal *ethos* and the ecclesiastic modes of the Middle Ages is the displacement of the *finale* or *primo tono*, which has a clear impact on the sonority aesthetic of a scale and the corresponding character or affect: while in the Greek conception the octave frame and the placement of the semitone were the reason for a character distinction between each mode, in the medieval notion the "respective pitch" was the foundation for the character attribution[48]. In the latter, the lower the *primo tono*, the closer to the earthly attributes; the higher the pitch, the closer to the "celestial joy"[49]. Nonetheless, there is a diversity of ordering systems to be acknowledged, according to different traditions. Further distinctions are to be found later in history as well, for instance between the Zarlino and the Gabrieli

[48] Cf. Ibid. *Vol. 65/3.* September 2012. P. 9–10.

[49] Cf. Ibid.

traditions[50]. It was Glarean who decisively influenced the development of the order systems of the Middle Ages towards the *Musica poetica* in 1600: this was notably done by expanding the modus system from eight into twelve different modus, with the so called "Dodecachordon"[51]. His significant contribution lies in the introduction of the dorian bemolles and lydian bemolles, which—as Müller explains—corresponds to the present-day major-minor system[52].

The Notre-Dame repertoire of the early polyphony (for instance with Leonin and Perotin) likewise reflected a similar concern: the chosen modus was in accordance with the affects described in the text[53]. It can thus be concluded, that "the concept of the modal *ethos* [from the ancient Greeks] represents the point of departure for the doctrine of the affects in the Middle Ages"[54] and that the antiquity concept has changed from its original ideal.

The shift towards the *Trivium* in the Renaissance was greatly influenced by the emerging intellectual movement, initiated in Italy in the 14th century, known as Humanism and which spread throughout Europe: there was the will to revisit the scriptures of antiquity. Authors such as Dante, Petrarca and Bocaccio had a direct impact on the emergence of the madrigal, the doctrine of the affects in music and the theories of the musical rhetorics[55]:

> "The classic rhetorics and its revival in the Humanism era served as a role model for the musical theories in the 16th and 17th century"[56].

---

[50] It is to be noted that also in the Zarlino tradition the soul's emotions should be conveyed through music. Cf. Müller, Jan. (2002). *Der Komponist als Prediger*. Sect.: 3.2.3.: „Modale Affektenlehre". P. 92.

[51] Cf. Ibid.

[52] Cf. Ibid.

[53] Cf. Krones, Hartmut. "Musik und Rhetorik". (2016). In: Laurenz Lütteken (Ed.). *MGG Online*. „Die Entstehung der musikalischen Rhetorik—b. Textausdeutung.".

[54] Arlettaz, Vincent: „L'expression dans la musique ancienne (I)". In: *Revue musicale de Suisse Romande. Vol. 65/3*. Septembre 2012. P. 11. (Trans. by the author). French expression: "le concept de l'ethos des modes est le point de depart de la doctrine de l'expression au Moyen Âge.".

[55] As Krones underlines, the majority of the humanist artists were poets and composers at the same time, as for example Francesco Landini (1335—1397) and Heinrich Glarean (1488—1563). Cf. Krones, Hartmut. "Musik und Rhetorik". (2016). In: Laurenz Lütteken (Ed.). *MGG Online*. "Die Entstehung der musikalischen Rhetorik—b. Textausdeutung, Affekt und Effekt seit dem Mittelalter.".

[56] Bartel, Dietrich. (2010). *Handbuch der musikalischen Figurenlehre*. P. 22. German expression: "Die klassische Rhetorik und ihre Wiederbelebung im Zeitalter des Humanismus diente für die Musiktheorie des 16. Und 17. Jahrhunderts als Vorbild.".

Nonetheless, a relatively early formulation of the affects is to be found already in 1473/74 with Johannes Tinctoris, who accounted 20 affects in his treatise *Complexus effectuum musices* (~1473/74)[57]. These principles, prior to have been systematized for the first time in the early 17th century, were naturally divulged and applied (probably orally diffused) during the medieval and Renaissance epoch across several musical genres—in greater lines explained, from the monody to polyphony, until the appearance of the madrigal in the Renaissance and the dramatic style, which preceded the opera genre. During this development—while the notion had always been present[58]—it had undergone some significant alterations, not only with its impact on interpretation (namely at the end of the 15th century with Conrad von Zabern)[59] but especially later through Nicola Vicentino (1511–1576) with the addition of dynamics and agogic notions, such as the use of the *accelerando*; their purpose being to emphasize the described emotions of the text[60]. These alterations reflect the evolution towards a gradually more precise musical notation[61].

An important impact of the Humanist movement, which had a crucial implication for the development of these notions later on, is to be found in the work of Claudio Monteverdi (1567—1643) with the madrigals and the elements of the *Seconda pratica,* such as the *stylo concitato.* He distinguished between the different emotional qualities of music[62] and categorized the music with the following epithets: excited ("concitato"), soft ("mole"), tempered ("temperato"); music that was capable of expressing anger ("ira"), moderation ("moderato") and humility ("humilità")[63]. Madrigalisms are to be understood as metaphors of natural phenomena put into music (descriptive aspect) and at the same time as reflections of the emotions depicted in the text. This compositional-technical device was used by composers of future generations, notably by Schubert.

The affect aesthetic as a concern in the choices of the modes and scales had not only their importance in Italy, but in whole Europe, also in the 16th century

---

[57] Cf. Krones, Hartmut. "Musik und Rhetorik". (2016). In: Laurenz Lütteken (Ed.). *MGG Online*. „Die Entstehung der musikalischen Rhetorik—b. Textausdeutung, Affekt und Effekt seit dem Mittelalter.".

[58] Cf. Arlettaz, Vincent: „L'expression dans la musique ancienne (I)". In: *Revue musicale de Suisse Romande. Vol. 67/1.* Mars 2014. P. 52.

[59] Cf. Ibid. *Vol. 66/1.* Mars 2013. P. 38.

[60] Cf. Ibid. *Vol. 66/4.* Decémbre 2013. P. 43.

[61] Cf. Ibid. *Vol. 67/1.* Mars 2014. P. 53.

[62] Cf. Floros, Constantin. (2008). *Hören und verstehen.* P. 39.

[63] These descriptions are to be found in: Ibid.

and the reformation movement in Germany and Switzerland, as Jan Müller's dissertation delineates[64]. The impact of the affect aesthetic on Protestant composers is explained by the fact that they, particularly those from the evangelist-Lutheran church, followed the Franco-Flemish di-Lasso school (1532–1594), characterized by their imitation of vocal polyphony (mainly four voiced masses and motets and three voiced profane chants), which, consequently, highly influenced the so-called Lutheran sermon motets[65]:

> "In the personal preparation of a musical motif, characterized by declamation and affect as the nucleus of elaborate motetic passages within a rhetorically grounded overall concept, the pan-European di-Lasso school has an effect above all on Lutheran composers."[66].

In the tradition of the Franco-Flemish school, music was seen as subordinated to the text and ought therefore to be adjusted to the text[67]. The "ethical" ground concern of music was still present for example in Josquin Desprez (1450–1521) and Orlando di Lasso (1532–1594)[68]. The development that the di Lasso school took under Germanic Protestant influence led, in turn, to "genre-specific aspects" of the sermon motets[69], including the formation of clauses and hierarchy, the modal affect doctrine and musical-rhetoric figures[70]. One of the Lutheran composer and theorist who contributed to the continuation of this line until the *Musica poetica*

---

64 Cf. Müller, Jan. (2002). *Der Komponist als Prediger.* Sect.: 3.2.3.: „Modale Affektenlehre".

65 The dispersion of this stylistic tradition can be, in turn, particularly due to the invention of Gutenberg's printing press in 1440.

66 Müller, Jan. (2002). *Der Komponist als Prediger*. P. 77. (Trans. by the author). German expression: "In der persönlichen Zubereitung eines durch Deklamation und Affekt geprägten musikalischen Motivs als Keimzelle elaborierter motettischer Abschnitte innerhalb eines rhetorisch fundierten Gesamtkonzeptes wirkt die gesamteuropäische di-Lasso-Schule vor allem auch auf die ev.-luth. Komponisten.".

67 Cf. Krones, Hartmut. "Musik und Rhetorik". (2016). In: Laurenz Lütteken (Ed.). *MGG Online*. „Die Entstehung der musikalischen Rhetorik—b. Textausdeutung, Affekt und Effekt seit dem Mittelalter".

68 Cf. Nettesheim, Agrippa von: "De vanitate et incertitudine scientiarum". (1532). In: Ibid. The "ethical ground concern" means the mission of music as a helpful means to best express the text and consequently have the desired impact on the listener.

69 Cf. Müller, Jan. (2002). *Der Komponist als Prediger*. Sect.: 3.1.3: „Erste deutschsprachige Predigtmotetten". It should be noted that motets are mainly a rhetorical grounded musical genre. Cf. Ibid. P. 82.

70 Cf. Ibid. P. 83–84.

was Gallus Dressler (1533–1580/89)[71]. Of particular note is the fact that Dressler wrote three treatises, including the *Praecepta musicae poëticae* in 1563/64, which was only published in 1914–15, and has recently received more research attention. The term of *Musica poetica* is hereby used: this terminology has been introduced for the first time with the treatise of N. Wollicks (1501) and became, due to N. Listenius, a discipline along with the *musica theorica* and *musica pratica* since 1537[72]. In Dressler's conception there was already an awareness of the affinity between the musical clauses and rhetorical sentences[73]. This consciousness was shared by other authors of *Musica poetica*[74].

As a conclusion to this subchapter, the following complementing statements can be summarized: (i) even though the first formulations on a therapeutic effect on the psyche can be traced back to the 15th and 16th century[75], the first approaches date back to the early Greeks—for them, it was commonly conscious that music had a significant impact on the psyche, and thus was respectively applied for educational purposes among others; (ii) apart from the character of the modes, being affect related and their conscious choice in relation to the text statements, the practical use of rhetoric figures in polyphonic music refers way back in history: after Schmitz "at least since Dufay"[76]; (iii) the madrigal can be understood as "an early high point in the practice of the rhetorical figures"[77], which soon spread out in all Europe; (iv) the heritage of the Franco-Flemish schools were of great significance for the development of the concept of *Musica poetica.*

---

[71] Dressler was a pupil of the Jena Academy, a city under the influence of humanism and the evangelist-Lutheran philosophies of Melanchthon. Cf. Heuchemer, Dane. (2008). "Gallus Dressler Praecepta musicae pöeticae (Percepts of Poetic Music)". In: Robert Forgács (Ed.). *Renaissance Quarterly, Vol. 61(1).* P. 266–267. Moreover, Melanchthon particularly emphasized the importance of the music-text relationship in the Lutheran schools. It should also be noted that for Luther the *Ars musica* belonged to the arts as well as to sciences. Cf. Krones, Hartmut. "Musik und Rhetorik". (2016). In: Laurenz Lütteken (Ed.). *MGG Online.*

[72] Cf. Krones, Hartmut. "Musik und Rhetorik". (2016). In: Laurenz Lütteken (Ed.). *MGG Online.* „Die Entstehung der musikalischen Rhetorik—c. ‚Rhetorisches' Bewusstsein".

[73] Cf. Müller, Jan. (2002). *Der Komponist als Prediger.* P. 95.

[74] Cf. Ibid.

[75] Cf. Krones, Hartmut. "Musik und Rhetorik". (2016). In: Laurenz Lütteken (Ed.). *MGG Online.* „Die Entstehung der musikalischen Rhetorik—b. Textausdeutung, Affekt und Effekt seit dem Mittelalter".

[76] Schmitz, Arnold: „Figuren, musikalisch-rhetorische". (1955). Cited after: Ibid.

[77] Krones, Hartmut. "Musik und Rhetorik". (2016). In: Laurenz Lütteken (Ed.). *MGG Online.* „Die Entstehung der musikalischen Rhetorik—b. Textausdeutung, Affekt und Effekt seit dem Mittelalter".

Musica Poetica: The Theory of the Affects and the Music Rhetoric Figures of the Baroque

6

As previously explained, the retrospective interest towards the ancient linguistic related rhetoric theories, originating in the 14th century Humanism, represented the springboard for the developments of the musical rhetorics of the baroque. There was a liberation from the medieval way of thinking, which consequently instigated the will to engage again on the theories of antiquity. In this way, the building blocks for the doctrine of the musical rhetorics are the ancient classical rhetoric theories[1]. Moreover, the *basso continuo*, a technique emerging in the 16th century, represented another catalyst for the musical rhetorics, since it implied or at least provided a basis for the employment of rhetoric rules[2]. Consequently, with the urge to institutionalize a system of categorized musical figures and the purpose to establish a doctrine, the structure of the speech with its rhetorics has thus found corresponding terms in the structure of a musical work.

Several musicologists have identified that the musical rhetoric figures remained a phenomenon particular to the German baroque[3]. Nevertheless, Descartes' *Les passions de l'âme*, seem to have impacted some music theoreticians of that time, e.g., Athanasius Kircher[4]. Consequently, the underlying motivation was the increasing interest towards a "rationalization of the affects"[5] characteristic of the 17th century doctrines of the affects.

---

[1] Cf. Bartel, Dietrich. (2010). *Handbuch der musikalischen Figurenlehre*. P. 23.

[2] According to Grimalt, „in musical praxis, the shift from polyphony to the *basso continuo* era involves a radical application of rhetoric rules to composition". Grimalt, Joan. (2021). *Mapping musical signification*. P. 45.

[3] Cf. Bartel, Dietrich. (2010). *Handbuch der musikalischen Figurenlehre*.

[4] Cf. Menke, Johannes. (2014). „Mehr als ‚Figurenlehre'. Giacomo Carissimi: Jonas und Jephte". In: Diergarten, Felix. *Musikalische Analyse*.

[5] Ibid. P. 23. (Trans. by the author). German expression: "Bekanntlich war man im 17. Jahrhundert an einer Rationalisierung der Affekte interessiert; stellvertretend seien hier nur

L. Dill, *Schubert's Metamorphoses*,
https://doi.org/10.1007/978-3-662-73476-6_6

There was a mutual interchange between the doctrine of the affects (music and affect) and the musical-rhetoric doctrine (music and language). Additionally, a paradigm shift is to be noticed within the doctrine of the affects and the formulations in the categorization of the musical rhetorical figures between the 17th and 18th century: while at first the affects were primarily to be communicated through the text, the emergence of the concept of "expression of feelings" ("Ausdruck der Empfindung") around the 1730 Germany brought along a new aesthetic movement[6]. Under this term there is a twofold difference in sense: on the one hand, the moving into the foreground of an idiosyncratic expression of feelings and on the other the "emancipation of an independently linguistic instrumental music"[7]. This led to the development of a variety of systematizations with different, even incompatible repertoire of figures[8], that are to be found along the distinctive formulations from 1601 until 1788. All these changes were the results of a changing society, with new moral and aesthetic values, which included new developments in church music through the protestant philosophy of Martin Luther[9].

These distinctive conceptualizations are subject to a critical view, especially regarding its methodological use for musical hermeneutics, as more recent research indicates. Further problems relate to the key-characteristics, tropes and topoi, which are all inherent topics in these doctrines. Slowly, with the transformations of concepts, the musical rhetorical figures lost their original function[10], which led eventually to the end of formularizations and categorizations. Still, it is of general consensus in literature that these doctrines prevailed and had great influence on composers from the so called Classic and Romantic period—an

die 1649 publizierte Schrift ‚Les passions de l'âme' von René Descartes und die zeitgleich entstandene Affektenlehre von Athanasius Kircher erwähnt, [...]".

[6] Cf. Greifenstein, Johannes. (2021). „'Affectus exprimere' und ‚Ausdruck der Empfindung'. Musik, Gefühl und Sprache im 17. und 18. Jahrhundert.". In: Stolzenberg, Jürgen. (2021). *Ausdruck in der Musik*. P. 145–146.

[7] Ibid. P. 146. (Trans. by the author). German expression: „[...] so läßt sich [...] die Emanzipation einer selbständig sprachförmigen Instrumentalmusik beobachten.".

[8] Cf. Klassen, Janina. (2001). „Musica poetica und musikalische Figurenlehre—ein produktives Missverständnis.". In: Wagner, Günther. (2001). *Jahrbuch des Staatlichen Instituts für Musikforschung Preußischer Kulturbesitz*. P. 73–83.

[9] Cf. Ibid.

[10] Cf. Ibid.

impact which extends until the present-day[11]. This statement indicates the sinking of the musical figures into the cultural unconscious. Schubert, was one of the composers who, consciously or unconsciously, used these concepts[12].

6.1 Introduction to the Musical Rhetorics and the Different Systematizations

The linguistic rhetorics and the musical rhetorics shared the same aim, which was to give a terminology to an underlying phenomenon[13]—a terminology which expresses or illustrates an underlying emotion with corresponding inner gestures or mental movements. As Bartel explains, the music theorists turned their attention towards the rhetoric lexicon, due to a restricted musical terminology[14]. This means that the linguistic rhetorics were taken as a basis from which the musical rhetorics developed independently.

The following digression will establish a foundation for improving understanding of musical rhetoric theories in different levels: firstly, it will clarify how linguistic rhetoric figures influenced musical rhetorics, and which contents were taken over in the 17th and 18th century. Secondly, it will help to realize how close the relationship is between the figure concept and C.G. Jung's archetypal theories—to see how the figure concept can fall into the cultural unconscious, acting as an unconscious effect on the transmission of the inner state of mind of composers to the listeners. Finally, it will permit the acknowledgement of the most relevant points in the developments of the musical rhetoric theories through time, which will ultimately allow for the recognition of the impact of them on composers from subsequent generations, such as Schubert.

The term *figura* was first used by Cicero (born c. 106 BC) as a technical stylistic terminology belonging to the linguistic rhetorics. In this manner, Cicero was responsible for the inclusion of the term as a technical word in the rhetorics[15]. For him the term *figura* means scheme ("Schemata") and styles of speech ("Stilarten der Rede"). With the poet and philosopher Lucretius (born c. 95 BC), a

[11] Cf. Krones, Hartmut. "Musik und Rhetorik". (2016). In: Laurenz Lütteken (Ed.). *MGG Online*. "Geschichtlicher Überblick—3. Weiterwirken.". and „"Geschichtlicher Überblick—4. Spätes Nachwirken (1821 bis heute)."

[12] Examples on the application of the affect doctrine and rhetoric figures in Schubert's compositions are to be found in various works in the analysis section in Part IV.

[13] Cf. Bartel, Dietrich. (2010). *Handbuch der musikalischen Figurenlehre*. P. 22.

[14] Ibid.

[15] Ibid. P. 13.

twofold subjacent meaning of *figura* was introduced: primordial image ("Urbild") and image imprint ("Abbild"). This understanding reflects the movement going from the form ("Gestalt") to *mimesis*[16].

Later, by Quintilian (born ca. 35) this nominalization was used in the context of the doctrine of figures and defined as creative speech ("Gestaltung der Rede")[17]. Thereby, the established etymological semantics of the word *figura* was twofold: *forma* (shape) and *imago* (primordial image)[18]. The main function of the figures slightly changed from Quintilian to Susenbrotus and to Gottsched, going, respectively, from (i) a means of slightly underlining the affects in the text (persuasive function) to (ii) a means of artistically shaping speech (decorative function) and finally (iii) a means of expressing and giving rise to affects (expressive function)[19]. The change from a practical ground principle to an artistic and poetical one is evident since Susenbrotus' conceptualization[20]. Similar divergences in the focus of their terminological functions are to be found in the music theories, which naturally varied according to the epoch-related stylistic necessities and the cultural environment. Observing these considerations in Jungian terms, the double distinction in meaning inherent in the word *figura* can indicate its close relation to symbols. Since symbols are manifestations of archetypal content, the word *figura* can therefore also translate different states of developments of an archetype (3.2). Schlesinger has drawn attention to the twofold meaning of symbol being primordial image ("Urbild") and imprint ("Abbild")[21]: "In any case, every symbol consists of two parts, two symbol halves, the tangible, present image and the mostly abstract, invisible archetype."[22]. In this way, they function—in the Jungian sense—as "*a priori* forms of perception

---

[16] Cf. Ibid. P. 13.

[17] Cf. Ibid. P. 14. Prior to Quintilian and Cicero, the term was already used by the roman poet Terence (born c. 195 BC). From then on, there was a development in the meaning of the *figura* terminology. The changes extended firstly from a grammatical understanding of the term by Marcus Terentius Varro (born c. 116 BC), who replaced the Aristotelian and Platonian term schema by *figura*, and subsequently with the poet and philosopher Lucretius (born c. 95 BC). Cf. Ibid. P. 13.

[18] Cf. Ibid. P. 14.

[19] Cf. Ibid. P. 21.

[20] Cf. Ibid. P. 19.

[21] Cf. Schlesinger, Max. (1912). *Symbolik in der Tonkunst*. P. 7.

[22] Ibid. (Trans. by the author). German expression: "Jedenfalls besteht jedes Symbol aus zwei Teilen, zwei Symbolhälften, dem faßbaren, anwesenden *Abbild* und dem meist abstrakten unsichtbaren *Urbild.*".

and organization of people's experience of the world"[23]. By the involvement of *mimesis*, not only imitation is sought, but the *movens* is accentuated, thus imitating, expressing or transmitting the inner movement related to the underlying emotion. Archetypes as previously explained (I), give form to psychic energy. Thus, their manifestations appeal to inner psychic movement.

In music, the twofold semantics of *figura* as primordial image ("Urbild") and an imprint ("Abbild") remained[24], i.e., figures have a form and content, capable of giving rise to affects. In this way, they induced the desired affect described in the text (effect function), by activating the unconscious mind in a synesthetic way. The distinctive functionalities that were related above also apply to the different systematizations that are to be noted in the musical rhetorics[25]. The first systematizations of these theories in music are due to Joachim Burmeister (1601) and the last attributed to Johann Nikolaus Forkel (1788). The latter is considered to be the successor of Johann Mattheson. As it will be described later, Mattheson's treatise *Der vollkommene Capellmeister* (1739) has majorly impacted the notion of the music rhetoric figures, especially in what concerns their independent use of the text, i.e., in purely instrumental music. He thus contributed to the development of this concept and emphasized the importance of instrumental music being able to transmit the state of mind of the composer[26]; up until then, the expression of the affects was bound to a leading voice and predominantly related to the text[27].

For the understanding of the musical rhetorics the ancient linguistic rhetoric terms *res* (thought/core idea) and *verba* (individual words) are to be introduced. For the compositional doctrines from the 16th—18th century, *res* refers to the content and the meaning of the text[28]. This text ought eventually to be put into

[23] Roesler, Christian. (2022). *The Archetype Concept of C.G. Jung*. (Trans. by Alexander Ulyet and Christian Roesler). Sect. 2.1. "Definition". P. 7.

[24] Cf. Bartel, Dietrich. (2010). *Handbuch der musikalischen Figurenlehre*. P. 23.

[25] Bartel examined the major systematizations from Burmeister to Nucius, Thuringus, Kircher, Elias Walther, Bernhard, Printz, Ahle, Janowka, Gottfried Walther, Vogt, Mattheson, Spiess, Scheibe and to Forkel. These are to be found in: Ibid.

[26] Cf. Mattheson, Johannes. (2020). *Der vollkommene Capellmeister*. P. 211.

[27] As it will be shown through the chapter, Mattheson and later Forkel were of particular importance, not only regarding the development of the doctrines of the musical figures, but also concerning their influential significance for composers of the subsequent century. Forkel's conception, in particular, can be related to the Jungian theories, as it will be described at the end of this chapter and elaborated later on (7).

[28] Cf. Krones, Hartmut. "Musik und Rhetorik". (2016). In: Laurenz Lütteken (Ed.). *MGG Online*. "Die Kompositionslehre der musikalischen Rhetorik—4. *Res* und *Verba*".

music, through specific musical tools, which bear a semantic. *Verba* refers to these individual elements of the musical speech and are understood as a creative means ("Gestaltungsmittel"), including the color of notes, scales, clauses, etc.[29]. The latter constitutes the musical vocabulary with their specific semantics.

In analogy with the doctrine of the affects, *res* consequently stands for the general affect of a text, which can be conveyed in music through key and time signatures[30]; while *verba* stands for the individual sense behind one specific word[31], which is set in music through tone painting means, using musical figures and madrigalisms[32]. These tone painting techniques, such as madrigalisms, were well-regarded means of expressing the reflection of nature (of what is on the outside) in the inner world, expressing the sense of unity between the individual psyche and nature (4). The topic of *Res* and *Verba* is of major importance when dealing with the word-tone relationship ("Wort-Ton Beziehung") during the analysis of songs but is also matter for deep thought during the compositional process. Ultimately, these rhetorical elements carry "different perspectives of the composer on the same content: either on the aspects that concern the whole, or on those that concern the individual."[33]. Said so, the words and the musical setting can be semantically congruent or, in contrary, express conflicting or non-related affects[34]. The handling of *res* and *verba* in a composition is inextricably tied with the continuous debate along music history over the priority of music or of the text[35].

---

[29] Cf. Ibid.

[30] Cf. Moßburger, Hubert. (2012). „'Res' oder ‚Verba'? Zum historischen Ursprung der Kontroversen über das Wort-Ton-Verhältnis und ihren analytisch-hermeneutischen Konsequenzen.". In: *Zeitschrift der Gesellschaft für Musiktheorie*, 5/9. P. 159–185.

[31] Cf. Ibid. Moßburger explains how the doctrine of the *verba* in music was introduced by Johannes Nucius in 1613. This tradition continued with Thuringus (1624), Schonsleder (1631), Herbst (1642) and Corvinus (1646). Cf. Ibid. P. 161.

[32] Cf. Ibid.

[33] Ibid. (Trans. by the author). German expression: „Bei ‚Res' und ‚Verba' haben wir es nicht mit verschiedenen Inhalten zu tun, die einer Vertonung zur Verfügung stünden, sondern mit unterschiedlichen Blickrichtungen des Komponisten auf denselben Inhalt: entweder auf die Aspekte, die das Ganze, oder auf diejenigen, die das Einzelne betreffen.".

[34] Cf. Ibid. P. 174–175. With Schubert being a relevant name in the history of the Lied, the text-tone relationship plays an important role when analyzing his songs, as it will be demonstrated in Part IV. In addition, psychologically it is significant to note the discrepancies inherent in a musical setting and analyze what these reveal about the composer's world.

[35] Cf. Ibid. P. 165.

Besides the five main categories of the musical rhetorics[36], the decorative quality of the linguistic rhetorics (*ornatus*) played a central role in the musical rhetorics, having been considered the "primarily relevant virtue"[37]. Its constituents are the tropes and the musical rhetoric figures[38]. Tropes—or topoi—may be synonymously used in linguistic rhetorics as metaphors, i.e., words that relate to a pictural subjacent meaning. In music, as fixed musical formula and image[39], this tool is often used as a descriptive element, belonging to the tone painting

[36] The five categories are: (i) *inventio*, (ii) *dispositio*, (iii) *elaboratio* (*decoratio*), (iv) *memoria* and (v) *pronuntiatio* (*actio, executio*). Cf. Krones, Hartmut. "Musik und Rhetorik". (2016). In: Laurenz Lütteken (Ed.). *MGG Online*. "Die Kompositionslehre der musikalischen Rhetorik—2. Hauptteile der musikalischen Rhetorik.". The *inventio*, meaning "the finding", was characterized by contrapuntal and *basso continuo* techniques. The so-called *loci topici* are part of the *inventio* and were seen as a "helpful means for invention". Cf. Mattheson, Johannes. (1739). „Der Vollkommene Capellmeister". Cited after: Ibid. (Trans. by the author). German expression: "bisweilen ziemlich artige Hülffs = Mittel zum Erfinden […] an die Hand geben". *Inventio* is to be firstly found in Glareans *Dodekachordon* and had an impact notably on Clement Janequin and G. Dressler. Mattheson contributed to further subcategorizations of this principle. Cf. Ibid.The *dispositio* is understood as the structure of a musical work (cf. Ibid), which included the *exordium* (the beginning of the melody), *narratio* (report), *propositio* (content or aim of the tone speech "Klangrede"), *confirmatio* (affirmation), *confutatio* (dissolution or refutation) and *peroratio* (resolution or the closing of the tone speech). Cf. Mattheson, Johannes. (1739). „Der Vollkommene Capellmeister". Cited after: Ibid. Compositions which feature a cyclical unity were also comprised. Improvisation, strict polyphony, imitation techniques (*mimesis*) were often used as means to develop the melodic material initially presented, for which the term *ricercar* is often applied and seen as a predecessor of the fugue genre. Cf. Ibid. *Pronuntiatio* refers not only to the actual performance but to the moment where the recitative style gained a central role. Being a component that adds on dramaticism it will remain a favored compositional tool in the following historic periods. It should also be highlighted that, back then, the executor of a musical piece was required to know and follow the rhetoric rules. For accentuating the expression of the affects described in the text, the singer ought to accompany the performance with additional gestures and movements. Cf. Ibid. "Kategorien der musikalischen Rhetorik—5. Deklamation und Vortrag". This was still a common practice in Schubert's time. Cf. Legler, Margit. (13.10. 2023). "Genre Conventions in the Early German Lied and the Declamatory Tradition". [Conference presentation]. *Combining the Arts. Multimedia Performances in the early 19th century Habsburg Empire*. Schubert Research Center. Vienna: University of music and performing arts (mdw).

[37] Cf. Krones, Hartmut. "Musik und Rhetorik". (2016). In: Laurenz Lütteken (Ed.). *MGG Online*. "Die Kompositionslehre der musikalischen Rhetorik—3. Virtutes elocutionis.".

[38] Cf. Ibid.

[39] Huovinen, Erkki. Kaila, Anna-Kaisa. (2015). „The Semantics of Musical Topoi: An Empirical Approach". *Music Perception: An Interdisciplinary Journal, 33(2)*. P. 217–243.

means. Not only can the color of a specific instrument have a symbolic undertone—as the oboe or shawm which is often used to sound paint the shepherd's lament—but also intervals, sounds, clauses, fugues[40] and individual movements.

From the point of view of the historic development of these doctrines, the first systematization of the music rhetoric figures is to be found in the work of Joachim Burmeister (1601). Burmeister's systematization led to initial subdivision of the (i) harmonic figures (*figurae harmonicae*), the (ii) melodic ones (*figurae melodiae*) and, belonging to both, (iii) *harmoniae quam melodiae.* In this initial conception, the task of the musical figures was to fulfill the mission of entertaining and moving the listener. This categorization was reviewed by Nucius, who grouped the figures as *figurae principales* and *figurae minus principales*[41]: they are content-filled figures with meaning, can express and evoke affects, as well as being carrier of images, feelings and emotions[42], belonging to the *stylo moderno.* With the harmonic advancements that the *stylo moderno* and *seconda practica* brought along, dissonances and the use of chromaticism gained increasing importance. Thus, dissonances and chromatic melodic movements were filled with a specific meaning and were used to express feelings (*pathos*), such as pain, sorrow, suffering, misfortune, etc. This semantic core seemed to have prevailed through music history, and many of Schubert's chromatic passages can be associated with similar emotions.

[40] Cf. Krones, Hartmut. "Musik und Rhetorik". (2016). In: Laurenz Lütteken (Ed.). *MGG Online.* "Die Kompositionslehre der musikalischen Rhetorik—3. Virtutes elocutionis—a. Tropes.".

[41] While Joachim Thuringus (1624), Athanasius Kircher (1650) and Thomas Janowka (1701) adopted Nucius terminology, Christoph Bernhard (1648) and later Johann Gottfried Walther (1708), used the terms *figurae fundamentales* and *figurae superficialis*, respectively. Nucius' fundamental differentiation between pure musical and musical rhetorical figures was later rescinded by Mattheson, who rather emphasized their equal characteristics. Cf. Bartel, Dietrich. (2010). *Handbuch der musikalischen Figurenlehre.*

[42] Cf. Krones, Hartmut. "Musik und Rhetorik". (2016). In: Laurenz Lütteken (Ed.). *MGG Online.* "Die Kompositionslehre der musikalischen Rhetorik—3. Virtutes elocutionis—b. Musikalisch-rhetorische Figuren.".

While Kircher strengthened the relationship between the figures and the affects[43], it was due to Johann Gottfried Walther that the term music rhetorical figures was introduced in the lexica for the first time in 1732[44]. Along with the *Pracepta* treatise of 1708, Walther established the most important source for the musical rhetoric figures of the Baroque[45]. In addition to Walther's importance for the development of the doctrine, Christoph Bernhard emphasized the interpretation of the text ("Textausdeutung") as being a function of the figures: he understood the figures being tied to the text and bearing the concept of form ("Gestalt") and imprint ("Abbild") with content[46]. His figure doctrine incorporated the use of dissonance only partially.

Johann Mattheson played a central role in the subsequent developments of the doctrine of figures. He was considered to be a "rational man of the Enlightenment"[47] and a representative of the concept of naturalness ("Natürlichkeit"). As an opposition to the rococo style of the baroque, this movement searched for the simplicity and the return to nature, to the natural[48]. *Der vollkommene Capellmeister* (1739) served as an encyclopedia with educational purposes for court and church musicians at that time[49], but which influenced later musicians as well. Consequently, when dealing with the subject of musical language, this book is of the utmost importance. Mattheson begins, addressing the historical fundamentals, establishing a first foundation for his thoughts. He tackles questions like the fundamentals of music, tone, the purpose of music, the relation of nature, morals, rhetorics and mathematics, the art of writing a melody, etc. While in vocal music, the expression of feelings is described in the text, Mattheson advocates for the importance of instrumental music expressing the state of mind:

---

[43] In his formulations, Kircher directly associates the figures with the effect of the church modes, which he called *toni*, a perception meeting the notions of antiquity and the early Christian music of the Middle Ages. Cf. Bartel, Dietrich. (2010). *Handbuch der musikalischen Figurenlehre.*

[44] Cf. Ibid. P. 52. Walther's figure understanding is nearer Printz's conception of the same, who understood the figures as decorative, unifying the terminology of *figura* with manierism, i.e., ornamentation and not giving rise to affects.

[45] Cf. Ibid. P. 50. His works consisted of exposing different conceptions of the figures according to several authors, such as Thuringus, Janowka, Printz and Ahles, into a dictionary format—thereby, he distanced himself from a doctrine. Cf. Ibid. P. 51.

[46] Cf. Ibid. P. 39. Moreover, Bernhard also differentiated the *stylus gravis* from the *stylus luxurians*, to which the groups of *communis* and *theatralis* are to be mentioned. Cf. Ibid. P. 40.

[47] Bartel, Dietrich. (1997). *Musica poetica.* P. 137.

[48] Cf. Michels, Ulrich. (2008). *Dtv-Atlas Musik.* P. 333: "Aufklärung und Natürlichkeit".

[49] Cf. Bartel, Dietrich. (1997). *Musica poetica.* P. 136.

> "Who, however, might be of the opinion that the intended *loco* would mostly depend on the meaning of certain words intended for music, would not have been particularly mistaken; the so-called text in vocal music serves mainly to describe the affects. However, one must know here that even without words, in pure instrumental music in general and in the case of a simple melody, the intention must be directed towards an idea of the governing emotional inclination, so that the instruments, by means of the sound, make, as it were, a speaking and comprehensible performance." [50].

Later, Forkel defended this perspective[51]. In the second part of the book, Mattheson dedicates the attention to musical rhetoric figures and affects and in the third he addresses harmony, polyphony and counterpoint. One of the distinctive elements of his thought is the strengthening of the connection between the rhetoric and the musical composing techniques, an attitude which reflected his own zeitgeist, by introducing new terms, such as "singing poem" (Sing-Gedicht) and redefining music as "tone speech"[52] ("Klang-Rede"). As such, he expressed his core idea by emphasizing the primal function of the melody: Mattheson encouraged the expression of subjective feelings and advocated the thesis that only melody, as a natural means, could fulfill the task of awakening, expressing feelings and move listeners[53]—a belief which was later argued by Forkel.

[50] Mattheson, Johannes. (2020). *Der vollkommene Capellmeister.* Kassel: Bärenreiter-Verlag Karl Vötterle. P. 211–126/127 §45. (Trans. by the author). German expression: "Wer aber in den Gedancken stehen mögte, es käme mit dem vorhabenden *loco* wol meistentheils auf die Bewandtniß einiger gewissen zur Music bestimmten Worte an, der hätte zwar nicht sonderlich gefehlet; angesehen der so genannte Text in der Vocal-Music hauptsächlich zu den Beschreibungen der Affecten dienet. Allein, man muss doch hiebey wissen, daß auch ohne Worte, in der blossen Instrumental-Music allemahl und bey einer ieden Melodie, die Absicht auf eine Vorstellung der regierenden Gemüths-Neigung gerichtet seyn müsse, so daß die Instrumente, mittelst des Klanges, gleichsam einen redenden und verständlichen Vortrag machen". This perspective impacted not only composers from the 18th century but also of the whole romantic period. On the one hand, instrumental music was increasingly in the foreground and gaining importance in the concert hall; on the other, expressing idiosyncratic emotions was a central preoccupation of the so-called romantic artist.

[51] Also Scheibe adhered to Mattheson's thinking, even though he underlined that they ought not to have a programmatic character but should restrain themselves to the pronunciation of the affects. Moreover, Scheibe viewed the difference between figures and ornaments from a different angle, outgoing from their structure only (and not their impact). Cf. Bartel, Dietrich. (2010). *Handbuch der musikalischen Figurenlehre.* P. 65–68.

[52] Cf. Ibid. P. 57.

[53] Cf. Greifenstein, Johannes. (2021). „'Affectus exprimere' und ‚Ausdruck der Empfindung'. Musik, Gefühl und Sprache im 17. und 18. Jahrhundert.". In: Stolzenberg, Jürgen. (2021). *Ausdruck in der Musik.* P. 153–154.

Mattheson distinguished twelve word-figures, seventeen speech-figures and thirty or more extension figures[54]. The latter are understood as a means of decoration, not necessarily affect-bounded and were named as "Manieren", which ought to be used with reservation. These musical flourishes, such as ornaments or embellishments, were to be added by the performer him-/herself[55].

Forkel was considered to have been the last theoretician of the Baroque era to have systematized the doctrines of musical rhetorical figures in 1788. He defended music's message function and understood music as capable of expressing an infinity of feelings, "where other languages no longer suffice, and where their ability to express comes to an end."[56]. The arising philosophical and theological developments bounded with, on the one hand, the arisen empirical thought in sciences (outgoing from Locke's Philosophy), the cartesian principles and the Enlightenment ideals, and on the other hand, with the reformation movement of the church, led to an increasing focus on the "individualization of general feelings"[57]—a characteristic of the sentimental style ("Empfindsamer Stil"), and which impacted composers throughout the romantic period.

> "The individual expression of a musician is constrained by fixed compositional means, by a schematized dogma of sensations (the doctrine of affects) that is binding for both composer and listener, as well as by the close relationship with an extra-musical art."[58].

---

[54] Cf. Krones, Hartmut. "Musik und Rhetorik". (2016). In: Laurenz Lütteken (Ed.). *MGG Online*. "Die Kompositionslehre der musikalischen Rhetorik—3. Virtutes elocutionis—b. Musikalische-rhetorische Figuren.".

[55] Cf. Bartel, Dietrich. (2010). *Handbuch der musikalischen Figurenlehre*. P. 60–61.

[56] Forkel, Johann Niklaus. (1778). „[Rez.] Über die Theorie der Musik". Cited after: Greifenstein, Johannes. (2021). „'Affectus exprimere' und ‚Ausdruck der Empfindung'. Musik, Gefühl und Sprache im 17. und 18. Jahrhundert.". In: Stolzenberg, Jürgen. (2021). *Ausdruck in der Musik*. P. 155–156. (Trans. by the author). German expression: "Musik fängt da an, 'eigentlich Sprache der unendlichen Grade von Empfindungen zu werden, wo andere Sprache nicht mehr hinreichen, und wo ihr Vermögen sich auszudrücken ein Ende hat', so Forkel [...]".

[57] Cf. Bartel, Dietrich. (2010). *Handbuch der musikalischen Figurenlehre*. P. 71.

[58] Ibid. P. 69. German expression: „Sie ist eine Lehre, welche die Mittel zum Ausdruck von Affekten festlegt und diese weiterhin in einem engen Zusammenhang mit einer anderen Disziplin, nämlich der Rhetorik, versteht. Dass dies dem neuen Zeitgeist entgegensteht, ist offensichtlich. Der individuelle Ausdruck eines Musikers wird durch festgelegte Kompositionsmittel, durch ein schematisiertes, für Komponist wie auch Zuhörer verbindliches Dogma der Empfindungen (die Affektenlehre) wie auch durch die enge Verwandtschaft mit einer außer musikalischen Kunst eingeschränkt.".

For Forkel the figure meaning contained again the original Lucretius meaning: by bearing the meaning of primordial image ("Urbild") and imprinted image ("Abbild"), figures are "deeply rooted in the human nature"[59]. He thus extended that primal thought, making his conception of the musical rhetorics a quite avant-gardist one for his time[60]. The function of the figures was not only to put feelings and emotions in music (expression function)[61], but also represent in music the primordial abstract impressions and notions ("Vorstellungen")[62]. The impressions would exist before any formulation and ought to be recognized through the senses. Furthermore, he believed on the transfer of impressions from one sense to the other[63]. Thereby, he seems to have been quite conscious of the complex inner nature of the human being and their emotions: in contrast to Mattheson, Forkel advocated for the use of harmony and polyphony as a means of emotional expression, since a simple melody would be too one-sided[64].

From this ground reasoning Forkel developed a system, in which there is a "quality gradation"[65] between the two types of musical rhetorics and where the figures were mainly at the service of the *movere,* i.e., of the expression of feelings[66]:

i. "Figures for the mind" ("Figuren für den Verstand"), which arise out of a direct comparison between music and speech, to which structure, outline,

---

[59] Forkel, Johann Nikolaus. (1788). „Allgemeine Geschichte der Musik". Cited after: Bartel, Dietrich. (2010). *Handbuch der musikalischen Figurenlehre.* P. 72. „Die Figuren ‚liegen daher tief in der menschlichen Natur, […]'".

[60] Cf. Krones, Hartmut. "Musik und Rhetorik". (2016). In: Laurenz Lütteken (Ed.). *MGG Online.* "Kategorien der musikalischen Rhetorik—1. Gesamtsicht.".

[61] Cf. Bartel, Dietrich. (2010). *Handbuch der musikalischen Figurenlehre.* P. 72.

[62] Cf. Ibid.

[63] Cf. Ibid.

[64] Cf. Greifenstein, Johannes. (2021). „'Affectus exprimere' und ‚Ausdruck der Empfindung'. Musik, Gefühl und Sprache im 17. und 18. Jahrhundert.". In: Stolzenberg, Jürgen. (2021). *Ausdruck in der Musik.* P. 157. Hereby, Forkel's theories reveal themselves to be of particular relevance for this dissertation. Chap. 7 will develop this topic more in depth by (i) dealing with the complexity and ambiguity of emotions that are expressed in music, notably through harmonic means, and (ii) relating these to the psychological equivalents of Jung's theories.

[65] Bartel, Dietrich. (2010). *Handbuch der musikalischen Figurenlehre.* P. 72. German expression: „qualitative Abstufung".

[66] Cf. Ibid. P. 71.

periodicity, time extension but also form, style, genre[67], and especially the "contrapunctual arts"[68] pertains. Here, Forkel might be the closest to the earlier formulations of the music rhetoric figures.

ii. "Figures of imagination" ("Figuren für die Einbildungskraft"), which in turn consist of a further twofold differentiation:
   a. "The external visible and audible figures"[69] with the aim to "(re)create the image of an [outer] object in the listener's imagination"[70]. This category belongs to the tone painting techniques, whereby the imitation (*mimesis*) of the movement is carried out through sound and rhythm[71].
   b. The "figures of inner sensation"[72], which are considered by himself to be the most important figures of expression: the feelings which emerge from the sensory experience are to be expressed. As such they are a "semantically charged (meta)-language with communication function"[73], where the widest range of sign systems, rhetorical figures and tone painting elements belong.

Consequently, Forkel expanded the meaning of music beyond its emotional resonance to include an intellectual component. In this process the listener's cognitive capacity and sensitivity co-determine the realization of the expressed affects[74]. Forkel's perspective, being a mirror of his own time, led to the decay of the musical-rhetorics systematizations in the baroque (no more dogmas and doctrines)—subsequently, a new music aesthetic was sought and emerged.

---

[67] Cf. Krones, Hartmut. "Musik und Rhetorik". (2016). In: Laurenz Lütteken (Ed.). *MGG Online*. "Kategorien der musikalischen Rhetorik—1. Gesamtsicht.".

[68] Cf. Bartel, Dietrich. (2010). *Handbuch der musikalischen Figurenlehre*. P. 72.

[69] Cf. Forkel, Johann Nikolaus. Cited after: Ibid. German expression: „die Figuren äußerer sichtbarer und hörbarer Gegenstände".

[70] Ibid. German expression: „[…] das Bild eines Gegenstandes in der Phantasie des Zuhörers entstehen zu lassen.".

[71] Cf. Ibid.

[72] Cf. Ibid. German expression: "Figuren innerer Empfindungen".

[73] Cf. Krones, Hartmut. "Musik und Rhetorik". (2016). In: Laurenz Lütteken (Ed.). *MGG Online*. "Kategorien der musikalischen Rhetorik—1. Gesamtsicht.".

[74] Cf. Greifenstein, Johannes. (2021). „'Affectus exprimere' und ‚Ausdruck der Empfindung'. Musik, Gefühl und Sprache im 17. und 18. Jahrhundert.". In: Stolzenberg, Jürgen. (2021). *Ausdruck in der Musik*. P. 157.

6.2 The "German Baroque Phenomenon" and its Impact on (Future) Composers

While Italian composers were more likely marked by madrigalisms—a tradition going back to Monteverdi and other composers of the madrigal—the subject of *Musica poetica,* as a systematized doctrine, is considered to be characteristic of the German baroque[75]:

> "The rigorous application of rhetorical terminology and methodology to musical analysis and composition remained a predominantly German Baroque phenomenon."[76].

The dichotomy that settled in between Germanic countries and Italy seems to have been firstly motivated by differences between Protestant and Catholic thinking in these countries. Thus, the "German baroque" was marked by the protestant theology of Martin Luther. In opposition to his contemporaries, Calvin and Zwingli, Luther followed Augustine's thoughts in what regards music in the church:

> "Luther's views on music reflect Augustine's synthesis of Greek music theory with Christian dogma: music not only mirrors the order of the created universe through its own numerical order but can positively affect individuals by audibly 'putting them in touch' with the greater order of Creation."[77].

He appealed to the concepts of the *ethos* doctrine and the rhetorical figures related to the affects. Additionally, the linguistic subjects received particular attention in the Lutheran Latin School ("Lateinschule"), as did the word and the rhetoric devices in services. These were purposefully employed as a means of persuasion, and, in this manner, the rhetorics fulfilled a didactic function[78]. Not only did the Protestant services start to be preached in German language, but also the sermon motets were performed in the vernacular. As already mentioned in the previous chapter, sermon motets made use of rhetorical devices. This brought as a consequence the popularization of rhetoric figures and the accessibility of their meaning to the people. Music had, in his perception, the capability to move

---

[75] Cf. Bartel, Dietrich. (1997). *Musica Poetica.* Part One—Chap. 2: "Toward Musica Poetica: The emergence of a German Baroque Music.".

[76] Ibid. Introduction. P. ix.

[77] Ibid. P. 5.

[78] Cf. Ibid. P. 7.

listeners and make them "receptible to the spoken words"[79]. Consequently, music incites oration and preaching, especially when paired with a sacred text[80]. While music had the power to turn "the invisible audible"[81], the rhetoric figures created, in turn, an "exegetic" basis for compositions and texts[82].

There is an evolution to be noticed regarding the developments of the affects doctrine and of the theories around the musical rhetoric figures through the time: the initial focal point with the Aristotelian concept of *mimesis* shifted progressively towards an individual expressiveness and the will to evoke emotions in the listener. This process happened gradually but especially gained on importance throughout the second half of the 18th century[83], which reflected the emotion-aesthetic of the sentimental style characteristic of the second half of the 18th century.

The individual language of each theoretician resulted in the great variety of systems, which implies that they were never uniform[84]—a conclusion which can be regarded as a natural consequence of the twofold, ambivalent etymological nature of the word *figura,* as stated above. Yet, their use for hermeneutic purposes in music analysis is quite popular, at least since Arnold Schering's Article "Die Lehre von den musikalischen Figuren im 17. und 18. Jahrhundert" of 1908[85]. Nevertheless, its hermeneutic use requires a careful application. Janina Klassen, along with other musicologists, draws attention to the dangers of their thoughtless application and, consequently, to the need of an in-context-wise examination of the figures:

> "It is necessary first to analyze their use in a historical context to be able to operate with figures."[86].

---

[79] Cf. Ibid. P. 8.

[80] Cf. Ibid. P. 7.

[81] Cf. Ibid. P. 3.

[82] Cf. Ibid. P. 9.

[83] Cf. Grimalt, Joan. (2021). *Mapping musical signification.* P. 47.

[84] Cf. Menke, Johannes. (2014). „Mehr als ‚Figurenlehre' Giacomo Carissimi: Jonas und Jephte". In: Diergarten, Felix. *Musikalische Analyse.* P. 19.

[85] Cf. Ibid.

[86] Klassen, Janina. (2006). „Figurenlehre und Analyse. Notizen zum heutigen Gebrauch.". In: *Zeitschrift der Gesellschaft für Musiktheorie 3/3.* P. 285–289. (Trans. by the author). German expression: "Um mit Figuren operieren zu können, müsste ihr Gebrauch im historischen Kontext zunächst analysiert werden.".

Johannes Menke emphasizes Janina Klassen's reasoning, and explains her idea that figures "[…] are based in collective musical affect experiences"[87], belonging however to a specific setting:

> "As isolated phenomena, figures can fulfill their purpose as ingredients in musical production in the context of the treatises in which they are listed. Although they are easily applicable as hermeneutic instruments for analysis, they have little informative value. Only within the context of a specific work with its genre tradition and with the interaction with other 'Satzmodellen' [i.e., compositional types and formulas] or even individual structures do figures form constellations which, for their part, as meta-figures so to speak, can certainly convey 'collective musical emotional experiences'"[88].

The same careful attention and contextualized analysis is required while decoding the semantic value of tropes or topoi, since they also translate the transformations of the cultural environment and are each time embedded in the specific framework of a composition. For instance, Grimalt observed that those topoi "tend to become increasingly abstract"[89]. The topic of key-characteristics is equally controversial since there is the problem of the different temperaments and also the sometimes-contradictory descriptions of each key. In this case, a contextualized perspective

---

[87] Klassen, Janina. (2010). "Figur und Rhetorik". Cited after: Menke, Johannes. (2014). „Mehr als ‚Figurenlehre' Giacomo Carissimi: Jonas und Jephte". In: Diergarten, Felix. *Musikalische Analyse.* P. 23. (Trans. by the author). German expression: „Sie [die musikalische Figuren] basieren auf kollektiven musikalischen Affekterfahrungen.".

[88] Menke, Johannes. (2014). „Mehr als ‚Figurenlehre' Giacomo Carissimi: Jonas und Jephte". In: Diergarten, Felix. *Musikalische Analyse.* P. 23. (Trans.by the author). German expression: "Als isolierte Phänomene können Figuren im Kontext der Traktate, in denen sie aufgeführt werden, ihren Sinn als Ingredienzen bei der musikalischen Produktion erfüllen. Als hermeneutische Instrumente zur Analyse sind sie zwar leicht einsetzbar, haben aber eine geringe Aussagekraft. Erst im Kontext eines bestimmten Werkes mit seiner Gattungstradition und im Zusammenspiel mit anderen Satzmodellen oder auch individuellen Strukturen bilden Figuren Konstellationen aus, die ihrerseits, gewissermaßen als Meta-Figuren durchaus ‚kollektive musikalische Affekterfahrungen' transportieren können.".

[89] Grimalt, Joan. (2021). *Mapping musical signification.* P. 83. Here Grimalt juxtaposes the examples of the horn fifths in Joseph Haydn's works as a hunting topos (exemplified by his early symphonies), mirroring the classical tradition, and the use of the horn in the romantic context of the 19th century Germany, rather recalling the image of an "idealized, pastoral Vaterland" (exemplified with the horn Trio op. 40 of Johannes Brahms). Ibid. However, the one epoch spanning requires caution too, since e.g., the romantic period, as seen in precedent chapters, is vast. Thus, the contextualization should ideally happen within one composer and the examination of each work individually, analyzing whether there is a matching with the contemporary common perspective or if it conveys a different message/imagery.

is also needed. Taking the thematic inherent meaning of the text in cases of lieder and operas as the semantic meaning of the chosen key can, however, reveal to be the most accurate method of dealing with key-characteristics[90].

The cross-epochal transformations of the original concept are a natural result of a society and culture in permanent development. Therefore, it is important to avoid generalizations and to prevent a universal view of the figures, since these concepts have gone through changes, mirroring the aesthetic demands of a constantly changing society and culture. On the contrary, a contextualized approach is absolutely necessary[91].

Even though no further systematizations and formulations seem to have been undertaken since Forkel, these theories prevailed and had an impact on the subsequent historic periods. These theories of the baroque, as Krones delineates, have influenced composers of the next generations, from J.S. Bach, Carl Philipp Emanuel Bach, Leopold and Amadeus Mozart, Christian Fr. D. Schubart, Jean-Jacques Rousseau, Joseph Haydn, Ludwig van Beethoven, Carl Czerny, Franz Liszt, Richard Wagner, Hugo Wolf, Robert Schumann, Anton Bruckner, Johannes Brahms, to composers of the so-called "Second Viennese school" and up until today[92].

For the particular case of Schubert, not only are specific rhetorical figures to be found in his vocal and instrumental works, but also the overall basic "procedure of 'translation' from the conceptual into the musical [which] recalls the baroque principle of musical-rhetorical figures"[93], as Eggebrecht elucidates. The application of the baroque musical-rhetorical devices of *inventio* and *elaboratio* is

---

[90] The following literature convey the mentioned method and shall be here cited as an example: Cf. Auhagen, Wolfgang. (1983). *Studien zur Tonartencharakteristik in theoretischen Schriften und Kompositionen vom späten 17. bis zum Beginn des 20. Jahrhunderts.* For Schubert cf. Böhm, Richard. (2006). *Symbolik und Rhetorik im Liedschaffen von Franz Schubert.*

[91] For this reason, since the semantic value of rhetorical figures needs a contextualized approach, the author will not list the rhetorical figures in this chapter. Examples of such figures are to be found directly in the analysis section, with the respective inherent meaning.

[92] Cf. Krones, Hartmut. "Musik und Rhetorik". (2016). In: Laurenz Lütteken (Ed.). *MGG Online.* "Geschichtlicher Überblick—3. Weiterwirken.". and „"Geschichtlicher Überblick—4. Spätes Nachwirken (1821 bis heute).".

[93] Eggebrecht, Hans Heinrich. (1970). „Prinzipien des Schubert-Liedes". In: *Archiv für Musikwissenschaft, Vol. 27, No.2.* P. 89–109. Citation to be found on P. 95. German expression: „Das Verfahren der ‚Übersetzung' vom Begrifflichen ins Musikalische erinnert hier [„ Täuschung" aus der *Winterreise*] an das barocke Prinzip der musikalisch-rhetorischen Figuren; [...]".

demonstrated by Schubert's compositional technique of introducing, at the beginning of the lied, a primordial motif which translates the overall tone of the poem; this core idea is then continually present throughout the musical setting, based on the principle of variation[94]. As it will be elaborated later, this compositional approach is to be identified in several instrumental works of Schubert as well (IV). These baroque terms find their equivalent in the musical theme, respectively its development quality, and further as its return. Eggebrecht refers that in Schubert's case they are strongly in tune with the statement of the text[95]. Seidel[96] and Hoffmann-Erbrecht[97] also expressed the high probability of Schubert having possessed a deep knowledge of the figures doctrine, which is of importance when considering a hermeneutic approach. These affirmations are grounded on the strong evidence that Schubert was a pupil of and influenced by Antonio Salieri. Schubert thus reveals a singular way by which poetry is incarnated as a musical construction:

> "[...] whereby the linguistic layer of poetry is elevated to the structural principle of music, poetry is realized as a musical structure"[98].

Consequently, especially in Schubert songs, the term of "musical poetry" ("musikalische Lyrik")[99] can be applied.

---

[94] Cf. Ibid. This kind of procedure is also known as motif metamorphose technique. The author will rather use the latter terminology in Part III and IV.

[95] Cf. Ibid. P. 90, 91, 92.

[96] Cf. Seidel, Elmar. (1969). „Ein chromatisches Harmonisierungs-Modell in Schuberts ‚Winterreise'". Cited after: Krones, Hartmut. "Musik und Rhetorik". (2016). In: Laurenz Lütteken (Ed.). *MGG Online*. "Geschichtlicher Überblick—3. Weiterwirken.". and „"Geschichtlicher Überblick—4. Spätes Nachwirken (1821 bis heute).".

[97] Cf. Hoffmann-Erbrecht, Lothar. (1989). „Vom Weiterleben der Figurenlehre im Liedschaffen Schuberts und Schumanns". Cited after: Ibid.

[98] Eggebrecht, Hans Heinrich. (1970). „Prinzipien des Schubert-Liedes". In: *Archiv für Musikwissenschaft, Vol. 27, No.2*. P. 89–109. Citation to be found on P. 91. German expression: "[...] womit die Sprachschicht der Lyrik zum Strukturprinzip der Musik erhoben, Lyrik als musikalische Struktur verwirklicht wird.".

[99] This term is proposed by Barbara Dobretsberger and is to be understood as a counterpart to Schönberg's concept of the musical prose ("musikalische Prosa"), namely presenting corresponding elements of a lyric poetry in the music, such as a lyrical-symmetrical form, structure and rhythm, as well as the principle of repetition. Cf. Dobretsberger, Barbara. (2019). *Formen der Vokalmusik*. P. 27.

Besides composers, also theoreticians and philosophers have expressed their concordant opinions in theoretical-aesthetical scriptures, including Christian Gottfried Krause, Friedrich Schlegel, Goethe, E.T.A. Hoffmann, Georg Wilhelm Friedrich Hegel, Arthur Schopenhauer, Eduard Hanslick, Ludwig Wittgenstein[100]. Schubart, who wrote the important treatise regarding the musical aesthetics in 1784 (published in 1806) *Ideen zu einer Ästhetik der Tonkunst* emphasized the rhetorical importance in music, the *mimesis* aspect of instrumental music and key-characteristics. He advocated that "the composer ought to know everything that a poet and rhetor knowns"[101]. Schlegel, states how the affects can only be expressed through music: "the infinite longing, melancholy and remembrance can only be awakened by music"[102]. Goethe and later Hegel addressed the dialog and the discourse quality of music: the former described how in a string quartet "four reasonable people talking among themselves"[103] is audible; the second, perceived instrumental statements in Mozart's symphonies "'as an art of dialogue' with 'replies'"[104]. Hegel was also "convinced about the rhetorical character of the music"[105].

All of these statements allow for the following concluding thoughts: being a means of expressing complex inner states and emotions, (i) the systematization of the baroque figures caused an overall spread consciousness among composers in regard to these principles, which increased on popularization with the use of them in Protestant services and sermon motets, (ii) the musical rhetorics contribute(d) to an unconscious communication of symbols, appealing to and activating all senses in a synesthetic way, and (iii) speaking in Jungian terms, the rhetorical figures have, with time, fallen in a collective matrix of a culture, i.e., in the cultural unconscious.

---

[100] Cf. Krones, Hartmut. "Musik und Rhetorik". (2016). In: Laurenz Lütteken (Ed.). *MGG Online.* "Geschichtlicher Überblick—3. Weiterwirken.". and „"Geschichtlicher Überblick—4. Spätes Nachwirken (1821 bis heute).".

[101] Schubart, Christian Friedrich Daniel. (1784/1806). „Ideen zu einer Ästhetik der Tonkunst". Cited after: Ibid. "Geschichtlicher Überblick—3. Weiterwirken.". German expression: „[…] alle Instrumente seien nur ‚Nachahmungen des Gesanges', und nicht zuletzt deswegen müsse der ‚Tonsetzer alles wissen, was Dichter und Redner kennen sollen'.".

[102] Schlegel, Friedrich. (1804). „Philosophische Lehrjahre". Cited after: Ibid. German expression: „die unendliche Sehnsucht, Wehmuth und Erinnerung kann nur durch Musik erweckt werden.".

[103] Goethe, Wolfgang, Johann. Letter to Carl Friedrich Zelter. (09.11.1829). Cited after: Ibid.

[104] Hegel, Georg Wilhelm Friedrich. (1818/1835). "Ästhetik". Cited after: Ibid. "Geschichtlicher Überblick—4. Spätes Nachwirken (1821 bis heute).".

[105] Ibid.

A great number of attempts at definition in the different areas and disciplines have resulted in a non-uniformed use of the term "symbol"[106]. In the linguistic field, this term is often used, under a semiotic perspective, as a synonym to signs. It is important to clarify that the author uses C.G. Jung's understanding of the concept "symbol" as an operational term. In this view, symbols differ from the term sign. The word "symbol", here consciously applied, is seen in opposition to the word "signs", referring to the meaning of primordial image and imprinted image inherent in the concept of figures. One figure can have more than one subjacent meaning and nuances, which is to be interpreted depending on the musical and text passage (the same variety in shades exists in key characteristics). This ambivalence corresponds to the nature of symbolic phenomena and therefore figures are not to be perceived as signs. The expression of affects, feelings and emotions is a further indicator of the underlying archetypal structures (3). In opposition, signs, addressed in the musical semiotics, have rather an immediate connotation. This represents the main difference between symbols and signs.

[106] Cf. Nünning, Ansgar. (2013). *Metzler Lexikon. Literatur- und Kulturtheorie*. P. 729.

7 Music as the Expression of the Ineffable

> "Every human being has their own language. Language is the expression of the spirit." – Novalis[1].

The equation of music being equivalent to language has given rise to many lines of discussion along different disciplines of musicology and music history. Language is a complex communication system of signs, which, when linked together, gain meaning and end up constituting syntax. Not only do the natural languages have an analyzable syntax, but so do mathematics and music. From this fact, terms such as "musical prose" and "musical lyric" emerge[2]. Semantic content led to the development of various methods of analysis, such as semiotics (the study of sign systems) and the semantics (the study of meaning), both valid in a linguistic context as in a musical one. Linguistics and sociologists have developed and used different models to explain how communication functions, e.g., the triangle model following the main three steps of addresser—message—addressee. This basic system of communication can be easily transferred to music, e.g., composer—musical work—listener/interpreter. Analyzing these three elements is a transdisciplinary task between the different subdomains of historical and systematic musicology. Being music an art of expression, its central purpose is

[1] Novalis. Fragmente I—Individuelle Sprache. Project Gutenberg. (Trans. by the author). German expression: "Jeder Mensch hat seine eigene Sprache. Sprache ist Ausdruck des Geistes.". In a similar way, Wilhelm von Humboldt understands the language as the "creative organ of thought" and as the expression of the "own unique worldview". von Humboldt, Wilhelm. (2016). *Über die Verschiedenheiten des menschlichen Sprachbaues.* Chap. 2: „Von der Natur der Sprache und ihrer Beziehung auf den Menschen im Allgemein.". German expression: „Die Sprache ist das bildende Organ des Gedanken", respectively, „[...] so liegt in jeder Sprache eine eigenthümliche Weltansicht.".

[2] Cf. Dobretsberger, Barbara. (2019). *Formen der Vokalmusik.* P. 27.

L. Dill, *Schubert's Metamorphoses*,
https://doi.org/10.1007/978-3-662-73476-6_7

the act of communicating/expressing emotions and states of mind artistically. Scholarly discussions around this topic are consequently abundant and intense, even today: some scholars advocate the close relationship of music and language accentuating a one-to-one approach; others highlight the differences with it and defend the thought that music is either more than a language or cannot simply be analogously compared[3]. However, this kind of analysis is often done without considering the creative process and therefore reveals itself to be insufficient in some respects, since emotions as part of the process of artistic expression require an investigation taking the creation process into account[4]. As a consequence, a reformulation is needed: music can communicate not only hidden messages, feelings and states of mind, deep anchored emotions, moods, but also (primordial) experiences, and especially psychic processes of an archetypal nature. This was already acknowledged at the beginning of the 20th-century in the domain of systematic musicology, e.g., in music philosophy or music psychology[5]. Applying these concepts in the framework of historical musicology, e.g., in music analysis, can be a fruitful endeavor (IV).

While music psychologists have the primary aim to decode the emotional effect of music on the listener, based mainly on empirical studies, they have recognized a lack of research attention nowadays on the emotional processes involved during the course of music creation (performing, improvising, composing, music learning, etc.)[6]. Music psychologists make the distinction between the cognitive and emotional positions, which resulted from the antagonistic debate between Hanslick and Hausegger, respectively[7]. Hausegger in *Music as expression* (1885) supported the thesis that music contains an emotional quality, which is based on experience and empathy of emotional expressive movements ("emotionale Ausdrucksbewegung"). Hausegger's position is understood as a reaction to Hanslick's statement in *On the musically beautiful* (1865), who in turn, advocated that "the meaning of music, including emotions, is only ascribed to it and does

---

[3] The author will develop this thought and refer these perspectives throughout this chapter. Furthermore, the report on the International Congress of the Society for Music Research in Freiburg im Breisgau 1993 serves as a point of reference for these discussion lines. Cf. Danuser, Hermann., Plebuch, Tobias. (Ed.). (1998). *Musik als Text.*

[4] The previous chapter has already shown the relationship between the rhetoric figures and emotional states, how the figures aim at or serve the expression of affects.

[5] In music psychology Ernst Kurth shall be cited as an example, for an advocate of the thought that music relates of psychic processes (7.2).

[6] Cf. Egermann, Hauke., Kreutz, Gunter. (2018). "Wirkung—Emotionen und ästhetische Gefühle". In: Lehmann, Andreas C., Kopiez, Reinhard. *Handbuch Musikpsychologie.* P. 618.

[7] Cf. Ibid.

not originate from it"[8]. In several passages, Hausegger mentions an impulsive force and an "inner expressive urge"[9] in relation to the creative activity, which should be understood in the context of his "expression movement" idea:

> "The artist creates unconsciously, and all the surprising correspondences between his composition and the movements that govern the expressive apparatus are not simply the result of external observation, but products of a direct expressive urge aroused within him which, with all the sensitivity and agility of the expressive medium, transfers all aspects of its nature to the tonal world at the artist's disposal. In all works that have a substantial dramatic effect, one may be sure that this effect is the product of the correspondence of the most significant aspects of the music with natural forms of expression of the human organism."[10].

On the other hand, music philosophers have identified different emotion-theories around the topic of musical expressivity: (i) the expression theory, which believe that music contains the emotions of its creator and eventually reflects a process of emotional transformation; (ii) the symbol theory, in which the symbolic and metaphorical characteristic of emotional expression inherent in music is defended; (iii) the "corded shell" theory ("Konturtheorie")[11], where the structural relationship between basal and complex emotions and music is examined, (iv) the Persona theory, where the expressed emotions perceived by the listener equals emotional experiences of an imagined person (unknown or from the historic-biographical and musical context); (v) evocation theory, which states that music evokes feelings as a reaction of emotional states from an imagined person, i.e., a theory which grounds itself on the concept of emotional contagion and on an empathetic attitude of the listener[12]. Even though, many of these theories can complement themselves, individually they also present problems that can be

---

[8] Hanslick, Eduard. (1865). "Vom musikalisch Schönen". Cited after: Ibid. P. 618. (Trans. by the author). German expression: "[…] dass jegliche Bedeutung von Musik, einschließlich etwaiger Emotionen, ihr [der Musik] nur zugeschrieben sei, keineswegs aber aus ihr hervorgehe.".

[9] Von Hausegger, Friedrich. (2018). *Music as Expression.* (Trans. by Robert J. Crow). P. 112.

[10] Ibid. P. 108.

[11] This term refers to the theories exposed in Peter Kivy's "Sound sentiment. An Essay on the Musical Emotions. Including the Complete Text of 'the Corded Shell'" and Stephen Davis "The Expression of Emotions in Music". Cited after: Ibid.

[12] Cf. Zwinggi, Stefan. (2021). "Ausdruck in der Musik als Thema der analytischen Musikphilosophie". In: Stolzenberg, Jürgen. *Ausdruck in der Musik.*

debated[13]. This points to the need, as Zwinggi underlines, to work in a synergistically and multidisciplinary fashion, a consensus to be found today among many scholars[14].

In terms of the philosophy of music, the concept of musical expression allows for a great differentiation in shades, e.g., feelings, affects, emotions, moods, etc. Zwinggi refers to Suzanne K. Langer (*Philosophy in a New Key* in 1942)[15] as one of the proponents of the aforementioned symbol theory, who had identified the noted diversity of meaning. These possible smooth distinctions in meaning confirms the different layers of musical expression in a psychological context, going from more superficial feelings to deep anchored emotions or moods—from concrete conscious feelings to abstract polyvalent moods, grounded in the unconscious.

These debates demonstrate (i) the communication principle of "music as a language", (ii) the manifold conceptions and meanings of the musical expressiveness, of the emotional core of music, and (iii) delineate some controversial thoughts in the matter, e.g., whether music contains emotions, which are capable of being transmitted and evoked in listeners, or not. From another perspective, Jung's theories demonstrate that emotions are the link between the inner and the outer world, between the personal and the collective, present in the addressor and in the message of music. Consequently, the three-fold communication model is explained, by highlighting the relation with the creative process and the relation with the inner world, where language is primarily to be understood as abstract and then symbolic: archetypes have an emotional core, which urge for (artistic) expression.

[13] Cf. Zwinggi, Stefan. (2021). "Ausdruck in der Musik als Thema der analytischen Musikphilosophie". In: Stolzenberg, Jürgen. *Ausdruck in der Musik.*

[14] Cf. Ibid.

[15] Cf. Ibid.

7.1 The Fourth Dimension of Music—the Archetypal Language

"Archetypes in practical experience are images and emotions at the same time."[16].

Emotions play a crucial role in Jungian Psychology[17]. Since Jung's first theories, namely his feeling-toned complex theory, he has been able to demonstrate how emotions are at the core of every complex. His association experiments showed how specific words could be charged with emotions[18], and were linked to a specific past experience. Consequently, Jungian psychologists are convinced that:

> "Human life is accompanied by emotionality from the beginning to the end – in the waking state as in dreams. Each experience is linked with emotion, each memory is tied with emotionality (or we do not remember). Transformation, change[,] need emotion."[19].

---

[16] Jung, Carl Gustav. "GW 18/I". Cited after: Kast, Verena. (2014). *Die Tiefenpsychologie nach C.G. Jung*. Chapter "Das kollektive Unbewusste und die Archetypen". (Trans. by the author). German expression: "Archetypen in der praktischen Erfahrung [...] sind Bilder und gleichzeitig Emotionen.".

[17] After C.G. Jung "Feeling is primarily a process that takes place between the ego and the given content, a process, moreover, that imparts to the content a definite value in the sense of acceptance or rejection ('like' or dislike). The process can also appear isolated, as it were, in the form of a 'mood', regardless of the momentary contents of consciousness or momentary sensations. The mood may be causally related to earlier conscious contents, though not necessarily so, since [...] it may equally well arise from unconscious contents. But even a mood, [...] implies valuation. [...] Feelings, therefore, is an entirely subjective process [...]. When the intensity of feeling increases, it turns into an affect, i.e., a feeling-state accompanied by marked physical innervations. Feeling is distinguished from affect by the fact that it produces no perceptible physical innervations [...]". Jung, Carl Gustav. (2014). "Psychological Types". In: *CW. Vol. 6*. (Trans. by Gerhard Adler and R.F.C. Hull). Chapter XI: "Definitions". The term "emotion" is used by Jung as a synonym for affects. Cf. Ibid.

[18] Following Jung's logic, words can be strongly affectively charged, have an archetypal background, and evoke an emotional response on the addressee. The analogical thought in music has already been demonstrated notably by Bernstein in his Harvard Lectures: if letters are individual notes, words can be musical motives. Cf. Bernstein, Leonard. (1976). *The unanswered Question.*

[19] Kast, Verena. (2014). *Die Tiefenpsychologie nach C.G. Jung*. Chapter "Die Affektivität als Grundlage der Persönlichkeit". (Trans. by the author). German expression: „Das menschliche Leben ist von Anfang bis zum Ende von Emotionalität begleitet—im Wachen und im Träumen. Jede Erfahrung ist verknüpft mit Emotion. Jede Erinnerung ist mit Emotionalität verknüpft, oder wir erinnern nicht. Wandlung, Veränderung benötigt Emotion.".

With this sentence, Verena Kast explains how emotion is omnipresent and is a common ground of the living beings; how it is part of the soul and how it forms the core of personality, how it establishes a connection between the outer world (waking state) and the inner world (dreams). It also highlights the essential function of emotions for individuation, which has an effect not only on the individual human being, but also works on a collective level, impacting an entire culture and society. Consequently, emotions contribute to the self-regulation process of the psyche[20].

Kast explains the origins and nature of emotions, namely that they arise unconsciously through the confrontation with specific existentially meaningful circumstances[21]. The deep unconscious nature of emotions is described by Jung himself in his memoirs, in the context of the creative act:

> "Insofar as I managed to translate the emotions that were stirring me into images, in other words to find the images that were hidden behind the emotions, inner peace set in. If I had let things remain on an emotional level, there is every reason to believe that I would have been torn asunder by the contents of the unconscious."[22].

This statement describes how emotions are intrinsically tied with the creative process. Following Verena Kast's reflections, Jung's *Red Book* contains no more than translations of his own emotions into pictures, with the purpose to bring the inner living images (archetypes) to consciousness and thus to process the active archetype and the correspondent emotion, to integrate them in the own personality. This is based on the same processing principle that happens in dreams and fantasies and can, therefore, also be applied to the compositional process in music. In other words, the archetypal content, the inner images—images, which can also be musically perceived in form of musical motives, musical phrases, harmonic progressions, etc.—give structure to emotions, which are then further processed and transformed through the creative act. Consequently, there is a

[20] Cf. Ibid. Chapter "Komplex, Symbol und Traum".

[21] Ibid. Chapter "Das kollektive Unbewusste und die Archetypen".

[22] Jung, Carl Gustav. (1961). *Ma vie*. P. 284. French expression: "Dans la mesure où je parvenais à traduire en images les émotions qui m'agitaient, c'est-à-dire à trouver les images qui se cachaient dans les émotions, la paix intérieur s'installait. Si j'avais laissé les choses demeurer sur le plan de l'émotion, il y a lieu de penser que j'aurais été déchiré par les contenus de l'inconscient.".

dynamic element which is inherent. Verena Kast describes this mechanism as follows: "Archetypal images permit emotions to be captured in a certain structural dynamic."[23]. In a similar manner, Christian Roesler formulates:

> "According to Jung, archetypes are strongly affectively charged, which means that when we experience them, they relate to specific and clearly traceable emotions. It could even be said that they structure and channel emotions."[24].

This can be exemplary substantiated with the experiences of the soul images Anima and Animus, which, when they happen, are characteristically accompanied by a high degree of emotionality[25]; the same occurs with every type of archetypal manifestations and the associated numinous experience[26]. Jung's thoughts on the emotional charge of archetypes find consensus in Analytical Psychology. Jung himself is straightforward in his formulation: "symbols transports and transforms emotions and insights"[27].

These statements bring the insight that not only artistic expressions emerge out of the confrontations with archetypes, which in turn have an underlying emotion, but also that any living symbol can and will affect another human being, especially if the same element finds an inner resonance. Out of this basic principle, the contents of the collective unconscious act as a conducting unifying vector between the composer, the interpreter and the listener; therefore, it occurs as a meta-level mediator for conveying emotions and archetypes, ultimately a narrative process characterized by its symbolic content.

Jung stated: "Emotions are contagious […]. Each emotional process immediately triggers similar processes in the other."[28]. These thoughts actually match

---

[23] Kast, Verena. (2014). *Die Tiefenpsychologie nach C.G. Jung*. Chapter "Das kollektive Unbewusste und die Archetypen".

[24] Roesler, Christian. (2022). *The Archetype Concept of C.G. Jung*. (Trans. by Alexander Ulyet and Christian Roesler). "Chapter 2.1. Definitions". P. 8.

[25] Verena Kast even says that the experience of Anima/Animus can only be qualified as such if accompanied by an intense emotion. Cf. Kast, Verena. (2014). *Die Tiefenpsychologie nach C.G. Jung*. Chapter "Anima und Animus".

[26] Christian Roesler mentions the numinous experience as proof for the strong emotional charge of archetypes. Cf. Roesler, Christian. (2022). *The Archetype Concept of C.G. Jung*. (Trans. by Alexander Ulyet and Christian Roesler). Chapter 2.1. "Definitions". P. 8.

[27] Jung, Carl Gustav. "GW 5". Cited after: Kast, Verena. (2014). *Die Tiefenpsychologie nach C.G. Jung*. Chapter "Das Symbol". (Trans. by the author). German expression: "Symbole transportieren und transformieren Emotionen und Erkenntnisse.".

[28] Jung, Carl Gustav. "GW 18/1". Cited after: Kast, Verena. (2014). *Die Tiefenpsychologie nach C.G. Jung*. Chapter "Das gemeinsame Unbewusste". (Trans. by the author). German

several above-cited philosophical theories of emotions. For instance, the evocation theory, which has gained increasingly on application since the last twenty years, and which are based on the principle of compassion[29]. It finds an early equivalent in Hausegger's musicological formulations as well:

> "In music, we are therefore dealing with the sensations of tone. The effect of these tones does not remain isolated. It is not confined to the sensory organ that receives them. It is transmitted to the whole nervous system and evokes certain states within this nervous system. It influences our feelings."[30].

There are several explanations for this phenomenon, nowadays[31]. The essential premise is that archetypes have an emotional core and music expresses emotions and inner states. Consequently, archetypes are expressed through music and can be perceived and reexperienced by the listener/interpreter on the basis of a resonance mechanism. This process functions pre-linguistically[32], which means that this process is more rapid and direct, and more abstract, since the procedure of formulation is slower. Consequently, Hanslick's argument and other theories claiming that music has no emotional basis or cannot evoke emotions is controversial, thus this argument can be debated, or even seen as refuted.

On the other hand, spinning Hausegger's thought further leads to the interpretation of the concept of movements of expression ("Ausdrucksbewegung") as spontaneous expressions of the inner world, i.e., abstract psychic movements between the "I" and the deep unconscious structures. These movements, on a

---

expression: "Emotionen sind ansteckend […]. Jeder emotionale Vorgang löst unmittelbar ähnliche Vorgänge im anderen aus.".

[29] Zwinggi mentions Stephen Davis concept of compassion as a contagious emotion. Cf. Davis, Stephen. (2011). "Infectious Music. Music-Listener Emotional Contagion". Cited after: Zwinggi, Stefan. (2021). "Ausdruck in der Musik als Thema der analytischen Musikphilosophie". In: Stolzenberg, Jürgen. *Ausdruck in der Musik*. P. 45.

[30] Von Hausegger, Friedrich. (2018). *Music as Expression.* (Trans. by Robert J. Crow). P. 98.

[31] Due to the high complexity of the various debates on this topic, which extends from psychology to neurosciences, and which surpasses the scope of this dissertation, these will not be developed here. For up-to-date state-of-the-art research covering the current lines of discussion and considerations on the topic of emotion theories please see: Roesler, Christian. (2024). "Emotion Regulation, Relationship and Therapeutic Change in Analytical Psychology and Contemporary Psychodynamic Approaches". *Journal of Analytical Psychology*, 2024, 69, 4, 1–18.

[32] Cf. Bauer, Joachim. (2005). "Warum ich fühle, was du fühlst: intuitive Kommunikation und das Geheimnis der Spiegelneurone.". Cited after: Roesler, Christian. (2016). *Das Archetypenkonzept C.G. Jungs.* Chapter 4.3.5. „Spiegelneurone und der 'intersubjektive geteilte Raum'".

synesthetic basis, recall not only speech melodic patterns but mainly primordial images, states or moods which carry in themselves a polarity and ambivalent moving qualities. These speech-like musical patterns, speech melodies or speech-like inflections, evoke an unconscious mimetic movement. Congruently, Karbusicky explains that the mimetic movement in musical structures are devoid of any conceptualization ("begriffslos")[33]. In this abstract manner, the musical language is more direct and nearer to the inner reality than any natural language. In other words, it can be said that music conveys artistically a deep psychic dynamic language, capable of expressing the inner archetypal stages and narrative processes.

As already stated, narrative processes can be found in myths, legends and fairy tales. Marie-Louise von Franz explained the distinction between them: while myths and legends are geographically bound to a specific culture, fairy tales have a more collective character[34] (3.1). Speaking of a narrative character in music and its symbolic content, it can be highly tempting to restrict this viewpoint to programmatic music. After all, program music is defined as instrumental music with an outer-musical content, following a specific storyline given by the title or program notes[35], while absolute music[36], on the other hand, is defined as the opposite of program music, lacking an outer musical content[37]. Nevertheless, music remains an act of the mind, of spiritual creation, where not only the "I" but also the Self is at work. Consequently, the inner movements can be found reflected in it. Analogously, absolute music could be compared to fairy tales, while program music is comparable, due to its specific character, to myths and legends.

---

[33] Cf. Karbusicky, Vladimir. (1986). *Grundriß der musikalischen Semantik*. P. 94. Additionally, Clemens Kühn hints at the characteristic of the musical language being devoid of any conceptualization: Cf. Kühn, Clemens. (2005). *Analyse lernen*. P. 194–195.

[34] Cf. von Franz, Marie-Louise. (1995). *L'interprétation des contes de fées*.

[35] The definition of program and absolute music used in this chapter is based on: Michels, Ulrich. (2008). *Dtv-Atlas Musik*. P. 143. For a more detailed definition, covering the problematics of the term see: Altenburg, Detlef. (2016). "Programmusik". In: Laurenz Lütteken (Ed.). *MGG Online*. (2016).

[36] This term is attributed to Edward Hanslick and to the so-called autonomous aesthetic.

[37] These outer musical contents are often inspired from sensory impressions or stimulated by emotions and moods, which are then conveyed in musical language through tone painting, tone symbolic means. However, musicologists have already recognized a large number of works that are close to a programmatic intention or have a hidden program, sometimes of autobiographical nature (e.g., Mahler's or Alban Berg's works). This idea can be found in Constantin Floros' analysis of Gustav Mahler's or Alban Berg's works.

Hans Zender, an advocate of the relationship between music and language, affirmed that for him music is part of the *logos*, a language that follows its own rules, similar to speech. Yet, he also confessed that music, in his opinion, narrates a process which is "Wortlos" ("wordless", i.e., ineffable). Being a great admirer of Japanese culture and Zen, he once compared music to Zen, through the following analogy:

> "Zen actually strives for a wordless experience, similar to music – music is also wordless in its primordial form."[38].

Returning to and extending Hausegger's thought still further—it could be assumed that these emotion movements ("Ausdrucksbewegung") emerge from the deepest layers of the unconscious and are of abstract nature; in other words, this conveys the primarily, ineffable nature of the musical language. It is the author's understanding that this category goes far beyond the attributable musical symbols that can be found as musical topoi, or tone-symbolism—it translates the abstract, it recalls the primordial movements or paths from the deep darkness of the unconscious to the light of consciousness, the flow from a past experience to the ephemeral present, from the oneiric reality to the ontic reality. These expressive movements can be perceived and attributed to the gestural ductus of a melodic line (tone-movement), which can translate not only "processes of movement in nature"[39], but also the inner movement of ambivalent/polyvalent emotional states. These relate to the primordial experiences stored in the deep unconscious; the movement recently described from darkness to light. A chain of sixteenth notes, for example, can be interpreted as the flowing of the psychic energy between the unconscious structures and the "I". This movement can, additionally, be underlined harmonically through the minor-major brightening[40] or through other meaningful harmonies. Being a melodic line, it contains intervals which stand in a tension relationship to each other, which can be more

[38] Zender, Hans. In: Moritz. Reiner, E. (2020). *Hans Zender—Mit den Sinnen denken.* [DVD]. Minutes: 37:56. (Trans by the author). German expression: „Zen strebt eigentlich nach einer wortlosen Erfahrung ähnlich wie Musik—Musik ist ja auch wortlos in ihrem Urbestand.".

[39] Schlesinger, Max. (1967). *Symbolik in der Tonkunst.* P. 41. German expression: "Bewegungsvorgänge in der Natur".

[40] Karbusicky already wrote about this specific harmonic shift in color, relating to the dark-light symbolism. Here, he highlights the emotional quality tied with the light symbol in Romanticism. Cf. Karbusicky, Vladimir. (1986). *Grundriß der musikalischen Semantik.* P. 264.

or less intense, depending on the level of their consonance or dissonance quality. The tension between opposites is an inherent quality of the archetypes. These interrelationships between intervals, on the other hand, can form a motif, or recall a rhetoric figure and gain therefore on specific semantic charge; in turn, this can awaken further archetypes (e.g., tritone as the *diabolus in musica*). The rhythm associated with the melodic line/gesture evokes the sensation of a primordial time, since rhythm is considered to be a primordial element of music ("Urelement")[41]; and can independently also create other, more specific patterns with a proper semantic of its own, such as rhythmic motifs (e.g., the fate motif of Beethoven's 5th Symphony). In addition, rhythm can underline the ephemeral time perception of music, the always changing nature of psychic states and moods or convey an inner sense of eternity[42]. It is the function of harmony and tone-colors ("Klangfarben") to translate the underlying emotion through special chords and harmonic progressions (e.g., the so-called painful chords, such as diminished seventh chords, ninth chords…).

Within the tonal system, harmonies maintain a certain relationship of tension, as intervals do. Heinz Acker, for instance, recognizes three major fields of tension: (i) the pole of rest, which in the functional harmony, corresponds to the tonic, providing a feeling of being "at home", (ii) the leading towards ("hinführende Kraft") or the "centripetal force"[43], relating to the dominant and (iii) its opposite pole, the leading away ("wegführende Kraft") or "centrifugal force"[44], being the characteristic of the subdominant. For this reason, closed cadential endings (dominant-tonic) are often associated with the feeling of a return home, e.g., one archetypal station of the hero-journey.

Modulations play an important role in this context. Hausegger, for example, sees modulation as the harmonic means capable to express emotional states[45]:

> "Modulation corresponds to different phases of mood. And it is my opinion that this is the significance of harmony for musical tone, in its formation of music as an art form that expresses human emotional states."[46].

---

[41] Schlesinger argues that rhythm has the capability, "the power to symbolize inner life". P. 38. Schlesinger, Max. (1967). *Symbolik in der Tonkunst*. German expression: "Da der Rhythmus diese Kraft hat, das Innenleben zu symbolisieren, […]".

[42] Cf. Schlesinger exemplified the eternity parabole with Haydn's use of organ points in *The creation.* Cf. Ibid. P. 39.

[43] Acker, Heinz. (2009). *Modulationslehre.* P. 19.

[44] Ibid.

[45] This idea is aligned with Forkel's thoughts mentioned in the previous chapter.

[46] Von Hausegger, Friedrich. (2018). *Music as Expression.* (Trans. by Robert J. Crow). P. 88.

Modulations can moreover hint at specific emotional processes, corresponding to the stages of "exposure, tension, entanglement and relaxation"[47], depending on the manner they occur:

> "[…] the type of modulation, whether hesitant or in rapid shifts, symbolizes the course of the emotional process."[48].

Similarly, Reinhard Amon explains the close relationship between the type of modulation and the semantic, syntactic and formal-structural context of a composition, hence allowing the formation of a rich symbolic network[49]. Consequently, if the composer opts for a modulation in rapid sudden shifts, or in contrary prioritizes a modulation sequence, "undertakes twisted paths"[50], or conveys "no clear goal, circling around over several tonalities"[51] can be a strong statement on what emotions and inner states are being conveyed. A rapid chromatic shift might, for instance, suggest a sudden change of mind, a sudden different perspective that proposes itself and ultimately, an inner change of state that might occur. The mediantic modulation allows for more rapid shifts to distant tonalities, which could convey a state of alienation or estrangement[52]. On the other side, a modulation sequence can already transmit a longer inner developmental process, or a process of spinning around, e.g., devil's mill ("Teufelsmühle")[53]. A succession of thirds or fifths steps, for example, can end up depicting a circle-like or spiral-like path, respectively; both processes finally leading to enharmonic relations. Enharmonic relations suggest the expression of a double, or illusory identity ("Doppelidentität" respectively "Scheinidentität")[54], which, in turn, can

---

[47] Schlesinger, Max. (1967). *Symbolik in der Tonkunst.* P. 48. (Tran by the author). German expression: „Exposition, Spannung, Verwicklung und Entspannung […]".

[48] Ibid. (Tran by the author). German expression: "[…] die Art der Modulation, ob zögernd oder in schnellen Rückungen, symbolisiert den Verlauf des Gefühlsprozesses […]".

[49] Cf. Amon, Reinhard. (2005). *Lexikon der Harmonielehre.* P. 173.

[50] Ibid. (Trans. by the author). German expression: "auf verschlungenen Wegen".

[51] Ibid. (Trans. by the author). German expression: „ohne klares Ziel über mehrere Tonarten kreisend".

[52] The type of modulation in thirds gains on popularity specially in the romantic period and represents a favored modulation technique of Schubert, as it will be demonstrated in Part IV.

[53] Literature examples, also in Schubert's music, can be found in: Acker, Heinz. (2009). *Modulationslehre.* P. 288–295.

[54] Friedrich, Siegfried. (2015). *Zu Funktion und Wirkung gradueller Tonhöhenänderungen in Johann Sebastian Bachs ‚Das Wohltemperierte Klavier' I und II sowie in Franz Schuberts ‚Die schöne Müllerin'".* Wien: Böhlau Verlag. P. 363.

hint at the intersection point of symbolic motives or archetypal structures, within the development line of the individuation process (similarly, also spiral-like).

The "potentiation" of the aforementioned centripetal and centrifugal tonality forces of the dominant and subdominant harmonies, respectively, is realized by the so-called double dominant and double subdominant[55]. These harmonies, as well as the secondary dominants ("Zwischendominante"), refer to a tonal center adjacent to the initial tone[56]. In this manner, several "fields of sense"[57]—to speak in Gabriel's language—are created, i.e., there is a simultaneity of happenings or of different (inner/outer) realities, which stand in a tension relationship to each another. Whether these harmonies are of short transitory nature, whereby the initial tonal center is still felt as being in the foreground, or whether these are used as a means of modulation, with which another key is achieved, can be a further psychological indicator of which reality is being reinforced. Based on these considerations, harmonies can be considered as archetypal carriers of moods, pointing to psychological processes, since also functional harmonic progressions, for instance, can express emotions.

Finally, the dynamics, the phrasing and the articulation contribute to an intensification of the musical statement. As such, Schlesinger describes the effect of dynamic ranges and the agogic of a musical phrase as "the depiction of the growth, development, fading and extinction of feelings."[58]. The simultaneity of motives often of antagonistic characters—as emotions are—is a strong indicator of the archetypal language. This fact led to the hypothesis that archetypes directly shape and influence the musical language[59]. This means that (i) everything emerges primarily out of that abstract expressive movement, (ii) that all manifestations of archetypes through musical topoi, leitmotivs, rhetorical figures, madrigalism, etc. correspond to another layer, superposed on the previous one, in which they gain in structure and form.

---

[55] Acker, Heinz. (2009). *Modulationslehre.* P. 26.

[56] Ibid.

[57] This concept has been introduced by Markus Gabriel in the framework of realistic ontology. Cf. Gabriel, Markus. (2013). *Warum es die Welt nicht gibt.* Also: Cf. Gabriel, Markus. (2016). *Sinn und Existenz.*

[58] Schlesinger, Max. (1967). *Symbolik in der Tonkunst.* P. 50. (Trans. by the author). German expression: „Die Wirkung der Dynamik und Agogik ist vor allem bedeutungsvoll für die Darstellung des Wachsens, Werdens, Verblassens und Erlöschens der Gefühle.".

[59] This hypothesis will be investigated in the analysis chapters of Schubert's compositions (IV): firstly, works will be individually examined, and, at a final step, put into the context of the individuation process. This last step will enable to see how the development of archetypes takes place, and how they shape and influence Schubert's musical language.

These musical elements sink into the cultural unconscious. The hereby described evolution of the emotional content of music corresponds thus to the archetypal transformations going from (i) the abstractedness and the experience of primordial wholeness (uroboros), to (ii) the form gaining of a specific archetype, which (iii) can subsequently be further split into other, more concrete symbolic forms (3.2). The transitions from one layer to the other is, however, smooth, as the archetypal transformations (3.2) and can therefore flow into one another. The language of the composer, being shaped by the cultural environment, gains individuality due to the idiosyncratic use of these musical elements.

All of these musical elements happen in music simultaneously[60] and are interconnected, often even superposed[61]. With the melodic line (creating space[62] and appealing to *mimesis*), the rhythmic pattern (recalling time perception), and the harmonies (translating states of mind and sensory experiences), a fourth dimension is achieved, where perceptions of time and space are transcended through the presence of archetypal structures; it is therefore possible to perceive and experience musically the polarity nature of archetypes.

Karbusicky hints to the duality nature of psychic states, moods or emotions, giving the example of "fearful joy" or "sorrow with hope"[63], already present in folk music. There is an immersion into a psychic or spiritual dimension, where transformations can take place and numinous experiences can happen. Karbusicky formulates this process as follows:

> "The unconscious is brought to a resonance because the archetype addresses the fundamental parameters of existence: Birth, security of the child in the womb, linking the cognitive elements to an 'aha-experience' […] fulfilled longing for 'confidentiality

[60] The simultaneity and superpositions of various musical elements are perceivable at least since polyphony. Hausegger understands the beginnings of harmony and the tonal system to the time when the "ear was […] confronted not only by groups of notes in succession, but also by groups of notes sounding at the same time.". von Hausegger, Friedrich. (2018). *Music as Expression.* (Trans. by Robert J. Crow). P. 87.

[61] Leonard Bernstein gives several, highly convincing examples of ambivalence in music. Cf. Bernstein, Leonard. (1976). *The unanswered Question.* Lecture 4: "The delights and dangers of ambiguity.".

[62] Schlesinger specifically compares the tone-movement of melody to the sense of space, while rhythm appeals to the sense of time. Cf. Schlesinger, Max. (1967). *Symbolik in der Tonkunst.* P. 40, respectively, P. 39.

[63] Cf. Karbusicky, Vladimir. (1986). *Grundriß der musikalischen Semantik.* P. 262. German expressions: "bange Freude" and "Kummer mit Hoffnung".

> and security', recognition of the primordial knowledge that was buried in consciousness. The discovery of the archetypal resembles […] a 'regaining of a long-lost and constantly sought-after consciousness'."[64].

Jörg Rasche understands the semantic of musical language as "a network of inner relationships"[65], where each individual piece of music has its own language. Moreover, he affirms that the concept of "expression movement" ("Ausdrucksbewegung") is capable of conveying much more than words; when archetypal gestures are developed into a high complex language and can express inner transformations[66]. In this manner Rasche introduces in the musical context C.G. Jung's concept of the participatory consciousness:

> "Music lies outside of what can be captured well with language. […] It is not about things, but about relationships. It expresses a participatory consciousness, […]. The unconscious is, after Jung's understanding participatory, it connects us with other beings and the timeless archetypal structures, which develop in us. We create music with our creative I, as such we elevate it into the realm of our consciousness. Because music is not bound to the linguistic semantic, because it speaks out of its own right, a kind of consciousness realizes itself in it, which includes the participatory quality of the unconscious."[67].

[64] Karbusicky here cites Wagner, since he examines his works, and links his statements with the thoughts of C.G. Jung. However, in the author's view, this can be applied to other composers and compositions. Cf. Ibid. P. 260. German expression: „Das Unbewusste wird zu einer Resonanz gebracht, weil der Archetypus die grundlegenden Existenzparameter anspricht: Geburt, Geborgenheit des Kindes im Mutterschoße, Verknüpfung der kognitiven Elemente zu einem ‚Aha-Erlebnis' […], erfüllte Sehnsucht nach ‚Vertraulichkeit und Sicherheit', Wiedererkennen des Urbekannten, das im Bewußtsein verschüttet war. Die Entdeckung des Archetypischen gleicht, […] einem ‚Wiedergewinn eines längst verlorenen und stets wieder gesuchten Bewußtseins.".

[65] Rasche, Jörg. (2014). *Das Lied des Grünen Löwen*. P. 345. (Trans. by the author). German expression: „als ein Netz von inneren Bezügen".

[66] Cf. Ibid. Chapter: „Musik und Sprache".

[67] Ibid. P. 388–389. (Trans. by the author). German expression: „Aus diesem Grunde liegt Musik tatsächlich außerhalb dessen, was sich mit Sprache gut erfassen lässt. […]. Sie handelt allerdings nicht von Dingen, sondern von Beziehungen. Sie drückt ein partizipierendes Bewusstsein aus, […]. Das Unbewusste ist nach dem Jung'schen Verständnis partizipierend, es verbindet uns mit den anderen Wesen und den zeitlosen archetypischen Strukturen, die sich in uns entfalten. Musik gestalten wir mit unserem kreativen Ich, damit heben wir sie in den Bereich unseres Bewusstseins. Weil Musik jedoch nicht an die sprachliche Semantik gebunden ist, weil sie aus eigenem Vermögen spricht, realisiert sich in ihr eine Art Bewusstsein, das die partizipierende Qualität des Unbewusstsein enthält.".

These lines express the inner dialogues that occur between consciousness and unconscious during, equally, the creative act of composing, the interpreting act of performing or the processes that unfold while listening.

7.2 The Inner Dynamic of Music—Excursus on Ernst Kurth's Ideas About Music

From the previous considerations it can be said that musical motives, rhythmic patterns and special harmonic chords, harmonic progressions or shifts in color can translate not only the state of mind and emotions but can be an indicator of archetypal manifestation carrying therefore the archetypal polarity of the opposites. Archetypes, with their emotional core, appear in the context of the individuation process (3.1), with the purpose of self-regulating the psyche by confronting and integrating the opposites, respectively the split elements of the personality. In the context of an individuation process, archetypal symbols mark the specific stages in the individuation process. If these are to be found in music, then, consequently, music can be perceived as storytelling, a narrative of the inner psychic processes, where these archetypal stages are musically identifiable. Subsequently, music reflects the creative and the individuation processes. This means that through the life of the composer there are recurrent archetypal motives which, with the unfolding of time, transform themselves and develop in a spiral-like manner[68]. This thought can be applied to either the composer (the creative and individuation of the composer himself), as to the performer[69] or the listener—after all, the addressee listens and/or perceives the (archetypal) content of the message through his own (inner) world as well. Hans Zender expressed a similar thought, saying that the process of becoming ("Werdensprozess") is strongly tied

[68] C.G. Jung himself has described this spiral-like recurrences and transformations of archetypal motives through the individuation process, by analyzing series of dreams: "We can hardly escape the feeling that the unconscious process moves spiral-wise round a center, gradually getting closer, while the characteristics of the center grow more and more distinct.". Jung, Carl Gustav. (2014). "Psychology and Alchemy". In: *CW. Vol. 12.* (Trans. by Gerhard Adler and R.F.C. Hull). Chap. 3: "IV. The Symbols of the Self.". The same thought is described in *Traumsymbole des Individuationsprozesses.* See also: Jung, Carl Gustav. (2019). *Dream symbols of the Individuation process.* Suzanne Gieser (Ed.). This thinking is well accepted in Analytical Psychology.

[69] It should be appended that the interpreter contributes to further developments and changes of the unconscious structures, as for instance a fairy teller, comparingly, does. Cf. von Franz, Marie-Louise. (1995). *L'interprétation des contes de fees.*

with the musical experience[70]; his main concern as a composer having been to contribute to an individuation process of the listener[71]. In this context, repetitions in a sonata form, for example, play an important role, since they show the necessity of the composer to go through similar inner experiences once again, in order to integrate the split elements. In this manner, the repetition allows the achievement of a higher stage in self-development. Other compositional techniques, such as the variation principle, the "motif metamorphosis technique"[72] or the cyclical form also have a similar function, in that they indicate the inner developments of musical and archetypal motifs (20).

The position of Ernst Kurth is, in this observation, significant since it stands close to depth-psychological points of view. They are close to the philosophical drive theories, which, in return, influenced the depth psychological currents[73]. By making hermeneutical use of psychodynamic models, Kurth shared the belief that the musical phenomenon is a result of unconscious forces, which relate to the inner movements, and consequently, is the psychic process itself[74]. He was also an advocate of the thesis that music has an inner dynamic, an emotional core. Wolfgang Krebs describes Kurth's theories with these lines:

> "For Kurth, the truly musical is the inaudible, the sensation of a pervasive tension in and between the sounds and tones. The theorist describes the interplay of congestion and the triggering of moments of movements as the potential and kinetic energy of the musical process. [...] For Kurth, it is not the tonal side of listening to music, but the inner dynamics of perception that make up the musical phenomenon. Music is a constant impression of movement, of impulse, release, development of power, fed from

---

70 Cf. Zender, Hans. In: Moritz. Reiner, E. (2020). *Hans Zender—Mit den Sinnen denken.* [DVD]. Minutes: 47:15.

71 Cf. Ibid. Minutes: 51:50.

72 Godel, Arthur. (1985). *Schuberts letzte drei Klaviersonaten (D958—960).* P. 19–20.

73 Wolfgang Krebs shows in his article that Ernst Kurth thoughts are sometimes closer to Jungian concepts than to a Freudian attitude. Additionally, Krebs explains how Schopenhauer's concept of the will has greatly impacted his theories. Particularly, Krebs hints at the understanding of the libido concept in Jungian terms. Cf. Krebs, Wolfgang. (2006). "Zwischen Schopenhauer und Freud. Ernst Kurths Musiktheorie als hermeneutisches Potenzial.". In: *Zeitschrift der Gesellschaft für Musiktheorie. Vol. 3/2*. P. 223–243. It must be added, that Kurth himself refers to Schopenhauer in his writings, e.g., cf. Kurth, Ernst. (1920). *Romantische Harmonik und ihre Krise in Wagners „Tristan"*. P. 4, footnote 1.

74 Cf. Krebs, Wolfgang. (2006). "Zwischen Schopenhauer und Freud. Ernst Kurths Musiktheorie als hermeneutisches Potenzial.". In: *Zeitschrift der Gesellschaft für Musiktheorie. Vol. 3/2*. P. 223–243.

> the sphere of the unconscious – these are the common dynamistic terms Kurth uses to describe the psychological phenomenon."[75].

Music has an energetical movement (kinetic energy[76]), inherent in the musical expression (composition). This statement reveals Kurth's sources of inspiration. Undoubtedly, as Freud and Jung, also Kurth was influenced by the collective fascination towards the unknown, the unconscious forces, which marked the beginning of the 20th century. Accordingly, Kurth understands, for instance, the "origin of all melody […] to take place in the unconscious"[77]. Furthermore, Kurth was impacted by the will concept of Schopenhauer and C.G. Jung's understanding of libido as a life energy[78].

> "Schopenhauer's view of the nature of music 'as a direct image of the will itself' is confirmed by the similarity of the character of the most primal musical tensions with sensations of movement, of psychic sensory energies with physical force processes."[79].

---

[75] Cf. Ibid. P. 224. (Trans. by the author). German expression: "Das wahrhaft Musikalische ist für Kurth das Unhörbare, die Empfindung einer durchgreifenden Spannung in und zwischen den Klängen und Tönen. Das Widerspiel von Stauung und Auslösung von Bewegungsmomenten bezeichnet der Theoretiker als potentielle und kinetische Energie des musikalischen Verlaufes. […] Nicht die klangliche Seite des Musikhörens, sondern die innere Dynamik des Empfindens macht für Kurth das musikalische Phänomen aus. Musik ist ein beständig aus der Sphäre des Unbewussten gespeister Eindruck von Bewegung, von Impuls, Entladung, Kraftentfaltung—so die geläufigen dynamistischen Vokabeln, derer sich Kurth zur Beschreibung des psychologischen Phänomens bedient.".

[76] Kurth himself describes what he meant with kinetic energy in music like follows: "Thus the fundamental content of every melodic movement, but also of every single note, is a living force, an intrinsic state of psychic tension that pushes out of the note […]". Kurth, Ernst. (1920). *Romantische Harmonik und ihre Krise in Wagners „Tristan"*. P. 6. (Trans. by the author). German expression: „Somit ist der tragende Inhalt einer jeden Melodiebewegung aber auch jedes einzelnen Tones, den sie durchstreift, eine lebendige Kraft, ein aus dem Tone herausdringender eigentümlicher psychischer Spannungszustand, den ich als ‚kinetische Energie' bezeichnet habe".

[77] Ibid. P. 5. (Trans. by the author). German expression: "Der Ursprung aller Melodik vollzieht sich im Unbewußten […]".

[78] Cf. Krebs, Wolfgang. (2006). "Zwischen Schopenhauer und Freud. Ernst Kurths Musiktheorie als hermeneutisches Potenzial.". In: *Zeitschrift der Gesellschaft für Musiktheorie. Vol. 3/2*. P. 223–243.

[79] Kurth, Ernst. (1920). „Romantische Harmonik und ihre Krise in Wagners Tristan". Cited after: Ibid. P. 229. German expression: „Schopenhauers Anschauung vom Wesen der Musik ‚als unmittelbaren Abbilds des Willens selbst' findet ihre Bestätigung in der Gleichartigkeit

From this basis he defended that the inner will urges for movement as a "primordial force" and that music expresses this movement. An essential statement of Kurth himself reads as follows:

> "[...] the archetypal form of musical volition [...] are psychic tensions that urge to be released in movement; all musical events are based on movement processes and their inner dynamics."[80].

Not only the will but the counter will ("Gegenwille")[81], as its opposite, enters as the other inner voice seeking expression[82]. At this point, the above stated relationship between different harmonic functions can be recalled once more: with each harmony having its own function in relation to one tonal center, harmonies can bear the principle of opposites (e.g., pushing vs. pulling forces); consequently, harmonically they can reflect the expression of will and counter will. Musical expression is a complex and interwoven network of outer influences and inner movements. It seems to be of common consensus that music remains a complex, probably the most complex form of artistic expression. This can be explainable through the ambivalent/polyvalent nature of music which lies in the ambivalent character of emotions and the polarity of the inherent archetypal structures. Consequently, the more complex the musical harmonies, the superposition of motives, or the structure of a work is, the more ambivalent they are. The fact that music is a language, but cannot be one-to-one compared to a language, and yet is more than a language, conveys its paradoxical character, namely that it is the closest to the "true" (language of the) inner nature. As such, music can express numinous experiences and the abstract unconscious elements of the Self.

---

vom Charakter der ursprünglichsten musikalischen Spannungen mit Bewegungsempfindungen, von psychischen Empfindungsenergien mit physischen Kräftevorgängen.".

[80] Kurth, Ernst. (1920). „Romantische Harmonik und ihre Krise in Wagners Tristan". Cited after: Ibid. (Trans. by the author). German expression: „Die Urform musikalischer Willensregung [...] sind psychische Spannungen, die nach Auslösung in Bewegung drängen; alles musikalische Geschehen beruht in Bewegungsvorgängen und ihrer inneren Dynamik.".

[81] For further literature concerning the concepts of the will ("Wille") and the counterwill ("Gegenwille") cf. Arendt, Hannah. (2016). *Vom Leben des Geistes*. Chapter: "Das Wollen".

[82] Examples of this statement can be found in the analysis section of Part IV, e.g., in the first movement of Schubert's string quartet *Death and the maiden* (16) or in the second movement of Schubert's piano sonata in A major sonata D 959 (17).

Even though ambivalent words in language exist, music demonstrates an intertwining of individual ambivalent elements superposed in time, which make up its abstract nature and have fascinated philosophers, composers, scholars or artists throughout history. Conclusively, its symbolic contents and archetypal manifestations can be individually identified and analyzed (formally, semantically or semiotically). The primordial abstractedness remains, however, ineffable, nonverbal, devoid of any conceptualization, being individually felt and perceived unconsciously or intuitively, making possible to recall and relive primordial experiences[83].

[83] This process remains dynamic, due to its transformational character.

Part III
Mosaics of Schubert's life and work

To interpret or analyze the music of Schubert it is important to understand the composer's world first (13). This includes the aesthetics of the time in which Schubert lived, the historical-political-cultural environment as well as biographical facts. "Mosaics from Schubert's life and work" are sidelights about certain aspects of his biography, characteristics of Schubert's musical language and creative process that seem particularly pertinent to consider, and in part contribute to prepare the reader for the analysis chapters that will follow (IV). Included are relevant and current lines of debate within the Schubert research community, such as topics concerning Schubert's religiosity, the "years of crisis" and the categorization of "early and late works". This chapter will include an overview of the current state of art as well as literature review concerning these topics. Furthermore, the main elements that constitute Schubert's archetypal language will be mentioned, creating a foundation upon which the analytical endeavor will then develop.

The (Viennese) Weltschmerz and the Search for him-Self

8

> "As a stranger I came, as a stranger I go once more […]"[1].

With this verse Wilhelm Müller opens his cycle of poems *Die Winterreise*, henceforth set into music by Schubert in 1827 as D 911. The particularly broad topic here addressed, includes an utterance of alienation and "desolation" of a primarily political nature[2] that is characteristic of Müller's poems. In addition to Müller, this sentiment might extend to how Schubert and his friends may possibly have perceived the Metternich censorship regime, which prevailed in Vienna during the Restoration time, namely as an "epochal ice age"[3]:

> "*Die Winterreise* […] a musical imagination of a hopeless state of burdensome persistence and unresolvable stasis"[4].

Vienna was an imperial city around 1810, considered the biggest German speaking city and seen as an ideal place for artists and musicians in particular, due to the cultural richness that reigned there[5]. This, however, did not necessarily

---

[1] Müller, Wilhelm. (1821). "Gute Nacht" from *Die Winterreise.* Müller, Wilhelm. (1991). *Die Winterreise und Die Schöne Müllerin.* Zürich: Diogenes Verlag. (Trans. by the author). German expression: „Fremd bin ich eingezogen, fremd zieh‘ ich wieder aus".

[2] Cf. Hinrichsen, Hans-Joachim. (2019). *Franz Schubert.* Chap. 6: „Spätwerk in jungen Jahren. Die großen Liederzyklen.".

[3] Ibid.

[4] Ibid. (Trans. by the author). German expression: „Die Trostlosigkeit der Winterreise hat in diesem Sinne durchaus auch eine politische Dimension: als musikalische Imagination eines ausweglosen Zustands von lastender Dauer und unlösbarer Erstarrung".

[5] Cf. Dürr, Walther: „Schubert in seiner Welt". In: Dürr, Walther., Krause, Andreas. (2020). *Schubert Handbuch.* P.2.

L. Dill, *Schubert's Metamorphoses*,
https://doi.org/10.1007/978-3-662-73476-6_8

correspond to Schubert's reality and concerns in particular the lack of recognition he received during his lifetime[6], at least on the part of publishers. Lieder and dances were generally well received, his instrumental works less[7]. As a vast metropolis, the implied sense of distance to nature[8] was particularly meaningful for the creativity of the Romantic composer. Therefore, there was a strong will to "humanize nature"[9], by understanding nature as a reflection of the human's needs, moods, etc.[10]. This is clearly apparent in Schubert's setting of *Die Winterreise.* Complementing these thoughts, it should also be mentioned the high expectations of the people towards the ideology of the French Revolution that preceded that time and the associated final outcome of deep disappointment and outrage, which was still hovering the air, and which was another source of critical expression in literature and in music—the "longing for an ideal world, but also for social participation"[11] is representative of that period and it particularly fits Schubert's world.

Although Schubert did not express himself much regarding political matters, there are several documents where he conveyed distress at life in Vienna. In Schubert's own words:

> "[…] 'the idle, insignificant life that characterizes our time.' (1824)."[12].

> "[…] 'how everything has now just petrified into bland prose, how most people quietly watch and even feel comfortable with, how they entirely leisurely glide over the mud into the abyss' (1825)".[13].

---

[6] Cf. Brendel, Alfred. (1989). "Schubert's last three piano sonatas". In: *RSA Journal, Vol. 137, No. 5395*, P.401–411.

[7] Cf. Brendel, Alfred. (1898). *Les trois dernières Sonates de Franz Schubert.* Akerman, Chantal (Director). [Programme].

[8] Cf. Dürr, Walther: „Schubert in seiner Welt". In: Dürr, Walther. Krause, Andreas. (2020). *Schubert Handbuch.* P.2.

[9] Ibid. (Trans. by the author).

[10] Cf. Ibid.

[11] Dobretsberger, Barbara. Correspondence between Barbara Dobretsberger and the author. Salzburg: February 16, 2023.

[12] Schubert, Franz: Letter to Schober. (1824). In: Deutsch, Otto Erich. (1964). *Schubert—Die Dokumente seines Lebens.* P. 258. (Trans. by the author). German expression: "[…] das Thatenlose, unbedeutende Leben, welches unsere Zeit bezeichnet.".

[13] Schubert, Franz: Letter to Spaun. (1825). In: Ibid. P. 296. (Trans. by the author). German expression: "[…] wie jetzt alles zur faden Prosa sich verknöchert, wie die meisten Leute ruhig zusehen oder sich gar wohl dabei befinden, wie sie ganz gemächlich über den Schlamm in den Abgrund glitschen.".

> "[…] Vienna 'although a bit large, it is devoid of warmth, openness, of real thoughts, reasonable words and, in particular, of spirited deeds' (1827)."[14].

According to Erickson, one major consequence of the reigning censorship was the "turning inwards" of the Viennese society, namely "[…] to innocent and nonpolitical activities"[15], resulting in the so-called Biedermeier society. This consisted of an arising bourgeois society, marked by a private, domestic musical life—for which the Schubertiades are seen as an example—and the predilection for the dance[16]. This important statement demonstrates a different Vienna between Schubert's hometown and the city where his contemporary father-figure, Beethoven, lived. The latter, in contrast, socialized in the aristocratic environment[17]. Moreover, it shows how Schubert's circle of friends were particularly important to him. They were practically to be considered as a second family[18]: more than giving him financial and logistical support, they were highly cultivated and literary people, artists, who introduced him to many writers, artists and musicians, with whom he could have a great intellectual and artistic exchange. They had the sense for "[…] the true art […]"[19], as Schubert himself writes in a letter to Schober during his first stay at the count Esterházy in Zseliz.

Beyond the above-mentioned political aspect, Müller's verse at the beginning of this chapter includes an omnipresent theme in Schubert's musical utterances,

---

[14] Schubert, Franz: Letter to Mrs. Pachler. In: Ibid. P. 451. (Trans. by the author). German expression: „[Wien]'s ist freilich ein wenig groß, dafür ist es aber leer an Herzlichkeit, Offenheit, an wirklichen Gedanken, an vernünftigen Worten, und besonders an geistreichen Taten".

[15] Erickson, Raymond. (1997). *Schubert's Vienna.* "Vienna in Its European Context". P. 25.

[16] Cf. Ibid.

[17] Beethoven composed for aristocracy, while Schubert was embedded in established middle-class society and composed rather for his group of friends and those who attended the Schubertiades. Hinrichsen works out several important aspects considered in that distinction, including the idea of Schubert as the first freelance composer. Cf. Hinrichsen, Hans-Joachim. (2019). *Franz Schubert.* Chap. 1: „Schuberts Wien".

[18] Dürr mentions how several circles of friends "replaced" so to say family and school, at the time when Schubert moved out of his parents' house in 1818 and would have experienced a life and creative crisis. Cf. Dürr, Walther: „Schubert in seiner Welt". In: Dürr, Walther Krause, Andreas. (2020). *Schubert Handbuch.* P.3.

[19] Schubert, Franz: Letter to Schober. (1818). Cited after: Brown, Maurice J.E.: "Franz Schubert". In: Sadie, Stanley. (1980). *The New Grove Dictionary of Music and Musicians. Vol. 16.* P.757.

reaching up to his Heine-setting from 1828[20] and definitely to his last instrumental compositions. Hans-Joachim Hinrichsen emphasizes that in his Heine settings, contrarily to Schumann, Schubert does not focus on Heine's "subtle irony" but rather on the "[…] tragic sarcasm of that existential uncertainty […]"[21], which he traced back to the aesthetic concept characteristic of the Romantic period: the "Weltschmerz" (Jean Paul). Psychologically considered, sarcasm is a means by which offended feelings are oppressed, even concealed from oneself[22]. These veiled feelings of the lyrical I are sensed in the piano accompaniment and mirrored in nature, the environment of the lyrical subject, meaning that the lyrical I does not want to perceive what his unconscious already knows[23].

The concept of the "Weltschmerz" is materialized, among other elements, through the Atlas-motif, i.e., a rhythmic motif which emerges especially on his latest compositions[24], and which appear often in compositions interrelated in tonalities[25]. This mythological figure of a titan was sentenced to carry the celestial vault, since he participated in the insurrection against the Olympic gods. He must carry the "entire world of pain" on his shoulders, as it is described in the Heine poem set into music by Schubert as D 957 in 1828. The semantic nature

[20] Cf. Hinrichsen, Hans-Joachim. (2019). *Franz Schubert.* Chap. 6: „Spätwerk in jungen Jahren. Die großen Liederzyklen.". Chap. 6: „Spätwerk in jungen Jahren—Die großen Liederzyklen". E-book.

[21] Ibid. (Trans. by the author). German expression: „In seinen großen Vertonungen von Heine-Gedichten reagiert [Schubert] nicht, wie später Schumann, auf deren feine Ironie, sondern auf den tragischen Sarkasmus jener existentiellen Verunsicherung, die man in der Literaturwissenschaft treffend als ‚Weltschmerz' bezeichnet hat.".

[22] Cf. Jung, Carl Gustav. (1958). "GW XI". Cited after: Wehr, Gerhard. (2014). *C.G. Jung Leben—Werk—Wirkung.* P. 328.

[23] This draws attention to an important aspect of the development of the German Lied, characteristic to Schubert and which will be addressed later.

[24] Examples can be found in: (i) *Drei Klavierstücke* Op. 946/1, where the motif appears for the first time in his last compositions (ii) the last three piano sonatas D 958—D 960, (iii) the String quintet C major D 956, (iv) the Heine-Lied "Der Atlas" D 957, (v) the Kyrie of the E-flat major Mass D 950. Cf. Godel, Arthur. (1985). *Schuberts letzte drei Klaviersonaten.* P. 28. Gülke complements this list, by mentioning for instance the F minor Fantasy for piano four hands D 940. Cf. Gülke, Peter. (2020). *Franz Schubert in seiner Zeit.* P. 300. All these works were written within the same period, i.e., during his last year of life, in 1828.

[25] Godel indicates how the character of a musical piece is tied to these inherent interconnections of tonalities. Cf. Godel, Arthur. (1985). *Schuberts letzte drei Klaviersonaten.* P.27. Godel also indicates how this rhythm can be traced back to Beethoven's Egmont ouverture. Cf. Ibid. P. 27–28. Additional references are to be found in Beethoven's Piano Sonata Op. 111. Cf. Gülke, Peter. (2020). *Franz Schubert in seiner Zeit.* P. 298.

of his name hints to the “bearer” or the “tolerator”[26] (18). In this last sense, a biblical parallel can be found not only in the figure of Hiob, to whom everything was taken away and who tolerated all pain that was inflicted to himself, but also in Christ’s calvary (18). In the Heine setting, Atlas’ resistance towards his destiny clearly comes to the fore, as it will be described in the analysis section (18). Starting from the Atlas song and the subsequent analysis of Schubert’s last instrumental works, the semantic core of this motif undergoes an important transformation, going from resistance in the Heine lied, to a “heroic” and at the same time “fearful” and “threatening” character in the C minor Sonata D 958 (first movement)[27], to a “Credo, ma con fuoco”[28] in the A major sonata D 959 (first movement), culminating in a “clairvoyant melancholy”[29] in the last B major sonata D 960 (second movement).

Additionally, Weltschmerz is to be found present in Schubert’s music in a much subtler way, going beyond the specific rhythmic figure: Gernot Gruber mentions how pain, loneliness and death, but also hope, love, friendship, solidarity and loyalty are more than mere themes in Schubert’s life: they are “[...] aesthetical objects seeking artistic resolution”[30], and which move osmotically between “utopia” and a “poetic nihilism”[31]. This means, on the one hand, (i) the hope for a better world, specifically for art[32], where music is perceived as a sacred art, having “salvation as a goal”[33], and, on the other hand, (ii) the despairing of that same hope[34], leading to a complete denial and to a “total annihilation of all illusions”[35]. Looking into the abyss can serve as an image for the latter. The merging of these two “explanatory models” generates the concept that Gruber named as

[26] Grant, Michael., Hazel, John. (2008). *Lexikon der antiken Mythen und Gestalten.* P. 81. (Trans. by the author).

[27] Brendel, Alfred. (1996). *Musik beim Wort genommen.* P. 136. (Trans. by the author). German expression: “Zugleich heroisch und angstvoll [...] bedrohlich und bedroht”.

[28] Ibid.

[29] Ibid. (Trans. by the author). German expression: “Hellsichtig-melancholisch“.

[30] Gruber, Gernot. (2010). *Schubert. Schubert?* P. 234. (Trans. by the author). German expression: „[...] Schmerz, Einsamkeit und der drohende Tod waren für ihn ästhetische Gegenstände, die zu künstlerischen Lösungen drängten.“.

[31] Cf. Ibid. P. 236. (Trans. by the author). German expression: “Poetischer Nihilismus“. See also „Einleitung“ p. 7–10 and „Gibt es ein Fazit?“, p. 260–264.

[32] Cf. Ibid. Chapter: „‘Liebe‘: Utopische Hoffnung in der Kunst.“. P. 223.

[33] Ibid. P. 215. (Trans. by the author). German expression: “Heil als Ziel“.

[34] Cf. Ibid. Chapter: “’Schmerz’: Das Nichts und der poetische Nihilismus”. P. 233.

[35] Ibid. P. 10. (Trans. by the author). German expression: “ein nihilistischer Zerstörer aller Illusionen“.

"the antithetic as a life and artistic principle"[36], which is nothing more than an expression of Schubert's dual nature[37] and the idea of parallel worlds[38] inherent in his music. This thought may find a Jungian parallel in what is understood in Analytical Psychology as a dialectical process. In the latter, the concept of enantiodromia is central (3.1). This process may ultimately result in a synchronicity of opposites, culminating in a "dissolving"[39] wholeness that characterises the creative process itself.

Gruber's concept of the antithetics can furthermore explain, among other aspects, Schubert's will for sociability but also his need for inner retreat, which permits to submerge into the unknown, into the center of him-Self[40], and thus to transcend to another sphere. Gruber's statements on the antithetic principles are significant, in particular when taking the creative and the individuation process into consideration. Jungians speak of the polar nature of archetypes (which could be understood in the light of Heidegger's two wills theory)—"psychic themes organized in opposite tension"[41]. By using the antithetic concept Gruber criticizes the unilateral interpretations of Schubert's nature up to this day and accentuates the ambivalent character of his music, with the aim of moving closer towards an integral image of Schubert and his music—a thought that goes along Jung's perception of the human as individuals.

---

[36] Ibid. Chapter: „Schuberts ‚Doppelnatur'—Antithetik als Lebens- und Kunstprinzip.". (Trans. by the author). German expression: "Antithetik als Lebens- und Kunstprinzip.".

[37] Cf. Ibid. P. 242.

[38] Cf. Ibid. P. 246.

[39] At this point, it seems of importance to make a clear distinction of the word "dissolve". In this context, i.e., in connection with the process of becoming whole and the integration of opposites, it is not to be understood as the elimination of one or the other force, i.e., not as resolution of the inner and outer world problems, which is inherent in this dualistic perception. It is rather to be perceived in terms of the transcendental function, a confrontation with the opposite forces, which is the creative process per se (the work of art or musical composition being the result). In Jungian terms the opposites do not stand in a conflictive way to each other, but rather in a dynamic, creative manner, even in a complementary, compensatory relationship. Cf. Vogel, Ralf T. (2017). *Individuation und Wandlung*. P. 42. Jung himself points to this fact, when he explains that the goal of wholeness is not the resolution, i.e., the elimination of the tension generated by the opposites, but the sustaining of the tensions that are created out of the confrontation with the opposites. Cf. Jung, Carl Gustav. "GW 16". Cited after: Ibid. P. 43.

[40] Cf. Gruber, Gernot. (2010). *Schubert. Schubert?* P. 242.

[41] Roesler, Christian. Personal communication between Christian Roesler and the author. Basel: January 12, 2023.

Schubert himself pronounced: "My art exists through my sense for music and through my suffering […]"[42]. This statement reflects at first the literary and philosophic topoi back then, to perceive pain as "an incentive to create"[43], i.e., a positive poetic state[44]. In the same way, the longing for death is another topos, which was particular to Schubert's time and of which Schubert was acquainted with[45]. These are all matters towards which, however, Schubert behaved ambivalently. The theme of death goes beyond the aesthetic question and extends to the biographical level. This refers not only to the fact that Schubert became aware of his own mortality early on, but also to the death of his mother, which was a traumatic event for Schubert—he was only 15 years of age at the time. The result was that death gained a plethora of different shades of meaning.

Alfred Brendel, in particular, draws attention to the dual-expression of death in his music, namely as: "death terror", "death warmth", "death allure" or even a "clairvoyant death clarity"[46]. Intriguingly, Brendel also recounts how for Schubert, death and the mother-figure became one, once his mother passed away, turning in this manner the "maternal bond" into a form of "death imprisonment"[47]. This is revealing, since in Jungian terms the archetype of the great mother embodies exactly these ambivalences, namely life and death (3.2)[48]. The ambivalent nature of the great mother archetype encompasses the characteristics of the good, nourishing mother and of a chthonic figure of the terrible

---

[42] Schubert, Franz: "Aus einem verlorenen Notizbuche Schuberts von 1824". In: Deutsch, Otto Erich. (1964). *Schubert—Die Dokumente seines Lebens.* P. 233. (Trans. by the author). German expression: „Meine Erzeugnisse sind durch den Verstand für Musik und durch meinen Schmerz vorhanden […]".

[43] Gruber, Gernot. (2010). *Schubert. Schubert?* P. 233. (Trans. by the author).

[44] Cf. Ibid.

[45] The contradictory treatment of the death thematic can be drawn along various of the Schubert works. Gruber refers specifically to the lieder "Der Jüngling und der Tod" D 545 and "Der Tod und das Mädchen" D 531 as an example, where there is the contradictory expression towards death and yet the "musical goal remains the same", namely death as consolation, respectively death as redemption. Cf. Ibid. P. 235.

[46] Brendel, Alfred. (2001). *Ausgerechnet Ich.* (Trans. by the author). German expression: „Todesschrecken", „Todeswärme", „Todesverlockung", „hellsichtige Todesklarheit".

[47] Brendel, Alfred. (1996). *Musik beim Wort genommen.* P. 143. (Trans. by the author). German expression: „Nach dem Tod seiner Mutter werden Tod und Mutter gleichsam identisch; Mutterbindung wird zur Todesverhaftung".

[48] In *Ausgerechnet Ich* Brendel additionally states how he recognizes death and life being expressed in an equally strong manner in his music. Cf. Brendel, Alfred. (2001). *Ausgerechnet Ich.* P. 160–161. German expression: „Ich empfinde in Schuberts Musik Tod und Leben gleich stark.".

mother, savage and destructive in character (3.2)[49]. Therefore, the great mother archetype can manifest itself in different forms[50]. Considered from a broader perspective, the great mother connects to nature: the "'primordial mother and 'mother earth'"[51]. In this broad sense, its presence in Schubert's music can be seen as a compensatory element that has a self-regulatory and balancing effect in relation to distant nature—a characteristic of the big city in which he lived. The great mother can be characterized by the heaven, the moon, etc., but also by the underworld, the death world, the devouring and the poisoning[52], etc.

Congruently, Gruber defends the view that Schubert frequently perceives death rather in nihilistic terms[53], where the nothingness means a "state as a goal"[54]. These "state" experiences can only happen spontaneously—the unconscious psychic structures may have the goal to reach such a state, a state which cannot be consciously induced. In this comprehension death can mean a "[...] dissolution into non-being or into the harmony of the all of nature"[55]. In a similar way to Gruber, Brendel sees in Schubert the image of the "wanderer at the abyss"[56]. Broadly seen the abyss stands for the unconscious powers, for "states that have

---

[49] Cf. Neumann, Erich. (2002). *The origins and history of consciousness.* Part A:" The creation myth", Chap. 2: "The Great Mother". The perception of this ambivalence or the recognition of the "overshadow day-night metamorphosis", to speak in Neumann's language, happens from the moment on that ego-consciousness begins to arise, when there is a "detachment" from the so-called "uroboric stage". Cf. Ibid.

[50] C.G. Jung has an extensive list of some of the different manifestations of the mother archetype in: Jung, Carl Gustav. (2020). *Archetypen. Urbilder und Wirkkräfte des Kollektiven Unbewussten.* Chapter: „Die psychologischen Aspekte des Mutterarchetypus". Subchapter 2: „Der Mutterarchetypus". P.101–105. Erich Neumann, Jung's pupil, also dedicated himself extensively to this archetype, notably in: Neumann, Erich. (2021). *Die Große Mutter.*

[51] Jung, Carl Gustav. (2020). *Archetypen. Urbilder und Wirkkräfte des Kollektiven Unbewussten.* P. 174. (Trans. by the author).

[52] Cf. Ibid. Chapter: „Die psychologischen Aspekte des Mutterarchetypus". Subchapter 2: „Der Mutterarchetypus". P.101–105. It is to be noted that in some cases, specifically in male psychology, the Anima can stand intertwined with the mother archetype. Cf. Ibid. P.103.

[53] Cf. Gruber, Gernot. (2010). *Schubert. Schubert?* P. 233.

[54] Ibid. P. 234. (Trans. by the author). German expression: "Seine Ästhetisierung [...], macht aus dem Nichts ein Etwas, einen Zustand als Ziel.".

[55] Ibid. P. 235. (Trans. by the author). German expression: „Welche Ruhe findet der Wanderer: den Tod als Auflösung ins Nichts-Sein oder in die Harmonie einer All-Natur ?".

[56] Cf. Brendel, Alfred. (1898). *Les trois dernières Sonates de Franz Schubert.* Akerman, Chantal (Director). [Programme].

not yet taken shape"[57]. It symbolizes the "becoming one with the Absolute in the *unio mystica*"[58]. By further deconstructing the symbolism of the abyss, the representation of the great mother comes to the fore[59], as both the loving and the terrible mother[60]. In terms of the creative process, this can point to a critical psychological turning point, namely the instant when something new can originate out of the nothingness of being (1). When nothingness "becomes", it is driven by a new impulse that arises spontaneously from the depths of the psyche—a self-driven archetypal urge and an innovative will to (re)create. Out of a momentary inertia of the Self, the psychic forces are set in motion again, becoming a kind of catalysator, and thus the being at the center becomes a new reality. In the same manner that for Schubert love shifts rather into the "utopic hope"[61], death tends to shift into a nihilistic state[62], in which, consequently, (re)creation is enabled[63].

A crucial representation of the great mother, which turns out to be of central expression in Schubert's individual musical thinking are the fate-goddesses[64], known as the morai[65] in Greek mythology or as norns, their Germanic equivalent.

[57] Mollwo-Oesterreicher, Marianne. (1978). *Herder Lexikon Symbole.* P. 9. (Trans. by the author). German expression: „Das Grund- u. Bodenlose symbolisiert Zustände, die (noch) nicht Gestalt gewonnen haben […]".

[58] Ibid. (Trans. by the author). German expression: „[…] aber auch das Einswerden mit dem Absoluten in der *unio mystica.*".

[59] Cf. Jung, Carl Gustav. (2020). *Archetypen. Urbilder und Wirkkräfte des Kollektiven Unbewussten.* Chapter: „Die psychologischen Aspekte des Mutterarchetypus", subchapter 2.: „Der Mutterarchetypus". P.102.

[60] Cf. Mollwo-Oesterreicher, Marianne. (1978). *Herder Lexikon Symbole.* P. 9.

[61] Gruber, Gernot. (2010). *Schubert. Schubert?* P. 228.

[62] Cf. Ibid. P. 234.

[63] Several examples can be found in the analysis section (IV).

[64] The power of fate appears to be an inherent core subject of the human being, which is moreover intertwined with individuation, as it is to be seen in Jung's biography. Ralf T. Vogel on the one hand draws attention to the nowadays neglection of this fact within the psychotherapy context, on the other hand stresses the crucial importance of this term for the individuation process. Cf. Vogel, Ralf T. (2017). *Individuation und Wandlung.* P. 35.

[65] The roman equivalent to the fate-goddesses are the *parcae* and are also known as *Fatae.* They are stated as being the daughters of Nix, the night, but also as the daughters of Zeus, the storm god and Themis, meaning order. Cf. Grant, Michael. Hazel, John. (2008). *Lexikon der antiken Mythen und Gestalten.*

These three female personifications of destiny are depicted as spinners, sometimes, illustrated at "[…] the well of Urd, at the origin of all becoming […]"[66]. There they continually spin the thread of life until it is cut off[67]; therefore, they symbolize "the rule of fate"[68]:

> "They spin the newborn people's life thread, and this determines their future fate. Klotho was the woman at the spindle, Lachesis assigned their life fortune, and Atropos finally cuts off the thread with her scissors, determining the date of death."[69]

In this depiction there are various symbolic contents to be revealed: (i) the spindle wheel itself, which "due to its uniformly rotating movement symbol[izes] the unchangeable law of the inexorable fate or also of the eternal return"[70], (ii) the thread symbol representing primarily time and life, in other words "[…] the mysteriousness of human existence […]"[71], but which can also mean union between this world and the world beyond[72] or indicate a "wanderer's" journey[73] and (iii) the scissors, which are responsible for cutting off the thread of life, a metaphor

---

[66] Betz, Otto. (2016). „Der Lebensfaden". In: *herder.de*. P.2. (Trans. by the author). German expression: "[…] saßen die Nornen an der Quelle Urd, am Ursprung allen Werdens, und webten das Netz des Schicksals.".

[67] Cf. Ibid.

[68] Cf. Mollwo-Oesterreicher, Marianne. (1978). *Herder Lexikon Symbole*. P.112. (Trans. by the author). German expression: „Schicksalsgöttinen, die durch ihr Handeln das Walten des Schicksals symbolisieren […]".

[69] Betz, Otto. (2016). „Der Lebensfaden". In: *herder.de*. P.1. (Trans. by the author). German expression: „Sie [die Moiren] spinnen den neugeborenen Menschen ihren Lebensfaden zu und dieser bestimmt ihr künftiges Schicksal. Klotho war die Frau mit der Spindel, Lachesis teilte dem Menschen sein Lebenslos zu, Atropos schnitt schließlich mit ihrer Schere den Faden ab und bestimmte damit das Todesdatum.".

[70] Mollwo-Oesterreicher, Marianne. (1978). *Herder Lexikon Symbole*. P.159. (Trans. by the author). German expression: „Spindel, wegen ihrer gleichmäßig drehenden Bewegung Symbol unabänderl. Gesetzmäßigkeit, des unerbittl. Schicksals oder auch der ewigen Wiederkehr; […]".

[71] Guardini, Romano. Cited after: Betz, Otto. (2016). „Der Lebensfaden". In: *herder.de*. P. 2. (Trans. by the author). German expression: "[…] dass die 'Fadensymbolik' die Rätselhaftigkeit menschlicher Existenz verstehbar machen kann.".

[72] Cf. Mollwo-Oesterreicher, Marianne. (1978). *Herder Lexikon Symbole*. P. 48.

[73] Cf. Betz, Otto. (2016). „Der Lebensfaden". In: *herder.de*. P. 3.

for the sudden death and a "symbol of 'man's' dependence on the powers that govern fate […]"[74].

> "As a result, life appears as something that is started and continued by unknown powers; of which one never sees what is coming but only what is; which can be smooth, but also have knots and be confused; which is weak, threatened by the tear, and yet withstands many tensions; and which is ultimately brought to an end by the same forces that have begun it. Through this image, existence is interpreted."[75]

These symbolic content around the fate-goddesses are present in many fairy tales. This is true also for Schubert's music and not only through the fate-motif, which can be traced back to Beethoven's 5th Symphony. In an attempt to decipher the most recognized feature of Schubert's musical language, the pianist Christian Zaccharias emphasizes the fact that the lied "Gretchen am Spinnrade" D 118 marks a turning point in his musical language and concludes that it reflects Schubert's own perception of time: Schubert spins and spins around[76], thus it is linked to fate. This lied was composed in 1814, when Schubert counted 17 years and it reveals already a decisive point in his individuation process (20). Two elements are integrated in the piano accompaniment: (i) the course of time with the regular *staccato* quavers of the left hand (followed by the silence) and (ii) the *circulatio* gesture of the semiquavers of the right-hand, sound-painting the movement of the spindle wheel. In Jungian terms, *circulatio* or *circumambulatio* points to the

---

[74] Mollwo-Oesterreicher, Marianne. (1978). *Herder Lexikon Symbole.* P. 141. (Trans. by the author). German expression: „In der griech. Mythologie Attribut der Moire Atropos, die damit den Lebensfaden durchschneidet: Symbol der Abhängigkeit des Menschen von den das Schicksal lenkenden Mächten u. Symbol für den plötzlichen Tod.".

[75] Guardini, Romano. Cited after: Betz, Otto. (2016). „Der Lebensfaden". In: *herder.de.* P. 2. (Trans. by the author). German expression: "Dadurch erscheint das Leben als etwas, das von unbekannten Mächten begonnen und fortgesetzt wird; von dem man immer nur sieht, was ist, und nicht, was kommt; das glatt sein, aber auch Knoten haben und sich verwirren kann; das schwach ist, von der Zerreißung bedroht, und doch viele Anspannungen aushält; das schließlich von den gleichen Mächten, die es begonnen haben, auch zum Ende gebracht wird. Durch dieses Bild wird das Dasein gedeutet.".

[76] Cf. Zacharias, Christian. (2019). *Why does Schubert sound like Schubert?* [Lecture-Recital]. Stagecast Ltd (Production). With this statement Zacharias also shows the difference with Beethoven's perception of time, who rather uses pulse as an energetic tool to express his clear direction striving towards a precise goal.

search for the Self[77]. The piano accompaniment emphasizes the spinning around and the course of fate. In opposition, the melodic line at the beginning contains the dactyl rhythm, known as the wanderer rhythm, which hints to the life journey. Finally, it is through the harmony that Schubert alters the light showing the inner changes of "Gretchen" taking place during this wander-journey.

[77] Cf. Jung, Carl Gustav. (2014). "Psychology and Alchemy". *CW. Vol. 12.* Chap. 3: "The Symbolism of the Mandala—II. The Mandalas in the Dreams". Jung explains how the wheel, as an important symbol in alchemy, features a circulating process. In: Ibid. Vol. 13: "Alchemical studies, 3. Fundamental concepts, B. The circular movement and the centre". C.G. Jung speaks of *circumambulatio* as the circular movement bringing an important inner movement: "Psychologically, this *circulatio* would be the 'movement in a circle around one-self', so that all sides of the personality become involved. 'The poles of light and darkness are made to rotate', that is, there is an alternation of day and night. The circular movement thus has the moral significance of activating the light and dark forces of human nature, and together with them all psychological opposites of whatever kind they may be. It is nothing less than self-knowledge by means of self-brooding […]". Ibid.

On His Roots, Education and Musical Paragons

9

Schubert was a precocious talent. This sometimes-overlooked fact is of great importance for the understanding of his works, the development of his musical language and his individuation process. His musical gifts were noticed at once, already by his father—a schoolmaster of Moravian descent[1]—and by his eldest brother Ignaz, who taught him the violin and piano, respectively. His musical education in violin, piano, singing and basso continuo started around 1807 at Lichtenthal with the organist of the local parish church Michael Holzer, to whom he later dedicated some vocal and church works. One year later, he was admitted at the imperial and royal city college, the "Wiener Stadtkonvikt", where he was engaged in several activities from singing in the choir, to playing in and conducting the orchestra, up to having lessons in piano, viola and basso continuo with Wenzel RuŽička.

His intellectual capabilities, moral qualities and commitment were equally highly praised[2]. The same applied to his musical talent, which was recognized as being of divine nature with the remark "[…] he got it from the good Lord"[3], and so Schubert was soon sent to be a pupil of the master Antonio Salieri in counterpoint and vocal compositions. This is a significant fact because, thanks to Salieri, Schubert was exposed to a rich heritage of musical tradition, and it can be assumed that it included knowledge in musical rhetorics and key characteristics

[1] Cf. Brown, Maurice J.E: "Franz Schubert". In: Sadie, Stanley. (1980). The New Grove Dictionary of Music and Musicians. Vol. 16. P. 752.

[2] Cf. Ibid. P. 753.

[3] Dürr, Walther. „Schubert in seiner Welt". In: Dürr, Walther. Krause, Andreas. (2020). Schubert Handbuch. P. 10. (Trans. by the author). German expression: "dem kann ich nichts lehren, der hat's vom lieben Gott".

L. Dill, *Schubert's Metamorphoses*,
https://doi.org/10.1007/978-3-662-73476-6_9

(6.2). Through him, Schubert was introduced to many musical works, which made a strong impression on him, as for instance the Gluck operas[4].

Schubert experienced the reported first "outburst of composition"[5] during these years, as a result of being exposed to a variety of resources and outer incentives[6]. Regarding his education, it is to be mentioned that Schubert enrolled in counterpoint lessons with the renowned Simon Sechter, two weeks before he died in 1828[7]. This information reveals his constant desire to improve and perfect himself, or at least to deal more closely with counterpoint techniques again. Such perfectionism and the will to incorporate new compositional elements, together with his peculiar "clairvoyant"[8] way of working without interruption, could be a possible reason for the existence of fragmentary works.

Schubert had many paragons who influenced him in a way or another. According to Brown, the influence of Salieri's tutelage is to be heard in some of his early works, especially in his vocal canons[9]. From friend's reports it is known that Schubert worshipped Händel, Gluck, Mozart, Haydn and Beethoven[10], each of them for a specific music genre: Händel especially for the ancient music and oratorios, Gluck and Mozart for their operas, and with regard to instrumental music Mozart, Haydn and Beethoven were the ones who captured his attention[11]. Furthermore, the names of Joseph and Michael Haydn for church music are to be mentioned[12].

---

[4] Cf. Ibid. P.13.

[5] Brown, Maurice J.E: "Franz Schubert". In: Sadie, Stanley. (1980). The New Grove Dictionary of Music and Musicians. Vol. 16. P. 754.

[6] Cf. Ibid.

[7] More recent literature confirms that Schubert received a single lesson from Sechter, to whom he left exercises in fugue expositions. Cf. Dürr, Walther: „Schubert in seiner Welt". In: Dürr, Walther. Krause, Andreas. (2020). Schubert Handbuch. P.15.

[8] Cf. Hilmar, Ernst. (1997). Franz Schubert. P. 32. See also: Vogl, Johann Michael. Citated after: Stadler, Albert: "Biographisches Material". (Begun on January 17th 1858). In: Deutsch, Otto Erich. (1983). Schubert. Die Erinnerungen seiner Freunde. P. 170. Vogl, Johann Michael. Citated after: Stadler, Albert: "Biographisches Material". (Begun on January 17th 1858). In: Deutsch, Otto Erich. (1983). Schubert. Die Erinnerungen seiner Freunde. P. 170.

[9] Brown, Maurice J.E: "Franz Schubert". In: Sadie, Stanley. (1980). The New Grove Dictionary of Music and Musicians. Vol. 16. P. 753.

[10] Cf. von Spaun, Joseph. In: Deutsch, Otto Erich. (1983). Schubert Erinnerungen seiner Freunde. P. 34.

[11] Cf. Dürr, Walther: „Schubert in seiner Welt". In: Dürr, Walther. Krause, Andreas. (2020). Schubert Handbuch. P. 12.

[12] Cf. Ibid. P.13.

Paragons for the German lied were composers such as Johann Rudolf Zumsteeg and those of the second Berlin school, like Friedrich Zelter and Johann Friedrich Reichardt[13]. Although emancipation with regard to the role of the piano in the lied had not yet been achieved, as it was later with Schubert, the developments brought along with the second Berlin School concerned primarily the importance of the folk lied and the folk tone ("Volkston") along with a lyric that conveyed subjective expression[14]. According to the paradigms of the second Berlin School, the piano accompaniment was only to sustain the overall affect and the singing voice, and never have priority over the text[15], i.e., "to serve the poem and not to illuminate it"[16].

When Rossini's operas were performed in Vienna, Schubert was equally enthusiastic[17] as he was in regard to Carl Maria von Weber's *Freischütz*[18]. In turn, Schubert's compositions of the *Impromptus* and *Moments musicaux* are believed to have been inspired by the tradition of two composers considered to be the fathers of the short lyric piano pieces, composed in three-part liedform, containing a contrasting middle section: Voříšek and Tomášek[19].

It was Beethoven, however, whom Schubert particularly revered. Beethoven was already a prominent figure both within and outside Vienna, while the young Schubert was still discovering his own voice. Taken into consideration the humble side of Schubert's personality in this regard, he lived so to say in Beethoven's shadow[20]. This might be one of the reasons why, despite being fellow city residents, they possibly met no more than once or twice[21]. The other plausible reason could be the different social milieus they used to frequent. Still, Beethoven

---

[13] Cf. Ibid. P.12–13.

[14] Cf. Schmierer, Elisabeth. (2017). Geschichte des Kunstliedes. Chapter: „Das Lied in der ersten Hälfte des 19. Jahrhunderts".

[15] Cf. Ibid.

[16] This point is referred to as one of Goethe's aesthetic ideals in: Brendel, Alfred. (2022). "Naivety and Irony. Goethe's musical needs". In: Publications of the English Goethe Society. Vol. 91, no.1, p. 75–87.

[17] Cf. Dürr, Walther: „Schubert in seiner Welt". In: Dürr, Walther. Krause, Andreas. (2020). Schubert Handbuch. P.14.

[18] Cf. Ibid. P. 16.

[19] Cf. Ibid. P. 18.

[20] Schiff, Andras. (2019). Sir András Schiff on The Music of Franz Schubert. [Recording Presentation].

[21] It is still not known with certainty at what extent they knew each other personally. Cf. Dürr, Walther: „Schubert in seiner Welt". In: Dürr, Walther. Krause, Andreas. (2020). Schubert Handbuch. P. 15–16.

was not indifferent to Schubert's music. Schubert dedicated and handed over to Beethoven a set of eight Variations on a French lied for piano four hands, a piece which Beethoven used to play with his nephew[22]. It is also known that Beethoven knew and appreciated some of Schubert's lieder.

In any case, Schubert devoted himself to studying Beethoven's œuvre in depth, particularly his chamber music and piano works, but also his symphonic compositions, which comprised the 3rd, 5th and 7th Symphonies[23] particularly—their motivic core is shown to be of importance in Schubert's own music. The Egmont ouverture could also be added to the list, for the same reason[24]. There are many examples where a reference to Beethoven can be made. Martin Chusid mentions two Beethovenian aspects that were particularly influential for Schubert. These refer to the cyclic unity and the variation form[25], which Schubert happened to use subsequently, and sometimes even in combined manner, as for example in the *Wandererfantasie* D 760 in C major (1822). In addition, Dürr's comment underlines Schubert's interest upon "[…] Beethoven's technique to amplify the piano sound, to give an orchestral coloration to it […]"[26]. This is again a musical feature to be found within the same example given, the *Wandererfantasie.*

Schubert's involvement with the work of Beethoven coincided precisely with the period of his life frequently referred to as the "years of crisis", often dated as 1818–1823. Brown attributes the noted "depression" strictly to personal causes and to the fact that Schubert had to resume teaching again, an activity which he apparently disliked[27]. According to this dating system, the beginning of the "crisis" would undoubtedly be linked to the end of Schubert's romantic relationship with the beloved teacher's daughter, Theresa Grob, for whom Schubert had confessed to having deep feelings. His love for her, according to Schubert's confession to Hüttenbrenner, was also reciprocated, but impossible[28]. Furthermore,

[22] Cf. Ibid.

[23] Cf. Ibid. P. 16.

[24] Cf. Godel, Arthur. (1985). Schuberts letzte drei Klaviersonaten. P. 27–28.

[25] Cf. Chusid, Martin: "Schubert's chamber music: before and after Beethoven". In: Gibbs, Christopher. H. (1997). The Cambridge Companion to Schubert.

[26] Dürr, Walther: „Schubert in seiner Welt". In: Dürr, Walther. Krause, Andreas. (2020). Schubert Handbuch. P. 16. (Trans. by the author). German expression: „Schubert übernimmt etwa Beethovens Techniken, den Klavierklang zu verstärken, ihn gar auch orchestral zu färben […]".

[27] Cf. Brown, Maurice J.E: "Franz Schubert". In: Sadie, Stanley. (1980). The New Grove Dictionary of Music and Musicians. Vol. 16. P. 757.

[28] According to Hüttenbrenner's report, Schubert would have said: " I loved someone very deeply and she loved me too. She was a schoolmaster's student, a little younger than I, and

1818 corresponds to his first stay abroad in Zseliz, where he served as the Count Esterházy's children's music master. From Schubert's writings it is known that, after a first agreeable impression of Zseliz and the Count's family (especially of the young Countess Caroline), he deeply longed for his hometown and most of all for the company of his friends. When he returned, he had to resume work as a teacher, which may also reflect probable financial concerns. From these facts it is to deduce that the reasons for his alleged crisis were manifold and not only of personal and financial nature. The reported creative crisis[29] could possibly be associated with his own confrontation with Beethoven's work[30] and the will to make progress in developing his own musical language, i.e., the urge to differentiate himself and to express his contribution to the world, fulfilling in this manner his feeling of "duty" as an artist. A comparative analysis, which has already been done by several authors, can actually reveal significant differences between both composers.

---

sang in a mass that I composed, the soprano solos most beautifully and with deep feeling. She wasn't pretty, had pox scars on her face; but she was good, good hearted. For three years she hoped that I would marry her; however, I could not find a job, which would have provided for us both. She married then someone else, according to her parents' will, which hurt me a lot. I still love her, and since then I haven't been able to like anyone else as much as her. She just wasn't meant for me.". Hüttenbrenner, Anselm: Letter to Liszt. (1854). In: Deutsch, Otto Erich. (1983). Schubert Erinnerungen seiner Freunde. P. 209. (Trans. by the author). German expression: „[…] ich habe Eine recht innig geliebt und sie mich auch. Sie war eine Schullehrerstochter, etwas jünger als ich, und sang in einer Messe, die ich komponierte, die Sopransoli wunderschön und mit tiefer Empfindung. Sie war eben nicht hübsch, hatte Blatternarben im Gesicht; aber gut war sie, herzensgut. Drei Jahre lang hoffte sie, daß ich sie ehelichen werde; ich konnte jedoch keine Anstellung finden, wodurch wir beide versorgt gewesen wären. Sie heiratete dann nach dem Wunsche ihrer Eltern einen anderen, was mich sehr schmerzte. Ich liebe sie noch immer, und mir konnte seither keine andere so gut und besser gefallen wie sie. Sie war mir halt nicht bestimmt.". For more insight into Schubert's relation to Theresa Grob: Steblin, Rita: "Schubert's relationship with women: an historical account". In: Newbould, Brian. (2017). Schubert Studies.

[29] A creative crisis does not necessarily mean a period of total cessation of work. For the artist the craft can also be his consolation, with which he might overcome the crisis, even if it is only for a few hours, while immersed in his creative work. This might result in fragmented compositions or drafts.

[30] Cf. Dobretsberger, Barbara. Personal communication between Barbara Dobretsberger and the author. Salzburg/Lisbon: November 25, 2021.

10 Impressions: the "Viennese" vs. "Cultural Appropriation"

The simultaneous "awakening of a national consciousness [taking place] within the European people at the beginning of the 19th-Century […]" led to " […] national dances being integrated into art music"[1]. Schubert himself wrote around 500 dances, many among them having emerged out of improvisations at the piano[2]. Consequently, these dances are anchored within a folk musical tradition, i.e., they present folk music characteristics, reflect musically the Austrian idiom and are strongly linked to societal values. In this sense, this gives them a collective character that is specific to Austrian culture. On the other hand, similarly to the procedure in fairy tales, where unconscious appropriation and inner transformations take place, Schubert narrates them musically adding his own personal undertone and giving them a distinctive character. In these dances not only the Viennese Weltschmerz is audible, it is in fact accompanied by the "longing for an

[1] Dobretsberger, Barbara. (2016). Formen der Instrumentalmusik. (Trans. by the author). German expression: „Als neuer Impuls für die Tanzkompositionen zeigt sich das mit Beginn des 19. Jahrhunderts erwachende Nationalbewusstsein der europäischen Völker; nicht nur die Pflege in der Volksmusik, sondern auch die Integration nationaler Tänze in die ‚Kunstmusik' löst das Interesse an stilisierten höfischen Tänzen ab.". P.193.

[2] Cf. Litschauer, Walburga: „Tänze und Märsche für Klavier—‚Halt's enk zsamm'". In: Dürr, Walther., Krause, Andreas. (2020). Schubert Handbuch. P. 437.

The title makes reference to Dobretsberger, Barbara. Main theme of the Analysis Seminar of the summer semester 2023: "Haltet den Dieb! Kulturelle Aneignung, Nationalcharakter, Abgrenzungsmanöver und Zuschreibungen in der Musik".

L. Dill, *Schubert's Metamorphoses*,
https://doi.org/10.1007/978-3-662-73476-6_10

ideal world, but also for social participation"[3], i.e., Schubert's "joy of conviviality"[4], an aspect which, according to Gernot Gruber, is often repressed within the history of reception and interpreters, especially in regard to the "late Schubert"[5].

Continuing this line of thought, it might be interesting to consider the metaphysical concept of "(true) being and (mere) appearance"[6] in relation to Schubert's dances, interpreting them as masked confessions which draw on the ball tradition of the Viennese Opera Ball[7]. These are stated as having become a legend following the festivals of the Vienna Congress in 1814–15 and which were prominent subsequently, especially around the 1820–30. These are still of international interest today[8]. By implication and stated promptly in mere Jungian terms: the dance may serve the purpose of a mask (Persona). With their fleeting charm, Schubert's dances touch lightly upon deeper veiled elements, i.e., concealed phenomena[9], which come to life in his other instrumental music, in a more dramatic or sombre manner, such as in piano sonatas, string quartets, etc. Examples can be found in several works, among others: the German Dance in A minor D 783, no.10, from which the same thematic material comes in the 12 German Ländler D 790 again and is used as derivation in the Piano Sonata in A minor D 784 as the opening material[10]. Another striking example is the G-sharp minor Ländler D 790 no.6 and the opening motif of the 3rd movement from the

---

[3] Dobretsberger, Barbara. Correspondence between Barbara Dobretsberger and the author. Salzburg, February 16, 2023.

[4] Gruber, Gernot. (2010). Schubert. Schubert? P. 234. (Trans. by the author). German expression: "Freude an Geselligkeit".

[5] Ibid.

[6] Cf. Arendt, Hannah. (2016). Vom Leben des Geistes. Part I, Chap. 2: „(Wahres) Sein und (bloße) Erscheinung: die Zwei-Welten-Theorie". German expression: "(Wahres) Sein und (blosse) Erscheinung".

[7] Cf. Wiener Staatsoper. „Die Geschichte des Wiener Opernballs". [Article].

[8] Ibid.

[9] Cf. Arendt, Hannah. (2016). Vom Leben des Geistes. Part I, Chap. 2: „(Wahres) Sein und (blosse) Erscheinung: die Zwei-Welten-Theorie".

[10] Cf. Krause, Andreas: „Die Klaviermusik—‚So frei und eigen, so keck und mitunter auch so sonderbar'". In: Dürr, Walther., Krause, Andreas. (2020). Schubert Handbuch. P. 410.

D minor string quartet D 810 "Death and the Maiden"[11], a thematic material of cyclical nature[12] (16). In regard to the dances, Litschauer already noted that there are certain melodic and dance patterns named as dance series ("Reihungen"), which Schubert liked most and used in several of the dances, sometimes even lending them a certain cyclical pattern[13].

Due to Austria's status as a Habsburg multinational state, a significant number of outside influences infiltrated Austrian culture, resulting in a merging of cultures. The "cultural appropriation" theme in regard to Schubert is therefore justifiable—it can be noticed that influences from other nations can be found in Schubert's music, despite the fact that he himself never traveled outside the Habsburg Empire. This topic represents a further area of debate among Schubert interpreters and musicologists.

Alfred Brendel argues that his music has more outer characteristics than it has of a Biedermeier Vienna:

> "Schubert was never the musical vernacular poet that even Busoni thought he was. Rather, he took his inspiration from beyond the confines of the city. We hear Hungarian in the finale of the B-flat major sonata, Bohemian (polka and sousedská) in the third of the posthumous piano pieces or even Spanish [traits] in the macabre finale of the C-minor sonata, which actually has a lot to do with Goya, who also died in 1828, and nothing at all to do with Kupelwieser or Schwind."[14].

Brendel's citation addresses different issues. The first sentence mirrors a controversial topic among interpreters still today: András Schiff, for instance, deliberately chooses a Bösendorfer to play Schubert, due to his firm conviction that this piano has the most suitable sound in regard to the Viennese dialect[15].

---

[11] Cf. Chusid, Martin: "Schubert's chamber music: before and after Beethoven". In: Gibbs, Christopher H. (1997). The Cambridge Companion to Schubert. Part II: "Schubert's music: style and genre". Part II: "Schubert's music: style and genre". Chap. 9.

[12] Cf. Ibid.

[13] Cf. Litschauer, Walburga: „Tänze und Märsche für Klavier—‚Halt's enk zsamm'". In: Dürr, Walther., Krause, Andreas. (2020). Schubert Handbuch. P. 439.

[14] Brendel, Alfred. (1992). Musik beim Wort genommen. P. 84. (Trans. by the author). German expression: „Schubert ist nie der musikalische Mundartdichter gewesen, für den ihn selbst ein Busoni gehalten hat. Eher holte er sich seine Anregungen jenseits der engeren Stadtgrenzen. Wir hören Ungarisches im Finale der B-Dur-Sonate, Böhmisches (Polka und Sousedská) im dritten der nachgelassenen Klavierstücke oder gar Spanisches im makabren Finale der c-Moll-Sonate, das ja tatsächlich mit dem ebenfalls 1828 verstorbenen Goya viel und mit Kupelwieser oder Schwind überhaupt nichts zu schaffen hat.".

[15] Schiff, Andras. (n.d.). Schiff András filmje Schubertről—András Schiff tells about Schubert. [Documentary]. Scorer Associates. Minutes 13:31 of 48:54.

In addition to Schiff, Harnoncourt expressed a similar thought, when he stated that Schubert had his own Viennese dialect[16]. As for his main argumentation he explains that the Viennese people tend to have a paradoxical attitude, wherein "[…] life, expressed through the energy of the dance and the vernacular language, is combined with the confrontation of pain and despair […]"[17]—which again refers to the Viennese Weltschmerz (8). However, one aspect does not necessarily invalidate the other, both can coexist. As seen above, Austria as a multinational state is a strong validating factor that speaks for Brendel's statement, while the dance and other Viennese mannerisms are also at the core of Schubert's own culture and musical language.

Brendel's allusions to the Hungarian colouring and the bohemian traits are quickly recognizable and can be heard in a variety of music pieces. From Hüttenbrenner's report it is known that Schubert had a special fascination to "gypsy music"[18]. Thereby it was foremost the "musical phenomena" that interested him, i.e., the overall mood, performance style, melodic line and inflections and not the direct arrangement of a folksong[19]. Starting with the Hungarian influence, following additional examples can be included: among others (i) the *Ungarische Melodie* D 817 related to (ii) the *Divertissement à la hongroise* D 818, (iii) the Impromptus Op. 142 D 935 no. 4[20], (iv) several passages out of the C major String Quintet D 956, like the 1st movement (mm. 42–51)[21], the Trio section of the third movement and the beginning of the last movement as well as the closing

[16] Cf. Harnoncourt, Nikolaus. In: Martínez Guzman, Fernando. (2021). „El legado religioso y sinfónico de Franz Schubert: Reflexiones de Nikolaus Harnoncourt". Humanitas 97, año XXVI, Septiembre 2021. P. 510–523.

[17] Ibid. (Trans. by the author). German expression: "A primera vista resulta paradójico que la afirmación de vida, expresada a través de la energía de la danza y el idioma vernáculo, esté combinada con el enfrentamiento del dolor y la desesperación, aspecto que Harnoncourt interpreta como el principal nivel expresivo del compositor.".

[18] Hüttenbrenner, Anselm: „Marburg, am 23. Hornung 1858". In: Deutsch, Otto Erich. (1983). Schubert Erinnerungen seiner Freunde. P. 78.

[19] Cf. Domokos, Mária. (1993). „Über die ungarischen Charakteristiken des Divertissement à l'hongroise D. 818". In: Schubert durch die Brille: Internationales Franz Schubert Institut—Mitteilungen / 11. P. 53–62.

[20] The Hungarian coloring noted here is notably referred to by William Kinderman who points in particular to rhythmic aspects such as "unpredictable accentuation", "alternations of duple and triple meter", "cadential trills […] emphasized by syncopated accents" and further "Hungarian rhythms". Kinderman, William: "Schubert's piano music: probing the human condition". In: Gibbs, Christopher H. (1997). The Cambridge Companion to Schubert. Part II: "Schubert's music: style and genre". Chap. 8.

[21] In particular Montgomery draws attention to a mannerism inherent in the C major String quintet, which is typical of the "Schrammelmusik" heard in the Austro-Hungarian cafés at

theme of the first movement[22], (v) the opening theme from the F minor Fantasy for piano duet D 940[23], (vi) the oboe solo which opens the second movement of Schubert's *Great* C major Symphony[24] (vii) the fourth movement of the string quartet in A minor D 804[25], (viii) the rondo theme of the fourth movement of the G minor string quartet D 173[26], (ix) the sixth movement of the Octet in F major D 803[27], (x) the third *moment musical* in F minor D 780[28].

---

the beginning of the 19th Century. Cf. Montgomery, David: "Franz Schubert's music in performance: a brief history of people, events, and issues.". In: Gibbs, Christopher H. (1997). The Cambridge Companion to Schubert. Part III: "Reception". Chap. 16.

[22] Among several rhythmic and harmonic aspects and instrumentally derived gestures, Jonathan Bellman highlights the drone fifths in low strings as specifically conveying a Hungarian tone colour in the third movement. Furthermore, the *alla zoppa* figure is recognized, which is used both in its pure rhythmic form in the fourth movement (opening), as well as melodically in the closing theme of the first movement. Cf. Bellman, Jonathan. (1991). "Toward a Lexicon for the Style hongrois". In: The Journal of Musicology. Vol.9 no.2. P. 214–237.

[23] In this particular example, Bellman refers to the *Kuruc*-fourth figure, which would be the equivalent to the horn fifths, and which opens the beginning of the F minor Fantasy for piano duet. Usually, this figure is played by the Hungarian shawm-like instrument called *tárogató* and associated with a Hungarian national hero figure. Cf. Ibid.

[24] Meant is again the instrumental reference of the *tárogató*. Cf. Ibid.

[25] Csilla Pethő particularly analyses the influence of the verbunkos—according to Csilla Pethő, a stylistic element of Hungarian national art music—in Schubert's music, mentioning several works, inter alia, the fourth movements of both the A minor string quartet D 804, the G minor string quartet D 173 (as an example of "Schubert's early Hungarian style") and the sixth movement of the Octet in F major D 803. Pethő, Csilla. (2000). ",Style Hongrois'. Hungarian Elements in the Works of Haydn, Beethoven, Weber and Schubert". In: Studia Musicologica Academiae Scientiarum Hungaricae, Vol. 41, No. 1/3. P. 199–284. The verbunkos is also defined as a type of dance of gypsy origins. Cf. Szabó-Knotik, Cornelia. "Zigeunermusik". In: Österreichisches Musiklexikon online. [Article]. Flotzinger, Rudolf. (Begr.). Barbara Boisits (Hg.).

[26] Cf. Pethő, Csilla. (2000). ",Style Hongrois'. Hungarian Elements in the Works of Haydn, Beethoven, Weber and Schubert". In: Studia Musicologica Academiae Scientiarum Hungaricae, Vol. 41, No. 1/3. P. 199–284.

[27] Cf. Ibid.

[28] Cf. Ibid.

The Hungarian influence stems mainly from Schubert's stay and visits in and around Zseliz, where both the folksongs and the gypsy music[29] had an impact on him, but also from Kupelwieser's paintings[30] and from Haydn's previous use of the "style hongrois"[31]. Typical are the displaced and unpredictable accents, bourdon bass, as well as the "alternations of duple and triple meter [...]"[32]. Mária Domokos notes more Hungarian features in Schubert's music like the cymbal tremolos, gypsy cadences, ornaments and appoggiaturas, influences from the *verbunkos* Hungarian folkdances, the *bokázó* closing formula and the *Rakóczi*-march drum roll rhythms[33]. Jonathan Bellman completes this list with the so-called *kuruc*-fourth figure derived from the traditional *tárogató* woodwind instrument and the *alla zoppa* rhythm[34]. For the connection to Bohemian and Czech musical influence, the *Fantasia* in C major for Violin and Piano D 934 can be taken as an example[35]. In more general terms, one could think of the major-minor shifts as a Slavic influence, coming from folk music, which may eventually be linked to Schubert's Moravian roots.

Brendel's reference of a Spanish affinity, is musically harder to comprehend at a first glance. The only direct Spanish references to be traced in Schubert's life and work are (i) his code name in the so-called "Nonsense society" ("Unsinngesellschaft"), being Schubert the "Ritter Juan de la Cimbala", in other words

---

[29] As basic features of Hungarian music, both the phrygian and aeolian key and the characteristic agogic, e.g., a certain type of rubato and holding back the tempo play an important role. Cf. Domokos, Mária. (1993). „Über die ungarischen Charakteristiken des Divertissement à l'hongroise D. 818". In: Schubert durch die Brille: Internationales Franz Schubert Institut—Mitteilungen / 11. P. 53–62.

[30] The drawing „Zrinyis Ausfall aus der Festung Szigeth" is specifically mentioned. Cf. Ibid.

[31] For more insight: Cf. Pethő, Csilla. (2000). "‚Style Hongrois'. Hungarian Elements in the Works of Haydn, Beethoven, Weber and Schubert". In: Studia Musicologica Academiae Scientiarum Hungaricae, Vol. 41, No. 1/3. P. 199–284.

[32] Kinderman, William: "Schubert's piano music: probing the human condition". In: Gibbs, Christopher H. (1997). The Cambridge Companion to Schubert. Part II: "Schubert's music: style and genre". Chap. 8.

[33] For more insight into the Hungarian coloring in Schubert's Divertissement à l'hongroise: Cf. Domokos, Mária. (1993). „Über die ungarischen Charakteristiken des Divertissement à l'hongroise D. 818". In: Schubert durch die Brille: Internationales Franz Schubert Institut—Mitteilungen / 11. P. 53–62.

[34] Cf. Bellman, Jonathan. (1991). "Toward a Lexicon for the Style hongrois". In: The Journal of Musicology. Vol.9 no.2. P. 214–237.

[35] McKay particularly highlights the major-minor dichotomy in this Fantasia in general and mentions the Czech dance-like theme of the faster main section of the first movement. Cf. McKay, Elizabeth Norman: "Schubert's string and piano duos in context". In: Newbould, Brian. (2017). Schubert Studies. Chap. 3. P. 102–103.

the Don Giovanni or the Knight of the Keyboard[36], (ii) the caricatures painted of Schubert, by his friend Leopold Kupelwieser, with the "Spanish rod"[37]—a symbol related to the figure of the schoolmaster, which was a commonly used device at that time and which may rather allude to Schubert's father, (iii) the libretto written by his friend Franz von Schober, for the singspiel *Alfonso und Estrella* D 732 from 1821/22. However, musically speaking, apart from the pavane rhythm[38] and the occasional use of the phrygian mode[39] in some of his works, there are not many significant musical features characteristic of the Spanish colouring. Furthermore, there is no evidence that Schubert actually knew Goya's work directly. It would seem logical to trace the finale of the C minor Sonata D 958 back to Italian influence, since it is a tarantella. This would take into consideration the heritage of Schubert's musical education.

Questioning this statement from another perspective, Brendel's subtle hint as an interpreter is probably thought much more as a parallel—i.e., synchronous archetypal theme(s) common to both contemporaries, but apart living, Goya and Schubert—than to be taken as a true occurrence (17). This synchronicity is naturally expressed in two different ways artistically and musically since each artist had their own lived experiences and come from different origins. Both address a theme common to all humankind. In another paper, Brendel specifically mentions Goya's "black fantasies"[40], which assumingly relates to the period when Goya painted topics related to horrific visions[41], undoubtedly artistic expressions of an (archetypal) shadow nature. Under the author's perception, Brendel's aim is possibly to pinpoint to Schubert's shadow side and even in a more collective

[36] More to this topic is to be found written by: Steblin, Rita: "Schubert: The nonsense society revisited". In: Gibbs, Christopher H., Solvik, Morten. (2014). Franz Schubert and his World. Chap. 1. Here, Steblin emphasizes the importance of conducting a more thorough analysis through the codified language present in the nonsense society's newsletters in order to learn more about Schubert himself.

[37] Cf. Steblin, Rita: "Schubert's relationship with women: an historical account". In: Newbould, Brian. (2017). Schubert Studies. Chap. 10. P.234.

[38] The pavane is a dance of Spanish origins that flourished in Europe during the Renaissance period. In Schubert's music, however, the dactyl rhythm characteristic of this dance is usually associated with the Wanderer semantic (the wanderer-rhythm) because of the connection with the song "Der Wanderer" D 493.

[39] Examples include the song "Der Wegweiser". Cf. Youens, Susan. (1991). Retracing a Winter's Journey. P.242.

[40] Cf. Brendel, Alfred. (1989). "Schubert's last three piano sonatas". In: RSA Journal, Vol. 137, No. 5395, P.401–411.

[41] Cf. Hagen, Marie-Rose and Rainer. (2012). *Francisco Goya.*

extent—to the fatefully recurring and human condition of destruction and annihilation recorded through the history of humankind; an impactful archetypal force coming from the depths of the psyche.

Based on this assumption, it is possible to understand "Weltschmerz" being both related to cultural matters, i.e., the cultural unconscious as expressed in the dances, but which is also to be taken as a thematic touching upon the *conditio humana.*

Schubert's Spontaneity and Archetypal Language 11

"Everything that lies in the unconscious wants to become an event […]"[1].

Arthur Godel explains in *Schuberts letzte drei Klaviersonaten*:

> "Schubert's compositions largely reflect the immediate course of the compositional process; the sketches are protocols of invention in which everything follows one another as it emerged in the act of composition. This is what characterises the spontaneity of Schubert's works, […]"[2].

This statement of Godel's, which reflects one of his major findings in regard to Schubert's creative process, emphasizes an aspect of Schubert's working process that will be explored in this chapter. A work of art or a musical composition does not only come into being through influence from (external) sensory perception[3] but also through the inner impulses of the unconscious. With Schubert it shows

[1] Jung, Carl Gustav. "Erinnerungen, Träume, Gedanken". Cited after: Vogel, Ralf T. (2017). *Individuation und Wandlung*. P. 89. (Trans. by the author). German expression: „Alles, was im Unbewussten liegt, will Ereignis werden […]".

[2] Godel, Arthur. (1985). *Schuberts letzte drei Klaviersonaten.* P. 41. (Trans. by the author). German expression: "Schuberts Kompositionen spiegeln denn auch weitgehend den unmittelbaren Verlauf des Kompositionsprozesses, die Entwürfe sind Erfindungsprotokolle, in denen alles so aufeinander folgt, wie es im Kompositionsakt entstand. Das macht die Spontaneität von Schuberts Werken aus, […]".

[3] It can be argued that perception is only one out of four different functions of the human psyche, namely the function of sensation. Each function (sensation, intuition, thinking and feeling) of Jung's outlined psychological types expresses one fundamental view of the human being and of the world perception. They are organized in a polar manner, tend toward self-regulation and therefore naturally play a role in the individuation and creative processes. Despite the natural unconscious stimulation of repressed functions, this concept allows the

L. Dill, *Schubert's Metamorphoses*,
https://doi.org/10.1007/978-3-662-73476-6_11

that the latter plays an important role. The aim of this chapter is to outline the main characteristics of this relationship during Schubert's creative process and to show how creativity and individuation are strongly intertwined concepts leading to a transcendent experience, fruit of the transcendental function of the Self, which consists of a "[...] dialog between consciousness and his opposite, the unconscious [...]"[4]. To investigate this relationship, it is compelling to address how the composer deals with the element of chaos and order in his compositions since it might give some indications on his creative process.

From the inquiry on this topic exposed in the subsequent chapter (11.1), it appears that Schubert revealed a peculiar relationship with chaos and order, which, generally speaking, would distinguish himself from other composers such as Mozart, Haydn or Beethoven—even when creating order through keys, thematic or motivic relations, Schubert seems to have been driven not only by reason but by unconscious powers. As described by his friends, he was immersed in a deep process while composing[5]. This is expressed by the manner that these motivic relations are inherent and developed along one or several compositions, namely through the technique of "motif-metamorphosis"[6]. Godel explains how this technique leads to a "[...] reminiscent unity and permanent transformation [...]"[7], expressing how Schubert's music "[...] lives from remembrance"[8]. This internal dialogue between the inner structures and his consciousness as a composer, for whom music is his primal language of expression, is enabled through the ego-Self axis and is activated by the confrontations with and the overpowering by certain archetypes.

How he dealt with his (inner) thoughts and how they changed in the course of a composition is expressed musically and can therefore be analysed. Within the next subchapters some archetypal aspects of his creative process will be laid out.

---

subject to consciously choose to activate the respective repressed function of his/her personality, with the intention of coming closer to wholeness. Cf. Vogel, Ralf T. (2017). *Individuation und Wandlung*. Chap. 5: "Individuation und die psychischen Grundfunktionen". P. 38–40.

[4] Ibid. P. 45. (Trans. by the author). German expression: „Die Transzendente Funktion übt den Dialog zwischen dem Bewusstsein und seinem Gegenüber, dem Unbewussten, ein [...]".

[5] The used words and sentences of Schubert's friends to describe his creative process were: a "state of clairvoyance", "divine inspiration", "the beauty of his music emerged unconsciously". Cf. Hilmar, Ernst. (1997). *Franz Schubert*. P. 32.

[6] Godel, Arthur. (1985). *Schuberts letzte drei Klaviersonaten*. P. 19.

[7] Ibid. (Trans. by the author). German expression: „[...] Technik der Motivmetamorphose: Sie garantiert dem Stück zugleich erinnernde Einheit und permanente Wandlung.".

[8] Ibid. (Trans. by the author). German expression: „[...] die vom Erinnern lebt.".

11.1 Chaos and Order. The Shadow and the Doppelgänger

"'In the work of art, chaos has to shine through the veil of order.'"[9].

"While composing there are surely unconscious processes taking place. There may be a plan, but what happens in detail is also—fortunately—sometimes left to chance."[10]

As the looking into the abyss is an important turning point in the creative act (8), so too is returning to the origins of existence, to the chaos state. Both elements, the abyss and chaos, are strongly intertwined in each other, the latter being the "renewal source"[11], the *prima materia*[12]. In a dialectic understanding, chaos is essential for order, as order is for chaos, both being united in a whole. Each composer deals with the relationship of chaos and order differently.

Brendel grasps this relationship in Schubert with the metaphor of the sleepwalker:

"Beethoven the architect and Schubert the sleepwalker. Which meant to say that Beethoven in his works keeps you always informed where he is and justifies every step. He builds as a good architect would build to produce something secure and lasting. Schubert doesn't give one that sense of security or inevitability."[13].

In the author's perception, Schubert as the "sleepwalker" is to be understood in as much as he composes out of a state, driven by the unconscious. Therefore, the unexpected turns that his music takes are not constructed but are rather accidental: "[…] Haydn springs his surprises, while Schubert is being surprised."[14]. This statement exemplifies what Jung meant, when speaking about the creative process, with the following sentence:

---

[9] Novalis. Cited after: McLellan, Joseph. (1988). "Alfred Brendel and the Schubert statement". The *Washington Post*. [Article].

[10] Brendel, Alfred. In: Brendel, Alfred. Gülke, Peter. (2020). *Die Kunst des Interpretierens*. P.43. (Trans. by the author). German expression: „Innerhalb des Komponierens gibt es natürlich auch unbewusste Vorgänge. Es mag zwar einen Plan geben, aber was im Einzelnen passiert, ist auch manchmal—zum Glück—dem Zufall überlassen.".

[11] Mollwo-Oesterreicher, Marianne. (1978). *Herder Lexikon Symbole*. P. 32.

[12] Ibid.

[13] Brendel, Alfred. In: McLellan, Joseph. (1988). "Alfred Brendel and the Schubert statement". The *Washington Post*. [Article].

[14] Ibid.

> "[...] the ego is swept along an underground current, becoming nothing more than a helpless observer of the events. [...]"[15].

Archetypal structures impose their will over the will of the composer itself, driving him through the creative process, influencing and shaping the artistic outcome.

For Schubert chaos "arises from [his] feverish hauntings of horrors"[16], whereas order is inherent through the thematic and motivic cohesion[17]. These horrific visitations are brought up by the shadow archetype, in the romantic period habitually personified by the figure of the doppelganger, with whom there is a confrontation during the so-called "night sea voyage" to the unconscious realm. The lied "Der Doppelgänger" D 957 from the Heine-setting can be seen as an example. In Schubert's musical utterances the doppelgänger is frequently accompanied with topics of pain, fate, and death[18]. In extreme cases, as the 2nd movement of the A major Sonata D 959 (IV 17), there is the frightening expression of the deepest shadow side through a rather chaotic and completely "irrational explosion"[19].

However, this chaos has an inherent Ariadne's thread through the interactions Schubert established between keys, themes, and motifs. The motivic interrelations are subtler in character because they are not a result of a "systematic thought" but rather emerge "in an arbitrary way"[20], based on the variation principle rather than literal quotations[21]. Therefore, it is to presume that these variations, which create order and the "inner unity"[22], are the result of unconscious processes—in fact of inner developments taking place intuitively during the act of composing,

---

15 Cf. Jung, Carl Gustav. (2014). "Spirit in Man, Art and Literature". In: *CW. Vol. 15.* (Trans. by Gerhard Adler and R.F.C. Hull). Part IV: "On the relation of Analytical Psychology to poetry—2. The artist".

16 Brendel, Alfred. (1996). *Musik beim Wort genommen.* P. 96. (Trans. by the author). German expression: Nichts ist typischer für Schubert als diese fiebernden Heimsuchungen des Grauens [...]".

17 Cf. Ibid.

18 Occasionally, the doppelganger can show itself with light characteristics as shown in the analysis section with the transformation taking place along the D minor string quartet D 810 "Death and the Maiden", third movement (16.).

19 Cf. Ibid. P.92.

20 Brendel, Alfred. In: Brendel, Alfred. (1898). *Les trois dernières Sonates de Franz Schubert.* Akerman, Chantal (Director). [Programme].

21 Cf. Ibid.

22 Cf. Brendel, Alfred. (1996). *Musik beim Wort genommen.* P. 96.

as "a matter of the blooming of the composer's imagination"[23]. These motivic cohesions can go far beyond the constraints of individual movements. They can create a cyclical unity, which might extend itself over several works, as there is a natural overlapping of material which occurs, while working on concurrent compositions[24]. As such, these transformations can indicate Schubert's own inner development, as it will be shown in the last analysis chapter (20).

Some aspects of this interplay between consciousness and the unconscious, between chaos and order can be traced by analyzing the musical scores and comparing the draft manuscript with the fair copy. Reference is made to this in the analysis section in each case. An impressive example can be found between the original and edited scores of the E-flat major piano trio D 929, more precisely, in the spontaneous reminiscences of motifs found in the original score and subsequently cut out by Schubert himself (19).

11.2 Schubert's (inner) Religiosity: The Great Mother and the Child Archetype

> "[...there is a passage,] here, wherein a horn calls as if from afar, seeming to me to have come down from another sphere. Here, everything hearkens too, as if a heavenly guest were sneaking around in the orchestra."[25].

> "'God is a primal experience of the human being'"[26].

> "Were the eye not sun-like, It could never behold the sun; Were God's own might not dwell within us, how could the divine enchant our sight!"[27]

---

[23] Brendel, Alfred. In: Brendel, Alfred. (1898). *Les trois dernières Sonates de Franz Schubert.* Akerman, Chantal (Director). [Programme].

[24] Cf. Ibid.

[25] These are Schumann's words on the second movement of Schubert's C major Symphony. Häusler, Josef (Ed): Schumann, Robert. (2010). *Schriften über Musik und Musiker.* Häusler, Josef (Ed). P. 179. (Trans. by the author). German expression: "In ihm findet sich auch eine Stelle, da, wo ein Horn wie aus der Ferne ruft, das scheint mir aus anderer Sphäre herabgekommen zu sein. Hier lauscht auch alles, als ob ein himmlischer Gast im Orchester herumschliche.".

[26] Jung, Carl Gustav. (1933). "Bruder Klaus". Cited after: Wehr, Gerhard. (2014). *C.G. Jung Leben—Werk—Wirkung.* P. 242. (Trans. by the author). German expression (stems from Jung's writings on Niklaus von der Flüe: „Gott ist eine Urerfahrung des Menschen.".

[27] Goethe, Wolfgang Johann. (1988). *Gedichte und Epen. Band 1.* P. 367. (Trans. by the author). German expression: "Wär' nicht das Auge sonnenhaft, die Sonne könnt' es nie erblicken; Läg' nicht in uns des Gottes eigne Kraft, Wie könnt' uns Göttliches entzücken!".

In his musical utterances, and especially in the later compositions, Schubert often expresses the sentiment of being trapped in fate, as if he would be a prisoner of fate[28]. This is often linked to the topic of the Weltschmerz and of death (8), which came to expression before his knowledge of his potential deadly illness[29]. Schubert's own religious experiences and the "crucial phase in the individuation process of coming to an acceptance"[30] have a significant role on how he individually deals with this challenge[31]. The acceptance of fate conveys a highly religious attitude. In Jungian thoughts, Christ's crucifixion is understood as a metaphor, pointing to the need to accept to carry one's own cross, and by doing so to set a process in motion (18). Finally, Schubert's religiosity is a highly debated question even today. There are scholars that advocate for the religious content of Schubert's music, others who dispute it. The main points that gave rise to the contrasting discussions will be presented now.

Several renowned interpreters hint at Schubert's deep religiosity. Brendel in his argumentation-lines addresses a harmonic aspect. He alludes in several of his writings to the plagal cadences and plagal progressions to be heard in Schubert's repertoire, for instance within the last trilogy of the piano sonatas D 958–960 (17) and the E-flat major mass[32]. These, so-called "Amen" cadences, can communicate the "feeling of 'resilience'"[33], as perceivable in the *Benedictus* or *Agnus Dei* of the fifth mass in A-flat major. The gradually abundant use of these plagal harmonic motions, notably in his later (instrumental) works, might be seen as evidence of being embedded in a religious-cultural context. The cross-reference connotations of a specific semantics between church music and instrumental music invoked by Brendel could also indicate that his faith was not necessarily tied to the church as an institution. This is the case in particular of Nikolaus

---

28 This makes a main contrast to Beethoven's perception of fate, which, in general terms, is more directed towards the sense of fighting for justice and transmitting hope. Cf. Pires, Maria João. (2012). "Maria João Pires". [Interview]. Kasica, Katarzyna (Direction). Mierzejewska, Agata (Interviewer). Beethoven seems to resolve this question based on the free will over fate.

29 Cf. Dobretsberger, Barbara. Personal communication between Barbara Dobretsberger and the author. Salzburg/Lisbon: November 25, 2021.

30 Roesler, Christian. Personal communication between Christian Roesler and the author. Basel: January 12, 2023.

31 This is, however, not a straightforward process at all, as it will be demonstrated in the analysis section of the thesis (20).

32 Cf. Brendel, Alfred. (1992). *Musik beim Wort genommen.*

33 Hilmar, Ernst. (1997). *Franz Schubert.* P. 90.

Harnoncourt, who saw in his two late masses true "acts of religious devotion"[34] and "[...] of a tremendous explosiveness and transcendental power"[35]. Andras Schiff emphasized Schubert's religiosity as an inherent trait of his musical language: "It [Schubert's music] is not music of an atheist [...]"[36]. Finally, Schubert himself wrote about faith:

> "Man enters the world with faith, it comes far before understanding and knowledge; for in order to understand something, I must first believe something; it is the higher basis on which the weak understanding plants its first pillar of proof. Understanding is nothing but analyzed faith."[37].

Badura-Skoda argues that composers do not set a religious text into music unless they are motivated firstly by "a basic religious attitude"[38]. Yet Schubert's masses are subject of debate among musicologists. His relation to the church and to religion is today a widely discussed subject within the Schubert research community, although no established consensus has yet been reached. The fact that there is no clear statement by Schubert himself led to the emergence of differentiated hypotheses. In literature, these discussions are based specifically on the following, most commonly cited evidences: (i) the written testimony of Ferdinand Walcher, who wrote to Schubert "*Credo in unum Deum*—not you, I know

[34] Harnoncourt, Nikolaus. In: Martínez Guzman, Fernando. (2021). "El legado religioso y sinfónico de Franz Schubert: Reflexiones de Nikolaus Harnoncourt". *Humanitas 97, año XXVI*, Septiembre 2021. P. 510–523. (Trans. by the author). Spanish expression: "Harnoncourt no solo considera sus dos Misas tardías como 'actos de devoción religiosa'; además, reconoce en ellas una música 'de tremenda explosividad y poder transcendental [...]'".

[35] Ibid. (Trans. by the author). Spanish expression: "Harnoncourt no solo considera sus dos Misas tardías como 'actos de devoción religiosa'; además, reconoce en ellas una música 'de tremenda explosividad y poder transcendental [...]'".

[36] Schiff, Andras. In: Schiff, Andras. (n.d.). *Schiff András filmje Schubertről—András Schiff tells about Schubert*. [Documentary]. Scorer Associates. Minutes 30:00 of 48:54.

[37] Schubert, Franz. „Aus einem verlorenen Notizbuche Schuberts von 1824". In: Deutsch, Otto Erich. (1964). *Schubert—Die Dokumente seines Lebens*. P. 233. (Trans. by the author). German expression: „Mit dem Glauben tritt der Mensch in die Welt, er kommt vor Verstand und Kenntnissen weit voraus; denn um etwas zu verstehen, muß ich vorher etwas glauben; er ist die höhere Basis, auf welche der schwache Verstand seinen ersten Beweispfeiler aufpflanzt. Verstand ist nichts als ein analysierter Glaube.".

[38] Cf. Badura-Skoda, Paul. „Messtexte". Cited after: Gülke, Peter. (2020). *Franz Schubert in seiner Zeit*. P.271. German expression: „Ein Komponist vertont einen Messtext [...] aus einer religiösen Grundhaltung heraus, [...]".

it well [...]"[39] (ii) the text omissions in his masses compositions, notably in the *Gloria* and in the *Credo* and (iii) Schubert's statement about a clergyman and his sermons, with the depreciative comment "brute like a buffalo"[40]. The statement of Walcher can lead to an atheistic interpretation, which, however, comes most probably from Walcher's dogmatic thinking, and can therefore be regarded as a misjudgment, as already suggested by Walther Dürr[41]. Equally, the third observation merely indicates a critical attitude of Schubert towards a clergyman and is for this reason entirely meaningless for the discussion. In opposition, the text omissions in his masses seem to lead to further speculations. A historical and aesthetical contextualization can be helpful to address these questions.

The term of Biedermeier era, in which Schubert lived, is considered to be highly problematic: generally, it is prejudicially loaded with derogatory connotations such as sentimentality and triviality, when in fact a "diversity of traditions"[42], a "stylistic pluralism"[43] and a "complex spiritual life"[44] can be noticed. All those features are reflected in the church music compositions. The former Josephinism and the catholic Enlightenment in Austria[45] had their musical impact on the so-called first Viennese school composers, particularly Schubert's paragons Michael and Joseph Haydn[46]. However, the above statement of Schubert about faith and reason points to his general attitude against this kind of thinking. He seemed to have been rather influenced by the so-called "popular

---

[39] Walcher, Ferdinand: Letter to Schubert. (1827). In: Deutsch, Otto Erich. (1964). *Schubert—Die Dokumente seines Lebens.* P. 403. (Trans. by the author). German expression: "'Credo in unum Deum!'—du nicht, das weiss ich wohl [...]".

[40] Peter, Mathias. „Schubert und sein Verhältnis zur Katholischen Kirche—Schubert, der Kirchenrevoluzzer?" Domradio. [Article]. German expression: "Roh wie ein Büffel".

[41] Cf. Dürr, Walther. (2002). „‚Die Allmacht' (D 852). Schubert, Schelling und der Pantheismus.". In: *Laudato Si, mi Signore, per sora nostra matra terra.* P. 103–116.

[42] Hrncirik, Peter: "Tendenzen der Kirchenmusik im Biedermeier. Historische und stilidiomatische Aspekte.". In: Harrandt, Andrea., Partsch, Erich Wolfgang. (2010). *Kirchenmusik im Biedermeier.* P. 23. (Trans. by the author). German expression: "Traditionsvielfalt".

[43] Ibid. P. 14. (Trans. by the author). German expression: "Stilpluralismus".

[44] Ibid. P. 10, respectively P.14. (Trans. by the author). German expression: "[...] dem komplexen Geistesleben [...]".

[45] This movement was notably shaped by the concept of freedom, the Kantian Enlightenment ideals and the Jansenism. The Jansenists were in turn moved by the will to return to an empirical based notion of faith and devotion, grounded on the church father Augustine.

[46] Cf. Jahrmärker, Manuela. „Die Kirchenmusik—Von der liturgischen Funktion zum persönlichen Bekenntnis". In: Dürr, Walther. Krause, Andreas. (2020). *Schubert Handbuch.* P. 346.

devotion" ("Volksfrömmigkeit")[47]. In particular, the growing weight of the bourgeoisie over church music regulations is explained by Gernot Gruber to lie on "the repercussion of the Napoleonic turmoil and the national bankruptcy"[48] since 1811, and reinforced from 1820 on, with the emergence of the church music associations. As a result, the focus turned towards a "soulfully, inner devotion"[49] and originated a conception of faith oriented towards "a bourgeois tone"[50]. This inflection can already be heard in Schubert's second mass in G major D 167[51].

From the perspective of the church music specialist Peter Hrncirik, Beethoven and Schubert are presented as revolutionary composers in their church music style tendencies, being mostly active in the genre of the instrumental masses: Romantic traits are audible in both composers, although—he specifies—in Beethoven still in a subtler way[52]. The latter was of foremost importance in the great symphonic masses and the *missae solemnes*[53]. The main characteristic of the post-classical era church music was the musical expression of a personal religiosity, which ought to be conveyed by the means of sound, through a variety of new compositional resources which included a potentially significant deviation in the treatment of the text:

> "[...] 'to grasp the realm of the personal religiosity and to interpret it tonally with increased harmonic means (chromaticism), the exploitation of instrumental timbres, motif formations similar to leitmotifs that characterize the textual content. The compositional peculiarities are: largely homophonic choral movements and a songlike themes of the solo parts. The general bass accompaniment is omitted when the orchestra is full; the organ, when used as an obbligato, is given an independent function. The Gloria and Credo are composed in the clear arch form of a-b-a. Yet it is precisely

---

47 Cf. Gülke, Peter. (2020). *Franz Schubert in seiner Zeit.* P. 268.

48 Gruber, Gernot. (2010). *Schubert. Schubert?* P. 108. (Trans. by the author). German expression: „Durch die Auswirkungen der napoleonischen Wirren und des Staatsbankrotts von 1811 hatten sich für die Kirchenmusikpflege die finanziellen und dann die institutionellen Voraussetzungen geändert.".

49 Ibid. (Trans. by the author). German expression: „ So bot sich auch für groß angelegten Messkompositionen der Anreiz, in die Repräsentation von Glaubenswahrheiten den ‚bürgerlichen' Ton einer gefühlvoll innigen Frömmigkeit hineinzubringen.".

50 Ibid. (Trans. by the author). German expression: "[...] den ‚bürgerlichen' Ton [...]".

51 Cf. Gülke, Peter. (2020). *Franz Schubert in seiner Zeit.* P. 268.

52 Cf. Hrncirik, Peter: "Tendenzen der Kirchenmusik im Biedermeier. Historische und stilidiomatische Aspekte.". In: Harrandt, Andrea., Partsch, Erich Wolfgang. (2010). *Kirchenmusik im Biedermeier*. P. 19, respectively P. 15.

53 Cf. Ibid. P. 21.

in these two movements that there are various deviations in the treatment of the text (omissions, shortenings or arbitrary additions)'."[54].

A further factor to cogitate is that "the individuality of a composition was in the foreground"[55]. These traits are not only to be found already in Beethoven's C major mass, but also in Schubert's mass compositions, which can explain Schubert's text omissions. While the exclusions in *Gloria* are understood as being of a pure musical order, those of the *Credo* are taken by its theological content[56]. Yet, apart from the dismissed "*et unam, sanctam, catholicam, et apostolicam Ecclesiam",* Otto Erich Deutsch accentuated that other passages from the liturgy text were "sacred to him"[57]. Conclusively, the mentioned exclusion merely indicates Schubert's reluctance to the dogmatic Catholic institution, which is finally an

[54] Scharnagl. „Anm.12". Cited after: Ibid. P. 34. (Trans. by the author). German expression: "[…] ‚mit gesteigerten harmonischen Mitteln (Chromatik), Ausnutzung instrumentaler Klangfarben, leitmotiv-ähnlichen, den textlichen Inhalt charakterisierenden Motivbildungen den Bereich persönlicher Religiosität zu erfassen und klanglich zu deuten. Als kompositionstechnische Eigenarten treten dabei hervor: weitgehend homophone Chorsätze und eine liedhafte Gestaltung der Solopartien. Die generalbassmäßige Orgelbegleitung entfällt bei vollbesetztem Orchester; die Orgel erhält, wenn sie obligat verwendet wird, eine selbständige Funktion. Gloria und Credo sind in der übersichtlichen Bogenform a-b-a komponiert. Doch kommt es gerade in diesen beiden Sätzen zu mancherlei Abweichungen in der Textbehandlung (Auslassungen, Kürzungen oder willkürliche Ergänzungen)'.".

[55] Jahrmärker, Manuela. „Die Kirchenmusik—Von der liturgischen Funktion zum persönlichen Bekenntnis". In: Dürr, Walther. Krause, Andreas. (2020). *Schubert Handbuch.* P. 346. (Trans. by the author). German expression: „[…] dass bei Komponisten wie Schubert, […] die Werk-Individualität im Vordergrund steht.".

[56] Cf. Dürr, Walther: „Schubert in seiner Welt". In: Dürr, Walther. Krause, Andreas. (2020). *Schubert Handbuch.* P.8.

[57] Deutsch, Otto Erich. (1964). *Schubert—Die Dokumente seines Lebens.* P. 403. (Trans. by the author). German expression: „Schubert hat zwar die Worte ‚Et unam, sanctam, catholicam, et apostolicam Ecclesiam' in seinen Messen ausgelassen, nicht aber die anderen Teile des Credo, das ihm heilig war.".

insignificant statement on his religiosity[58]. Gruber suggests considering both reasons: "Genre-related historical background"[59] as well as "a personal, emotional confession of Schubert's private devotion"[60]. This can further suggest that Schubert used other resources to express his own religiosity, namely through specific musical tools. Ulrich Michels gives the example of Schubert's use of sound as a means for the expression of the divine presence in the *Credo* of his fifth Mass in A-flat major D 678[61]. He explains: "Schubert no longer uses only the melodic motif as a means of expression, but sound itself. In this context, sound relates to melody in the same way that universal fulfillment and pure being relate to individual manifestation"[62]. Peter Gülke's analysis of this same mass brings more insight into the symbolic tools Schubert used musically: he established through harmony and key relations his symbolic means to express the mystery of God's incarnation and associated these with a juxtaposition between contrapunctual techniques (fugue) and *a-capella* sections[63]. Gülke speaks of a mixture between "modern harmonics" and "archaic" components[64], which correspond to the simultaneous use of *stile antico* and *stile moderno*[65]. Specifically in the *Credo* of his fifth mass in A-flat major D 678 Schubert places a lot of emphasis on the number twelve,

58 Hilmar's two comments stated below can highlight Schubert's general undogmatic attitude in life: "Constraints were obviously [...] abhorrent to him [Schubert].". Hilmar, Ernst. (1997). *Franz Schubert.* P. 19. (Trans. by the author). German expression: „Zwänge waren ihm offensichtlich schon damals zuwider [...]". Later he writes: „[...] the careful elimination of this passage in all his church works was not a matter of religiosity, but should be understood as a criticism of the church and its practices, that is, of its worldly behavior and dogmatism. The phrases of the church dogmas were simply rejected by Schubert.". In: Ibid. P. 111. (Trans. by the author). German expression: „Die sorgfältige Eliminierung dieser Textpassage in allen seinen Kirchenwerken war aber keine Frage der Religiosität, sondern als Kritik an der Kirche und ihren Praktiken zu verstehen, das heißt an ihrem weltlichen Verhalten und ihrer Bigotterie. Die Phrasen der kirchlichen Dogmen wurden von Schubert schlichtweg abgelehnt.".

59 Gruber, Gernot. (2010). *Schubert. Schubert?* P. 108. (Trans. by the author). German expression: „[...] gattungsbedingten historischen Hintergrund [...]".

60 Ibid. (Trans. by the author). German expression: „[...] ein persönliches emotionales Bekenntnis [,] auf Schuberts private Frömmigkeit [...]".

61 Cf. Michels, Ulrich. (2008). *Dtv-Atlas Musik.* P. 427.

62 Ibid. (Trans. by the author). German expression: „Schubert setzt nicht mehr nur das melodische Motiv, sondern den Klang als Ausdrucksmittel ein. Dabei verhält sich dieser Klang zur Melodie wie universale Erfüllung und reines Sein zu individueller Erscheinung.".

63 Cf. Gülke, Peter. (2020). *Franz Schubert in seiner Zeit.* P. 272—277.

64 Cf. Ibid. P. 274.

65 A further characteristic of Schubert's style in church music is the conjunction of the *amoroso* gesture and the *marcato* gesture, giving the mass a "Biedermeier tone", as for

since not only the word *Credo* is repeated twelve times, but also the key relations between the *et homo factus* and the *crucifixus* are related by twelve fifths[66]. Biblically the number twelve is loaded with the semantic of completeness and wholeness[67]. The *Sanctus* of the same mass is equally rich in symbolic content: the trinity symbolism is featured in the three *Sanctus* calls[68]. The mediantic key relationship (the third steps) seem of additional importance, since with these relations Schubert achieves to form a closing circle[69], which is another image for wholeness (Self, I 3). Later in *Pleni sunt coeli* the number four gains in importance, "returning to the earthly dimension"[70]. It can be added that the number four is also significant for alchemy[71] and consequently for C.G. Jung. According to the latter, the inclusion of the fourth element (*Quaternio*) results in wholeness.

Walther Dürr observes that Schubert's doctrinal hesitancy is indicated to be mostly prominent towards the Holy Trinity, the Catholic dogmas of the Immaculate conception, and the resurrection[72]. It seems that Schubert's Catholic background is significant in so far that church music and masses were amongst the music genres for which he was required to create[73].These statements, rather directed to the Catholic church and its dogmas[74], might lead to interrogating whether the Protestant Reformation thinking—which was being divulged and spread throughout Europe, communicating a new conception of faith—had an impact on Schubert. Interestingly, Schubert showed a special attention in setting

instance Schubert's G major mass D 167, as Hrncirik explains. Cf. Hrncirik, Peter: "Tendenzen der Kirchenmusik im Biedermeier. Historische und stilidiomatische Aspekte.". In: Harrandt, Andrea., Partsch, Erich Wolfgang. (2010). *Kirchenmusik im Biedermeier*. P. 57.

[66] Cf. Peter Gülke highlights these facts within his analysis of Schubert's fifth mass. Cf. Gülke, Peter. (2020). *Franz Schubert in seiner Zeit.* P. 275.

[67] Cf. Mollwo-Oesterreicher, Marianne. (1978). *Herder Lexikon Symbole.* P. 190.

[68] Cf. Gülke, Peter. (2020). *Franz Schubert in seiner Zeit.* P. 276.

[69] Cf. Ibid.

[70] Ibid. P. 277.

[71] In fact, in the alchemy the number four is related with the four classical elements, i.e., fire, water, air and earth. The number three are the alchemistic ground principles, i.e., salt, sulfur and mercury, and the number twelve contains both numbers. Cf. Mollwo-Oesterreicher, Marianne. (1978). *Herder Lexikon Symbole.* P. 190.

[72] Cf. Dürr, Walther: „Schubert in seiner Welt". In: Dürr, Walther. Krause, Andreas. (2020). *Schubert Handbuch.* P.8.

[73] Cf. Ibid. P.9.

[74] Cf. Ibid. P. 8.

poems of Protestant poets into music and had himself written a poem conforming the Klopstocks ode-style[75]. However, there are no further areas of alignment which could substantiate that supposition. In fact, musically there are also counter examples, as the *Ellens Gesang* "Ave Maria" D 839 for instance, which will be matter for discussion later on.

Hans Küng states that since Johann Sebastian Bach there was a paradigm shift taking place in regard to the relation between the composer and the church, when composers began to be more independent from the church and to compose to a lesser extent under commission[76]. While this may be the case in general terms, commissioned works can still be traced back to the Classical period and even into the Romantic period. Two main examples include Schubert's first mass, the F major Mass D 105 and possibly his second mass in G major D 167. Küng's statement about the growing connection to nature that emerged and the increasing intention to create from self-experience, from true feelings and sensations cannot be denied[77]. This corresponds to the understanding that Schubert's extra musical and inner poetic inspiration would rather arise from a general basic mood or atmosphere, than linked to a particular text passage[78]. This is valid for his song compositions but can also be taken into consideration while examining his masses.

Beethoven is considered to be crucial for this shift. Particularly to mention are his words in his *Missa solemnis* "From the heart—might it return again—to the heart", which can be understood as a "legacy for [the coming] generations"[79], as Nestler suggests. Reflecting his music in general, this statement ought to reveal a "new subjective, humanistic religiosity"[80]. In that perspective, Schubert can be perceived as being as much a revolutionary as Beethoven, since both Beethoven's *Missa solemnis* (1819–23) and Schubert's A-flat major mass (1819–22) were concurrently composed, and both are considered to convey an identical message: "in

[75] Cf. Dürr, Walther. (2002). „‚Die Allmacht' (D 852). Schubert, Schelling und der Pantheismus.". In: *Laudato Si, mi Signore, per sora nostra matra terra.* P.105.

[76] Cf. Küng, Hans. (2012). „Komponisten und ihr Glaube". In: Der Neue Zürcher Zeitung. [Article].

[77] Cf. Ibid.

[78] Cf. Michels, Ulrich. (2008). *Dtv-Atlas Musik.* P. 435.

[79] Nestler, Gerhard. (1979). *Geschichte der Musik.* P. 437. (Trans. by the author). German expression: „Dieses Wort, auf Beethoven's Musik in ihrer Gesamtheit bezogen, ist für Generationen ein Vermächtnis gewesen.".

[80] Ibid. (Trans. by the author). German expression: „Im Hinblick auf die Musik der Missa solemnis mag es als der Begriff einer neuen ichbezogenen, humanen Religiosität gelten.".

a personal, confessional way, a musical statement [that] take[s] on a weight of its own"[81].

This novel standpoint here addressed can be strongly linked to a pantheistic view. There are countless examples of pastoral and pantheistic musical statements throughout Beethoven's works, being the sixth symphony a striking example. The belief in the imprint of the divine in nature, rather than the liturgically transmitted image of God, seems to have been an idea that resonated in Schubert's mind. Walther Dürr has studied this topic in his article "Schubert, Schelling und der Pantheismus"[82]. Schubert's relation to pantheism and to Schelling's idealistic philosophy is revealed to come from his circle of friends, specifically the circle which emerged around 1819/20, which included Schubert, Schober, Bruchmann and Senn. By exploring the relationship between the text and the music of "Die Allmacht" D 852, Dürr was able to draw this parallel. He concludes from his analysis that, despite Pyrker's lack of pantheistic conduct in the poem, Schubert behaves very much so in his musical language[83], which makes a double interpretation possible. Schubert's pantheistic expression was not only achieved by the dynamics used, but particularly by the choice of tonalities and of the harmonic progression that he undertook, i.e., a wandering around, revealing a circle-like process. In addition, the arrival on A-flat major in m. 32 is particularly emphasized: Dürr explains that although this tonality is traditionally associated with death, in Schubert it is specifically linked to "the connotation of redemption and of suspension of all contradictions"[84]. The so-called "star chords", a topos already used by Zumsteeg and Beethoven[85], is, as a primordial motto, omnipresent throughout the song, upon which certain (rhetorical) figures are added, as a means of tone painting[86]. Complementarily, Michels mentions the "romantic tone painting" intentions of nature in Schubert's *Sanctus* in the A-flat

---

[81] Gruber, Gernot. (2010). *Schubert. Schubert?* P. 108. (Trans. by the author). German expression: „In Werken wie Beethovens Missa solemnis oder Schuberts As-Dur-Messe wird die liturgische Funktion zweifellos strapaziert, denn die musikalische Aussage neigt in einer persönlich-bekenntnishaften Weise dazu, Eigengewicht zu erlangen.".

[82] Dürr, Walther. (2002). „‚Die Allmacht' (D 852). Schubert, Schelling und der Pantheismus.". In: *Laudato Si, mi Signore, per sora nostra matra terra.*

[83] Cf. Ibid.

[84] Cf. Ibid. P. 114. German expression: „[…] As-Dur, der Tonart des Todes, bei Schubert allerdings grundsätzlich mit der Konnotation von Erlösung, Aufhebung der Widersprüche.".

[85] Cf. Ibid. P. 113.

[86] Cf. Ibid.

mass[87], which can further substantiate the meaningful connection between nature and religiosity for Schubert.

As Dürr indicates, the musical pantheistic setting in Schubert's composition can be related to Schelling's notion of transcendentalism. In particular to the thought of the subject as creator, who—speaking in Jungian terms, within an uroboric stage with nature—becomes self-conscious through the act of creation:

> "The I as becoming and the infinitely producing [I], who becomes conscious of itself. The expression of this shudder, however, is the art, which reflects the unconscious through the product."[88].

Goethe, whose poetry Schubert chose to set into music on several occasions, was a renowned pantheist. This can be understood as a further hint that this pantheistic view was meaningful to Schubert. In Pyrker's poem "Die Allmacht", as Dürr mentions, Schubert reacts to the process of unification with nature as a religious experience, equating God with nature.

This association between nature and religiosity—as a basic attitude in life—can be traced in Schubert's lieder repertoire and in his instrumental works as well, due to a common motivic ground. From the impetus to research for signs of Schubert's religiosity in his compositions, Peter Gülke made key discoveries, which are significant for this dissertation. To mention is the finding of a "four-tone archetype"[89] (Fig. 11.1), which arose from the *Kyrie,* the *Credo* and *Dona nobis pacem* of his first mass in F major D 105 (1814) and which constitutes a common ground motif for several subsequent compositions (Fig. 11.2 and Fig. 11.3). The works mentioned are *inter alia*: (i) the *Credo* of his second mass in G major D 167, (ii) the "Wanderers Nachtlied" D 768, (iii) "Im Abendrot" D 799, (iv) the *Sanctus* of the *Die Deutsche Messe* in F major D 872, (v) the second movements of the piano sonatas A major D 959 and B-flat major D 960, (vi) the second theme of the first movement of the C major string quintet D 965, (vii) the chiasmus or cross-motif from the Heine song setting "Der Doppelgänger" D 957 and (viii) the *Agnus Dei* from his E-flat major mass D 950. The core element inherent in all these motifs is the falling second and the ambitus of the minor third. Out of that ground motif, there is the emergence of a new one

---

[87] Cf. Michels, Ulrich. (2008). *Dtv-Atlas Musik.* P. 427.

[88] Cf. Dürr, Walther. (2002). „„Die Allmacht' (D 852). Schubert, Schelling und der Pantheismus.". In: *Laudato Si, mi Signore, per sora nostra matra terra.* P. 110. German expression: "Das Ich als Werdendes und unendlich Produzierendes seiner Selbst bewusst wird. Ausdruck dieses Schauders aber ist die Kunst, die ‚das Unbewusste durch Produkte reflektiert'".

[89] Gülke, Peter. (2020). *Franz Schubert in seiner Zeit.* P. 267.

creating a novel semantic value in "Der Doppelgänger"—a shadow aspect—and the *Agnus Dei* of Schubert's sixth mass in E-flat major. The minor third transformed itself into the diminished fourth, equivalent to the tritonus interval, which is also known as the *diabolus in musica.* From these detailed cross-references presented between masses, lieder and instrumental music, it is to be deduced that the words *Kyrie eleison, Credo, Dona nobis pacem,* and *Agnus Dei* have a rich semantic connotation[90] and are in a way omnipresent in an important number of his works.

Fig. 11.1 The original "four-tone archetype" in the Kyrie and the Credo of Schubert's first mass in F major D 105. (Figure taken from: Gülke, Peter. (2020). *Franz Schubert in seiner Zeit.* P. 267. © 2020 Laaber Verlag, Laaber.)

In addition, Gülke brings into focus E.T.A. Hoffmann's arguments, that through the creation of art there is a strong connection with the inner spiritual feeling of devotion, "a union with the Eternal"[91]:

> "No other art emerges so purely from the ongoing spiritualization of the human being, no other art requires such purely spiritual, aesthetic means as music. The notion of the Highest and of the Holiest, of the spiritual power, which ignites the spark of life in all nature, is audibly expressed in sound and thus the music, the singing, becomes the highest and fullest expression of existence—creators praise!—therefore, in its intrinsic peculiar nature, music is a religious cult and its origins are to be sought and found solely in religion […]"[92].

[90] Harnoncourt already hints at the manyfold meaning of the word *eleyson* in Schubert's fifth mass. Cf. Harnoncourt, Nikolaus. In: Martínez Guzman, Fernando. (2021). "El legado religioso y sinfónico de Franz Schubert: Reflexiones de Nikolaus Harnoncourt". *Humanitas 97, año XXVI*, Septiembre 2021. P. 510–523.

[91] Hoffmann, E.T.A. (1988). "Alte und neue Kirchenmusik". Cited after: Gülke, Peter. (2020). *Franz Schubert in seiner Zeit.* P. 270. (Trans. by the author). German expression: "der Vereinigung mit dem Ewigen […]".

[92] Ibid. (Trans. by the author). German expression: "Keine Kunst geht so rein aus der inneren Vergeistigung des Menschen hervor, keine Kunst, bedarf so nur einzig reingeistiger, ästhetischer Mittel als die Musik. Die Ahnung des Höchsten und Heiligsten, der geistigen Macht, die den Lebensfunken in der ganzen Natur entzündet, spricht sich hörbar aus im Ton, und so wird

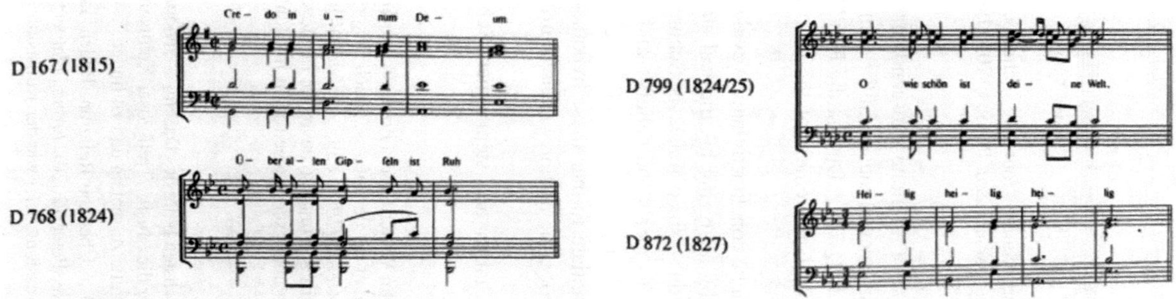

Fig. 11.2 Further examples for the common ground between Schubert's compositions. (Figure taken from: Gülke, Peter. (2020). *Franz Schubert in seiner Zeit.* P. 269. © 2020 Laaber Verlag, Laaber)

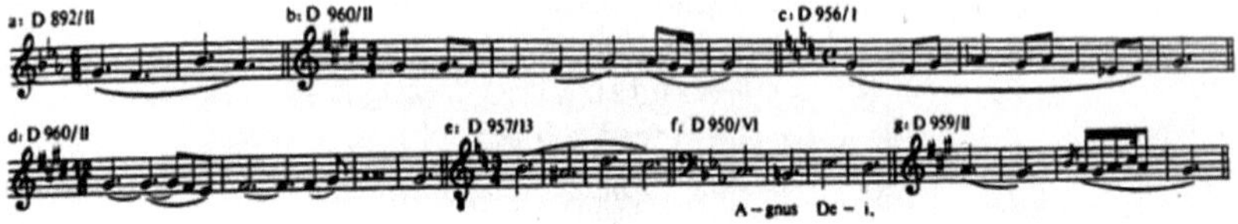

Fig. 11.3 Motives derived from the original "four-tone archetype". (Figure taken from: Gülke, Peter. (2020). *Franz Schubert in seiner Zeit.* P.319. © 2020 Laaber Verlag, Laaber)

To better illustrate how "the sense of art alone transcends into religion"[93] present in both Schubert's lieder and instrumental music, Gülke mentions the "Wanderers Nachtlied" D 768, "Im Abendrot" D 799, "Du bist die Ruh" D 776, the G major piano sonata D 894 and the Adagio movement of the C major string quintet D 956[94].

Out of these indications it can be concluded that: (i) evidences for his personal religiosity can be found rather by analyzing his musical statements and less by accentuating the textual omissions—since music is Schubert's mother tongue, with which he can best express his ideals and beliefs—and (ii) that for Schubert nature, art (i.e., music) and religiosity are powerfully interrelated to each other. In order to elucidate and substantiate further these hypotheses, and relate them with C.G. Jung's archetypal theory, the author will now turn towards Schubert's own utterances.

In a letter addressed to his father and stepmother, Schubert expressed the following thought:

> "In particular, my new songs, from Walter Scott's *Fräulein vom See* [op. 52], pleased a lot. People were also marvelled at my devoutness, which I expressed in a Hymn to the Holy Virgin [meant is *Ellens Gesang III*, D 839, "Ave Maria! Jungfrau mild"], and which, as it seems, seizes all spirits and tunes to devotion. I believe that is so, because I never force myself to devotion and, except when I am involuntarily overcome by

---

Musik, Gesang der Ausdruck der höchsten Fülle des Daseins—Schöpferlob!—Ihrem innern, eigentümlichen Wesen nach ist daher die Musik… religiöser Kultus und ihr Ursprung einzig und allein in der Religion, in der Kirche zu suchen und zu finden.".

93 Schleiermacher, Friedrich. (1799). „Über die Religion. Reden an die Gebildeten unter ihren Verächtern". Cited after: Gülke, Peter. (2020). *Franz Schubert in seiner Zeit.* P. 270. (Trans. by the author). German expression: „[…] wie der Kunstsinn für sich allein übergeht in Religion […]".

94 Cf. Gülke, Peter. (2020). *Franz Schubert in seiner Zeit.* P. 270.

it, I never compose such hymns or prayers, but then it is usually the right and true devotion."[95].

Schubert's language in this letter reveals his basic attitude—a religious experience of existence. Reading it through in Jungian terms, it is possible to interpret Schubert's statement as a confession of how the expression of the great mother archetype took possession of himself in the shape of the Virgin Mary. It was a spontaneous experience which arrived and towards which Schubert could only be receptive. In fact, the symbol of the Virgin indicates "the receptiveness of the soul towards God"[96]. In this perspective, the religious experience arises from within and realizes itself as a numinous experience of unity, namely through immersion in his creative Self and musical craft—the spiritual component is explained by Jung through his idea of the transcendent function, inherent notably in his archetypal theories and individuation process[97]. Such a transcendental or numinous experience stands out of Schubert's own formulation that he was "involuntarily overcome by [devotion]"[98] during the act of composing. The adverbial choice of the "involuntarily" ("unwillkürlich") can be taken here as a proof of the impulsive nature of unconscious psychic elements. Jung himself said that religion is "a kind of relationship to the '*numinosum*', towards what deeply moves"[99]. He further explained that "to be seized by something in an overwhelming way, is the

---

[95] Schubert, Franz: Letter written to father and stepmother. 1825. In: Deutsch, Otto Erich. (1964). *Schubert—Die Dokumente seines Lebens.* P. 299. (Trans. by the author). German expression: Besonders machten meine neuen Lieder, aus Walter Scott's Fräulein vom See [op. 52], sehr viel Glück. Auch wunderte man sich über meine Frömmigkeit, die ich in einer Hymne an die heil. Jungfrau ausgedrückt habe [gemeint ist Ellens Gesang III, D 839, »Ave Maria! Jungfrau mild«], und, wie es scheint, alle Gemüther ergreift und zur Andacht stimmt. Ich glaube, das kommt daher, weil ich mich zur Andacht nie forcire, und, außer wenn ich von ihr unwillkürlich übermannt werde, nie dergleichen Hymnen oder Gebete componire, dann aber ist sie auch gewöhnlich die rechte und wahre Andacht.".

[96] Mollwo-Oesterreicher, Marianne. (1978). *Herder Lexikon Symbole.* P. 83. (Trans. by the author). German expression: „Die christl. Mystiker verglichen auch die gegenüber Gott aufnahmebereite Seele mit einer J[ungfrau].".

[97] Cf. Roesler, Christian. (2024, October 4–6). *The process of transformation.* [Conference abstract]. Catholic University of Applied Sciences: Freiburg im Breisgau.

[98] Schubert, Franz: Letter written to father and stepmother. 1825. In: Deutsch, Otto Erich. (1964). *Schubert—Die Dokumente seines Lebens.* P. 299. (Trans. by the author). German expression: „[…] wenn ich von ihr unwillkürlich übermannt werde […]".

[99] Jung, Carl Gustav. (1960). *Das Einzelne, das Religiöse und das Transzendente. Gerster, Georg.* [Interview]. (Trans. by the author). German expression: "Religion ist eine Art Beziehung zum Numinosen, zu dem was mich ergreift". Minutes: 23:41/36:47.

phenomenon God"[100], when something "intercedes" for the ego, when the "'I' get[s] overwhelmed by the unconscious with an emotion"[101], when something is "imposed", to which the ego has to "succumb"[102]. The overwhelming power is the inherent nature of the archetype and is per se emotional[103]. The religious manifestation of the great mother archetype can itself manifest symbolically in different forms, as the image of the paradise and the river of paradise, as "the goal of longing for redemption"[104], etc. which are to be found in several of his works.

The same process is valid for the emergence of other archetypes, such as e.g., the divine child archetype. Through this archetype the creative "I" is overcome by the powers of the child archetype and its *pueritia conditio*, meaning a reconnection with "the primordial, unconscious and instinctive state"[105]. The child stands not only for the unbiased and innocence, but as "[…] a symbol for the beginnings and the fullness of possibilities"[106]. Being nearer wholeness, a place where the bond with the hidden powers of nature and of the Self is still strong, it exerts a connecting function to the primordial, the unifying role with the Self, which ultimately leads to transcendence (16). Indeed, the child archetype (especially in the Christian sense) classically manifests itself in transformational processes and habitually acts as a symbol of new hope[107]. Musically, it reappears in several compositions, such as the "Der Erlkönig" D 328 (16), *Unfinished* Symphony in B minor D 759[108] and the D minor string quartet D 810 "Death and the Maiden" (16).

---

[100] Ibid. (Trans. by the author). German expression: "Immer wenn ein Mensch […] ergriffen wird von Etwas, in überwältigender Weise, dann ist es das Phänomen Gott […]". Minutes 30:57/36:47.

[101] Ibid. (Trans. by the author). German expression: "Ich werde vom Unbewussten her mit einer Emotion überschüttet." Minutes: 32:45/36:47.

[102] Cf. Ibid.

[103] Cf. Ibid.

[104] Jung, Carl Gustav. (2020). *Archetypen. Urbilder und Wirkkräfte des Kollektiven Unbewussten.* P.101. (Trans. by the author). German expression: „[…] das Ziel der Erlösungssehnsucht (Paradies, Reich Gottes, himmlisches Jerusalem) […]".

[105] Ibid. P. 148. (Trans. by the author).

[106] Mollwo-Oesterreicher, Marianne. (1978). *Herder Lexikon Symbole.* P. 87. (Trans. by the author).

[107] Cf. Roesler, Christian. (2022). *Development of a Reconceptualization of Archetype Theory.* Report to the IAAP. P. 49.

[108] Cf. Schering, Arnold. (2012). *Franz Schuberts Symphonie in H-Moll („Unvollendete") und ihr Geheimnis.*

Some years prior to Schubert addressing his father and stepmother on the topic of *Ellens Gesang,* Schubert wrote down a dream "Mein Traum", which is a further source that might explain, or at least shed some light into his relation to religiosity:

> [I] "I was a brother to many brothers and sisters. Our father and mother were good. I was devoted to all of them with deep love.—Once my father took us to a feast. There the brothers became very happy. But I was sad. Then my father came to me and ordered me to enjoy the delicious food. But I could not, and my father was angry and banished me from his presence. I turned my steps and with a heart full of infinite love for those who spurned it, I wandered into faraway places. For years I felt the greatest pain and the greatest love dividing me. Then I heard of my mother's death. I hurried to see her, and my father, softened by grief, did not prevent my entry. There I saw her corpse. Tears flowed from my eyes. I saw her lying there like in the good old past, the way the deceased want to be remembered, as she once was, I saw her laying there.
>
> And we followed her corpse in mourning and the grave sank.—From that time on I stayed at home again. Then my father took me to his favourite garden once again. He asked me if I liked it. But I did not like the garden at all and did not dare to say anything. Then he asked me a second time, furiously: if I do like the garden?—I denied tremblingly. Then my father hit me and I fled. And for the second time I turned my steps, and with a heart full of infinite love for those who spurned me, I wandered again into faraway places. I sang songs for long, long years. When I wanted to sing love, it became pain. And if I only wanted to sing pain again, it became my love. So the greatest pain and the greatest love divided me.
>
> [II] And once I heard of a pious virgin who had just died. And a circle was drawn around her tomb, in which many young men and old men walked for ever as if in bliss. They spoke softly, not to wake the Virgin.
>
> Heavenly thoughts seemed to be constantly spraying out of the Virgin's tomb onto the young men like light sparks, which made a gentle noise. I longed to walk there too. But only a miracle, said the people, would lead into this circle. But I walked slowly, with devotion and firm faith, with lowered eyes towards the tomb, and before I knew it, I was in the circle, which emitted a miraculous sound; and I felt eternal bliss as if condensed in an instant. I also saw my father reconciled and loving. He embraced me in his arms and wept. But I wept even more."[109].

[109] Schubert, Franz: „Allegorische Erzählung von Schubert—‚Mein Traum'". 1822. In: Deutsch, Otto Erich. (1964). *Schubert—Die Dokumente seines Lebens.* P. 158–159. (Trans. by the author). German expression: [I.] Ich war ein Bruder vieler Brüder und Schwestern. Unser Vater und unsere Mutter waren gut. Ich war allen mit tiefer Liebe zugethan.—Einstmahl führte uns der Vater zu einem Lustgelage. Da wurden die Brüder sehr fröhlich. Ich aber war traurig. Da trat mein Vater zu mir, und befahl mir, die köstlichen Speisen zu genießen. Ich aber konnte nicht, worüber mein Vater erzürnend mich aus seinem Angesicht verbannte. Ich wandte meine Schritte und mit einem Herzen voll unendlicher Liebe für die,

As Schering appropriately remarked, this "dream" is structured into two parts, the first belonging to the "personal earth sorrow"[110] written in sonata form[111], and the second part to "heavenly visions"[112], i.e., all psychic elements that are presented in the first part of the dream become spiritualized in the second part[113]. This dream structure and dream motifs reveal how much of personal aspects might

---

welche sie verschmähten, wanderte ich in ferne Gegend. Jahre lang fühlte ich den größten Schmerz und die größte Liebe mich zertheilen. Da kam mir Kunde von meiner Mutter Tode. Ich eilte sie zu sehen, und mein Vater von Trauer erweicht, hinderte meinen Eintritt nicht. Da sah ich ihre Leiche. Thränen entflossen meinen Augen. Wie die gute alte Vergangenheit, in der wir uns nach der Verstorbenen Meinung auch bewegen sollten, wie sie sich einst, sah ich sie liegen. Und wir folgten ihrer Leiche in Trauer und die Bahre versank.—Von dieser Zeit an blieb ich wieder zu Hause. Da führte mich mein Vater wieder einstmahls in seinen Lieblingsgarten. Er fragte mich ob er mir gefiele. Doch mir war der Garten ganz widrig und ich getraute mir nichts zu sagen. Da fragte er mich zum zweitenmahl erglühend: ob mir der Garten gefiele?—Ich verneinte es zitternd. Da schlug mich mein Vater und ich entfloh. Und zum zweitenmal wandte ich meine Schritte, und mit einem Herzen voll unendlicher Liebe für die, welche sie verschmähten, wanderte ich abermals in ferne Gegend. Lieder sang ich nun lange, lange Jahre. Wollte ich Liebe singen, ward sie mir zum Schmerz. Und wollte ich wieder Schmerz nur singen, ward er mir zur Liebe. So zertheilte mich die Liebe und der Schmerz.

[II.] Und einst bekam ich Kunde von einer frommen Jungfrau, die erst gestorben war. Und ein Kreis sich um ihr Grabmahl zog, in dem viele Jünglinge und Greise auf ewig wie in Seligkeiten wandelten. Sie sprachen leise, die Jungfrau nicht zu wecken. Himmlische Gedanken schienen immerwährend aus der Jungfrau Grabmahl auf die Jünglinge wie leichte Funken zu sprühen, welche sanftes Geräusch erregten. Da sehnte ich mich sehr auch da zu wandeln. Doch nur ein Wunder, sagten die Leute, führe in diesen Kreis. Ich aber trat langsamen Schrittes, innen Andacht und fester Glaube, mit gesenktem Blicke auf das Grabmahl zu, und ehe ich es wähnte, war ich in dem Kreis, der einen wunderlieblichen Ton von sich gab; und ich fühlte die ewige Seligkeit wie in einen Augenblick zusammengedrängt. Auch meinen Vater sah ich versöhnt und liebend. Er schloß mich in seine Arme und weinte. Noch mehr aber ich.

[110] Schering, Arnold. (2012). *Franz Schuberts Symphonie in H-Moll („Unvollendete") und ihr Geheimnis.* P.15. (Trans. by the author).

[111] Cf. Ibid. Interestingly, Schering not only compares the dream to its musical equivalent of the unfinished Symphony in B minor (being structured in two part and two movements, respectively), but also draws attention to its relatedness to other early lieder, all dealing with the death, love, mother, loneliness and wandering thematic such as: (i) "Der Wanderer" D 489 (1816), (ii) "Der Grablied für die Mutter" D 616 (1818), (iii) "Der Unglückliche" D 713 (1821), (iv) "Ihr Grab" D 736 (1822), (v) "Todesmusik" D 758 (1822).

[112] Ibid. The heavenly visions are already contained in the expression of "speaking softly". The ***p***-dynamic hints at some mysterious happening to come about to the "unearthly". Cf. Ibid. P. 36. (Trans. by the author).

[113] This can substantiate the fact that for Schubert the pious virgin here is connected with the mother archetype (cf. first part of the dream).

be linked to archetypal ones. Consequently, the first part is to be considered rather within the personal domain, tied to his personal complexes and difficulties, whereas the second section belongs rather to a narration of a collective sphere, conveying archetypal motifs and an inner urge that seeks towards the middle of the Self.

Schubert's dream expression of 1822 reveals how pain, sorrow, oppressiveness, death, fate, love and loneliness are intertwined in his mind, how the childhood condition of innocent love and openness is deceived and how wandering and turning into the arts, into music are presented as a pivotal moment at the end of the first part, leading to self-observation, self-expression. Lastly, in the second part, it turns into self-development, self-empowerment. Here lies the transformational evolution between both fragments. The symbol of the garden, which is at first rejected due to the connection to his father[114] and to certain aspects of society[115], might hint at "the difficulties and obstacles which have to be overcome"[116], to the heavenly sphere and "the higher level of spiritual development"[117] taking place in the second section.

Of special interest is the second part of the narration (Table 11.1). In hermeneutic terms, the "miraculous sound" has something to do with a pure, primordial tone, which again is tied with the experience of the great mother archetype: through her Schubert comes to the experience of eternal bliss. He overcomes all problems and transcends to another sphere, which then leads to reconciliation with the father figure and to unification. Again, the great mother archetype is expressed in different ways, leading him to a religious-musical experience: the virgin's grave acts as an angel's call to cross the threshold. This awakens the will to go through a transformation, to go towards the middle of the circle, being the "magic circle" another manifestation of the great mother archetype[118], but also of the Self (3). Through the virgin's symbolism, as already

---

[114] It is to be noticed that the father wanted his sons to follow his steps as schoolmasters, which is interwoven with the schoolboard, church and religion. Cf. Dürr, Walther: „Schubert in seiner Welt". In: Dürr, Walther. Krause, Andreas. (2020). *Schubert Handbuch.* P. 7.

[115] When interpreting the garden, from the subjective level, and as being a place outside the house—the house representing here the own psyche—then the garden could possibly hint at outer elements, as e.g., be associated with the societal values, in a censorship regime, that are expected to be fulfilled.

[116] Mollwo-Oesterreicher, Marianne. (1978). *Herder Lexikon Symbole.* P. 59. (Trans. by the author).

[117] Ibid. (Trans. by the author).

[118] Cf. Jung, Carl Gustav. (2020). *Archetypen. Urbilder und Wirkkräfte des Kollektiven Unbewussten.* P. 102.

described above, Schubert is empowered with the great mother archetype and is able to cross the threshold with devotion and faith. The gentle, quiet and pure tone equals the symbol of eternal bliss, of the "numinosum", indicating how, for Schubert, art is the medium to transcend to a religious experience and self-development.

Table 11.1 Archetypal motifs from the second part of Schubert's 1822 dream

Dream key-motifs	Underlying Archetypal motifs/processes	Further explaining notes
Pious virgin	Great mother (Feminine principle).	The "just died" refers to the death of Schubert's own mother (cf. first part of the dream).
Circle/bliss	Symbol of the Self/ numinosity of the Archetype.	
Miracle, devotion, faith	Spiritual component of the dreamer.	
The leading into the circle	Crossing the threshold.	
Miraculous sound/eternal bliss	Numinous experience/ Transcendental function (→Transformation)	
The figure of the father (reconciled and loving, embracing him)	Effect of numinous experience—noted transformation	Father motif stems from the first part of the dream and might be related to his biography
Weeping	Emotional reaction, tied to the archetypal experience.	

Under these findings, it can be stated that those archetypes emerge impulsively and act as mediators, during the creation act, for a religious inner experience, which enables arriving at a transcendental state, where all contradictions are unified, and all earthly problems resolved. Nature plays an important role (4). It is about a religious experience which, psychologically speaking, is analogue to the process of becoming one-Self[119]. Schubert, in his own words, referred to the unknown realm of the psyche as the source of inspiration. He spoke of fantasy

[119] Cf. Wehr, Gerhard. (2014). *C.G. Jung Leben—Werk—Wirkung.* P. 241.

and imagination, i.e., a mental activity which is nourished from the unconscious, as if it were personified and foremost as the well of creativity:

> "O fantasy, thou highest jewel of man, thou inexhaustible spring, from which both artists and scholars drink! Oh remain with us, even if only acknowledged and revered by a few, to save us from that so-called Enlightenment, that ugly skeleton without flesh and blood!"[120].

11.3 The Wandering Journey to him-Self

Reiterating a few incidents in Schubert's life and the time period they occurred can be helpful for the development of this chapter: (i) Schubert's apparent years of crisis[121] dating from 1818 to 1823 and his involvement with Beethoven's works; (ii) the diagnosis of his potentially fatal disease and the awareness of his own mortality dating from 1822/23; (iii) Schubert's unattainable romance towards the teacher's daughter Theresa Grob, (iv) Schubert's above mentioned dream of 1822, i.e., one year before the end of the alleged crisis, which coincided with the composition of the *Unfinished* Symphony and features motifs such as the wanderer, the primordial tone and the great mother; (v) the subsequent abundance of creative work which lasted straightforwardly until his death; and (vi) the fact that in the male psychology the mother archetype and the anima are strongly interconnected[122], making their distinction challenging to discern at times. The following information ought to be added to these reiterations: (i) the death of Schubert's mother, when Schubert counted 15 years, which was described to be a traumatic episode in his life and (ii) the genesis of the C major *Wandererfantasie* D 760, which was written in November 1822.

---

[120] Schubert, Franz: "Aus einem verlorenen Notizbuche Schuberts von 1824". In: Deutsch, Otto Erich. (1964). *Schubert—Die Dokumente seines Lebens.* P. 233. (Trans. by the author). German expression: „O Phantasie du höchstes Kleinod des Menschen, du unerschöpflicher Quell, aus dem sowohl Künstler als Gelehrte trinken! O bleibe noch bey uns, wenn auch von Wenigen nur anerkannt und verehrt, um uns vor jener sogenannten Aufklärung, jenem häßlichen Gerippe ohne Fleisch und Blut, zu bewahren!".

[121] The Schubert biographer and specialist Ernst Hilmar had already suggested to perceive the so-called years of crisis, actually as "[…] years of highly significant spiritual change.". Hilmar, Ernst. (1997). *Franz Schubert.* P. 31. German expression: „Es waren weniger ‚Jahre der Krise' […] als vielmehr Jahre eines hochbedeutenden geistigen Umbruchs.".

[122] Cf. Jung, Carl Gustav. (2020). *Archetypen. Urbilder und Wirkkräfte des kollektiven Unbewussten.* Chapter: „Die psychologischen Aspekte des Mutterarchetypus", subchapter 2.: „Der Mutterarchetypus". P.103.

As a first consideration it can be affirmed that Schubert's dream of 1822 reflects a processing mechanism, having a strong positive effect and inducing the breaking out of the "crisis". Additionally, the *memento mori*—the moment of becoming aware of one's own mortality—can have led in Schubert to an acceleration of his own individuation path[123], i.e., functioning as a reminder of the need to fulfill his "duty" as an artist. Therefore, it can be seen as the source to an important outflow of creativity[124], which truly occurred in Schubert's creative process in the unfolding of the subsequent years. In fact, it can be understood as a moment where he allowed himself to get involved in a confrontation with the unconscious, by undertaking a wander-journey into the inner and the outer world:

> "A 'farewell life' (Kast 2017, p.105), a 'transience-sensitive receptivity' (Boothe 2014, p.234), which does not ward off the many small and large deaths, but 'thinks life from the end [in order] to derive its actions from it' (to Salm 2014, S.9), has many useful consequences for individuation. It confronts with the question of meaning and conveys meaning, it makes the banal visibly banal (Yalom 2000) and it is a source of creativity (e.g., in art, Forde 2007)."[125].

This journey began at first in a manner quite unusually Schubertian, namely extravagantly in his *Wandererfantasie*. The crucial impetus for this composition was not only the commission he received by a Johann Nepomuk Hummel's pupil to write a virtuosic piece[126], but especially the formerly composed lied "Der Wanderer" D 493 (1816), from which the lines of Lübeck still strongly echoed in Schubert's mind[127] and from which he retrieved the core primordial motif of the entire fantasy. In the *Wandererfantasie* (19) Schubert, possibly (un)consciously, disassociated himself initially from the rather introverted wanderer of the previous

---

[123] Cf. Roesler, Christian. Personal communication between Christian Roesler and the author. Basel: January 13, 2023.

[124] Cf. Kast, Verena. (2003). "Diese vorüberrauschende blaue einzige Welt.". Cited after: Vogel, Ralf T. (2017). *Individuation und Wandlung*. P. 80.

[125] Vogel, Ralf T. (2017). *Individuation und Wandlung*. P. 80. German expression: "Ein ‚abschiedliches Leben' (Kast 2017, S.105), eine ‚vergänglichkeits-sensible Empfänglichkeit' (Boothe 2014, S. 234), die die vielen kleinen und großen Tode nicht abwehrt, sondern ‚das Leben vom Ende her denkt, [um] daraus seine Handlungen abzuleiten' (zu Salm 2014, p. 9), hat viele individuationsnützliche Folgen. Es konfrontiert mit der Sinnfrage und vermittelt Sinn, es macht das Banale sichtbar banal (Yalom 2000) und es ist eine Quelle der Kreativität (z.B. in der Kunst, Forde 2007).".

[126] Cf. Massin, Brigitte. (1977). *Franz Schubert*. P. 975.

[127] Cf. Gülke, Peter. (2020). *Franz Schubert in seiner Zeit*. P. 202.

lied[128], loaded with sorrow and despair to an adventurous spirit of a hero, who is willing to confront himself with the darkest side of his psyche. This could have been done in an attempt to integrate the less expressed aspects of his personality.

In accordance to Neumann's life phases description of the development of the human being, the hero has to undergo the so-called "dragon battle"[129]. In his quest, Schubert musically incorporates a richness of contrapuntal techniques in the last movement, e.g., a fugue theme, the subsequent fugato passage and an unmistakable orchestral tone—features, already mastered by Beethoven. This prompts the consideration of parallels between the dragon-battle episodes and Beethoven, who is often regarded as a father-like figure and a master of contrapuntal techniques—it is as if he is attempting to emancipate himself and to conquer highly considered forms in composition techniques. These passages are frequently counterbalanced by more lyrical passages, which may point to an archetype with a specific function.

The feminine principle, now in form of the Anima as the second theme, will come as the helper in these confrontations (dragon-battles), acting as a redemption motif[130]. From the musical standpoint, this theme recalls some biographical elements: it is as if it is accompanied by the reminiscence of the primordial tone,

---

[128] The wanderer from whom the "sigh ever asks where?", who is "a stranger everywhere", in search of the hopeful green land: "[…] I wander quietly, I'm hardly joyous, and the sigh ever asks where? Forever where? The sun hither methinks so cold, the blossom withers, the life's old, and what they say, a deaf sound, I am a stranger everywhere.". (Trans. by the author). German expression: "Ich wandle still, bin wenig froh, und immer fragt der Seufzer wo? Immer wo? Die Sonne dünkt mich hier so kalt, die Blüte welk, das Leben alt, und was sie reden, tauber Schall, ich bin ein Fremdling überall". He ends his lament stating on his own ontological tragedy, that happiness is everywhere where he is not. As Krause describes, the question about a hopeful "utopic land takes a brutal turn" at the end of the song. Krause, Andreas: „Die Klaviermusik—'So frei und eigen, so keck und mitunter auch so sonderbar'". In: Dürr, Walther., Krause, Andreas. (2020). *Schubert Handbuch*. P. 403. German expression: "Nimmt die Frage nach dem Land der Utopie im Lied eine wenig hoffnungsvolle, wenn nicht sogar brutale Wendung […]". The hopeful green here mentioned, becomes later the dearest color of the miller's beloved in *Die Schöne Müllerin,* therefore can be seen in the Jungian perspective in relation with the Anima (15).

[129] Neumann, Erich. (1949). "Ursprungsgeschichte des Bewusstseins.". Cited after: Vogel, Ralf T. (2017). *Individuation und Wandlung*. P. 65.

[130] This motif appears in many of Schubert's musical utterances (20). Moreover, these archetypes are typically recurrent motives. After C.G. Jung, the redemption or salvation motif is to be found in all religions. Cf. Wehr, Gerhard. (2014). *C.G. Jung Leben—Werk—Wirkung*. P.242. Cf. Jung, Carl Gustav. (2020). *Archetypen. Urbilder und Wirkkräfte des Kollektiven Unbewussten*. P. 174. Their recurrence will be taken into consideration in the analysis section.

which Schubert heard in his dream (III Table 11.1, 19). Curiously enough, this note (the B in m.47 and later the B-flat note in m. 112) turns out to be the perfect fifth of the respective harmony in question (E major, respectively, E-flat major), which, being a consonant interval, may symbolically allude to the pure tone from the dream and to a spiritual function of this note. In this sense, the Anima-note fulfills here its archetypal role of a mediator between consciousness and the unconscious (3.1). Schubert's inner search for the feminine principle, the Anima, might have been accentuated by the death of his mother on the one hand, and the unfulfilled love towards the teacher's daughter on the other. Being a through-composed fantasy, written in a cyclical form and tied to the variation form, all motifs are intrinsically interrelated. As a result of this compositional technique, the wanderer reflects his adventurous character, his hopes, his torments, but he also melts with his counterpart, his lyrical Anima side (19).

At first sight, it may seem enigmatic why Schubert rapidly abandons the fugato style in the last movement and returns to the dragon battles until the very end—this aspect of the composition shares a striking parallel with Schubert's first performance of this work, during which he abruptly ceased playing and uttered "Let the devil play that stuff!"[131]. The answer may lie in a phenomenon, specific to artists, that was observed by Neumann—the artist would not be able to go through a full dragon battle, or at least not in the usual unfolding of Campbell's Hero journey (3), since the artist would always need a strong connection to the source of creativity, which is in the unconscious, i.e., the feminine principle or the Great Mother[132]. This would explain why he remains on the level of the dragon battles and drops the fugato style. Jung himself already explained in *Psychology and Literature* the following thought:

> "The creative process has a feminine quality and the creative work arises from unconscious depths—we might truly say from the realm of the Mothers. Whenever the creative force predominates, life is ruled and shaped by the unconscious rather than by conscious will, and the ego is swept along on an underground current, becoming

[131] Leopold Kupelwieser to Kreissle. Deutsch, Otto Erich. (1983). *Schubert Erinnerungen seiner Freunde.* P.224. (Trans. by the author). German expression: "Das Zeug soll der Teufel spielen!". The non-willingness of Schubert to finish the performance and this cited statement rather reflects how this unconscious situation affects him, namely not only during the act of composing (abandoning the fugato style) but even during the performance (leaving the piano and interrupting his playing).

[132] Cf. Neumann, Erich. (1959). *Der schöpferische Mensch.* Zürich: Rhein-Verlag. See also: Neumann, Erich. (2004). *Kunst und schöpferisches Unbewussten.*

> nothing more than a helpless observer of events. The progress of the work becomes the poet's fate and determines his psychology."[133].

Hence, the need of the composer to succumb to the inner forces.

Further consequent examples of the emergence of the Anima can be accounted, among other works, in the second theme of the D minor String quartet D 810 of 1824 (16) and in the lied "Der Lindenbaum" from the song cycle *Die Winterrreise.* Apart from being understood as the feminine principle in general terms, the linden tree is, in the music historical context of the Romantic period, tied with the symbol of love and the redemption semantic[134], which, as understood above, is also a characteristic inherent of the feminine principle. Additionally, it appears that there is an akin musical gesture present in both "Der Wanderer" and "Der Lindenbaum", which supports the aforementioned argument[135]. The further different shapes that the Anima takes will be a matter of closer investigation in the analysis section (IV).

---

[133] Jung, Carl Gustav. (2014). "Spirit in Man, Art and Literature". In: *The Collected Works of C.G: Jung. Vol.15.* (Ed. and trans. by Gerhard Adler and R.F.C. Hull). Chapter IV: "Psychology and Literature, Introduction—2. The Artist".

[134] Cf. Dobretsberger, Barbara. Personal communication between Barbara Dobretsberger and the author. Salzburg: May 25, 2023.

[135] Meant are the similarities of the musical gestures between the phrases „Ich wandle still" in „Der Wanderer" and the „so manches liebe Wort" in „Der Lindenbaum" pointed out by Krause. Cf. Krause, Andreas: „Die Klaviermusik—‚So frei und eigen, so keck und mitunter auch so sonderbar'". In: Dürr, Walther., Krause, Andreas. (2020). *Schubert Handbuch.* P. 402.

12 Pre-Analytical Considerations on Schubert's Musical Language

> "He [Schubert] gave tones (sounds) to poetry (art of poetry) and language (discourse) to music. He ascribed the art of poetry to sounds and discourse to music."[1].
>
> "He has tones for the most subtle sensations, thoughts, even events and states of life"[2].

In the following chapter some of the key characteristics of Schubert's musical language will be presented, acting as an introduction to the analysis section (IV). This will include some of the on-going debates in the Schubert's research community on peculiarities of his musical language and the categorization of different creative periods. By doing so, the intention is to investigate what these elements could possibly say about his creative process and to establish the connection with the Jungian perspective. This will enable a better elaboration of the existing intrinsic interrelations between the idiomatic aspects of his music and their semantic connotations, later on. In view of the richness of symbolic elements present in Schubert's music and their individual semantic value, these parallels will finally be revealed in the respective analysis chapter.

---

[1] Grillparzer, Franz: „Grillparzers Entwürfe für Schuberts Grabschrift". In: Deutsch, Otto Erich. (1964). *Schubert—Die Dokumente seines Lebens*. P. 580. (Trans. by the author). German expression: „Er gab der Poesie (Dichtkunst) Töne (Klänge) und Sprache (Rede) der Musik. [...] Er hieß die Dichtkunst tönen u. reden die Musik.".

[2] Schumann, Robert. (1854). *Gesammelte Schriften über Musik und Musiker.* Vol. 1. P. 206. (Trans. by the author). German expression: „Er hat Töne für die feinsten Empfindungen, Gedanken, ja Begebenheiten und Lebenszustände.".

L. Dill, *Schubert's Metamorphoses*,
https://doi.org/10.1007/978-3-662-73476-6_12

It seems that all the discussed aspects elaborated in the previous chapters can be found reflected in Schubert's musical language. As mentioned in the preceding section, music can be considered Schubert's mother tongue, the means by which he is able to express and convey his state of mind—as also the above-mentioned citation of Schumann's scriptures translates. Thereby, the inherent unconscious structures play an important role, carrying the listener to another realm of the primordial, i.e., the (collective) unconscious:

> "But that the outside world, as it shines today, darkens tomorrow, often reaches into the interior of the poet and musician, [...] lies hidden in this [C-major] symphony [...], indeed that it leads us into a region where we seem to have been, yet cannot remember [...]"[3].

Schubert was long perceived as the lied composer, with the song-like themes and who featured the small form. The lied[4] is for Schubert the genre wherein the unconscious structures can be traced more precisely, due to the text-tone relationship. In turn, Schubert's own lied aesthetics had a great impact on his instrumental works. The technique of direct or indirect self-quotations and the allure of a song's ground atmosphere are to be found in a great number of instrumental compositions. For instance, Andras Schiff accounts for references to *Die schöne Müllerin* in Schubert's D major sonata D 850, elements of "Der Atlas" and "Erlkönig" in the C minor sonata D 958, the atmosphere of "Am Meer" in the opening theme of the B-flat major sonata D 960[5]. This means that Schubert's songs can be used as substantiating evidence when analyzing semantically or hermeneutically his instrumental works. Each song is musically linked to the text and therefore loaded with semantic connotations, towards which the composer refers to in his instrumental compositions. This also indicates that, on the one hand, the basic atmosphere of individual songs echoed in Schubert's mind throughout the years, and on the other, that the ground song themes and motifs used underwent a transformation through Schubert's life. These twofold indicators can be noted when analyzing the lieder and instrumental works comparingly

[3] Ibid. Vol. 3. P. 200. (Trans. by the author). German expression: „Aber dass die Außenwelt, wie sie heute strahlt, morgen dunkelt, oft hineingreift in das Innere des Dichters und Musikers, [...] in dieser Symphonie [...] verborgen liegt, ja dass sie uns in eine Region führt, wo wir vorher gewesen zu sein uns nirgends erinnern können [...]".

[4] From all musical genres the lied, alongside with the piano sonatas, accompanied him throughout his entire life.

[5] Cf. Schiff, Andras: "Schubert's piano sonatas: thoughts about interpretation and performance". In: Newbould, Brian. (2017). *Schubert Studies*. P. 207.

(IV). Beyond creating this semantic carpet of interrelations—a rich foundation for hermeneutical interpretations—Schubert's music can be generally perceived as being a poetic language, reflecting a "new colorful way of treating the piano"[6].

This innovative style of piano accompaniment, developed by Schubert, proved to be crucial for the development of the lied genre in the History of music. Contrary to Salieri's desire of a full dedication to Italian masters[7], Schubert had the great inner urge to set German poetry into music, such as that of Goethe, Schlegel and Schiller. To a certain degree, his role models for this genre are considered to be Zumsteeg, Reichardt and Zelter, who were composing in the style conforming the Second Berlin School. They were mainly "poetically newly oriented"[8] (comparingly to the First Berlin School composers), for which not only the folksongs played a role, as with Herder, but also their lyrics were to convey subjective expression, as with Klopstock, Goethe and Schiller[9]. Thereby, the function of music and specifically of the piano accompaniment was still a subservient one— it followed the criteria advocated by Goethe. For him, the music ought: (i) "to be derived directly from the words and the verbal melody"[10], (ii) "to remain undisturbed by the attempts to illustrate or interpret the poem"[11], (iii) "to serve the poem and not illuminate it"[12]. Despite the fact that these paragons influenced Schubert to a certain extent[13], he opposed himself to their aesthetic

[6] Brendel, Alfred. In: Brendel, Alfred. Gülke, Peter. (2020). *Die Kunst des Interpretierens.* P. 39. (Trans. by the author). German expression: „Es ist eine ganz neue farbige Art, das Klavier zu behandeln.".

[7] Von Spaun reported that Salieri disapproved of such a great enthusiasm from Schubert's side in regard to Mozart's and Beethoven's works and specifically of the musical setting of German poetry. Cf. Von Spaun, Joseph. In: Deutsch, Otto Erich. (1983). *Schubert Erinnerungen seiner Freunde.* P. 26.

[8] Schmierer, Elisabeth. (2017). *Geschichte des Kunstliedes.* Chapter: „Das Lied in der ersten Hälfte des 19. Jahrhunderts". P. 77. (Trans. by the author). German expression: „Die Komponisten der Zweiten Berliner Liederschule waren dichterisch neu orientiert.".

[9] Cf. Ibid. P. 78.

[10] Goethe, Wolfgang. In: Brendel, Alfred. (2022). "Naivety and Irony: Goethe's Musical Needs". In: *Publications of the English Goethe Society. Vol. 91 (no.1).* P.78.

[11] Ibid.

[12] Ibid.

[13] Specifically to mention is the influence of Reichardt for the "declamatory style [and] the recitativ-arios", as Dürr specifically accounts in "Prometheus" D 674 or "Grenzen der Menscheit, D 716. Dürr, Walther: „Schubert in seiner Welt". In: Dürr, Walther., Krause, Andreas. (2020). *Schubert Handbuch.* P. 13. This dramatic stylistic tool was common to Zumsteeg as well. Cf. Dittrich, Marie-Agnes. "Die Lieder. 'Für Menschenohren sind es Harmonien'". In: Ibid. P. 148.

ideals, by giving the piano an expressive role and an egalitarian treatment, i.e., the piano "accompaniment" becomes as important as the text[14]. Schubert often used form, melodic gestures, rhythmic motives, rhetoric figures, harmony and harmonic progression as a means to emphasize the text or react to it—to Goethe's dissatisfaction[15]. As Dittrich explains:

> "He juxtaposes them with the text, often reinforcing it, but sometimes also in an idiosyncratic interpretation or even ironic contradiction."[16].

In particular, the introductory bars of the piano gained on significance, often tone painting the nature phenomena and the surroundings of the lyrical subject:

> "In 'Der Lindenbaum" we have the rustling of the leaves, the breeze and the murmur of the well; 'Im Dorfe' [he] combines the rattling of the chains, the barking of the dogs, and the snoring of the sleepers; the beginning of 'Erlkönig' with its bold repeated octaves conjures the night, the wind, and the galloping of the horse; and 'Gretchen am Spinnrade' opens with the spinning wheel, the foot that keeps it in motion, and the restlessness of the heart."[17].

---

[14] Due to this characteristic, the term "collaboration" would seem more adequate, even though the piano part in a song is traditionally addressed as the piano "accompaniment". The suggested term would emphasize not only the equal treatment of piano and voice, but also their mutual interactions.

[15] Goethe disapproved of Schubert's setting of his own poem "Der Erlkönig". Only years later and under the influence of Wilhelmine Schröder he came to appreciate it. Although as a poet Goethe behaved ambivalently (and even felt a double nature in himself), for his "musical needs" he searched for the type of simplicity mentioned above, which was to be found in the second Berlin school composers, in particular with Zelter and Reichardt. Cf. Brendel, Alfred. (2022). "Naivety and Irony: Goethe's Musical Needs". In: *Publications of the English Goethe Society. Vol. 91 (no.1).* P.75–87.

[16] Dittrich, Marie-Agnes. „Die Lieder. 'Für Menschenohren sind es Harmonien'". In: Dürr, Walther. Krause, Andreas. (2020). *Schubert Handbuch.* P. 149. (Trans. by the author). German expression: "Er stellt sie dem Text gegenüber, oft ihn verstärkend, bisweilen aber auch in eigenwilliger Interpretation oder gar in ironischem Widerspruch. Wesentlich ist dabei der neuartige Klavierpart.".

[17] Brendel, Alfred. (2022). "Naivety and Irony: Goethe's Musical Needs". In: *Publications of the English Goethe Society.* Vol. 91 (no.1). P.83.

Introductory bars are already to be found in lieder of the "Wiener Liederschule"[18] to which Mozart, Haydn and Beethoven belonged—composers that Schubert venerated (again, to Salieri's discontentment)[19]. The emergence of this particular song tradition was affected by the fusion and interaction of instrumental music, the singspiel and the opera genre, wherein an instrumental prelude, interlude, and postlude measures, as well as melismatic and Arie-like melodic lines were integrated[20]. The recitative style that Schubert inherited from Reichardt, Zumsteeg, Mozart and Gluck, was propitious to achieve the intended dramatic effect—Schubert used it often for musical monologs, as a means of creating a contrast to the lied-like melodies[21], as e.g., "Die Post" of *Die Winterreise.* In "Erlkönig", Dittrich notes how the "fainting" declamatory voice conveys the tragic nature of the child's death, when the final verse "In his arms, the child—was dead!"[22] ("In seinen Armen das Kind war tot") is declaimed. This aspect has impressed Liszt very much, who saw in Schubert "the dramatic lyricist"[23]. Examples can be found beyond his lied compositions: the second movement of the A major piano sonata D 959 can be seen as one striking example, where the transition to the A' section consists of a dialogue with his inner voices, featuring a recitative-like style. Another compositional tool that Schubert combined with the declamatory tone was the use of tremolo[24], equally taken from the operatic repertoire. This stylistic device was most effective to convey feelings such as fright, danger, shivering, etc. Schubert came to increasingly explore this technique in his later works, specifically since the *Quartettsatz* in C minor D 703 (1820). Dobretsberger observes a personal tonal language in the latter, specifically alluding to the

---

[18] This term is firstly associated with Josef Anton Steffan (1726–1797), who supplied the first examples of this particular tradition. Cf. Schmierer, Elisabeth. (2017). *Geschichte des Kunstliedes.* Chapter: „Das Lied in der ersten Hälfte des 19. Jahrhunderts". P. 85.

[19] Cf. von Spaun, Joseph. In: Deutsch, Otto Erich. (1983). *Schubert Erinnerungen seiner Freunde.* P. 26.

[20] Cf. Schmierer, Elisabeth. (2017). *Geschichte des Kunstliedes.* Chapter: „Das Lied in der ersten Hälfte des 19. Jahrhunderts". P. 85.

[21] Cf. Dittrich, Marie-Agnes. "Die Lieder. 'Für Menschenohren sind es Harmonien'". In: Dürr, Walther. Krause, Andreas. (2020). *Schubert Handbuch.* P. 148.

[22] Cf. Ibid. (Trans. by the author).

[23] Cf. Ibid. (Trans by the author). German expression: "Franz Liszt, der in Schubert den ‚dramatischen Lyriker' bewunderte […]".

[24] Cf. Ibid.

use of tremolos and of the melody that bear resemblance to his language in the "late" years[25].

In the first song cycle accounted in the History of music—Beethoven's *An die ferne Geliebte* of 1816—where the simplicity of the melodies could be comparable to Reichardt's melodic typology[26], tone painting elements are to be found as echoes or as comments to the voice, sometimes preceding the entry of the singer, e.g., (i) the pastoral invocation with the horn calls in "Wo die Berge so blau", which have the function of "remembrance" of the beloved[27], (ii) the triplets suggesting the movement of the brook in "Leichte Segler in den Höhen", (iii) the mordents and trills conveying the chirping of the birds in "Diese Wolken in den Höhen". The through-composed form and the cyclical unity were innovative characteristics for this genre, which probably captivated Schubert. Nevertheless, Beethoven in his last song "Nimm sie hin denn diese Lieder", already insinuates a Romantic feature[28], which Schubert takes to the extreme: Charles Rosen mentions how "the memory of the distant beloved [turns into] a memory of grief and absence"[29] and that "Romantic memories are often those of absence, of that which never was."[30], by which the sense of hope and "Sehnsucht" are implicit.

[25] Dobretsberger, Barbara. Personal communication between Barbara Dobretsberger and the author. Salzburg/Lisbon: December 2, 2021.

[26] Cf. Rosen, Charles. (1998). *The Romantic Generation.* P. 174.

[27] Cf. Ibid. P. 166–167.

[28] The word "insinuates" was deliberately used here. Beethoven conveys a closed form, as Elmar Budde advocates. Cf. Budde, Elmar. (2003). *Schuberts Liederzyklen.* P.21. This can be musically heard through the decisive tone the ending takes, i.e., specifically through the forte dynamic and the *sf* in the last piano chord. However, by using an ending motif that derives from the same thematic material from the beginning of the cycle, Beethoven "suggest[s] the incomplete". Rosen, Charles. (1998). *The Romantic Generation.* P. 174. In addition, the fermata on this last chord can also suggest the willingness of remaining in the search, in the unknown, as the words "On the hill I sit peering" can indicate. Whether "Schubert took another path [than Beethoven]" as Budde defends, or whether Schubert took Beethoven's insinuation further in an idiosyncratic way, Schubert song cycles musically rather convey an open form, i.e., they tend to "lead into the uncertainty". Budde, Elmar. (2003). *Schuberts Liederzyklen.* P.21. (Trans. by the author). German expression: "[…] seine Zyklen sind nicht kompositorisch geschlossen, sie münden ins Offene, ins Ungewisse.".

[29] Rosen, Charles. (1998). *The Romantic Generation.* P. 174.

[30] Ibid. P. 175.

Another feature which Beethoven here addressed, and which is common to Schubert's nature, is the theme of the distant beloved, which—to speak in Jungian terms—suggests the expression of the Anima[31].

Nonetheless, the piano function in Schubert's song compositions is not merely to describe the atmosphere through tone painting elements, but also to communicate the inner experiences and to "give voice to the feelings"[32]. Schubert distanced himself from certain former "rules" of the lied genre, by using the piano accompaniment as a statement to the text:

> "The piano now does not only play the bass and harmony, but it reacts psychologically and poetically to the text and temporarily subordinates it to the musical events"[33].

In this manner, Schubert revolutionized the lied aesthetic of his time:

> "With the advent of Schubert, lieder were elevated from the status of an everyday commodity to masterpieces in their own right, and to one of the peak achievements of the nineteenth-century music"[34].

With this particular trait, the piano acquired an identity of its own, being able to express the unconscious elements of the lyrical I. Edward T. Cone discussed how voice and piano reflect two personae, where the piano itself "symbolically suggests both the impingement of the outer world on the individual represented by the vocal persona, and the subconscious reaction of the individual to this impingement"[35]. In this manner, Schubert was able to express the ambivalences,

---

[31] The distant beloved can be paraphrased as the unknown beloved—in this sense, archetypally, it refers to the inner image of the own counterpart (Anima).

[32] Dittrich, Marie-Agnes. „Die Lieder. 'Für Menschenohren sind es Harmonien'". In: Dürr, Walther. Krause, Andreas. (2020). *Schubert Handbuch.* P. 149. German expression: „Mitsprache des Gefühls".

[33] Brendel, Alfred. In: Brendel, Alfred. Gülke, Peter. (2020). *Die Kunst des Interpretierens.* P.35. (Trans. by the author). German expression: „Das Klavier spielt jetzt nicht nur den Bass und die Harmonien, sondern es reagiert psychologisch und poetisch auf den Text und ordnet ihn zeitweilig dem musikalischen Geschehen unter.".

[34] Brendel, Alfred. (2022). "Naivety and Irony: Goethe's Musical Needs". In: *Publications of the English Goethe Society.* Vol. 91 (no.1), P.75–87. Routledge Taylor & Francis Group. P.82.

[35] Cone, Edward T. (1974). "The composer's voice". Cited after: Ferris, David: "Dissociation and Declamation in Schubert's Heine Songs". In: Bodley, Lorraine Byrne., Horton, Julia. (2016). *Rethinking Schubert"*. P. 400.

the discrepancies, and the romantic split of the lyrical subject through his musical discourse (e.g., with the use of tremolos, rhetorical figures, but specifically through harmonic means). This characteristic, a part of Schubert's poetic language, is quite obvious already in his early songs but is to be found frequently, especially in his Müller cycles and Heine settings.

Having been considered as the "song prince" ("Liederfürst"), the lied-like themes are taken as a recognizable feature of Schubert in all of his musical genres:

> "Endless melodies seem to burst out of this creative genius. […] His melodies fall into beautifully natural phrases that are always singable […]"[36].

Schumann described Schubert's musical thoughts in the last piano sonatas as conveying a permanent musicality and songful trait[37]. Among other musicians and musicologists, Thomas Schmidt-Beste features the lied-like themes as the first "typical" characteristic of Schubert's sonata form[38]. While this may be true—and countless examples of song-like melodies could be cited here—it is also to be highlighted that the integrity of a lied or of any instrumental composition is often achieved by Schubert out of a motif, a particular musical gesture or ground character, which can then be metamorphosed through the variation principle[39]. This can be a musical gesture, which he interchangeably used as self-quotations in other instrumental compositions, e.g., the *circulatio* of the spinning wheel in *Gretchen,* a gesture that can be found in other works, as for instance in the beginning of the A minor string quartet *Rosamunde* D 804. It often appears that a specific rhythmic motif is the core element providing for inner unity. This reflection might represent a counterpoint to the idea of Schubert as being (solely) a lyrical composer.

---

[36] Schiff, Andras: "Schubert's piano sonatas: thoughts about interpretation and performance". In: Newbould, Brian. (2017). *Schubert Studies.* P. 204.

[37] Cf. Schumann, Robert. (1854). *Gesammelte Schriften über Musik und Musiker.* Vol. 2. P. 240.

[38] Schmidt-Beste, Thomas. (2006). *Die Sonata.* P.138.

[39] Cf. Budde, Elmar. (1991). „Berlin und die Schöne Müllerin". Cited after: Dittrich, Marie-Agnes. "Die Lieder. 'Für Menschenohren sind es Harmonien'". In: Dürr, Walther. Krause, Andreas. (2020). *Schubert Handbuch.* P. 151.

Not only several musicologists such as Marie-Agnes Dittrich[40] and Elmar Budde give that proclamation, but also interpreters such as Alfred Brendel[41] and Andras Schiff[42]. Additionally, these rhythmic patterns can semantically allude to an explicit basic atmosphere or mood, e.g., the dactyl or spondee rhythm of the wanderer. The original motif from the lied "Der Wanderer" D 493 is to be found in several subsequent pieces, from the closely-related *Wandererfantasie* (11.3, 19), to e.g., "Der Wanderers Nachtlied", the A minor string quartet D 804 and the associated *Impromptu* D 935 no.3, the lied "Der Tod und das Mädchen" D 531 and the related D minor string quartet D 810, and in the song cycle *Die Winterreise.* The fate-motif, with reference to Beethoven's fifth symphony, but also to the fate-goddesses as the underlying archetypal principle (8), belongs to this sphere as well. Among others, examples of the latter are to be found in the *Unfinished* symphony, the D minor string quartet and the last piano sonatas. The Atlas-motif[43] is another rhythmic motif which justifies being restated here, due to its importance and coherent appearance in his "late works", expressing the "Weltschmerz" (8, 18).

Schumann, who described the songful character inherent in Schubert's language, advocates for Schubert's use of his own dances as a model for other compositions[44]. It is a fact that Schubert was also a greatly appreciated dance composer—another genre wherein he made use of the same compositional proceedings of self-quotations[45]. It can be deduced that specific rhythms had special connotations for Schubert, as did the melodic gestures that are semantically linked to the poems he set to music (lieder). Furthermore, Schubert occasionally used the rhythm to merge two contradictory emotions: the lightlessness of the dance and the heaviness of a sorrowful sigh, e.g., in Schubert's *Andantino* of the A

---

[40] Cf. Dittrich, Marie-Agnes. „ Die Lieder. 'Für Menschenohren sind es Harmonien'". In: Dürr, Walther. Krause, Andreas. (2020). *Schubert Handbuch.* P. 151.

[41] In particular, Brendel points to the long non-melodic passages in some of his piano sonatas, such as the A minor D 845, the C minor D 958 and the A Major D 959, and the C major symphony. In this statement he emphasizes the importance of the rhythmic component in his works. Furthermore, he explains the abundance of singable melodies due to Schubert being a vocal composer. Cf. Brendel, Alfred. (2001). *Ausgerechnet Ich.* P. 162.

[42] Cf. Schiff, Andras: "Schubert's piano sonatas: thoughts about interpretation and performance". In: Newbould, Brian. (2017). *Schubert Studies.*

[43] Cf. Godel, Arthur. (1985). *Schuberts letzte drei Klaviersonaten.* P.27–28.

[44] Cf. Krause, Andreas: „Die Klaviermusik—'So frei und eigen, so keck und mitunter auch so sonderbar'". In: Dürr, Walther., Krause, Andreas. (2020). *Schubert Handbuch.* P. 417.

[45] Some of the cross-references found between motifs of dances and his other instrumental works were already listed (10).

major sonata D 959 (17). This leads to the conclusion that it is always dangerous to follow a one-sided image of a composer, and that a versatile, more inclusive view comes closer to the authentic nature of Schubert's music. To use Schiff's formulation: "In Schubert's music melody, harmony and rhythm co-exist in perfect equilibrium."[46].

In Schubert's time, the lied, for which he was most recognized, was still considered to be a genre of minor importance[47], featuring the small form. His dances, for which he was greatly appreciated and his character pieces such as the *Impromptus* and the *Moments musicaux* were also written in the ternary form[48]. In terms of sonata form, Schubert's earlier compositions included a significant number of fragmentary works. The reason might lie in his rather independent learning process. In addition to the already mentioned crisis and the in-depth study of Beethoven's works, the only instructional insight he had acquired regarding the usual sonata form and the structural model of his time, was through his early lessons with Michael Holzer, prior to the "Konvikt" time[49]. Hinrichsen devoted an entire book solely to the "diversity of forms"[50], peculiarities and deviations he noted in Schubert's conception of the sonata form. Among other aspects, which will be tackled later in the chapter (e.g., modulation processes), the beginning of the re-exposition in the subdominant[51] is considered to be a particular Schubertian trait, observed *inter alia* not only by Hinrichsen but also by Thomas Schmidt-Beste[52]. Cited examples for a subdominant re-exposition are, in each case related to the first movements, the following: the symphonies D 125 and D 485, the piano sonatas D 279, D 459, D 537 and D 575, the violin sonata D 385,

---

[46] Schiff, Andras: "Schubert's piano sonatas: thoughts about interpretation and performance". In: Newbould, Brian. (2017). *Schubert Studies.* P. 197.

[47] Cf. Gülke, Peter. In: Brendel, Alfred. Gülke, Peter. (2020). *Die Kunst des Interpretierens.* P.35.

[48] Schumann, however, perceived the individual pieces of the "later" composed Impromptus D 935 (with the exception of the 3rd piece, composed as a theme and variations), as singular movements out of a sonata for piano. Cf. Schumann, Robert. (1854). *Gesammelte Schriften über Musik und Musiker.* Vol. 3. P. 37–40.

[49] Cf. Hinrichsen, Hans-Joachim. (1994). *Untersuchungen zur Entwicklung der Sonatenform in der Instrumentalmusik Franz Schuberts.* P. 31.

[50] Ibid. P. 39. German expression: „Formenvielfalt".

[51] This harmonic characteristic is often called "Transpositionsreprise", a term to be reported back to Felix Salzer. Cf. Ibid. P. 124. Due to its problematic connotation, Hinrichsen suggests limiting the general use of this term to the re-exposition of the B major sonata D 575 specifically and otherwise speaking solely of a subdominant re-exposition. Cf. Ibid. P. 129.

[52] Cf. Schmidt-Beste, Thomas. (2006). *Die Sonata.* P.138.

the piano quintet D 667, among others[53]. However, it seems that this technique had an "experimental"[54] character, featured in his "earlier" works. According to Hinrichsen, this practice was abandoned since 1819, due to its "simplicity", being the *Forellenquintett* and the piano sonata D 664 two compositions of a "farewell" of that use[55]. Later, for his piano sonatas D 840 and D 845, Schubert features the so-called "veiled beginnings of the re-exposition"[56], which "presumably" started a tradition leading to Brahms and Bruckner[57].

Schubert was creating a new path into the big instrumental form, which had a great impact on the coming generations. Additionally, inherent musical gestures and rhythmic motives play a crucial role in the structure of his compositions. One of the first attempts to create a new musical form, brought to its conclusion, can be found in the origins of the *Wandererfantasie,* as Krause implies[58]. This piece was considered a "bravour" piece, which naturally pleased the audience for its virtuosic character:

> "The Fantasy has always been recognized as the genre of musical pieces in which the composer's art, freed from the fetters of form, can unfold most clearly and fully prove its worth. Mr. Schubert proved his mastery in this latest work, in which he showed that he not only possesses the gift of invention, but also knows how to execute his happy motifs according to all the demands of art."[59].

[53] The complete listing is to be found in: Hinrichsen, Hans-Joachim. (1994). *Untersuchungen zur Entwicklung der Sonatenform in der Instrumentalmusik Franz Schuberts.* P. 125.

[54] Ibid. P. 146.

[55] Cf. Ibid. P. 131–132.

[56] Ibid. P.142. German expression: "Verschleierung des Reprisenbeginns".

[57] Ibid. P.147.

[58] Cf. Krause, Andreas: „Die Klaviermusik—'So frei und eigen, so keck und mitunter auch so sonderbar'". In: Dürr, Walther., Krause, Andreas. (2020). *Schubert Handbuch.* P. 392.

[59] Announcement of the work publication in the Viennese newspaper. "Aus der amtlichen 'Wiener Zeitung' vom 24. Februar 1823". In: Deutsch, Otto Erich. (1964). *Schubert—Die Dokumente seines Lebens.* P. 186. (Trans. by the author). German expression: „Die Fantasie ward von jeher als jene Gattung der Tonstücke anerkannt, in welcher die Kunst des Tonsetzers sich, von den Fesseln der Form befreit, am deutlichsten entfalten, und ihren Wert ganz erproben kann. Herr Schubert bewährte seine Meisterschaft in diesem neusten Werke, in welchem er zeigte, dass er nicht nur die Gabe der Erfindung besitzet, sondern auch seine glücklichen Motive nach allen Forderungen der Kunst durchzuführen versteht. [...]".

The genre of the fantasy, as described in the above citation, is most propitious to the creation of a new form since it allows a certain freedom of imagination[60]. In Jungian terms, imagination, similarly to dreams, allows unconscious structures to arise. In the midst of a creative process, this can mean to find the archetypal structures expressed creatively by means of a direct transmission from the unconscious. Verena Kast explains that through fantasies and through imagination "in a highly creative person, there is a spontaneous revival of the unconscious"[61], where a resonance with these symbolic structures takes place; thereby time and space are transcended[62].

Other characteristics of the fantasy genre which pleased Schubert particularly were the use of diminished 7th chords—a chord, bearer of a special rhetoric and semantics. Being linked with the affect of pain, it was used to achieve a dramatic effect in the classic period. Clemens Kühn clarifies that "the interest of the Romantics [in these chords] lay in their gloomy colouring and tonal shimmer"[63]. After the *Wandererfantasie*, Schubert composed the following sonatas with his new form conception in mind, featuring traits of the fantasy genre, as the research findings of Andreas Krause reveal[64]. Apart from the obvious examples of the *Fantasie* for violin and piano in C major D 934 and the F minor *Fantasie* for piano four hands D 940, among others, Krause points in particular to two examples taken from Deutsch's *Schubert—Dokumente seines Lebens*: the piano sonata in A minor D 845 and the sonata in G major D 894, both of which have been described as reflecting the fantasy genre[65].

Schubert's personal note in his big sonata form compositions is particularly recognizable through (i) the stating of more than two contrasting themes within the exposition section, which are all distinct in character, (ii) the wandering

[60] Fantasies belong to the genre of character pieces, which flourished in the Romantic period. The reason mainly being because they perfectly convey the aesthetic ideals of that time. Examples can be found earlier in History, e.g., in Mozart's and Beethoven's works.

[61] Kast, Verena. (2014). *Die Tiefenpsychologie nach C.G. Jung.* Chapter: "Schöpferische Haltung durch schöpferische Methoden.". (Trans. by the author). German expression: „Bei hochschöpferischen Menschen ist, […] eine spontane Belebung des Unbewussten auszumachen.".

[62] Ibid.

[63] Kühn, Clemens. (2005). *Analyse lernen.* P. 74. (Trans. by the author). German expression: „[…] die Romantik interessiert eher seine düstere Färbung und sein tonales Schillern.".

[64] Cf. Krause, Andreas: „Die Klaviermusik—'So frei und eigen, so keck und mitunter auch so sonderbar'". In: Dürr, Walther., Krause, Andreas. (2020). *Schubert Handbuch.* P. 392.

[65] Both full articles can be found in: Deutsch, Otto Erich. (1964). *Schubert—Die Dokumente seines Lebens.* P. 348 and 422 respectively.

around to the most remote harmonies within the constraints of this form[66] and (iii) the spinning-forth character of the single themes and motives through the motif-metamorphosis technique. However, in an attempt to create a novel big form in instrumental music, Schubert was not always fully understood. As evidence, it may be stated, that his last piano sonatas only begun to be integrated in the pianistic repertoire in the 20th century, through the hands of Schnabel (encouraged by his teacher Leschetizky) and Erdmann[67]. This fact occurred despite the admiration of Schumann, Mendelssohn, Liszt, Anton Rubinstein, Dvořák and George Grove[68]. Schubert's ideal was long believed to have been driven to an extreme in his last piano trilogy, termed with the comment of the "heavenly lengths" by Schumann:

> "And his heavenly lengths of the [C-major] Symphony, like a thick novel in four volumes, as for instance of Jean Paul, who also could never end, and for the best reasons, to let the reader also create afterwards."[69].

Schumann's connotation of the "heavenly lengths" is to be positively understood, not only due to the association with one of his favorite novel-authors Jean Paul, but also in connection with his description of Schubert's last three piano sonatas, where he states:

> "Be that as it may, these sonatas seem to me strikingly different from his others, namely by a much greater simplicity of invention, by a voluntary resignation to brilliant novelty where he otherwise sets himself such high standards, by spinning out certain general musical thoughts instead of weaving new threads period after period. As if there could be no end to it, never at a loss for a sequence, always musical and rich in song, it trickles on from page to page, interrupted here and there by individual more violent impulses, which, however, quickly calm down again."[70].

---

[66] The novel harmonic peculiarities will be addressed more in depth at a later point.

[67] Cf. Brendel, Alfred. (1996). *Musik beim Wort genommen.* P. 85.

[68] Cf. Ibid.

[69] Schumann, Robert. (1854). *Gesammelte Schriften über Musik und Musiker*. Vol. 3. P. 201. (Trans. by the author). German expression: „Und diese himmlische Länge der Symphonie, wie ein dicker Roman in vier Bänden etwas von Jean Paul, der auch niemals endigen kann und aus den besten Gründen zwar, um auch den Leser hinterher nachschaffen zu lassen.".

[70] Ibid. Vol. 2. P. 240. (Trans. by the author). German expression: "Wie dem sei, so scheinen mir diese Sonaten auffallend anders als seine andern, namentlich durch eine viel größeren Einfalt der Erfindung, durch ein freiwilliges Resignieren auf glänzende Neuheit, wo er sich sonst so hohe Ansprüche stellt, durch Ausspinnung von gewissen allgemeinen musikalischen Gedanken, anstatt er sonst Periode auf Periode neue Fäden verknüpft. Als könne es gar kein Ende haben, nie verlegen um die Folge, immer musikalisch und gesangreich rieselt es von

This statement is not to be taken as a depreciative comment on Schubert's works, precisely due to the link with Jean Paul. Here, Schumann indicates a main difference between his "younger" and "later works", alluding to Schubert's nature and willingness to dwell in the moment, in opposition to stating contrasting ideas one after the other[71]. These moments are constantly transfiguring, reflecting a change in color and a change of his inner states. With this technique, the "heavenly lengths" and the never-ending ends are created, but also the sense for unity[72], which Schumann might have actually appreciated. Particularly, Charles Rosen highlighted some points in common between both composers in his following statement: "[...] Schubert and Schumann, both of whom often settled for literal repetition at great length [...]"[73].

The lengths of Schubert's instrumental compositions, specifically of the sonata form, can, furthermore, be associated with his own creative process: Schubert was reported to have rarely revised his works[74]. This way of working consequently lent to his works a spontaneous and primordial character, whichcan henceforth express the archetypal structures within. In his records, Spaun specifically hints to the following characteristic:

> "It is true that Schubert did not go through his compositions anymore, did not work on them afterwards with a file, whereby lengths or deficiencies arose here and there, but on the other hand they have something original and fresh about them, which is very often lost through much filing"[75].

Seite zu Seite weiter, hier und da durch einzelne heftigere Regungen unterbrochen, die sich aber schnell wieder beruhigen.".

[71] Wolfgang Boetticher links Schubert's tendency to monothematic constellations as a feature of the "romantic spinning-forth" with the "Technique of dwelling without a structural constraint.". Boetticher, Wolfgang. (1983). *Einführung in die musikalische Romantik.* P. 36. (Trans. by the author). German expressions: "Züge romantischen Weiterspinnens", respectively, "Technik des Verweilens ohne strukturellen Zwang.".

[72] Brendel suggests understanding Schumann's word choice of "Einfalt" not as "simplicity [of invention]" but rather as "unity". This reading goes conjointly with the author's thoughts. Cf. Brendel, Alfred. (1996). *Musik beim Wort genommen.* P. 86.

[73] Rosen, Charles. (1998). *The Romantic Generation.* P. 458.

[74] Only occasionally there are to be found statements in literature referring to a revision or to a change that Schubert would have made, respectively, accepted from his brother's suggestions. Gülke mentions such occurrences notably in the A-flat major mass and the G major mass. Cf. Gülke, Peter. (2020). *Franz Schubert in seiner Zeit.* P. 269. A similar occurrence led Schubert to restructure the fourth movement of the Piano Trio in E-flat major D 927 (19.).

[75] Von Spaun, Joseph: „Aufzeichnungen über meinen Verkehr mit Franz Schubert (1858)". In: Deutsch, Otto Erich. (1983). *Schubert Erinnerungen seiner Freunde.* P. 163. (Trans. by the author). German expression: „Wahr ist es, daß Schubert seine Kompositionen nicht mehr

> "Schubert can be accused of one mistake, namely that he never reworked his compositions and polished them, which is why here and there there are individual lengths or incorrectnesses; but the question is whether this was really a mistake and whether the resulting freshness and originality of his compositions did not far outweigh the lack of polish."[76].

This "new" form that Schubert created, can be understood as having been crucial for the development of this genre in music History: having already been recognized by Brahms[77], this might have inspired the next generations of composers[78], i.e., particularly the post-Romantic composers, such as Bruckner and Mahler. Peter Gülke explained that through the three-theme exposition and through the harmonic paths that Schubert undertook, he was generating a new perception of space—of "tone-spaces"—wherein the harmonic spaces would be metaphors for "life-spaces" and the different themes and motives would correspond to "living beings"[79].

It is relatively widespread that musicologists identify and subdivide the life of a composer into different, commonly three distinct creative phases, in which the composer displays contrasting compositional styles, sometimes conveying a changed message. These follow the pattern of early, middle and late periods, respectively, a young style, a development phase and a mature style. The latter, which can be seen as expressing a death message, a highly spiritual sphere, conveying a transcendental tone, habitually features a still incomprehensible language for their contemporaries. Regarding Schubert's life, this topic is matter for vast

---

durchging, nicht nachträglich mit der Feile daran arbeitete, wodurch hie und da Längen oder Mängel entstanden, dagegen aber haben sie etwas Ursprüngliches und Frisches an sich, das sich sehr oft durch vieles Feilen verliert.".

[76] Von Spaun, Joseph: „Einige Bemerkungen über die Biographie Schuberts von Herrn Ritter von Kreißle-Hellborn". In: Ibid. P. 418. (Trans. by the author). German expression: "Einen Fehler kann man Schubert vorwerfen, nämlich daß er seine Kompositionen nie nochmals vorgenommen und daran gefeilt habe, daher hie und da einzelne Längen oder Inkorrektheiten vorkommen; allein es fragt sich, ob das wirklich ein Fehler war und ob nicht die dadurch veranlaßte Frische und Ursprünglichkeit seiner Kompositionen den Mangel der Feile weit überboten haben.".

[77] Cf. Gülke, Peter. In: Brendel, Alfred. Gülke, Peter. (2020). *Die Kunst des Interpretierens.* P.41.

[78] Cf. Rosen, Charles. (1998). *The Romantic Generation.* P. 21.

[79] Gülke, Peter. In: Brendel, Alfred. Gülke, Peter. (2020). *Die Kunst des Interpretierens.* P.42. The equivalent German words used were respectivelly: „Tonräume", „Lebensräume" and „Lebewesen".

discussion within today's Schubert community research, which include the legitimacy of the terms "early" and "later" works in Schubert's 31 years of life[80]. Some advocate the unfeasibility of speaking of a late work[81], while others confidently speak of three periods[82]. In the case of the former, the supporting explanations mainly focus on his young life, which is seen as interrupted. In contrast, the latter focuses on his enormous productivity, the concept of "Todessehnsucht" and the indication of certain stylistic characteristics. The motivation for such distinct positions might firstly lie in Grillparzer's epitaph.

> "The art of sound buried a rich possession here, but even more beautiful hopes. Franz Schubert lies here. Born on XXXI. January MDCCXCVII. Died on XIX. Nov. MDCCCXXVIII. XXXI years of age."[83].

Grillparzer's words originated a twofold discussion: interpreters, such as Brendel, put the emphasis on the "higher hopes". This means that Schubert's last works do not convey a final death message, but rather point to a development to come, leaving an immense potential behind:

> "The style of the year 1828 is no 'late style', as I see [...] in the late Mozart. A new, solemn, tenderly hymnal note can be found in the first two movements of Schubert's B-flat major sonata or the Adagio of his C-minor sonata; [...]"[84].

Others, such as Andras Schiff rather accentuate Schubert's Homeric testament and bring forward the idea that he was actually awaiting "and even welcoming

[80] Discrepancies in opinions are also to be found in the so-called years of crisis and its time-framing fixation years being 1818–23—a topic which will be developed subsequently.

[81] Cf. Brendel, Alfred. (1996). *Musik beim Wort genommen.* P. 80.

[82] Cf. Schiff, Andras: "Schubert's piano sonatas: thoughts about interpretation and performance". In: Newbould, Brian. (2017). *Schubert Studies.* P. 192.

[83] Grillparzer, Franz: „Inschrift auf Schuberts Grabmal (Herbst 1829)". In: Deutsch, Otto Erich. (1964). *Schubert—Die Dokumente seines Lebens.* P. 580. (Tran by the author). German expression: „Die Tonkunst begrub hier einen reichen Besitz, aber noch viel schoenere Hoffnungen. Franz Schubert liegt hier. Geboren am XXXI. Jaenner MDCCXCVII. Gestorben am XIX. Nov. MDCCCXXVIII. XXXI Jahre Alt.

[84] Brendel, Alfred. (1996). *Musik beim Wort genommen.* P. 80. (Trans. by the author). German expression: "Der Stil des Jahres 1828 ist kein ‚Altersstil', wie ich ihn [...] beim später Mozart wahrnehme. Eine neue, feierliche, zart-hymnische Note läßt sich in den ersten beiden Sätzen von Schuberts B-Dur-Sonate oder im Adagio seiner c-Moll-Sonate freilich konstatieren; [...]".

death"[85]. A similar position was already advocated by Schumann, who wrote the following statement upon Grillparzer's verse:

> "And if the words written on his tombstone buried 'a beautiful possession, but even more beautiful hopes', let us gratefully remember only the former. To ruminate on what he could have still achieved leads nowhere. He has done enough, and praise ought to be those who, like him, have striven and achieved."[86].
>
> "[…], where the imagination is now filled with the thought of the near parting, through the sad 'very last'"[87].

These two latter positions can lead to the interpretation of perceiving his last piano sonatas, the C major string quintet, and the Rellstab, Heine and Seidl settings as a testimony or as a "Schwanengesang"[88]—another appreciated discussion. As Schiff stated, the "Todessehnsucht" (Novalis) was an aesthetic ideal from that time[89], as already mentioned in previous chapters. Beyond that, he was conscious of his illness (the latest since his stay in the hospital in 1823). Additionally, it should be underlined that Schubert augmented his productivity in his last year and months, possibly indicating his consciousness upon his coming death and all the unsaid elements he wanted to express. However, Brendel states that life and death are equally strong in Schubert's life. He advocates that the string quintet and "Der Hirt auf dem Felsen" D 965 are two examples of works which do not convey a death message[90]. Psychologically observed, these can be seen as the result of a compensation of an absence, or an expression of

---

[85] Schiff, Andras. In: Schiff, Andras. (n.d.). *Schiff András filmje Schubertről—András Schiff tells about Schubert.* [Documentary]. Scorer Associates. Minutes 35:20 of 48:54.

[86] Schumann, Robert. (1854). *Gesammelte Schriften über Musik und Musiker.* Vol. 2. "Schubert's letzte Compositionen.". P.240. (Trans. by the author). German expression: "Und wenn auf seinem Leichenstein die Worte stehen, dass unter ihm ,ein schöner Besitz, aber noch schönere Hoffnungen' begraben lägen, so wollen wir dankbar nur des ersteren gedenken. Nachzugrübeln, was er noch erreichen können, führt zu nichts. Er hat genug getan, und gepriesen sei, wer wie er gestrebt und vollendet.".

[87] Ibid. P. 239–240. (Trans. by the author). German expression: „[…] wo die Phantasie durch das traurige 'Allerletzte' nun einmal vom Gedanken des nahen Scheidens erfüllt ist.".

[88] This notion was actually brought forward by the Viennese publisher Tobias Haslinger, who grouped and named these last songs mentioned as the "Schwanengesang" cycle. This concept is often transferred to other "late works", such as his last piano trilogy.

[89] Cf. Schiff, Andras. In: Schiff, Andras. (n.d.). *Schiff András filmje Schubertről—András Schiff tells about Schubert.* [Documentary]. Scorer Associates. Minutes 35:20 of 48:54.

[90] Cf. Brendel, Alfred. (2001). *Ausgerechnet Ich.* P. 160–161.

the inner projections, of one of his inner wills. It can be the result of a self-regulatory mechanism, as Jung frequently mentioned, or, theologically speaking, of a phenomenon of rapture (18).

The piano trilogy D 958—960, the E-flat major mass, the C major string quintet, the Heine settings were among Schubert's last musical sayings. Even Brendel, who does not acknowledge a late style in Schubert, recognizes the existence of a "hymnal tone"[91]. Would it not be possible that Schubert could have intuitively had a premonition about his terminal state and expressed this artistically, or symbolically, in his music? While this can be regarded as just a speculation, this view in general can be supported from the Jungian perspective. For Jungians, dreams are overall understood as "[...] the voice of nature within [...]"[92]. These can fulfill the function of preparing death, whereby there may be a prediction of a terminal situation as the physical death itself[93] but, more importantly, "a profound transformation and a continuation of the life process"[94] communicated by the unconscious. According to Marie-Louise von Franz, there is a great affluence of dream symbols that spiritually prepare to this transformation[95]. Although Schubert's last dreams are unknown, the "hymnal tone" and the archetypal structures present in his music could thus reflect the development of these inner processes already taking place. Consequently, this could also explain his inner urge to compose as much as possible and the growth in musical production within the last year of his life. This hypothesis will be verified in accordance with the results gained from the analytical chapters (20).

Returning to the debate of the existence and the subdivision of the composer's life in different phases, there are different ways and angles of analyzing this question, which can lead to distinct "conclusions". If his age is taken as the orientation mark, it is impossible to speak of a late style, even taking into account the fact that, at that time, life expectancy was generally much shorter, especially due to insufficient medical knowledge. In contrast, by examining the development

---

91 Brendel, Alfred. (1996). *Musik beim Wort genommen.* P. 80.

92 Von Franz, Marie-Louise. (1984). *Traum und Tod.* P.7. (Trans. by the author). German expression: „Träume lasse sich bekanntlich nicht manipulieren, sie sind gleichsam die Stimme der Natur in uns. Deshalb stellt sich die Frage, wie die Natur selbst uns auf den Tod vorbereitet.".

93 Cf. Ibid. P. 9–10.

94 Ibid. P.203. (Trans. by the author). German expression: "Die Träume vor dem Tod stehender Menschen zeigen alle, daß das Unbewußte, [...] das Bewußtsein nicht auf ein totales Ende vorbereitet, sondern auf eine tiefgehende Verwandlung und auf eine irgendwie beschaffene Fortsetzung des Lebensprozesses, [...]".

95 Cf. Ibid. P.9.

of Schubert's musical language within the constraints of his 31 years lifespan, some significant pillars of changes can be identified, which could substantiate using the term "late works"[96]. As Krause points out, Schumann in his "Schriften über Musik und Musiker" already acknowledged a break in style between his so-called "middle" piano sonatas and the "late" trilogy[97].

To base a conclusion solely upon the development of Schubert's musical language led to contrasting arguments among musicologists regarding the split into different styles or periods[98]. This reflects, after Hilmar, "[...] a certain uncertainty in the identification of stylistic features"[99]. To resume Hilmar's 1997 research: (i) Alfred Einstein established the year 1825/1826 as the beginning of the last phase, (ii) Brown perceived three "late phases", the first beginning in 1825, a middle section going 1826–1827 and the last year standing per se, while (iii) Chochlow sees *Die Winterreise* D 911 (1827) as the beginning of a new idiom, having the Heine setting as its climax[100]. This situation becomes more complicated, when, additionally, there is no agreement on the so-called "years of crisis", which is also a highly polemic discussion, especially with regard to the time frame of the years involved.

Gernot Gruber hints at this problem in particular[101]. Firstly, he encourages questioning the fixation on time-framing; secondly, it is implied in his text the need for a cautious and deeper observational attitude, where a differentiation between the personal sphere, Schubert's healthwise condition and artistic fields[102]

---

96 The author suggests to use this term in inverted commas when related to Schubert or to use the formulation "late works in young years", as Hinrichsen does. Hinrichsen, Hans-Joachim. (2019). *Franz Schubert. Chapter 6:* „Spätwerk in jungen Jahren. Die großen Liederzyklen.". This position seems to have been influenced by Herman Grimm's formulation "All works by Schubert are early works.". Grimm, Herman. (1872). "Das Leben Raphael's". Cited after: Hinrichsen, Hans-Joachim: "Is there a late style in Schubert's oeuvre?". In: Bodley, Lorraine Byrne., Horton, Julian. (2016). *Rethinking Schubert.* Oxford: Oxford University Press. P. 17.

97 Cf. Krause, Andreas: „Die Klaviermusik—'So frei und eigen, so keck und mitunter auch so sonderbar'". In: Dürr, Walther., Krause, Andreas. (2020). *Schubert Handbuch.* P. 417.

98 Cf. Hilmar, Ernst. (1997). *Franz Schubert.* Chapter: "Die 'späten' Jahre (1824–1828). Die Liederzyklen.". P. 76–104.

99 Cf. Ibid. P. 78. (Trans. by the author). German expression: „Die unterschiedliche Auffassung der einzelnen Entwicklungsstufen in dieser letzten Schaffensperiode dokumentiert aber zugleich eine gewisse Unsicherheit bei der Festlegung stilistischer Merkmale.".

100 Cf. Ibid. P. 78.

101 Cf. Gruber, Gernot. (2010). *Schubert. Schubert?* Chapter: "Künstlerische Krise?" and Chapter: "Und nach der Krise?". P. 93–108 and P. 115–126, respectively.

102 Cf. Ibid. P. 93.

should be made. Hilmar paraphrased the conceived term of 1985 as "years of spiritual upheaval"[103]. Congruently, Andreas Krause understands the years of crisis as a "paradigm shift"[104], especially within the context of his piano sonatas composed during those years and understands them as a bridge to the greater form: "The path to the great Symphony"[105]. From the depth psychological point of view, these two latter statements can be explained: a crisis can represent a turning point, of an inner revolution and of discovering new creative reformulations to the perceived difficulties. This indicates that there might exist an interaction between several factors, personal and artistic, that played a role, and that should be taken into consideration.

Visibly, no firm consensus appears to have been established in these matters so far. A crisscrossing and overlapping of knowledge might, therefore, be helpful to arrive at a new perspective. Particularly, the intertwining of the information gained from (i) the most recent research concerning the analysis of musical features, which might point to identifiable changes and to a differentiated use of stylistic elements with (ii) the identified main archetypal stages and psychological processes that may have shaped Schubert's individuation process and his creative process, might be valuable. The outcome of the realized analysis will be resumed in the form of an illustration (20). The first suggested procedure will now be outlined in an introductory manner.

Schubert's distinctive and "paradoxical"—to use Brendel's own formulation—relationship towards the major-minor modes shall be initially cited, as a main characteristic of his musical language:

> "As a rule, one could say that the minor [mode] signifies reality for him, that is, the difficulty and struggle of life; and that the major [mode] expresses longing, the unattainable, the utopian need for happiness—'there where you are not, there is happiness', as it says in the 'Wanderer'"[106].

---

[103] Hilmar, Ernst. (1997). *Franz Schubert.* Chapter: "Die 'späten' Jahre (1824–1828). Die Liederzyklen.". P. 31. (Trans. by the author). German expression: „[...] Jahre eines hochbedeutenden geistigen Umbruchs".

[104] Krause, Andreas: „Die Klaviermusik—'So frei und eigen, so keck und mitunter auch so sonderbar'". In: Dürr, Walther., Krause, Andreas. (2020). *Schubert Handbuch.* P. 390.

[105] Ibid. (Trans. by the author). German expression: „[...] den Weg zur großen Sinfonie".

[106] Brendel, Alfred. (2001). *Ausgerechnet Ich.* P. 163. (Trans. by the author). German expression. „In der Regel könnte man sagen, daß Moll für ihn die Realität bedeutet, also die Schwierigkeit und den Kampf des Lebens; und daß das Dur die Sehnsucht, das Unerreichbare, das utopische Bedürfnis nach Glück ausdrückt—‚dort, wo du nicht bist, dort ist das Glück', wie es im ‚Wanderer' heißt.".

The major and minor mode can convey the sense of harmonic color. Hinrichsen notes how the juxtaposition of major and minor is used not only as a means to express a certain atmosphere but also as a "form-defining"[107] device. As an example, he cited the first movement of the G major string quartet D 887. This unique understanding of both modes can, psychologically observed, express manifold inner states, including the inner-outer world problem. Sometimes, the turn to major may signify an important inner transformation. Particularly, in the case of the B-flat major sonata D 960, the turning to major at the end exemplifies how pain is always existent, yet how it transforms itself, e.g., into a redemptive light—a process that occurs after an inner acceptance of fate (18).

The mediantic key relationship was a propitious means for Schubert to create a certain harmonic color. Clemens Kühn gives several examples, from Beethoven and Schubert, where the third-related keys modulation technique—marked as a Romantic stylistic device[108]—is used to "reinforce harmonic color"[109]. Among them the following works are cited: Schubert's *Zwanzig Walzer* D 146 no.18 and "Sei mir gegrüßt" D 741. The same change in color and—to put in other words—change of inner perception occurs when there is a restatement of the same theme in another harmony[110], another technique dear to Schubert. To illustrate this point, Kühn cited the *Andantinò* of the A major Sonata D 959. This practice, depending on the context, can psychologically hint to a shift into another reality plane, a moment of regression or to a pretence of a certain mood or feeling (as e.g., IV 17). This technique can also allow for the communication of an intended sense of distance to "home". This distance, as a "metaphor of absence"[111], may reflect the concepts of "the sublime and the melancholy"[112], i.e., the "Sehnsucht", and the notion of "Weltschmerz" (8). It may also translate the succumbing to the paths of his unconscious, as the wanderer would: to follow the brook and letting himself get lost during the wander-journey[113] (15). This alludes to the concept of the path

---

[107] Hinrichsen, Hans-Joachim. (1994). *Untersuchungen zur Entwicklung der Sonatenform in der Instrumentalmusik Franz Schuberts*. P. 352.

[108] Cf. Kühn, Clemens. (2005). *Analyse lernen*. P. 81.

[109] Ibid. P. 82. (Trans. by the author). German expression: „Terzverwandschaft lockert Verbindungen. Mit der Lockerung wird die harmonische Farbe verstärkt.".

[110] Cf. Ibid.

[111] Rosen, Charles. (1998). *The Romantic Generation*. P. 135.

[112] Cf. Ibid.

[113] Cf. Zacharias, Christian. (2019). *Why does Schubert sound like Schubert?* [Lecture-Recital]. Stagecast Ltd (Production).

as an archetypal notion, a path that leads from the "periphery to the center"[114]. The concept of direction, of orientation and disorientation, which could also be applied to the wanderer archetype, is derived from this particular archetype[115]. Merging these procedures with Schubert's concept of form, Schubert creates a peculiar sense of space and time, by juxtaposing the created distance to home with his tendency to monothematic or monomotivic sonata-form constructions[116] and circular motions: moving within a stillness, within a dwelling in the moment.

Schubert enjoyed surprising the listener; this was not only achieved by the aforementioned minor-major brightenings but also through the contrasts between regular and irregular phrase constructions to extensions in the re-exposition and the later exposition of a first theme, sometimes appearing only in the coda section (e.g., first movement of the D minor string quartet D 810, IV 16). Asymmetrical phrase constructions are typical of Schubert. With this tension and surprise creating device, Schubert renders an additional uncertainty and instability to his phrases, which could also translate an inner condition or state of mind. Schubert employs all of these structural elements and in particular the sudden harmonic shifts, in order to express the romantic "Zerrissenheit" (i.e., to be torn asunder) and the inner search for wholeness, particular to the wanderer archetype. As Kinderman explains:

> "Musically, Schubert uses a combination of heightened thematic contrast, juxtaposition of major and minor keys, and abrupt modulation to reflect [the] duality between

[114] Neumann, Erich. (2015). *The Great Mother.* P.9. (Trans. by Ralph Manheim). The origins of such an archetypal experience can be firstly traced back to the "prehistoric men of the ice age", where the path led to the caves in the mountains. These caves, were sanctuaries with animal pictures, were "hidden" and its inside difficult to reach. Cf. Ibid. The pathway leading there was experienced as a ritual: "In a ritual that was still in large part unconscious, the way led these early men into mountain caves, in whose hidden and almost inaccessible recesses they established 'temples' adorned with representations of animals […]". Ibid. P.8. A further differentiation of this archetype is the "Christ's Calvary" ("Leidens-Weg Christi"), which achieves of "a new, wholy inward, and symbolic level" through "Christ's conscious utterance 'I am the way'"—going from "way of destiny" ("Schicksalsweg") to the "way of redemption" ("Erlösung"). Ibid. P. 9.

[115] Cf. Ibid.

[116] This propensity to monothematic constructions is not only to be found in his "late" compositions but is already to be found in some of his earlier works, in particular in the earlier string quartets, as Hinrichsen points out. Cf. Hinrichsen, Hans-Joachim. (1994). *Untersuchungen zur Entwicklung der Sonatenform in der Instrumentalmusik Franz Schuberts.* P.34.

internal and external experience, or imagination and perception—between the beautiful, bright reams of the protagonist, on the one hand, and a bleak external reality, on the other."[117].

Schubert's "younger compositions" are considered to reflect a more Haydnesque or Mozartian tone quality, even though the earliest works can already hint at distinctive Schubertian traits, which he would come to develop. This is the case especially in what concerns the deviations of the commonly used structural models, as highlighted by Hinrichsen[118]. The "Sonatensatz" piano trio B-flat major D 28 (1812) can be taken as a good example, featuring still the classicist language of his paragons, yet with the characteristic Schubertian inspirations. Hinrichsen points to the similarities with Mozart's B-flat major piano trio KV 502[119]. This parallel can be especially noted, in what concerns the melodic ductus and the classic oriented piano notation, i.e., a piano part featuring accompaniment-like character, with alternations between tonic and dominant chords and the symmetrical phrase construction of the beginning of the exposition. Yet, the sigh from the 5th bar of the cello, already lends his personal color to the piece. Often in Schubert's repertoire, sigh motives (as the musical rhetoric figure of the *suspiratio*) appear conjointly in their two forms: the falling second with the semantics of a sorrowful sigh and the arising second as an *interrogatio*[120]—a rhetorical figure, which depending on the musical context, can be further differentiated. These are particularly abundant in *Die Schöne Müllerin* (15)[121]. However, the sigh motif is a recurring motif throughout his compositions, being still greatly present in his later works, as for instance in the last piano sonatas (17 and 18).

In regard to the form, the stating of the re-exposition in the subdominant is, as seen above, a trait, present specifically in his "earlier" works. From Schubert choices of modulation paths, he opted for a more "stepwise" conservative one in

[117] Kinderman, William: "Schubert's piano music: probing the human condition". In: Gibbs, Christopher H. (1997). *The Cambridge Companion to Schubert.* Part II: "Schubert's music: style and genre". Chap. 8. E-book.

[118] Cf. Hinrichsen, Hans-Joachim. (1994). *Untersuchungen zur Entwicklung der Sonatenform in der Instrumentalmusik Franz Schuberts.* Chapter: „Die Aneignung der Sonatenform im Frühwerk".

[119] Cf. Ibid. P.40.

[120] Cf. Amon, Reinhard. (2005). *Lexikon der Harmonielehre.* P.126.

[121] This characteristic in the mentioned song cycle was notably referred to by Elmar Budde. Cf. Budde, Elmar. (2003). *Schuberts Liederzyklen.*

his "youth" compositions, the so-called "evolutionary" modulations[122]. These are especially to be found in the transitions to the second theme of a sonata.

In his lieder, he seemed to have found a symbolic element to his personal language, since *Gretchen*—the characteristic trait of the circular movement of the spinning wheel, which he used for subsequent instrumental works. As already worked out semantically (8), its symbolism is tied with the fate-goddesses, a form of expression of the great mother archetype. Comparing this early and developing phased language to that of subsequent works, it is thenceforth possible to recognize a development in the contrasting musical elements. To these shifts in language, Xavier Hascher particularly notes the moving away from "classical-like turns of phrases and stock accompaniment figures [...]"[123] and the turning to an "[...] entirely new and idiosyncratic material which Schubert is able to draw from his experience with the lied [...]"[124]. This meant turning away from his "classical models" such as Haydn and Mozart, as also noted by Walther Dürr[125]. Thereby, Beethoven had become an important reference for Schubert to discover new pathways[126].

The *Quartettsatz* D 703 from 1820 played an important role in this transition phase. Especially so, in what concerns his treatment of the melody and the use of tremoli[127], which already hint at some of the features to be found more recurrently in his "late works". While, according to Carner Mosco, already the 5th Symphony (1816) among his symphonic works is mentioned as Schubert's "conscious farewell to the two masters of his youth [Haydn and Mozart]"[128], others, such as Xavier Hascher, observe this change in the *Unfinished* symphony of 1822[129]. In view of (i) the creative events of more personal nature, researched and elucidated previously (11.2 and 11.3), and (ii) his development in

[122] Cf. Hinrichsen, Hans-Joachim. (1994). *Untersuchungen zur Entwicklung der Sonatenform in der Instrumentalmusik Franz Schuberts.* P.52.

[123] Hascher, Xavier: "Narrative dislocations in the first movement of Schubert's 'Unfinished' Symphony". In: Bodley, Lorraine Byrne. Horton, Julian. (2016). *Rethinking Schubert.* P. 127.

[124] Cf. Ibid.

[125] Cf. Dürr, Walther: "Compositional strategies in Schubert's late music". In: Ibid. P. 38.

[126] Cf. Ibid.

[127] Cf. Dobretsberger, Barbara. Personal communication between Barbara Dobretsberger and the author. Salzburg/Lisbon: December 2, 2021.

[128] Carner, Mosco. "The orchestral music". Cited after: Wollenberg, Susan. (2011). *Schubert's Fingerprints: Studies in the instrumental works.* P. 135.

[129] Cf. Hascher, Xavier: "Narrative dislocations in the first movement of Schubert's 'Unfinished' Symphony". In: Bodley, Lorraine Byrne. Horton, Julian. (2016). *Rethinking Schubert.* P. 127.

other genres as the close in time written string quartet (*Quartettsatz*), the latter composition (*Unfinished*) would seem more appropriate to be seen as a mark sign for an accomplished change, at least amongst his symphonic works. This, however, does not invalidate the existence of occasional novel elements in the 5th Symphony, and other earlier works (as his 1817 piano sonatas show) since change can be part of a longer process.

Research in these earlier works reveal that they already hint at an inner processing of new elements. Particularly to mention is Schubert's B major sonata D 575. Radcliff describes this sonata as "intriguingly [bearing an] unsettled air, as though Schubert was aware that his idiom was changing"[130]. The "unsettled air" begins already with the introductory 14 bars, which present, in spite of its "classical" writing appearance, already some destabilizing elements such as asymmetrical phrases and tonal distance to the home key of B major, with the C major chords in m. 10. Striking is the surreal dream-like world that Schubert enters through the sudden shift in m.15, i.e., through the modulation to the minor sixth G major (a common proceeding in his later works): "[…] it seems as if the tonal ground is continually slipping away beneath our feet."[131]. Schubert accentuates this sensation of estrangement with the foreign notes to the harmony, each time, in the last beats of each bar. Radcliff's use of the past progressive verbal tense in "his idiom was changing" indicates an ongoing process. This ought to be considered in the sense that all boundaries should be regarded as flowing smoothly into each other. The earlier indexes of a development to come, reflect a rather natural functioning of the creative psyche. As individuation occurs in a spiral-like manner, so does the musical thinking process unfold. Other examples constitute the four-handed sonata in B-flat major D 617, the so-called "little A major" sonata D 664 and the A major *Forellenquintett* D 667 from which on, Krause notes, his typical use of mediantic related tonalities increased ever since[132].

Going from a "youthful Haydnesque idiom to a new scale of massive architectural sophistication"[133], his late style would reflect, according to Joe Davis, "disjunctive moments" such as "abrupt modal shifts", sudden "interruptions" either by suspended silences, rhetorical figures or by "gestural intrusions",

---

130 Radcliffe, Philip. (1967). "Schubert Piano Sonatas". In: *BBC Music Guides*. P.14.

131 Sacre, Guy. (1998). *La musique de piano. Vol. J-Z.* P. 2479. (Trans. by the author). French expression: „[…] on dirait que le sol tonal se dérobe continuellement sous nos pas.".

132 Cf. Krause, Andreas: „Die Klaviermusik—'So frei und eigen, so keck und mitunter auch so sonderbar'". In: Dürr, Walther., Krause, Andreas. (2020). *Schubert Handbuch.* P. 390.

133 Howatt, Roy: "Architecture as drama in late Schubert". In: Newbould, Brian. (2017). *Schubert Studies.* P. 166.

"structural fractures" and "harmonic dislocations"[134]. This statement might be complemented with Walther Dürr's findings of "surprising fermatas and discontinuations"[135]. These sudden breaks and silences can possibly reflect psychologically a sudden annulment of identity or a moment of inflation, as if symbolically an abyss would open in front of the protagonist, who powerless succumbs to the engulfment of an archetype—these can be the paths of the creative, dynamic psyche. It can also express a solidification or a freezing after a shock-moment, of a returning to the void, the center of the origins, whereupon recreation is enabled again (e.g., IV 17). This kind of expression is recurrently found in the rhetorical figure known as *interruptio* or *aposiopesis.* Archetypically speaking this could also refer to the emergence of the great mother archetype—to be precise: of the negative form of the great-mother archetype (3.2).

While "the concept of sonority as an independent parameter"[136] was a trait already present in Schubert's "early works", Walther Dürr identifies a new manner Schubert treated this factor in conjunction with the structure of a movement[137] in his subsequent works. As the main examples the following works and features were cited: the beginning of the G major sonata as well as of the string quintet and the use of trombones in the C major symphony. As some less striking examples, but still presenting this new conception of sonority, the piano trio in E-flat major, the second movement of the string quintet and the B-flat major sonata D 960 were concurrently mentioned.

The few pedal markings to be found in Schubert's manuscripts can also reflect a specific sound effect. Sometimes these are used as a means to achieve a fusion[138] between the past and the present, a distant remembrance and a closer feeling, between an outer reality and an inner one (18). In this manner Schubert

---

134 All of these here stated and in inverted commas marked aspects, are to be found in: Davies, Joe: "Stylistic disjuncture as a source of drama in Schubert's late instrumental works". In: Davies, Joe. Sobaskie, James William. (2019). *Drama in the music of Franz Schubert.* P. 303.

135 Dürr, Walther: "Compositional strategies in Schubert's late music". In: Bodley, Lorraine Byrne. Horton, Julian. (2016). *Rethinking Schubert.* P.33.

136 Ibid. P. 36. In Dürr's statement a broader definition of sonority is meant: sonority not only as timbre, but also in relation to dynamics, where Schubert creates specific sonority fields: "Sonority extends to specific characteristics of dynamics, for example to the dynamic range of sections (*Klangstärkeflächen*)" and "implies the use of specific instruments in passages where one would least expect them". Cf. Ibid. Dürr accordingly cites musical examples such as the G major sonata D 894 and the beginning of the String Quintet D 956. Cf. Ibid.

137 Cf. Ibid. P. 36.

138 Cf. Godel, Arthur. (1985). *Schuberts letzte drei Klaviersonaten.*

conveys a poetic language, narrative in character. Musicologists refer to a prominent epic character[139] which stands out—this can be particularly felt in the slow movements, of e.g., the late string quartets, the C major string quintet and the last piano trilogy D 958–960. Such narrative and epic character in these "late" compositions could, in opposition to the drama genre, psychologically mean a slight distancing from the felt tragic event, an estrangement or as if the "I" would take a step back. This attitude can be psychologically beneficial to overcome a difficult situation or to gain a new vision about the present situation.

Schubert's recurrent concept of emphasizing the meaning of the second movements (especially in his "later" works) was, historically seen, a novelty in the conception of the form[140]. This trait can be heard in e.g., the A minor D 804 and the D minor D 810 string quartets, which found its climax with the C major string quintet, and all three last piano sonatas. Being the center of a work, they presented thematic ideas of crucial importance for the outer and adjoined movements. Linked to the core importance of the second movements, Schubert often and simultaneously used the technique of juxtaposing self-quotations, i.e., motifs of previously composed lieder, with the variation form. Examples include: the second movement of the *Wandererfantasie* (19), the fourth movement of the *Forellenquintett* (14), and the *Death and the maiden* string quartet (16).

As for harmonic questions, David Beaches particularly investigated the "modulations involving minimal or no preparation […] and enharmonic modulations […]"[141] in works such as the B minor Symphony D 739, the C major quintet D 956, the Piano Trio in B-flat major D 898, the *Moment Musical* no.6 D 780, *inter alia*. The just mentioned sudden shifts ("Rückungen"), known as "non-evolutionary modulations"[142], are described by Susan Wollenberg as conveying to the new key a "quality of a revelation"[143]. These increasingly frequent

[139] The epic quality was already observed by Dahlhaus and has been discussed notably in Korstvedt, Benjamin M. "'The prerogative of the late style': thoughts on the expressive world of Schubert's late works". In: Bodley, Lorraine Byrne. Horton, Julian. (2016). *Schubert's Late Music.*

[140] Cf. Godel, Arthur. (1985). *Schuberts letzte drei Klaviersonaten.*, e.g. P.21.

[141] Beach, David. (2017). *Schubert's mature instrumental music. A theorist's perspective.* Rochester: University of Rochester Press. P.30.

[142] The term was suggested by Wilhelm Keller. Cf. Hinrichsen, Hans-Joachim. (1994). *Untersuchungen zur Entwicklung der Sonatenform in der Instrumentalmusik Franz Schuberts.* P. 51.

[143] Wollenberg, Susan: "Schubert Transitions". Cited after: Wollenberg, Susan. (2011). *Schubert's Fingerprints: Studies in the instrumental works.* P. 47.

shifts might, in psychological terms, strongly reflect an inner change of perception or feeling, as if "the I takes on a shift in perspective"[144]. In this regard, Max Schlesinger explains that "the type of modulation, whether hesitant or in rapid shifts, symbolizes the course of the emotional process."[145] (7). The second mentioned enharmonic aspect is a particularly captivating device to express an ambivalent aspect. By audibly perceiving the "same" sound experience, the chords carry another meaning and therefore fulfill another function[146] (7). The application of enharmonic equivalences can hint to an "illusory identity"[147], to an inner double attitude or nature.

In regard to Schubert's choice of keys in his "late works": Wollenberg[148] cites "commentators" having noted a "penchant" for keys such as C-sharp minor[149] and F-sharp minor[150]. This statement, however, should be further questioned or refuted, since it is possible to find a great number of major tonalities in his later works, such as both piano trios, i.e., the B-flat D 898 and E-flat major D 929, the cantanta "Mirjams Siegesgesang" D 942 in C major, "Auf dem Strom" D 943 in E major, the C major Symphony D 944, the E-flat major mass D 950, the String quintet D 956 in C major, "Die Taubenpost" in G major D 957, the A major D 959 and B-flat major D 960 piano sonatas, "Der Hirt auf dem Felsen" D 965 in the same tonality as the last piano sonata.

---

[144] Dobretsberger, Barbara. Correspondence between Barbara Dobretsberger and the author. Salzburg/Lisbon: December 17, 2021.

[145] Schlesinger, Max. (1967). *Symbolik in der Tonkunst.* P. 48. (Trans. by the author). German expression: „Die Art der Modulation, ob zögernd oder in schnellen Rückungen, symbolisiert den Verlauf des Gefühlsprozesses.".

[146] Cf. Amon, Reinhard. (2005). *Lexikon der Harmonielehre.* P.67.

[147] Friedrich, Siegfried. (2015). *Zu Funktion und Wirkung gradueller Tonhöhenänderungen in Johann Sebastian Bachs "Das Wohltemperiert Klavier" I und II sowie in Franz Schuberts "Die schöne Müllerin"*. P.363. German expression: "Scheinidentität".

[148] Cf. Wollenberg, Susan. (2011). *Schubert's Fingerprints: Studies in the instrumental works.* P.90.

[149] While the tonality of C-sharp minor was described as a "repentance lament", as a sigh or as an "intimate conversation with God" by Schubart, Krause and Böhm rather advocate its death tone or death wish semantic, perceiving death as redemption. Additionally, Böhm finds a relation to the wander and pilgrimage subject. Cf. Böhm, Richard. (2006). *Symbolik und Rhetorik im Liedschaffen von Franz Schubert.* P. 81.

[150] F-sharp minor is, according to Schubart dark in color and conveying "resentment". Krause describes it the "ghostlike" key as the tonality of the laments. After Böhm's comparingly research on key characteristics tied to certain lied-themes, F-sharp minor is linked to the past and to tears. Cf. Ibid. P. 80.

Robert Hatten acknowledges in the "late" Schubert a "[...] more profound spiritual depth [...] mov[ing] from traditional communicative signs to more ineffable symbols of interiority"[151], where the "[...] symbolic takes on mythic dimensions [...]"[152]. Hatten particularly researched about Schubert's use of the instrument reverberations and the use of overtones which, after him, can "[...] capture the 'resonance' of a spiritual association"[153]. Relatedly, Laura Tunbridge, by referring to Ian Bostridge, describes an "emotional immediacy—a direct line between feeling and expression"[154], while Su Yin Mak, by referring to Adorno and Kinderman, speaks of "narratives of an outsider protagonist alienated from external reality"[155].

The abundance of plagal harmonies, already previously cited in reference to Alfred Brendel (11.2), have been noted by further musicologists, such as Xavier Hascher[156]. The increasing major and minor fluctuations, chromaticism and Neapolitan relations are further traits of Schubert's harmonic language[157]. These features are considerably more present in his "later works", in comparison to his "early works". To this list, the increase used of tone repetitions and ambivalent, dissonant chords and intervals might be added, such as diminished 7th chords, augmented 6th chords, 9th chords, the Neapolitan sixth chords, and the use of the tritone interval (*diabolus in musica*)—all of which musically have a semantic connotation on the emotional, creative and psychic level. Schubert consciously or unconsciously appropriates the semantics of these harmonies and of several rhetorical figures, rendering an archetypal and symbolic colour to a certain passage, which can correspond to certain stages in the individuation process, respectively, creative process. These ought to be addressed and revealed in the analysis section only, in connection with the respective passage or musical

---

151 Hatten, Robert: "Schubert's alchemy: transformative surfaces, transfiguring depths". In: Bodley, Lorraine Byrne. Horton, Julian. (2016). *Schubert's Late Music.* P.110.

152 Ibid.

153 Hatten, Robert. (2004). *Interpreting Musical Gestures, Topics, and Tropes.* P. 186.

154 Tunbridge, Laura: "Singing against late style: the problem of performance history". In: Bodley, Lorraine Byrne. Horton, Julian. (2016). *Schubert's Late Music.* P.426. This mentioned aspect might be related to Spaun's above stated statement of Schubert's discontinuing the revision of the works composed.

155 Mak, Su Yin: "Formal ambiguity and generic reinterpretation in the late instrumental music". In: Ibid. P. 282.

156 Hascher, Xavier: "Narrative dislocations in the first movement of Schubert's 'Unfinished' Symphony". In: Bodley, Lorraine Byrne. Horton, Julian. (2016). *Rethinking Schubert.* P. 140.

157 Cf. Brendel, Alfred. (2001). *Ausgerechnet Ich.* P. 163.

example, to avoid many reiterations and above all to respect the individuality of expression of these symbolic elements.

These tone qualities, which are subsequently going to be analyzed, show a development in his creative and individuation process, pointing to the direction of wholeness and the center of the Self (20). Intriguingly, Schumann had already acknowledged this point. He expressed this thought, in his own manner, when he referred to the returning to the center in relation to Schubert's form conception:

> "[…] he gives us a work in the most beautiful form, and in spite of that in a newly devoured way, never straying too far from the center, always returning to it."[158].

[158] Schumann, Robert. (1854). *Gesammelte Schriften über Musik und Musiker.* Vol. 3. P.202. (Trans. by the author). German expression: " […] er gibt uns ein Werk in anmuthvollster Form, und trotz dem in neuverschlungener Weise, nirgends zu weit vom Mittelpunkt wegführend, immer wieder zu ihm zurückkehrend.". Schumann's utterance refers to a "later" composition, namely the C-major Symphony.

Part IV
Analysis

Review of Existing Music Analytical Literature and Presentation of the Method

13

One of the aims of a music analytical endeavor is to look for the meaning of the musical text, with the further objective of uncovering the intentions of the composer and gaining insight into his/her world, and applying the gained knowledge for interpretative purposes. There are several methods that have been applied so far which not only encompass a certain bandwidth within musical analysis itself, but also reach beyond it to models from humanistic-cultural or philological studies. These include *inter alia* hermeneutical, phenomenological or semiotic models[1]. It is also evident that there is an increasing need to draw on interdisciplinary approaches[2]. This dissertation undertakes such an integrative attempt, striving to achieve synergy between the two fields of musicology and Analytical Psychology. Therefore, to master the technical language of each domain is necessary to undertake such an analysis. The aim with this method is to answer the five main research questions that have already been enumerated in the Introduction, and are now to be restated: (i) what are the emerging archetypes and how do they change in their semantics from one work to the other (metamorphoses), (ii)

[1] There is an extensive list of literature on each domain and sub-domain of music analysis, which therefore cannot be covered in this dissertation. For an overview of methods in music analysis see, e.g., Redmann, Bernd. (2002). *Entwurf einer Theorie und Methodologie der Musikanalyse.* Or: Diergarten, Felix. (2014). *Musikalische Analyse.*

[2] As noted, the range of such methods is extensive. Examples include, for instance, approaches linking musicology and linguistics, semiology, semantics, etc., which provide productive results and new insights, e.g., Mihailo Antovič (his field of studies include theories of categorization in cognitive semantics, the study of music and language from an evolutionary standpoint and approaching the connection of musicology with linguistics with regard to the emergent conditioning and spatial cognition), Lawrence Zbikowski (who includes both fields of cognitive linguistics and cognitive psychology), Michael Spitzer (intersection of music with philosophy, psychology, biology and religion).

L. Dill, *Schubert's Metamorphoses*,
https://doi.org/10.1007/978-3-662-73476-6_13

what are the inherent psychological processes and (iii) idiosyncrasies of Schubert's musical language; finally, (iv) how do these archetypal manifestations and psychological processes coincide with specific and important biographical events. The answer to these questions will be presented in 20.

By working with music analysis and Analytical Psychology, two operational levels can be recognized (Figure 13.1). These encompass (i) the knowledge to be gained from an objective-theoretical oriented examination of the musical phenomenon itself, respectively, of Schubert's musical language (first upper half of the illustration). To tackle this task, the author drew on biographical documents, that were already presented in part III., and to existing music analytical literature, which will subsequently be subject to a concise review. The second operational level refers to (ii) the composer's inner spiritual world[3] (second lower half of the illustration). The latter can only be methodologically approached with depth-psychological knowledge and the application of the language and methodological tools of this field—with Jungian methods and the application of C.G. Jung's concepts. The literature review that refers to the first mentioned level will now follow.

Of the scholars whose works were consulted as part of this research, the most cited authors and their analytical methods will be briefly addressed[4]. In more general terms a survey of literature on Schubert's biography, historical background, and aesthetic aspects that is used in the analysis section has already been presented in the corresponding part III: primary sources to this category include Otto Erich Deutsch Collections: *Dokumente seines Lebens* and *Erinnerungen seiner Freunde* and Schubert's musical scores. As for the analytical side—although the author aims to carry out a primary analysis of the five main works in question—the use of secondary literature was particularly important for works or movements that were examined in an introductory manner in each of the main analysis chapters. Drawing on several analytical texts had the advantage of (i) indicating aspects prone to a psychological analytical perspective (ii) substantiating the

[3] Ralf Vogel speaks of the "spiritual inner space". Vogel, Ralf T. (2024). *Das Geheimnis der Seele.* Sect. 3.5. "Die Tiefenpsychologische Perspektive—Imaginology". (Trans. by the author). German expression: "Seeleninnenraum".

[4] Since the analytical literature is vast, the literature review presented here is in respect to the scholarly works used for the analytical section of this dissertation. For further literature regarding Schubert and music analytical literature see the discussion lines in Part III with the respective footnote references or the bibliographic list. For the category in respect to Jungian literature used in the analysis chapters, an overview was already given in Part 3.1. Mostly the author reached to Jung's own writings, the works of Jung's disciples such as Jolande Jacobi or Erich Neumann and to current scholarly Jungian literature such as from Christian Roesler, Verena Kast, Ralf Vogel, and others.

author's psychological interpretation and lastly (iii) gaining an overview of analytical methods used. In doing so, the author concentrated primarily on relevant literature to be found within the Schubert Research Community, with the major compendiums of Walther Dürr and Andreas Krause's edition of *Schubert Handbuch*[5], Christopher Gibb's edition of *The Cambridge Companion to Schubert*[6], Lorraine Byrne Bodley and Julian Horton's edition of *Rethinking Schubert*[7], as well as individual works such as Susan Wollenberg's *Schubert's Fingerprints*[8], and Brigitte Massin's book entitled *Franz Schubert*[9]. These sources deal not only with the first category mentioned (historical and biographical elements) but also offer an overview of the variety of analytical approaches to several of Schubert's works.

From the mentioned literature, and especially in respect to the performed song analysis, a particular attention was given to Marie-Agnes Dittrich's analytical contributions in *Schubert Handbuch* „Die Lieder. 'Für Menschenohren sind es Harmonien'"[10]. Apart from the introduction laying out the steppingstones for the main analytical aspects with which Dittrich later works (e.g., the role of piano part in lieder, components of Schubert's music such as rhythm, melody, harmony, compositional technique and key characteristic, or recurring themes, such as the death theme, etc.), the implemented analysis by Dittrich highlights the interconnection between textual and the musical levels, emphasizing the word-tone relationship, key characteristics, tonal and formal structural concerns. From the second cited compendium, Martin Chusid's contribution "Schubert's chamber music: before and after Beethoven"[11] is characterized by a comparative analytical approach[12] and includes observations on the formal aspects of works around the alleged "years of crisis" (1818–1824).

---

[5] Dürr, Walther. Krause, Andreas. (2020). *Schubert Handbuch.*

[6] Gibbs, Christopher. (1997). *The Cambridge Companion to Schubert.*

[7] Bodley, Lorraine Byrne., Horton, Julia. (2016). *Rethinking Schubert.*

[8] Wollenberg, Susan. (2011). *Schubert's Fingerprints: Studies in the Instrumental Works.*

[9] Massin, Brigitte. (1977). *Franz Schubert.*

[10] Dittrich, Marie-Agnes. „Die Lieder ‚Für Menschenohren sind es Harmonien'". In: Dürr, Walther. Krause, Andreas. (2020). *Schubert Handbuch.*

[11] Chusid, Martin. "Schubert's chamber music: before and after Beethoven". In: Gibbs, Christopher. (1997). *The Cambridge Companion to Schubert.*

[12] Chusid addressed motivic interchanges within Schubert's own works, e.g., the material of the G-sharp minor Ländler D 790, nr.6 (mm.1–8) and the opening material of Scherzo from the D minor string quartet D 810, but also punctually with works of Beethoven. Cf. Ibid.

While Chusid addressed formal aspects of Schubert's music in relation to Beethoven's, Bodley's and Horton's edition, *Rethinking Schubert*, features discussion lines around the "late style" and its characteristics. These considerations have been useful for this dissertation since a stylistic shift after 1824, respectively, 1825 is confirmed notably by Hans-Joachim Hinrichsen[13] and by Cameron Gardner[14]. In addition, Leo Platinga's contribution "Schubert, Social Music and Melancholy"[15] to this compendium, contextualizing Schubert's works in his environment and highlighting the importance of the dance in Schubert's more "elevated genres"[16], invited to a Jungian psychological reading of this phenomenon, e.g., the ländler rhythm in Schubert's *Andantino* of the A major piano sonata D 959 (17).

Susan Wollenberg's diversified approach in *Schuberts Fingerprints*[17] points to distinct elements that make up Schubert's idiosyncratic language, addressing not only formal concerns (e.g., Schubert transitional procedures notably in sonata form, threefold constructions, "poetic transitions") but also covering harmonic ones (e.g., minor-major brightening, the tonal colour of the Neapolitan minor and its importance in the coda section of the D minor string quartet D 810). Furthermore, Wollenberg drew analogies, which were prone to Jungian application, e.g., the mentioned parallels between the transition from the B-section to the A'-section of the A major's *Andantino* (D 959) with Gluck's opera *Orfeo* and the chorus of furies (17). Besides analytical thoughts of a more personal nature, Wollenberg refers to other authors, which permitted gaining an overview of several analytical concepts. Brigitte Massin's book *Franz Schubert*[18], still considered a reference despite the older date of publication, is marked by biographical contextualization and an analysis synthesizing a great amount of works in several genres. Massin's overview alludes to numerous interconnections of works and motivic material between instrumental works and songs, for instance. Her explanations, coming from a formal analysis approach, allows the reader to concentrate on the above-mentioned motivic interchanges.

---

[13] Hinrichsen, Hans-Joachim. "Is there a late style in Schubert's Œuvre?". In: Bodley, Lorraine Byrne. Horton, Julia. (2016). *Rethinking Schubert.*

[14] Gardner, Cameron. "(Re-)Theorising Schubert's 'Reliquie': Precedents, the 'Great' Symphony, and Narrative". In: Ibid.

[15] Platinga, Leo. "Schubert, Social Music and Melancholy". In: Ibid.

[16] Ibid. P. 240.

[17] Wollenberg, Susan. (2011). *Schubert's Fingerprints: Studies in the Instrumental Works.*

[18] Massin, Brigitte. (1977). *Franz Schubert.*

In addition to the above-mentioned literature, authors with more specific methodological approaches or interpretations were consulted. These include Arthur Godel's *Schuberts letzte drei Klaviersonaten*[19] and Arnold Feil's *Franz Schubert Die Schöne Müllerin—Winterreise*[20]. Both of them have remained a reference up until today, featuring constructive perspectives on different levels. Arthur Godel's mediation of Schubert as an artist of transformation[21], his comparison of Schubert's music to a life process[22], as well as his acknowledgment of Schubert's creative spontaneity[23], *inter alia,* was particularly inspiring for the author and supports her hypothesis. It concerns specifically the hypothesis (i) of a psychic transformational process occurring during the creative act (the individuation process), as well as (ii) of the impact of archetypal structures on Schubert during the creative process. In relation to the last point, for instance, Godel identifies an idiosyncratic way of working, which can certainly be viewed from a Jungian perspective:

> "He creates coherence and context not through consistent deduction and final alignment, but through associative linking and reminiscent circling. The association follows a kind of 'dream logic'. It abandons itself to the unpredictable consequences of the images generated by the stream of mental processes. They develop a life of their own, a momentum of their own, in which the subject has to follow without volition. Moments stretch into eternities."[24].

Particularly important in this regard was Godel's identification of the "motif-metamorphose technique"[25] as a means of Schubert to create cyclical unity,

---

[19] Godel, Arthur. (1985). *Schuberts letzte drei Klaviersonaten (D958—960).*

[20] Feil, Arnold. (1996). *Franz Schubert.*

[21] Godel, Arthur. (1985). *Schuberts letzte drei Klaviersonaten (D958—960).*

[22] Ibid. P. 256. This life process is characterized of being „temporary, changeable and transient": Ibid. (Trans. by the author). German expression: "Schuberts Musik ist wie der Lebensprozess: vorläufig, veränderlich, vergänglich.".

[23] Cf. Ibid. P. 41.

[24] Ibid. P. 238. (Trans. by the author). German expression: "Er schafft Stimmigkeit und Zusammenhang nicht durch konsequente Deduktion und finale Ausrichtung, sondern durch assoziatives Verknüpfen und erinnerndes Umkreisen. Die Assoziation folgt einer Art ‚Traumlogik'. Sie überlässt sich der unvorhersehbare Folgen der Bilder, die von dem Strom psychischer Prozesse erzeugt werden. Sie entwickeln ein Eigenleben, eine Eigendynamik, bei der das Subjekt willenlos zu folgen hat. Augenblicke dehnen sich zu Ewigkeiten.".

[25] Ibid. *Inter alia*, P. 19–20.

whereby the motif is prone to constant transformations. In addition, Godel's allocation of the Atlas motif[26] as one unifying rhythmical element across the piano trilogy prompted the author to create a mythical analogy with the Atlas myth and his daughters, the Hesperides (18). Apart from these specificities, Godel not only discussed the formal and tonal structure of each movement, both in text and through visual representations, but above all laid out a comparative analysis between Schubert's first draft of the piano sonatas and the definite version, both of which were helpful to delineate particularities of the creative process. Arnold Feil's rhythmic studies on *Die Schöne Müllerin* have also incited a Jungian interpretation of certain passages, which substantiates the reading presented in 15.

In terms of specific approaches, the author includes Gernot Gruber's more recent considerations of a more philosophical nature in *Schubert. Schubert?*[27]:

> "'Utopias', the 'nothingness' or the principle of the 'antithetic' thus become potential fields of identification that can determine both artistic interpretation and scientific exegesis."[28].

Gruber's deliberations encouraged further reflection on these themes from a Jungian viewpoint, which especially found echo in the examination of the *Andantino* from the A major piano sonata (17). In the first part of his book Gruber lays the biographical foundation upon which he subsequently operates.

Coming from a background in formal analysis, and as a musicologist who is also proficient in German philology, Barbara Dobretsberger offers an analysis of the song "Die Forelle" in her music analysis handbook *Formenlehre der Vokalmusik*[29], placing Schubart's poem in its historical and political context and linking it to Schubert's own comparable reality. Beyond addressing several specific and detailed technical elements both concerning text and music, her approach gave light to a differentiated analytical interpretation of such a popular song, which was thought-provoking for the analysis of the *Forellenquintett,* encouraging the establishment of psychological parallels (14). In addition, Dobretsberger's textbook points out the historical origins of musical elements, providing a basis on which symbolic meanings in musical forms can subsequently be discerned.

---

[26] Cf. Ibid. P. 27–28.

[27] Gruber, Gernot. (2010). *Schubert. Schubert?*

[28] Ibid. P. 261. (Trans. by the author). German expression: „'Utopien', das 'Nichts' oder das Prinzip der 'Antithetik' werden so zu potenziellen Feldern der Identifikation, die die künstlerische Interpretation wie die wissenschaftliche Exegetik bestimmen können.".

[29] Dobretsberger, Barbara. (2019). *Formen der Vokalmusik.*

For the specific analysis of key characteristics in Schubert's œuvre, Richard Böhm's *Symbolik und Rhetorik im Liedschaffen von Franz Schubert*[30] permitted approaching and deciphering the symbolic aspect of his music. Böhm not only gives a historic overview on the topic of musical rhetorics and key characteristics but his book also contains reasoning as to a methodology of investigation in this field. His core research on the creation of song databases and their juxtaposition with ancient studies in key characteristics (e.g., Christian Friedrich Daniel Schubart's *Ideen zu einer Ästhetik der Tonkunst*) are to be highlighted. The fact that Böhm based his research on the lied repertoire to attribute to each key its own characteristics, has the advantage that (i) it is tailored to Schubert's œuvre and (ii) the meaning of the key is directly tied to the word semantics inherent in the song's poetic source, which lends more credibility to the problematics of key characteristics. In more general terms, but still in regard to symbolic contents of music, Max Schlesinger's *Symbolik in der Tonkunst*[31] was equally relevant for the psychological and symbolic reading of musical elements such as rhythm, melody, dynamics or modulation processes.

Further secondary sources that have been consulted and occasionally used in this analysis section included *Schubert Liedlexikon*[32] (edited by Walther Dürr and Michael Kube), Reinhard Amon's *Lexikon der Harmonielehre*[33], Clemens Kühn's *Analyse lernen*[34] and Heinz Acker's *Modulationslehre*[35]. As for the specific field of music as a language, the classic *Handbuch der musikalischen Figurenlehre*[36] by Dietrich Bartel or Hartmut Krones' *MGG Article* "Musik und Rhetorik"[37] on musical rhetorical figures were essential to identify the rhetorical figures in Schubert's music and attribute the respective term or description.

In addition to the selected scholarly literature, a further concern was to bring the fields of musicology and interpretation closer together, by juxtaposing analytical observations of interpreters (or their performances) with those of musicologists. With this motivation, the author hopes to emphasize the importance of increasing collaboration between scholars, musicologists and performers. The

[30] Böhm, Richard. (2006). *Symbolik und Rhetorik im Liedschaffen von Franz Schubert.*

[31] Schlesinger, Max. (1967). *Symbolik in der Tonkunst.*

[32] Dürr, Walther., Kube, Michael. [et al.]. (2013). *Schubert Liedlexikon.*

[33] Amon, Reinhard. (2005). *Lexikon der Harmonielehre.*

[34] Kühn, Clemens. (2005). *Analyse lernen.*

[35] Acker, Heinz. (2009). *Modulationslehre.*

[36] Bartel, Dietrich. (2010). *Handbuch der musikalischen Figurenlehre.*

[37] Krones, Hartmut. "Musik und Rhetorik". (2016). In: Laurenz Lütteken (Ed.). *MGG Online.*

analytical contributions from Alfred Brendel deserve special mention. In *Musik beim Wort genommen*[38], Brendel carried out a philosophically oriented analysis of the three last piano sonatas, understanding them through the Hegelian perspective of thesis-antithesis-synthesis. Alban Berg Quartet's interpretation of the D minor string quartet D 810[39], or Christian Zacharias Lecture-Recital on Schubert[40], were also considered. The latter pointed in particular to the important meaning of Schubert's *circulatio* gesture, which was a vital discovery for the entire psychological interpretation of Schubert's individuation process.

Moving from the general to the specific, it is now important to address the analytical concepts that present a similar connection between psychology and Schubert's music. Subsequently, the main methodological differences with these perspectives will be pointed out, emphasizing the particular elements that make the Jungian view of an artistic (or musical) work special. Lastly, the methodological process as illustrated in Fig. 13.1 will be briefly explained.

Especially since the last century, there is a growing interest in the more obscure side of Schubert's œuvre, which is a natural reaction to the long-preserved unilateral image of Schubert being a lyrical and melancholic composer. Such interest impacted not only musicologists but also interpreters[41] and led to several scholarly texts, in which the personality of the composer is thematically addressed, entering thereby the domain of psychology. In general, several sources were found in which musicologists either connected a musical phenomenon to a personality trait of Schubert's or applied clinical terms to diagnose psychic conditions. Such interpretations can be read, for example, in Hugh MacDonald's "Schubert's volcanic temper"[42], Elizabeth McKay's "Two natures" in *Franz Schubert*[43], David Ferris' "Dissociation and Declamation in Schubert's Heine

[38] Brendel, Alfred. (1996). *Musik beim Wort genommen.*

[39] Monsaingeon, Bruno. *The Alban Berg Documentary.* (1996). [Documentary/Masterclass].

[40] Zacharias, Christian. (2019). *Why does Schubert sound like Schubert?* [Lecture-Recital]. Stagecast Ltd (Production).

[41] One example of an interpreter who advocates for the dark, chaotic or irrational side of Schubert is Alfred Brendel. In one of his writings Brendel compared, for instance, the middle section of Schubert's *Andantino* of the A major piano sonata D 959 with the paintings from the dark period of Francisco Goya (10, 17). Cf. Brendel, Alfred. (1989). "Schubert's last three piano sonatas". In: *RSA Journal, Vol. 137, No. 5395*, P. 401–411.

[42] MacDonald, Hugh. (1978). "Schubert's volcanic temper". In: *Musical Times. Vol. 119, No.1629.* P. 949–952.

[43] McKay, Elizabeth Norman. (2001). *Franz Schubert: A Biography.*

songs" in *Rethinking Schubert*[44], Susan Wollenberg's "Schubert's violent nature" in *Schubert Fingerprints*[45] or Giuseppina La Face Bianconi's *Das Haus des Müllers*[46].

In Ferris' contribution, the doppelganger phenomenon in Heine's setting "Der Doppelgänger" D 957 is explained as a reflection of a psychological disorder (narcissism) and to Freud's idea of the "uncanny"[47]. From a further point of view and influenced by Elizabeth McKay's hypothesis, Susan Wollenberg reached to the term of "bipolar condition"[48] when speaking of Schubert's personality in a music analytical context. Giuseppina La Face Bianconi continued a similar line of research in her book *Das Haus des Müllers*[49], although featuring a more specific analytical approach and focusing on the lied cycle *Die Schöne Müllerin.* Bianconi understands the song cycle as a "depiction of a psychological process in the form of a sung monodrama"[50]. Yet, the hermeneutic method of Bianconi is rather marked by the use of music analytical observations[51], with a focus on music psychology field[52], which she then linked to the application of concepts from the fields of phenomenological Psychopathology[53]. Her reading reflects a Freudian view, and close links to cognitive musicology[54]. In the last part, Bianconi establishes direct parallels with Schubert's "own experiences with psychic

[44] Ferris, David. (2016). "Dissociation and Declamation in Schubert's Heine songs". In: Bodley, Lorraine Byrne. Horton, Julia. (2016). *Rethinking Schubert.*

[45] Wollenberg, Susan. (2011). *Schubert's Fingerprints: Studies in the Instrumental Works.* Chap. 6: "Schubert's violent nature".

[46] Bianconi La Face, Giuseppina. (2013). *Das Haus des Müllers.*

[47] Ferris, David. (2016). "Dissociation and Declamation in Schubert's Heine songs". In: Bodley, Lorraine Byrne. Horton, Julia. (2016). *Rethinking Schubert.* P. 383.

[48] Wollenberg, Susan. (2011). *Schubert's Fingerprints: Studies in the Instrumental Works.* Chap. 6: "Schubert's violent nature". P. 161–162.

[49] Bianconi La Face, Giuseppina. (2013). *Das Haus des Müllers.*

[50] Ibid. P. 31. German expression: "In der vorliegenden Abhandlung befasse ich mich mit der *Schönen Müllerin* jedoch […] in der Form eines gesungenen Monodramas gefassten Schilderung eines psychischen Prozesses.".

[51] For the music analytical observations, Bianconi especially relied on the interpretations of Thrasybulos Georgiades, Arnold Feil, Hans Heinrich Eggebrecht and Susan Youens. Cf. Ibid. "Vorwort".

[52] In this field, Bianconi particularly highlights models from Irène Deliège. Cf. Ibid. "Vorwort".

[53] Cf. Ibid. "Vorwort".

[54] Cf. Polzonetti, Pierpaolo. "La Casa Del Mugnaio: Ascolto e Interpretazione Della Schone Mullerin: Com l'edizione Del Ciclo Liederistico Secondo la Neue Ausgabe Schubert-Ausgabe.". [Review]. In: *Music Library Association, Notes, vol.62, no.1.* (2005). P. 130–33.

difficulties and specially with the problem of depression"[55]. Even if Bianconi expresses her non-intention to arrive at a medical diagnosis, her vocabulary and application of concepts specific to psychopathology convey a divergent picture—as such, Bianconi's overall hypothesis relies on understanding the song cycle as a "depression, which […] develops into a psychosis and leads to suicide"[56] and on Schubert's apparent intention to draw a "psychopathological image by means of his music"[57]. Consequently, the musicologist looks out for "indications and symptoms"[58]. This approach, however, rather contradicts her defensive statement regarding her primary aim.

Although these studies also contain other compelling considerations[59], the specific pathological conclusions mentioned are often derived from potentially premature borrowings of terms from clinical psychology. In addition, there seems to be the prejudice about the need to understand the "volcanic" eruptions in Schubert's music as representative of Schubert himself as a person[60], or even

[55] Bianconi La Face, Giuseppina. (2013). *Das Haus des Müllers.* P. 32. German expression: "[…] Schuberts direkte persönliche Erfahrung mit psychischen Schwierigkeiten und speziell mit dem Problem der Depression […]".

[56] Ibid. P. 32. German expression: "Mit ihrer Hilfe stellt Schubert in der *Schönen Müllerin* eine Depression dar—die Depression des Müllers, die sich im Hin und Her zwischen melancholischer Bedrückung und euphorischer Verzückung zu einer Psychose entwickelt und in den Selbstmord mündet.". *De facto*, the mentioned musicologists used the following keywords throughout her book: clinical picture, depression, narcissism (e.g., Ibid, p. 82 or p. 112), masochistic (Ibid, p. 66). Polzonetti accounted for further keywords such as: compulsion, autistic closer, and bipolar. Cf. Polzonetti, Pierpaolo. "La Casa Del Mugnaio: Ascolto e Interpretazione Della Schone Mullerin: Com l'edizione Del Ciclo Liederistico Secondo la Neue Ausgabe Schubert-Ausgabe.". [Review]. In: *Music Library Association, Notes, vol.62, no.1.* (2005). P. 130–33.

[57] Cf. Bianconi La Face, Giuseppina. (2013). *Das Haus des Müllers.* P. 49. (Trans. by the author). German expression: "[…] dass Schubert hier mit musikalischen Mitteln ein psychopathologisches Bild entworfen hat, […]".

[58] Ibid. German expression: "Indizien und Symptomen".

[59] For instance, David Ferris' development and application of Edward T. Cone's reflections on the important psychological role of the piano in Schubert's songs should be considered in this regard. Equally to mention is Ferris' specific approach relating tonal structures and phrase rhythm, suggesting what the author understands—to speak in Jungian terms—as moments of synchronicity between the musical events and inner processes: "[…] the most dramatic change in declamation corresponds to the most unusual moment in the tonal form, the arrival of the raised mediant, and thus to the moment of psychological dissociation depicted in the poem.". Ferris, David. (2016). "Dissociation and Declamation in Schubert's Heine songs". In: Bodley, Lorraine Byrne. Horton, Julia. (2016). *Rethinking Schubert.* P. 392.

[60] Cf. MacDonald, Hugh. (1978). "Schubert's volcanic temper". In: *Musical Times. Vol. 119, No.1629.* P. 949–952.

related to his physical illness[61], instead of clearly separating the composer from the "creative process that moves him"[62]. Turning to C.G. Jung's conception of the psyche (being antagonistically structured) and specifically to the archetypal theory allows for the explanation of the musical phenomenon in question (e.g., the volcanic eruptions) without the need (as a musicologist) to draw on any medical terms or attribute a pathological condition to Schubert.

As just suggested, all of the above-mentioned interpretations greatly differ from the Jungian method of examining a work of art. For instance, the analytical approaches of La Face Bianconi contrasts quite drastically from a Jungian perspective[63], not only in the way biographical facts are used and how to approach a symbol, but also in the overall ideology. In Freudian terms the symbol is rather synonymously used as a sign or a symptom[64]. The reading of the mirror symbolism in "Thränenregen" is an instructive example of how the author's and Bianconi's interpretations diverge. Bianconi comprehends this symbol as a symptom of a pathological condition, referring to the miller-lad's narcissistic side[65]. In contrast, in Jungian psychology, the mirror is understood as a symbol of insight[66], which leads to a completely different interpretative outcome[67] (15).

Unlike Bianconi, for whom a pathological reading is in the foreground, the Jungian perspective advocates a world view based mainly on the concept of the

61 Such an approach can be read in: Youens, Susan. (1997). *Schubert, Müller, and "Die Schöne Müllerin"*. Her final interpretative considerations in "Lilies that fester" resulted primarily from her reading of the mill as "places of transformations, both spiritual and erotic", albeit the emphasis is put by Youens on the latter aspect.

62 Jung, Carl Gustav. (2014). "Spirit in Man, Art and Literature". In: *The Collected Works of C.G. Jung. Vol. 15.* (Trans. by Gerhard Adler and R.F.C. Hull). Chapter: "On the relation of analytical psychology to poetry". Paragraph 112.

63 It must be acknowledged that, despite the different approaches and interpretations, Bianconi and the author herself have come to identify three similar psychological phenomena: Bianconi also identified a disavowal in "Mein!" (cf. Bianconi La Face, Giuseppina. (2013). *Das Haus des Müllers.* P. 64 and P. 80), a psychic regression (cf. Ibid. P. 93) and also associated the last song with the mother womb (Cf. Ibid. P. 115).

64 Cf. Jung, Carl Gustav. (2014). "Spirit in Man, Art and Literature". In: *The Collected Works of C.G. Jung. Vol. 15.* (Trans. by Gerhard Adler and R.F.C. Hull). Chapter: "On the relation of analytical psychology to poetry". Paragraph 105.

65 Cf. Bianconi La Face, Giuseppina. (2013). *Das Haus des Müllers.* P. 115.

66 Cf. Mollwo-Oesterreicher, Marianne. (1978). *Herder Lexikon Symbole.* P. 158.

67 Similar observations regarding discrepancies between a Freudian or a Jungian analysis of a symbol and of a work of art have been revealed by Jung's disciple Erich Neumann. Cf. Neumann, Erich. (2004). *Kunst und schöpferisches Unbewusstes.*

soul[68], which emphasizes the importance of analyzing the work of art solely for the creative process itself:

> "Only that aspect of art which consists in the process of artistic creation can be a subject for psychological study [...]"[69].

> "In order to do justice to a work of art, analytical psychology must rid itself entirely of medical prejudice; for a work of art is not a disease, and consequently requires a different approach from the medical one."[70].

In this case, it is not the composer "Schubert" who is at work. It is a higher instance within him. This thought refers to the unique character of Jungian psychology, that has been previously clarified (I). It is necessary to elucidate beforehand, that due to this reason, all the processes and terminologies that will be used in the subsequent analysis chapters are to be exclusively understood in these terms: to describe psychological processes symbolically in a composition does not equal to attribute a pathological condition to the composer—nor are the terminologies applied to inherit such a function in forthcoming research. When operating with the two fields, it was a necessity in the methodological process to make use of the language and terms of Analytical Psychology. This step was essential in order to analyze the psychic processes during the creative act and to support the analogies elaborated. Apart from the literature sources mentioned above, to best of the author's knowledge (issued from a vast literature review), there is no other analytical literature on Schubert that feature the methodological approach used by the author (Fig. 13.1)[71]. The following paragraphs will elucidate the methodological procedure illustrated in Fig. 13.1.

---

[68] Cf. Vogel, Ralf T. (2024). *Das Geheimnis der Seele.*

[69] Jung, Carl Gustav. (2014). "Spirit in Man, Art and Literature". In: *The Collected Works of C.G. Jung. Vol. 15.* (Trans. by Gerhard Adler and R.F.C. Hull). Chapter: "On the relation of analytical psychology to poetry". Paragraph 97.

[70] Ibid. Paragraph 107.

[71] As was mentioned previously, Jung himself left publications on his analysis of works of art and literature, however, he did not deal with music. In addition, his above cited scriptures permitted the author to discern how such an analysis should be approached and what the critical points are when applying a psychological interpretation to a work of art. For the work mentioned by C.G. Jung see: Ibid. Going beyond Schubert's repertoire, the book of Jörg Rasche addresses the psychological processes underlying works of Bach, Beethoven, Schumann and Chopin, applying the alchemical model for his musical interpretation. Cf. Rasche, Jörg. (2014). *Das Lied des Grünen Löwen.*

The composer's world is made of several elements which have a direct impact on the composition (opus). These elements consist of the (i) the aesthetic characteristics of Schubert's zeitgeist, (ii) the historical-political and cultural context (collective), (iii) biographical leitmotifs, events and facts (personal) which include religious orientation, ideologies, etc., and ultimately (iv) the inner spiritual world, which consists of the personal and the collective unconscious. For the unveiling of these elements, the above-mentioned primary sources such as correspondences of Schubert himself and contributions of Schubert's friends played an important role not only for the biographical-historical questions but especially to gain insight into the inner world of Schubert[72]. Particular attention was given to Schubert's dream report[73] (11.2, 19) and several of Schubert's correspondences (e.g., 16 or 17).

As stated above, these aspects constitute the musical language of the composer, which can be objectively analysed. Thus, the musical phenomenon is examined analytically using several tools of music analysis. These include formal analysis, motivic and harmonic analysis, identification of figurative contents such as musical rhetoric figures, madrigalisms, topoi, key characteristics, etc., as well as taking into consideration the circumstances of creation (genesis) of the composition in question, which is then seen again within the context of the biographical and historical background. To address the unconscious realm, the application of Jungian concepts—especially from the archetypal theory—and Jungian methods are essential. These include the application of the amplification method previously described (2.6). In practice, the analysis process unfolds as follows: once the musical motifs and symbolic content have been identified, they are attributed with epitomes, which are then linked to the corresponding Jungian terms or concepts (archetypal structures and/or psychic processes).

As music is the art of expression of ambivalent/polyvalent emotions perceivable primarily intuitively—due to the resonance mechanism (7)—and by the sense of hearing, the analysis without the score plays also an important role in the

[72] As Eugen Drewermann stated, every utterance of a person reveals unconscious states or feelings. Several of Drewermann's *Sommervorlesungen 2023* refer to this idea: Cf. Drewermann, Eugen. (2023). „Sommervorlesung 2023: Märchen zeigen den Weg zur Liebe, wo Sehnsucht Realität wird". [Lecture]. The author thus understands the importance of the biographical and historical events as catalysators, i.e., as outer objects or events that activate, on the basis of a resonance-mechanism, an inner archetype. In this sense these aspects do influence creative work.

[73] Schubert, Franz: „Allegorische Erzählung von Schubert—‚Mein Traum'". 1822. In: Deutsch, Otto Erich. (1964). *Schubert—Die Dokumente seines Lebens*. P. 158–159.

unveiling process of the "un-known" realm. This type of aurally based analysis—which is also a common approach in music analysis—is then assisted with the Jungian method of active imagination performed by the author herself. In order to gain a more objective outcome, the findings resulting from the latter process are always to be verified with the above-mentioned means of an impartial music analysis. Through this approach, the analyst arrives at a possible interpretation of meaning, which is carried out as objectively as possible by substantiating it with (i) the musical facts and (ii) through analogies of the psychic processes to be found reported in Jungian technical literature. Despite its systematic nature, this approach entails a continuous exchange of information during the process of gaining insight into the archetypal content, psychic processes and the musical language of the composer[74]. It is also important to bear in mind that, when coming close to hermeneutic approaches, the conclusions presented should rather be understood as substantiated interpretation possibilities.

With this description, it becomes clear how this method represents a sharp counterpoint to previous music psychological approaches mentioned in the literature review. Using the theory of the archetypes in a music analytical context represents a new attempt to get to the heart of Schubert's music itself on the one hand and to unravel the composer's creative process on the other. Ultimately, this means a new approach in music understanding. The findings gained from this method not only generate new knowledge in regard to the music of Schubert and his creative or individuation process[75], but also greatly impacts interpretation and performance. The latter, in turn, has a direct effect on the listening and perception process—which may bring about a numinous experience of transformational nature since the vehicle of the emotional expression lies in the archetypal structures that are being particularly emphasized in such an informed performance practice. This statement relates to the last aspect illustrated in Fig. 13.1 which has to do with a temporal aspect: the analyst or the listener, is transported back to past aesthetics but at the same time is affected by an atemporal element, which

[74] In addition, the analysis chapters have shown several times how an over-systematization can sometimes be deceptive or even misleading as far as the symbolic content of the music is concerned.

[75] Although this method allows for an approach shedding light on new aspects in Schubert's music and creative process, the respect towards the primordial "I" of the composer prohibits the author from adopting any apodictic tone or attitude. For this reason, the author sought cautious formulations or even occasionally opted to leave some questions open, where it was considered necessary (e.g., 16).

is present due to the archetypes and which comprehends the emotional unifying structures between composer-interpreter/analyst-listener: "For only in the archetypes and in the emotions lies the unifying and connecting element [...]"[76].

Given Schubert's prolific nature as a composer, it is impossible to include the entirety of his œuvre within the scope of this dissertation. For this reason, particular compositions were chosen, which, in the author's understanding, may better reveal psychological turning points. A choice with regard to the time span was equally necessary, establishing eventually the period of time covering the years 1814–1828. The reason why the author did not begin with earlier works lies in the fact that 1814 marked the year of Schubert's independence (Schubert had left the city college and begun working at his father's school). Psychologically, this was an important step in his own development, which can also be observed on a musical level in the composition "Gretchen am Spinnrade" (1814)—a moment revealing a synchronicity. This lied especially marks Schubert's self-awareness revealing a particular idiosyncratic language, which explains the reason why the author did not choose 1816 (the year in which Schubert actually stopped taking lessons from Salieri). Each of the five chosen compositions *Forellenquintett* D 667, *Die Schöne Müllerin* D 795, the string quartet *Der Tod und das Mädchen* D 810, and the second movements of the piano sonatas A major D 959 and B-flat major 960 will be first analyzed individually with the respective interrelated songs. An analytical supplement featuring the *Wandererfantasie* D 760 and the Piano Trio in E-flat major D 920 will complement the analytical findings with two important archetypes, the wanderer and the "Dümmling". The concluding chapter of part IV features then a summary of the analytical interpretations, in which gathered musical and psychological information are overlapped and correlated, enabling an overview on the individuation process (20). The last chapter will also feature the author's reflections on areas for future research.

[76] Drewermann, Eugen. (1991). *Tiefenpsychologie und Exegese. Band I.* P. 71.

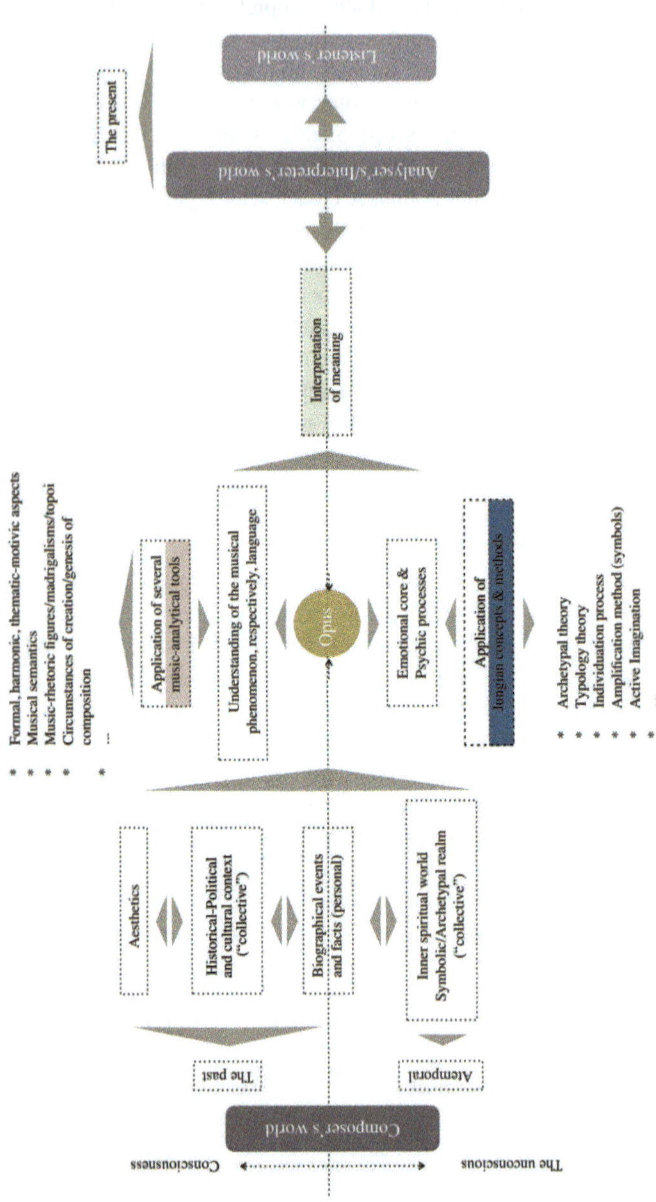

Fig. 13.1 Outline of an integrated approach based on the theory of the archetypes and music analytical tools for a new understanding of music

Forellenquintett D 667: The Theriomorphic and Anthropomorphic Manifestation of the Self and the "Enlargement of the Personality"

14

Before composing the *Forellenquintett* D 667, Schubert had set the poem "Die Forelle" by Christian Friedrich Daniel Schubart to music several times. Taking into consideration the circumstances of Schubart's environment and his own political engagement—which, in some measure, were comparable to Schubert's background—this poem was recently recognized as bearing a political statement[1], criticizing the absolutist, respectively, the censorship regime that had once ruled. Observed from a psychological perspective, such regimes have an effect on society and consequently give rise to mental conflicts that impact the Self. Such themes include C.G. Jung's often discussed Persona-shadow dialectic. According to his concept, the Persona aspect of the ego (mask) may become overdeveloped, especially when it is strongly influenced by or embedded in a society with strict rules of conduct[2]. Since the psyche is structured in a relationship of tension between the opposites, this historical fact can thus have immediate consequences on the unconscious, which under certain circumstances can lead the shadow to

[1] Cf. Dobretsberger, Barbara. (2019). *Formen der Vokalmusik.* Sect. 5.5.3.: "Liedanalyse am Beispiel von Schuberts ‚Die Forelle' D 550". See also: Cf. Schick, Hartmut. (2007). "Christian Friedrich Daniel Schubart: Der Dichter-Musiker, Nördlingen und Wallerstein". In: *Rosetti-Forum. Mitteilungen der Internationalen Rosetti-Gesellschaft.* Nr. 8. P. 15–26.

[2] Cf. Jung, Carl Gustav. (2023). *Die Beziehung zwischen dem Ich und dem Unbewussten.*

Jung, Carl Gustav. (2011). *Four Archetypes.* (Trans. by R.F.C. Hull). P. 54. The music analytical and psychological findings developed in this chapter were presented by the author herself in public for the first time under the title "Franz Schubert: Das *Forellenquintett* D 667. 'Musikalische Lyrik' in der Instrumentalmusik. Eine Analyse aus einer Tiefenpsychologische Sicht" in the form of a one-and-a-half hour and slide-assisted lecture in the frame of a music analysis seminar at the University Mozarteum, Salzburg (November 23, 2023), under the supervision of Barbara Dobretsberger.

L. Dill, *Schubert's Metamorphoses*,
https://doi.org/10.1007/978-3-662-73476-6_14

take the upper hand, causing an inflation[3]. As part of a transformation these processes can possibly lead to an "enlargement of the personality"[4]. For these reasons, musical analysis pointing to the connections with the historical-political context can bring some insights for psychological interpretation.

The lied "Die Forelle" D 550 was particularly well received among Schubert's circle of friends and became a popular song[5]. Amidst the admirers of Schubert's song was the music patron and amateur cellist Sylvester Paumgartner, who gave Schubert the special assignment of integrating the song into his chamber music composition—the piano quintet D 667. So doing, the work has not four but five movements, in which the variation movement featuring the song's thematic material corresponds to the fourth movement. However, this is not the only particularity of this work. While piano quintets were amongst the traditional genres during Schubert's time, the instrumentation usually featured a common string quartet plus piano, whilst here a contrabass is added. Such peculiarities that strikingly stand out from the common particularly stimulate reflection. Musicologists thus seek explanations by e.g., searching for possible paragons. One hypothesis that is often mentioned in literature, and that originated from a statement by Schubert's friend Stadler, consists of seeing Hummel's septet op. 74 (published in 1816) and/or his piano quintet op. 87 (composed in 1802 and published in 1821) as models[6]. Hummel was then considered a celebrity, and his works were regularly performed. Therefore, the counter argument from Brigitte Massin that the 1802 composed work had a posterior publishing date (1821) in relation to the genesis of Schubert's piano quintet[7] (1819) is not entirely infallible. Massin suggested looking for further explanations in the ancient Italian traditions of *musica da camera* or to understand this choice in relation to Paumgartner's

[3] Cf. Ibid. Jacobi also deals with the contrast structure of the psyche in: Jacobi, Jolande. (2006). *Die Psychologie von C.G. Jung*. P. 58–60.

[4] Jung, Carl Gustav. (2011). *Four Archetypes*. (Trans. by R.F.C. Hull). P. 54.

[5] Several comments from Schubert's friends can attest this statement, e.g., Stadler, Albert (1858). In: Deutsch, Otto Erich. (1983). *Schubert Erinnerungen seiner Freunde*. P. 173. Similarly, also Hüttenbrenner referred to this lied as the „marvelous song ‚Die Forelle'". Hüttenbrenner, Anselm: "Anselm Hüttenbrenner für Liszt: Bruchstücke aus dem Leben des Liederkomponisten Franz Schubert". (1854). In: Ibid. P. 208. (Trans. by the author). German expression: „[…] das wunderliebliche Lied ‚Die Forelle' […]".

[6] In his report, Stadler exposes Paumgartner's wish that Schubert would integrate the song D 550 in the piano quintet and would follow Hummel's model of the above-mentioned chamber music works. Cf. Stadler, Albert. (1858). In: Ibid. P. 173.

[7] Cf. Massin, Brigitte. (1977). *Franz Schubert*. P. 873.

personality and the musical-technical abilities of an amateur musician[8]. Taking into consideration Schubert's education, the first statement could also be conceivable if regarded as a distant influencing factor. A further possibility might lie in a sound experiment: the tone quality gained from the fusion of cello and contrabass not only generates more depth of sound, but also emancipates the cello from its original bass function, assigning the instrument a more melodic role[9]. This sound density might be a characteristic that appealed to Schubert, which he later took up again and developed further, e.g., in his C major string quintet D 956 composed in 1828.

Even though the variation movement of the piano quintet was a special assignment from the music patron Sylvester Paumgartner, the fact that Schubert had involved himself time and again with this subject, i.e., the lied, from 1816/17–1821 has equally given rise to further considerations. The simplest interpretation for the several song compositions is that Schubert might have merely rewritten the well-appreciated melody for several of his friends[10], each version presenting minor differences. However, the possibility that the veiled content of the text appealed to Schubert is substantial[11]. There is evidence that the piano quintet may support this theory, as it will be elaborated in the analysis. The transcription of this song into the piano quintet features not only some deviations but, above all, transformations on the motivic level since all five movements are interrelated by a core motivic cell. Furthermore, as it will be demonstrated in due course, the quintet contains a moment of resolution in the narration that is absent in the song, which confirms this reading.

The main difference in the song versions concerns the prelude measures added in the 1821 version, i.e., by dating, they refer to the song version composed after the piano quintet. It could therefore also be possible that an archetypal theme underneath the subject presented on the text level might have been particularly active and seeking expression. The fact that the piano quintet is pure instrumental music and not a composition inextricably tied to a text source like the song itself, enables the composer to react more to its abstract aspect, i.e., to the inherent

[8] Cf. Ibid.

[9] Cf. Hinrichsen, Hans-Joachim. „Die Kammermusik: 'Bergendes Gehäuse' und ‚Hang ins Unbegrenzte'". In: Dürr, Walther., Krause, Andreas. (2020). *Schubert Handbuch.* P. 480–481.

[10] Cf. Massin, Brigitte. (1977). *Franz Schubert.* P. 776.

[11] Cf. Dobretsberger, Barbara. (2019). *Formen der Vokalmusik.* P. 105.

unconscious archetypal elements. From this perspective, it can be of interest to question the impact of the poem's symbolic content, respectively of the song on the "I" and how this is processed in the *Forellenquintett.* In order to gain this overview, the song will be the subject of a brief introductory analysis, which includes first some concise background information on Schubart's life and the origins of the poem. The formal analysis of the variation movement in the piano quintet will be carried out by pointing to the interchange of motivic material with the lied and by comparing the narrative ductus of both. Lastly, the psychological reading will follow, in which the motivic level and the musical elements will be associated with the corresponding symbols and archetypal manifestations, pointing to the path of a possible psychological process expressed in the music.

14.1 Introduction: The Content of the Poem and the Song "Die Forelle" D 550 in the Context of the Historical-Political Environment

The poem that gave origin to Schubert's musical setting of "Die Forelle" D 550 seems at first to have an innocuous content; it involves a trout that is caught and killed by a fisherman. The last stanza, not set to music by Schubert, gives the poem an apparent moralistic turn: young girls are cautioned about possible seducers; the latter corresponding to the fisherman. The story line is described from the perspective of a third observer as the lyrical "I", whereby the first stanza rather depicts the scenario and the nature idyll. Apart from anaphors, assonances and alliterations, which enrich the tone level of the poem, and besides rhythmical changes that coincide with turning points in the plot (e.g., semicolons and colon in the third stanza), the poem is revealing for its hidden content. The poem bears a biographical undertone and a concealed political critique[12], which needs to be understood in the context of Schubart's environment.

[12] Cf. Dobretsberger, Barbara. (2019). *Formen der Vokalmusik.* P. 105–108.

The poet and music theoretician Christian Friedrich Daniel Schubart, having lived in the age of Absolutism, was imprisoned for ten years, in reason of having been a supporter of the Enlightenment[13]. During his incarceration from 1777–1787, Schubart accomplished several writings, including the theoretical treatise *Ideen zu einer Ästhetik der Tonkunst*[14] and amongst several other literary works, the poem "Die Forelle". After being smuggled out of prison, the latter was released for publishing in 1785[15]. Several interpretations of Schubart's verses have been made, ranging from the portrayal of a nature idyll to a symbolic reading, in which the trout is identified with a girl and the fisherman with a male protagonist[16]. However, as Dobretsberger has already pointed out, both possibilities remain rather surface-level[17], since these two readings appeal to the seemingly inoffensive matter of the poem. In contrast, Dobretsberger draws attention to the political content of the poem, which is concealed by the use of metaphorical language and the moral content of the last stanza, which veils the poet's actual political criticism towards the absolutist regime[18]. Hartmut Schick defended the same opinion, having ascertained that Schubert certainly understood the poem's political meaning[19]. After all, Schubert experienced a similar oppressive censorship regime, having lived in the Metternich era, and certainly must have related to Schubart's experiences[20]. This perspective is particularly prone to Jungian considerations, which will be elaborated later.

---

[13] Cf. Ibid.

[14] Here, Schubart refers *inter alia* to key characteristics and to the importance of the German theory of the affects, as mentioned previously in 6.2.

[15] Schubart, Christian Friedrich Daniel. (1785). *Gedichte aus dem Kerker.*

[16] Cf. Dobretsberger, Barbara. (2019). *Formen der Vokalmusik.* P. 105–108.

[17] Cf. Ibid.

[18] Cf. Ibid. In this perspective the last stanza is understood as having been an "essential measure for survival". Cf. Ibid. P. 105. (Trans. by the author). German expression: "Das Hinzufügen der vierten Strophe, die mehr eine moralisierende Reduktion des Geschehens auf die Warnung vor dem ‚Verführer mit der Angel' ist, vor dem sich die Mädchen hüten sollten, war für Schubart überlebensnotwendig.".

[19] Cf. Schick, Hartmut. (2007). "Christian Friedrich Daniel Schubart: Der Dichter-Musiker, Nördlingen und Wallerstein". In: *Rosetti-Forum. Mitteilungen der Internationalen Rosetti-Gesellschaft.* Nr. 8. P. 15–26. Cited after: Ibid.

[20] There were arrests within Schubert's social circle, which Schubert himself experienced in 1820 together with his friend Johann Chrisostomus Senn. Cf. Gibbs, Christopher H. (1997). *The Cambridge Companion to Schubert.* „Chronology". For the source document see: Deutsch, Otto Erich. (1964). *Schubert—Die Dokumente seines Lebens.* P. 87.

"In einem Bächlein helle,	"In a bright little brook,
Da schoß in froher Eil	here, in a joyful rush
Die launische Forelle	the mirthful trout
Vorüber, wie ein Pfeil:	like an arrow it swifts:
Ich stand an dem Gestade,	On the shore I stood,
Und sah' in süsser Ruh	and watched in sweet serenity
Des muntern Fischleins Bade	the merry little fish's bath
Im klaren Bächlein zu.	in the clear little brook.
Ein Fischer mit der Ruthe	A fisherman with the rod
Wohl an dem Ufer stand,	there on the shore he stood,
Und sah's mit kaltem Blute	and watched it with cold blood,
Wie sich das Fischlein wand.	how the fishlet twistingly moves.
So lang dem Wasser Helle,	So long the water clear,
So dacht' ich, nicht gebricht,	so long I thought, not broken,
So fängt er die Forelle	so long he catches not
Mit seiner Angel nicht.	the trout with his rod.
Doch endlich ward dem Diebe	But at last, time for the thief
Die Zeit zu lang; er macht	had turned too long; treacherously
Das Bächlein tückisch trübe:	he stirs the brooklet muddy:
Und eh' ich es gedacht,	And ere I could ween,
So zuckte seine Ruthe;	so twitched his rod;
Das Fischlein zappelt dran;	the fishlet squirms;
Und ich, mit regem Blute,	and myself, with lively blood,
Sah die Betrogne an.	at the betrayed I looked.
[Ihr, die ihr noch am Quelle	[Thee, who still linger at the source
Der sichern Jugend weilt,	of secure youth,
Denkt doch an die Forelle;	do think of the trout;
Seht ihr Gefahr, so eilt!	if danger is at sight, so hasten!

Meist fehlt ihr nur aus Mangel	For mostly it only lacks
Der Klugheit; Mädchen, seht	wisdom; maidens, beware of
Verführer mit der Angel –	the seducers with the rod –
Sonst blutet ihr zu spät.]"[21].	or else, late you may bleed.]"[22].

As Dobretsberger explains, the key to understanding the political statement beneath the poem lies in the allegory of the "clear brook" representing the Enlightenment ("Bächlein helle" as "die Helle der Aufklärung") and the fisherman representing the opponents of Enlightenment (the fisherman is entitled "Diebe", i.e., thief), who "deliberately attracts the fish into the trap by muddying the water"[23]. The fact that Schubert omitted the last moral stanza in his musical setting is to be understood as an indication pointing to Schubert's alertness in spirit in regard to socio-political matters[24]. His general critical attitude towards such subjects is traceable not only through the analysis of several documents[25] (17), but also through the musical setting of another political text—*Die Winterreise* of Wilhelm Müller[26]. In addition, the fact that Schubert repeatedly dealt with this subject from 1816 to 1821, and that he disregarded the fourth, ending moral strophe in all versions, speaks for the importance of its political content for Schubert[27]. This can be extended to an underlying archetypal subject that could be linked to the impact of the political environment and cultural context on Schubert, and that was activated and addressed here—this thought will be presented in the analysis of the piano quintet (14.2). First, however, a concise analysis of the lied is first requisite for a better comprehension of the motivic interrelations between the works in question.

The first musical setting of Schubart's poem was composed at the end of 1816, beginning of 1817, subsequently forming the basis for no fewer than five versions.

[21] Schubert, Franz. (1821). "Die Forelle" D 550. *Petrucci Music Library* (*IMSLP*).

[22] Ibid. (Trans. by the author).

[23] Dobretsberger, Barbara. (2019). *Formen der Vokalmusik.* P 105. (Trans. by the author). German expression: „Die „Helle" des noch ungetrübten frischen Wassers steht als Metapher für die Aufklärung. Durch das vom Angler mutwillig getrübte Wasser wird der Fisch vom Feind der Aufklärung in die Falle gelockt.".

[24] Cf. Ibid.

[25] Cf. Documents 207, 258, 296 and 451 in: Deutsch, Otto Erich. (1964). *Schubert—Die Dokumente seines Lebens.*

[26] Cf. Dobretsberger, Barbara. (2019). *Formen der Vokalmusik.* Sect. 5.5.3.: "Liedanalyse am Beispiel von Schuberts ‚Die Forelle' D 550".

[27] Cf. Ibid.

The last version was written two years after the *Forellenquintett* had been composed. All of the song versions bear great similarities among themselves. Apart from minor changes, the most striking difference that is to be recognized between them is the addition of five prelude bars in the piano accompaniment of the latest version from 1821[28]. Brigitte Massin's assumption that the description of nature in the poem might have awakened earlier melodic memories in Schubert is revealing for the genesis of the melodic material of "Die Forelle": the trout's theme shows indeed some correspondences with the earlier song "Daphne am Bach" D 411 on a text by Stolberg[29]. These melodic interrelations might have arisen out of free association of Schubert, due to the similarities already to be found on the textual level between Schubart's and Stolberg's poems[30].

Schubert's "Die Forelle" particularly stands out for the plethora of tone painting means he uses and the manner he employs them with the main objective of underlining the message of the text. Broadly speaking, the apparent luminous sound quality of D-flat major veils its own shadow counter side: the fact that it is a complex tonality might be a masked indication of the problematic and pernicious subject underneath[31]. Looking at the motivic level, the most striking example for the tone painting means used here is the sixteenth-sextuplet motif, that dominates almost the entire lied and musically conveys the babbling of the brooklet and/or the joyful bathing of the trout[32]. This motif will slightly change in shape and will even cease to exist for a short period of time (mm.37–42). In order to better make the distinction between the several shapes, these differences should now be exposed accordingly: at the beginning the sextuplet motif is marked by a chromatic succession of notes in a rising gesture culminating in an accent and a subsequent falling note (Fig. 14.1). However, as soon as the singing voice enters, the diastematics of this motif increases, featuring a broken-up, yet chaotically ordered major triad, equally leading to an accent and a subsequent falling note (Fig. 14.1).

Dobretsberger attributes the first mentioned chromatic version to the observer who describes the peripeteia of the trout, since it is to be found consequently

---

[28] Since this is the version that is usually performed nowadays, the author opted to choose this version for examination. For a comparative analysis between the different song versions and their interpretations see: Zilkens, Udo. (2000). *Franz Schubert. Vom Klavierlied zum Klavierquintett.*

[29] Cf. Massin, Brigitte. (1977). *Franz Schubert.* P. 776.

[30] Cf. Ibid.

[31] Cf. Dobretsberger, Barbara. Personal communication between Barbara Dobretsberger and the author. Salzburg: November 9, 2023.

[32] Cf. Dobretsberger, Barbara. (2019). *Formen der Vokalmusik.* P. 105–108.

linked to the verses relating to the lyrical "I" (mm.14–25, mm. 44–51, as well as the prelude, interlude and postlude bars)[33]. Contrastingly, the second triadic ductus rather relates to the trout's reality[34].

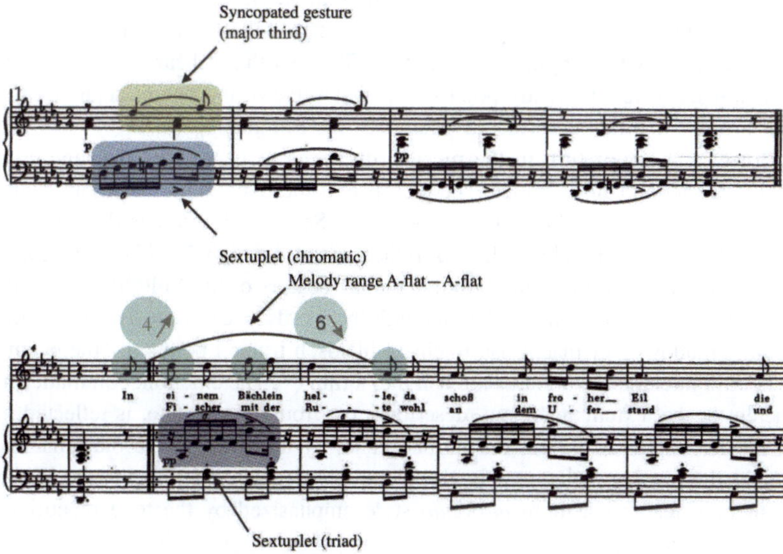

Fig. 14.1 Sextuplet motif featuring the chromatic ductus vs. the triad motif. The melodic range depicts a return to the initial note (circling around). The importance of the triad and the fourth and sixth interval in the thematic material. (Sheet music excerpt taken and adapted from *IMSLP*)

The major tone colour can easily be associated with the trout's joyful state of being in his life element. The brief melismas that are to be found in the singing voice (e.g., m.8, m.12, m. 16) emphasize the trout's lively and joyful nature. When examining the phrase structures of the two initial A-sections (mm.6–29), it becomes clear that it is congruently conveying the textual statement by its regular structure, i.e., no particular tension is created for the time being, at least in this

33 Cf. Ibid. P. 107.

34 Cf. Ibid.

regard. This section is constructed featuring two successive periods and a repetition of the last consequent phrase. A further noteworthy aspect of the melody is its shape, depicting a closing circle by its constant return to the note A-flat[35] (Fig. 14.1). However, more subtle examples of tone painting means can be noted. For instance, the syncopated gesture featuring an ascending major third interval that is assigned to the piano prelude bars introduces the triad-motif (Fig. 14.1) that is retaken by the singing voice (m.6)[36]. The fact that it bears the interval of the major third might already point to the first verse of the poem, depicting the clear brook and alluding to the advocators of the Enlightenment[37].

However, a major turn in the musical ductus is to be perceived in the contrasting B-section (mm.29b-42). The presence of the B-flat minor harmony alone is significant (mm.30–31), which according to Schubart himself is described as "eccentric", being a tonality "clothed in the garb of the night"[38]. If the preceding major tonality stood metaphorically for the advocators of the Enlightenment, the fact that this harmonic change befalls with the words "treacherously he stirs the brooklet muddy" ("er macht das Bächlein tückisch trübe") points to "the enemy of the Enlightenment who lures the fish into a trap"[39]. The emotional dramaticism inherent in the textual statement, describing the trout's tragic fate, is reflected in the music. This is achieved, on the one hand, by a change in the diastematics, both in the singing voice and in the piano accompaniment (Fig. 14.2). While the melody features a more *parlando* style emphasized by the tone repetitions

[35] Cf. Dobretsberger, Barbara. Personal communication between Barbara Dobretsberger and the author. Salzburg: November 9, 2023.

[36] Even though the prelude bars are missing in the earlier versions, the same gesture is to be found in the interlude or postlude bars.

[37] Cf. Dobretsberger, Barbara. Personal communication between Barbara Dobretsberger and the author. Salzburg: November 9, 2023.

[38] Cf. Schubart, Christian Friedrich Daniel. „Ideen zu einer Ästhetik der Tonkunst". Cited after: Böhm, Richard. (2006). *Symbolik und Rhetorik im Liedschaffen von Franz Schubert.* P. 89. German expression: "Schubart: B moll: Ein Sonderling, mehrentheils in das Gewand der Nacht gekleidet. Er ist etwas mürrisch, und nimmt höchst selten eine gefällige Miene an.".

[39] Dobretsberger, Barbara. (2019). *Formen der Vokalmusik.* P. 105. (Trans. by the author). German expression: „Durch das vom Angler mutwillig getrübte Wasser wird der Fisch vom Feind der Aufklärung in die Falle gelockt.".

(increased dramaticism)[40], the piano's sextuplet motif exhibits an increasingly constrained range, later getting stuck in the *circulatio* figure (mm.34–36), and ultimately ceasing to exist (mm.37–42). Once again, the music rhetorical figure is used as a means to convey the circling around gesture, depicting, in this context, the hopeless situation and the condition of getting trapped[41]. In addition to this evolution, the falling gesture with the accentuated note tied with the sextuplet motif, is also missing from the beginning of the B-section. The coincidence of these two facts regarding the sextuplet motif indicates a "reduction of the range of motion"[42], simultaneously foretelling that the liveliness of the trout (sextuplet triad motif + accent) will be taken away. On the other hand, the imminent tragedy is also suggested by the irregular phrase structures and the moments of standstills of the B-section. The latter are to be recognized by the shortness of breath characteristic of the phrase structures and the brief, yet long felt pauses that interrupt each short phrases (mm.29b–38).

These musical events are sustained by an increased use of chromaticism and tension-filled chords. From the harmonic standpoint, not only the tonality turned to the B-flat minor key, but also an increased use of chromaticism is noticeable. Equally, the second pendulum in mm.34–36 is striking[43] (Fig. 14.2): the E-flat dominant seventh chord (m.34 first beat) is followed by the B-flat half-diminished seventh chord, i.e., a highly dissonant chord, which includes the tritone interval (*diabolus in musica*). This harmonic event is linked to the words "treacherously he stirs the brooklet muddy" ("er macht das Bächlein tückisch trübe"); thus, the semantic of the diminished fifth refers to the fisherman and his character. The latter, being a particular highly dissonant chord, is placed on the light beat of the measure, reflecting all the more the conflictual situation in which the trout finds itself: the special colouration achieved, highlights the terrifying emotional

---

40 Such recitativ-like passages were intentionally used as a means to underline dramaticism (12). Cf. Dittrich, Marie-Agnes. " Die Lieder. 'Für Menschenohren sind es Harmonien'". In: Dürr, Walther. Krause, Andreas. (2020). *Schubert Handbuch.* P. 148.

41 Cf. Dobretsberger, Barbara. (2019). *Formen der Vokalmusik.* P. 105–108. Psychologically, it is also possible to read the *circulatio* differently, originating a further possible interpretation, that will be exposed later (14.3).

42 Ibid. P. 108. (Trans. by the author). German expression: "[...] eine weitere Reduktion des Bewegungsspielraums [...]".

43 Cf. Dobretsberger, Barbara. Personal communication between Barbara Dobretsberger and the author. Salzburg: November 9, 2023.

condition of the fish in view of the fisherman's act of muddying the brooklet. The fact that these harmonies are obsessively repeated for three consecutive measures especially emphasizes the feeling of being stuck or trapped. Following this highly emotional charged passage, the piano accompaniment ceases with the sextuplet motif and turns to chord repetitions (Fig. 14.2). The latter, generally have a special semantics in Schubert's works, being associated with death[44]. While this is applicable in the context of this song, this motif is also tied with an additional semantic, derived from the Beethovenian repertoire—the succession of four notes, with the last being held longer, referring to the fate-motif (Fig. 14.2).

By using these tone painting means and by referring to Beethoven's motif, Schubert, musically and emotionally, foretells the tragic fate of the trout. The chromatic descending line as the *lamento* figure (bassline of the piano in mm.39–41) confirms this destiny. The horrifying moment illustrating the trout's death is dramatized by the dense chord repetitions (mm.41–42), here functioning as pure madrigalism, i.e., depicting the squirming of the little fish that has been hooked. The particularly low register that Schubert chose for the chords lends the passage its dark tone-colour (mm.41–42). Once the *climax* is achieved, the music returns to the initial motivic material and to the corresponding major tonality (m.43). The reprise of the A-section at the end points to the aaba-form, a variant of the barform, in German terminology known as "Reprisenbarform". Dobretsberger interprets this return to the A-section as a "throwback to the [initial] idyll"[45].

[44] Cf. Dittrich, Marie-Agnes. "Die Lieder. 'Für Menschenohren sind es Harmonien'". In: Dürr, Walther. Krause, Andreas. (2020). *Schubert Handbuch.* In: Dürr, Walther. Krause, Andreas. (2020). *Schubert Handbuch.* P. 165.

[45] Dobretsberger, Barbara. (2019). *Formen der Vokalmusik.* P. 107. (Trans. by the author). German expression: "T.44 bringt die Rückblende in die 'Idylle' des a-Teils [...]".

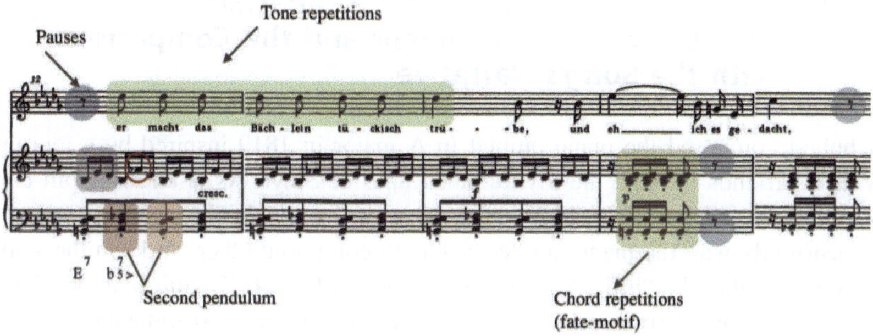

Fig. 14.2 B-section: The change in the melodic ductus from great diastematics to tone repetitions. The chordal repetitions featuring the Beethovenian reference of the fate-motif. In the piano: the change of the sextuplet motif towards the circulatio figure, depicting the narrowing of the trout's space and the act of getting caught. The pauses and the shorter, irregular phrases heighten the expectation and create tension. Harmonically, the passage expresses also great tension with the second pendulum and the half-diminished seventh chord. (Sheet music excerpt taken and adapted from *IMSLP*)

In conclusion, it can be observed that, although the piano accompaniment and singing voice are harmonically and motivically connected (e.g., through the triad motif), Schubert succeeds in creating the same two sensory levels present in the poem. The first concerns the observer level (the lyrical I), already noticed in the poem, which corresponds to the chromatised version of the sextuplet motif[46]. The second, refers to the depiction of the landscape and the reality of the trout[47]. The latter is expressed by the broken triadic element of the sextuplet motif. These two sensory levels can be observed due to the dialectic that is existent in the song. As Barbara Dobretsberger has pointed out, the song features a dualistic contrasting structure between the A-section and the B-section at various musical levels, such as: (i) major vs. minor tonalities, (ii) a strophic vs. a non-strophic tendency, (iii) regular vs. irregular phrase constructions, (iv) a diatonic vs. a chromatic ductus, (v) significant diastematics of the melodic line vs. tone repetitions[48]. As it has been examined, the madrigalisms and the linked word-tone relationship are particularly rich here and will be of relevance for the subsequent analysis of the variation movement of the piano quintet.

---

[46] Cf. Dobretsberger, Barbara. (2019). *Formen der Vokalmusik*. P. 105–108.

[47] Cf. Ibid.

[48] Ibid. P. 107.

14.2 The Piano Quintet—a Formal Analysis of the Variation Movement and the Comparison with the Song's Narrative

Schubert composed the piano quintet in A major in 1819 inspired by a journey with his friends through the idyllic landscapes of Steyr. As is known from correspondences, Schubert greatly valued moments of conviviality with his friends. Concurrently with the piano quintet, Schubert composed other works in the same tonality, notably the "little A major" piano sonata D 664. Brigitte Massin relates both works and their common ground tonalities to the above-mentioned biographical fact[49]—both convey a rustic undertone and associations with a water landscape in the countryside easily emerge. Their luminous character is indeed often mentioned in literature. However, the song and the quintet are often misinterpreted for their seemingly light character. Even though this is also a character trait of theirs, the dark side is often repressed or at least lightened[50]. In fact, the seemingly light character of this piece is often used as a counter argument to question the thesis that 1819 was considered to be a critical time in Schubert's life (12). As it will be mentioned in the last chapter (20), this concept is now being reconsidered or at least reformulated[51]. The psychological interpretation that will be given at the end of the *Forellenquintett* analysis may shed some light into this debate. It is necessary to undertake a formal analysis of the quintet, with the aim of establishing the interrelations between all of its movements and those of the previously analysed song.

As previously mentioned, there is a great exchange of motivic material between the song and the quintet. The sextuplet motif from the lied, which presents a rising gesture culminating on an accent, is to be identified in the first movement of the quintet, although repurposed in form of the triplet opening

---

[49] Cf. Massin, Brigitte. (1977). *Franz Schubert.* P. 874.

[50] Even Alfred Brendel, who habitually defends Schubert's dark side, uses this luminous and light character of the piano quintet as an argument to object the predominance of the thematic of death in Schubert's œuvre: "Nevertheless, there are also masterpieces by Schubert that are completely devoted to life. I have already mentioned the 'trout quintet'". Brendel, Alfred. (2001). *Ausgerechnet Ich.* P. 161. (Trans. by the author). German expression: „Dennoch gibt es bei Schubert auch Meisterwerke, die völlig dem Leben zugewandt sind. Das ‚Forellenquintett' habe ich schon genannt.". Prior to that statement, Brendel already described the *Forellenquintett* as the expression of a naïve gaiety. Cf. Brendel, Alfred. (1996). *Musik beim Wort genommen.* P. 150.

[51] Cf. Linke, Cosima. (2023). "Arabella Pare, Franz Schubert. The fragmentary Piano Sonatas (= Schubert: Perspektiven—Studien, Bd.7), Stuttgart: Steiner 2022". In: *Zeitschrift der Gesellschaft für Musiktheorie. Vol. 20/1.* P. 111–115.

motto (Fig. 14.3). It should be noted that the rising gesture features one connecting element between both motifs, besides the fact that sextuplets and triplets are related rhythms. There is a second core component that links all the movements of the piano quintet and that is derived from the song, that is the triad motif, including the fourth and sixth interval (Fig. 14.3, Fig. 14.4, Fig. 14.5). Apart from these main motifs, the tone repetitions are also retaken from the song and equally featured or converted into chords or into a tremolo. However, two further cells are to be recognized as new and as a cross reference in the piano quintet: (i) the dotted rhythm and (ii) the *staccato* falling scale that is initiated with a long note preceding it, often being ornamented (Fig. 14.4). Both play an important role in the variation movement of the piano quintet. The following illustrations shall better depict these interrelations[52].

As far as the formal structure is concerned, the variation movement consists of the theme followed by five variations. The latter is characterized by the *Allegretto* section (m.128), which concludes the movement, and in which the song is unexpectedly quoted with its original sextuplet motif. If an analogy would be drawn between the piano quintet and the song's apparent plot, the tonal disposition and the variations of the motifs that are presented in each tonal section are revealing (Fig. 14.6). Comparing these observations with the narration of the piano quintet, it becomes clear how the fifth variation represents new material in the narrative ductus, that was not necessarily existent in the song. While in the poem the story ends with a brief negative remark from the part of the observer

[52] Alfred Einstein's remark about the similarities between the song *Die Forelle* D 550 and Mozart's *Das Veilchen* KV 476 (composed in 1785 to a poem by Goethe) is thought provoking. Cf. Einstein, Alfred. (1952). *Schubert: Ein musikalisches Porträt*. P. 170. It is evident that the poems are thematically close to each other. Additionally, there are also correspondences in the piano quintet that even surpass the theme and variations movement. Particularly, the phrase twist in the mm.48–52 from the fifth movement evokes associations with the Mozart's song; cf. *Das Veilchen* mm.12–14 "it was a sweet violet" ("es war ein herzigs Veilchen"), which features the same ascending fourth, followed by the descending fifth interval, then a rising major third and a subsequent consecutive descent with passing note within the same major third interval ambit (Fig. 14.5). There is a high probability that Schubert might have known this song since it was published in 1789 alongside *Das Lied der Trennung* KV 519 as part of *Zwey Deutsche Arien*. For the publishing date see: Arthur, John. Schachter, Carl. (1989). "Mozart's 'Das Veilchen'". In: *The Musical Times, Vol.130, No. 1753*. P. 149–164. It is also known from reports by Schubert's friends that Schubert was "highly familiar" with the works of Haydn, Mozart and Beethoven, always having a great enthusiasm towards them. Cf. Spaun, Joseph von. (1829). "Über Schubert". In: Deutsch, Otto Erich. (1983). *Schubert Erinnerungen seiner Freunde*. P. 26, respectively, P. 34. The question of whether this hypothesis was a conscious reference or an unconscious association on the part of Schubert requires further investigation, which is beyond the scope of this dissertation.

("with lively blood, at the betrayed I looked", i.e., "mit regem Blute, sah ich die Betrogne an"), the new material present in the piano quintet would correspond to a moment of resolution of the story. This means that Schubert adds a *lysis* with the fifth variation[53] (Fig. 14.6). Even though the moment in which the observer looks at "the betrayed" could be pinpointed to the D-flat note of the cello (m.103), the variations in the thematic material and the development of the entire fifth variation rather correspond to the presentation of a resolution (*lysis*), as it will be evident in the following analysis.

The theme and the subsequent three variations are harmonically quite straightforward, remaining in the tonal domain of the D major key (Fig. 14.6). It is striking that Schubert chose to exclude the piano for the theme's presentation—only the strings are to be heard in the softest dynamics (***pp***), which lends the passage an atemporal and spaceless sensation. For this reason, it is possible to classify the theme's presentation as the *illud tempus* (Fig. 14.6). The trout melody is announced by the first violin (theme), taking over the melismatic writing of the song (e.g., m.3, m.7, m.9, m.11, m.17). The other string instruments accompany the melody in chords or passing notes. The chords, in turn, feature tone repetitions and the dactyl rhythm (m.1). In the first variation, the flowing sextuplet motif of the song is introduced in the viola, this time with a perfect *circulatio* figure (m.21), while the first violin and cello alternately pass on the sixteenth-note triplet motif, thus reinforcing the viola's statement. However, these are kept in the initial ***pp*** dynamics. The piano makes its appearance retaking the theme and embellishes it with humorous trills and mordents (referring to the violin of m.16). Its high register and double octave voicing are particularly eye-catching. The contrabass is kept quite simple, fulfilling a supportive harmonic role, nearly like a *basso continuo.* It is striking how the trills and mordents accumulate throughout the variation, ultimately featuring a dialogue-like gesture between violin and piano for the second part of the variation (mm.29–40). The fact that (i) the piano makes its *debut*, that (ii) the flowing sextuplet motif and (iii) the ornamental embellishments of the theme predominantly stand out, contributes to the descriptive character of this variation in regard to the trout's scenario. Due to these reasons, if the attention is drawn to the narrative ductus, this first variation could be the equivalent to the *dramatis personae.*

---

[53] The identification of the narrative's structure follows Marie-Louise von Franz method of fairy-tales (and dream) interpretation, which are based on the different phases that an archetypal story presents. Cf. Franz, Marie-Louise. (1995). *L'interprétation des contes de fées.* P. 55–57.

Fig. 14.3 Motivic interrelations between the trout's theme and the thematic-motivic material of the piano quintet's first movement. (Sheet music excerpt taken and adapted from *Henle digital edition* © 2016 G. Henle Verlag, Munich)

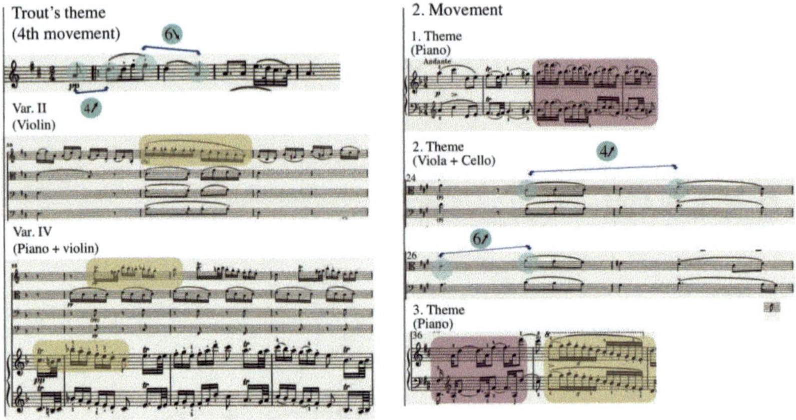

Fig. 14.4 Motivic interrelations between the fourth movement and the thematic-motivic material of the piano quintet's second movement. (Sheet music excerpt taken and adapted from *Henle digital edition* © 2016 G. Henle Verlag, Munich)

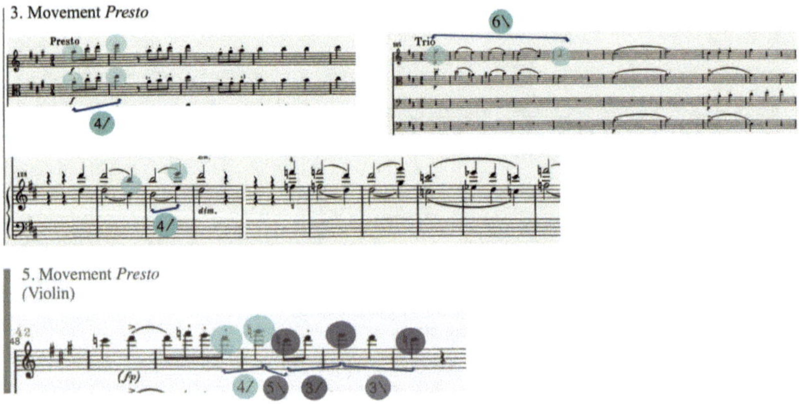

Fig. 14.5 Motivic interrelations between the fourth movement and the thematic-motivic material of the piano quintet's third and fifth movements. (Sheet music excerpt taken and adapted from *Henle digital edition* © 2016 G. Henle Verlag, Munich)

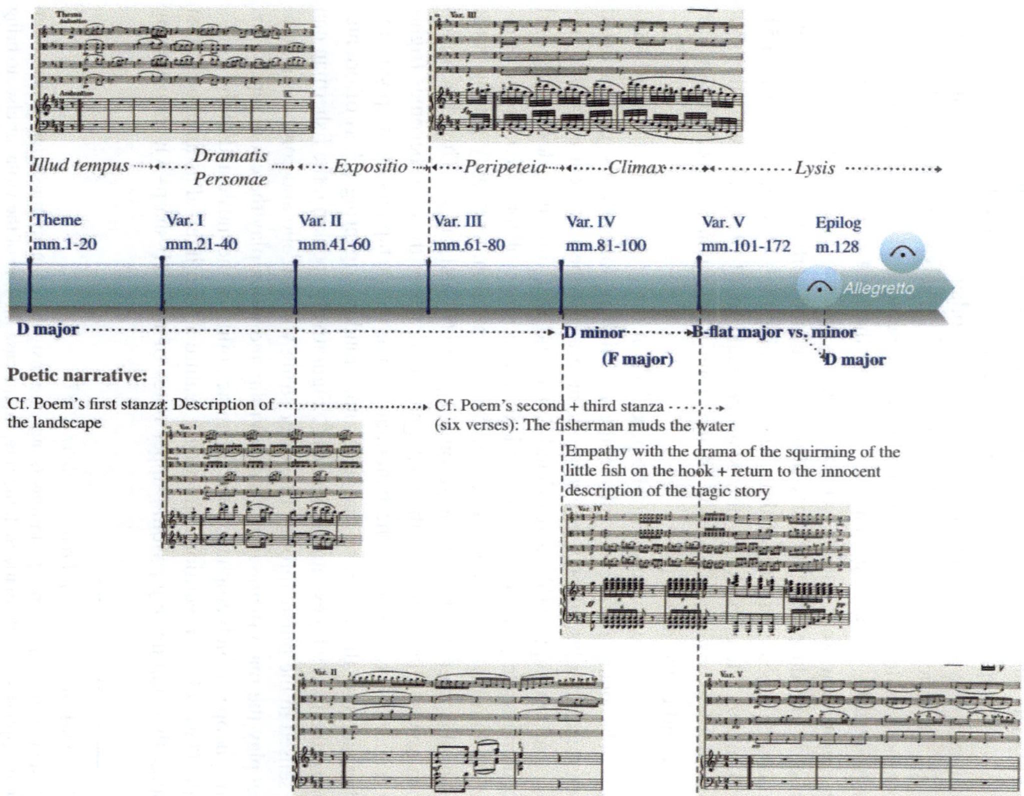

Fig. 14.6 Formal and harmonic structure of the piano quintet's fourth movement, by drawing an analogy to the narrative of the poem. (Sheet music excerpt taken and adapted from *Henle digital edition* © 2016 G. Henle Verlag, Munich)

In the second variation, the sextuplet motif is present, no longer in the circling around form, but featuring "garland"[54]-like scales and arpeggios that are played by the first violin. While the viola retakes the entire theme, both cello and piano are only left with the head motif of the theme. This fragmentary writing is even more intriguing, since it seems to be of Schubert's intention to bring the piano part forward by ***mf*** dynamic markings (while all other instruments, including the viola's thematic line, remain in the ***p*** dynamic)[55]. The split theme thus becomes more noticeable. This fact can anticipate an element of conflict. This is then emphasized by the accents that are placed on the light beats of the measure in the violin's part (e.g., m.44). The new falling *staccato* scale motif, mentioned above, is introduced by the first violin in the second part of this variation (m.49) and is then repeated a total of three times bringing the variation to an end (m.51, m.55, m.59). Here, both the new *staccato* scale motif alongside with the split trout motif expose the condition of the trout. Consequently, this variation can correspond to the *expositio.*

A first dynamic contrast is to be perceived at the beginning of the third variation. The piano initiates a trill in the ***f*** which is followed by uninterrupted thirty-second notes, always in unisono. These are shaped as clear *circulatio* figures that are kept within a restricted range and that flow into descending and ascending scale patterns (e.g., mm-61–62). The range of the *circulatio* is strikingly becoming shorter and shorter across the variation, ultimately getting stuck within the interval of a minor second (e.g., m.67 and m.71). This description alone revives the moment in the poetic narrative, where the trout becomes frightened and tries to flee from the fisherman. Using the metaphors of the poem, the fisherman stirs the water, so that it becomes muddy, triggering a loss of orientation of the fish, who eventually panics[56]. Figuratively speaking, the fisherman can be sensed in the music through the lower string voices (cello and contrabass), that now play the main theme in *pizzicato.* Violin and viola, play the chord repetitions and syncopes which emphasize the unpredictability of the music and of the trout's path. These chord repetitions punctually feature a third interval as an upbeat, first rising, then falling, e.g., violin, upper notes of m.61 (F-sharp–A); transitioning

---

[54] Massin, Brigitte. (1977). *Franz Schubert.* P. 876.

[55] Listening to various interpretations brings the insight that many musicians in fact often opt to emphasize the thematic melodic line, in this case the line of the viola, or else, to bring out the first violin, while the piano part is rather interpreted in retreat. So doing, however, Schubert's intentions of bringing to the fore the split fragmentary aspect of the theme through the ***mf*** dynamics, are in fact attenuated.

[56] Cf. Dobretsberger, Barbara. (2019). *Formen der Vokalmusik.* P. 105–108.

to m.62 (A–F-sharp). The third interval is familiar from the song's prelude measures. However, introduced as the right hand syncopes in the lied, it is actually presented as a major third, featuring the fundamental note and the third of the D-flat major chord (D-flat–F). As previously seen, this gesture metaphorically stood for the clear brook, respectively the Enlightenment. The fact that in the quintet, the violin plays (as its top notes) the third and the fifth of the D major chord, makes the minor third of the major chord to be emphasized, possibly pointing to the act of stirring and muddying the water. In a veiled manner, this indicates the imminent danger. Again, from the structural point of view of the narrative, these aspects point to the peripeties of the main character (*peripeteia*), the trout (Fig. 14.6).

While the third variation brought a dynamic contrast, the fourth not only emphasizes this (*ff*), but also turns harmonically over to D minor—a key often associated with the death semantics, particularly in Schubert's repertoire[57]. The content of the music confirms this reading: the theme is now solely rudimentary. The piano as well as the violin and viola play chord repetitions as sixteenth-note sextuplets, which convey a similar sound effect as a tremolando. The latter, as previously explained in the song analysis, can be interpreted as a madrigalism (here, depicting the squirming of the fish); yet, they also bear in Schubert's repertoire the meaning of death, as seen above. This highly dramatic moment in the storyline is equally intensely set in music by a means of dense writing. Analogously with the narrative structure, this section undoubtedly refers to the dramatic height of the action (*climax*). Congruently, Brigitte Massin compared the fourth variation with the third stanza of the song[58]. However, the imminent turn to the major key, that brings with it the *staccato* descending scale motif (mm.89–91), is rather surprising—the psychological interpretation developed later will provide some insights.

The flowing gesture is initially featured in the lower voices, first as sixteenth triplets, then as a rising sextuplet (mm.81–84). Subsequently, there is a change of roles to be noted: the flowing motif is retaken by the first violin, while all other three voices adopt the tone repetitions together with the piano (m.85). This change of roles is preceded by a short caesura which triggered the abrupt key change to the relative major key (mm.84–88). The piano eventually joins the flowing triplets and the first section of this variation ends in F major. Being in

[57] In Richard Böhm's song databases, D minor is described *inter alia* as the tonality in connection with transience, grave and death. Cf. Böhm, Richard. (2006). *Symbolik und Rhetorik im Liedschaffen von Franz Schubert.* P. 82. German expression: "Vergänglichkeit, Grab und Tod".

[58] Cf. Massin, Brigitte. (1977). *Franz Schubert.* P. 876.

the F major tonality, which relates to "memories of a beautiful past"[59], the second part of this variation congruently evokes the *staccato* scale motif initiated by a humorous-effective trill. This motif is presented here in a soft dynamic and featuring the imitation technique. This technique appeals to the ancient *caccia* traditions (mm.89–92)[60]. The ending of this section is marked by a modulatory character, in which harmonies such as G minor (m.94 and m.98), D minor (mm.95–96) or B-flat major (m.97) are to be punctually perceived. In this oppressive passage, an ambivalent diminished seventh chord emerges (the second half of m.93), conveying—if the analogy with the song is pursued further—the trout's death. The *lamento* line of the violin (m.94 and m.98) always leading back to the D minor key (m.95, respectively, m.99), confirms the tragic fate of the trout. This modulatory passage led back to the D minor key (m.99), closing in this manner the fourth variation. However, the forthcoming variation offers some melodic and harmonic surprises.

The F note with which the cello initiates the fifth variation presupposes a continuation in the D minor sphere. However, the unfolding immediately reveals the shift to the third related B-flat major. Almost as a consequence, the thematic material of the melody, played here by the cello, undergoes a metamorphosis in that it extends the range of the melody a third higher. The "new" note of the melody is emphasized by an accent. One measure later, a further note is accentuated, bringing a change in the tonal colour: B-flat major slides into its counter pole, B-flat minor (m.103), clouding the general hopeful idyllic mood of the B-flat major key[61]. The next four bars head to the dominant key, F major (m.107–108). In the background to these harmonic shifts, there is a new element to be acknowledged in the first violin, namely the dotted rhythm mentioned above, present from the first bar (m.101) and which is symbolically significative[62].

The second part of this variation is shaped even more by noticeable harmonic shifts and moments of suspension of the musical ductus. While the theme's melody played by the cello rises in the heights (mm.108–112), Schubert turns to B-flat minor (m.110) and subsequently to the third related key of D-flat major (m.112), the original key of the song. To reformulate this harmonic path in the

---

[59] Cf. Böhm, Richard. (2006). *Symbolik und Rhetorik im Liedschaffen von Franz Schubert.* P. 64. German expression: "Erinnerungen an schöne Vergangenheit.".

[60] The importance of this compositional technique will be revealed in the next sub-chapter.

[61] For the key characteristics of B-flat major see: Böhm, Richard. (2006). *Symbolik und Rhetorik im Liedschaffen von Franz Schubert.* P. 66.

[62] This thought will be examined in the next sub-chapter.

figurative sense, it conveys the feeling of rising into the celestial heights. The latter harmony of D-flat major lends a whimsical atmosphere to the passage. Once arrived in D-flat major the musical ductus remains suspended in this peaceful key. Böhm describes this tonality as "peace and tranquility (even in death)"[63] which seems to suit this passage. The off-beat repeated chords featured in the piano emphasizes the related feeling of suspension in time, simultaneously creating a musical sound carpet beneath the melody (e.g., mm.113–116). This feeling of being in suspension is also given by the tone repetitions and the octave repetitions that are to be noticed throughout the entire passage, which have the effect of a long-held note. The same four bars are repeated again (mm.117–120), with a minor variation in the thematic material (cello, m.117). The end of the variation is marked by a modulation sequence structured by two bars (mm.121–122, mm.123–124, mm.125–126). This sequence conveys the descending from the previously achieved heights of D-flat major, passing by unexpected harmonies such as the D-flat minor harmony in m.122 and the turn towards the dark harmony of F-sharp minor in m.126. One measure is subsequently appended featuring the dominant seventh chord of D (m.127)—as if the descent could be continued further. However, Schubert places six organ points on this measure, which not only suspends the musical ductus but also increases the expectation of the listener enormously. This makes the return of the theme in its original song form and in D major all the more surprising.

With the return of the original theme of "Die Forelle" (*Allegretto*, m.128), Schubert retakes exactly the same piano accompaniment figure as in the lied, i.e., introducing, for the first time, the original rising sextuplet motif, characterized by the broken triad and leading to an accentuated note. Meanwhile, the left-hand jumps in a light and playful manner, giving harmonic support. The violin is given the central role with the theme and is embellished by grace notes. Once the theme is announced, the equivalent of the first periodic phrase construction of the song is repeated by the cello in m.136—a dialogue between violin and cello establishes itself. The second periodic antecedent phrase consequently begins in m.144 with the violin. The consequent phrase of this period is like the song, being subsequently repeated one octave higher (mm.152–155). If Schubert would have followed the exact same pattern of construction as in the lied, the movement would have ended here with the corresponding five postlude bars. However, this is not what Schubert did.

---

[63] Böhm, Richard. (2006). *Symbolik und Rhetorik im Liedschaffen von Franz Schubert.* P. 73. (Trans. by the author). German expression: "Friede und Ruhe (auch im Tod)".

The cello quite unexpectedly reassumes the thematic material related to the second period (m.156ff.), while the violin plays the sextuplet motif. The latter is now performed with the chromatic ductus that corresponds to the prelude, interlude and postlude bars of the song. Striking is the fact that the piano accompaniment is entirely discontinued for the measures associated with the respective cello's presentation of the theme. For the last repetition of the consequent phrase, however, violin and cello play the melody in unisono, while the piano retakes the sextuplets motif in its original prelude form, featuring the chromatic ductus. The syncopated rising third interval that characterised the song's prelude bars are to be heard, also in unisono and in major, in the last measures of the movement (mm.169–170). The movement ends with a prolonged D major chord (*fermata*) that lasts two whole measures.

The movement was just formally described, highlighting the musical facts and making metaphorical associations with the corresponding song "Die Forelle". The previously used means, in which the quintet was analysed in comparison with the programmatic undertone of the poem's narrative was helpful insofar as a transformation[64] could be observed—especially, in regard to the fifth variation. The change in the thematic material at the beginning of the fifth variation, the significant harmonic modulations that occur, the resuming of the theme and ultimately, the fusion between the two instruments at the end, that have previously been in dialogue with each other, confirms the above raised hypothesis that the quintet brings a resolution (*lysis*) to the trout's story. This consideration is now of interest for the psychological interpretation that follows. The next subchapter will deal with the abstract aspect of the music, addressing the possible inner psychic processes, eventually relating them with the historical and political background mentioned above. First, however, the motifs should be presented accordingly in association with the corresponding archetypal principles.

14.3 An Analysis of the Inherent Psychological Processes

If it is assumed that it was the ground atmosphere of the poem/song that captivated Schubert, then all elements featuring in there should be understood in more abstract terms. Considering the brooklet as the life environment of the

[64] Even though Schubert retakes the melody of the song at the end of the piano quintet, the entire narrative ductus of the fifth variation has a new colour, which implies a psychological transformation.

trout, it can represent two principles (Fig. 14.7): the *libido*, i.e., the underneath life force or the inner motivating force (positive aspect), but also the destructive *Thanatos* energy (negative aspect). The positive aspect of it is epitomized by the transparency of the water quality—in musical terms, by (i) the original sextuplet motif, with the inherent (ii) major triad motif, which is in turn related with (iii) the tonal quality of the D major key, and (iv) the heartbeat motif. The negative aspect is symbolically represented by the muddy water—in musical terms, by the (i) tone repetitions or chord repetitions, (ii) the tremolo, and (iii) the minor tonality or minor triad. These are the overarching elements of the two principles, which are then to be considered for their sub-elements. For instance: the above-mentioned sextuplet motif manifests itself consequently in different ways, which are interconnected with the emotional condition of the "I" but also with the counter principle. These manifestations include (Fig. 14.7): the chromatic and triadic sextuplet motif, the garland motif, the triplets, but also the *circulatio* and the repeated chords as a sextuplet motif. The triadic motif, associated above with the wild behaviour of the fish, can psychologically point to the still unstructured chaotic aspects of the personality, whereas the chromatic line, conveying order and linearity can stand for the structured personality (Fig. 14.7). Since the variation movement ends with the chromatic version it presupposes a process of transformation or an "enlargement of the personality"[65].

The two above-mentioned life-death principles, as the two fundamental drives, have thus an effect on the "I" and the inner protagonists. The light side of the Self is here theriomorphically symbolised by the fish[66]—musically it is represented by the theme featured in the high range, i.e., performed by the instruments of higher pitch (violin) and the higher range of the piano (Theme + Var. I). The shadow, as the dark side of the Self is in this context anthropomorphically projected into the fisherman's figure—musically, associated with the lower register of the theme's instrumentation (Var. III, cello and contrabass). This approach in which all motifs are seen as intrinsically connected with each other is based on the amplification method and dream interpretation technique of C.G. Jung[67], where all elements are considered in an intertwining network and sub-divided into further sub-elements and their associations, as opposed to a detached chain of associations leading to a

[65] Jung, Carl Gustav. (2011). *Four Archetypes*. (Trans. by R.F.C. Hull). P. 54.

[66] In *Aion* C.G. Jung addresses several manifestations forms of the Self and particularly deals with examples concerning the theriomorphic manifestation of the Self, whereby the fish symbol takes significant attention. Cf. Jung, Carl Gustav. (1970). *Aion*.

[67] Cf. Jacobi, Jolande. (2006). *Die Psychologie von C.G. Jung*. P. 88 or P. 90.

rather reductive outcome[68]. The following figure shall depict the just-formulated analytical concept (Fig. 14.7).

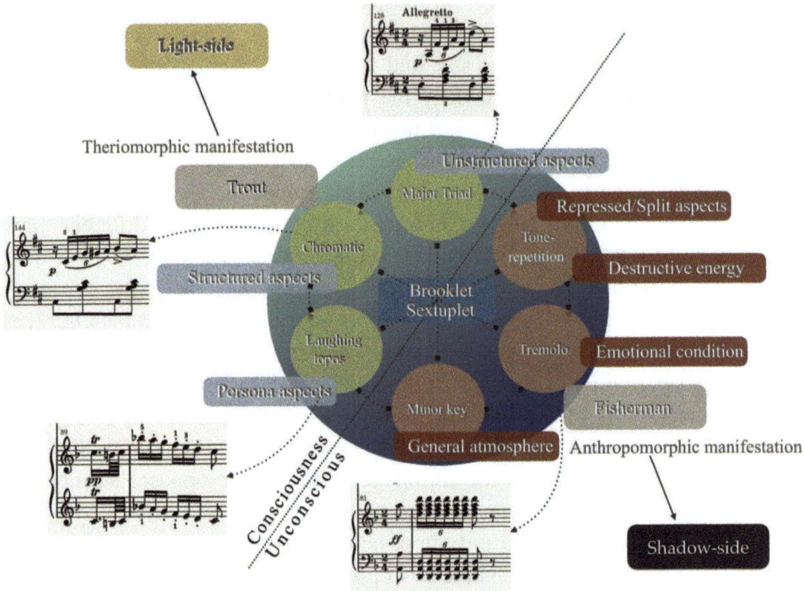

Fig. 14.7 The sextuplet motif and its differentiations in the piano quintet's variation movement. The two overarching principles governing and influencing the "I". The trout as the theriomorphic manifestation of the Self and the fisherman as its anthropomorphic manifestation. (Sheet music excerpt taken and adapted from *Henle digital edition* © 2016 G. Henle Verlag, Munich)

The psychological process that is about to be described throughout the variations is based on the phenomena inherent in the theories of ego-development (3. 1): the shadow aspects are often experienced first by the "I" as an outer object of estrangement, which are consequently repressed. Once repressed, these aspects grow in significance, gaining in this way, a life of their own, by which the "I" is set out to the constant danger of being overwhelmed by them, i.e., exposed to processes such an inflation.

In view of these reflections, the theme and first variation can be understood as expressing the Self, whereby the "I" is still immersed in its natural environment.

[68] Cf. Illustrations in pp. 90–91 in: Ibid.

The theme, played by the violin, is symbolically understood as representing the trout, i.e., the Self. As previously seen, the brooklet features the figuration of the sextuplet motif in the form of the *circulatio* in the first variation. The *circulatio* in turn, may point here to the primordial unity (uroboros) that represents the first condition of the human being[69]. The trills and mordents are understood as madrigalisms, emphasizing the primordial condition of the "I", i.e., the state of being in harmony with nature. The association of chirping birds that arises in this context is especially given by the trills and mordents. Being in the uroboros state points to a still undifferentiated state of consciousness (Fig. 3.6 of 3.1).

As noted earlier, the sextuplet motif changes its form in the second variation. The "garland"[70]-like shape of rising and descending scale patterns may convey the flowing or exchanging of psychic energies between the unconscious and consciousness. Hence, this observation points to a development that is occurring in relation to the previous condition—it presupposes that the "I" is gradually detaching itself from an undifferentiated state (uroboros state) into developing an ego consciousness (Fig. 3.6 of 3.1). The split or the dialectic that emerges during the process of ego-development is congruently expressed by the fact that the theme presents itself fragmentarily (piano part). The identified musical motif of the falling *staccato* scale that emerges in this variation can be understood as a laughing topos, representing the Persona aspect of the "I" (mask) or the idyll that once existed. That means that only one aspect of the personality is put in the foreground or accepted by the "I", while the other is rather repressed, consequently falling into the shadow. To counterbalance this unilaterality, the archetypal antagonistic principle (shadow) is consequently activated.

In the following third variation, the theme incorporates the shadow aspect of the "I" and of society, conveyed by the low register of the theme (cello and contrabass as the fisherman). In turn, the sextuplet motif subsequently transmutes into the virtuosic thirty-two-note chains, featuring the *circulatio* figure, thus expressing here the emotional condition of the "I" in search of the lost wholeness. The panic identified above is recognised through the fearful flight of the "I" when confronted with the shadow aspect. The note repetitions and the rhythmic syncopations (violin and viola) emphasize the emotional conflict that lies in this ambiguity. Once again, the sextuplet motif transforms itself (variation IV), into the complete opposite of its original semantic, i.e., embodying *Thanatos* energy.

---

[69] In Jungian psychology, as already previously seen (I.) the circle symbolism points to wholeness, respectively to a primordial state of oneness (uroboros).

[70] Massin, Brigitte. (1977). *Franz Schubert*. P. 876.

The latter is to be identified by the chord repetitions that are featured in the violin, viola and piano and its commonly attributed meaning in Schubert's literature. Due to the dramatic inner occurrences, the positive sextuplet motif is broken into sixteenth-note triplet groups (cello and contrabass). There is a change of roles to be noticed and a clear overwhelming of the negative death drive, which can also be interpreted as an overpowering of the shadow aspect.

As far as the theme of variation IV is concerned (Self), it is now provided only in a rudimentary form. This fact points to the process of inflation, whereby the "I" uncritically approached the negative pole of the archetype[71] (3.2), which will consequently lead to annihilation. Accordingly, this destructive energy needs to be counter balanced again. This occurs subsequently through the change to F major which triggers a throwback, allowing the emergence of "memories of a beautiful past"[72] (second part of variation IV). This can be identified in the passage featuring the trills followed by the laughing topos in a *caccia* manner (mm.89–92)—as if the "I" would be pursued[73] by the reminiscences of the joyous time it was once embedded in, i.e., recalling the primordial unity with nature (uroboros). This observation also shows musically what is inherent in the Jungian concept of the Persona and shadow, being a pair of opposites (3.1). The moment of painful insight or return to reality is given by the diminished seventh chord and the modulation path returning to D minor (mm.93–100), which ultimately confirms the symbolic death of the "I".

The fact that the "I" has undergone a psychic transformation process involving the symbolic experience of death[74], triggers the activation of the opposite pole of the archetype again. Such dynamic processes are a result of the antagonistically structured human psyche, which led C.G. Jung to conceptualize the archetypes as polarized. The self-regulatory process, which runs autonomously, is seen in relation to the complementary and compensatory behavior of the psyche[75]. As a result, the "I" subsequently enters the idyllic realm of the B-flat major tonality.

---

[71] Cf. Jung, Carl Gustav. (2023). *Die Beziehung zwischen dem Ich und dem Unbewussten.*

[72] Böhm, Richard. (2006). *Symbolik und Rhetorik im Liedschaffen von Franz Schubert.* P. 64. (Trans. by the author). German expression: "Erinnerungen an schöne Vergangenheit.".

[73] This interpretation is based on the ancient traditions of the *caccia* that particularly point to the act of pursuing and fleeing. Cf. Dobretsberger, Barbara. (2019). *Formen der Vokalmusik.* P. 124.

[74] The symbolic death is described by Jung as being part of the rebirth mysteries, i.e., as part of a transformation process. Cf. Jung, Carl Gustav. (2011). *Four Archetypes.* P. 62–63.

[75] Cf. Jacobi, Jolande. (2006). *Die Psychologie von C.G. Jung.* P. 58–60. Jung himself has described these processes in: Jung, Carl Gustav. (2023). *Die Beziehung zwischen dem Ich und dem Unbewussten.*

The transformation process is confirmed by two musical facts: (i) the emergence of the dotted rhythm (m.101), as the heartbeat motif, relating to the life force, and (ii) the melodic change in the thematic material (m.103), raising the melodic line a third higher. The fact that the "I" is now in a parallel world (*Elysium*) assists for the integration of the split shadow elements[76]. Consequently, B-flat major is constantly being juxtaposed with its harmonic opposite pole, B-flat minor. The musical narration here corresponds psychologically to what C.G. Jung called a dialectic process[77]. The same dialectic process is taken to extremes in the following passage (mm.113–127), whereby the "I" rises into the transcendent realm of D-flat major and subsequently descends into the dark realm of F-sharp minor. The fact that these tonalities represent antagonistic principles is given by the fact that the one is a flat key, the second a sharp key. Key characteristics can assist this interpretation. D-flat major is described by Böhm as the key of "peace and tranquility" ("Frieden und Ruhe"), having been associated with "the union with Aurora, freedom, love, to 'shine down as a star'"[78] in the song "Memnon" D 541 (mm.40–57). In turn, F-sharp minor is, according to Schubart, the key of "resentment and displeasure" ("Groll und Missvergnügen")[79].

The several organ points placed in m.127 can be understood as representing psychologically a moment of immobilization which triggers a turning point. This process can find its equivalent in what Erich Neumann called a "phenomenon of reversal"[80]. Similarly, already C.G. Jung had used Heraklit's concept of "Enantiodromia" (I.) to describe the process of turning into the opposite[81]. This moment arrives with the unexpected recovery of the lied's citation in D major (m.128). This presupposes a prior successful dialectic process, which may lead to the

[76] Eugen Drewermann mentioned this psychological fact in the context of a fairy tale analysis. Cf. Drewermann, Eugen. (2023). „2. Sommervorlesung 2023: Märchen als Therapie. Auslegung von Grimms ‚Das Mädchen ohne Hände'". [Lecture]. Minutes: 01:07:45.

[77] C.G. Jung deals with this process in several of his works, notably in Jung, Carl Gustav. (2023). *Die Beziehung zwischen dem Ich und dem Unbewussten.* In addition, Jacobi features this process as a sub-chapter of its own in: Jacobi, Jolande. (2006). *Die Psychologie von C.G. Jung.* P. 72–73.

[78] Böhm, Richard. (2006). *Symbolik und Rhetorik im Liedschaffen von Franz Schubert.* P. 73. (Trans. by the author). German expression: "Vereinigung mit Aurora, Freiheit, Liebe, als 'Stern herab zu scheinen'".

[79] Cf. Ibid. P. 80.

[80] Cf. Neumann, Erich. (2021). *Die Große Mutter.* For the theoretical fundamentals exposed in this dissertation see 3.2.

[81] Roesler, Christian. Personal communication between Christian Roesler and the author. Freiburg im Breisgau: June 18, 2024. The definition of Enantiodromia is to be found in: Cf. Jung, Carl Gustav. (2013). *Kleines Lexikon der Analytischen Psychologie.*

assimilation of the split elements, ultimately a "return" to the Self. Now, the theme is presented once on the violin (consciousness/light element), once in the cello (unconscious/shadow element). This suggests the just mentioned process of incorporation of the shadow, which means that the "I" takes a critical look at the shadow aspects, integrating them[82]. It should be noted that the sextuplet motif is firstly presented in the original triadic motif. However, from m.144, which corresponds to the second period phrase construction of the lied, the sextuplet motif changes into the chromatic form, remaining so until the end. The proceeding of the theme in the cello part of m.156, which lacks musical necessity or logic, will lead to a synchronized restatement of the trout theme in m.164. This means that it functions as an archetypal principle for the "enlargement of personality"[83]. This fusion of violin and cello together with the original sextuplet motif may therefore indicate the ultimate transformation of the "I". If the triadic sextuplet representation is taken as the unstructured part of the personality, and the chromatic form as the structured part of the personality (Fig. 14.7), then the fact that it ends with the chromatic form synchronized with the light and shadow aspect of the theme consequently substantiates the "positive" transformation process.

This reading can be understood on the subjective or on the collective level, as an expression of the emotional conditions in the face of a society shaped by a censorship regime. Following C.G. Jung's thoughts, if the "I" is immoderately influenced by a society that is solely driven by mere appearances (Persona), it experiences an inner conflict or one-sidedness[84]. The light side of the Self and the positive life drive is experienced indirectly through a theriomorphic symbol, in this case the fish; while its annihilation drive is experienced through an anthropomorphic projection, in this case the fisherman. It should be enhanced that Jung described and elaborated on the fish's symbolism as a representation of Christ and the Self in his work *Aion*[85]. How this dichotomy is felt by the "I", when it emancipates from the undifferentiated/uroboros state (Theme and variation I), comes to expression through the splitting of the theme (variation II). Thereby, the shadow aspect, having been repressed, takes a life of its own, becoming autonomous and exerting a great power over the "I" (variation III). The latter, not possessing enough ego-strength (yet), eventually undergoes a process of inflation, i.e., it is engulfed by the shadow (variation IV). This inner conflict, which resulted from the repression of the shadow side in favour of the world of appearances

[82] Cf. Jung, Carl Gustav. (2023). *Die Beziehung zwischen dem Ich und dem Unbewussten.*

[83] Jung, Carl Gustav. (2011). *Four Archetypes.* (Trans. by R.F.C. Hull). P. 54.

[84] Cf. Jung, Carl Gustav. (2023). *Die Beziehung zwischen dem Ich und dem Unbewussten.*

[85] Cf. Jung, Carl Gustav. (1970). *Aion.*

(society), triggered the inflation (shadow overpowered); thus, a symbolic death is experienced (end of variation IV). As the psyche is structured in poles of opposite tensions, a counter world is created by an autonomous self-regulatory mechanism. Consequently, an idyllic world emerges (variation V). Being in this *Elysium*—a place prone to the integration of split elements—there is a juxtaposition of the contrasting tonalities (the pair of key opposites: B-flat major vs. B-flat minor). This is an expression of a psychological dialectic process, in which the light aspect is constantly being juxtaposed with the shadow aspect:

> "[…] a process which, by bringing the contents of the conscious mind closer to the contents of the unconscious, i.e., the ego and the non-ego, brings about a confrontation between these two psychic realities […], which aims to bridge the two in something third, i.e., a synthesis, and leads to this."[86].

Through this dialectic procedure, the split or repressed shadow element, which had previously gained a life of its own, has now been assimilated again, which leads back to the Self (*Allegretto*). The theme is presented again, yet it reappears in its original form, featuring the triadic sextuplet motif, as the expression of the chaotic unstructured condition it once was. In turn, the structured element arises imminently in the form of the chromatic sextuplet motif. Consequently, through assimilation there is an "enlargement of the personality"[87] to be noted. The theme is now performed both by the light side, represented by the violin, and shadow side, represented by the cello—which substantiates the interpretation of the integration of opposites. The fact that the cello retakes the *élan* in m.156, leads to a unisono synchronization between the two. The unisono factor thus speaks for a compliance between consciousness and the unconscious, expressing how the "I" ultimately arrives at transcending the outer reality (Fig. 14.8).

---

[86] Jacobi, Jolande. (2006). *Die Psychologie von C.G. Jung*. P. 72. German expression: "Es ist auch in sich dialektisch, als ein Prozeß, der durch die Heranführung der Inhalte des Bewußtseins an die Inhalte des Unbewußten, also des Ego an das Non-Ego, eine Auseinandersetzung zwischen diesen beiden psychischen Realitäten hervorruft, die eine Überbrückung der beiden *in etwas Drittem*, also in eine *Synthese* bezweckt und in diese mündet.".

[87] Jung, Carl Gustav. (2011). *Four Archetypes*. (Trans. by R.F.C. Hull). P. 54.

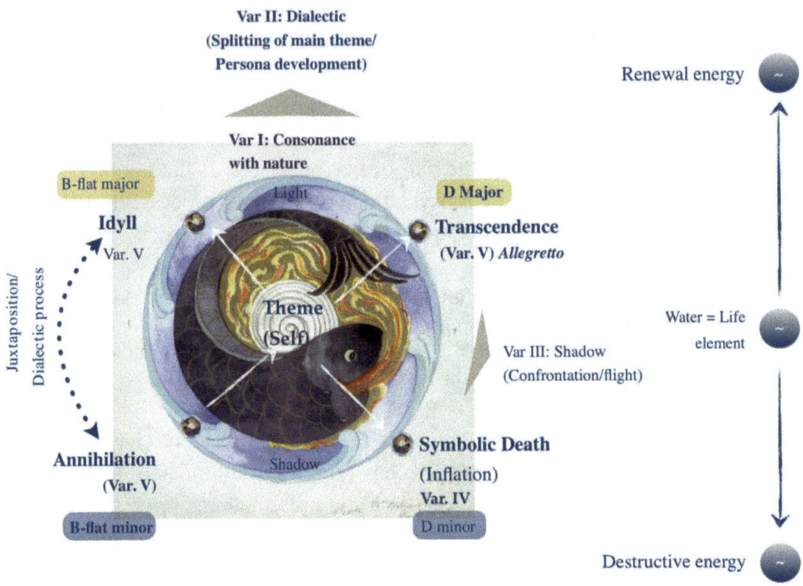

Fig. 14.8 Representation of the psychic processes inherent in the variation movement of the piano quintet in A major D 667. (Illustration used: "008 AHAF, Anonymous picture of a patient". Property of the image archive of the C.G. Jung Institut Zürich-Küsnacht and reproduced with its permission)

With these psychological observations, the importance of the new material in variation V is clear: Schubert presents a resolution (*lysis*) by critically looking at the shadow aspects and integrating them. This last concluding thought can equally indicate an integration of some split elements which, with regard to the years of introspection (or the so-called "years of crisis") shows a positive development (cf. 20).

Die Schöne Müllerin D 795. The miller-lad's journey (in)to him-Self

15

Die Schöne Müllerin, composed in 1823 (possibly in the fall[1]), represents the first song cycle that Schubert wrote. It is based on the poems of Wilhelm Müller (1794–1827)—a German poet, politically aware, who opposed the social order and politics of his time. His idiom reflects the nature aesthetics of the Romantic period and the characteristics of folk poetry[2]. It seems to be of general consensus that Wilhelm Müller remains in the shadow of Schubert[3], although in his lifetime he was also known for his *Griechenlieder*. Details of a biographical nature and of Wilhelm Müller's œuvre cannot be dealt with here, since it would go beyond the scope of this dissertation. The most substantial information regarding the genesis

[1] There are some controversial opinions about the actual dating of the composition, though, the most recent literature suggests that it was highly probable to date it back to the fall of 1823. Cf. Dittrich, Marie-Agnes. "Die Lieder. 'Für Menschenohren sind es Harmonien'". In: Dürr, Walther. Krause, Andreas. (2020). *Schubert Handbuch.* Chapter: „Werkbesprechungen. Die Schöne Müllerin".

[2] Cf. Allen, Philip S. (1899). "Wilhelm Müller and the German Volkslied. I.". In: *The Journal of Germanic Philology. Vol. 2, Nr.3.* P. 283–322.

[3] Cf. Cottrell, Alan. (1970). *Wilhelm Müller's Lyrical Song-cycles.* P. 1. See also: Ritter, Hans Martin. (2014). „Winterreise. Wilhelm Müller entdeckt das lyrische Monodram". In: *Musik und Text. Band 3.*

The music analytical and psychological findings developed in this chapter were presented by the author herself in public for the first time under the title 'Franz Schubert: Der Müller und der Bach. Der Dialog des Müllers inneren Stimmen—eine Analysemethode anhand C. G. Jung's Archetypenlehre' in the form of one-and-a-half hour and slide-assited lecture in the frame of a music analysis seminar at the University Mozarteum, Salzburg (March 23, 2024), under the supervision of Barbara Dobretsberger.

L. Dill, *Schubert's Metamorphoses*,
https://doi.org/10.1007/978-3-662-73476-6_15

of these poems will be given first, followed by the circumstances of origin of Schubert's musical setting.

As it will be elaborated in the introductory chapter (15.1), Wilhelm Müller's *Die Schöne Müllerin* is based on elements of folk poetry, i.e., it narrates a story based on folk tales[4]. As such, archetypes and archetypal stations are to be found in the poems and in Schubert's musical setting. This chapter attempts to decipher the archetypal core of this story line and the possible effect of these structures on Schubert's inner processes during its creation. Once the general characteristics of this narration are mentioned, the analysis follows the developments of the archetypal stages inherent in the song cycle. In order to preserve the clarity of the complex inner processes and not to interrupt the flow of the psychic narrative, the songs have been musically examined in varying degrees of detail, with some being mentioned *en passant*. This method was chosen particularly for this song cycle to contextualize the songs, since it bears a narrative quality that conveys a psychological transformation process. The aim of the musical analysis is to focus on the psychological core statement as the Ariadne's thread across the chapter and to work out the musical details in this sense. For the same reason, the songs were subsequently assembled in groups according to the identified main psychic stations. A special emphasis is given to "Der Müller und der Bach", since (i) this lied stands between the two crucial inner events ongoing in "Trockne Blumen" and "Des Baches Wiegenlied", (ii) unveiling important symbolic contents that are essential for the psychological outcome.

15.1 Introduction to the genesis of *Die Schöne Müllerin*. The general characteristics of the cycle and of its protagonists examined under a Jungian perspective

Literary circles were common during Schubert's and Müller's lifetime. Like Schubert with his circle of friends and the *Schubertiaden*, Wilhelm Müller himself was member of a literary circle in Berlin, together with other important personalities, such as the poet Ludwig Rellstab, Clemens Brentano, the painter Wilhelm Hensel and his sister Luise Hensel[5]. They held regular meetings in the house

[4] Deutsch, Otto Erich. (1915). *Das Urbild der "Schönen Müllerin"*.

[5] Cf. Braun, Christiane. Berke, Dietrich. „Die Schöne Müllerin op. 25 (D 795)—Liederzyklus Wilhelm Müller". In: Dürr, Walther. Kube, Michael. [et al.]. (2013). *Schubert Liedlexikon*. Brigitte Massin accounts additionally the poet Achim von Arnim. Cf. Massin, Brigitte. (1977). *Franz Schubert*. P. 1025.

of the Berlin state Councilor von Stägemann. Ludwig Berger—a composer who belonged to the so-called third Berlin school along with e.g., Felix Mendelssohn Bartholdy[6]—was the piano teacher of Luise Hensel[7] and a friend of the members of this literary circle[8], having occasionally attended these meetings[9].

Such informal gatherings between personalities as poets, painters, and composers, established a place for vivid exchanges, certainly including discussions on political and social matters *inter alia*. More importantly, they undoubtedly unleashed creative forces and can be seen as a great source of inspiration. This is especially true for the genesis of Wilhelm Müller's miller-girl poems: after a report of Ludwig Rellstab, these personalities gave each other specific artistic assignments[10]. A particular "Liederspiel" assignment was given during one of the gatherings around 1816/1817. The main literary incentive for such a project came from several sources: on the one hand, from the topic inherent in Giovanni Paisiellos' opera buffa *La molinara,* which had just been performed in Europe and had found a German adaptation in Christoph Friedrich Bretzner's version *Die Schöne Müllerin*; on the other hand, several of Goethe's œuvre seem to have been the springboard, such as *Der Edelknabe und die Müllerin, Der Junggesell und der Mühlbach, Der Müllerin Verrat* and *Der Müllerin Reue*[11]. The "Müllerlieder" from *Des Knaben Wunderhorn* were a source of inspiration as well[12]. Writing the plot, acting, and performing constituted the activities in which all participants engaged actively, thereby exerting a profound mutual influence on each other[13]. The composer Ludwig Berger was asked to collaborate in this "Liederspiel" project and was the one responsible for the musical setting[14]. This means that Wilhelm Müller used to exchange ideas with Ludwig Berger and vice-versa. According to the reports of Rellstab, this collaboration was apparently not that straightforward and undemanding[15]—still, they reciprocally influenced each other

---

[6] Cf. Schmierer, Elisabeth. (2017). *Geschichte des Kunstliedes.* P. 75.

[7] Cf. Youens, Susan. (1991). "Behind the scenes: 'Die schöne Müllerin" before Schubert". In: *19th Century Music, Vol. 15, Nr. 1*, P. 3–22.

[8] Cf. Massin, Brigitte. (1977). *Franz Schubert.* P. 1025.

[9] Cf. Ibid.

[10] Cf. Feil, Arnold. (1996). *Franz Schubert.* P. 24.

[11] Cf. Braun, Christiane. Berke, Dietrich. „Die Schöne Müllerin op. 25 (D 795)—Liederzyklus Wilhelm Müller". In: Dürr, Walther. Kube, Michael. [et al.]. (2013). *Schubert Liedlexikon.*

[12] Cf. Ibid.

[13] Cf. Feil, Arnold. (1996). *Franz Schubert.* P. 24.

[14] Cf. Ibid.

[15] Cf. Youens, Susan. (1991). „Behind the scenes: 'Die schöne Müllerin' before Schubert". In: *19th Century Music,* Vol. 15, Nr. 1, P. 3–22. JSTOR, https://doi.org/10.2307/746295.

in their versions of *Die Schöne Müllerin*[16]. The storyline is based on folk lied tradition, following the popular story of the beautiful miller-girl, named Rose, who had several suitors: a gardener, a hunter, and the miller-lad. The dramatic point lies in the fact that Rose, having rather a volatile character, preferred the hunter to the miller-lad—the hunter figure, was regarded as the highest symbol of masculinity, and was, unlike the miller-lad, devoid of any sensitive abilities.

Having its roots in folk tradition, this story bears an archetypal core. The inherent collective, archetypal character seemingly resonated in Wilhelm Müller, who subsequently slightly changed the storyline to a love triangle, wherein the gardener character is withdrawn. So doing, Wilhelm Müller unveils another underlying motivation of a rather biographical core: he nurtured an unfulfilled love towards Luise Hensel, who was courted by Clemens Brentano—the latter, was characterized by the hunter figure in the storyline[17]. Although bearing folk tone traits, this autobiographical story was published in the form of a series of poems under the title of *Sieben und siebzig Gedichte aus den hinterlassenen Papieren eines Waldhornisten* in 1821. These poems were a source of inspiration for several composers[18], including Schubert.

Schubert—possibly unaware of Ludwig Berger's prior musical setting—composed the music according to Wilhelm Müller's published version of 1821[19], making a selection of poems. The ones excluded were the prologue and epilogue of the poet, as well as "Das Mühlenleben", "Erster Schmerz, letzter Schmerz" and "Blümlein Vergißmein". There are several possible reasons why Schubert did not set these poems to music. On the one hand, it could be caused by a special structural concern, related to the dramaturgical construction of the composition[20]. On

---

16 Ludwig Berger's lied compositions, comprising ten songs, are entitled *Gesänge aus einem gesellschaftlichen Liederspiele „Die schöne Müllerin"* and were published in 1819 by E.H.G. Christiani as op. 11.

17 Cf. Feil, Arnold. (1996). *Franz Schubert.* P. 24.

18 Susan Youens gives an overview on the several existent versions prior to and after Schubert: Cf. Youens, Susan. (1997). *Schubert, Müller, and 'Die schöne Müllerin'.*

19 Cf. Dittrich, Marie-Agnes. "Die Lieder. 'Für Menschenohren sind es Harmonien'". In: Dürr, Walther. Krause, Andreas. (2020). *Schubert Handbuch.* Chapter: „Werkbesprechungen. Die Schöne Müllerin".

20 As Bianconi explained, there is consensus about the fact that the song cycle consists of two parts. Cf. Bianconi, Gioseppina La Face. (2013). *Das Haus des Müllers.* P. 30. Footnote 44. This type of construction, in turn, reveals its dramaturgical arc. However, for the latter, there are several differing theories for the possible reason of Schubert's omissions of the above-mentioned poems. As already noted by Bianconi, for Capell and Daverio, "Pause" is understood in its literal sense, thus clearly marking the beginning of the second half. In turn, Georgiades rather advocates for "Thränenregen" being the end of the first part. Ibid. For

the other hand, these omissions could hint at topics that were either too hurtful to engage with emotionally, or that Schubert considered irrelevant. It may also be a combination of these distinct motives.

From biographical facts, it is known that the time of composition of Schubert's *Die Schöne Müllerin* (and the year of 1823 in general), was particularly characterized as having been a time of great distress: (i) not only because he was diagnosed with a potential fatal illness, which led to his hospitalization and during which Schubert felt a decrease in his work flow[21], (ii) but also because his latest works in the opera genre were not well received[22]. Moreover, Schubert, who was having great financial issues at that time, eventually made a poor business decision at the beginning of that year: he felt compelled to relinquish his rights in the publication of some works (op. 1–14) in favour of Cappi & Diabelli, which he subsequently regretted, later severing his relationships with those publishers[23]. In addition to these concurrently existing matters, earlier traumatic events might still have had an impact on him—especially so, if Schubert's general state of mind was stricken due to the coexisting mentioned issues. Two events should be recalled here: (i) the traumatic event for Schubert related to his mother's death and (ii) the unfulfilled love towards Theresa Grob, who despite nurturing feelings for Schubert, was obliged to marry someone else, due to his low income. All of these facts could have been present at the time of origin of the miller-lad's song cycle.

Psychologically observed, it is plausible that, while composing the miller-lad's songs, Schubert could have found some kind of consolation both, in dealing with this storyline and in expressing, processing his sorrow through his music,

Georgiades direct source see: Georgiades, Thrasybulos. (1967). *Schubert Musik und Lyrik.* P. 253. As it will be explained later, the analytical findings of the author rather point to the latter opinion. To be more specific, "Thränenregen" is here comprehended as the turning point in the dramaturgical arc. Coincidingly, due to the above-mentioned omissions, "Thränenregen" represents the exact midpoint of the song cycle, being the tenth song out of a total of twenty.

[21] Cf. Schubert, Franz: Letter to Schober. (30.11.1823). In: Deutsch, Otto Erich. (1964). *Schubert—Die Dokumente seines Lebens.* P. 207. Here, Schubert uttered: "Since the opera, I have not composed anything, but a few Müller lieder.".

[22] For instance, the one-act operetta *Die Verschworenen* D 787, completed in April 1823 was not performed. Similarly, the production of the opera *Fierabras* D 796, finished in September/October 1823, was rejected. Prior to those two attempts, *Alfonso und Estrella* D732, composed between September 1821 and February 1822 had had the same destiny. Cf. Brown, Maurice J.E.: "Franz Schubert". In: Sadie, Stanley. (1980). *The New Grove Dictionary of Music and Musicians.* P. 761–763.

[23] Cf. Ibid. P. 761.

by giving it an artistic shape. Schubert himself confessed the relation between his emotions and experiences, and his creative work: "My creations are existent through the understanding of music and through my pain"[24]. As already explained (7), emotions have an archetypal core seeking expression. Nevertheless, outward stimuli can emotionally affect as well, due to the resonance or confrontation with the inner psychic reality. Considering his biographical facts, some archetypes might have been specially charged at the time of creation, e.g., Anima and Great Mother—archetypes, that are also present, playing an important role in the storyline of Wilhelm Müller's *Die Schöne Müllerin*, as it is to be elaborated.

In general terms, it can be recognized that the poems and the song cycle deal with the romantic fantasy of the wanderer archetype, who goes on a journey into nature and lets himself be guided by nature's elements. Nature is humanised [25]. This observation implies that the processes of nature are experienced mythologically, that nature itself and all its elements—brooks, plants and stones, etc.,—are believed to have a soul. Hence, nature is perceived to be closely tied to the human being. In this sense, this journey evokes primordial experiences and a specific way of living in tune with nature, which meets the beliefs attributed to animism (4). Restating this in Jungian terms, nature and psyche are experienced as a unity by the inner primordial reality. This thought, which is also specific to the aesthetics of German Romanticism (e.g., Schelling), is present in C.G. Jung's conception of the Self (4). In this sense, wandering can be understood as an individuation process: by observing the outer landscapes the wanderer in fact looks within. Consequently, occurrences in nature find resonance in the unconscious, being lived by the individual as metaphors of the inner reality. Thus, this wandering journey narrates the inner developments taking place. It is about a process of transformation, i.e., an individuation process, while reflecting at the same time the artist's quest to dissolve the dialectic between the inner and outer world (4).

---

[24] Cf. Schubert, Franz: "Aus einem verlorenen Notizbuche Schuberts von 1824". In: Deutsch, Otto Erich. (1964). *Schubert—Die Dokumente seines Lebens*. P. 233. (Trans. by the author). German expression: „Meine Erzeugnisse sind durch den Verstand für Musik und durch meinen Schmerz vorhanden […]".

[25] Cf. Dürr, Walther. „Schubert in seiner Welt". In: Dürr, Walther. Krause, Andreas. (2020). *Schubert Handbuch*. P. 2.

During the journey (in)to him-Self, the wanderer gets confronted with the shadow, meets (and possibly integrates) the Anima figure, who will allow a deeper descent in the unconscious, finally encountering the mana-personality of the Great Mother. The mentioned process reflects the archetypal stages present in C.G. Jung's classic theory of the archetypes (3.1). This interpretation will present a different shade in the understanding of the narration in relation to the consensual reading of this poem/song cycle that, in turn, tends to remain on the surface in terms of content. The latter, in a nutshell, describes a miller-lad, unluckily in love with the miller's daughter, who, in his depressive state, finds redemption in ending his life by drowning himself in the brook.

As the song cycle is based on a given text, featuring characters and personified elements of nature, the analysis should follow the same methodological approach as fairy tales or dream interpretations. All characters appearing in the storyline, including the elements of nature, should be analysed from the subject-level perspective, since they are, in fact, subpersonalities, i.e., are all part of the own psyche (Fig. 15.13). In addition to C.G. Jung's descriptions of the archetypal stages, the author draws also on the archetypal model of Erich Neumann for this chapter, where the archetype is presented as four-poled (3.2). This is due to the fact that water is one central symbol of the cycle, integrating the feminine forces of the unconscious, i.e., the Anima and the Great Mother, which are inextricably linked. Punctually, some parallels can also be drawn with Campbell's model of the hero's journey[26] (3.1).

The miller-lad as the lyrical "I" is the narrator of all lived experiences during this journey. It can generally be assumed that his singing voice represents his consciousness, while the piano reflects his unconscious voice[27]. From the poems it is known that the miller-lad is also a wanderer, a poet and a musician. His personality is especially characterized by the fact that the thinking and sensation functions are charged[28]: he judges through his thinking and perceives the outer world through his senses. The latter describes his connection to the outer nature, which in fact, is a reflection/projection of his inner nature: "I heard a brooklet roaring […]" ("Ich hört' ein Bächlein rauschen")[29]. The way he reacts to the outer

[26] Cf. Campbell, Joseph. (1993). *The Hero with a Thousand Faces.*

[27] This is based on the observations of Edward T. Cone, already presented in III, who emphasized the importance of the piano role in Schubert's lieder, relating it to the unconscious.

[28] The author is aware that—as already C.G. Jung drew attention to the following fact—these typological observations are only to be taken as a bare orientation line and not as a fixed characteristic of the individual's personality, since these qualities have a changing nature due to the self-regulating process of the unconscious itself.

[29] Müller, Wilhelm. (1991). *Die Schöne Müllerin.* P. 45. (Trans. by the author).

stimuli constitutes his tendency to the introverted typology[30]; however, the song cycle begins with a rather progressive energetic movement: "[…] each conscious act of will is the expression of the progressive energy […]. The progression is in the need to adapt to the outside world […]"[31]. It is important to recall that both, types and functions, stand always in a compensatory relationship to each other, as the unconscious is to consciousness[32]. For this reason, the piano, symbolizing the miller-lad's unconscious, will often reveal characteristics of the feeling and intuitive function, through e.g., harmonies and motivic interrelations. Furthermore, his personality possesses the characteristic naivety, timidity and the capacity of deep feelings and faithful love.

After having examined some general characteristics of the work and its genesis in relation to biographical facts, the chapter will continue with the musical and psychological analysis of the selected songs.

---

30 Vogel explains: "In extraverted mode, a function grasps the object quickly and can also let it go again quickly; contact with the object is relatively free. The person concerned can—to put it colloquially—distance themselves again; the content of such a function does not get 'under their skin'. If, on the other hand, a function is introverted, the person is personally affected by the content, it gets under their skin, 'touches them'". Vogel, Ralf T. (2017). *Individuation und Wandlung*. P. 39–40. (Trans. by the author). German expression: „Im extravertierten Modus greift eine Funktion das Objekt schnell auf und kann es auch schnell wieder loslassen, der Kontakt zum Objekt ist relativ frei. Der Betreffende kann sich—umgangssprachlich ausgedrückt.—wieder abgrenzen, Inhalte einer solchen Funktion gehen ihm nicht sehr ‚unter die Haut'. Ist eine Funktion dagegen introvertiert eingestellt, ist der Mensch persönlich von den Inhalten betroffen, sie gehen ihm ‚unter die Haut', ‚berühren ihn'".

31 Jacobi, Jolande. (2006). *Die Psychologie von C.G. Jung*. P. 61–62. German expression: "[…] jeder bewußte Willensakt ist ein Ausdruck der Progression der Energie […]. Die Progression ist in der Notwendigkeit der Anpassung an das Außen […]".

32 Jacobi, for instance, formulates: „Extraversion and Introversion also behave towards each other in a compensatory way.". Ibid. P. 29. (Trans. by the author). German expression: "Extraversion und Introversion verhalten sich zueinander ebenfalls kompensatorisch.".

15.2 "Das Wandern" and "Wohin?": The *prima materia* and the negative Anima as an autonomous complex

"[...] the path of the soul that leads to the water."[33].

In "Das Wandern" (no.1) the journey of the miller-lad begins—the journey (in)to him-Self. The march-like character is accentuated by Schubert's choice of measure (2/4) and the spondaic rhythm of the left hand (the wanderer rhythm). By choosing B-flat major as the starting key, Schubert points to the initial inner mood of the miller-lad: his journey is started with "devoted faith, [with] confidence and surrender to the will of Divine providence"[34]; his inner driving force is his thirsty condition of his soul, the longing ("Sehnsucht") of the unknown, of the yet to be explored[35]. The harmonic disposition is rather simple since there is an alternation between tonic and dominant. The "simplicity" hereby conveyed may already point to the characteristics of the miller-lad's personality mentioned above. In addition to this "naïve" harmonic disposition with which the song begins and which reflects a tendency to the folk tone[36], Schubert emphasizes some of the words of the poems through repetition and accents. However, the rhythmic structure is not as innocent as it appears. Schubert creates already a first rhythmic contradiction (Fig. 15.1) by adding the alternated intervals of the third and sixth in the semiquavers figure of the right hand on the light beat of the measure[37]. This

[33] Jung, Carl Gustav. (2020). *Archetypen. Urbilder und Wirkkräfte des Kollektiven Unbewussten.* P. 23. (Trans. by the author). German expression: "[...] de[r] Weg der Seele, der zum Wasser führt.".

[34] The cited description of the B-flat major tonality is taken from Schillings Encyclopedia, that reads as follows: "The psychic expression of this tonality B-flat major is [...] devouted faith, confidence, that calmly surrenders to the will of divine providence.". Schilling, Gustav. (1974). *Encyclopädie der gesammten musikalischen Wissenschaften oder Universal—Lexikon der Tonkunst.* Nachdruck der Ausgabe Stuttgart 1835. Band I. P. 489. (Trans. by the author). German expression: "Der psychische Ausdruck dieser Tonart B-Dur ist [...] und der fromme Glaube, das Vertrauen, das sich ruhig dem Willen der göttlichen Fügung überläßt.".

[35] Schubart described this tonality as the "key of Sehnsucht". Cited after: Braun, Christiane. Berke, Dietrich. „Die Schöne Müllerin op. 25 (D 795)—Liederzyklus Wilhelm Müller". In: Dürr, Walther. Kube, Michael. [et al.]. (2013). *Schubert Liedlexikon.* P. 638. Böhm complements with Schubart's description of "looking towards a better world". Böhm, Richard. (2006). *Symbolik und Rhetorik im Liedschaffen von Franz Schubert.* P. 66.

[36] The melodic character conveys a character recalling the yodelling traditions. Cf. Georgiades, Thrasybulos. (1967). *Schubert Musik und Lyrik.* P. 222.

[37] Cf. Feil, Arnold. (1996). *Franz Schubert.* P. 60–61.

ambiguity is accentuated by placing the dominant chord on the strong beat[38] (the dominant seeks resolution in the tonic, i.e., it strives for the tonic). Employing Feil's analytical discoveries regarding the harmony and the generated rhythmical off-beat emphasis for an archetypal reading, leads to a revealing observation: this indistinctness can point to the still unstructured or underdeveloped parts of the miller-lad's personality (the *prima materia*), which seeks to be addressed and which will be developed through his active attitude of starting a wandering journey.

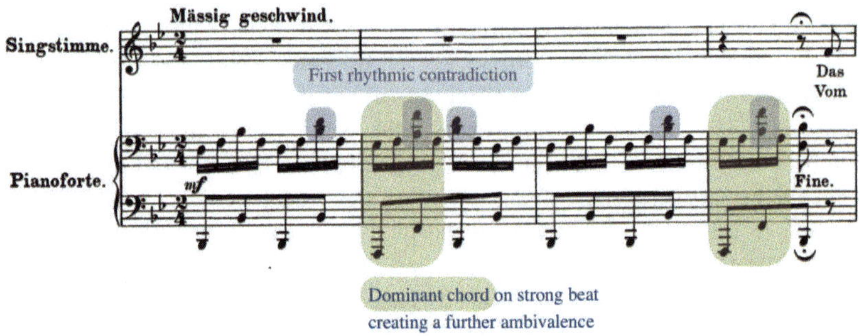

Fig. 15.1 Ambivalences and rhythmic contradictions in "Das Wandern", pointing to the unstructured parts of the miller-lad's personality (prima materia). (Sheet music excerpt taken and adapted from *IMSLP*)

After stating the initial (inner) situation, the brook appears in "Wohin?" (no.2). The brook fulfills several functions throughout the cycle, which will be gradually uncovered in the course of the analysis. For the time being, the brook recalls the archetype of the path[39], since the miller-lad orients himself by the brook: "O, brooklet, speak! Whereto?" ("O Bächlein sprich wohin?"[40]. Suddenly, he hears an inner call, which sends him down into the valley—symbolically speaking, down into the unconscious realm: "I must go down too with my wandering pole. Down and ever forth [...]" ("I musste auch hinunter mit meinem Wanderstab. Hinunter und immer weiter [...]")[41]. With the gradual descending movement

[38] Cf. Ibid.

[39] The archetype of the path has been dealt with previously (4). Erich Neumann describes the importance of this archetype and the roots of it in: Neumann, Erich. (2021). *Die Große Mutter*.

[40] Müller, Wilhelm. (1991). *Die Schöne Müllerin.* P. 46. (Trans. by the author).

[41] Ibid. (Trans. by the author).

towards the brooklet, the miller-lad's senses get clouded. This process of an inner voice calling and intoxicating the senses, driving the "I" towards the valley, to the water of the unconscious can be read in C.G. Jung as following:

> "The path of water, which always leads downwards, must be travelled if we want to recover the treasure [...]"[42].

Examining the musical score so far, the pastoral landscape narrated by the lyrical "I" is musically described by the G major tonality (which, by all means, can point to an illusory idyll as well[43]). The right-hand semiquavers-sextuplet motif tone paints the shimmering water movement of the brook. This madrigalism as a motif can be termed accordingly, as the brooklet motif. Precisely in key moments, Schubert makes use of certain compositional techniques to emphasize what the text conveys or to comment on it. For instance, the *colla voce* in mm. 23–26 between the singing voice and the piano left hand, depicting a falling line, is striking: "Down and ever forth, and ever along the brook" ("Hinunter und immer weiter, und immer dem Bache nach")[44]. The same happens later in mm.42–45, which underlines the revelation of his clouded emotional state as a consequence of the roaring brooklet. A change of diastematics is to be identified, where the senses of the miller-lad are getting clouded: by using tone repetitions in mm. 35–39, the miller-lad conveys his emotions. With this *parlando*-style passage Schubert conveys, in a direct manner, the inner emotional state of the miller-lad, due to the closeness with the tone colour of human speech. Dittrich's observation emphasizing the fact that Schubert often reached back to the recitativo style to increase dramaticism should be recalled here (III). This is emphasized by the musical phrases which are now shorter in structure, i.e., 2 bar-structure instead of 4-bar structure (mm.35–41). These alterations not only increase the dramaticism but also express a sense of disorientation, present at the textual level.

This emotional state and loss of direction is additionally expressed through Schubert's increased use of chromaticism, e.g., mm.11–12 "I know not, what befell on me, nor who gave advice to me" (Ich weiß nicht, wie mir wurde, nicht wer den Rat mir gab")[45]. A more striking example is the passage from mm. 35 "Is this then my lane? O brooklet speak whereto? Thou have with thy roaring

---

[42] Jung, Carl Gustav. (2020). *Archetypen. Urbilder und Wirkkräfte des Kollektiven Unbewussten.* P. 24. (Trans. by the author). German expression: "Den Weg des Wassers, der immer nach unten geht, muss man wohl gehen, wenn man den Schatz, […], wieder heben will".

[43] Cf. Böhm, Richard. (2006). *Symbolik und Rhetorik im Liedschaffen von Franz Schubert.*

[44] Müller, Wilhelm. (1991). *Die Schöne Müllerin.* P. 45. (Trans. by the author).

[45] Ibid. (Trans. by the author).

entirely bewildered my senses" (Ist dies denn meine Straße? O Bächlein sprich wohin? Du hast mit deinem Rauschen, mir ganz berauscht den Sinn")[46]. The urgent question of "O brooklet speak whereto?" in mm.38–39 is chromatised and set to music in an ascending manner, which points to the musical rhetorical figure of the *interrogatio.* The insisting repeated questions about "where to" in the following measures (mm. 40–41) are again chromatised, however, combined now with a falling gesture (E"–D-sharp"). This descending mimetic movement within the ambit of a second recalls the *suspiratio* figure, which utters his desperate state of disorientation and his appeal for direction. Noteworthy is the fact that the musical motif of "wohin?" ends subsequently with a falling third (D-sharp–B), which corresponds to the same interval under the words "Rauschen" and "Sinn"[47] in mm. 42–43, respectively, mm.44–45: "Thou have with thy roaring entirely bewildered my senses". This means that Schubert musically anticipates the revelation of the miller-lad's clouded senses[48]. Intriguingly, the downward movement of the "wohin?" motif emphasizes the direction he ought to follow—the path leading downwards to the water, to the unconscious. It is as if the miller-lad had already an inkling that the answer to that question would lie in the downward direction[49]. This is to be understood psychologically as an inner force acting upon him, i.e., an unconscious force that intoxicated his senses and takes the leading position over the "I". Out of the reason that the journey along the water drives him downwards, it is impossible then to proceed with the ascending *interrogatio* figure[50] (Fig. 15.2).

[46] Ibid. (Trans. by the author).

[47] Cf. Dobretsberger, Barbara. Personal communication between Barbara Dobretsberger and the author. Salzburg/Noiraigue: March 29, 2024.

[48] Cf. Ibid.

[49] Cf. Ibid.

[50] Cf. Ibid.

Fig. 15.2 The change of diastematics and the increasing use of chromaticim setting musically the inner state of disorientation of the miller-lad. Rising *interrogatio* figure vs. the falling *suspiratio* and the falling third as the motivic bound between "wohin?", "Rauschen" and "Sinn". (Sheet music excerpt taken and adapted from *IMSLP*)

The fascinating unconscious voice, that was just musically analysed, is to be attributed to one of the "treasures" living within the water and that C.G. Jung, in the above-cited statement, mentions: symbolically speaking, water represents not only the unconscious but also the "feminine forces"[51]. At this point, it can be said that there are two feminine forces within the brook symbolism that are acting over the miller-lad. Firstly, there are the daughters of the brook, the nymphs[52]. Archetypally, they are the manifestation of the negative Anima figure[53]—they are seductive, enchanting and desire to bewitch or to cloud the senses of the miller-lad, to speak in Müller's language: "Surely, the nymphs are singing deep down their round" ("Es singen wohl die Nixen tief unten ihren Reihn")[54]. Denoting

[51] Mollwo-Oesterreicher, Marianne. (1978). *Herder Lexikon Symbole.* P. 179. (Trans. by the author). German expression: „Die Psychoanalyse sieht im W. vorwiegend ein Symbol des Weiblichen u. der Kräfte des Unterbewußten.".

[52] The appearance of this mythological feminine water creature can be seen as an example for the folk poetry influence and character of Wilhelm Müller's poems. In German Romanticism, this theme was adopted from the French literature on *La belle melusine* from the Middle Ages. In the German Romantic conception, the nymphs endowed with a combination of magical healing powers and tragic death or a regressive death drive that is projected and achieved through the rebirth properties of water. Cf. Meier-Seethaler, Carola. "Nixe". In: Symbolonline.de. [Article].

[53] This analogy can be found in several writings of C.G. Jung. Cf. Jung, Carl Gustav. (2020). *Archetypen. Urbilder und Wirkkräfte des Kollektiven Unbewussten.*

[54] Schubert altered Müller's original text which read: „[...] down there their round" ("[...] dort unten ihren Reihn"). Müller, Wilhelm. (1991). *Die Schöne Müllerin.* P. 46. (Trans. by the author).

that the nymphs can act out of themselves and have a great impact on the miller-lad's senses, these Anima personifications, can function as, what Jung called, an autonomous complex[55]. Secondly, the other inherent feminine power relates to the fate goddesses[56], who will show him his path of Destiny towards the mill. The fate goddesses, also designated as norns (8), are possible manifestations of the Great Mother archetype, which include both opposite poles, the positive and the negative. The symbol for the fate goddesses is the spinning wheel. The wheel in itself is a symbol of wholeness, due to its circular shape. In a further step of the analytical consideration, it is significant to examine how this symbolic content is translated in musical terms in relation to the poem, and to understand which proportions it takes in the first songs of the cycle.

Schubert achieves the analogy with the norns and the wheel, as a symbol of wholeness, through tone painting means, i.e., by using the rhetorical figure of the *circulatio,* inherent in the brooklet motif. This circular movement is already present since the very first song "Das Wandern", depicted by the semiquaver shape of the right hand and underlined by the repetition of certain key words of the poem such as "the wandering" ("das Wandern"), "the water" ("das Wasser"), "the wheels" ("die Räder") and "the stones" ("die Steine"). Through the recurrence of these words and through the strophic form of the song a circular perception of time[57] is conveyed, musically creating a movement recalling an eternal return, present in the circle symbolism, i.e., a constant return to a centre. By replacing the key words of each stanza "the wandering"—"the water"—"the wheels"—the "stones" with the corresponding underlying symbolism, in the same four-step manner, results the following formulation: the "journey"—through the "unconscious"—to the "Self"—leading to "eternity". The first and second steps have been addressed in "Das Wandern" and in "Wohin?", respectively. Subsequently, as the third step, the "wheels" should follow as the symbol for the Self in "Halt!".

---

[55] Cf. Jung, Carl Gustav. (2023). *Die Beziehung zwischen dem Ich und dem Unbewussten.* Chapter: "Anima und Animus".

[56] It should be recalled that the norns are often depicted by the water, at river edges. Cf. Betz, Otto. (2016). „Der Lebensfaden". In: *herder.de.*

[57] From the philologist's point of view of Alan Cottrell the transformed word repetitions are seen as an inner driving force, pushing forwards and unleashed by the wandering movement. He emphasizes the bridging function of the first and the last stanza through the word "gaiety" ("Lust"). Cf. Cottrell, Alan. (1970). *Wilhelm Müller's Lyrical Song-cycles.* P. 10.

15.3 "Halt!" and "Danksagung an den Bach": The Norns and the Path of Destiny to the Mill. The Mill as a Symbol of Wholeness. The Acceptance of "I" Towards its Purpose

When approaching this song analytically, it can be generally observed that the musical motifs present at the beginning of the third lied play an important role in the course of its development. These comprise the following elements (Fig. 15.3): (i) the *circulatio* figure (m.1), followed by (ii) a repeating sixteenth note motif (m.2), which is characterized by the *tremolando* effect, and (iii) the *exclamatio* figure with which the singing voice begins (m.12). The prominent role of these three motifs in this lied becomes evident due to their intensification in the course of the song. In addition, (iv) the menacing rising half tone step marked by an accent on the first up-beat note of the piano left hand (mm.2–3) bears an important symbolic meaning, underlining the emotional expression caused by or inherent in the previously mentioned motifs, as it will be examined later. For this reason, the main motivic particularities will be analysed first, in order to juxtapose them with the psychological explanation in a second step.

The piano opens this song with the mentioned *circulatio* motif, featured in parallel octaves (unisono) and played in the *f* dynamics (marked with a diminuendo hairpin). The recurrence of this figure is to be identified first within the range of four bars, extending itself, for its third appearance in m.11, to six bars—this irregularity can be explained from the harmonic standpoint by the fact that Schubert needs the added two bars (mm.9–10) to return to the home key C major after the unexpected shift to G minor of m. 5[58]. From m.11 on, however, an increasing insistence on the *circulatio* figure becomes visible: initially, it is repeated every two bars until m.23; then, it appears within a one-bar structure, with minor exceptional outbursts of the quavers motif (e.g., m. 25 or m. 29)—this motif is derived from the piano left hand from m.3 and tone paints the clatter of the wheels. What is noteworthy about this passage (m.23) is that the *circulatio* coincides with the phrase beginning of the singing voice for the first time. This is musically understandable, given that the singing phrase does not begin with an upbeat, as the beforehand phrases did. This exception is only to be identified in connection to the words "Hey welcome, sweet mill melody!" (Ei willkommen! Süßer Mühlengesang!")[59]—a passage characterized by the tone repetitions in the high register and the pendulum motion, which musically tone paints the

---

[58] This analytical observation will be examined in more detail at a later point.

[59] Müller, Wilhelm. (1991). *Die Schöne Müllerin.* P. 47. (Trans. by the author).

diphthong "Ei" (between the notes D–A and D–B in m.23), achieving consequently a lullaby-like rhythm[60]. The intensification of the *circulatio* continues and culminates in the final page of the song, where the quavers motif, depicting the clattering of the wheels, gradually disappears (m.45f.). Furthermore, the postlude measures of the piano (mm.57–58) reveal the presence of two *circulatio* figures within a single bar structure. This means that Schubert escalates this motif until the end of the lied through the principle of repetition and by increasing its recurrences within shorter periods of time.

Following the opening motif, a second motif is immediately introduced bringing along a dynamic contrast: the repeating sixteenth note motif of the piano right hand (m.2 with upbeat). Through the alternated tone repetitions inherent in this motif, Schubert creates a *tremolando* effect, which can be understood here as a madrigalism. It is striking to observe that this motif is omnipresent throughout the entire song, creating a sort of ostinato that will also be increased in tension. It is over this sound carpet, that the singing voice enters with the observation "A mill I see blinking, out of the alder trees, through roaring and singing, cracking the clatter of wheels" ("Eine Mühle sehe ich blinken, aus den Erlen heraus, durch Rauschen und Singen bricht Rädergebraus")[61]. Schubert underlines the significance of the first word semantically, by providing it with the *exclamatio* connotation. This rhetorical figure has a prominent role in this lied, due to its recurring appearances. In key moments, the expression of this figure is either softened or intensified, either by reducing the range of the interval to a fourth (e.g., m.31 under the words "and the house", i.e., "und das Haus") or by expanding its range to an octave (m.40 under the word "sky", i.e., "Himmel"). This intervallic change of the *exclamatio* coincides with a crucial harmonic passage. In the first mentioned case, Schubert creates a harmonic contradiction with the text: under the words "and the house, how so homely" ("und das Haus wie so traulich")[62], he places the dominant seventh chord, which is left unresolved (m.33). Instead of resolving it to the expected tonality of C major, Schubert shifts to the key of D minor in m.34: "and the windows, how blank!" (und die Fenster, wie blank!")[63]. Only afterwards, Schubert returns to C major (m.38), where the reference to the

[60] Cf. Dobretsberger, Barbara. Personal communication between Barbara Dobretsberger and the author. Salzburg: March 29, 2024. The 6/8 metric indication of Schubert can underline this interpretation. Cf. Ibid.

[61] Müller, Wilhelm. (1991). *Die Schöne Müllerin.* (Trans. by the author). Again Schubert altered Müllers original word „at glance" („blicken") to "blinking" ("blinken").

[62] Ibid. P. 47. (Trans. by the author).

[63] Ibid. (Trans. by the author). Already Arnold Feil pointed to that harmonic peculiarity of the mentioned measures. Cf. Feil, Arnold. (1996). *Franz Schubert.* P. 55.

sun and the heaven is to be found, alongside with the mentioned expansion of the *exclamatio.*

After reaching the seemingly victorious and harmless C major, the miller-lad asks: "so was that thou meant?" ("war es also gemeint?")[64]. The same question is repeated by Schubert four times, in all, successively, while Wilhelm Müller only sets the question once. The organ point C in the piano part is striking, especially for the two last questions, at the end of the song (e.g., from m. 53). Equally noteworthy is the constant return to the note C in the singing voice while the miller-lad is posing the questions, alongside with the reminiscences of the *interrogatio* motif of "Wohin?"[65]—however, this time he remains always in the ascending gesture, featuring a rising melancholic sigh (*suspiratio*). The harmony is darkened in colour with the note of A-flat in the first, third and last repetition[66], while the singing voice lingers on the word "so" ("also"). This cloudiness in the harmony could be an indicator of an emotional conflict with the tenacious expression of C major. A similar emotional utterance, in the state of unclearness, can be found in the harmonic colours, existent in the passage comprising mm. 31–38, which lends a specific atmosphere of uncertainty or expresses the fearful inhibited state of the miller-lad. These emotions are predicted by the motif mentioned in the beginning of this subchapter: the menacing rising half tone step marked by an accent on the first up-beat note of the piano left hand (mm.2–3). From the standpoint of the initial tonality of this song—C major—the accentuated F-sharp note in the bass register of the piano represents the tritone interval (i.e., the *diabolus in musica*). In order to develop this thought further, the motives that were just elaborated musically will now be examined from a Jungian perspective.

---

[64] Müller, Wilhelm. (1991). *Die Schöne Müllerin.* P. 47. (Trans. by the author). This question addressed to the little brook is a further fact that substantiates the typological reading above mentioned, of the miller having his sensation function especially charged up.

[65] Cf. Dobretsberger, Barbara. Personal communication between Barbara Dobretsberger and the author. Salzburg/Noiraigue: March 29, 2024.

[66] Cf. Braun, Christiane. Berke, Dietrich. „Die Schöne Müllerin op. 25 (D 795)—Liederzyklus Wilhelm Müller". In: Dürr, Walther. Kube, Michael. [et al.]. (2013). *Schubert Liedlexikon.* P. 639.

Fig. 15.3 The leading motifs of "Halt!". (Sheet music excerpt taken and adapted from *IMSLP*)

As just seen, the *circulatio* motif bears an underlying semantic core of great importance, which is emphasized by Schubert's intensification throughout the lied: this figure, as suggested above, is a tone painting means of Schubert to depict the mill wheels, which can be understood as a reference to the norns and as the symbol of the Self, due to the circular shape they present[67]. The fate goddesses are therefore the underlying force in this lied, guiding the miller-lad on the path to individuation and indicating the direction to the Self (represented by the mill). After all, it is in the mill where a transformation takes place: the corn is processed into something edible[68]. This suggests that, once in the mill

[67] Cf. Butzer, Günter. Jacob, Joachim (Ed.). (2012). *Metzler Lexikon literarischer Symbole*. P. 278–279. Congruently, see the symbols of the circle or of the Wheel in: Mollwo-Oesterreicher, Marianne. (1978). *Herder Lexikon Symbole.*

[68] Cf. Roesler, Christian. Personal communication between Christian Roesler and the author. Basel: March 7, 2024.

individuation can begin, i.e., the processing of unconscious elements into consciousness can take place and subsequently, a higher state of consciousness can be achieved[69]. The dynamic contrast that separates the two initial musical motifs can emotionally be seen as a phenomenon of synchronicity: the process of individuation, which is about to begin, comprises a change towards a deep realisation coming ahead. This is by no means a banal experience and can generate a state of excitement and expectation but at the same time also of restlessness and fear. Exactly this ambivalent reaction can occur when the "I" resonates with a symbol of wholeness, as the mill (*circulatio* motif). This emotional condition is musically mirrored in the *tremolando* motif. The word itself *tremolando* translates the state of shivering and conveys the extent to which the miller-lad is emotionally and physically affected[70]. With its appearance in the ***p***-dynamic, Schubert generates a contrast to the aforementioned *circulatio* figure, underlining the inner emotional reaction to the opening *circulatio* motif. At this point the menacing nature of the left-hand motif in mm.2–3 can also be revealed psychologically: this note, functioning as a *diabolus in musica* as above mentioned, can be pointing to the (unconscious) dangers and threats (shadow side) that he must confront himself with during his journey to the mill (to the Self). In turn, the subsequent unexpected and abrupt shift to G minor in m.5—the tonality of "restless and aimless wandering around"[71], of "displeasure and resentment"[72]—emphasizes the miller-lad's intuition. These emotions, expressing his unconscious fears, are then confirmed in mm.31–36 through the previously analysed harmonies and the way Schubert renders the *exclamatio*.

In contrast, the eight welcoming measures, mentioned above in due brevity (from m.23 on), convey a lighter tone colour and a more inward character. This change of character and the piano ***p***-dynamics could reflect the miller-lad's inner

[69] Analogically, a similar process can be read in Lévi-Strauss *Le cru et le cuit*, namely the process of passing from the state of nature to the civilization state. Roesler, Christian. Personal communication between Christian Roesler and the author. Basel: March 7, 2024. Cf. Lévi-Strauss, Claude. (1990). *Das Rohe und das Gekochte.*

[70] From another perspective, the tremolando figure could also tone paint the standing still or the act of lingering in reference to the poem's title "Halt!" and to the psychic conditions of the miller-lad after "Wohin?". This interpretation is to be found in: Braun, Christiane. Berke, Dietrich. „Die Schöne Müllerin op. 25 (D 795)—Liederzyklus Wilhelm Müller". In: Dürr, Walther. Kube, Michael. [et al.]. (2013). *Schubert Liedlexikon.* P. 638–639.

[71] Böhm, Richard. (2006). *Symbolik und Rhetorik im Liedschaffen von Franz Schubert.* P. 84. (Trans. by the author). German expression: „Umherirren, ruheloses, zielloses Wandern".

[72] This description is in accordance with Schubart, cited after: Ibid. (Trans. by the author). German expression: „Groll und Unlust".

voice—in hermeneutic terms describing a whisper of the fate-goddesses. Congruently, the punctual lullaby character that is given to these measures can be understood as an attitude of the miller-lad of letting himself be cradled by the rushing of the brooklet, its inherent singing voices, and the clattering of the wheels[73], i.e., as a moment where the "I" is under the hypnotic spell of the unconscious structures and welcomes his path to destiny. Subsequently, after recovering his senses through the metaphor of the sun-light and the bright C major tonality, the "I" seems to want to remain within this "harmless" tonality, by the insistent return and willingness to remain in C. This means, that the "I" wants to remain in the light and wants to perceive the mill as a symbol of hope, prosperity, and abundance[74]. However, his hesitation, which points to the perils and the shadow side, is audible through the opacity of the harmony: it is as if, simultaneously, another voice within the "I" would hesitate or reject his fateful duty (a voice acting as a counter-will). The expression of the counter-will can be, in turn, a common unfolding of the process and can be encountered in the description of the hero's journey[75], especially at the beginning of individuation. Here, the double meaning of the *tremolando* motif together with the menacing left-hand motif (mm. 2), examined above, can be confirmed: there are two wills within him expressing contradictory emotions. Simultaneously, the unconscious forces—or the norns—are acting upon the "I", making the miller-lad ask the brooklet a total of four times about his destiny. It shall be recalled that the number four refers to wholeness[76]. This may be an allusion to the aim of the unconscious, directing him towards the exploration of the unconscious realm and to seeking wholeness.

"Halt!" ends with an inquiry about his path to destiny. Subsequently, Wilhelm Müller begins "Danksagung an den Bach" with the same questions and remains almost the entire poem in the questioning ductus. In fact, this poem lives from questions. It is worthwhile to see how Schubert deals with these and what they communicate emotionally from a psychological point of view. Elmar Budde draws attention to the importance of the *interrogatio* figure in Schubert's

[73] Cf. Dobretsberger, Barbara. Personal communication between Barbara Dobretsberger and the author. Salzburg/Noiraigue: March 29, 2024.

[74] Antagonistic characteristics are to be found within the mill symbol, as it is the case of all symbols in general (they bear always the opposites). This light-side aspect specific of the watermill symbolism can be read in: Cf. Butzer, Günter. Jacob, Joachim (Ed.). (2012). *Metzler Lexikon literarischer Symbole*. P. 278.

[75] In Campbells description of the hero's journey, for instance, there is a first rejection of the hero in regard to the task that he is given to solve. Cf. Vogel, Ralf T. (2017). *Individuation und Wandlung*. P. 52–53.

[76] Cf. Jung, Carl Gustav. (1961). *Ma vie*. P. 315.

songs composition[77]. From the analysis of this specific lied, it becomes apparent that Schubert not only sets the questions in musical form through the musical rhetorical figure, but even emphasizes them, often with the principle of repetition. Essentially, however, Schubert extends the miller-lad's questioning attitude beyond that seen in Wilhelm Müller's work, namely through the use of modulations. These harmonic deviations can contribute to a possible psychological interpretation of the miller-lad's (inner) attitude. In order to unveil these emotional utterances, a bare observation of how the questioning-answer ductus is created can be helpful.

As suggested above, the miller-lad's questions refer at first to his path to destiny in reference to the previous poem/song: three times "so was that thou meant?" ("war es also gemeint") is repeated (mm.4–5, mm.8–9, mm.9–10). The *interrogatio* motif functions herein not only as a bridge between these two lieder[78], but also as a reminiscence of previous manifestations. This can be musically substantiated by the intervallic ambit and the downward vs. upward gesture. For these three repetitions the miller-lad remains in the ascending gesture of the phrase beginnings and stays within the range of a third (notes B–D of mm.4–5). In its second repetition, this figure is even highlighted by the extension to an *exclamatio* ambit (B–G). After posing the third question, which remains in the tonical domain of G (mm.9–10), the long-awaited answer is then given by his senses: "to the miller-girl!" ("Zur Müllerin hin!"[79]. Precisely on these responding words (mm.12–15), Schubert not only remains in the rising *interrogatio* ductus (C-sharp–G), but also modulates, providing to this reply a rather searching undertone. By doing so, Schubert extends the questioning ductus of Wilhelm Müller, simultaneously foretelling his doubting attitude of "have I understood it?" ("hab' ich's verstanden?"). This conveys a specific emotional state of the miller-lad: what in fact ought to be an answer, is transformed into another question, as if he would grope around in an inner uncertainty. The following two inquiries of "have I understood it?" maintain the same nature as the initial three, in terms of the content it refers to (path to destiny), since these are not yet resolved. These are constructed as a sequence from m.15 and m.16, with each one beginning with a falling fourth interval and ending with a rising third. Only with the return to G major, the response "to the miller-girl!" is musically congruent with the text as a valid response.

[77] Cf. Budde, Elmar. (2003). *Schuberts Liederzyklen.* P. 58.

[78] Cf. Feil, Arnold. (1996). *Franz Schubert.* P. 56.

[79] Müller, Wilhelm. (1991). *Die Schöne Müllerin.* P. 48. (Trans. by the author).

As the first questions seem to be answered, the nature of the consequent ones in terms of content are related to the response he had just received, i.e., related to the miller-girl: "has she sent thee? Or did thou beguile me?" (Hat sie dich geschickt? Oder hast mich berückt?"[80] (mm.21–22, mm. 22–23, mm.24–25 and m.26). This will remain an unanswered question for some time within the poem cycle. However, the harmony of the piano part can already reveal some emotional aspects: the turning to the opposite pole, the G minor key (mm.22), unveils his inkling in regard to the sought response—as an intuition that the "I" does not want to admit as truthful. It should be reminded that, according to Schubart, G minor is the tonality of "displeasure and resentment"[81]. At the same time, it can reveal a state of confusion and the intertwining relationship between the nymphs and the miller-girl. The emotional expression behind these harmonies is subsequently contrasted by his one will.

His desire to receive an affirmative answer is reflected by the turn to the hopeful and idyllic B-flat major[82] key (mm.25–26), concurrently with the *interrogatio* figure (the rising third interval under the word "[has] she [sent thee]" ("[hat] sie [dich geschickt])" in the singing voice). Finally, the last repetition of this question, by which Schubert creates a five-bar phrase, can be taken as an echo (mm.26). This emotional attitude, mirrored in Schubert's harmonic choices, shows the naïve character of the miller-lad, who is driven by his own "participation mystique"[83]—to speak in Jungian manner—the utopia of reciprocal love. The projection of feelings and the refusal of confronting her directly with the question is a typical attitude of this miller-lad. He lives in a platonic world:

---

[80] Ibid. P. 48. (Trans. by the author).

[81] This description is in accordance with Schubart, cited after: Böhm, Richard. (2006). *Symbolik und Rhetorik im Liedschaffen von Franz Schubert.* (Trans. by the author). German expression: „Groll und Unlust".

[82] The semantic of the B-flat major key stated above is in accordance with Richard Böhm's findings and song database. Cf. Ibid. P. 66. The B-flat major sonata D 960 can be taken as an example.

[83] Jung, Carl Gustav. (2023). *Die Beziehung zwischen dem Ich und dem Unbewussten.* P. 33. The term „participation mystique" refers to Lévy-Bruhl, whereby C.G. Jung understands it as the primordial sense of oneness, i.e., a psychic state where the ego-consciousness does not distinguish itself from unconscious structures. Cf. Definition of „participation mystique" in: Jung, Carl Gustav. (2013). *Kleines Lexikon der Analytischen Psychologie.*

> "His 'participation mystique' allowed him to assume without further ado that his emotion was naturally also the emotion of the other person, which is usually the case at the deepest levels of human psychology"[84].

For the last stanza of the poem, Schubert returns and remains in the brooklet's tonality, G major. Decisively, the miller-lad now accepts his fate and goes towards the mill: "Well, however it may be, I give myself in: what I've sought, have I found, whatsoever it may be" ("Nun wie's auch mag sein, ich gebe mich drein: was ich such hab'ich funden, wie's immer mag sein")[85]. Once there is an acceptance of the "I" towards his purpose, the peripeties of the individuation process can begin to unfold: the next archetypal station of the meeting with the shadow.

15.4 From "Feierabend" to "Thränenregen": The Persona-Shadow Conflict—the Inner *Force Motrice* as the Positive Anima and the Consequent Insightful Moment

By accepting his fate, the first difficulties are stated in "Am Feierabend" (no.5). From the poetic level, the fear that he might not be attractive to the miller-girl, from his physical constitution, becomes for the first time visible: his last hope is that his loyalty and his deep feelings towards her would be acknowledged. At the beginning, Wilhelm Müller uses the conditional verbal form, to accentuate what he wished to be, which is then juxtaposed in the second stanza, where all verbs are stated in the present tense.

Once again, the hectic mood of the poem is present in Schubert's musical setting at different levels. First, the contrast between the calmly flowing semiquavers of the preceding lied with the short-articulated *f* chords opening the fifth song is striking. Promptly, a rush of frenetic sounding semiquavers follows in the piano (mm.4–6), emotionally pointing to the inner turmoil of the miller-lad. This scale motif, first ascending and then descending, will merge into the *circulatio* figure in the right hand of the piano in m.7. Once the *circulatio* is established, it will

---

[84] Jung, Carl Gustav. (2023). *Die Beziehung zwischen dem Ich und dem Unbewussten.* P. 33. (Trans. by the author). German expression: "Seine primitive 'participation mystique' ließ ihn ohne weiteres annehmen, dass seine Ergriffenheit selbstverständlich auch die Ergriffenheit des andern sei, was auf den tieferen Stufen menschlicher Psychologie natürlicherweise meistens der Fall ist.".

[85] Schubert altered some parts of Müller's text. The original in German reads: "was ich such ist gefunden". Müller, Wilhelm. (1991). *Die Schöne Müllerin.* P. 48. (Trans. by the author).

persevere until m.25, expressing the obsessive circling around and the qualities he wished to possess. The intense affections of the miller-lad are emphasized by the *exclamatio* with which the singing voice begins (mm.7–8) and are coloured with the choice of the A minor tonality, the key of turmoil[86]. The same pattern of beginning was found in "Halt!", which started with an *exclamatio*[87], and in which the rhythmical cell pertaining to the *exclamatio* motif was congruent, i.e., both conveyed the rhythm: short-short-long. As soon as the attention is drawn towards the miller-girl and he expresses his desire that the "sweet miller-girl would heed the leal spirit of mine" ("daß die schöne Müllerin, merkte meinen treuen Sinn")[88], Schubert changes the atmosphere congruently with the shift to the A major key (mm.16–19). The majorization of the key lends it a shining quality, expressing his inner desire. This is emphatically underlined by the fact that the singer begins the phrase with the C-sharp note (m.16), i.e., the third of the A major scale[89]. This phrase begins on the strong beat of the measure and no longer with an upbeat. A major, however, bears a counter pole character in itself: as the tonality of the "pretence of positive moods"[90], it also provides these words with a colour of illusion. The reintroduction of the hectic chords from the beginning coincides with the moment of change in the poem towards the present tense. This change in musical texture provokes an even shorter-breathed melodic line than the beginning (mm.26–36). Analogously, in psychological terms, his desires can hint at the components that constitute the Persona of the miller-lad. On the other hand, this causes a gain of consciousness in regard to counter-pole of the miller-lad's mask, i.e., he becomes aware of his personal shadow side: "oh, how is my arm so weak" ("Ach, wie ist mein Arm so schwach")[91]. With the scattered, short-breathed phrase construction, Schubert hints at the still not integrated, split elements of his personality, elements that want to be recognized by the unconscious.

---

[86] Cf. Böhm, Richard. (2006). *Symbolik und Rhetorik im Liedschaffen von Franz Schubert.* P. 74–75.

[87] Already Marie-Agnes Dittrich noted the importance of the *exclamatio* figure in the beginnings of several lieder, including the above-mentioned one. Cf. Dittrich, Marie-Agnes. "Die Lieder. 'Für Menschenohren sind es Harmonien'". In: Dürr, Walther. Krause, Andreas. (2020). *Schubert Handbuch.* Chapter: „Werkbesprechungen. Die Schöne Müllerin".

[88] Müller, Wilhelm. (1991). *Die Schöne Müllerin.* (Trans. by the author).

[89] The third of a chord is the note lending the major or minor coloration to the harmony.

[90] Cf. Böhm, Richard. (2006). *Symbolik und Rhetorik im Liedschaffen von Franz Schubert.* P. 57. (Trans. by the author). German expression: „[…] Vortäuschung positiver Stimmungen […]".

[91] Müller, Wilhelm. (1991). *Die Schöne Müllerin.* (Trans. by the author).

To increase the dramatic situation, Schubert turns to the recitativ/*parlando* style towards the end of the lied, when the master, i.e., the miller-girl's father[92], enters the scene (m.46). By giving the master a monotonous and lower tone colour Schubert creates a further contrast in the diastematics, which, together with the long chords in the piano, increases expectation. When the girl suddenly enters the scene and wishes "all" ("Allen") a good night, Schubert emphasizes the torn emotions with a painful chord. As the result of the girl's indifference towards him, Schubert shifts from the shortly precedent modulation to F major (the master's speech) towards the D minor key and subsequently places a Neapolitan sixth chord in m.56 under the word "all" ("Allen"). In Schubert's music in particular the D minor key has the connotation of death, e.g., *Death and the maiden* (16)[93]. Uninterruptedly, the lied returns to the feverish mood of the beginning (m.59), marked now with the indication "slightly faster" ("Etwas geschwinder"). To spell the last words "leal spirit" ("treuen Sinn"), Schubert uses the *lamento* figure, which the piano immediately takes over in a chain of falling quavers (mm.84–88) in the form of a *catabasis* figure. The final *f* chords are psychologically telling: the perfect cadence in A minor affirms the outer reality, as if the "I" would be fatefully condemned to that reality.

While "Am Feierabend" expressed a great output of energy, the following poems, and songs—"Der Neugierige" (no.6), "Morgengruss" (no.8) and "Des Müllers Blumen" (no.9)—are more introverted in character, with the one exception of "Ungeduld" (no. 7). Both poetically and musically these songs bear a soft or quiet tone level. His belief in love, symbolized by the blue flower, appears time and again, but is specially referred to in the three aforementioned poems. As the so-called *rosa mystica*, this symbol of longing for wholeness[94] acts as a motivating force, the *force mortice,* which helps him to enter the emotional world of the unconscious[95]. The blue flower as a symbol, bearing this semantic connotation, is an archetypal manifestation that can be associated with the positive

[92] The father figure is inhere positively represented, as the one who recognizes the work of the miller-lad. If transferring this symbolic characterization into Schubert's life, interestingly, this positive father figure description would be congruent with the outcome of the 1822 dream of Schubert and the transformation that is there narrated—the reconciliation with the father figure, through the archetype of the (Great) Mother (cf. 11.2).

[93] For further comparative examples in Schubert's repertoire see: Böhm, Richard. (2006). *Symbolik und Rhetorik im Liedschaffen von Franz Schubert*. P. 82–84.

[94] Cf. Jung, Carl Gustav. (2019). *Dream Symbols of the Individuation Process.* Gieser, Suzanne. (Ed.). P. 135. "the blue flower [...] a wonderful thing they were seeking" P. 135.

[95] Cf. Roesler, Christian. Personal communication between Christian Roesler and the author. Basel: March 7, 2024.

Anima figure. It is due to this positive inner force, fairly paradoxically, that the miller-lad, while neglecting the reality, he simultaneously seeks the truth, e.g., "Der Neugierige" (no.6), "Ungeduld" (no.7), "Des Müllers Blumen" (no.9). To reformulate this philosophically: another will is at hand. This urge shows the unconscious force within himself that aims to balance his emotional state by confronting him with the truth.

He is only able to see the truth in "Thränenregen" (no.10), which intriguingly begins with a fantasy. A fantasy, observed in Jungian terms, translates a gradual immersion of the "I" into a state of oblivion[96], out of which elements of the unconscious emerge autonomously, eventually providing moments of insight or numinous experiences—leading to the path towards the middle[97]. The narrated imagination begins with an intimate depiction of being with his beloved under an alder roof. On the symbolic level of the poem, Wilhelm Müller conspicuously presents various symbols that, *de facto,* point to an inner imminent transformation. First, the brooklet functions here as a mirror. The mirror symbol is understood in Jungian sense as being a symbol of insight and realization[98] and it is important not to confound this symbol with a narcissistic attitude[99]. By looking into the brooklet, he searches for the image of his beloved, the eyes of the miller-girl: "I gazed at her image, at her eyes alone" ("Ich schaute nach ihrem Bilde, nach ihren Augen allein")[100]. In the folk's understanding, the eyes are understood as the mirror of the soul[101]. Psychologically interpreted: the miller-lad was searching for his inner soul image, the Anima. The fact that heaven is mirrored in the brooklet indicates his inner desire to become one with his counterpart, the Anima: "And sunk in the brooklet, the whole sky shined" ("Und in den Bach versunken,

[96] C.G. Jung referred to this state as an "abaissement du niveau mentale" in referrence to Pierre Janet. Cf. Jung, Carl Gustav. (2014). "Psychology and Alchemy". In: *The Collected Works of C.G. Jung. Vol. 12.* Chapter: "Initial dreams". A striking musical example of this psychic phenomenon is to be found in the middle section of the A major sonata D 959, 2nd movement (cf. 17).

[97] The middle is, in Jungian literature, found always in relation to the center of the personality, i.e., the Self. Jung, Carl Gustav. (2023). *Die Beziehung zwischen dem Ich und dem Unbewussten.* P. 145.

[98] Mollwo-Oesterreicher, Marianne. (1978). *Herder Lexikon Symbole.* P. 158.

[99] There are several passages in C.G. Jung's work dealing with the symbol of the mirror or with the act of gazing into the depths of the waters. This process is often mentioned by him in connection with an insight, which permits the recognition of the true being and ultimately leading to an experience of transformational nature, e.g., P. 24, P. 27 or P. 32–33 in: Jung, Carl Gustav. (2020). *Archetypen. Urbilder und Wirkkräfte des Kollektiven Unbewussten.*

[100] Müller, Wilhelm. (1991). *Die Schöne Müllerin.* P. 6 0. (Trans. by the author).

[101] Cf. Mollwo-Oesterreicher, Marianne. (1978). *Herder Lexikon Symbole.* P. 19.

der ganze Himmel schien")[102]. Consequently, an inner force drags him into an introspective state. At that precise moment, his eyes are filled with tears (i.e., he is emotionally seized—a characteristic reaction to an archetypal experience), and the image in the brooklet's mirror becomes "rippled" ("kraus"). In that instance, the miller-lad's feelings were so strong, that his inner state reflected itself in nature—the rain is used as a metaphor for his inner state of being. The aforementioned mirror interpretation is substantiated by the moon allegory in the second stanza of the poem, being itself the symbol of transformation, of "the becoming and of the fading"[103]. A transformation can only occur after a moment of insight.

In Schubert's musical setting, this lied, which represents the path that possibly leads to the centre of the personality, remarkably falls in the middle-point of the entire cycle (15.1, footnote 20.)—this is a direct consequence of Schubert's withdrawal of the poem "Das Mühlenleben" and the latter omitted ones. The symbolic content of the poem "Thränenregen" is rendered musically in a subtle, yet direct way. Schubert chose the tonality of A major, as the key of the "pretence of positive moods" to describe the miller-lad's fantasy. Nevertheless, the harmonies of the prelude (mm.1–4) veil this harmonic key. The piano, being his intuitive voice, opens the song with particularly dissonant chords, with an "augmented chord that resolves itself in a dominant second degree, which in turn, is veiled by an appoggiatura"[104]. It is worth noting, that (i) augmented chords as "wandering/floating chord[s]" ("vagierender Akkord")[105] had a particular significance in Romanticism due to their particularly high striving nature[106], and to the fact, that (ii) they bear the interval of the augmented fifth. Schubert placed this augmented chord as an upbeat, yet marked with an accent, engendering a rhythmical ambiguity. The polyphonic writing of Schubert in the opening piano measures also points to the complex inner emotional state of the miller-lad. All three voices of the piano are here interwoven in themselves, breaking any sense of measure line, and taking any sense of pulse away.

---

102 Müller, Wilhelm. (1991). *Die Schöne Müllerin.* (Trans. by the author).

103 Mollwo-Oesterreicher, Marianne. (1978). *Herder Lexikon Symbole.* P. 113. (Trans by the author). German expression: „allg. mit jedem Werden u. Vergehen.".

104 Dittrich, Marie-Agnes. "Die Lieder. 'Für Menschenohren sind es Harmonien'". In: Dürr, Walther. Krause, Andreas. (2020). *Schubert Handbuch.* P. 225. (Trans. by the author). German expression: „[…] einem übermäßigen Dreiklang, der sich dominantisch in die II. Stufe auflöst, die wiederum durch einen Vorhalt verschleiert wird.".

105 Amon, Reinhard. (2005). *Lexikon der Harmonielehre.* P. 33. The chord designation "vagierender Akkord" goes back to Schönberg's *Harmonielehre.* Cf. Schönberg, Arnold. (1986). *Harmonielehre.* P. 293.

106 Cf. Ibid. P. 34.

The formulation by Marie-Agnes Dittrich, cited above, referring to the harmonic complexity of the opening measures, is revealing with regard to the unconscious core of this passage. These musical facts, when psychologically analysed, reflect the "slackening of conscious tension"[107], also referred to an "abaissement du niveau mentale"[108] which is typical of being in a fantasy-like state. On the one hand, the polyphonic writing can point to the multiplication of personality centres also characteristic of such a process. The described lack of pulse orientation together with the harmonic vagueness present in these opening measures, conveys a particular sense of time and perfectly expresses the unconscious reality—a state, which represents the miller-lad's psychic condition at that precise moment. On the other hand, the appoggiaturas contribute to expanding the temporal perception by decelerating the moment of resolution. The unfolding of the miller-lad's imagination, as described above, leads to a moment of insight, naturally linked to a subsequent transformation. It is noteworthy to observe now how this transformation is set to music by Schubert.

When the moment of realization arrives, Schubert shifts the key to A minor (m.25) and places two, rather camouflaged, tritone intervals at once in the piano, in m.28, between the G natural (first beat) and the C# note (second beat) of the left hand, and between the E (first beat) and B-flat note (second beat) of the right hand. The B-flat note is doubled in the singing voice. This interval surrounds the words: "hither the mirror has gone rippled; she spoke: a rain's coming" ("Da ward es im Spiegel so kraus; Sie sprach: es kommt ein Regen")[109]. It shall be recalled that this interval (*diabolus in musica*) is, in psychological terms, semantically charged with the shadow side[110]—in this context, with the shadow side of the Anima. The madrigalistic influence on Schubert is to be heard in this poem particularly in the instant when the rain is announced—many thoughtful pianists choose at this point to play the quavers (inner voices) in a light *staccato* manner, which renders this (inner) nature experience in music[111]. The painful diminished seventh chord under the word "rain" ("Regen") underlines once more the miller-lad's inner feelings. Although the piano postlude begins

---

107 Jung, Carl Gustav. (2014). "The Practice of Psychotherapy". In: *The Collected Works of C.G. Jung. Vol.16.* (Ed. and Trans. by Gerhard Adler and R.F.C. Hull). Part II: "Specific problems of Psychotherapy", Chapter 7: "The ascent of the soul".

108 Ibid.

109 Müller, Wilhelm. (1991). *Die Schöne Müllerin.* P. 61. (Trans. by the author).

110 In the A major piano sonata D 959, for instance, the tritone interval introduces the descent to the realm of Hades (cf. 17).

111 Cf. Schubert, Franz. (1962). *Schubert: Die Schöne Müllerin D 795.* [Album recorded by Dietrich Fischer-Dieskau. Gerald Moore].

in the same way as the prelude measures, it shifts again to the minor sphere. His disillusioned state after the painful realization is brought to the fore by the lingering on the A minor atmosphere, with which this song concludes.

15.5 From "Mein!" to "Eifersucht und Stolz": The Negation of the „I" Towards the Outer Reality and the Resulting Flooding of the Shadow. The Characteristics of the Miller Lad's Persona and Shadow

At this point of the narration, it is meaningful to see how the miller-lad responds to this painful revelation. To do so, a short examination of the poem "Mein!" (no.11) is necessary, especially in regard to its content. Wilhelm Müller points here to a cross reference with the sixth poem "Der Neugierige"[112], where the miller-lad was asking the brooklet for only one word, which would describe the feelings of the miller's girl towards him: yes ("ja") and no ("nein"). He added that his world would be made of these two words, which psychologically observed, means that he, literally, lives within these two antagonistic spheres. In "Mein!" the miller-lad obsessively repeats: "The beloved miller-girl is mine, is mine!" ("Die geliebte Müllerin ist mein, ist mein")[113] ("Mein!" no.11). All endings of verses are made of internal rhyme, always closing with the syllable "-ein". It becomes clear now that Wilhelm Müller is using a figure of speech, the *paronomasia.* By repeating the word "mine" ("Mein") and ending all verses in "-ein", he is in fact giving "Mein" the semantic core of "nein" ("no"), which is in itself a contradiction[114]—a contradiction that exists between his consciousness and unconscious.

In Schubert's musical setting, this conflict is expressed through the oscillation between two opposing tonalities: D major, as the key of triumph and victory, and its counter pole, D minor, the key of melancholy and death[115]. His hopeful state of another ("springtime") reality is given by the B-flat major tonality, the key of hope and idyll[116] when the last stanza of the poem is sung. To emphasize

[112] Cf. Cottrell, Alan. (1970). *Wilhelm Müller's Lyrical Song-cycles.*

[113] In the original: "Die geliebte Müllerin ist mein! Mein!". Müller, Wilhelm. (1991). *Die Schöne Müllerin.* P. 62. (Trans. by the author).

[114] Alan Cottrell pointed already to this word play. Cf. Ibid.

[115] Cf. Böhm, Richard. (2006). *Symbolik und Rhetorik im Liedschaffen von Franz Schubert.*

[116] Cf. Ibid.

the imaginative character, both Müller and Schubert make use of rhetorical questions. Schubert's *interrogatio* figure can be identified by the ascending phrase endings (mm.41–46): "Springtide, are these all thy tiny little flowers?" ("Frühling, sind es alle deine Blümelein?"[117]. So doing, he emphasizes the words "springtide" ("Frühling"), "little flowers?" (Blümelein"), "sun" ("Sonne"), and "shine"("Schein"). From these summarised analytical observations, the following psychological conclusion can be drawn: the miller-lad does not want to face this reality gained from the insight in "Thränenregen" and flees from it[118]. Simultaneously, he expresses the typical congruent uncontrollable behaviour, which characterizes the influence of the obsessive nature of the Anima as an autonomous complex, i.e., the Anima acts out of its own[119]. This passionate song is contrasted with the following one, which characterizes a moment of "Pause" (no. 12), functioning as an instant of introspection and reflecting the enantiodromia phenomenon (3).

The two subsequent songs "Der Jäger" and "Eifersucht und Stolz" can be understood as two simultaneous inner occurrences. Herein, the hunter is depicted as the miller-lad's defiant rival and is evidently in the foreground. Following the Jungian method of dream or fairy tales' interpretation, the figure of the hunter is to be understood as a part of the miller-lad's personality, i.e., components of his personality which are repressed (subject-level). These elements thus represent the miller-lad's own shadow side. As it will be elaborated in shortness, the "I" is described in both poems as being trapped in obsession and despair, yet also in indecision towards the two wills that inhabit his soul; or to use Jungian terms: trapped in the Persona-Shadow dialectic. It can already be predicted that the "I", tending towards inflated states, will be overflooded by his shadow side[120]. This

---

[117] Müller, Wilhelm. (1991). *Die Schöne Müllerin.* P. 63. (Trans. by the author).

[118] Here too, the reference to a first denial attitude mentioned in Campbell's Hero's journey can be recognized—it is as if the miller-lad is trapped in this state. On the other hand, it seems that this reaction rather suits the introverted typology of the miller-lad. Jacobi explains: "In a given situation, this type of person [the introverter] withdraws for the first moment,'as if he would secretly say no', and only then does he come to the actual reaction.". Jacobi, Jolande. (2006). *Die Psychologie von C.G. Jung.* P. 28. (Trans. by the author). German expression: "Dieser Menschentypus zieht sich in einer gegebenen Lage im ersten Moment zurück,'wie wenn er leise Nein sagte', und erst dann kommt es zum eigentlichen Reagieren.".

[119] This important observation will be dealt with again and more in depth later in the chapter.

[120] It should be recalled that the process of individuation includes the necessity of raising awareness of the repressed shadow elements of the personality, integrating them and thus

is an expected consequence resulting from the proportions that the shadow side takes in these two songs, which translates that the "I" of the miller-lad is not strengthened enough to face the dark elements of his own psyche[121]. The emotional level of the poem is pronounced by the feelings of anger, complaint, and frustration existent in "Der Jäger" (no. 14) and the emotions of jealousy and pride in "Eifersucht und Stolz" (no. 15). To better delineate the psychological meaning of these two songs, the symbolic content of the poems and the inner protagonists shall be firstly addressed, followed by some specific musical observations, which underline the expression of the poem.

From the symbolism existent in "Der Jäger", Müller alludes to several aspects. As stated above, the hunter is perceived by the miller-lad as his defiant: "So stay, you defiant hunter, in the grove" ("Drum bleibe, du trotziger Jäger, im Hain")[122]. In turn, the miller-girl, representing the image of the Anima is here positively embodied with the symbol of the "little deer, a mild one" ("ein Reihlein, ein zahmes")[123]. This means, that the deer points to the characteristics of the miller-lad's inner female image, i.e., tame, shy and of innocent character[124]. In the narration, the deer must not be hunted by the huntsman, but ought to be destined for the miller-lad alone. On the contrary, symbolically speaking, the hunter is only entitled to have a wild boar. This statement expresses how the miller-lad's shadow side is perceived by himself, namely as primitive, animalesque, impure, immoderate, excessive, and violent[125]. In addition, the barking dogs—symbolically standing for the guardians of the realm of the dead (shadow/unconscious)[126]—should rest at home, suggesting the perception of the "I" that the unconscious

becoming whole. The integration process can be achieved through the transformation of the negative energy of the shadow content towards a positive one. During this process, inflations may happen.

[121] Jung has pointed out to the dangers of facing the shadow side with an unstrengthen "I". Jung, Carl Gustav. (2023). *Die Beziehung zwischen dem Ich und dem Unbewussten.*

[122] Müller, Wilhelm. (1991). *Die Schöne Müllerin.* P. 66. (Trans. by the author).

[123] Ibid. (Trans. by the author). German expression: "Hier wohnt nur ein Rehlein, ein zahmes, für mich.".

[124] For the literary symbolism of the deer and the respective qualities described above see: Butzer, Günter. Jacob, Joachim (Ed.). (2012). *Metzler Lexikon literarischer Symbole.* P. 340.

[125] For the symbolic meaning of the wild boar see: Mollwo-Oesterreicher, Marianne. (1978). *Herder Lexikon Symbole.* P. 150.

[126] Cf. Ibid. P. 79.

elements should not arise to consciousness: "and leave thy barking dogs at home" ("und laß deine kläffende Hunde zu Haus")[127].

Musically, the hunter/shadow is depicted by the hunting topos, i.e., the motif of the horn fifths but also through a specific composition technique: in "Der Jäger" Schubert makes use of the fugato style. This tradition is related to the ancient *caccia* practices, which were used to depict the action of hunting and fleeing[128]. However, in this reading, the choice of this compositional technique is not only to be understood as a tone painting means to describe the figure of the hunter, as already Braun and Berke suggested[129], but to musically express the pursuit of the shadow, which literally follows him (Fig. 15.4). Through these means, Schubert achieves to set in music the above-mentioned inflated state of the "I". The raising of despair of the miller-lad is emphasized by the breathless syllabic declamation, the lack of pauses, and the tension achieved by the increasingly higher top notes of the melody[130]. The general atmosphere is given by the choice of tonality: C minor mirrors the miller-lad's emotions, since this key expresses despair, separation, pain, death, and anger[131].

---

[127] Müller, Wilhelm. (1991). *Die Schöne Müllerin.* P. 66. (Trans. by the author).

[128] Cf. Dobretsberger, Barbara. (2016). *Formen der Instrumentalmusik.* P. 124.

[129] Cf. Braun, Christiane. Berke, Dietrich. „Die Schöne Müllerin op. 25 (D 795)—Liederzyklus Wilhelm Müller". In: Dürr, Walther. Kube, Michael. [et al.]. (2013). *Schubert Liedlexikon.* P. 652.

[130] The same analytical conclusions were found by Marie-Agnes Dittrich. Cf. Dittrich, Marie-Agnes. "Die Lieder. 'Für Menschenohren sind es Harmonien'". In: Dürr, Walther. Krause, Andreas. (2020). *Schubert Handbuch.* P. 226.

[131] Cf. Böhm, Richard. (2006). *Symbolik und Rhetorik im Liedschaffen von Franz Schubert.* P. 86.

Fig. 15.4 The hunting topos and the *caccia* style standing for the hunter, respectively, for the fleeing from the shadow. (Sheet music excerpt taken and adapted from *IMSLP*)

In "Eifersucht und Stolz", the above-described affective condition of the miller-lad is given by several musical details. The torn feelings are expressed by the constant harmonic oscillations[132]. From the motivic level, this is to be identified especially by the use of the *circulatio* motif, and the subsequent ferocious ascending and descending semiquaver chain of notes. These are practically omnipresent throughout the song. The one exception when this ductus is interrupted concerns mm.36–50, where the piano part is reduced to the hunting topos. With the successively interruptions through pauses, the text comprehensibility is especially underlined in this passage. Striking however, is the fact that singing voice and piano part are fairly independent from each other[133], which can be an important indication for a psychological statement.

The will of the unconscious evidently strives autonomously as can be noted in the fiercely and self-driven piano writing. This observation leads to the conclusion that there is a split between the "I" and the shadow elements. By enforcing its own power over the "I", the unconscious compels the "I" to face the own shadow side,

[132] Dittrich, Marie-Agnes. "Die Lieder. 'Für Menschenohren sind es Harmonien'". In: Dürr, Walther. Krause, Andreas. (2020). *Schubert Handbuch.* P. 226. (Trans. by the author). German expression: „[…] ein ständiger Wechsel der Tongeschlechter die zerrissenen Gefühle des Müllers an [zeigt].".

[133] Marie-Agnes Dittrich already pointed to the piano part as conveying a self-sufficient, independent character in relation to the singing voice. Cf. Ibid. P. 227.

since only by integrating these aspects, can the individual become whole. This behaviour refers to the self-regulation process of the psyche. This exemplifies C.G. Jung's statement that the unconscious creates purposefully a loss of psychic equilibrium with the further aim to find the middle point of the personality again:

> "I therefore regard the loss of equilibrium as something expedient, because it replaces the failing consciousness with the automatic and instinctive activity of the unconscious, which aims to establish a new equilibrium and also achieves this goal – provided that consciousness is able to assimilate, i.e., understand and process, the content produced by the unconscious."[134].

How the "I" is struggling with the Persona-Shadow problematic can be perceived also in the poetic level with the words: "Whereto so fast, so rippling and wild, my dear brook? Are thou hurrying full of rage after the rude brother hunter?" (Wohin so schnell, so kraus und wild, mein lieber Bach? Eilst du voll Zorn dem frechen Bruder Jäger nach?")[135]. Immediately, his fearful and indignant attitude is to be heard: "turn around, turn around and scold thy miller-girl, for her light, loose, fluttering sense" (Kehr um, kehr um, und schilt erst deine Müllerin, für ihren leichten, losen, kleinen Flattersinn")[136]. This statement reflects psychologically how he perceives the shadow side of the girl and how he reprimands it vehemently—the Persona of the miller-lad is here speaking and judging.

From these reflections the above-mentioned hypothesis is confirmed: the "I" is trapped in the Persona-Shadow problematics. At the end, the miller-lad will not accept his own shadow side. Consequently, he does not dare to realize his true Self. This will lead to his own despair since this means that he turns away from the aim of life[137]. These aspects are foretold musically on the one hand, by the empty octave sound at the end of "Der Jäger", i.e., the musical rhetorical figure

---

[134] Cf. Jung, Carl Gustav. (2023). *Die Beziehung zwischen dem Ich und dem Unbewussten.* P. 53–54. (Trans. by the author). "Ich betrachte daher den Gleichgewichtsverlust als etwas Zweckmäßiges, denn er ersetzt das versagende Bewusstsein durch die automatische und instinktive Tatigkeit des Unbewussten, welche auf die Herstellung eines neuen Gleichgewichts abzielt und dieses Ziel auch erreicht—vorausgesetzt, dass das Bewusstsein imstande ist, die vom Unbewussten produzierten Inhalte zu assimilieren, das heißt, zu verstehen und zu verarbeiten.".

[135] Müller, Wilhelm. (1991). *Die Schöne Müllerin.* P. 68. (Trans. by author).

[136] Ibid. (Trans. by author).

[137] Individuation is seen in Jungian terms as the aim of life, to fulfill the true Self: "Thus is the Self also the aim of life". Jung, Carl Gustav. (2023). *Die Beziehung zwischen dem Ich und dem Unbewussten.* P. 147. (Trans. by the author). German expression: „So ist das Selbst auch das Ziel des Lebens.".

of death, and on the other hand, by the perfect cadential statement at the end of "Eifersucht und Stolz". With the final affirmation of the G minor reality, he expresses the miller-lad's torn feelings and simultaneously foretells his fate[138].

15.6 "Die liebe Farbe" and "die Böse Farbe": The Enantiodromia at the Turning Point from the Blue Flower to the Colour Green after "Thränenregen"—the Antagonistic Forces Inherent in This Colour

At this stage, it should be noted that "Thränenregen" represented an impactful turning point in the song cycle. After the moment of revelation in the tenth song, there is a change of the symbolic focus: the focus of the blue flower as a positive force shifts and transforms itself into an obsession with the colour green, which becomes the defining experience at this point of the cycle. From a psychological perspective, such an occurrence marks a symbolic transformation. Jung spoke of Enantiodromia; Erich Neumann designated this experience as a "phenomenon of reversal" (3.2). A brief overview of the archetypal process may be beneficial: in "Thränenregen" the "I" experienced a significant insight; through the rejecting of the reality in "Mein!", the "I" was overflooded by the power of the shadow, symbolically represented by the hunter and the green colour ("Der Jäger"), musically by the imitation technique and the hunting topos. In such a position, the "I" is inevitably in danger because, lacking its own will, it is powerfully attracted to one of the poles of the archetype (3.2). When that point is reached, a phenomenon of reversal (enantiodromia) can happen (3.1). A similar process is to be noted with the two symbols mentioned above: the manifestation of the blue flower, as the positive Anima, was in the foreground up to "Thränenregen" and acted as a motivating force. Subsequently, the predominance of the green colour is striking, starting in "Der Jäger" and achieving its *climax* in the duet "Die liebe Farbe" (no. 16) and "Die böse Farbe" (no.17)[139]. As the title of both juxtaposed

---

[138] Böhm notes the use of G minor tonality in several songs conveying the theme of death or death pain, as well as aimless wandering. Cf. Böhm, Richard. (2006). *Symbolik und Rhetorik im Liedschaffen von Franz Schubert*. P. 84.

[139] It should be pointed out that the color green has in itself a light side, bearing the semantic of hope and that something is germinating, or bringing something to life. Cf. Riedel, Ingrid. (1990). *Farben.* However, here the folk symbolism and the dark green colour rather point to another semantic that is about to be unveiled.

songs suggests, a great ambivalence lives in this colour, which shall promptly be analysed symbolically.

Similarly to "Der Jäger" and "Eifersucht und Stolz" these two poems are also built as a duet and as such they can be understood as two simultaneous inner realities. It shall be recalled, that in the folk traditional readings, the colour green is symbolically attributed to the hunter[140]. The green colour represents, therefore, the miller-lad's shadow side and is experienced as a foreign aspect to the "I" (his defiant). In contrast, the white colour stands for the miller-lad and stands for the light side of his personality. However, as a wanderer, he is after all embedded in the green. The miller-lad's conflictual feelings towards his two colours, green (shadow side) and white (light side) can be perceived in both poems, since he often argues with one of the opposite colours. So doing, he enters—what is called in Jungian literature—a dialectical procedure. This kind of archetypal process is a typical development in the individuation process:

> "Since the archetypes are relatively autonomous, as all numinous contents, they can therefore not be integrated rationally, but demand a dialectic process, which means an actual confrontation, often performed […] in form of a dialogue, with which the [person] realizes, without knowing, the alchemical definition of meditation, […] as an inner dialogue [...]"[141].

Observing the poetic level of both songs, the dialogue is led by the expression of his two wills and his conflictual attitude towards his two colours. In "Die liebe Farbe" the green colour is described as being the beloved colour of the miller-girl (Anima). On the one hand, this means that she is attracted to the huntsman, but on the other hand, this also points to the fact, that she, under the eyes of the miller-lad, becomes associated with the colour green (negative drive) and not anymore with the blue flower (positive inner drive). Consequently, the green represents, in this context, the negative characteristics and the drive of the shadow, in contrast to the motivating function it once had (blue flower). Outstandingly, the trees existent in the poem are mainly those that are either permanently (dark) green and/or bearing a painful semantic, e.g., the word play "Thränenweiden" referring to the "Trauerweiden" (i.e., weeping willow), the rosemary and the cypresses, a

[140] Cf. Cottrell, Alan. (1970). *Wilhelm Müller's Lyrical Song-cycles.*

[141] Jung, Carl Gustav. (2023). *Die Beziehung zwischen dem Ich und dem Unbewussten.* P. 53. (Trans. by the author). German expression: „Da die Archetypen relativ autonom sind, wie alle numinosen Inhalte, so können sie nicht einfach rational integriert werden, sondern verlangen ein dialektisches Verfahren, das heißt eine eigentliche Auseinandersetzung, die von dem Patienten häufig in Dialogform durchgeführt wird, womit er, ohne es zu wissen, die alchemistische Definition der Meditation verwirklicht […], als inneres Zwiegespräch […]".

tree which is associated with cemeteries. It is as if he is trapped in the dark green world—a colour that dominates over the light side of his personality.

The same symbolic character of the green colour is mirrored in the musical means Schubert uses to emphasize such an oppressed atmosphere. The form with a ritornello is meaningful in this regard since it conveys a circling within itself. The fact that Schubert places the horn fifths, the hunting topos, in the ritornello passage "My sweetheart is so fond of green" ("Mein Schatz hat's Grün so gern")[142], marks the association with the green colour, bearing the shadow's quality (hunter), with the miller-girl, the Anima (Fig. 15.5). Furthermore, the monotonous rhythm, and the hypnotic ostinato of the F-sharp note[143] play an important role, lending this song its circling around character (Fig. 15.5). The torn feelings are set in music, e.g., through the appoggiaturas present in the piano prelude and postlude, symbolizing the difficulty of dealing with the topic, and special musical rhetorical figures[144] such as the *passus duriusculus* or even the *saltus duriusculus*[145], e.g., the augmented second in m.8 left hand of the piano part (Fig. 15.5). Particularly noticeable is the use of the *saltus duriusculus* under the word "heather" ("Heide"), e.g., the seventh jump in mm. 16–17. So doing, the heather—which can be understood as an idyllic place providing redemption for the suffering "I", as it is a natural landscape unaltered by humans—bears here the semantic core of death[146].

Being immersed in the hypnotic effect of "Die liebe Farbe" psychologically points to the possible danger of falling into a one-sidedness. Therefore, the "I" needs to (re)enter a dialectical procedure. The first verses of the poem "Die böse Farbe" reveal his two contradictory wills again: "I want to go out into the world, out [there] into the wide world" ("Ich möchte ziehn in die Welt hinaus, hinaus in die weite Welt")[147]. Translated into Jungian terms this statement would mean "I want to find my own Self"—which implies the difficult task of facing and integrating the shadow element. The two contradictory wills of the miller-lad are perceivable in the musical setting. In addition, the above-mentioned danger of

[142] Müller, Wilhelm. (1991). *Die Schöne Müllerin.* P. 71. (Trans. by the author).

[143] Cf. Dobretsberger, Barbara. Personal communication between Barbara Dobretsberger and the author. Salzburg: March 23, 2024.

[144] Cf. Ibid.

[145] These two rhetorical figures refer to a hard step, whereby *passus* is linked with chromatic or small steps, while *saltus* means a hard jump. Cf. Bartel, Dietrich. (2010). *Handbuch der musikalischen Figurenlehre.* P. 222, respectively, p. 239.

[146] Cf. Dobretsberger, Barbara. Personal communication between Barbara Dobretsberger and the author. Salzburg: March 23, 2024.

[147] Müller, Wilhelm. (1991). *Die Schöne Müllerin.* P. 73. (Trans. by the author).

one-sidedness is congruent with the tone-world B: the note B, as the last tone in the scale system, bears an eschatological effect[148]. His indecision regarding the tonality of B major vs. B minor is a sign of him being trapped within a dialectic. The singing voice opens the song decomposing the B chord as a rising arpeggio, surpassing the ambit of an octave (e.g., D–F m.5). This musical gesture tone paints the movement of going out into the wide world and is congruent with the text statement. It underlines the one-will. This will is contrasted immediately by the frequent minorizations which, as Marie-Agnes Dittrich has already shown[149], mostly occur at the end of each stanza, e.g., "If only it weren't so green, so green wouldn't be, out here in the woods and fields" ("Wenn's nur so grün, so grün nicht wär, da draußen in Wald un Feld!")[150]. The Neapolitan sixth chord, as a painful chord, emphasizes his feelings towards certain words, e.g., "pale as death" ("totenbleich", m.20), "farewell" ("Ade", m.39) and "hand" ("Hand", m.60). Braun and Berke interpret the constant shift towards the minor as bearing a sense of irony[151]. It shall be recalled that the Romantic irony is a means to address aspects that are particularly painful[152]. Schubert possibly even conveys a sarcastic undertone which, read psychologically, means to conceal or oppress the hurt feelings[153].

As Alan Cottrell has pointed out, the miller-lad understands it as his mission to say farewell to this love[154] now, e.g., "Die böse Farbe": "Oh unbind from thy brow, the green, green ribbon. Farewell, farewell!" ("O binde von der Stirn dir ab, das grüne, grüne Band. Ade, Ade!")[155]. So doing, he also represses the green colour, i.e., his shadow side. With the words "I want all the green grasses, fully

---

[148] Cf. Dobretsberger, Barbara. Personal communication between Barbara Dobretsberger and the author. Salzburg: March 23, 2024.

[149] Cf. Dittrich, Marie-Agnes. "Die Lieder. 'Für Menschenohren sind es Harmonien'". In: Dürr, Walther. Krause, Andreas. (2020). *Schubert Handbuch.* P. 227–228.

[150] Müller, Wilhelm. (1991). *Die Schöne Müllerin.* P. 73. (Trans. by author).

[151] Cf. Braun, Christiane. Berke, Dietrich. „Die Schöne Müllerin op. 25 (D 795)—Liederzyklus Wilhelm Müller". In: Dürr, Walther. Kube, Michael. [et al.]. (2013). *Schubert Liedlexikon.* P 656.

[152] Cf. Dobretsberger, Barbara. Personal communication between Barbara Dobretsberger and the author. Salzburg: March 23, 2024.

[153] Cf. Jung, Carl Gustav. "GW XI". Cited after: Wehr, Gerhard. (2014). C.G. Jung Leben—Werk—Wirkung. P. 328.

[154] Alan Cottrell saw the core of this cycle being the theme of farewell. Cf. Cottrell, Alan. (1970). *Wilhelm Müller's Lyrical Song-cycles.* P. 24–25.

[155] Müller, Wilhelm. (1991). *Die Schöne Müllerin.* P. 74. (Trans. by the author).

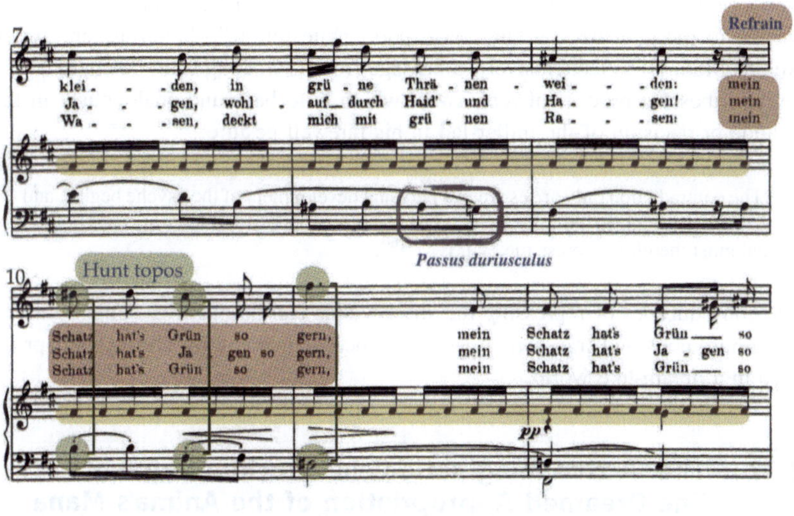

Fig. 15.5 "Die liebe Farbe". The refrain line pointing to the association of the green colour (being the colour of the shadow) with the Anima and referring to the hunt topos. The omnipresent hypnotic tone of F-sharp functioning as an ostinato. (Sheet music excerpt taken and adapted from *IMSLP*)

wept pale as death" ("Ich möchte die grünen Gräser all', weinen ganz totenbleich")[156] it is as if he would like to (re)paint the green environment (his shadow side) with his own light side (ego/Persona), namely the colour white. Simultaneously, it is as if he would perceive himself to be condemned to death, since this act would—psychologically observed—lead to a one-sidedness again. As already suggested above, this reflexion can be applied to both, the precedent lied as the present one since in "Die Liebe Farbe", the last verse before the refrain "Green, all green so round and round" (Grün, Alles grün, so rings und rund")[157] points to how the shadow side can be oppressive[158], if his light side would be negated. Subsequently, in "Die böse Farbe" the white colour, as the miller-lad's characteristic colour, is perceived by himself as painful. This is expressed in the musical setting of "Die böse Farbe" by (i) the Neapolitan coloration under the

[156] Ibid. P. 73. (Trans. by the author).

[157] Ibid. P. 72. (Trans. by the author).

[158] Cf. Dobretsberger, Barbara. Personal communication between Barbara Dobretsberger and the author. Salzburg: March 23, 2024.

words "fully wept pale as death" ("weinen ganz totenbelich") and (ii) with the *suspiratio* motif in mm.29 "me poor, poor white fellow" ("mich armen, armen weißen Mann")[159]. Conclusively, a passage from C.G. Jung shall be cited, where he describes the process of repression, which is to be found analogously in the attitude or decision of the miller-lad in his farewell gesture:

> "The contradiction only arises when a personal development of the psyche begins, and the *ratio* recognizes the irreconcilable nature of the opposites. One wants to be good and must therefore repress the evil; [...]"[160].

The consequences of repressing the shadow side can be massive—unless the "I" has a numinous and transformative experience, which can by all means happen, even in a dream-like world.

15.7 The "Active Imagination" in "Trockne Blumen": The Dreamed Appropriation of the Anima's Mana Power and its Powerful Effect on the Archetypal Process of the Miller-Lad

It should be observed that the miller-lad seems to have adopted a rather inactive attitude towards his beloved up to this point. As former scholars[161] have already observed, he has never openly confessed his love for her; rather, he asked the nature to do so for him, e.g., in "Eifersucht und Stolz" (no.15): "Go brooklet,

---

[159] Schubert repeats the adjective "poor", while Müller only states it once. Müller, Wilhelm. (1991). *Die Schöne Müllerin.* P. 73. (Trans. by the author).

[160] Jung, Carl Gustav. (2023). *Die Beziehung zwischen dem Ich und dem Unbewussten.* P. 39. (Trans. by the author). German expression: „Der Widerspruch erhebt sich erst, wenn eine persönliche Entwicklung der Psyche anhebt und dabei die Ratio die unvereinbare Natur der Gegensätze erkennt Die Folge dieser Erkenntnis ist der Verdrängungskampf. Man will gut sein und muss darum das Böse verdrängen; [...]".

[161] See, for example: Braun, Christiane. Berke, Dietrich. „Die Schöne Müllerin op. 25 (D 795)—Liederzyklus Wilhelm Müller". In: Dürr, Walther. Kube, Michael. [et al.]. (2013). *Schubert Liedlexikon.* The mentioned authors point to this fact in the seventh song "Ungeduld". This attitude of the miller-lad is visible also in the above-mentioned song "Eifersucht und Stolz".

thither, and tell her that" ("Geh, Bächlein, hin und sag' ihr das")[162]. It is only at this moment in the cycle, that the miller-lad becomes involved in an active imagination in "Trockne Blumen" (no. 18), in which the positive Anima figure re-emerges and sets an important inner movement back in motion again[163]. In order to unveil the complex psychic process inherent in "Trockne Blumen", it is necessary to look psychologically at some crucial signs mirrored both in the poetic and musical level. The respective analytical observations will be interpreted by directly drawing the respective psychological parallels.

In the poetic narrative the "lyrical I" shows an active behaviour for the first time, when the miller-lad fantasizes about the miller-girl's change of attitude. This occurs when in his imagination the miller-girl acknowledges his loyal and deep feelings: "And when she walks past the hill, and weens in her heart: he means it leal! Then all thou little flowers, come forth, come forth! May has come, winter is gone" (Und wenn sie wandelt am Hügel vorbei, und denkt im Herzen: Der meint' es true! Dann Blümlein alle heraus, heraus! Der Mai ist kommen, der Winter ist aus")[164]. From the linguistic level, the lyrical "I" gradually loses on its presence as the poem progresses[165], which, to translate in Jungian terms, depicts the ongoing immersion in deeper layers of his imagination ("abaissement du niveau mental", 3.1 Fig. 3.4). This transformation of the psychic state can be heard musically evolving throughout the song and is achieved through the contrasts created in the musical textures.

The initial death march rhythm (2/4 measure) is conveyed by short quavers, followed by pauses and the repetition of the same chords. This motif fulfills the function of an ostinato/organ point (mm.1–10 and later mm.17–24). The same shortness of breath is to be found reflected in Schubert's initial short four bars periodic phrase construction, which is organized in 2 + 2 measures in parallel construction. From these musical indications it can be said that this opening psychologically represents an inner stagnation of the miller-lad in relation to the outer reality, i.e., it represents the initial situation in which he finds himself. This musical ductus is subsequently slightly varied with the appearance of the dotted rhythm in mm.11–15. Slowly, movement is given by this rhythmical element when the symbol of the flowers is addressed for the second time. However, this

---

[162] Müller, Wilhelm. (1991). *Die Schöne Müllerin.* P. 68. (Trans. by the author).

[163] The positive function of the Anima and its eventual integration is described in the archetypal theory of C.G. Jung. Cf. Jung, Carl Gustav. (2023). *Die Beziehung zwischen dem Ich und dem Unbewussten.*

[164] Müller, Wilhelm. (1991). *Die Schöne Müllerin.* P. 78. (Trans. by the author).

[165] Dobretsberger, Barbara. Personal communication between Barbara Dobretsberger and the author. Salzburg: March 23, 2024.

does not last long at first (mm.11–15), since the feeling of being trapped in the atmosphere of a death march is still evidently in the foreground. These rhythmical variations in the musical ductus could point to the gradual loss of the ego consciousness, respectively, to the arising of unconscious elements ("abaissement"), which is mirrored in the poetic level.

To return to the musical observations—this rhythmical motif reappears again in mm. 25–29. Suddenly, under the words: "all the little flowers that she gave me" ("Die Blümlein alle die sie mir gab")[166], Schubert possibly places an *exclamatio* to emphasize that the attention is now fully turned to the miller-girl. So doing, the word "she" ("sie") has an accentuated character. Precisely in that moment, Schubert suspends the musical ductus in a dominant chord (B major). Having a powerful effect of arising expectation, this musical suspension on the dominant chord functions almost as an unwritten fermata—as observed in the musical analysis of other works, fermatas can point to psychological turning points (7, 12). Surprisingly, Schubert then changed key signature (mm.27–29). Interpreting these musical phenomena, the sudden turning point induced by the key change, can express a turning inwards, triggered by the reminiscence of the little flowers given by the girl. Congruently, in the psychological reading this can indicate a consequent change of perspective, i.e., a turning point which will lead to the miller-lad leaving the key of death (E minor) and entering its opposite pole (E major). In other words, this could be seen as a further musical example of the psychological "phenomenon of reversal"[167] or enantiodromia, discussed in previous chapters. This time, the recall of the flowers acts as a reminiscence of the positive Anima figure, restoring his life force again.

This reversal phenomenon, encouraged by the moment of suspension, is translated on the musical level with a clear change of ductus from m.30 on: immediately, the dotted rhythm suggested before is clearer in the foreground and is over-punctuated. Now, it underlines the statement of the text, which refers to the heart: "And when she walks past the hill, and weens in her heart: he means it leal!" ("Und wenn sie wandelt am Hügel vorbei, und denkt im Herzen er meint' es treu!")[168]. The dotted rhythm can therefore be addressed here as the heartbeat motif or life motif since the heartbeat stands for life. This means that the

[166] Müller, Wilhelm. (1991). *Die Schöne Müllerin.* P. 80. (Trans. by the author).

[167] Cf. Neumann, Erich. (2021). *Die Große Mutter.*

[168] Müller, Wilhelm. (1991). *Die Schöne Müllerin.* P. 80. (Trans. by the author).

semantic level of this motif has abruptly changed from an initial death march to a life motif, which confirms the psychological phenomenon of reversal mentioned above. To speak in Jungian terms, this sudden recovery of life energy can be attributed to an archetypal force with which the "I" has engaged himself in its fantasy. More precisely, it refers to the (possible or partial) integration of the Anima. By becoming active, the "I" has appropriated the mana-power of the Anima—or at least imagined that it has done so. The excitement of the positive Anima mana-force appropriation is clearly felt, being expressed by the euphorically ascending melodic lines and the *fp* accents in the piano (mm.35–38 and the following respective measures). This is especially noticeable in the march of the variations for flute and piano on the theme of this song. Additionally, the dactyl rhythm of the "Wanderer", present in mm.37–38, underlines the forward motion and an outwardly directed energy. The miller-lad repeats this fantasy twice entirely in his mind and the singing voice ends the final phrase with a heroic interjection in E major: "the winter is gone" ("Der Winter ist aus")[169]. However, the harmonic colours of Schubert's setting seem to express a different statement.

The ending of this song is in effect marked by a harmonic cloudiness. Furthermore, the piano, symbolizing his unconscious, repeats the motif twice in E major, but then it turns to the deep register of the piano (reminding a *catabasis* gesture) and repeats it a total of three times in the harmonic opposite pole (E minor). This not only marks a change of spheres[170] but these musical elements also point to another psychological verdict: the overjoyed exclamation of the lyrical "I" was misleading and, *de facto*, the appropriation of the mana-power of the Anima was barely an illusion of the "I"[171]. Despite the imaginative nature of the Anima's integration, this psychological process is meaningful for the individuation process.

169 Ibid. (Trans. by the author).

170 Dobretsberger, Barbara. Personal communication between Barbara Dobretsberger and the author. Salzburg: March 23, 2024.

171 Such process is described e.g., in: Jung, Carl Gustav. (2023). *Die Beziehung zwischen dem Ich und dem Unbewussten.*

The moment he became active by ordering all flowers to bloom again is to be understood as a crucial inner experience. Following the typical unfolding of individuation with the classic archetypes (3.1), this psychic occurrence will subsequently permit the encounter with the Great Mother. It should be recalled that the Great Mother is a mana-personality and as such exists directly in the environment of the Self, i.e., exerts a massive power of fascination on the "I". This process can occur, even if the Anima's mana appropriation was only imaginary[172]. This aligns with C.G. Jung's description of the process in which the Anima transforms itself, shifting from being an autonomous complex to fulfill the function of a mediator between the conscious "I" and the unconscious:

> "They [Anima and Animus] cannot be integrated into consciousness as long as their contents are unknown. The confrontation with them should bring their contents to light, and only when this task has been completed and the conscious mind has become sufficiently familiar with the processes of the unconscious reflected in the Anima, will the Anima really be perceived as a mere function."[173].

[172] This reading of this song can bring some additional insights to the unexplained heroic march in the *Variations for flute and piano on the theme of "Trockne Blumen"*, namely standing in connection with this active imagination and alluding to a possible appropriation of the "I" of the Anima's mana force.

[173] Jung, Carl Gustav. (2023). *Die Beziehung zwischen dem Ich und dem Unbewussten.* P. 113. (Trans. by the author). German expression: "Sie [Anima und Animus] können nicht dem Bewusstsein integriert werden, solange ihre Inhalte unbekannt sind. Die Auseinandersetzung mit ihnen soll ihre Inhalte ans Licht führen, und erst, wenn diese Aufgabe vollendet und eine genügende Bekanntschaft des Bewusstseins mit den in der Anima abgespiegelten Vorgängen des Unbewussten vorhanden ist, wird die Anima auch wirklich als bloße Funktion empfunden.".

The integration of the Anima means a functional transformation:

> "Through this process the Anima lost her demonic power of an autonomous complex, meaning, she cannot exert any kind of obsession anymore, since she is depotentiated. She is not anymore guardian of unknown treasures, [...] but a psychological function of intuitive nature."[174].

This elucidates the reason for the miller-lad's profound obsession in "Mein!" with the Anima figure: the Anima, then an autonomous complex, was acting out of its own. Remarkably, the fact that the little brook speaks to the miller-lad for the first time in the following song, can confirm this reading.

15.8 "Der Müller und der Bach": The Dialogue with the Miller-Lad's Inner Voice

"Der Müller und der Bach" (no. 19) conveys the dialogue between the miller-lad and his brooklet. It is structured in three parts: (i) the lament of the miller-lad, (ii) the brooklet's answer and (iii) the expression of the miller-lad's last will. The brooklet's speech conveys an important message which will impact the miller-lad's state of mind. First, the poem and its symbolic content are going to be examined, followed by an analysis of the musical elements present in this song. The psychological reading will be provided in the course of the analysis.

[174] Ibid. P. 132. (Trans. by the author). German expression: "Durch diesen Prozess verliert die Anima die dämonische Macht des autonomen Komplexes, das heißt, sie kann keine Besessenheit mehr ausüben, da sie depotenziert ist. Sie ist nicht mehr die Hüterin unbekannter Schätze, sie ist nicht mehr Kundry, die dämonische Gralsbotin von göttlich-tierischer Natur, nicht mehr die ‚Herrin-Seele', sondern eine psychologische Funktion intuitiver Natur, [...]".

15.8.1 The Golden Flower of Alchemy as the Brooklet's Promised Treasures

"Der Müller Wo ein treues Herze In Liebe vergeht, Da welken die Lilien Auf jedem Beet.	**"The miller** Where a loyal heart fades away in love, hither the lilies wither in every flowerbed.
Da muß in die Wolken Der Vollmond gehn, Damit seine Thränen Die Menschen nicht sehn.	Hither the full moon must wend through the clouds, so that its tears are by men unseen.
Da halten die Englein Die Augen sich zu, Und schluchzen und singen Die Seele zu Ruh'.	Hither the little angels hold their eyes closed, and sob and sing the soul to rest.
Der Bach Und wenn sich die Liebe Dem Schmerz entringt, Ein Sternlein, ein neues, Am Himmel erblinkt.	**The brook** And when love is from pain unchained, a little star, a new one, twinkles in the sky.
Da springen drei Rosen, Halb roth, halb weiß, Die welken nicht wieder, Aus Dornenreis.	Hither three roses spring, half red, half white, they wither no longer, from thorny twigs.
Und die Engelein schneiden Die Flügel sich ab, Und gehn alle Morgen Zur Erde [hinab][3].	And the little angels cut off their wings, and wend every morning down to Earth.
Der Müller Ach, Bächlein, liebes Bächlein, Du meinst es so gut: Ach, Bächlein, aber weißt du, Wie Liebe thut?	**The miller** Oh brooklet, dear brooklet, you mean it so well: Oh, brooklet, but do you know, what love can do?

Ach, unten, da unten,	Oh, down, down there,
Die kühle Ruh'!	the cool tranquillity!
Ach, Bächlein, liebes Bächlein,	Oh, brooklet, dear brooklet,
So singe nur zu."[175].	so sing sing along."[176].

The poem is constructed in eight strophes, each of them containing four verses, disposing the rhyme scheme abcb and a dimeter metric[177]. The ending cadences of the poem consist of a regular alternation between feminine and masculine endings. From the text alone, each character presents a tone colour of its own: the miller-lad's speech contains an abundance of darker vowels, like "o" or "u", which translate his state of spirit; while the brooklet's words feature brighter vowels, often including "e" and "i". On the tone painting level, diphthongs can be recognized in the brooklet's speech, e.g., "drei", "weiß", "-reis", "Englein", "schneiden". The alliteration of the "u" vowel in the last stanza is striking, which can be interpreted as the allusion to the depths of the water. Alan Cottrell understands the repetition of this vowel as establishing a rhythmic rocking movement and functioning as a bridge to the last poem's initial words "Rest well, rest well!" ("Gute Ruh, gute Ruh!"[178])—these are related to the lullaby's motif of the brooklet[179]. The onomatopoetical level of a poem is particularly significant for the musical setting. As such, it is of great interest to examine how the composer sets the tone painting elements to music. In general terms, Schubert achieves the analogy with the darker vs. lighter vowels through the choice of tonalities: the miller-lad is attributed with the harmonic colour of G minor, as the tone of "expression of bitter feelings"[180], while the brooklet sounds in G major, the tone of connection with nature (eclogue, pastoral tone colour)[181]. As it will be explained later, the diphthong coincides with a change in the rhythmical level of the music.

---

[175] Müller, Wilhelm. (1991). *Die Schöne Müllerin.* P. 81–82. The referred and used edition by the author is based on the published version of 1830 by F.A. Brockhaus in Leipzig, a five-band edition of works by Wilhelm Müller.

[176] Ibid. (Trans. by the author).

[177] Cf. Braun, Christiane. Berke, Dietrich. „Die Schöne Müllerin op. 25 (D 795)—Liederzyklus Wilhelm Müller". In: Dürr, Walther. Kube, Michael. [et al.]. (2013). *Schubert Liedlexikon.* P. 658–659.

[178] Müller, Wilhelm. (1991). *Die Schöne Müllerin.* P. 83. (Trans. by the author).

[179] Cf. Cottrell, Alan. (1970). *Wilhelm Müller's Lyrical Song-cycles.* P. 28.

[180] Dittrich, Marie-Agnes. "Die Lieder. 'Für Menschenohren sind es Harmonien'". In: Dürr, Walther. Krause, Andreas. (2020). *Schubert Handbuch.* P. 228.

[181] Cf. Böhm, Richard. (2006). *Symbolik und Rhetorik im Liedschaffen von Franz Schubert.*

The poem features a rich network of symbols, grounded in folkloristic topoi[182]. This will subsequently be analysed in a Jungian manner. Some of the motifs seem to have a more central meaning than others in the overall message that the poem conveys. These are: the lily flower, the moon, the angels, and three half red half white roses. The latter three elements appear in the brooklet's speech, pointing to the importance of its utterance. Even if the lily flower is found associated with a feminine sexual symbol in folk poetry or connected to death[183], in Jungian terms, it is rather understood spiritually, as an expression of one aspect of the Anima and its pureness of spirit, innocence and virginity[184]. In the context of the poem, the wilting of the lily could possibly be an allusion to the unfulfilled love. The full moon, in turn, as already mentioned (e.g., "Thränenregen"), can be interpreted as a symbol of an imminent transformation, a transformation from one state to another: "Hither, the full moon must wend through the clouds, so that its tears are by men unseen" (Da muß in die Wolken der Vollmond gehn, damit seine Thränen die Menschen nicht sehn")[185]. Yet, this textual statement, illustrating the weeping full moon hiding behind the clouds, could possibly express a (momentary) reluctance of the "I" to undergo that transformation, or at least how painful such a process may be. At such moments, it is meaningful to see if Schubert, in his musical setting, responds to the symbolic content of the poem, hinting at interpretative possibilities, and whether there is congruency or, on the contrary, a contradiction with the poet's statement. At first sight, the answer to this doubt lies in the harmonic path with which Schubert shapes the phrase in question. At precisely this point, as it will be elaborated later in more detail, the harmonic path leads to D major, the triumphal dominant key of G. This phrase is extended as if there were an inner will to linger in that harmony. At first sight, this observation would prioritize the second hypothesis, that Schubert's harmonization would rather be in contradiction with Müller's statement. However, it could also be argued that this harmonic level plays in the unconscious realm (i.e., the piano accompaniment as the expression of the miller-lad's unconscious,

---

[182] Cf. Cottrell, Alan. (1970). *Wilhelm Müller's Lyrical Song-cycles.* P. 26.

[183] Cf. Butzer, Günter. Jacob, Joachim (Ed.). (2012). *Metzler Lexikon literarischer Symbole.* P. 245–246.

[184] Cf. Mollwo-Oesterreicher, Marianne. (1978). *Herder Lexikon Symbole.* See also Marie-Louise von Franz' interpretation of Brother Klaus' visions, e.g., specifically the vision of the "About the horse that eats the lily". von Franz, Marie Louise. (1987). *Die Visionen des Niklaus von Flüe.* Guido Ferrari (Director). [Documentary/Interview]. Minutes: 28:53/ 02:00:00.

[185] Müller, Wilhelm. (1991). *Die Schöne Müllerin.* P. 81. (Trans. by the author).

cf. 12) and in this sense, it does not necessarily contradict Müller's utterance but rather complements it (Fig. 15.11).

Angels, being light beings and messengers between this world and the Beyond permit the return to the paradise (on earth)—what is being searched in heaven, will descend down to earth[186]. With the act of cutting off their wings (present in the brooklet's speech), angels are able to connect the two spheres, heaven and earth[187]; such is the brooklet's promise. It should be appended that staying in a place like the sacred garden (paradise on earth)—even if it were only real in his imagination, i.e., an illusion—would psychologically provide for the necessary sense of security for the "I" to integrate the split elements[188]. Fascinatingly, the symbolism of the three roses, half red and half white, which appear in the brooklet's speech just before the angels are mentioned, refers to a symbol to be found in ancient alchemical manuscripts. The alchemical golden flower is described as being half red and half white (Fig. 15.6)[189]:

[186] Cf. Drewermann, Eugen. (2023). „2. Sommervorlesung 2023: Märchen als Therapie. Auslegung von Grimms ‚Das Mädchen ohne Hände'". [Lecture].

[187] Cf. Roesler, Christian. Personal communication between Christian Roesler and the author. Basel: March 7, 2024.

[188] Cf. Drewermann, Eugen. (2023). „2. Sommervorlesung 2023: Märchen als Therapie. Auslegung von Grimms ‚Das Mädchen ohne Hände'". [Lecture].

[189] As described previously (2.5), the central aim in alchemy was not the bare transmutation of metals, but the symbolic significance of these transformations, standing for a spiritual transformation. C.G. Jung and Marie-Louise von Franz have studied in depth alchemical manuscripts in this sense. The different states of metals to be found in alchemy represent the different psychic states, where the achievement of the golden state is "linked to the search of the philosopher's stone" and to the "striving for purification of the soul". Mollwo-Oesterreicher, Marianne. (1978). *Herder Lexikon Symbole*. P. 62. (Trans. by the author). German expression: "Die G.macherei der Alchimisten, die mit der Such nach dem Stein der Weisen zusammenhing, muß urspr. in enger Beziehung zum Streben nach Läuterung der Seele [...] gesehene werden.".

Fig. 15.6 Left image: "Anonymous, colored manuscript, around 1550". Universitätsbibliothek Basel, L IV, P. 293. Picture taken from: Historisches Lexikon der Schweiz HLS (online). Right image: "The red-white Rose, the 'golden flower' of alchemy, as the birthplace of '*Filius philosophorum*' (Ripley, Scrowle, 1588)". (Picture and corresponding description taken from: Jung, C.G. (2001). *Traum und Traumdeutung*. Image no.24. © 1971–1990 Walter Verlag, Olten. (Trans. by the author). German expression: "Die rot-weiße Rose, die 'Goldblume' der Alchemie, als Geburtsstätte des ‚*filius philosophorum*')

From these sources the golden flower is understood as the symbol of wholeness, from which *Filius philosophorum*, i.e., the divine child, is born[190]. The coloured manuscript shows the sun as the symbol of the male, and the moon as the symbol of the female. The conjunction is to be found in the uroboros symbol within the circle, which includes the opposites. The corresponding description of C.G. Jung for the coloured manuscript presented here reads as follows:

> "The 'tale-eater' (Ouroboros) as the starting material of the alchemical process with the red and white rose, the 'flos sapientum'; below: 'coniunctio solis et lunae'; in the center: the 'lapis philosophorum' as the son. (Pandora, 1588)."[191]

---

190 Congruently, this symbol of the rose is often associated with the mandalas, which is another symbol for wholeness, and is used in traditions of Christian mysticism. Cf. Roesler, Christian. Personal communication between Christian Roesler and the author. Basel: March 7, 2024.

191 Jung, Carl Gustav. (2001). *Traum und Traumdeutung*. Image no.6. (Trans. by the author). German expression: "Der 'Schwanzfresser' (Ouroboros) als Ausgangsstoff des alchemistischen Prozess mit der rot-weißen Rose, dem 'flos sapientum'; unten: 'coniunctio solis et luna'; in der Mitte: der 'lapis philosophorum' als der Sohn. (Pandora, 1588). The same image presented above is to be found as a black-and-white copy in: Ibid.

In folk tradition, the name of the miller-girl being Rose is assigned the same corresponding colour, while the colour of the miller-lad, as already previously seen, is white.

Based on these considerations, the brooklet, by speaking in the aforementioned symbolic terms, might be suggesting an important transformation to come, if the miller-lad would allow the opposites to form a union. In other words—it is as if the brooklet would be promising unreachable wealth, as if he would want to persuade the lyrical "I" to allow the integration of the opposites, by promising the paradise on earth and the arrival of the divine child, as the result of being whole[192]. How Schubert reacts musically to this symbolic ground requires a closer and deeper investigation of the musical elements, which will be unveiled in the following subchapter.

15.8.2 Unveiling the Brooklet's Function as the Great Mother Archetype

As the poem presents a threefold structure, Schubert congruently composes this song in the ABA' lied form. The 3/8 measures and the rhythm present in the two initial piano bars, with the weight on the second beat, convey the iambic rhythm. The emotional state of the miller-lad being heavy and tired is expressed through the limping iambic metric of the piano accompaniment[193]. In a next step, it is significant to reveal the purpose of this rhythmic motif in each section of the song, which also includes comparing the piano prelude and the postlude measures.

The function of these two opening measures is the one of an ostinato, which will be omnipresent in the entire A-section (mm.1–28). In contrast, it shifts to the background in the A'-section (mm.62–89). For the B section (mm.29–61) it is only sparingly existent, and its character transformed (Fig. 15.7). The main element that constitutes this motif is the interval of the "empty" fifth (perfect fifth). This interval recalls two concurrent meanings: (i) the sound of the lyre,

---

[192] This statement brings another perspective on the reading of the brook's stanzas, viewing them as a persuasion to avert suicide. Cf. Cottrell, Alan. (1970). *Wilhelm Müller's Lyrical Song-cycles*. P. 26.

[193] Dobretsberger, Barbara. Personal communication between Barbara Dobretsberger and the author. Salzburg: March 23, 2024.

as the miller-lad's instrument[194] and (ii) the horn fifths as the hunting topos, symbolizing the hunter. This fact alone can be used as a musical substantiation for the psychological interpretation elaborated above: the hunter is, as the lyre, part of his personality (the lyre, representing his light, poetic side, while the hunting topos standing for the shadow, his aggressive side). The bridge function of the postlude measures, in contrast, can represent both the turning towards the brooklet and the reception of the same, as being the main events in the brooklet's lullaby (no. 20). These last measures of no.19 are characterized by the brooklet's motif and the downwards direction towards the darker register of the piano, as a metaphor for the depths of the water (Fig. 15.7). The semiquaver sextuplets motif is, in this song, introduced by the brooklet's speech in the B-section. The iambic limping rhythm of the prelude is entirely absent in the postlude measures[195]. In turn, the brooklet is given the leading word both in the B-section and postlude measures.

Comparing the phrases structures between the miller-lad and the brooklet, the following structure can be identified: for the miller-lad's first lament (i) an initial regular eight bar phrase, made of 4 + 4 measures, corresponds to the first poem's strophe (mm.1–8); (ii) followed by an irregular phrase construction as the second strophe, in which an additional measure is added in the consequent phrase (mm.11–19). This coincides with the modulation path going through the hopeful idyllic B-flat major tonality arriving at the dominant key of G minor, i.e., unconsciously lingering in the desired triumphant D major harmony (Fig. 15.11); (iii) the last strophe of the miller-lad remains regular again (mm.20–27). In the second miller-lad's speech the only irregular construction refers to the first consequent phrase (mm.66–70) and coincides with the question "oh brooklet, but do you know, what love can do?" ("Ach Bächlein, aber weißt du, wie Liebe thut?")[196], which is emphasized by the painful Neapolitan sixth chord.

For the brooklet's speech, phrases are regular *per se*, but feature some particularities. After the first consequent phrase, the same repeats itself, creating an echo effect (mm.33–40). Interpreting these details in psychological terms, it is as if the unconscious is trying to connect the inner and outer world, projecting something into the outside in order to hear it as a clear return (4). This phenomenon happens when the following words are sung: "a little star, a new one, twinkles in the sky"

---

[194] References to the lyre are made in the poems "Pause" and "Mit dem grünen Lautenbande". Further comments to the fellow's musicality are to be noticed in e.g., the ending of "Eifersucht und Stolz".

[195] Cf. Dobretsberger, Barbara. Personal communication between Barbara Dobretsberger and the author. Salzburg: March 23, 2024.

[196] Müller, Wilhelm. (1991). *Die Schöne Müllerin.* P. 82. (Trans. by the author).

("Ein Sternlein, ein neues, am Himmel erblinkt")[197]. The same happens in the last stanza of the brooklet, which corresponds to the descent of the little angels (mm.53–60). Differently is the brooklet's second stanza, where the consequent phrase actually merges with the new antecedent phrase in m.48. The psychological meaning of the merging of consequent with a new antecedent phrase could lie in the brooklet's possible intention to persuade, as if emphasizing the important meaning of its message.

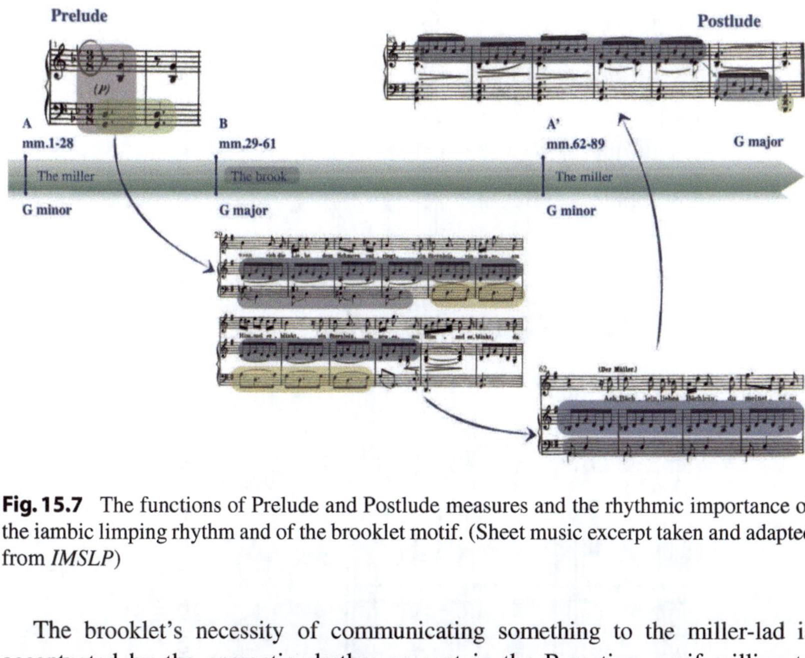

Fig. 15.7 The functions of Prelude and Postlude measures and the rhythmic importance of the iambic limping rhythm and of the brooklet motif. (Sheet music excerpt taken and adapted from *IMSLP*)

The brooklet's necessity of communicating something to the miller-lad is accentuated by the energetic rhythm present in the B-section, as if willing to return the life energy back again. As Arnold Feil had already demonstrated, there is an inversion that happens on the rhythmical level. The rhythm is transformed into a slight Waltz-like rhythm (Fig. 15.8). Through these means, Schubert translates musically the above-identified diphthong of the poem.

[197] Ibid. P. 81. (Trans. by the author).

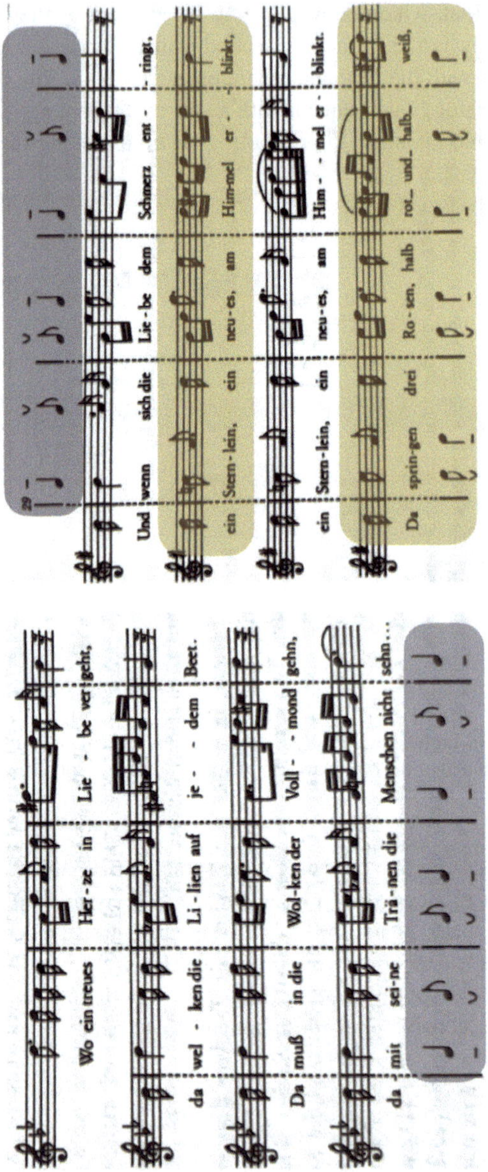

Fig. 15.8 Analysis of the rhythmical structure. (Picture taken and adapted from: Feil, Arnold. (1975). *Franz Schubert*. P. 94–95. © 1975 Philipp Reclam jun. GmbH & Co., Stuttgart)

The A'-Section shows that the miller-lad is not indifferent to the brooklet's message. This can be substantiated by the fact that the brooklet motif continues to sound when the miller-lad resumes his speech at the end, as well as by the shifting into the background of the iambic piano accompaniment (Fig. 15.7). The absence of the iambic metric in the postlude measures, as mentioned before, also supports this reading. So doing, both, the miller-lad and the brooklet, fuse together in the A'-section; this can be taken as an indicator of the miller-lad's receptiveness towards the brooklet's message; or—applying the archetypal theory—as the unconscious expression of the Great Mother's overpowering character. If this would be the case, then, the promised treasures of the brooklet's speech could only be an illusion, since it is the expression of the Great Mother's *fascinosum*, i.e., its mana power. This would confirm that the Anima appropriation of the "I" in "Trockne Blumen" was of illusory nature and that in fact, it was the brooklet, i.e., the Great Mother who had appropriated the mana force of the Anima:

> "It was an illusion: the 'I' did not overcome the Anima and therefore its mana-force was not integrated. [...] The ['Great Mother'] could therefore take possession of the 'I', because the 'I' had dreamed about the victory over the Anima. That was an assault, and every assault of the 'I' is followed by an assault of the unconscious [...]"[198].

Returning to the music analytical findings: there is a transformation in diastematics, to be noted between the miller-lad's lament and the brook's answer (Fig. 15.9). The melody of the miller-lad (antecedent phrase) begins with a *lamento* figure[199], i.e., a descending fourth interval, followed by an *exclamatio*, i.e., an ascending sixth interval, and ending with a falling tritone (*diabolus in musica*). Psychologically, his melody expresses a circling around a centre that

---

[198] Jung, Carl Gustav. (2023). *Die Beziehung zwischen dem Ich und dem Unbewussten*. P. 134–135. (Trans. by the author). German expression: "Es war eine Täuschung: Das Ich hat die Anima nicht überwunden und ihr Mana daher nicht erworben. [...] Der ‚Zauberer' [Die Große Mutter] konnte nur darum Besitz vom Ich ergreiffen, weil das Ich von einem Sieg über die Anima träumte. Das war ein Übergriff, und jeder Übergriff des Ich ist gefolgt von einem Übergriff des Unbewussten [...]". The Magician is as another Mana-Personality, like the Great Mother. Therefore, it can be substituted for here by the Great Mother. C.G. Jung himself describes the same process and refers to the equivalence between the Magician and the Great Mother in: Ibid. P. 133.

[199] This descending line could also be interpreted as the music rhetorical figure of the *catabasis*. Cf. Dobretsberger, Barbara. Personal communication between Barbara Dobretsberger and the author. Salzburg: March 12, 2024. While the madrigalism of the *lamento* places the torn feelings of the miller-lad as the focal point, which corresponds to the choice of tonality and harsh harmonies existent in the A section, the *catabasis* figure, in this context, would rather convey the gesture of turning inwards. The latter is also congruent with the text statement. This shows the two possible readings of this downward musical gesture.

conveys his obsessive thoughts or his state of being trapped in these recurring thoughts. Together with the iambic rhythm, it transmits a monotonous, obsessive state, even though the melody is not made of tone repetitions. This melodic disposition experiences a transformation with the brooklet's speech, which completely changes the character of the "same" melody (this motivic interrelation is a further indicator that the brooklet is part of his personality). The first interval becomes a falling major third. The *exclamatio* figure remains, but the subsequent interval is no longer a tritone but a falling perfect fifth, which gives a sense of security (and removes the dissonance). The diastematic of the brooklet motif contributes to the change in the inner energetic level. By leaving the *exclamatio* figure under the words "love" ("Liebe"), Schubert underlines the focal point of the message.

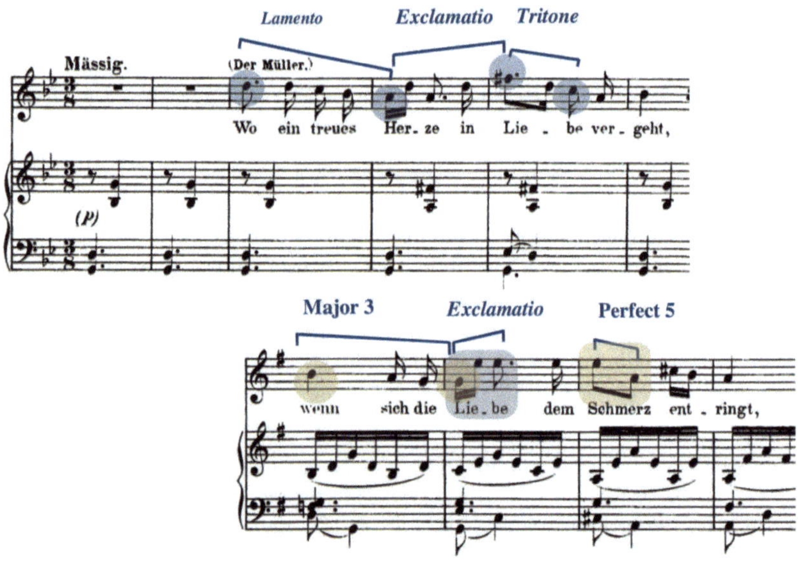

Fig. 15.9 Interval metamorphosis between the miller-lad's lament and the brooklet's answer; between the "I" and the unconscious or the Great Mother Archetype. (Sheet music excerpt taken and adapted from *IMSLP*)

Harmonically, this song is rich in particularities. The first to mention occurs right in the fifth measure: over the organ point of G, creating a tonal carpet, Schubert generates a harsh dissonance by placing the F-sharp note in the melodic line, a strange note to the harmony, and by adding an appoggiatura, i.e., the E-flat note, which resolves to the D (Fig. 15.10). Interpreting this harmonic observation, this harsh dissonance reflects the torn emotions of the miller-lad, since its recurrences coincide with the words: "love" ("Liebe") and "eyes" ("Augen") in m.5 and m.22, respectively. It ought to be recalled that symbolically, the eyes are in the popular understanding the windows to the soul. Remarkably, in the same spot in the A'-Section, i.e., after the brooklet's speech, the appoggiatura is withdrawn, softening the initial harmonic dissonant tension (m.64). The painful Neapolitan sixth chord is especially emphasized in this song since it appears three times in the entire A-section (m.8, m.16, m.25). The words that are expressed under this harmonic light are special ones, namely "lily" ("Lilien"), tears ("Tränen"), and sing ("singen"), i.e., "hither the little angels hold their eyes closed, and sob and sing the soul to rest", ("Da halten die Englein die Augens ich zu, und schluchzen und singen die Seele zu Ruh")[200]. The soothing effect of the brooklet's words can be also identified by the fact, that in the A'-section, the Neapolitan sixth comes not more than once (m.67), under the question "oh brooklet, but do you know, what love can do?" ("Ach, Bächlein, aber weißt du, wie Liebe thut?")[201] right in the beginning when the miller-lad resumes his lament.

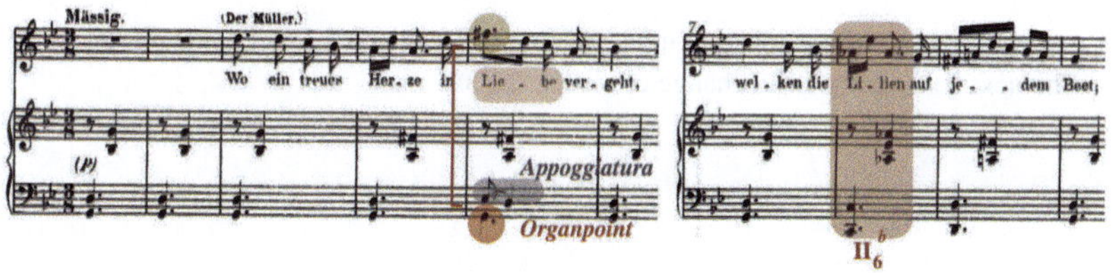

Fig. 15.10 Harmonic special features and the word-tone relationship in mm.5 and mm.8. (Sheet music excerpt taken and adapted from *IMSLP*)

The means that Schubert used to modulate in this song are (i) through the majorization (the typical major brightening), respectively, minorization of the third—this type of modulation occurs in the moments referring to the protagonist's change m. 29, respectively, m. 62; (ii) by giving the direction to the relative major tonality, i.e., B-flat major, e.g., mm.11–19 (Fig. 15.11), which coincides with the asymmetrical phrase of the miller-lad expressing his momentarily hopeful state; (iii) by a sudden third shift in m.75 under the words "Oh, brooklet, dear brooklet, so sing sing along" (Ach, Bächlein, liebes Bächlein, so singe nur

200 Müller, Wilhelm. (1991). *Die Schöne Müllerin.* P. 81. (Trans. by the author).

201 Ibid. P. 82. (Trans. by the author).

zu")[202]. At that moment, the harmonic path includes the modulation to B-flat major (as in the A-part), but then the shift to G major, the key of the brooklet, occurs. Explaining this phenomenon in the light of archetypal theory, and from the comparison between the A-section and the A'-section, the following formulation presents itself: the miller-lad's first speech points to the inner (unconscious) longing for triumph; a triumph, however, felt by the "I" as a distant reality—this could be understood from the perspective of the Great Mother, as the active inner instance willing to triumph and acting upon the "I"; while his second discourse, in response to the brooklet's words, points to the longing of the "I" for the Great Mother and to her overpowering influence on the "I". The synthesis is given in the A'-section by the fusion of the miller-lad's lament with the presence of the brooklet's motif which is in the foreground. Philosophically enhancing, the third step shift from B-flat major to G major can, in the words of Markus Gabriel, indicate the turning towards another "field of sense"[203], namely towards the brooklet, i.e., to another reality, world or state—in the archetypal language, this means a return to the searched primordial experience of being one with the Great Mother. Similarly, C.G. Jung identified a shift in perspective as a resulting effect of such a process:

> "Apparently, the energy leaving the conscious mind has revitalised the unconscious. The next consequence is a change of senses."[204].

[202] Ibid. P. 82. (Trans. by the author).

[203] Gabriel, Markus. (2016). *Sinn und Existenz.*

[204] Jung, Carl Gustav. (2023). *Die Beziehung zwischen dem Ich und dem Unbewussten.* P. 53. (Trans. by the author). German expression: "Offenbar hat also die das Bewusstsein verlassende Energie das Unbewusste belebt. Die nächste Folge ist eine Sinnesänderung.".

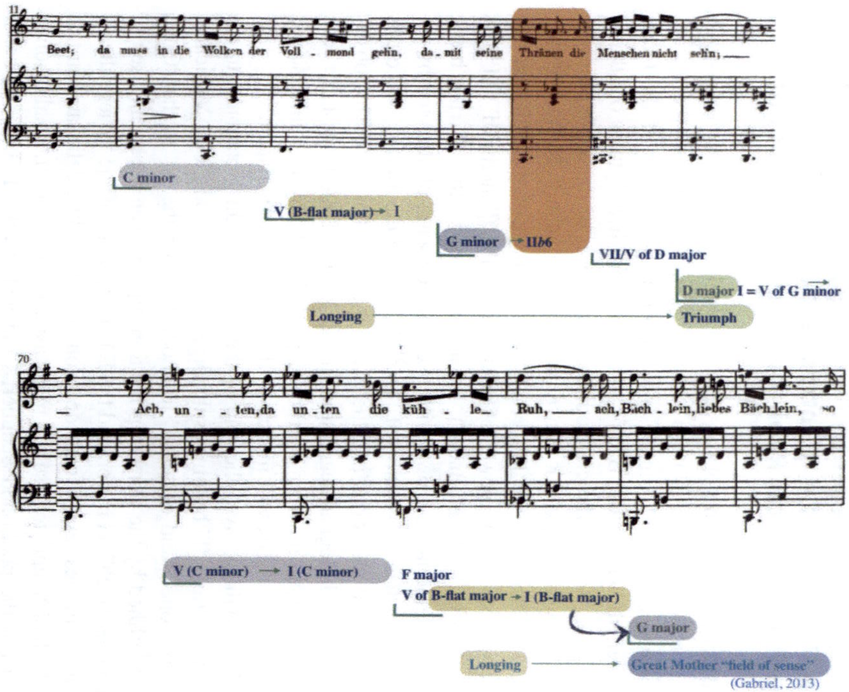

Fig. 15.11 Modulations and key characteristics mm.11–19 vs. mm.70–76: The longing for triumph vs. the longing for the primordial feeling of unity with the Great mother (brooklet reality). The third step modulation, characteristic of Schubert, is here indicated by the arrow. (Sheet music excerpt taken and adapted from *IMSLP*)

The last archetypal function of the brooklet has thus been unveiled: the underground overarching feminine force behind the brooklet symbolism is the archetype of the Great Mother, which comes especially to light in the "Wiegenlied".

15.9 "Des Baches Wiegenlied": Immersion in the Self as a Process of Deep Introspection Leading to a Psychological Rebirth. Concluding Thoughts

Due to the illusory appropriation of the Anima's mana power in the miller-lad's active imagination in "Trockne Blumen", the gates of the depth of the unconscious were opened and the "I" finally met the mana-personality of the Great Mother[205] in "Der Müller und der Bach". In the previous lied, it turns out that it was in fact the Great Mother who claimed the mana-power of the Anima for herself and not the "I", which gave her an overpowering dominance. In "Der Müller und der Bach" she, being in the immediate surroundings of the Self, exerted her *fascinosum* and bewitching power of attraction on the ("uncritical") "I" (B-section of "Der Müller und der Bach"). As a consequence, the "I", not being enough strengthened and lacking own will, is enchanted with, or attracted by the return to an uroboric state (A'-section of "Der Müller und der Bach"), since this state revives primordial memories and the experience of wholeness. This observation points to a psychological regression linked to an inflation; the latter, can be described as an engulfment or overflooding of the "I" by the unconscious structures[206]. This hypothesis will mature in the course of the chapter.

Hence, Wilhelm Müller gives the role of the poem's main protagonist to the brooklet, while the lyrical "I" becomes submerged in the unconscious. Musically, the transition from one "field of sense" to another—from the "I" to the "Great Mother"—is underlined by the third-step relationship between the ending key of "Der Müller und der Bach", G major, and the E major reality of the "Wiegenlied". This interpretation implies several considerations which will be delineated in this chapter, and which differentiates itself in many aspects from conventional reading, both with regard to the poem and Schubert's musical setting. In order to better

[205] This psychological process can be found described in: Ibid.

[206] This psychological event could correspond to the longing for the death aesthetic characteristic of Müller's and Schubert's epoch ("Todessehnsucht"). However, death is to be understood as a transformation from one state to the other (not necessarily as a physical death), as it will be developed throughout the chapter.

present the proposed interpretation, the poem in question and the music shall be concisely analysed in terms of their symbolic and motivic content.

There seems to be a widespread consensus among scholars that Wilhelm Müller's poem "Des Baches Wiegenlied" has the meaning of a lullaby into death. The same congruent attribution can be found in the musicological literature regarding the semantic interpretation of Schubert's setting (no.20). Consequently, death is given a negative connotation, which led to numerous theories of interpretation, including pathological readings[207]. However, the allusion to death is by no means to be taken literally. Alan Cottrell has pointed to the fact that death is seen by Wilhelm Müller as a moment of (spiritual) transformation from one state to another:

> "The poem 'Des Baches Wiegenlied' portrays death not as the obliteration of consciousness but as a transformation from one state into another. The brook itself remains conscious and ministers to the needs of the sleeper in anticipation of a future awakening ('Bis alles wacht') which is prefigured in the metaphor of the rising moon. From this vantage point Müller's deeper awareness of the theme *Wandern* begins to reveal its significance. Life itself as *Wandern* was for him in the deepest sense a journey into *self-knowledge.* [...] the moment of death is the highest moment of self-knowledge, the goal of the 'Wanderschaft' through life, when '...das Meer will trinken die Bächlein aus' ('Des Baches Wiegenlied'). At this moment the spiritual essence of the individual destiny rises as the moon into the cosmic ocean, as a seed of new life. [...] Despite inner desperation and even the possibility of suicide, death held for Müller a mystery which points to an inner kernel of freedom in the workings of destiny. [...] The 'Reis' aus uns heraus' represented for Müller the greatest enlivening of the process of self-knowledge, in which the free will of man awakens to new life."[208].

This view can be confirmed by a Jungian analysis of the poem. The metaphor of the dark night together with the moon allegory, taken from the richly symbolic setting, stands for a process of metamorphosis, as previously seen. The occurrence of transformation itself is suggested by the merging phenomenon of heaven and earth in the last stanza of the poem: "The full moon rises, the mist recedes, and heaven above, so wide is it" ("Der Vollmond steigt, der Nebel weicht, und der Himmel da oben, wie ist er so weit")[209]. The observations resulting from the analysis of the characteristics of the brooklet, or the Great Mother, leads to the following findings: the Great Mother conveys protection and redemption but,

---

[207] Cf. Youens, Susan. (1997). *Schubert, Müller, and 'Die schöne Müllerin'.* A further example is Bianconi, Gioseppina La Face. (2013). *Das Haus des Müllers.*

[208] Cottrell, Alan. (1970). *Wilhelm Müller's Lyrical Song-cycles.* P. 33–34.

[209] Müller, Wilhelm. (1991). *Die Schöne Müllerin.* P. 84. (Trans. by the author).

simultaneously, is capable of engulfing through her containing drive (3.2). From all the positive and negative qualities given to the role of the brooklet, it can be deduced that the Great Mother is to be seen as neither the good mother nor the bad mother but embodies both aspects. If Neumann's formulation is applied in this context: both characteristics, the "elementary" and the "transformative" of the Great Mother archetype are inherent in the brooklet[210].

In Schubert's musical setting, the soothing function and the feeling of redemption expressed in this song, are underlined on the one hand, by the typical rocking rhythm of a lullaby and on the other hand, by the harmonic oscillation between tonic and dominant. The protective character is equally emphasized by the choice of the strophic lied type. This typology is characterized by a constant repetition of the same musical material for each strophe. Symbolically speaking, it conveys the sensation of a closing circle[211]. In congruence with the archetypal language, the symbolic content of this song type matches the typical traits attributed to the elementary character of the Great Mother ("the great round"[212]). However, Neumann himself elucidates that both characters, the elementary and the transformative, are not necessarily "antithetical"—to use his own words—but rather interact with or are integrated in each other[213]. While the type of the lied points to the elementary character of the Great Mother due to the circle symbolism, the same can also indicate the transformative character, since the semantics of the music and its symbolic content change with each strophe (7). As a result, the above-stated merging phenomenon between heaven and earth expressed in the last strophe of the poem coincides with the fifth repetition of this strophic lied. Interpreting this detail: with each repetition, other states in the transformation are achieved, culminating in the union of heaven and earth. It should be noted that Analytical Psychology places significant emphasis on the symbolic meaning of the number five. Following Marie-Louise von Franz, this number is understood as the alchemical *quinta essentia*, the centering of the four—in other words, it corresponds to the moment of approaching the centre of the personality, i.e., the Self[214]. A further indication, regarding Schubert's setting, should be given:

---

210 Cf. Neumann, Erich. (2021). *Die Große Mutter.* For further details on Neumann's archetypal theory of the Great Mother see 3.2.

211 This circling around characterizes, as previously seen, Schubert's musical language (8). Also Zacharias emphasized this element in: Zacharias, Christian. (2019). *Why does Schubert sound like Schubert?* [Lecture-Recital]. Stagecast Ltd (Production).

212 Neumann, Erich. (2015). *The Great Mother*. (Trans. by Ralph Manheim, P. 25).

213 Cf. Ibid. P. 29.

214 Cf. von Franz. (1990). Cited after: Seifert, Ang Lee. "Fünf" In: Symbolonline.eu. [Article].

there are two rhythmical motifs that also imply the transformation character. The piano prelude of the "Wiegenlied" presents the dotted rhythm (m.2 and m.4) and the dactyl rhythm (mm.16–20). Both rhythmic cells refer to the previous song of "Trockne Blumen" (mm. 35–38). Therein, they bear the semantic core of "then all thou little flowers, come forth, come forth, May has come, winter is gone" ("Dann Blümlein alle, heraus, heraus! Der Mai ist kommen, der Winter ist aus")[215]. This rhythmical citation can evoke the meaning of renewal, which is again consistent with the given psychological interpretation.

As far as the poem is concerned: with the information on the symbolic content stated so far, Wilhelm Müller emphasizes the elementary character through the description of the over-protective Great Mother, and the transformative character through, e.g., the analogy with the full moon. This way of reading can be confirmed by the symbols inherent in the following phrase: "Allegiance is hither, shall thou lay by my side, 'til the sea will drain the brooklet out" ("Die Treu ist hier, sollst liegen bei mir, bis das Meer will trinken die Bächlein aus")[216]. At this point, it shall be noted that the symbolic meaning of water is not that straightforward and needs amplification. Generally speaking, it is associated with the unconscious. Due to the feminine forces inherent in water, the archetype of the Great Mother (positive and negative) is also attributed to the water symbolism, as previously noted. This includes both, the brooklet and the sea analogy just cited. In the Christian tradition, however, water refers to the water of life motif[217]. In this reading, water is a healing agent, capable of leading to (psychological) rebirth[218]. On the other hand, the sea can also stand for the "infinity and merging with God"[219]—a reading that underpins the turning towards the Self and towards the primordial state of unity with the mother, with nature, with the cosmos. These symbolic readings are not mutually exclusive, but truly complementary.

---

[215] Müller, Wilhelm. (1991). *Die Schöne Müllerin.* P. 80. (Trans. by the author).

[216] Ibid. P. 83. (Trans. by the auhor).

[217] Cf. Drewermann, Eugen. (2024). „Vortrag Grimms Märchen ‚Das Wasser des Lebens'. Konflikte überwinden.". [Presentation].

[218] This symbolic reading of water is to be found in the fairy tale of Grimm "The water of life", which bears a Christian parallel. Cf. Ibid.

[219] Mollwo-Oesterreicher, Marianne. (1978). *Herder Lexikon Symbole.* P. 108.

From these symbolic considerations, "Des Baches Wiegenlied" appeals to a specific type of psychological regression, bounded with a phenomenon of inflation[220]. A regression, as the term itself suggests, points to a retreat of the "I" (3.1 Fig. 3.4) and it arises from the "[…] need to adapt to the inner self, thus, to conform to the individual's own inner law"[221]. It is important to underline that this process is not necessarily to be taken negatively: a momentary return to this primordial state permits the incorporation and the working out of the split elements. As Jolande Jacobi elucidates, regressions occur every day during sleep[222]. C.G. Jung himself described several myths in which a regression, as a "very profound state of introversion"[223], is achieved[224]. This specific state of mind will lead to a subsequent process of rebirth and to a consequent transformation or expansion of the personality. In addition, other psychoanalytic traditions have developed a constructive idea about regression—in the Freudian lineage, Michael Balint was a pioneer in differentiating between a benign and a malignant type of regression[225]. In his work on the theory and therapeutic aspects of regressions[226], Balint drew attention to the investigations of Ernst Kris, who had discovered the particular

220 This concurrent psychological phenomenon is to be found described in: Jacobi, Jolande. (2006). *Die Psychologie von C.G. Jung*. P. 61–62.

221 Ibid. P. 62. (Trans. by the author). German expression: "[…] die Regression [ist] in der Notwendigkeit der Anpassung an das Innen, also an die Übereinstimmung mit dem eigenen inneren Gesetz des Individuums begründet.".

222 Cf. Ibid. P. 62.

223 Cf. Jung, C.G. (2014). "Symbols of transformation". In: *The Collected Works of C.G. Jung. Vol. 5.* Part II. Chapter VII: "The Dual Mother". Here, he was referring to the Indian myth of Hiawatha, however tracing some parallels with the Christian traditions.

224 Drewermann points out a similar phenomenon in the fairy tale "Brüderchen und Schwesterchen", namely the tree sojourn: "[…] one closes in one-Self, one naturally seeks out a place where one is protected, alike a cave in the own mother's womb, one regresses in a zone that one has sought to oneself […], in order to, in a longing manner, create a home for oneself,". (Trans. by the author). German expression: "[…] man schließt sich in sich selber ein, man sucht naturgegeben ein Ort auf, in dem man geschützt ist, wie eine Höhle im Mutterschoß; man regrediert in einer Zone, die man selber aufgesucht hat, […] um sich selber ein Zuhause schaffen, sehnsüchtig". Drewermann, Eugen. (2023). „5. Sommervorlesung 2023: Heilende Märchen. Drewermann deutet das Märchen Brüderchen und Schwesterchen.". [Lecture]. Minutes: 00:28:54/1:30:24.

225 Roesler, Christian. Correspondence between Christian Roesler and the author. Freiburg im Breisgau/Noiraigue: February 2, 2025.

226 Cf. Balint, Michael. (1987). *Regression*.

kind of regression "in the service of the 'I'"[227] notably in the context of artistic creativity[228].

An inflation, in turn, refers to the identification with the contents of the collective unconscious[229]. This psychic phenomenon manifests itself in the form of an imbalance. However, according to C.G. Jung—and as previously mentioned—the unconscious can purposefully induce such a state, with the long-term aim to reencounter the middle point of the personality[230]. This detour to one-Self, as part of the self-regulating process, implies the necessity for the "I" to properly work out and integrate the autonomous archetypal elements, consequently transforming them from autonomous complexes into a psychic function. The following C.G. Jung's case description is an example of an inflation process, which, intriguingly, bears several parallels with the miller-lad's experiences:

> "So, he built up a rapturous fantasy of love, which was abruptly shattered when he discovered that the girl wanted nothing to do with him. He was so desperate that he went straight to the river to drown himself. It was late at night and the stars twinkled at him out of the dark water. It seemed to him, as if the stars were swimming down the river in pairs, and a wondrous feeling took hold of him. He forgot his suicidal intentions and stared in fascination at this strange, sweet spectacle. And gradually he realised that each star was a face and that these couples were lovers, embracing each other and floating in a dream. Then a completely new realisation dawned on him: everything had changed, including his fate, his disappointment and his love had fallen away from him, the memory of the girl was distant and indifferent, but he was promised – he felt it clearly – untold treasures. [...] What had happened to him? [His mind] had seen a Dantean image whose beauty he would have never been able to express in verse. But he saw it, and it transformed him. What had been his greatest pain now lay in the distance; the moment he stepped onto the 'threshold of Proserpinas', a new, undreamt

---

227 Ibid. P. 163. (Trans. by the author). German expression: "Im Dienste des Ichs".

228 Cf. Ibid. P. 163–164.

229 Cf. Jacobi, Jolande. (2006). *Die Psychologie von C.G. Jung.* P. 39. There are several types of (psychological) inflations possible, that shall be here shortly recalled: (i) through an overwhelming reaction of the "I" (the exemplified below with the case description of C.G. Jung), (ii) through believing or through (iii) rejecting the unconscious emerging elements. These different reactions of the "I" towards the unconscious structures can be read in: Jung, Carl Gustav. (2023). *Die Beziehung zwischen dem Ich und dem Unbewussten.* P. 55.

230 Cf. Ibid. P. 53–54.

> world of stars had opened up to him, travelling their silent orbit far beyond his miserable earth. The premonition of an untold wealth [...] came to him like a revelation. [...] He was not drowning in the river, but in an eternal image [...]"[231].

Schubert's "Des Baches Wiegenlied" could thus be understood as an immersion into the Self, which in turn, refers to a spiritual transformation process of great importance: by returning to the womb of the Great Mother, this experience will permit the "I" to undergo a process of rebirth, allowing further developments in the individuation process that are yet to come. To return now to the thought mentioned at the beginning of this subchapter: the change of roles that has already been noted in the poetic level is equally identifiable in the musical language of Schubert. The loss of consciousness can be musically substantiated by the motif of the "bare" fifths (perfect fifths), which is omnipresent in the piano part. The overall ambience of this lied is created by the tonal quality of this motif. It should be reminded that this motif represents the antagonistic characteristics of the miller-lad, meaning that the shadow element of the hunting topos is present in the accompaniment of the piano almost throughout the entire lullaby, but also that his light side is inherent, through the association with the lyre, which stands for his poet-musician side. It should also be recalled that the piano fulfills the

---

[231] Ibid. P. 33–34. (Trans. by the author). German expression: "So baute er eine schwärmerische Liebesphantasie auf, die aber jäh zerbrach, als er entdeckte, dass das Mädchen überhaupt nichts von ihm wissen wollte. Er war dermaßen verzweifelt, dass er geradewegs zum Flusse ging, um sich zu ertränken. Es war spät in der Nacht, und die Sterne funkelten ihm aus dem dunkeln Wasser entgegen. Es schien ihm, als ob die Sterne Paaren den Fluss hinunterschwämmen, und ein wundersames Gefühl erfasste ihn. Er vergaß seine selbstmörderische Absicht und starrte fasziniert auf das seltsame, süße Schauspiel. Und allmählich wurde er gewahr, dass jeder Stern ein Gesicht war und dass diese Paare Liebende waren, die, sich umschlungen haltend, träumend vorbeitrieben. Da dämmerte ihm eine ganz neue Einsicht: Alles hatte sich gewandelt, auch sein Schicksal, seine Enttäuschung sowohl wie seine Liebe waren von ihm abgefallen, die Erinnerung an das Mädchen war fern und gleichgültig, dafür war ihm—er fühlte es deutlich—unerhörter Reichtum versprochen. [...] Was war ihm geschehen? Der arme Kopf hat ein Dante'sches Bild er-blickt, dessen Schönheit, in einem Verse ausgedrückt, er wohl nie hätte erfassen können. Aber er sah es, und es verwandelte ihn. Was eben größter Schmerz war, lag jetzt in der Ferne; eine neue ungeahnte Welt der Sterne, die weit jenseits dieser jammervollen Erde ihre stille Bahn ziehen, hatte sich ihm im Augenblick, da er die»Schwelle Proserpinas betrat, eröffnet. Die Ahnung eines unerhörten Reichtums [...] ging ihm auf wie eine Offenbarung. [...] Er ertrank nicht im Flusse, sondern in einem ewigen Bilde, [...]".

role of the unconscious sphere, which consequently suggests that the lyrical "I" is submerged in the unconscious. This being the case, it becomes striking how the actual melody of this lullaby lives in the inner voices of the piano part—an observation that speaks for the psychological reading of the "I" being immersed in the Self. In addition, the rhythmic level of the melodic material carries a primordial undertone, since this rhythmic cell (short-short-long as an anacrusis[232]) is to be found in previous songs—for the first time, in "Halt!", bearing the semantic of "A mill" ("Eine Mühle"). As explained before, the mill can be taken as a symbol of the Self due to the circular shape of the wheels. Consequently, in the "Wiegenlied" the "I" is immersed in the Self. Possibly, this was already predicted in the first lied with the four emphasized key words, the last ones being "the wheels" ("die Räder")—"the stones" ("die Steine"), standing for the symbols of the Self and eternity (15.2). What also particularly stands out and contributes to the general tone-colour of this lied, is the hypnotic tone repetitions of the B note, which fulfils the function of an ostinato, often associated with a death knell[233]and bearing the eschatological effect[234] (Fig. 15.12).

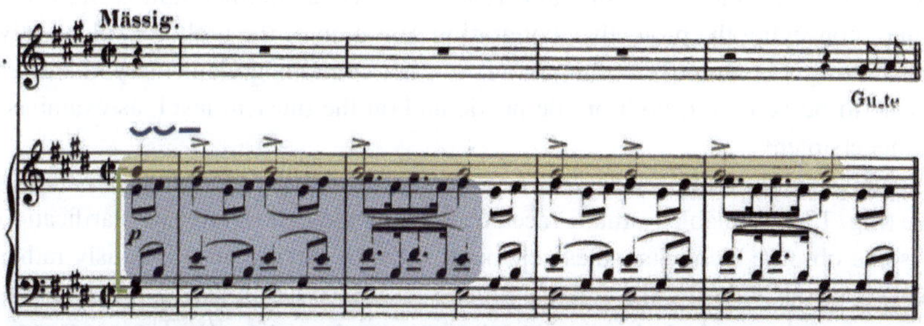

Fig. 15.12 The ostinato on the note B conveying the eschatological effect. The melody in the inner voices of the piano conveys the psychological phenomenon of immersion in the Self. The rhythmical references of "Halt!". (Sheet music excerpt taken and adapted from *IMSLP*)

[232] This rhythm is inverted in mm. 16–20, beginning in the strong beat of the measure and featuring the dactyl wanderer rhythm. Emotionally, the falling second gesture conveys the *suspiratio* figure.

[233] Other authors also speak of these tone repetitions as bells. See, for example: Braun, Christiane. Berke, Dietrich. „Die Schöne Müllerin op. 25 (D 795)—Liederzyklus Wilhelm Müller". In: Dürr, Walther. Kube, Michael. [et al.]. (2013). *Schubert Liedlexikon.* P. 660.

[234] Cf. Dobretsberger, Barbara. Personal communication between Barbara Dobretsberger and the author. Salzburg: March 23, 2024.

The understanding of death as a transformation inherent in Wilhelm Müller's statement, mentioned in the introduction, seems to find a parallel and identical reading in Schubert's setting, speaking for the fact that both artists possibly shared similar views on spiritual matters. Schubert focuses on the transformative character and not on death itself—this contrasts with the first musical setting by Ludwig Berger, who, despite having worked with Wilhelm Müller, puts the focus on the phenomenon of death itself, creating the respective atmosphere through the monotonous tone of the singing voice, the dark register of the piano and the funeral march rhythm. Moreover, the lullaby character intentionally given by Wilhelm Müller's title, to which Schubert was faithful, was peculiarly but consciously amended by Ludwig Berger to "Des Baches Lied" ("The brook's song"), retrieving not only the term of endearment, but essentially the archetypal core of a lullaby.

The archetypal essence of lullabies seems to be common to many cultures[235]. Their primordial melodies and rhythm are reminiscent, on the one hand, of the rocking movement of the mother holding her child and transmitting a primordial feeling of wholeness, on the other hand, of the intrauterine sensory experience of the heartbeat pulsation[236]. The archetype of the Great Mother fulfills the function of conveying the protective, comforting sensation of the uroboros, ultimately transmitting a redemptive feeling. However, her containing elementary character is also to be perceived both on the poetic and on the musical level, as examined in this chapter.

Analysing the song cycle *Die Schöne Müllerin* from the Jungian perspective (Fig. 15.14), enables a multi-faceted reading which allows for the clarification of some obscure elements—these elements seem to emerge unconsciously rather than consciously during the creative process. It is also worth noting that two fantasies were the catalysts for an inner turning point: (i) no. 10 "Thränenregen", which worked as the insight moment in the middle point of the cycle, and (ii)

---

[235] Cf. Pistone, Pascale. In: Goblot, Pascal. (2020). Sapiens, et la musique fut. Pérès, Guillaume (Producer). [Documentary]. Minutes: 00:49:44.

[236] Cf. Sloterdijk, Peter. (2015). *Der ästhetishe Imperativ.* Berlin: Suhrkamp. Chapter: „I. Klangwelt—La musique retrouvée".

no. 18 "Trockne Blumen", which brought inner movement through the active attitude of the "I". The latter was of particular importance since it enabled the encounter with the mana-personality of the Great Mother. These can be seen as two moments, in which the "I" detached itself from the demands of the Persona in the form of a fantasy and engendered key moments of transformation or expansion of the personality. The fact that the Great Mother exists in the immediate surrounding of the Self, exerted an overpowering effect on the I ("Der Müller und der Bach"), and in this way, induced the process of inflation linked to a psychological regression ("Des Baches Wiegenlied"). This return to an uroboric state means that all elements of the personality are undifferentiated and fused in an organic wholeness. If taking the two artistic forms of expression, the poem and the lied simultaneously as one artistic statement, then all archetypal motives are inherent in the "Wiegenlied": the light and shadow side of the miller-lad, the negative and positive Anima and the elementary and transformative characters of the Great Mother archetype. The shadow is also present through the tritone relationship established between the tonality of the first song B-flat major and the key of the last one, E major. The fact that the *diabolus in musica* (negative Anima) is here indirectly present is intriguing. Possibly, this background tonal relationship alludes to the intended attempt to integrate the negative aspect of the Anima by returning to the womb of the mother (a secure place).

"Des Baches Wiegenlied", which appeals to the healing properties of the water will, psychologically speaking, permit a rebirth. *Die Schöne Müllerin* coincides with Schubert's supposedly last year of crisis 12. This could be a revelation that needs to be examined more closely in accordance with the findings of the following music analysis (16, 20). Will the negative aspect of the Anima be integrated in forthcoming compositions?

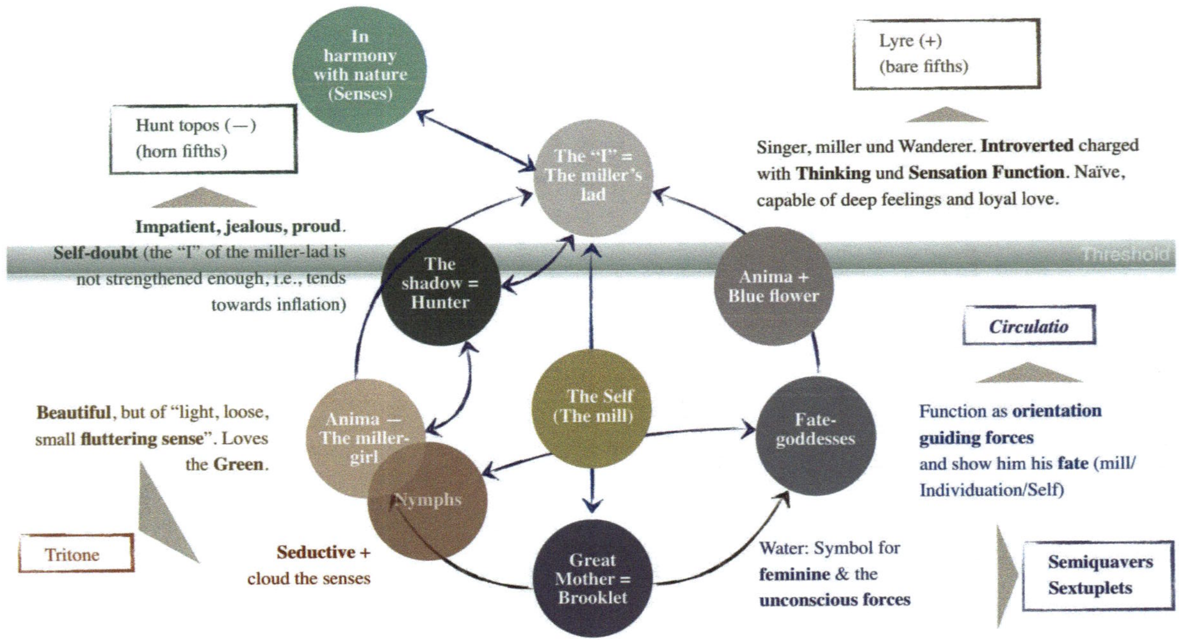

Fig. 15.13 The inner protagonists of *Die Schöne Müllerin* and the correspondent symbols and musical motif

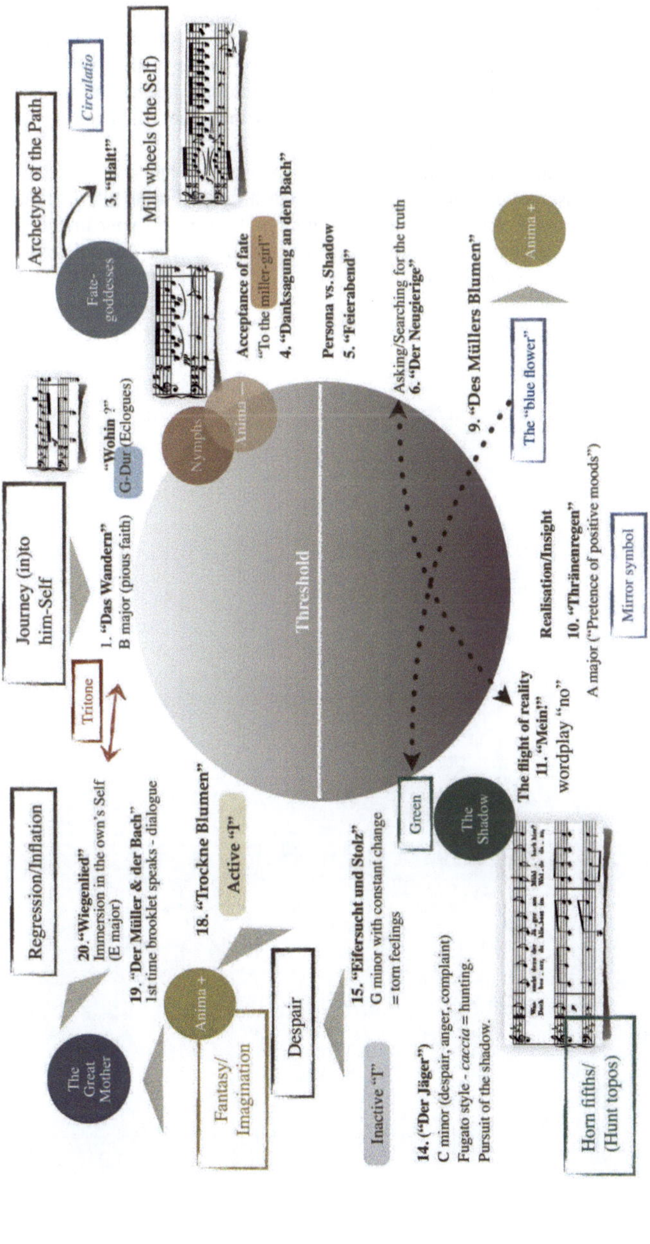

Fig. 15.14 Representation of the inner processes inherent in *Die Schöne Müllerin*'s musical narration featuring a transformational process. (Sheet music excerpt taken and adapted from *IMSLP*)

The D Minor String Quartet D 810 *Der Tod und das Mädchen*: From an Introverted State to the Birth of the New "I". 16

Schubert's D minor string quartet D 810, entitled *Der Tod und das Mädchen,* was composed in March 1824, after an alleged prolonged crisis 1818–1823 (12). Schubert had financial and health difficulties, as has been previously highlighted. He left many of his compositions unfinished during that period, which led some musicologists to assume that Schubert might have experienced the mentioned creative crisis[1]. This hypothesis has been lately increasingly questioned or reformulated. For instance, Arabella Pare attributes the existence of Schubert's fragmentary compositions to form- and instrument-specific concerns and to the development of his own style[2]. Nevertheless, this apparent moment of personal or creative reflection coincided with a time when Schubert was deeply engaged in

[1] Unfinished works included the genres of piano sonatas, symphonies and string quartets (e.g., the *Quartettsatz* in C minor).

[2] Cf. Linke, Cosima. (2023). "Arabella Pare, Franz Schubert. The fragmentary Piano Sonatas (= Schubert: Perspektiven—Studien, Bd.7), Stuttgart: Steiner 2022". In: *Zeitschrift der Gesellschaft für Musiktheorie. Vol. 20/1*. P.111–115. For the original text see: Pare, Arabella. (2022). *Franz Schubert: the fragmentary Piano Sonatas.*

The music analytical and psychological findings developed in this chapter were presented by the author herself in public for the first time under the title "Franz Schubert: Streichquartett *Der Tod und das Mädchen* D 810 d-Moll—1. Satz. Ein Musikanalyseansatz mit der Archetypenlehre von C.G. Jung" in the form of a one-and-a-half hour and slide-assisted lecture in the frame of a music analysis seminar at the University Mozarteum, Salzburg (April 28th, 2022), under the supervision of Barbara Dobretsberger. In addition, the topic was cursorily presented in a conference with the following publication to be published: Dill, Leonor. (2022). „Die Natur (in) der Musik Schuberts—Das Quartett 'Der Tod und das Mädchen' im Lichte des Archetypenkonzepts von C.G. Jung". In: *Eros und Thanatos*. Hofbauer, Gerhard (Ed.).

L. Dill, *Schubert's Metamorphoses*,
https://doi.org/10.1007/978-3-662-73476-6_16

studying Beethoven's work[3]. Investigating Schubert's biographical circumstances around 1824—the year of origin of the quartet—and subsequently comparing these facts with analytical findings, can reveal significant insights into Schubert's creative and individuation processes. This evidence mainly comprises the two following letters, the first addressed to his friend and painter Leopold Kupelwieser, dated 31st of March (Fig. 16.1), the second to his brother Ferdinand:

> "In one word, I feel like the most unhappy, miserable person in the world. Think of a person whose health never wants to get better, and who, out of despair, makes things worse instead of better, think of a person, I say, whose brightest hopes have come to nothing, to whom the happiness of love and friendship offer nothing but pain, at best, to whom enthusiasm (at least the stimulating kind for beauty) threatens to fade, and ask yourself whether this is not a miserable, unhappy person?—'My peace is gone, my heart is heavy, I can never find it and never again', so I can probably sing every day now, because every night when I go to sleep, I hope not to wake up again, and every morning only announces yesterday's grief to me. So joyless and friendless I spend my days, [...].
>
> I have done little new of songs, but I have tried my hand at several instrumental works, for I have composed two Quartets for violins, viola and violoncello and an Octet, and I want to write another quartet; in fact I want to pave my way to the great symphony in this way.—The latest news in Vienna is that Beethoven is giving a concert in which he will perform his new symphony, three movements from the new Mass and a new Ouverture.—If God wills, I am also destined to give a similar concert next year"[4].

[3] Dobretsberger, Barbara. Personal communication between Barbara Dobretsberger and the author. Salzburg/Lisbon: December 2, 2021.

[4] Schubert, Franz: Letter to Leopold Kupelwieser. (31.03.1824). In: Deutsch, Otto Erich. (1964). *Schubert—Die Dokumente seines Lebens*. P. 234–235. (Trans. by the author). German expression: "Mit einem Wort, ich fühle mich als den unglücklichsten, elendsten Menschen auf der Welt. Denk Dir einen Menschen, dessen Gesundheit nie mehr richtig werden will, u. der aus Verzweiflung darüber die Sache im[m]er schlechter statt besser macht, denke Dir einen Menschen, sage ich, dessen glänzendste Hoffnung zu Nichte geworden sind, dem das Glück der Liebe u. Freundschaft nichts biethen als höchstens Schmerz, dem Begeisterung (wenigstens anregende) für das Schöne zu schwinden droht, und frage Dich, ob das nicht ein elender, unglücklicher Mensch ist?—Meine Ruh ist hin, mein Herz ist schwer, ich finde sie nim[m]er u. nim[m]ermehr', so kann ich wohl jetzt alle Tage singen, denn jede Nacht, wen[n] ich schlafen geh, hoff ich nicht mehr zu erwachen, u. jeder Morgen kündet mir nur den gestrigen Gram. So Freude- u. Freundelos verbringe ich meine Tage, [...]. In Liedern habe ich wenig Neues gemacht, dagegen versuchte ich mich in mehreren Instrumental-Sachen, denn ich componierte 2 Quartetten für Violinen, Viola u. Violoncelle u. ein Octett, u. will noch ein Quartetto schreiben, überhaupt will ich mir auf diese Art den Weg zur großen Sinfonie bahnen.—Das Neueste in Wien ist, d[a]ß Beethoven ein Concert gibt, in welchen er seine neue Sinfonie, 3 Stücke aus der neuen Messe, u. eine neue Ouverture producieren läßt.—Wen[n] Gott will, so bin auch ich geson[n]en, künftiges Jahr ein ähnliches Concert zu geben.".

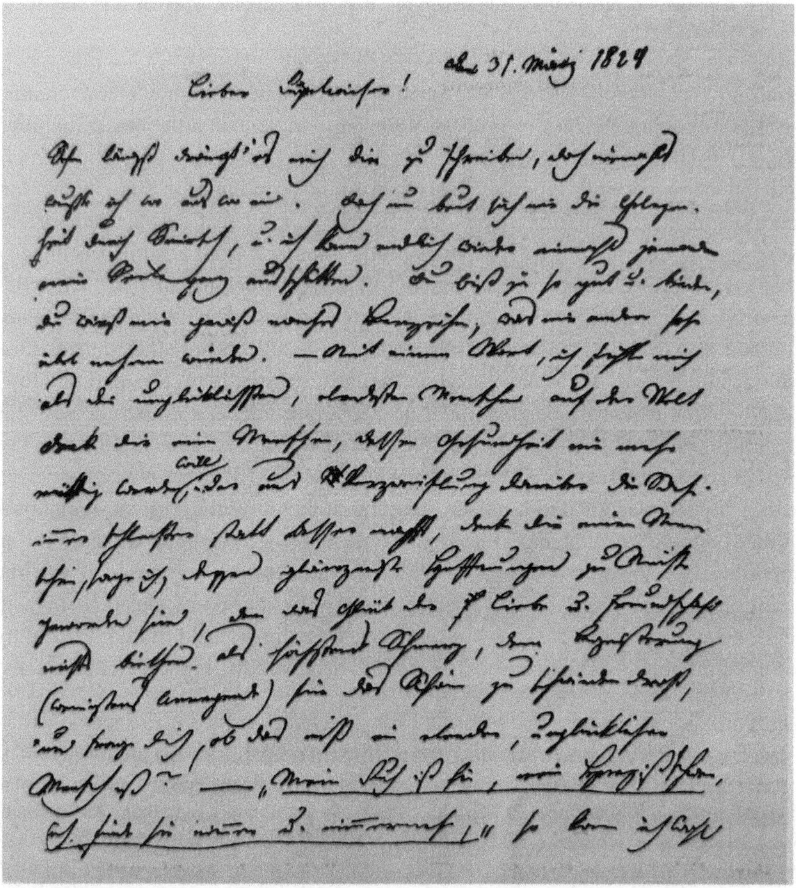

Fig. 16.1 Letter autograph from Schubert to Leopold Kupelwieser, dated March 31, 1824. (Picture taken from: Hilmar, Ernst. (2008). *Franz Schubert.* P.79. © 1997 Rowohlt Taschenbuch Verlag GmbH, Reinbek bei Hamburg)

"So that these lines do not perhaps tempt you to believe that I am not well or not in a cheerful mood, I hasten to assure you of the opposite. Of course, it is no longer that happy time in youthful glory, but that fatal realisation of a miserable reality which I try to embellish as much as possible with my imagination (thank God). One believes that happiness hangs in the place where one was once happier, whereas it is only in ourselves, [...]"[5].

From a psychological perspective, Schubert's last statement shows how creativity was important for him to process sufferings, trials and situations of conflict. While the latter document shows the positive effect of his creative engagement and reflects a possible tone of acceptance of his condition or fate, in the former document, Schubert expresses himself in a tone of real despair and sorrow. As Eugen Drewermann explains, behind any utterance from a human being lies a veiled cause of an unconscious nature[6]. If these letters are analysed from this perspective, then Schubert's statements refer not only to his physical health condition, but also to the psychological consequences. It reflects how the confrontation with death and fate might have been particularly substantial in this period. However, he simultaneously demonstrated an active attitude as a composer with his great aspirations of following in the footsteps of his father figure Beethoven. The cited quartets, the A minor D 804 and the D minor D 810[7], were hence conceived with a higher plan in mind, as the stepping stones towards a great symphonic work. It should be explained that composing a great symphony represented an important step towards being successfully recognized as a composer. It was the ambition of most composers, at least in that specific period of music History, to achieve such a milestone. Beethoven, in turn, was already held in high esteem by his contemporaries as the composer who had achieved the highest in this art and

[5] Schubert, Franz: Letter to his brother Ferdinand. (18.07.1824). In: Deutsch, Otto Erich. (1964). *Schubert—Die Dokumente seines Lebens*. P. 250. (Trans. by the author). German expression: "Damit Dich diese Zeilen nicht vielleicht verführen, zu glauben, ich sey nicht wohl, oder nicht heiteren Gemüthes, so beeile ich mich, Dich des Gegentheils zu versichern. Freylich ists nicht mehr jene glückliche Zeit, in der uns jeder Gegenstand mit einer jugendlichen Glorie umgeben scheint, sondern jenes fatale Erkennen einer miserablen Wirklichkeit, die ich mir durch meine Phantasie (Gott sey's gedankt) so viel als möglich zu verschönern suche. Man glaubt an dem Orte, wo man einst glücklicher war, hänge das Glück, indem es doch nur in uns selbst ist, [...]".

[6] Cf. Drewermann, Eugen. (2023). „Sommervorlesung 2023: Märchen zeigen den Weg zur Liebe, wo Sehnsucht Realität wird". [Lecture]. Minutes: 0:08:28/1:23:20.

[7] Martin Chusid has observed that Schubert's chamber music works, especially those for strings, were usually primarily aimed at a *Hausmusik* moment of making music together. Schubert himself used to play together with his family. Cf. Chusid, Martin. "Schubert's chamber music: before and after Beethoven". In: Gibbs, Christopher H. (1997). *The Cambridge companion to Schubert*. Part. II: "Schubert's music: style and genre. Chapter 9". However, the two mentioned quartets were conceived with a further purpose, described in Schubert's letter.

other genres[8]. In view of this context, it is justified to speak of Schubert, living in the same city as Beethoven, as having lived in Beethoven's shadow[9].

Several musicologists point to Schubert's great involvement with Beethoven's works, especially around this period[10]. According to Martin Chusid, Schubert seems to have been mostly concerned with two particularities of Beethoven's compositional technique, the cyclical unity and the variation form (12)[11]. These aspects happen to be embodied and processed in the two concurrently written quartets, the A minor D 804 *Rosamunde* and the D minor D 810 *Death and the maiden*. The same quartets feature a further peculiarity that is specifically Schubertian. This concerns the thematic ideas of the second movements which form the core and climax of the compositions[12], having represented a new aspect of composition compared to the earlier works of Haydn, Mozart or even Beethoven. In addition, Schubert was explicitly fond of using self-quotations to shape the thematic material. These were often taken from earlier lied compositions.

In the case of the D minor quartet, the second movement features the theme of the lied "Der Tod und das Mädchen" D 531 (1817)—a musical setting of the poem of Matthias Claudius. It was due to this quotation that the quartet owed its name. The analogies between the two works go, however, beyond the thematic construction of the second movement, as it will be shown in this chapter. Further song references are to be found in other movements of D 810. As Brigitte Massin acknowledged, "Der Erlkönig" also plays a role in this quartet[13]. Further analogies can be drawn with "Der Jüngling und der Tod" D 545. The string quartet as well as the songs are characterised by an extra-musical idea and a deep poetic imagination.

On account of these reasons, the archetypal core of the extra-musical aspects will be addressed firstly. Then, a concise analysis of the previously composed songs is performed. The chapter will proceed with an in-depth analysis of the first movement of the quartet, followed by a more general analysis of the remaining three movements with the aim of emphasizing the cyclical, transformative

[8] As a sidenote: not only Schubert, but also Brahms and Schumann struggled with the symphonic genre.

[9] Cf. Schiff, Andras. (2019). *Sir András Schiff on The Music of Franz Schubert*. [Recording Presentation].

[10] As an example, Martin Chusid shall be cited. Cf. Chusid, Martin. "Schubert's chamber music: before and after Beethoven". In: Gibbs, Christopher H. (1997). *The Cambridge companion to Schubert*. Part. II: "Schubert's music: style and genre. Chapter 9".

[11] Cf. Ibid.

[12] Cf. Godel, Arthur. (1985). *Schuberts letzte drei Klaviersonaten (D958—960).*

[13] Massin, Brigitte. (1977). *Franz Schubert.* P.1060–1064.

and transcendent semantics inherent in this quartet. To gain an overview of the creative process reflected in the quartet, it is advantageous to consider looking at the three last movements with a focus on the musical elements that are specifically informative for a psychological reading of it, i.e., to directly juxtapose both readings.

16.1 Death and the Maiden from a Mythological Perspective. Some Features of "Der Tod und das Mädchen" D 531. Further Song Influences on the String Quartet: "Der Jüngling und der Tod" D 545 and "Erlkönig" D 328

The network of symbolic or mythical elements inherent in the theme of death and the maiden is significant. In general terms, this topic—which notably influenced the visual arts from very early on—finds its parallel in the ancient myths and legends. The Persephone myth is particularly instructive in this context: in one of the most widely read versions, Persephone was described as the daughter of Zeus and Demeter (the goddess of harvest). She was abducted by her uncle Hades and sent to the underworld, where she eventually adopted the role of the queen of the underworld[14]. In Demeter's narration[15], she embarked on a search for her child Kore (Persephone) after realising that her daughter had been abducted. Eventually, Persephone was still allowed to arise to the upperworld (often said to have happened in springtime), which was symbolically understood as spiritual resurrection[16], but was predestined to return to the depths of the earth. Due to this reason, this myth is sometimes analogically compared to the origins of the seasons[17]. According to a second tradition, Persephone was the daughter of Styx (the river of the nether world) and was considered to be the queen of the dead[18].

Following the Jungian thought that Olympian gods and goddesses as well as other creatures are to be understood as epitomes of an inner psychic reality or

---

[14] Cf. Grant, Michael. Hazel, John. (2009). *Lexikon der antiken Mythen und Gestalten.* 1. Auflage. Berlin: List Taschenbuch (Ullstein Verlag). P.330–331.

[15] Cf. Ibid, 115–119.

[16] Cf. Ibid. P.330.

[17] Cf. Bellamy, Olivier. "Le quatuor 'La jeune Fille et la Mort' de Schubert: découvrez sa signification profonde. [Article].

[18] Cf. Grant, Michael. Hazel, John. (2009). *Lexikon der antiken Mythen und Gestalten.* P.332.

process (which is based on the phenomenon of projection)[19], the mythical aspect related to the first just-described transmission of the myth, points to a process of a transformational nature. At the same time, it bears the Nietzschean idea of the eternal return, which depicts the cyclic laws of nature. Viewed psychologically, the rising and descending gesture, up to the conscious realm, respectively, down to the unconscious, not only points to resurrection but also to the flow and interchange of psychic energies between the two psychic realms within the ego-self axis. Archetypally, this movement, which is also to be found in the hero-myth, means to descend to the underworld (unconscious) to find the hidden treasures in order to subsequently bring them to the upper world (consciousness)[20]. When narrating about the underworld and resurrection, this myth addresses two archetypal poles of the feminine, i.e., life and death[21].

Erich Neumann in *Die Große Mutter* provides some clarification of this myth, particularly with regard to the psychological phenomena underlying it, which are linked to the so called Eleusinian Mysteries: in short, the Persephone myth deals with the mother-daughter unity (mother-child relationship), which represents the core of the feminine principle (two poles of the archetype of the feminine)[22]. Thereby, "Kore's resurrection from the earth—the archetypal spring motif—signifies her finding by Demeter, from whom Kore had 'died' and her reunion with

[19] Cf. Neumann, Erich. (2021). *Die Große Mutter.* Jung himself described this phenomenon in several of his works: "I have often been accused of personifying the anima and animus as mythology does, but this accusation would be justified only if it could be proved that I concretize these concepts in a mythological manner for psychological use. I must declare once and for all that the personification is not an invention of mine but is inherent in the nature of the phenomena.". Jung, Carl Gustav. (2014). "Alchemical studies". In: *The Collected Works of C.G. Jung. Vol. 13.* (Ed. and trans. by Gerhard Adler and R.F.C. Hull). Chapter I: "Commentary on 'The secret of the golden flower". Subchapter 4: "Phenomena of the Way—B. Animus and Anima".

[20] Roesler, Christian. Telephonic communication between Christian Roesler and the author. Freiburg im Breisgau/Noiraigue: October 24, 2024.

[21] The fact that the Anima and the Great Mother, are both being united by the overarching feminine principle is not only addressed by Jung but also by Neumann. The latter explained that the life principle is to be linked to the "transformative character" ("Wandlungscharakter") of the feminine principle, while death is seen as its containing "elementary principle" ("Elementarcharakter") (3.2). Hence, these themes are to be accounted in several myths, legends or fairy tales. Cf. Neumann, Erich. (2015). *The Great Mother*. (Trans. by Ralph Manheim).

[22] Cf. Ibid. Chapter: "The woman's experience of herself and the Eleusinian Mysteries". P.305–325.

her."[23]. This re-union with the mother Demeter represents the transformation of Persephone herself, from Kore (virgin) to mother (i.e., maiden-mother):

> "But the true mystery, through which the primordial situation is restored on a new plane, is this: the daughter [i.e., Kore] becomes identical with the mother; she becomes a mother and is so transformed into Demeter. Precisely because Demeter and Kore are archetypal poles of the Feminine is susceptible to endless renewal."[24].

In Persephone's mythical context, Neumann highlights the part of the myth, in which the divine-child is born, the "Phanes-Eros" (Fig. 16.22), son of Persephone. The childbearing of the light son alludes to the transformative character of the feminine[25]. Accordingly, the archetype of the divine child appears in moments of profound transformations.

Although the Eleusinian Mysteries primarily relate to the feminine, they equally have an impact on masculine psychology: Neumann explains this fascination as a two-step process in which the "I" first identifies itself on an emotional and unconscious basis with its own feminine counterpart (Demeter) and then experiences itself as the newborn child[26], "the luminous son"[27]. In this context, Neumann refers to the identification with Triptolemus, who, in these mysteries is given the ear of grain with the task of distributing it throughout the world and teaching people how to cultivate it[28]. Symbolically, the golden seed represents Triptolemus himself[29], which is to be "sowed in the earth-womb of the Great Mother, where it dies and whence, transformed, it is resurrected"[30]. The underlying principle is a development that corresponds, in alchemical terms, to the process of maturation of the "'green stone' into gold"[31]. If the meaning of the psychological phenomena narrated here is transferred to the male psyche, then it can be ascertained that this myth speaks about the great inspirational source of

[23] Ibid. P. 308. (Trans. by Ralph Manheim).

[24] Ibid. P. 308–309. (Trans. by Ralph Manheim).

[25] Cf. Ibid. P. 319.

[26] Cf. Ibid. P. 323–324.

[27] Ibid. P. 320. (Trans. by Ralph Manheim).

[28] Cf. Ibid. P. 321. See also: Grant, Michael. Hazel, John. (2009). *Lexikon der antiken Mythen und Gestalten*. P.413.

[29] Cf. Neumann, Erich. (2015). *The Great Mother*. P.321.

[30] Ibid. (Trans. by Ralph Manheim).

[31] Ibid. P. 323. (Trans. by Ralph Manheim).

the Anima, when the latter is integrated and fulfills its "function as a mediator between the Ego and the inner world"[32].

As explained in the introduction, death represented a theme that was particularly active in Schubert's life, especially at the time of the quartet's genesis. Following the phenomenon of projection of the human psyche described above, this difficult subject could have been projected onto an outer object of symbolic nature, which would enable the "I" to deal with it and better process the split aspect. Returning to the ancient Greek legends—death was personified by Thanatos, the son of Nyx (the night) and the sibling of Hypnos (sleep). Thanatos fulfilled the function of the angel of death, who delivered mortals to Hades[33]. Having this family background, Thanatos is also ascribed "the power to regenerate"[34]. In one legend, Thanatos is portrayed as acting together with his brother Hypnos[35]. The latter inhabited a dark cavern in the isle of Lemnos, where the "stream of oblivion" was located. Legends narrate how he transformed into a nightjar to sing Zeus to sleep[36].

Symbolically, Jean Chevalier and Alain Gheerbrant elucidate that death has a transformational character and, psychologically, "releases the negative and regressive forces, materialises and liberates the ascending forces of the spirit."[37]. Cooper formulates similarly: "Death is also the change from one mode of being to another, the reunion of the body with the earth and the soul with the spirit."[38]. The fact that Thanatos and Hypnos are siblings might suggest that they are to be understood psychologically as one chthonic deity with a double nature, i.e., incorporating a doppelgänger[39]. From this perspective, death can be understood as bearing an undertone of reconciliation. This latter aspect might have possibly

32 Roesler, Christian. (2022). *The Archetype Concept of C.G. Jung.* (Trans. by Alexander Ulyet and Christian Roesler). "Chapter: 2.5.4. The image of the soul: Anima and Animus.". P.28.

33 Cf. Grant, Michael. Hazel, John. (2009). *Lexikon der antiken Mythen und Gestalten.* P.395.

34 Chevalier, Jean. Gheerbrant, Alain. [et. al.]. (1982). *Dictionnaire des Symboles.* P.751. (Trans. by the author). French expression: "le pouvoir de régénérer.".

35 Cf. Grant, Michael. Hazel, John. (2009). *Lexikon der antiken Mythen und Gestalten.* P.395.

36 Cf. Ibid. P. 213. German expression: „Er [Hypnos] flog zum Berg Ida, wo Zeus saß […] und ließ sich in Gestalt einer Nachtschwalbe auf einer Pinie nieder. Zeus liebte Hera, und dann sang Hypnos ihn in den Schlaf.".

37 Chevalier, Jean. Gheerbrant, Alain. [et. al.]. (1982). *Dictionnaire des Symboles.* P.751. (Trans. by the author). French expression: "[…] elle délivre des forces négatives et régressives, elle dématérialise et libère les forces ascensionnelles de l'esprit.".

38 Cooper, Jean C. (1978). *An illustrated Encyclopedia of Traditional Symbols.* "Death".

39 This reflection will be of particular importance for the analytical considerations later.

led to the romantic conception of death as a friend, stimulating the characteristic longing for the death ideal (III).

The aesthetic trait of the "Todessehnsucht" can be found reflected in the poetry of the "Sturm und Drang" epoch and of Schubert's time. Examples include the poem of Matthias Claudius "Der Tod und das Mädchen", set in music by Schubert in February 1817 (D 531), and the verses of Schubert's friend, Joseph von Spaun, which gave origin to the musical setting of "Der Jüngling und der Tod" D 545, composed one month later. In both poems, a dialogue arises between death and the maiden, respectively, the youth. Death is herewith personified and portrayed as a friend or even as a redeemer. Schubert uses harmonic means to render this aesthetic musically, e.g., through the harmonic brightening to the major key or the typical sudden harmonic shifts. To better exemplify these observations, a brief look at some aspects of both settings can be helpful.

In Matthias Claudius' poem "Death and the Maiden", the lyrical I is initially frightened of death. This is made clear due to the maiden's supplication for Death to disappear. The dialogue, which is featured by the poem's twofold structure, mirrors the speech of the desperate maiden and the persuasive tone of the personified death.

Das Mädchen:
Vorüber! Ach, vorüber!
Geh wilder Knochenmann!
Ich bin noch jung, geh Lieber!
Und rühre mich nicht an.

Der Tod:
Gib deine Hand, du schön und zart Gebild!
Bin Freund, und komme nicht, zu strafen.
Sei gutes Muts! ich bin nicht wild,
Sollst sanft in meinen Armen schlafen![40]

The Maiden:
"Fade away! Ah, fade away!
Go wild Death!
I am still young, go Dear!
And touch me not.

Death:
Give me thy hand, thou, lovely and tender creature!
I am thy friend and come not to punish.
Be of good courage! I am not wild,
Sleep gently in my arms!"[41]

The dualistic structure that composes the poem is musically created by Schubert through the great contrast in texture between the two sections. The dactyl rhythm, with which the piano prelude bars open the song, foretells what is imminent: this rhythm is bound with tone repetitions, which, as already previously

[40] Claudius, Matthias. (1774/1775). „Der Tod und das Mädchen" *Sämtliche Werke I./II.* In: *Claudius-Gesellschaft.*

[41] Ibid. (Trans. by the author).

stated (14), are attributed to the semantics of death in Schubert's music[42]. For this reason, as Susan Wollenberg suggested, two principles or motivic cells can be recognized in this musical theme that was named accordingly as Death theme, motif a and motif b (Fig. 16.2):

> "At the motivic level, it is helpful to identify the two primary cells contained in the 'Death' theme, the repeated note-pattern and the three-note conjunct motif that follows it, as 'a' and 'b'"[43].

The junction of these two motivic characteristics in the theme is sometimes designated in the literature as the "oracle topos" (with reference to Mozart's opera *Don Giovanni*)[44]. This semiotics-orientated approach is also open to a more differentiated interpretation—another perspective on these aspects will be given in the quartet's analysis.

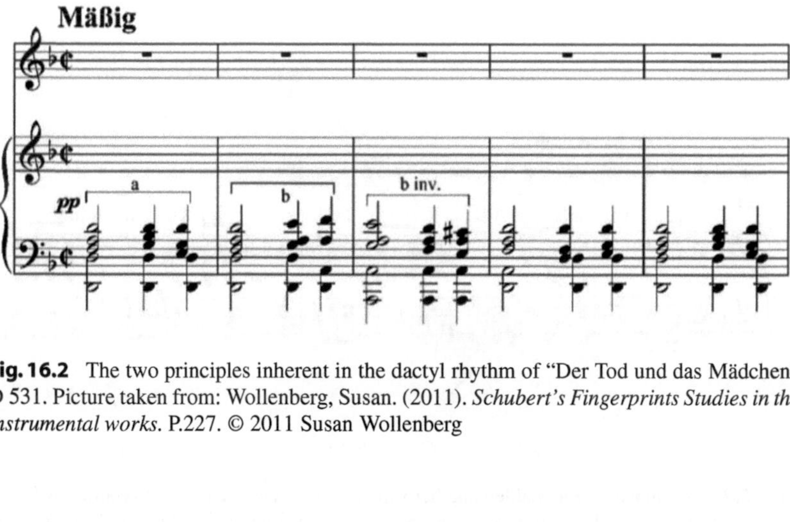

Fig. 16.2 The two principles inherent in the dactyl rhythm of "Der Tod und das Mädchen" D 531. Picture taken from: Wollenberg, Susan. (2011). *Schubert's Fingerprints Studies in the instrumental works*. P.227. © 2011 Susan Wollenberg

[42] Cf. Dittrich, Marie-Agnes. "Die Lieder. ‚Für Menschenohren sind es Harmonien'". In: Dürr, Walther. Krause, Andreas. (2020). *Schubert Handbuch*. P.165.

[43] Cf. Wollenberg, Susan. (2011). *Schubert's Fingerprints Studies in the instrumental works*. P. 226.

[44] Wolff, Christoph. (1982). "Schubert's 'Der Tod und das Mädchen': analytical and explanatory notes on the song D 531 and the quartet D 810". Cited after: Ibid. P.226.

Subsequently, faster rhythmic cells characterize the right hand of the piano accompaniment and are featured as upbeat quavers and off-beat chord repetitions, e.g., mm.9–15 (Fig. 16.3). This element, could also be associated with Beethoven's fate motif of the fifth Symphony in C minor op. 67—tone paints the maiden's inner condition of fear and restlessness. As a madrigalism, these fast rhythmic cells containing tone repetitions illustrate the act of quivering from fear and express how the maiden is strongly affected by the occurrence. The pauses in between the individual words of the melodic line emphasize the maiden's shortness of breath (Fig. 16.3). The maiden's supplicating tone is musically perceptible through the rising half tone step that characterises her appeal: A–B-flat–A "Vorüber", m.8–9; subsequently varying, whereby the first interval transforms itself into an interval of a minor third A–C–B-flat "Ach vorüber, m.9–10 (Fig. 16.3). A *lamento* figure (F–E–D–C-sharp) in the piano two bars interlude (mm.20–21) establishes the bridge to the corresponding second stanza of the poem (B-section).

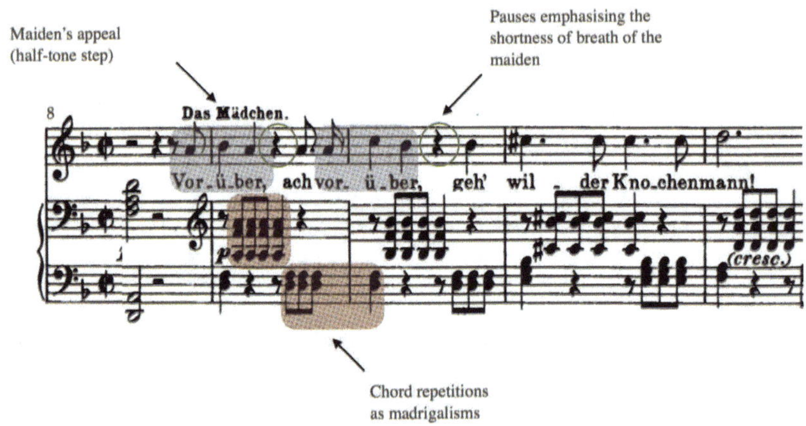

Fig. 16.3 The appeal of the maiden and her shortness of breath. The chord repetitions function here as a madrigalism, conveying the maiden's fearful attitude in face of death. (Sheet music excerpt taken and adapted from *IMSLP*)

The second part (mm.22–43), corresponding to the verses of Death and in which the wild bone man ("Knochenmann") presents himself as a friend, is composed in a monotonous tone, conveying a *parlando* style through the tone repetitions and referring to the material of the piano prelude bars. Due to this musical occurrence, the dactyl rhythm—which previously appeared as the wanderer rhythm in "Der Wanderer" D 493 (1816, 19)—incorporates the semantic of (a wandering to) death.

In terms of the formal structure, the music corresponding to the second stanza of the poem, i.e., to death's verses (16 bars) is longer than the first one corresponding to the maiden's verses (11 bars). It also bears regular phrase structures in contrast to the maiden's part. Schubert creates a harmonious and calmer mood for the B-section, which is also given by the low deep tone repetitions of the voice. So doing, Schubert might be alluding to the soothing side of Thanatos, i.e., his brother Hypnos. The turn to major in the postlude bars of the piano is rather surprising, bearing a luminous quality. This tonal brightening conveys death as being a soothing friend. The fact that the dactyl rhythm is continued for the postlude measures emphasizes that death has the upper hand. Similarly, Ellis Kohs described the dualistic atmosphere and style as intended to "[...] symbolise the dualism of life and death, with death having the last word."[45]. These elements give the last measures a specific perception of time, transmitting the atmosphere of "eternal rest"[46]. This time perception also brings the association with the image of the bone man depicted with an hourglass[47]. A look back at the poem shows the difference in relation to Schubert's song. The reader is left to assume the maiden's tragic fate, yet her reaction to Death's verses is not clearly expressed in the poem, leaving it with an open end. In contrast, Schubert's setting wordlessly expresses the maiden's surrender and the death conception of Romanticism through the harmonic and rhythmic means that have been elaborated above.

The rather optimistic view of death as a redeemer is particularly evident in the "Der Jüngling und der Tod". According to the poem of Spaun, youth smiles at Death and begs it to take him to the "dreamed land"—once more, the dreamed land lets associations with the aforementioned mythological relationship between Thanatos and Hypnos arise, being understood as two facets of the same figure. The different attitudes of the lyrical "I" towards death between the above-examined song and this one are obvious.

[45] Kohs, Ellis. (1976). *Musical Form.* P.306.

[46] Hirsch, Marjorie Wing. (1993). "Schubert's Dramatic Lieder". Cited after: Wollenberg, Susan. (2011). *Schubert's Fingerprints Studies in the instrumental works.* P.230.

[47] Cf. Mollwo-Oesterreicher, Marianne. (1978). *Herder Lexikon Symbole.* P.155.

"Der Jüngling: Die Sonne sinkt, o könnt' ich mit ihr scheiden! Mit ihrem letzten Strahl entfliehen! Ach diese namenlosen Qualen meiden Und weit in schön're Welten zieh'n.	"The Youth: The sun sinks, oh could I depart along! To flee away with its last ray! Oh avoid this nameless woe and move afar into more beautiful worlds.
O komme, Tod, und löse diese Bande! Ich lächle dir, o Knochenmann, Entführe mich leicht in geträumte Lande, O komm' und rühre mich doch an.	Oh come, death, and loosen these bonds! I smile at thee, oh Death, Seize me gently into the dreamed land! Oh do come, and do touch me.
Der Tod: Es ruht sich kühl und sanft in meinem Armen, Du rufst! Ich will mich deiner Qual erbarmen."[48].	Death: There is a cool and gentle rest in my arms, Thou plead! I will have mercy on thy woe."[49].

In Schubert's musical setting, which begins with a funeral march-like rhythm[50] in the key of C-sharp minor, the longing for death ("oh come, death, and loosen these bonds") is composed through the "colourful light of E major"[51]. However, the harmonic light suddenly changes when the bone man is addressed: E major "suddenly becomes the colourless 'white' sound of C major"[52] (Fig. 16.4). The juxtaposition of these harmonies and especially the turn to the latter tonality indicates how the bone man (Death) is, in youth's eyes, perceived and associated with the tonal quality of a C major chord: C major functions as the musical epitome of the bone man (Death) which, in mercy, is willing to redeem youth of his earthly burdens and sufferings.

[48] Von Spaun, Joseph. (1827). „Der Jüngling und der Tod". In: *The LiederNet Archive.*

[49] Ibid. (Trans. by the author).

[50] Waidelich, Till Gerrit. „Der Jüngling und der Tod (D 545). Joseph von Spaun.". In: Dürr, Walther. Kube, Michael. [et al.]. (2013). *Schubert Liedlexikon.* P.444–445.

[51] Acker, Heinz. (2009). *Modulationslehre.* P.189. (Trans. by the author). German expression: „im farbigen Licht von E-Dur".

[52] Ibid. (Trans. by the author). German expression: „[…] der schlagartige Wechsel zum farblosen ‚weißen' C-Dur Klang, […]".

Fig. 16.4 The juxtaposition of the "colourful" E major as the expression of the longing for death ("Todessehnsucht") and the contrast created by the "white" C major chord. (Figure taken and adapted from: Acker, Heinz. (2009). *Modulationslehre.* P.190. © 2009 Bärenreiter Verlag Karl Vötterle GmbH & Co. KG, Kassel)

Still from the harmonic point of view, it is curious to note how Schubert changed the final tonality path in the two existing versions of this lied. In the one version, Death is represented by the G minor tonality and the dreamed land by B-flat major (end); in the other version, the personified death sounds in D minor (the same tonality as the lied of "Death and the maiden"), and the realm of the dreamed land, closing the song, in F major[53]. In both cases the tonal relationship is established by the fact that these are, in each case, the corresponding relative major keys. If the final tonalities reached are considered comparatively

[53] Cf. Waidelich, Till Gerrit. „Der Jüngling und der Tod (D 545). Joseph von Spaun.". In: Dürr, Walther. Kube, Michael. [et al.]. (2013). *Schubert Liedlexikon.* P.444–445.

from the perspective of key characteristics, this would translate, for the first B-flat major the "looking towards a better world"[54] (i.e., the "dreamed land"), while the second end of F major would rather convey "complaisance and serenity"[55] in death. Even though the first-mentioned ending is often taken as the first version, Brigitte Massin questions which version came first and suggests to understand "Der Jüngling und der Tod" as a response to the prior composed lied "Death and the maiden" D 531[56].

Motivically, in "Der Jüngling und der Tod", the half tone step does play an important role, however, it is used differently than in "Der Tod und das Mädchen", and it bears a changed semantic (Fig. 16.5). Here, the descending *suspiratio*—tone painting the sinking of the sun and youth's desire to depart along with it—could stand for the description of youth's burden (e.g., mm.5–6 or m.10). Later, it appears bound to a rising gesture, yet still as sighs of longing (*suspiratio*). It features a tone of supplication for redemption rather than transpiring fear or a tone of appeal. One example can be found in the setting of the words "Oh, come Death" ("O komme Tod", mm.15–16). This half tone step is then expanded to a third interval ("seize me", i.e., "entführe mich" mm.19–20) and further extended into a phrase ascending to the celestial heights in the "dreamed land" ("geträumte Lande", m.20). On the rhythmical level, the dactyl (known as pavane, wanderer or wandering rhythm)—which played an important role in the D 531 song—functions as a bridge between youth's supplication and death's response (mm.24–26), being retaken subsequently in the piano postlude bars (mm.33–35). This rhythm, which is in fact dance-related (pavane)[57], is the link that unifies both songs as well as the thematic core of the quartet.

---

[54] Schubart, Christian Friedrich Daniel. „Ideen zu einer Ästhetik der Tonkunst". Cited after: Böhm, Richard. (2006). *Symbolik und Rhetorik im Liedschaffen von Franz Schubert.* P.66. (Trans. by the author). German expression: „Hinsehen nach einer bessern Welt".

[55] Schubart, Christian Friedrich Daniel. „Ideen zu einer Ästhetik der Tonkunst". Cited after: Böhm, Richard. (2006). *Symbolik und Rhetorik im Liedschaffen von Franz Schubert.* P.64. (Trans. by the author). German expression: „Gefälligkeit und Ruhe".

[56] Cf. Massin, Brigitte. (1977). *Franz Schubert.* P. 772–773.

[57] Marjorie Hirsch drew the parallel between the pavane dance rhythm and the song D 531. Cf. Hirsch, Marjorie Wing. (1993). "Schubert's Dramatic Lieder". Cited after: Wollenberg, Susan. (2011). *Schubert's Fingerprints Studies in the instrumental works.* P.226.

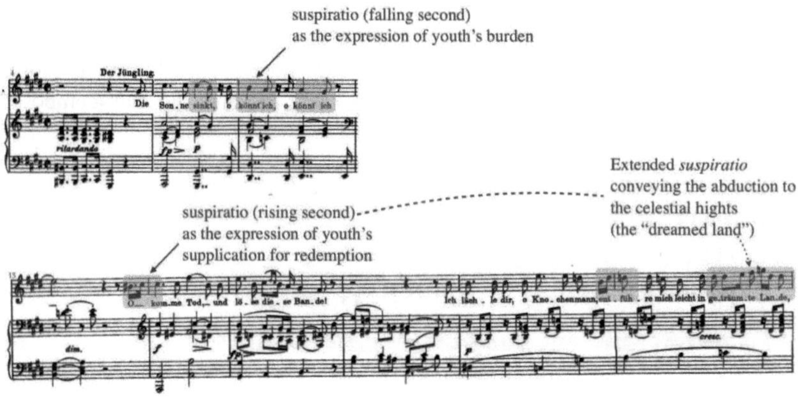

Fig. 16.5 The half-tone step motif in "Der Jüngling und der Tod" and its different semantic from "Der Tod und das Mädchen". (Sheet music excerpt taken and adapted from *IMSLP*)

Several aspects that are featured in the two lieder just discussed find an earlier parallel in Schubert's song compositions, in "Der Erlkönig" D 328 of 1815[58]. Nonetheless, the transcendent view of a soothing death, expressed by the final turn to the major tonality in the two previously analysed songs, is missing here; instead, death is personified as an evil spirit of an elf, that, following the folk legends, inhabits the alder trees. The core message of Goethe's ballad and Schubert's setting is highly dramatic in expression. The ground tonality is G minor; yet, it is not stable but moving[59]. The major tonalities featured in the song are used, however, not to depict death as a friend but rather to render the persuasive tone of "Erlkönig" (Fig. 16.6), pointing to his two-faced, knavish, and wicked nature.

The keys used for Erlkönig's verses are B-flat major (m.58), C major (m.87) and E-flat major (m.117). The last one, as Walther Dürr elucidated, is achieved by a half-tone shift from D minor to E-flat major which musically expresses Erlkönig's willingness to use violence, as described on the textual level[60]

---

58 It is noteworthy to mention that Schubert composed four versions of "Erlkönig", one after the other, with each version featuring small modifications. Cf. Massin, Brigitte. (1977). *Franz Schubert.* P.632. This fact must undoubtedly speak for the impact that Goethe's verses had on Schubert.

59 Cf. Ibid. P. 633.

60 Cf. Dürr, Walther. „Der Erlkönig op. 1 (D 328). Johann Wolfang von Goethe". In: Dürr, Walther. Kube, Michael. [et al.]. (2013). *Schubert Liedlexikon.*

(Fig. 16.6). The imminent modulation returning to D minor confirms the use of this tonality in the context of the moment of death. From these brief remarks on the tonal disposition of the song, it becomes apparent that there are some affinities between the keys used in "Erlkönig" and those in the later-composed songs.

Fig. 16.6 Erlkönig's verses in the different tonalities B-flat major, C major and E-flat major. (Sheet music excerpt taken and adapted from *IMSLP*)

Interrelations between the mentioned works are also presented at the motivic level. On the one hand, the rising half tone step, featured in the recitative-like maiden's supplication, was retaken from "Erlkönig" (Fig. 16.7). As Wollenberg stated[61], the similar *parlando* style is to be identified in the child's verses "My father, my father, do thou not hear, the dulcet vows of the Alder King?"[62] ("Mein Vater, mein Vater, und hörest du nicht, was Erlenkönig mir leise verspricht?"). Brigitte Massin rightly observed that by each intervention of the child appealing

---

[61] Cf. Wollenberg, Susan. (2011). *Schubert's Fingerprints Studies in the instrumental works.* P.227.

[62] Goethe, Wolfgang. (1782). „Der Erlkönig". The Project Gutenberg.

to his father, his tone voice level is literally raised by a half degree (the half-tone steps in mm.72–73: D-E-flat, mm.97–98: E-F, mm.123–124: F-G-flat)[63]. On the other hand, the dactyl rhythm, already identified in the two later songs, is used precisely in the most dramatic passage of "Erlkönig", namely, as Wollenberg pointed out[64], in the final recitative, when the father became aware of the child's death: "[In his] arms the child [was dead]" ("[In seinen] Armen das Kind [war tot.]").

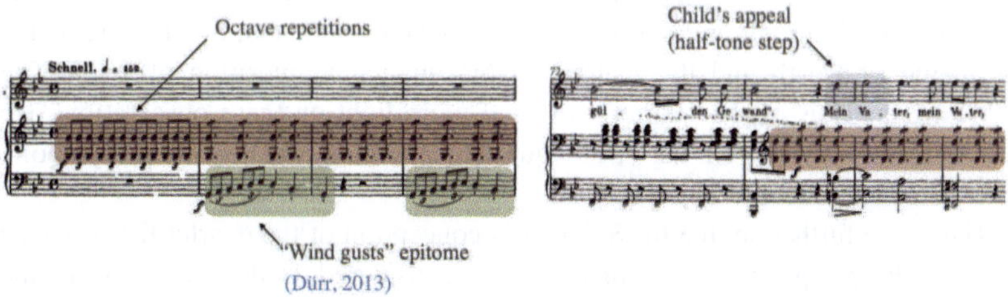

Fig. 16.7 On the left: The octave repetitions functioning as a tone carpet and the "wind gusts" motif featured in the left hand of the piano's prelude bars and functioning as a connecting motivic element throughout the song. On the right: The child's appeal in Erlkönig (mm.73–74). (Sheet music excerpt taken and adapted from *IMSLP*)

Within "Erlkönig" itself there are connecting elements that can be noted. These include *inter alia* the octave repetitions recalling a tremolando effect and functioning as a "tone carpet"[65] (Fig. 16.7). Brigitte Massin considers this element as the one giving the song its unifying dramaticism, not only depicting the outer landscape but conveying, as a madrigalism, the "inner anguish"[66] of the child facing "Erlkönig". The piano's left hand returning motif also establishes the motivic

[63] Cf. Massin, Brigitte. (1977). *Franz Schubert.* P.633.

[64] Cf. Wollenberg, Susan. (2011). *Schubert's Fingerprints Studies in the instrumental works.* P. 226.

[65] Dürr, Walther. „Der Erlkönig op. 1 (D328). Johann Wolfang von Goethe". In: Dürr, Walther. Kube, Michael. [et al.]. (2013). *Schubert Liedlexikon.* P.269–272.

[66] Massin, Brigitte. (1977). *Franz Schubert.* P.633.

unity of the song. Walther Dürr uses the epitome of "gusts of wind"[67] (Fig. 16.7), which symbolically speaking is revealing: the wind archetypically tells about the power, the effect or the expression of deities[68]—a reading which corresponds to the dominant presence of "Erlkönig" throughout Goethe's ballad and Schubert's setting.

Even if there would be a plethora of further analytical observations to be made in each of the examined songs, these brief analytical observations suffice to acknowledge a transformation of the meaning of death within the two years span that separate the three songs "Erlkönig" D 328, "Der Tod und das Mädchen" D 531 and "Der Jüngling und der Tod" D 545. Seven years later, Schubert revisited the theme of Death and the maiden in his quartet composition of 1824. The following analysis of the quartet will shed more light on these observations. To introduce the analysis of the string quartet, a brief return to a final symbolic reflection is pertinent.

There is a further source for Schubert's conception of the quartet that is based on a popular perspective, and which must be considered. In the folk tradition, the *danse macabre* plays an important role early on in History, as suggested by the mural paintings from the 14th or 15th century (Fig. 16.8). In this vision, the dance is seen as an "epiphany of death"[69]. When dance is linked to death, it transcends the moment of destruction, pointing to new creation and to liberation[70].

---

[67] Dürr, Walther. „Der Erlkönig op. 1 (D328). Johann Wolfang von Goethe". In: Dürr, Walther. Kube, Michael. [et al.]. (2013). *Schubert Liedlexikon*. P.271. (Trans. by the author). German expression: „Windstöße".

[68] Cf. Mollwo-Oesterreicher, Marianne. (1978). *Herder Lexikon Symbole*. Freiburg im Breisgau: Herder Verlag. P.184.

[69] Dobretsberger, Barbara. Personal communication between Barbara Dobretsberger and the author. Salzburg/Lisbon: December 2, 2021.

[70] Cf. Cooper, Jean C. (1978). *An illustrated Encyclopedia of Traditional Symbols*. "Dance/ Dancing". This description strongly reminds of the view in some cultures, where death is symbolized by a dancer incorporating the two principles—this is the case for instance in Hinduism. Shiva is the God of dance and death. Cf. Ibid. In European culture, as stated above, similarities with this conception are to be found in the so-called *danse macabre* or death dance ("tarantella").

Fig. 16.8 Feyerabend, Johann Rudolf. (1806). [Watercolour drawing]. Basel, Historical Museum. This painting was inspired by the late medieval mural of the Predigerkloster and depicts various people dancing with death in a hierarchical order (from the pope to the peasant). (Picture taken from: Official Website of Kanton Basel-Stadt. Trans. by the author)

The string quartet conveys death as a fateful condition. Hence, the fateful aspect associated with death finds a further mythological parallel. In Germanic mythology, death and fate are incorporated in a single figure: the norn responsible for cutting the thread of life, Atropos (8)[71]. These reflections will play an important role in the course of the quartet's analysis, more specifically of the fourth movement.

---

[71] Cf. Betz, Otto. (2016). „Der Lebensfaden". In: *herder.de.*

16.2 The First Movement Examined in Detail: General Observations and Preliminary Thoughts on the Formal Structure and Harmonic Path. Presentation of the Main Musical Motifs and the Corresponding Archetypes

The first movement of the D minor string quartet is composed in sonata form and begins with great contrasts between the themes and motifs presented, each distinct in nature. The quality of *pathos* is given through a plethora of musical parameters, which include (i) contrasting dynamics going from ***ff—pp***, (ii) madrigalism and rhetorical figures, including interruptions and caesuras, (iii) asymmetrical phrase-structures, (iv) rhythmical ambivalences and conflicts, including hemiolas, and (iv) special harmonies that enrich the harmonic colour palette of the first movement, ranging from diminished seventh-chords up to Neapolitan chords, augmented sixth chords or even ninth chords. These aspects will be analysed and treated individually in due course. Beethovenian traits can also be recognized, especially regarding the rhythm. Two core rhythmic cells that predominate in all movements can be related to the corresponding motifs of two Beethoven symphonies in particular: one the one hand, the fate motif of the fifth symphony, which opens Schubert's quartet; on the other hand, the dactyl rhythm in the *Allegretto* of the seventh symphony, which characterises the main theme, "death and the maiden". These are idiosyncratically integrated into Schubert's own musical language.

Before analysing the motivic level of the movement and attributing the associated archetypes, it is valuable to look at the formal structure of the opening movement, including the overall harmonic path, since it presents some peculiarities that should first be clarified and labelled accordingly. Some psychological comments, which will be elaborated in detail later, will be added occasionally for better orientation later on.

The exposition consists of an opening motto (mm.1–14) and two large sections. These are the thematic group A (mm.15–60) featuring the first theme, and the thematic group B (mm.61–140) featuring the secondary theme. Of the two main themes present in this sonata form movement, it is evident that the secondary theme predominates. Its "behaviour", featuring an obsessive musical thought of archetypal nature and being omnipresent throughout the movement while undergoing several transformations, suggests that this movement could have possibly been conceptualized as a monothematic sonata movement. Each thematic group can be subdivided as follows (Fig. 16.9):

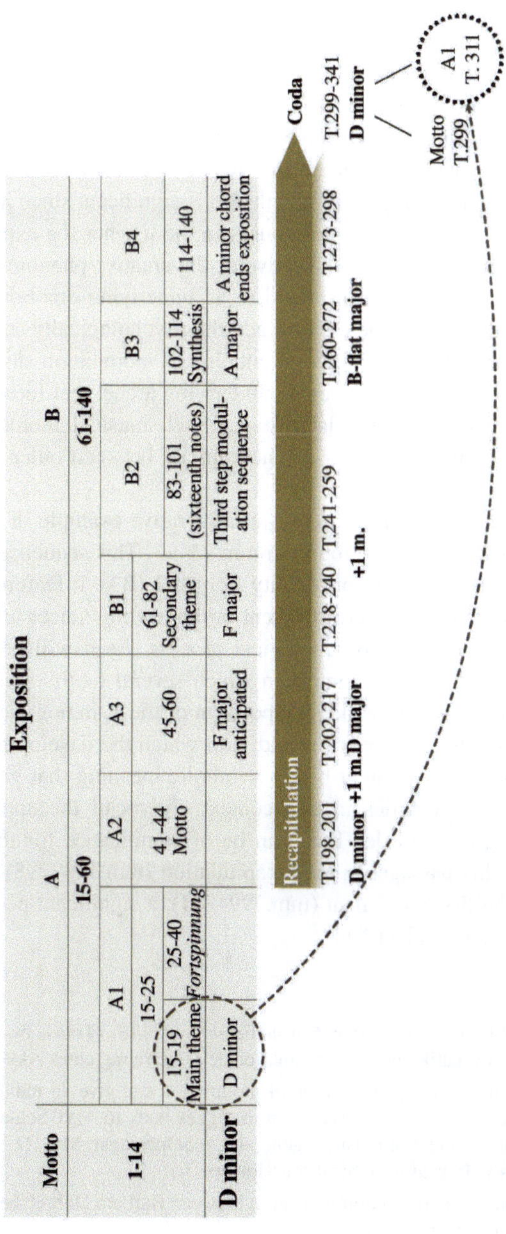

Fig. 16.9 Particularities of the formal structure: Comparative analysis between Exposition and Recapitulation

From Fig. 16.9, a first particularity of the exposition stands out, which refers to the harmonic path. While it is common to modulate to the major relative key for the presentation of the second subject in a minor tonical movement, Schubert introduces an element of surprise by anticipating the modulation to F major by ten measures and having it happen in m.51 instead of m.61. This results from a sudden chromatic shift, which is perceivable in the line of the second violin in mm.51–52 (D–D-flat–C). This type of modulation is significant since it musically causes a "functional recolouring"[72] and arouses in the listener the expectation of a new imminent subject. From the perspective of the creative phenomenon itself, this sudden shift can be revealing in regard to an underlying emotional process (7)[73]. Due to the spontaneity of the creative act, the psychologically substantiated hypothesis is reasonable that this choice of anticipated modulation shift occurred rather unconsciously. Therefore, it bears an underlying archetypal force imposing itself, which will be revealed at a later stage. Such musical moments in the creative process can be understood as a synchronicity between outer events and an inner change of mind[74].

Still from the harmonic point of view—an illustrative example of Schubert's typical modulation in thirds can be found in mm.93–97. This sequenced modulation passage will lead to the A major tonality in m.102 (B3). It features a longer harmonic process, bearing a countermovement in the leading voices and is therefore revealing of the underlying psychological process. As it will be explained later, it marks the transition to a moment in which several motifs merge. A further harmonic contrast is given by the juxtaposition of the A minor chord, ending the exposition, and the bright C major sound with which the development begins (mm.141–197). This harmony might bear a symbolic meaning that goes beyond the traditional key characteristics in this context. To recall the application of this key in "Der Jüngling und der Tod" can be of significance for the archetypal interpretation of this passage. In the recapitulation (mm.198–298) and in the coda, at the end of the first movement (mm.299–341), a significant peculiarity of the formal structure can be identified.

---

[72] Amon, Reinhard. (2005). *Lexikon der Harmonielehre*. P. 178. (Trans. by the author). German expression: "Chromatik bewirkt die funktionale Umfärbung eines Akkordes [...]".

[73] It has already been mentioned that the type of modulation can give an indication of the course of the emotional process—an observation that goes back to Max Schlesinger, who investigated the symbolic content of music in general. Cf. Schlesinger, Max. (1967). *Symbolik in der Tonkunst*. P. 48. To return to this discussion see 7.1.

[74] Dobretsberger, Barbara. Personal communication between Barbara Dobretsberger and the author. Salzburg/Lisbon: December 17, 2021.

The analytical comparison between the exposition and the recapitulation reveals a special structural feature: the recapitulation starts directly with the corresponding passage of the A2 section (m.198), instead of beginning with the main theme A1 (cf. m.15), as it would be common (Fig. 16.9). The long-awaited main theme A1 is only reintroduced in the coda section in m.311 (Fig. 16.9), which again heightens the expectation of the listener. Thereby, it takes an unexpected turn: through a modulation in thirds, the main theme is repeated in B-flat major (m. 316), instead of being repeated an octave higher as it was the case in the exposition (cf. m. 20). This type of unforeseen spontaneous act can be revealing in regard to the compositional or underlying archetypal processes. Once the major idiosyncrasies regarding the overall formal structure have been clarified, the main musical motifs and the corresponding archetypal manifestations are to be now presented.

In the subsequent music analysis, the musical motifs are assigned a qualitative term (epitome) and then related to an archetypal manifestation. Due to the given title and the thematic interconnections with the lied "Der Tod und das Mädchen", this quartet bears a strong poetic or extra-musical character. Out of this reason, it is tempting, or even helpful, to first understand the motifs in relation to the lyrical "I", i.e., from maiden's perspective. Yet, this quartet should not be confused with programmatic music. Since it is pure instrumental music, it is recommended to understand the motifs and the corresponding archetypal manifestations ultimately from an intramusical perspective ("Schubert's perspective"), as a possible utterance of Schubert's own unconscious that comes to light during his creative act[75]. Essentially, it is about the impact of these archetypes on the "I" and how the "I" experiences them. The following Fig. 16.10 intends to illustrate this approach and the interrelationship between each motif.

[75] It should be highlighted that depending on the choice of perspectives, i.e., depending on whether a passage is analysed considering the maiden's parallel world or seen from the perspective of Schubert's reality, can lead to different possible interpretations.

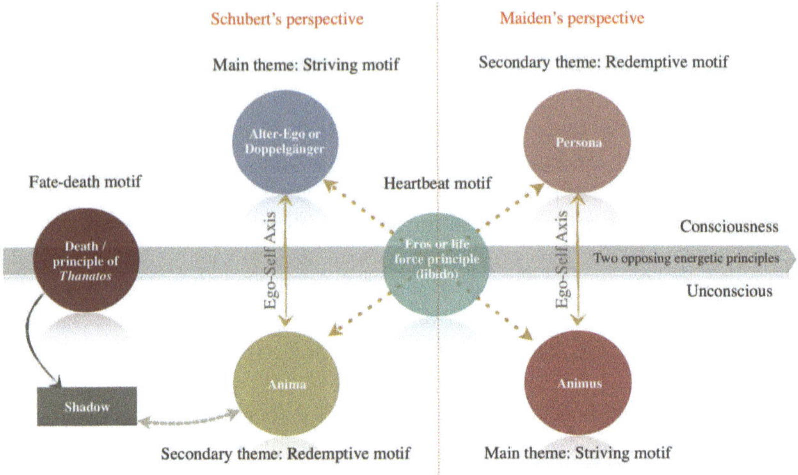

Fig. 16.10 The main musical themes and motifs with the corresponding archetypal manifestations. The two opposing energetic principles: Eros and Thanatos

There are four archetypes as the main musical motifs that can be identified (Figs. 16.10 and 16.11), each of them bearing further symbolic elements with which they can be associated. These are presented here in general lines and from the perspective of the maiden as a lyrical "I": (i) the death archetype (Thanatos) for the musical material of the opening motto, embodying the destructive principle (*Thanatos*)[76] and bounded with the fateful *conditio humana*; this motif is here labelled as fate-death motif (ii) the Animus for the first theme, symbolised by a striving musical gesture standing for the desire to rise into consciousness (striving

[76] The italicised spelling of *Thanatos* is used here whenever the principle of the destructive energy of death is to be emphasized; otherwise, the author refers to a specific form that this energy adopts and that functions as a projected shadow aspect (3.2): the personified death, Thanatos, the mythological figure of the ancient myths.

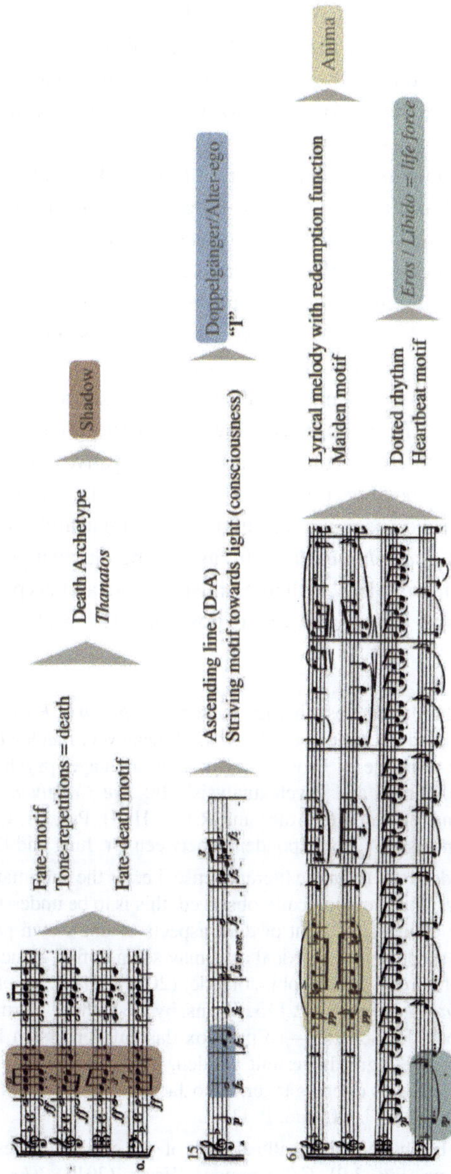

Fig. 16.11 Musical motifs and the corresponding archetypal attribution. (Sheet music excerpt taken and adapted from *IMSLP*)

motif); (iii) the Persona, belonging to the maiden's ego consciousness, which corresponds to the secondary theme and finally (iv) her life force (*libido* or *Eros*[77]), which is inherent in the maiden's theme in the musical form of the cello's over-dotted rhythm (also referred to as the heartbeat motif). With regard to "Schubert's perspective", these respectively correspond to: (i) the shadow archetype (death); (ii) Schubert's alter-ego[78], conveying the "I" and its own doppelgänger; (iii) the positive Anima, functioning as a redemptive motif and linked to the latter (iv) the life force principle of *Eros* (as the opposite pole of death), that simultaneously emerges with the Anima in form of the mentioned over-dotted rhythm. In a nutshell, the quartet is predicated on the interplay between these two counterforces acting upon the "I": *Eros*, understood in the Jungian sense as the motivating force or *libido*, and *Thanatos*, the destructive energy (as a shadow). Understanding these motifs from Schubert's perspective is revealing for the structure of the archetype of the Anima. As previously seen (3.2), it has two opposite poles, a light aspect (positive, i.e., *Eros*) and a shadow aspect (negative, i.e., *Thanatos*). From this reasoning, death can be understood as the negative pole of the Anima archetype, and life as the positive pole[79]. Consequently, the main psychological theme of the quartet can be seen as a succession of similar archetypal processes previously addressed in *Die Schöne Müllerin,* as will be elucidated later.

The next subchapter will deal with the musical and archetypal phenomena occurring in the opening motto and the exposition. The archetypal elements

---

[77] It should be recalled that in Jungian psychology the terms of *libido* or *Eros* are to be understood as life energy. Jung stated: "As you know, by *libido* I mean very much what the ancients meant by the cosmogonic principle of Eros, or in modern language, psychic energy". Cf. Jung, Carl Gustav. (2014). "Freud and Psychoanalysis". In: *The Collected Works of C.G. Jung. Vol. 4.* (Ed. and trans. by Gerhard Adler and R.F.C. Hull). Part III, Chapter: "Some Crucial Points in Psychoanalysis: A Correspondence between Dr. Jung and Dr. Loy.

[78] The term alter-ego is understood (i) in the literary sense, i.e., as the sublimating element of the composer's personality. (ii) Psychologically observed, this is to be understood as another ego, that encompasses the elements of light or dark aspects of one's own personality: "As an alter-ego, however, the shadow—paradoxical as it may seem at first glance—can also be represented by a positive figure, [...]". Jacobi, Jolande. (2006). *Die Psychologie von C.G. Jung. Eine Einführung in das Gesamtwerk.* P. 113. (Trans. by the author). German expression: "Als 'alter-ego' kann jedoch der Schatten—so paradox das auf den ersten Blick aussehen mag—auch durch eine positive Figur dargestellt werden, [...]". For this reason, this musical motif can also be designated as doppelgänger. Also Jacobi explains that the shadow can be understood as the "dark brother". Cf. Ibid. P. 111.

[79] This reasoning follows Erich Neumann's illustration of the opposite poles of the Anima and Great Mother archetype (Fig. 3.9). Cf. Neumann, Erich. (2015). *The Great Mother.* (Trans. by Ralph Manheim).

will be explained by relating them to the musical structures they are embedded in and with the corresponding psychological process. So doing, the process of assigning epitomes to the musical motifs and the association with the aforementioned archetypes will be outlined and explained in detail. With regard to the two archetypal poles or characters, it should be anticipated that the exposition will particularly deal with the effect of these two characters on the "I"—as Neumann would explain: the "elementary" and the "transformative" character of the archetype[80]. It is important to understand that both are existent with one predominant at certain stages[81]. Typically, however, the elementary character initially dominates the transformative character[82].

16.2.1 Opening Motto and Exposition: The Confrontation with Thanatos and Fate. The "I" Trapped Between its Two Wills. Experiencing the Two Poles of the Anima Archetype. The Failed Attempt at Assimilation

The opening motto (mm.1–14) is rhythmically characterised by a significant similarity to Beethoven's fate-motif (fifth Symphony, first movement) and is accordingly presented in the powerful *ff* unisono. This section is in itself irregularly structured (Fig. 16.12): the four initial bars are presented in a *catabasis* manner, i.e., in a falling scale within an octave range (D–D, mm.1–4). Subsequently, a first contrast is to be recognized, both in dynamics as in terms of sound density: the motto, which now appears only in one voice, is presented fragmentarily in the ***pp*** dynamics, and evokes rather an *interrogatio* gesture due to the rising movement at the end of each cell and the pauses in between (mm.4–5/mm.5–6). These disjointed elements are then followed by a longer line, consisting of four measures, which are then repeated, and which convey, again contrastingly, a lyrical or melancholic ductus (mm.7–14). There are three musical elements that constitute the motif of the opening motto: firstly, the tone repetitions of the outer voices (death semantic), which represents a common trait with the previously analysed songs; secondly, the triplet rhythm appended with a longer note (i.e., fate motif), and thirdly, the descending gesture of the inner voices. Psychologically, the different shapes that the fate-death motif incorporates throughout

[80] Cf. Ibid.

[81] Cf. Ibid.

[82] Cf. Ibid.

the course of the movement correspond to the form of appearance it respectively takes, whether as an outer projected image (death itself as Thanatos) or as an inner (abstract) form conveying instead its inherent *Thanatos* energy and shadow character[83]. Given the fact that this rhythmic element will run through the entire movement (even across the entire quartet) as its chthonic rhythmic drive, it is only natural that it appears in various musical and emotional roles. These three elements, which will now be subject of a closer musical and psychological examination, emerge simultaneously or alternately throughout the movement.

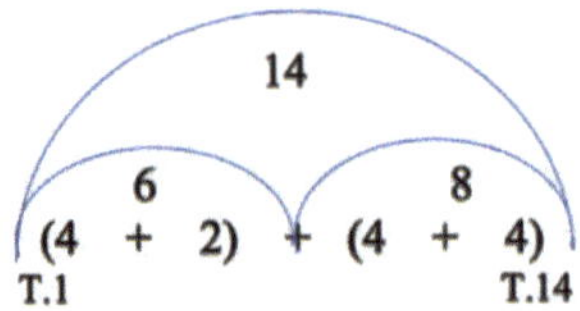

Fig. 16.12 Phrase structures of the opening motto material

Beginning with the triplet element, a development or transformation of this motif can be observed: the opening of the quartet has a "raising the curtain effect", which, however, is musically and emotionally closer to the meaning of "the ripping the curtain apart", described in the Gospel of Mark 15:38 or Matthew 27:51: a moment of shock that makes the underlying horror visible or, in this case, audible[84]. The semantics of this cross-reference explains why this basic motif of the "ripping the curtain apart" is retained throughout the rest of the movement[85]—it appears subsequently in the form of an accompanying figure (from m.15 on) and finally, it becomes incorporated into the melody (m.25). This illustrates the initial moment of shock or the confrontation with Thanatos (outer form of death), followed by a behaviour that equals the presence of a shadow (inner

83 These two types of archetypal manifestations are described in Jolande Jacobi's synopsis of C.G. Jung's psychological concepts. The outer form of an archetype corresponds to an outwardly projected inner image, while the inner form of an archetype often manifests itself in dreams, fantasies or visions. Cf. Jacobi, Jolande. (2006). *Die Psychologie von C.G. Jung.* P. 112.

84 Dobretsberger, Barbara. Correspondence between Barbara Dobretsberger and the author. Salzburg/Noiraigue: October 26, 2024.

85 Ibid.

form, *Thanatos*, m.15)[86]. If the first violin were to be seen as the voice of consciousness, due to its higher register and its bright tone quality, the incorporation of the triplets in the melody could possibly suggest an undifferentiated attitude of the "I" towards the shadow. Further musical examination of this motif reveals a first development that merits attention when the motto reappears quite unexpectedly in m.41. When comparing the initial measures with m.42 and m.44, it can be recognized that the original rests are now filled or replaced by the triplets of the fate-death motif. However, it is exceptionally featured here as an ascending movement—if this occurrence were to be described metaphorically, then it could be interpreted as a cry from the depths of the soul. A similar example of semantics can be heard in the cello voice (mm.45–50), where the rising gesture of the triplets has a threatening effect. From a psychological perspective, this recalls the increasing power of the omnipresent shadow element, death.

Continuing with the aforementioned aspect of the tone repetitions: from a rhythmic standpoint these undergo a transformation in that they appear (i) in augmented form in m.19, respectively, m.24 (violin and cello parts) and (ii) in the tremolos from m.25 on (inner voices). The latter (ii), as a madrigalism, depicts the act of trembling of fear and the inner restlessness—or, described psychologically, conveying the powerful emotional effect of death's presence on the "I". The first (i) musically convey a standstill—or, again paraphrased in psychological terms, express a counter force that withholds the "I". This statement is to be understood in the context of the musical phrase in which it is now embedded, i.e., belonging to the main theme. As it will be elaborated in the following paragraphs, this standstill might express the "I" trapped in its two wills. Before beginning with the analysis of the main theme it is important to understand the psychic dynamis inherent in the opening motto since it has an unequivocal impact on the emotional utterance of the first theme.

The motif of the opening motto is here justifiably linked with Thanatos, i.e., the archetype of death, respectively, the shadow archetype. This association is due to the musical and thematic framework, in which the motif is embedded ("Death and the Maiden")—on a subjective level of observation, Death, as an element of the maiden's own psyche, can represent a shadow aspect of herself. In Schubert's personal context, the negative connotation of the themes death and fate is given by Schubert's early confrontation with his own death (III), which possibly caused

---

[86] Analogously, in Goethe's "Erlkönig", death is at first invisible or only present as a shadow. The word *Thanatos* is here italicized due to the inner form of manifestation of the archetype, as previously explained. Therefore, when referring to the personified Thanatos, as the outer form manifestation of the archetype, the word Thanatos will not be italicized.

this aspect to split into the shadow[87]. There is a further key association that connects the biographical with the archetypal sphere: since the death of Schubert's mother, death and the mother figure have become intertwined[88] (III). This experience can also be explained in terms of the structure of the mother archetype, in which regression, death, disintegration, pain, annihilation are part of the negative pole of this archetypal principle, all aspects belonging to the shadow sphere (I, Fig. 3.9)[89]. The vehement character of the opening motto, given by the dynamics and the unisono writing, emphasize the power of this chthonic motif. The fate-death motif is omnipresent throughout the quartet, bearing sometimes a shadow character. Following C.G. Jung's concept of the psyche, which is dynamic by nature[90], i.e., bearing two poles of opposite forces, this rhythmic motif conveys the *Thanatos* energy as one of the inner *force motrice* of this movement. This naturally predisposes that an *Eros*-like energy or life energy will manifest itself. However, in the beginning of the movement, the "I" is still trapped in this conflictual *Thanatos* energy. Consequently, it attempts to liberate itself from it—a desire that comes musically to light with the main theme.

While the triplets of the fate-death motif run ghostly beneath the main theme, passing from the viola part down to the cello register, the theme (first violin, m.15–19) is presented in the ***p*** dynamic, featuring the dactyl rhythm, that was discussed in the song analysis. The tension phrase of five-bars—caused by the tone repetitions of m.19—features a countermovement between the first violin and the viola-cello lines. This phrase is subsequently repeated and sequenced an octave higher. The melody consists of an ascending, striving line, encompassing the fifth interval (D to A, Fig. 16.13). The rising line of the first violin represents a motivic connection with the previously examined lied "Der Tod und das Mädchen" since the bassline from m.9–14 features the similar pattern D–E–F–F-sharp–G–A. The first violin, even though playing in the soft dynamic, is dominating in character. This observation is due to the accents on each note of the melody, which emphasize the vehement, decisive and energic character. This translates to what in more traditional analysis literature would be termed as a "masculine" first theme. This traditional terminology is useful in that it allows for a more differentiated perspective of C.G. Jung's concept of the psyche, in

[87] The devastating effect of this confrontation is expressed in several of Schubert's letters, e.g., the letter cited above, dated 31st March 1824 (16).

[88] Cf. Brendel, Alfred. (2001). *Ausgerechnet Ich.*

[89] Cf. "Scheme III" and the corresponding elucidations of Neumann in Neumann, Erich. (2015). *The Great Mother.*

[90] Cf. Jacobi, Jolande. (2006). *Die Psychologie von C.G. Jung.* P.58–60.

which he understands that every individual bears a counterpart soul-image within themselves. This reflection explains the first step in the procedure of ascribing this motif to the maiden's Animus or ultimately to Schubert's alter-ego. Additionally, the irregular five-bar structure noted above encourages the psychological interpretation of a conflictual energy within. With the ascending gesture, there is clearly an inner force striving towards the light of consciousness.

At this point, it can be advantageous to crisscross the analytical findings on the fate-death motif with the main theme in mm. 15–19 since, psychologically, this passage conveys the expression of opposite forces operating simultaneously: on the one hand, there is the fate-death motif, which urges downwards into the depths of the unconscious (Fig. 16.13); on the other hand, this gesture is synchronized with the movement of the "I" as a doppelgänger that is striving upwards towards consciousness (Fig. 16.13)[91]. This means that there is a synchronized countermovement that psychologically conveys the flowing of psychic energies in the ego-self axis[92]. In this regard, the above-mentioned m.19, expressing a moment of standstill, gains on meaning: the "I" is striving upwards, yet there is another active counter-will withholding the "I" (*Thanatos*) and leading to a moment of impasse (Fig. 16.13). It is particularly striking how the repeated notes are musically effective both in the first violin (as an "I") and in the low cello voice (as the shadow/*Thanatos*), which can substantiate the psychological reading of the passage in question. It is as if the dark cello voice of the unconscious is trying to stop the ascending line of the first violin from entering the consciousness. This explains the above-mentioned interpretation of understanding the "I" trapped between the two wills. The generally striving character, including the struggle with fate and the inherent contradictions of the psyche, is being expressed here.

In comparison to the fate-death motif, also the alter-ego motif undergoes a transformation. However, this only becomes perceptible at the end of the analysis since this motif needs more time to process the inner occurrences. In other words, the musical metamorphoses corresponding to an underlying psychic transformation can be seen diachronically across all four movements of the quartet and will be addressed in the later subchapter (16.3).

[91] This can be taken as a musical example of the simultaneous existing and intertwining archetypal manifestations that are present in the music. In addition, the striving upwards to the light of consciousness (emancipation) is congruent with the current psychological state of the "I", i.e., being under influence of the elementary character of the Anima archetype.

[92] Jörg Rasche has noted and used a similar description of this psychological phenomenon in other musical works. Cf. Rasche, Jörg. (2014). *Das Lied des grünen Löwen*. P.91.

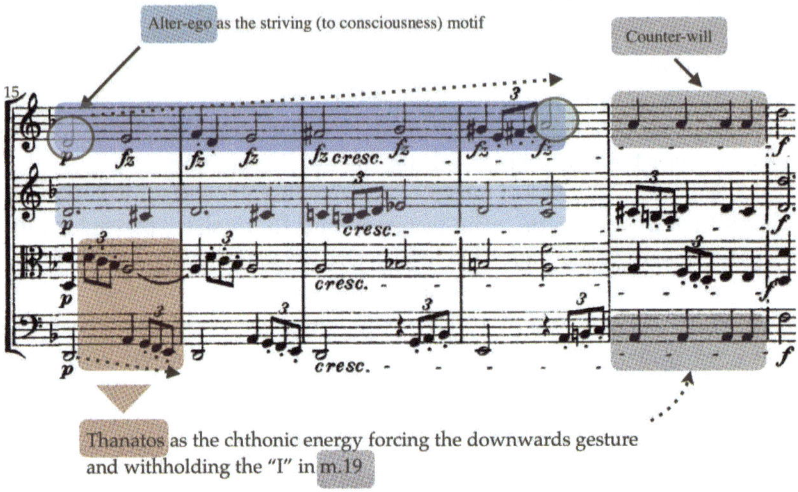

Fig. 16.13 The "I" trapped in the two wills: Thanatos forcing the downwards gesture and stopping the "I" in its striving upward gesture. The dominance of the elementary character or the negative pole of the Anima archetype on the "I". (Sheet music excerpt taken and adapted from *IMSLP*)

This music has an unpredictable character and features an extreme amount of tension as well as a changing harmony, e.g., the diminished seventh chord in m.28 and m.32. The extended dominant function of mm.32–40 and the unstable falling chromaticism in the cello part (A—A-flat –G—G-flat—F and then C-sharp—C—B—A-sharp—A) reinforce the impulsive character of this music. The aforementioned chromaticism is meanwhile taken over by the violin (mm.36–40), creating in contrast a counter-tension with its ascending gesture (F—F-sharp—G—G-sharp—A). This passage is underlined by the madrigalism of the tremolo which creates an underlying sound carpet and conveys the act of trembling. This harmonic tension and the inner restlessness hereby expressed are extended for more than ten measures, finally leading to the reappearance of the opening motif in m.41 (A2).

The triplet element of the fate-death motif is taken here as the core motif, subsequently derived compositionally. Apart from the opening motto, the triplets have appeared as an accompaniment or as part of the melodic line of the first violin so far. Incidentally, the fact that the latter coincided with the tremolo figure as a shadow can not only substantiate the above-raised hypothesis but above all psychologically determine the degree of closeness between the shadow archetype and the "I", that is strongly affected by it. Proceeding with the musical reading of the score: with the reappearance of the opening motto in m.42 the triplets are overpowered, in that they now fill the original silences and sound across all voices in an ascending manner. Simultaneously, a new element is discreetly introduced in m.42. The dotted rhythm, that heralds the upward gesture of the triplets, emerges rather camouflaged and possibly introduces the counter-principle of death that should soon be activated, i.e., the life energy. The antagonism between both archetypal forces seems to be emphasized musically by the additional ***sf*** marking on each triplet, separating one musical motif from the other and, metaphorically speaking, accentuating the overpowered *Thanatos*. This new rhythmic motif will play an increasingly important symbolic role that will be discussed in due course.

Schubert's music reveals a play with the tension relationship of phrase-structures which highlights the mentioned feeling of uncertainty. After the opening motto has been restated in its regular four bar structure (mm.41–44), an asymmetrical passage (A3) introduces the forthcoming secondary theme. First, there is a chromatic sequence to be noted which is initially structured by two bars repetition, then reduced to one bar (mm.45–51). Subsequently, a periodic like construction follows (mm.52–60), featuring a seemingly novel melodic material, which is derived from the core motif, that has just been developed (mm.45–51, also related to the earlier passage of m.25). This phrase is again antagonistically built, featuring a calm, symmetrical phrase of four-bars (mm.51–55) followed by a tension-phrase encompassing five measures (mm.56–69), leading to the first great caesura (*aposiopesis*). This rather extemporaneous stop in the musical ductus occurs through the unattended arrival on the strong affective B diminished chord of m.59 (Fig. 16.14), marked by a ***sf***. This chord is triggered by the simultaneous upward gesture of the first violin and cello, *crescending* in sound intensity. From a psychological point of view, the *aposiopesis* (Fig. 16.14) functions as a turning point, since the material that is subsequently presented is new.

After a brief one-bar introduction, the secondary theme is introduced in the *pianissimo* dynamics. As it is lyrical in nature, a great contrast with the first theme, that was in turn more vehement in character, is to be recognized. It can be valuable for a depth-psychological interpretation to refer in a differentiated way to the qualitative denominations of themes in a sonata movement, which have often been used in the past and sometimes even today: instead of an underlying "masculine" energy, this theme incorporates the attributes of what would be called "feminine" qualities, i.e., it expresses grace and delicacy—for this reason and from the perspective of the archetypal theory, this theme was previously assigned to the expression of the Anima (maiden's theme). In addition, the dotted rhythm in the cello is intrinsically linked to this theme. This involves the heartbeat motif, in turn, incorporating the *Eros* principle of the positive Anima. The shift in landscape, which is to be noted between the first thematic group and the secondary thematic group, is also emphasized by the F major tone quality—according to Böhm, it is the key of idyll and memories of a beautiful past[93]. It seems pertinent now to explain that as Thanatos has an outer and inner form of appearance, the same phenomenon occurs with the soul-image[94]: the maiden theme thus corresponds to the outer manifestation and the heartbeat motif to the inner form of appearance. The tonality of F major substantiates the positive aspect of this archetype. These considerations are important to bear in mind for the conclusive interpretation of this thematic group.

Continuing with the harmonic observation—the key of the secondary theme had already been introduced previously. The nine-bar irregular structured phrase (from mm.52–60), which fulfilled the function of a bridge to the secondary theme, was already in the tonality of the latter. This anticipation of the secondary's theme tonality occurred by the sudden chromatic shift of the second violin in m.51. Symbolizing the course of the emotional process, this change of perspective can be interpreted psychologically as the inner need to experience the atmosphere of F major, i.e., the reality of the maiden/Anima (Fig. 16.14). It is striking that the dotted rhythm, symbolizing the heartbeat motif, had appeared more frequently in the precedent measures (e.g., mm.52–57)—in any event, it coincides with the arrival in the F major key (in the A3 section), i.e., with the positive's Anima and its general presence. These observations rather speak in favour of the following interpretation: the positive Anima is felt as a redemptive motif, which would explain its musical recurrence throughout the movement. Consequently, the maiden's theme seemingly acts as the positive pole of the archetype. This interpretation bases itself on the traditional Jungian concept that the soul images

93 Böhm, Richard. (2006). *Symbolik und Rhetorik im Liedschaffen von Franz Schubert.* P.64.

94 Cf. Jacobi, Jolande. (2006). *Die Psychologie von C.G. Jung.* P. 116.

function as a bridge to the inner world and fulfills the purpose of a supernatural aid[95], assisting the "I" with the integration of the split aspects of the personality (e.g., the role of the Anima in the hero myth). Continuing this line of thought, the shadow aspect must be somehow present in this section, so that both poles would exist concurrently. To unravel its background presence, it is necessary to return to the musical level and examine the important changes in textures, characterizing this passage.

The light elements of the secondary theme, mentioned above, are juxtaposed with contradictory elements. These concern (i) rhythmic ambivalences, resulting from the omnipresence of the triplet motif in the viola, and (ii) the irregular phrase structures of the theme. These aspects are now to be considered in more detail. To directly juxtapose the musical facts with a Jungian interpretation here can be particularly helpful to unravel the musical and psychological phenomena and to understand them as a unity of expression. The fact that the triplet element of the fate-death motif is in the background (viola), functioning musically as a *perpetuum mobile* (Fig. 16.14) is the reason for a superposition of different layers. Psychologically observed, this motif points to the presence of a dark side. The shadow presence conveys the knavish omnipresence of death and the intransigence of the fateful *conditio humana.* Here, the shadow is active not as an outer manifestation (projected into a specific shape) as it was the case in the opening motto, but only in its inner form of appearance (an abstract almost indistinctly triplet motif as an inner voice in the ***pp*** dynamics). Strangely enough, the musical motif corresponding to the shadow is still the underlying motif that sets the musical direction (*perpetuum mobile*). Possibly, this might psychologically predict how the movement will end—as the shadow gaining the upper hand. A further possible interpretation would be that the negative Anima tries hereby to destabilize or take possession of the "I"[96], albeit the positive, transformative aspect seems to predominate here. The analysis of the rhythmic conflicts and phrase structures could shed light on the most likely psychological process.

[95] Cf. Roesler, Christian. Personal communication between Christian Roesler and the author. Basel: January 12, 2023.

[96] Such a process is e.g., described in Jacobi, Jolande. (2006). *Die Psychologie von C.G. Jung.* P.117.

The existent rhythmic conflict is to be heard by the fact that the fate-death motif is juxtaposed with the maiden's theme, which is in turn structured binarily. The interweaving between the triplet motif and the melodic material together with the heartbeat motif would archetypally reflect the two inner active forces of opposite nature: the Anima's shadow side, i.e., the *Thanatos* motif versus its light essence (*Eros*). A further musical element that could substantiate this hypothesis concerns an observation regarding the phrase structure of the maiden's melody, which can offer an additional psychological insight. The theme is musically shaped in a restless manner, being internally torn[97]. This is due to an irregular phrase construction (five bar structure), which *per se* stands in contradiction with the lyrical tone of the melody already identified. The musical tension thereby created can emphasize the inner emotional state, reflecting nothing less than the impact of the omnipresent shadow on the "I". It could however also indicate how the shadow aspect of the Anima is in itself not fully integrated in the "I" (cf. 15).

The synthesis of the gathered analytical information, and the consideration of the various hypotheses put forward on the maiden's theme passage, leads to the following conclusion: the (outwardly) projected Anima, in form of the maiden's melody (Persona), is here reinforced by its vital (inner) light element *Eros*, i.e., the musical dotted rhythm emerging in the cello part and symbolizing the heartbeat. From this observation, it can be deduced that the Anima, embodying both positive principles, is being reinforced here, helping the "I" to overcome the inner struggle with the shadow (viola). However, viewed from the triplet's perspective, this bass rhythm stands in a contradiction to it. This rhythmical ambivalence, alongside with the noted tension of the irregular phrases, could possibly be explained by the impact of the negative pole of the Anima (death), which is omnipresent in the background, on the "I"; in other words, these juxtapositions and the interweaving of contradictory elements result in the "I" experiencing the two opposite poles of the same archetype (Anima), which explains the musical contradictory elements (irregular phrase structures and rhythmic conflict).

[97] Dobretsberger, Barbara. Personal communication between Barbara Dobretsberger and the author. Salzburg/Lisbon: December 2, 2021.

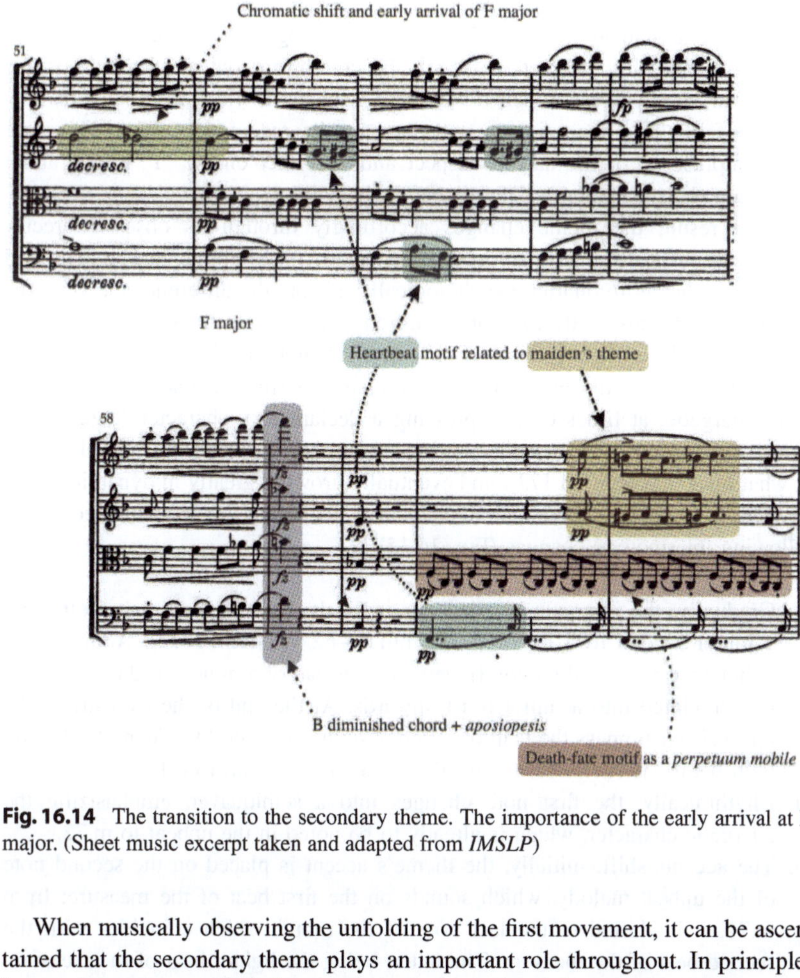

Fig. 16.14 The transition to the secondary theme. The importance of the early arrival at F major. (Sheet music excerpt taken and adapted from *IMSLP*)

When musically observing the unfolding of the first movement, it can be ascertained that the secondary theme plays an important role throughout. In principle, its omnipresence would allow analytical discussion of a monothematic sonata movement, in which the main theme does not appear centrally, but instead the secondary theme. The musical fact that the secondary theme is close to fulfilling the function of a monothematic theme could possibly unveil the original extra-musical intention—being the maiden the main character. In psychological terms, this is explained by the central role the positive Anima has for the psychological process (redemption and helper). The soothing impact of this theme on the "I" is expressed by its circling character, always repeating and transforming itself—the circling around as a *circulatio* points psychologically to the search of the Self[98]. Archetypally observed, it is as if, by coming in contact with the positive Anima, an inner process of self-regulation is triggered, which also explains how this motif can be unconsciously perceived for its redemptive effect. However, the omnipresence of the shadow aspect and its effect on the "I" brings about significant transformations of the maiden's thematic material.

As a result, the theme changes accordingly through its obsessive recurrency. The musical transformation of the thematic material that can be identified throughout the entire quartet, psychologically mirrors the different aspects of the Anima, possibly also reflecting the condition of the "I". In the general lines presented here, the metamorphosis of this musical motif evolves in the following way: it begins lyrically and gracefully in character (m.62), gradually becoming more energetic, at times even expressing a declamatory character (e.g., m.83), punctually expressing a more lamenting undertone or expressing reminiscences of what once was (e.g., m.173), and eventually growing greatly in dynamics (e.g., m.90, m.176, m.248). These overall character fluctuations are accompanied by the following intermotivic changes (Fig. 16.15):

i. Gradually, the intervals become continuously larger, going first from e.g., a minor second to a minor third (mm.61–62 vs. mm.71–72). Additionally, Schubert varies the direction (inversion): instead of a minor third downwards, it is modified into a minor third upwards. At the end of the exposition, the intervals encompass the leap of a minor sixth, followed by a leap of a fourth, both being the rhetorical figure of the *exclamatio* (mm.134–137).
ii. Rhythmically, the first note changes into a semiquaver, emphasizing the energetic character, which is already to be noted in the upbeat to m.72.
iii. The accents shift: initially, the theme's accent is placed on the second note of the upbeat melody, which sounds on the first beat of the measure; from m.72, it is shifted to the last note of the motif, which coincides with the second beat of the measure. The latter, being the lighter beat of the measure, creates a musically ambivalent statement. Similarly in m.102, the accent falls on the last note of the motif, which here is placed, however, on the first beat of the measure. At the end of the exposition, the accent comes on the

[98] Cf. the brief analysis of "Gretchen am Spinnrade" undertaken in part 8. Also the *Forellenquintett* deals with this thematic. Cf. Part 14. For Jung's reference on this term see: Cf. Jung, Carl Gustav. (2014). "Psychology and Alchemy". In: *The Collected Works of C.G. Jung. Vol. 12.* (Trans. by Gerhard Adler and R.F.C. Hull). Chapter 3: "The Symbolism of the Mandala—II. The Mandalas in the Dreams".

fourth note, with an additional ***sf*** marking in the last note (mm.133–134), which emphasizes the emotional utterance of the aforementioned intervallic transformation, respectively, the intervallic expansion to *exclamatio* figures (the sixth and the fourth).

iv. The articulation is altered from mm.83–92 onwards, which underlines the change from a *cantabile legato* to a more declamatory character.

v. The entire motif develops into a rocking motif (mm.128–132). Simultaneously, it embodies hemiolas that contrastingly bring the unstable character, once more, into the foreground.

These transformations (Fig. 16.15) are to be understood in the frame of the imminent musical and psychological occurrences that will follow. For this reason, they will now be further examined and contextualized.

The maiden's theme is irregularly structured into five-bar phrases, encompassing a total of ten bars. An outstanding harmonic feature is particularly striking in this passage, which permits supplementing the psychological interpretation of this passage: the melody ends deceptively on a diminished seventh chord[99], immediately triggering the triplet fate-death motif to emerge from the depths (m.71). A new attempt is initiated on m.72, but this time, the antecedent phrase does not succeed. Instead, it similarly slides back again into a new diminished seventh chord, similarly triggering the ascension of the fate-death motif from the depths (m.76). Only by adding two bars to the consequent phrase, i.e., only in the fourth repetition (mm.81–82) does the theme finally thrive forward and the new B2 section can subsequently begin. This musical phenomenon speaks in favour of the above raised psychological hypothesis: the "I" is experiencing the two opposite poles of the same archetype (Anima: life and death). The interplay of the positive and negative aspects, and its impact on the "I" is perceptible through (i) the incorporation of the negative aspect (triplets in the violins, m.66), (ii) the mentioned trials with the consecutive deceptive regressions[100] and a final striving forward. It is curious that the latter movement was the result of four consecutive

[99] This deceptive quality can also be a characteristic of the diminished seventh chord. Hartmut Krones lists this chord being a harmonic musical rhetorical figure (*ingano*), as a representation of doubt, fallacy or deceit. Cf. Krones, Hartmut. "Musik und Rhetorik". (2016). In: Laurenz Lütteken (Ed.). *MGG Online.* Subchapter: "Musikalisch-rhetorische Figuren—Harmonische Figuren". Beyond this, this chord in particular is also acknowledged as expressing feelings such as grief or pain. Cf. Amon, Reinhard. (2005). *Lexikon der Harmonielehre.* P.100.

[100] The term regression is here used due to the fact that death embodies a rather regressive energy. Cf. Roesler, Christian. Personal communication between Christian Roesler and

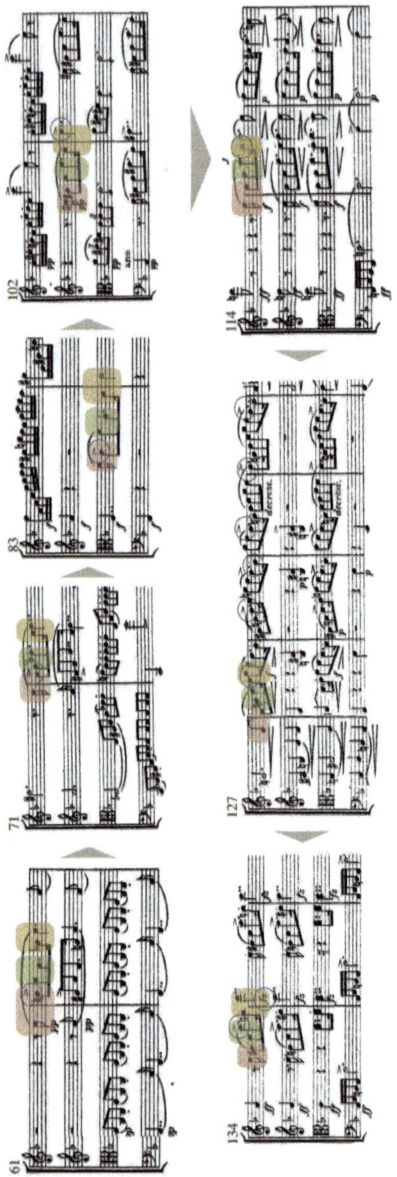

Fig. 16.15 The Maiden's Motif-metamorphosis through the exposition. (Sheet music excerpt taken and adapted from *IMSLP*)

repetitions of the theme: bearing in mind Jung's symbolic concept of the number four as a symbol of wholeness (2.2), this fact may point to the intention of the "I" to head in direction to the Self. With the last, fourth attempt it finally succeeded in bringing about an important inner movement.

This inner movement can be musically perceived through the sixteenth note chains (B2), symbolizing the exchange of energies between consciousness and the unconscious in the ego-self axis. Musically, the maiden's theme is immediately split into small motivic elements. This means that only the head of the theme (maiden's motif) is henceforth to be heard; initially, it crosses all three lower voices of the quartet (mm.83–89), in a dialogue-like fashion and features a declamatory tone. Simultaneously, the violin is given the leading, soloistic role here and thereby introduces the new motif: the sixteenth notes. The musical fact that the maiden's motif is traversed[101] through the different voices of the quartet in this section (mm.83–92) speaks in favour of the psychological interpretation that several aspects of the Anima (positive and negative) are being differentiated. Also, the dialogue-like feature psychologically translates the dialectical process that commonly occurs in such moments[102]. Such a formulation does correspond to an important step in the individuation process—to an attempt of assimilation or integration[103]. This process extends over several bars, even pages, and leads to the passage of the modulation in thirds, mentioned in the introduction to this chapter.

Schubert's third modulation process (mm.93–96) is revealing with regard to the mentioned underlying psychological process. Remarkably, this expressive passage corresponds to the moment in which the maiden's theme, or the derived fragmentary motif, is absent. This omission lasts a total of nine bars. Thereby, a synchronicity of counter-movements takes place: an ascending bass line beginning in m.93 will meet the concurrent descending line of the first violin at the vanishing point of m.97, to speak figuratively (Fig. 16.16). Observed from a Jungian perspective, such a process can depict an inner transformation, or at least

the author. Freiburg im Breisgau: June 18, 2024. For further insights into this psychological "energetic movement" see: Jacobi, Jolande. (2006). *Die Psychologie von C.G. Jung*. P.61–62.

[101] In musical technical terms, this passage conveys the compositional technique of imitation. The author has opted to refrain from employing the technical term and instead has chosen to adopt a metaphorical formulation in order to lay the groundwork for the psychological observation that is subsequently developed.

[102] The dialectical process that Jung described is to be read in: Jacobi, Jolande. (2006). *Die Psychologie von C.G. Jung*. Chapter: „Das dialektische Verfahren". P.72–73.

[103] Accordingly, this process can be read in: Cf. Jung, Carl Gustav. (2023). *Die Beziehung zwischen dem Ich und dem Unbewussten.*

an inner movement, in which there is an interchange or renewal of psychic energies flowing in the ego-self axis: on the one hand, the movement of the "I" that descends to meet the unconscious structures, on the other, the archetypes that emerge simultaneously. Such a phenomenon, in which ego-consciousness diminishes, is described by Jung as an *abaissement du niveau mental* and is congruent with a transformation process which has been initiated[104]. Such a state can "[...] narrow the mental horizon"[105] since it augments egocentricity[106]. This is by no means to be understood as a pathological condition, but it can explain the musical obsessive character of the maiden's motif throughout the movement. As a following analytical question, it is of special interest to see how this situation will develop musically and psychologically.

At the end of this sequenced section (mm.93–97), two harmonies are particularly revealing in terms of their emotional content. Both occur in the same bar 96 and emotionally express the painful psychological process: the Neapolitan sixth chord and the augmented sixth chord (Fig. 16.16). Once arrived at the dominant chord in m.97, the music begins to stagnate. This is particularly noticeable in mm.99–100. The lost sense of orientation expressed musically could lead to the following interpretation: it is as if the "I" was momentarily in the nothingness. Such moments can be understood as psychological turning points, i.e., being the equivalent to what Neumann termed as the "phenomenon of reversal"[107] (3.2). Jung used Heraklit's concept of Enantiodromia to describe such a process[108]. This inner need of turning towards a contrasting realm habitually occurs when the "I" gets closer the one archetypal pole[109]. From this psychological experience, the following section (B3) could be particularly enlightening.

---

[104] It should be noted that C.G. Jung actually listed this process in the frame of a subjective transformation, which pertains to one phenomenological group of the rebirth mysteries. Cf. Jung, Carl Gustav. (2011). *Four Archetypes*. P.53–54.

[105] Ibid. P.54.

[106] Cf. Ibid.

[107] Neumann, Erich. (2015). *The Great Mother.* (Trans. by Ralph Manheim). P.75.

[108] Roesler, Christian. Personal communication between Christian Roesler and the author. Freiburg im Breisgau: June 18, 2024. The definition of Enantiodromia is to be found in: Cf. Jung, Carl Gustav. (2013). *Kleines Lexikon der Analytischen Psychologie*.

[109] Cf. Neumann, Erich. (2021). *Die Große Mutter.*

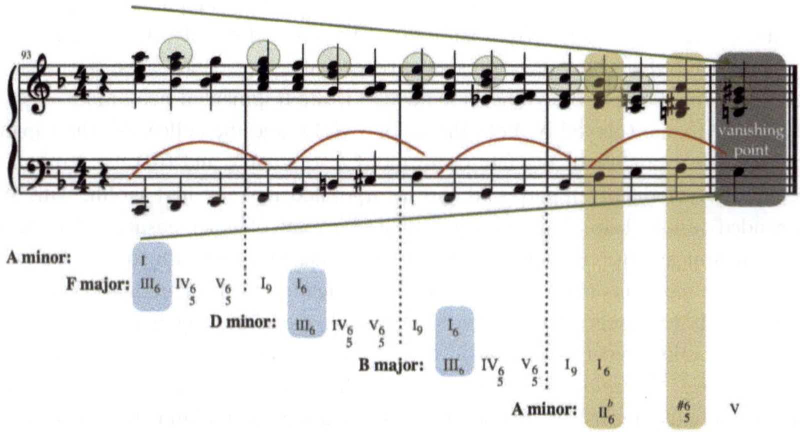

Fig. 16.16 Third modulation technique. Counter-movement leading to vanishing point. In psychological terms this passage can be analogously compared to what Jung termed as an "abaissement du niveau mentale"—a process featured in processes of transformation.

This psychological condition of being in the nothingness persists until m.101—the moment in which the harmonic direction of the music gradually becomes clearer through the leading G-sharp note (m.101): the harmonic path is now heading towards the luminous key of A major. The key characteristics can confirm the luminous character of this tonality[110]. These theories can also pinpoint another important trait of this key, that of being the "pretence of the positive moods"[111]. Psychologically speaking, this means that the latter aspect of the A major tone colour is only unconsciously known and indicates the illusory nature of the imminent B3 section.

---

[110] Cf. Böhm, Richard. (2006). *Symbolik und Rhetorik im Liedschaffen von Franz Schubert.* P.57.

[111] Ibid.

Once arrived in A major (B3, m.102), the "I" enters another realm, where reminiscences or memories from an idyllic past arise. Musically, there is an overlapping of motifs, which were presented beforehand, and which gave rise to this reading. This moment of synthesis includes: (i) the fragmented head motif of the secondary theme (played by both the second violin and the cello), (ii) the triplet and tremolo elements of the fate-death motif (viola part), and (iii) the semiquavers, now melodically repurposed and incorporated into the first violin, with an appended falling leap. This passage endures a total of ten measures. An energetic unison ascent, characterized by the semiquaver's rush, illustrates the two subsequent measures (mm.112–113) as a densification of the semiquaver's motif, which leads to a second *aposiopesis* in m.114. Once the top note is achieved (*ffz*), the cello interrupts the music with a motif ending in an upwards jump of a bare octave[112] (*exclamatio*). To paraphrase the A major passage (mm.102–114) in psychological terms: the maiden's motif is featured as its light (second violin) and shadow aspect (cello), which congruently speaks in favour of a synthesis or union of the several aspects of the personality. It should not be forgotten that, due to the key characteristic of A major, this occurs in an imaginary realm, i.e., this integration is self-illusory. After the dialogue of all the inner elements, a *unisono* gesture personifying the energy of an archetype rising from the depths of the unconscious seems to gain the upper hand once more (mm.112–114). Applying the traditional meaning of the musical rhetoric figures, the *exclamatio* figure, bearing the bare octave jump that is featured in the cello in m.114, symbolizes death. Consequently, this figure permits the association with the personified archetype of death (Thanatos), which literally frightens and brings the music to a stop, i.e., there is a new moment of standstill (m.114).

Typically, after an *aposiopesis*—which psychologically is here equivalent to a moment of shock—there is a gesture of groping around. The tension that is created is achieved musically by the long pedal points in the cello line of the following passage, conveying simultaneously the sensation of a longer perception of time. Looking at the pedal line alone on a larger scale, a gradual descent can be identified from m.114 until m.128 (F–F-flat–E-flat–D-C-sharp–B–A–G-sharp–E).

[112] The author consciously chose the term "bare octave" instead of the factual term "perfect octave" due to its symbolic association—using "bare octave" tends to emphasize the inherent semantics of the interval, since it is a rhetorical figure that encompasses Death. For this reason, the author will always refer to the latter formulation ("bare octave") where applicable.

In the meantime, the other three voices concurrently retake the maiden's motif in the *f* dynamic, featuring a descending line and a retreat into a ***pp*** dynamic (mm.115–117). Two attempts to resolve the shock moment of m.114 are made by these three voices in the intervening time: the first attempt in mm.115–119, the second in mm.120–133. At first sight, the second attempt seems to lead further. The music finally turns out to become even more indefinite and ambivalent due to the presence of the hemiolas (mm.129–132). In fact, the "wrongly" placed accents result in a loss of the bar's centre of gravity, causing more instability and restlessness—this loss of the gravity centre can be transferred analogously into the realm of the "I".

In m.134, a third and final attempt is made, this time only by the two violins. The passage in question begins in a similar way to the two preceding ones, with a first outburst from the cello, featuring the *exclamatio* (m.134) that emerges quite unexpectedly out of nowhere, and creating a great dynamic contrast (from ***p*** to a sudden ***ff***). Thereby, this last outburst now introduces the final measures of the exposition, in which the head motif of the maiden's theme is uttered in a high register (*exclamatios*, m.134–137). Psychologically interpreted, these three struggling attempts can be seen as if the "I" was again trying to integrate the mana-power of the Anima[113] (15), thereby being constantly interrupted by the dreadful chthonic structure (shadow) and consequently losing the sense of being centred (hemiolas). However, if the Anima is not fully integrated by the end of the exposition, possibly, it will not be able to succeed in its function to help the "I" to integrate the shadow part in the development (*peripeteia*)—which may already foretell the "tragic" ending of the first movement.

Musically, the last measures of the exposition depict the *climax* in the evolution of the maiden's theme, achieving its major intervallic metamorphoses (mm.134–137). The exposition then ends rhythmically with an energetic intensification of the dotted motif (m.138) and harmonically on a stable, yet A minor, chord.

---

[113] Such a process can be read in: Jung, Carl Gustav. (2023). *Die Beziehung zwischen dem Ich und dem Unbewussten.*

16.2.2 Development: The Descent into the Realm of the Unconscious and the Psychological Inflation as a Result of the Confrontation with and Pursuit of the Shadow. A Resurgence Attempt

Considering the classical conception of the sonata form according to which the formal function of the exposition is to exhibit the themes and motifs that are subsequently processed in the development section, the rhetorical figure of the *exclamatio*, expressed at the end of the exposition in the maiden's motif, is of particular psychological importance for the forthcoming development. The achieved metamorphoses of the maiden's motif, which have just culminated in the *exclamatio*, functioned symbolically as an "inner call of the soul"[114]. Hence, the development section of a sonata form can be analogously compared, at least in a hermeneutical approach, to the archetypal process of the descent into the underworld, where the "I" has to wrangle with the inner demons (shadow) and emancipate itself from the elementary character of the archetype (Anima). It is particularly compelling to see how this factor is translated into musical terms from the first measure of the development.

Observing the entrance to the development section from the harmonic point of view can be revealing in that regard. Schubert ended the exposition with a clear statement in A minor (Fig. 16.17). Subsequently, he opens the development with the tonic parallel key with the C major chord. Although it is a common harmonic choice, following the harmonic structure of a sonata movement in Schubert's time, this C major chord has a particular effect on the listener. This may be due to the motifs with which it is associated: the cello motif identified in m.114 contains the bare octave jump symbolising death, and the imminent *aposiopesis* that follows it. In this way, the C major harmony gains a new shade of meaning and can be felt by the listener as being unexpected, as a great harmonic contrast (Fig. 16.17). Such a musical statement reflects an emotional declaration, which suggests that there might be an additional semantics underlying the C major tone-colour.

---

[114] Dobretsberger, Barbara. (2016). *Formen der Instrumentalmusik*. P. 27. (Trans. by the author). German expression: „Die emphatische Sexte [ist hier] Sinnbild für den ‚Ruf' der Seele".

At this point, a systematic approach would suggest turning towards the key characteristics to investigate the quest concerning this harmonic meaning. However, in this case this tactic proves to be insufficient for determining the underlying emotional utterance. On the contrary, it is possible to find a suitable response by unveiling a harmonic cross-reference. It is conceivable that with the shift to C major initiating the development Schubert might be pointing to an earlier equivalent: the semantics of the C major from “Der Jüngling und der Tod” D 545. While in the key characteristics, C major is described as the tonality of innocence, positive contents, love and nature[115], in the aforementioned song, C major is conceived as the white colour of death, i.e., creating a synesthetic experience, as Acker described it[116]. The analogy described here explains why the tonic parallel key of C major, as a habitual procedure, feels estranging to the listener[117]. This approach is similar to Böhm’s method (13), which is to analyse the lieder work and thereby connect the harmonic semantics with the text’s words in order to unveil the characteristics of a key. This observation confirms the need for a differentiated and contextualized approach in the application of key characteristics in a musical analytical context, where a strong systematic methodology would obviously disappoint in this regard (6.2).

Beginning the development with this reference, Schubert foretells its psychological content: it reflects (i) a descent into the unconscious, (ii) the confrontation of the “I” with the shadow and the struggles with fateful death, (iii) finally, the inner battle with the two opposite energies (*Eros* and *Thanatos*). The following music analysis will demonstrate how this psychological reading can be discerned. In order to achieve symbolic clarity about the musical occurrences, a metaphorical description might occasionally be necessary.

---

[115] Cf. Böhm, Richard. (2006). *Symbolik und Rhetorik im Liedschaffen von Franz Schubert.* P.48–49. In this context, the Marc-Antoine Charpentier’s description in which C major is seen as the fiercely key, that evokes warlike emotions, might be the closest to the action present in this development, as it will turn out. Cf. Tobisch, Léopold. "Le pouvoir expressif et affectif des tonalités". (2020). [Article]. The analogy to Schubert’s own previous song seems to be more adequate here, inasmuch as the question of whether Schubert was aware of the French composer’s treatise remains unanswered.

[116] Cf. Acker, Heinz. (2009). *Modulationslehre.* P.189.

[117] It must be highlighted that such an understanding of a musical passage has a direct influence on the interpretation: the beginning of the development section with the C major harmony should serve as an example. It should therefore not be played as a usual unfolding of the sonata form, but the interpreter himself/herself must be seized by this shudder at the moment of the performance.

Fig. 16.17 End of exposition and beginning of the development with a great harmonic contrast. (Sheet music excerpt taken and adapted from *IMSLP*)

After the announcement of a shudder through the C major chord and the emotional reaffirmation of the unstable condition of the "I" caused by the shock (hemiolas, mm.146–149, Fig. 16.17), the "I" initiates the descent into the underworld (descending scale of mm.152–154). This musical image is unconsciously imposed on the listener through the use of the *catabasis* rhetorical figure (Fig. 16.18), identifiable in the cello voice (mm.152–154). This descent is marked by a significant contrast in dynamics, which is given by the sudden *ff* dynamics and the accent mark on the bass. It should be emphasized that, from a psychological perspective, this descent may indicate an autonomously imposed counter will[118], that induced this downwards movement.

Fig. 16.18 The descent into the underworld (*catabasis*). (Sheet music excerpt taken and adapted from *IMSLP*)

Once arrived in the realm of Hades (metaphorically speaking), there is a great exchange of motifs, and an inversion of roles to be noted in the music (mm.156–175). The following three musical main motifs and their corresponding archetypes are to be noted in the forthcoming passage: (i) the head motif of the maiden's theme, symbolizing the Anima and its two opposite forces (i.e., the two archetypal opposite poles), which include (ii) the triplet motif standing for the element of the shadow (*Thanatos*), (iii) and the heartbeat motif representing the life-force of the Anima (*Eros*). In general, the passage comprising mm.156–176 can be musically subdivided into two subsections: the first, going from m.156 to m. 165, and the second from m.166 to m.175.

In each of the two sections, there is an exchange of the mentioned motifs across the external "voices" of the quartet, i.e., the register of the first violin and cello. In m.156 the lower voices start this section with the triplet's motif. In the middle of the measure, the first violin enters as an upbeat and the maiden's motif. Before long, however, the first violin will eventually incorporate the triplets into its own voice (m.157, Fig. 16.19). Immediately, the maiden's motif is to be

[118] Jacobi explains how the power of the shadow can affect one's own will: "[…] often we go against our own will […]". Jacobi, Jolande. (2006). *Die Psychologie von C.G. Jung*. P.112. (Trans. by the author). German expression: "[…] gehen wir, oft ganz gegen unseren Willen, […]".

heard in the dark register of the cello (m.157, Fig. 16.19). In mm.160–162 there is a densification of the heartbeat motif in the ***ff*** dynamics, emanating from a *unisono* statement of the maiden's theme (m.160). The first section ends with the triplets in the dark cello register (***pp*** dynamics), featuring tone repetitions, and the restatement of the maiden's motif in the first violin. All voices are maintained in the softest dynamics here. This section is then repeated again up to m.176. Harmonically, appoggiaturas and suspensions (mm.157–160, Fig. 16.19, respectively mm. 167–170) provide for dissonances and harmonic tension.

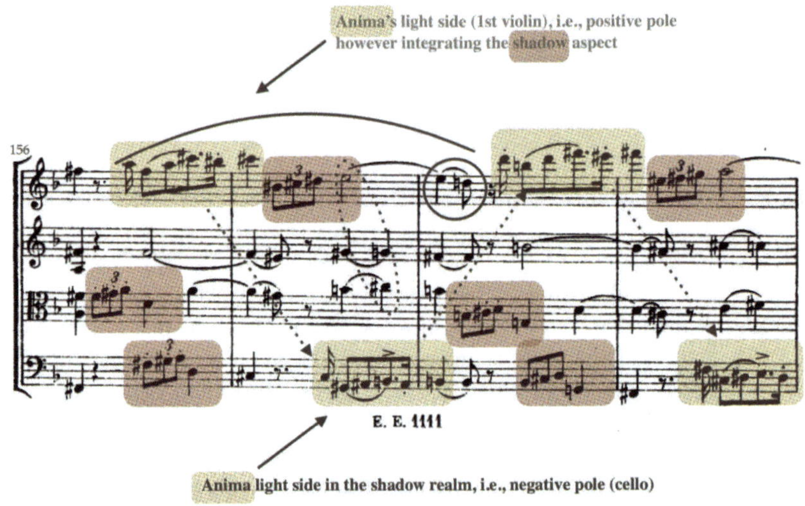

Fig. 16.19 The maiden motif incorporating the shadow aspect pointing to an attempt of integrating the shadow or to inflation. The suspensions create harmonic tension. (Sheet music excerpt taken and adapted from *IMSLP*)

Psychologically, the two identified musical sequences illustrate two inner battles whereby the two principles of the Anima, the *Eros* and *Thanatos*, as the positive and negative pole of the archetype, merge together. It is important to recall that these occurrences have an impact on the "I" and should ultimately be observed from this perspective. Transferring these events to the realm of the "I", this psychological situation can represent an inner conflict of an emotional-spiritual nature: if the violin line is understood as the "I", the musical phenomenon could also emphasize a psychological inflation taking place, which would correspond to the fact, identified above, that the "I" is immersed in the underworld (development-section), constantly being exposed to such a threat. This interpretation would explain the musical detail that the first violin integrates the destructive *Thanatos* energy, resulting in the noted psychic union of the two opposite poles. This phenomenon can be understood as having been an attempt of the "I" to integrate the shadow aspect of the Anima (negative pole, Fig. 16.19), whereby the "I" was not strong enough to differentiate ego-consciousness from unconscious structures, suffering such a fate (inflation). The elementary, negative pole of the archetype gains the upper hand. The fact that the maiden's motif begins to behave, psychologically speaking, like a shadow, subsequently sounding in the deep registers of the cello voice (m.157), confirms this interpretation.

The struggle character of this psychological process is expressed in the music through harmonic means by the above identified appoggiaturas and suspensions. Subsequently, the densification passages could possibly point to the dialectic process of juxtaposing contrasting elements. As part of the self-regulating mechanism of the psyche the densification of the heartbeat motif that is clearly tied here with the maiden's motif in mm.160–162, reinforces the *Eros* energy as the opposite force within being reactivated. In contrast, in mm.163–165 the shadow element is to be heard again, however, featuring a more threatening tone by taking its personified form of Thanatos. It simultaneously recalls the semantics of death, through the tone repetitions, and of fate, due to the rhythmic correspondence. In the meantime, the first violin, featuring the maiden's motif, utters her lamentation in a whispering tendency (***pp*** dynamics) and in a higher register—as if in a tone of reminiscence (mm.163–165, or mm.173–175).

How difficult this process is[119] can be perceived by the harmonic events and by the application of revealing compositional techniques in the following passage: in m.176 a sudden ninth chord imposes itself and a canonic imitation based on the maiden's motif follows during the next eight measures (mm.176–183). Finally, this section is closed once more with the densification of the heartbeat motif in mm.184–195. The mentioned ninth chord, which is known for its sombre nature, can be interpreted here as the "stroke of fate"[120]. This chord illustrates the dread towards the present reality of becoming one with the shadow (inflation).

[119] Jung has repeatedly described this process as a difficult task. Jacobi also underlined that the confrontation and integration of one's own shadow elements is characterized by great resistance and fear. Cf. Jacobi, Jolande. (2006). *Die Psychologie von C.G. Jung*. P.115. However, it is by means of projection that the shadow can be best confronted with and worked out. Cf. Ibid.

[120] Günter Pichler. In: Monsaingeon, Bruno. *The Alban Berg Documentary.* (1996). [Documentary/Masterclass]. Minuten: 18:10/22:07. (Trans. by the author). German expression: "Schicksalschläge".

The semantics behind the canonic imitation unveils the associated symbolic content: due to the relation with the ancient traditions of the *caccia*, the use of this compositional technique refers to the act of chasing. It musically depicts one voice being pursued by another[121]. This analogy is instructive for the purpose of reformulating the musical passage in Jungian terms: from one perspective, it can illustrate the dual nature of the "I". From a slightly different perspective, but not excluding the aforementioned hypothesis, this could also point to the chasing act of the shadow (Fig. 16.20). Applying a symbolic reading in regard to the instrument's range can be helpful here: if the two higher and the two lower voices would be seen as standing for consciousness, respectively, for the unconscious, then it becomes apparent that this process results in a play of the light and shadow elements, i.e., the dualistic juxtaposition of the opposite poles of the Anima. This is to be understood as a typical phenomenon that may occur due to the ambivalent nature of the psyche[122]. Transferred into the perspective of the "I", this passage may relate to the wrangling of the "I" in the face of the dualistic predisposition of the psyche.

After a brief pause, introducing a scenario change, a bridge section is to be noted which subsequently leads to the recapitulation. In this passage (mm.187–197) all three motifs are juxtaposed again, however, by different means: the pulsation of the heart, as the underlying life propulsive force, is to be heard as tone repetitions and as a *continuum* in the deep shadow registers of the cello (Fig. 16.20). The metamorphosed maiden's theme is interiorized in the voice of the viola, while the two violins, again in a *caccia* manner, introduce the triplet element (of the shadow) one after the other (Fig. 16.20). Musically, a well-defined ascending line is noticeable in the first and second violins. The first violin plays the following notes: A–B-flat–C-sharp–D–E (Fig. 16.20), which are subsequently repeated one octave higher and extended to A. The second violin precedes this line a fourth lower. The sequence of the last four notes leading to A is condensed in time, which conveys a (possibly forced or imposed) motion of striving forward (m.195–197). Alongside, the rhythmical diminution of the heartbeat motif

[121] Cf. von Fischer, Kurt. „Caccia". In: Sadie, Stanley. (1980). *The New Grove Dictionary of Music and Musicians. Vol. 3.* P.574–576.

[122] Similar descriptions of this phenomenology can be read in: Jacobi, Jolande. (2006). *Die Psychologie von C.G. Jung.* P.58–60. A similar phenomenon was identified in the fifth variation of the *Forellenquintett* (14).

in m. 197 emphasizes the energetic struggling upward movement. Depicting a gradually rising gesture, from the chthonic world of the unconscious towards the light of consciousness, this entire passage reflects the rising to the upperworld. This gesture might be termed as a resurgence attempt. However, the fact that the heartbeat motif is held in the lower register and the fate-death motif dominates in sound (violins) is an intriguing factor. Conceivably, this points still to an over-dominance of the shadow (Thanatos), due to the inflated state of the "I". With this long emergence process lasting for a total of eleven measures, the recapitulation is enforced—possibly by Thanatos.

Fig. 16.20 The rising towards the upper world (transition towards the recapitulation). (Sheet music excerpt taken and adapted from *IMSLP*)

Just as the development section of a sonata form can be understood as the moment of processing the musical and archetypal motifs, the recapitulation can be conceptualized as the return "home"—or psychologically speaking—to a previous reality or condition. In view of the important confrontations that the "I" had just undergone, it can be assumed that the "I" returns home transformed. However, the fact that Thanatos was the leading force, in this bridge passage, is alarming.

16.2.3 Recapitulation: A Regressive Return Home and the Imaginary Realm. The Process of Introverted Inflation as a Result of Regression

The recapitulation of this sonata form features some particularities. Coming right out of the depths of the soul (development), the fact that Schubert begins the recapitulation with the A2 motto instead of the main theme (alter-ego), can psychologically point to the overwhelming character of the personified shadow element, Thanatos. Consequently, this also suggests the lost condition of the "I". This corroborates that the "I", while in the underworld (development) has gone through a process of inflation (mm.156–175), ultimately bringing about a modification in the internal structure of the personality[123]. This indicates that the resurgence into the upperworld of consciousness was not fully achieved, in the sense that the "I" may not have emancipated itself from the overdominance of the shadow. This also explains the intriguing factor in the bridge section mentioned above.

Jung himself addresses this change of internal structure as a result of the phenomenon of possession[124]:

> "We now come to changes of personality which imply neither enlargement nor diminution but a structural alteration. One of the most important forms is the phenomenon of possession: some content, an idea or a part of the personality, obtains mastery of the individual for one reason or another. The contents which thus take possession appear as peculiar convictions, idiosyncrasies, stubborn plans, and so forth."[125].

Furthermore, Jung explained that there are different factors that can take hold of the "I", one of them being the "inferior function"[126], which relates to the shadow side of the personality. According to Jung, this process is seen as part of the subjective transformation:

> "The darkness which clings to every personality is the door into the unconscious and the gateway of dreams, from which those two twilight figures, the shadow and the anima, step into our nightly visions or, remaining invisible, take possession of our ego-consciousness."[127].

---

[123] This modification of personality is to be understood merely as part of a transformation process as Jung describes in Jung, Carl Gustav. (2011). *Four Archetypes.*

[124] Cf. Ibid. P.56.

[125] Ibid.

[126] Ibid. P.57.

[127] Ibid.

Some unpredicted elements in the musical score not only attract attention but also convey the different state of the "I" after having been exposed to the dreadful faces of its own shadow. Such moments are, for instance, the added m. 208, conveying a moment of suspension of the musical ductus, and the harmonic turn into the minor tone later in m.240. The harmonic path of the recapitulation slightly differs from the exposition and presents some unattended harmonic majorizations.

The F major melody, part of the A3 (m.52) is now to be heard in the "pure" D major key (m.209). This tonality may elicit a special pictorial effect on the listener here. In hermeneutic terms, this musical passage could be associated with a field of lilies[128] since it incorporates the essence of the positive Anima and expresses a glimmer of hope. This metaphor, which refers to the "lilies of the field" from the Gospel of Matthew 6:28, evokes a visual association that overarchingly transmits the feelings of tranquillity, faith and trust. Lastly, the importance of this amplification for this musical passage is the ground emotional expression linked to this image. Such interpretation is possible due to the transcendental nature of the D major tone colour, being the opposite pole of the death tonality, D minor[129]. Reinhard Amon for instance described D major as the tonality "meaning the transcendental, the connection between this world and the beyond"[130]. In a similar way, the A major section, termed here as synthesis (B3, cf. m.102), sounds now in the idyllic B-flat major tonality (m.260)—a key that also alludes to the beyond[131]. From these considerations, this phenomenon of sliding into the opposite, creating a parallel positive realm, might allude to the psychological process

[128] As already discussed in previous chapters (15), lilies are, in Jungian terms, to be associated with the spiritual component of the Anima. This hermeneutic observation results, on the one hand, from the application of the method of active imagination, which Jung himself used to approach the content of the unconscious and which is now applied to music analysis, and, on the other hand, from the amplification method to approach the symbol mentioned here (2.6).

[129] Cf. Böhm, Richard. (2006). *Symbolik und Rhetorik im Liedschaffen von Franz Schubert.*

[130] Amon, Reinhard. (2005). *Lexikon der Harmonielehre.* P. 289. A similar semantic is to be found in the lieder databases of Richard Böhm, who described D major as a key relating to the beyond, *inter alia.* Cf. Böhm, Richard. (2006). *Symbolik und Rhetorik im Liedschaffen von Franz Schubert.* P.54. The mentioned semantic can be substantiated by further analogies from the music literature: D major symbolises the resurrection in J.S. Bach's mass in B minor. The luminous hymnal element can be found furthermore in Beethoven's final movement of the ninth symphony (more precisely, after the fanfare passage).

[131] Cf. Böhm, Richard. (2006). *Symbolik und Rhetorik im Liedschaffen von Franz Schubert.* P.66. A further example in the musical literature stems from Schubert himself and his last piano sonata, which is widely considered as a swan song conveying a tone of acceptation of fate and, as the analysis chapter has shown, relating to the phenomenon of rapture (the beyond). See 18.

of "Enantiodromia"[132]. Combining these symbolic findings with the fact that the alter-ego theme is missing in this recapitulation, and that the changes in tonality point to luminous realms, may indicate that the "I" is "lost" in a fantasised world.

The recapitulation ends with a surprising cease of the musical ductus in m.297. The cello voice 'lonesome' holds the note D in its lower registers for two full measures. The coda section subsequently begins in a threatening undertone (m.299). The triplet element (*Thanatos*) continuously repeats itself for four bars until a ninth chord emerges (m.303). One measure later, the fate motif pronounces itself in the cello voice, softly, yet clearly due to the *staccato* articulation. In addition to the use of meaningful chords that lend to the passage a specific atmosphere, the accent markings of Schubert also underline the emotional condition of the "I": with the ***fp*** accent on the ninth chord the frightful emotions of the "I" in relation to his fate are emphasized. The imminent repetition of the same ninth chord in m. 307 has an even more frightening and ghostly effect by being accentuated within the ***ppp*** dynamics. After this terrifying moment in which time seems to standstill, the main theme is finally restated in m.311. However, the reappearance of the first theme so late in the storyline comes all the more unexpected. Psychologically observed, this could possibly point to a regressive return "home", to the original drama—the "I", having been overpowered by the shadow side at the beginning of the recapitulation, could not return "home" positively transformed, as it would have done if the first theme had been restated at the beginning of the recapitulation. The unfolding of the theme can bring some more insights.

As previously stated, the alter-ego theme is repeated here, not an octave higher as it happened in the exposition, but by a surprising sudden shift towards B-flat major in m. 316. Such uncommon structural-harmonic procedures are especially prone to background questionings of interpretative nature. To decipher the psychological meaning of such an act, the key characteristics can be instructive: B-flat major points to an idyllic world[133]. The fact that B-flat major coincides with the alter-ego theme can point to a creation of a parallel world with the

[132] Roesler, Christian. Personal communication between Christian Roesler and the author. Freiburg im Breisgau: June 18, 2024. The definition of Enantiodromia is to be found in: Cf. Jung, Carl Gustav. (2013). *Kleines Lexikon der Analytischen Psychologie.*

[133] This reading is based on the key characteristics of the B-flat tonality described in: Böhm, Richard. (2006). *Symbolik und Rhetorik im Liedschaffen von Franz Schubert.*

semantics of the B-flat major qualities, i.e., conveying a rather positive environment. This light modification may help the alter-ego theme to a final attempt to free itself from the constraints of the shadow aspect—an endeavour which dates back to its first appearance in the exposition, though, failed. Thus, the "I" tries once more to rise to consciousness and to deal with the two inner wills from the different B-flat major perspective. The mentioned third-step modulation shift (D minor to B-flat major), if contextualized in this thematic material (alter-ego), can confirm the sliding of the "I" into a parallel or fantasized world. These events increase the sense of expectation.

In mm.320–325, the shadow (*Thanatos*) takes once again possession of the "I", overflooding the "I". This is musically perceptible through the chaotic recurrence of the triplet motif cell, rising with each repetition in the upper register, and featuring the withheld energy of the tone repetitions (m.321 and m.323). This is then musically brought to a *climax* in mm.324–325. This newly reproduced inflation, in connection with the regression state, is pictorially rendered in the music in the following measures: the heartbeat motif, standing for the life energy (*Eros*), reappears in its augmented form and musically conveys the slowing down and the cessation of the heartbeat (m.326). This process is accentuated by Schubert's indication of a *ritardando* (m.327). At this point, the painful moment of the tragedy is emotionally intensified by the harmonies: Schubert places the Neapolitan sixth chord (Fig. 16.21) as the symbol of pain and death[134], with a ***fp*** in m. 328, immediately followed by an augmented sixth chord (m.329, Fig. 16.21). Susan Wollenberg interprets the Neapolitan episode in the coda section as a tonicized Neapolitan minor with an "extremely sinister"[135] effect, metaphorically associating as "glimpses [into] the abyss"[136]. The last reminiscences of the fate motif are to be heard in the shadowy bass until the long D minor chord settles

---

[134] The Neapolitan sixth harmony is seen as a "lamentation chord" ("Klageakkord") until the Romantic period inclusive. Cf. Kühn, Clemens. (2005). *Analyse lernen.* P. 76. Hartmut Krones described the Neapolitan sixth chord more emphatically as a harmonic musical rhetorical figure representing death or the longing for death. Cf. Krones, Hartmut. "Musik und Rhetorik". (2016). In: Laurenz Lütteken (Ed.). *MGG Online.* Subchapter: "Musikalisch-rhetorische Figuren—Harmonische Figuren".

[135] Wollenberg, Susan. (2011). *Schubert's Fingerprints: Studies in the Instrumental Works.* P. 40.

[136] Ibid. P.40.

into the total silence of death. Paraphrasing these musical events in C.G. Jung's words: the "I" undergoes a process of transformation, more specifically a symbolic death[137] (Fig. 16.21). The mentioned process psychologically points to a regressive movement. This musical phenomenon can be seen as a consequence of the late re-introduction of the main theme in the coda, instead of appearing in the recapitulation section. The regressive return "home" indicates that the "I" was not strong enough to deal with the confrontation with the chthonic structures (cf. IV 15). This movement expresses one phase of the individuation process.

When comparing this quartet movement with the earlier song settings, featuring a thematic parallel, it can be stated that Schubert does not end the movement in the major key, as he has done in the earlier song compositions. Instead, he returns to D minor, which archetypally underlines the phenomenon of the "I" being engulfed by the shadow. Psychologically analysed, this process corresponds here to an inflation combined with a regression, i.e., an intense state of introversion has been achieved, whereby death has been symbolically experienced by the "I"[138] (15). This latter process in fact occurred in *Die Schöne Müllerin,* which leads to the following reasoning: thematically, the first movement might refer to a continuation of the psychological challenges experienced in *Die Schöne Müllerin,* i.e., the attempt to incorporate the shadow element of the Anima. Both times the "I" had had the same fate of being engulfed. The fact that the quartet does not end here may point to an imminent development. The next movements can unravel further steps in this transformation process, which are of great importance for Schubert's creative development and individuation process.

---

[137] Congruently, in the rebirth myth, this is described by Jung as a "magical procedure". Jung, Carl Gustav. (2011). *Four Archetypes.* (Trans. by R.F.C. Hull). P. 62–63.

[138] Such a process of regression linked to an inflation can be read in: Cf. Jung, Carl Gustav. (2014). "Symbols of transformation". In: *The Collected Works of C.G. Jung. Vol. 5.* Part II. Chapter VII: "The Dual Mother".

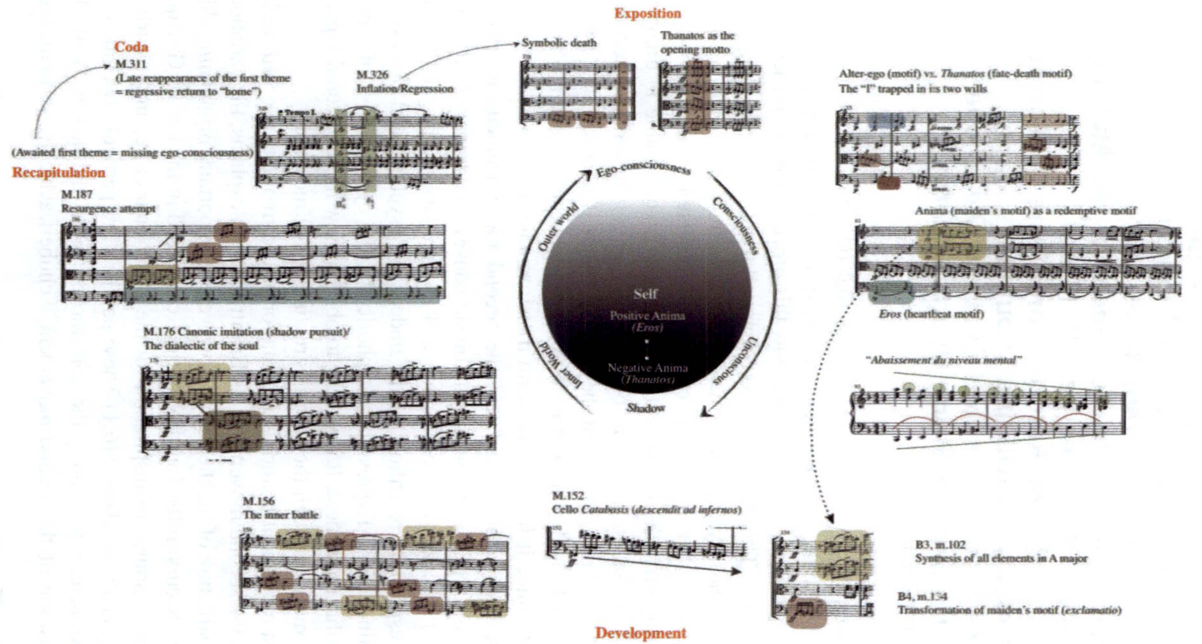

Fig. 16.21 Illustration of the psychic processes and archetypal stations of the first movement of the D minor String quartet D 810. (Sheet music excerpt taken and adapted from *IMSLP*)

16.3 A Brief Diachronic Overview of the Subsequent Movements: The Introverted Condition of the "I" and the Inner Metamorphoses (Second Movement)—the Reinforcement of the Alter-ego and the Birth of the new "I" (Third Movement)—the Resurrection of the "I" (Fourth Movement). Concluding Thoughts on the Interconnections Between *Die Schöne Müllerin* and the String Quartet *Death and the Maiden*

In view of the dramatic psychological process that occurred by the end of the first movement, where the "I" has entered a state of meaningful introversion, it is of great psychological interest to examine how this process will unfold across the following movements. This diachronic overview will focus on the most important aspects relevant to the psychological process. As previously explained, it is necessary to limit the number of musical details to be presented; the intention rather lies in highlighting only the fundamental points in order to be able to draw the archetypal parallels that are essential for the analytical conclusion. The recourse to direct metaphorical descriptions of the musical events is consequently a must. Thereby, the second movement will be highlighted to a greater extent than the other movements since it features the main transformation processes.

In general terms it can be said that the second movement characterizes a further typical aspect of Romanticism: the music conveys the (inner) landscapes, which are linked to space-time perception and to light-shadow play (4.3). The latter aspect is especially revealing for the underlying psychological process, as it will be explained later. Expressed metaphorically, the cyclical laws of nature can be heard in this movement. It is worthy to observe how these pictorial aspects are rendered in music through the formal structure of the movement.

After the first movement featuring a sonata form, a form of a theme with variations follows in the second movement. As Brigitte Massin explains, the variations retain the main structure of the theme[139]. However, an important, brightening shift to the major key occurs in the fourth variation, composed in the key of G major. The main (motivic) source of inspiration for the string quartet lies in the earlier-composed songs analysed above (16.1) These parallels are particularly evident in the second movement, representing the core movement of the quartet. With the harmonic disposition of the second movement, Schubert achieves an immediate

[139] Cf. Massin, Brigitte. (1977). *Franz Schubert.* P.1062.

tonal reference with the "Erlkönig" lied insofar the tonality chosen here is G minor[140]—the fundamental key of the setting of Goethe's ballad. In terms of the motivic level, it is the lied "Death and the maiden" that remains the main reference. As previously seen, the motivic core of the lied D 531 is retaken here in its original form and appears as "the choral [theme] of Death"[141]. The reference is made to the second stanza of the poem, featuring the bone-man's verses, i.e., death is placed in the foreground. Apart from the initial thematic material, the major ending of the song is to be heard in the theme's conclusion (mm.23–24), pointing to the laws of nature, i.e., to the cycle of nature's "reawakening". Referring to Persephone's myth, this possibly alludes to the arrival of spring. After the theme's presentation, a total of five variations will follow. The variations are conceived in such a way that the above-mentioned light-shadow play is to be noted in the juxtaposition of the variations. This reveals what in psychological terms would be termed as a dialectic process.

Still in regard to the theme's presentation, the archetypal shadow element, previously attributed to the musical tone repetitions, is to be found in the outer voices of the main theme (first violin and cello). Thereby, the G minor tone colour emphasizes the predominance of death[142]. Its dark tone colour is especially given by the "Erlkönig" tonal reference. These monotonous voices reframe the melodic line, which in contrast is to be found immersed in the inner voices (second violin and viola) at the very opening of the movement. Characteristic is again the double almost identical melodic line of both inner voices. From these analytical observations it becomes psychologically apparent how the "I" has been engulfed by the shadow (Thanatos), remaining now in its introverted condition for the theme's presentation. The observation of the double line substantiates the earlier attribution of this musical motif to the archetypal equivalent of the doppelgänger or the alter-ego. The fact that the boundaries between the Thanatos motif and the alter-ego motif are smooth, marked by an osmotic interchange of roles, only emphasizes the inflated state identified above. This interchange of roles could be described as an identification with Thanatos, perceivable in m.2.

---

[140] Cf. Ibid. P.1061.

[141] Ibid. P.1062. (Trans. by the author). French expression: "le choral de la Mort". Furthermore, Massin draws a parallel to the concurrent written quartet in A minor and the motivic interrelationship of the motifs inherent in both *andantes* of D 804 and D 810. Cf. Ibid.

[142] Cf. Böhm, Richard. (2006). *Symbolik und Rhetorik im Liedschaffen von Franz Schubert.* P.84–85.

Subsequently, while the thematic cell continues camouflaged in the inner voices of variation I (m.25), it coincidingly embodies the tremolo element (*Thanatos*) which functions as a madrigalism—rephrased psychologically, it may convey the fearful state of the "I", that is still possessed by Thanatos. Meanwhile, the shattered melodic line of the first violin is in the foreground. Characterized by a shortness of breath and a light *staccato* line it strongly recalls the maiden's breathlessness in the song. This is especially emphasized by the pauses placed on the strong beats of the measures. The cello part gives the pulsation of the dactylic pavane rhythm throughout the entire variation. Due to these observations, this first variation remains rather in the shadow realm.

Variation II conveys a great horizontal vastness and a sense of timelessness. This is especially rendered by the long cello line as the leading voice. Having surrendered the *pizz.* and passing to a *con arco* playing, the cello's lyric melody is underlined by a regular periodic phrase construction (made of 4 + 4 bars). The rhythmic heartbeat motif is discretely introduced in variation II (m.49) and presented in the second violin, bringing more inner movement (*Eros*). Additionally, the life energy that is to be sensed is supported by the sixteenth notes of the first violin, which, even though they still feature a shortness of breath due to the pauses, they gradually allow for a detachment from the previously installed monotony (tone repetitions of the theme and tremolo of the first variation). The dactylic pavane rhythm is featured in the melody (cello) and, in a light *staccato* manner, in the viola. Metaphorically described, this variation conveys a light aspect and the cyclical laws of nature, in that it appeals to the life element and to the renewal of energies. The latter is particularly perceptible due to the flowing sixteenth notes, recalling associations with the water.

A first major contrast is given by variation III, which returns to the shadow realm. Characterized by the synchronized rhythmic cell featuring the dactyl rhythm in diminution form, the original pavane dance rhythm changes in semantics. In hermeneutic terms it could be interpreted as expressing a chthonic energy and the intransigence of death (during the first four measures, the outer voices are congruently marked by tone repetitions). In this regard, Brigitte Massin draws a parallel, evoking the rhythm from the final dance of *Rosamunde*'s ballet, describing it, however, as more grotesque, cruel, desperate and violent[143]. This

[143] Cf. Massin, Brigitte. (1977). *Franz Schubert.* P.1063.

dynamism inherent here is especially perceivable due to the energetic *sforzatti* placed on each beat within a *ff* dynamic. An atmospheric counterpoint is given by the fragile line that is suddenly introduced in the first violin (m.77). Once again, metaphorically speaking, it is as if another light exposure sets in within a shadowy yet wide landscape, almost alluding to a world in the beyond. Eventually, this melody dissolves in sweet pain with the top note G (m.80). Another antagonistic element to acknowledge in this passage (mm.77–80) is the contrast of the strict dactyl, providing for a clear sense of time, against the long-held note of the violin, which conveys the wideness of the landscape (or spacelessness) and timelessness. The second part of this variation (m.81f.) is characterized by a telluric expression. There are two elements which are noteworthy: on the one hand, there are the inner voices, which are composed in a *caccia* manner, featuring the imitation technique—translated into psychological terms, it is possible again to speak of a shadow pursuit. On the other hand, the outbursts that are to be observed, first in the violin, then in the cello (as a response) might musically depict an inner emotional laceration. This latter association is especially due to the second element of this cell, i.e., the large broken chords placed on the second, respectively, first main beat. The torn emotions of the "I" come to the foreground together with the wild *Thanatos* (tone repetitions and imitations). The variation ends with a *crescendo* (mm.93–96). Thereby, the top note becomes increasingly higher until it reaches the top note G again.

The second major contrast is to be noted with the beginning of variation IV. This change is perceptible on various musical levels and is psychologically equivalent to an important inner transformation that takes place here. The majorization of the tonality is of great importance for the overall mood that is being transmitted. According to Böhm, G major is associated with nature and idyll[144]. Additional examples in Schubert's musical repertoire, suggest a further possible association: from *Die Schöne Müllerin*, this tonality is symbolically linked to the brooklet and archetypally associated with the Great Mother (15). The musical key characteristics and the symbolic aspects of the brooklet are to be found in the variation in question. This specifically refers to the flowing river and the

[144] Cf. Böhm, Richard. (2006). *Symbolik und Rhetorik im Liedschaffen von Franz Schubert.* P.51–52.

symbolic healing properties of water[145]. Musically, these aspects can be found in the calmly running triplets of the first violin, often embellished through brief mordents. The harmonic major tone quality gives the variation its overall light property. In addition, the "innocent" sounding ornaments are also responsible for creating a childlike atmosphere. These musical facts alongside the melodic material indicate the emergence of a further archetype.

The melody, being a variation of the theme, is derived from the alter-ego motif. Consequently, the melody is semantically tied with the "I". Taking into consideration the psychological and symbolic context in which it is embedded, it is as if the Great Mother is incubating an inner hero that is yet to be born—after all, the "I" is in an introverted state[146]. Therefore, the child archetype (Fig. 16.22) is suggested here, however, still in an abstract form, i.e., as a mere overall atmosphere. According to C.G. Jung and Erich Neumann, the archetype of the Anima and the Great Mother are structurally interconnected by the overarching feminine principle[147]. The symbolic death attributed to the introverted state transpires the related regressive energy attributed to the negative pole of the Great Mother. On the other hand, the latter as the "Great Round" is responsible for nurturing and providing healing[148]. In turn, the child archetype—especially in the Christian sense—appears in moments of significant transformation processes, having an effect of conveying new hope, as Christian Roesler's findings in regard to dream analysis suggest[149].

---

[145] These properties have been discussed in 15.

[146] Being motivically still close to its original form, the melody transmits the minor transformations that the "I" undergoes while in an introverted state. This is musically congruent with the variation genre.

[147] For C.G. Jung's reference: Cf. Jung, Carl Gustav. (2020). *Archetypen. Urbilder und Wirkkräfte des Kollektiven Unbewussten.* For Neumann: Cf. Neumann, Erich. (2021). *Die Große Mutter.*

[148] For this description of the Great Mother see Neumann's work: Cf. Ibid.

[149] Cf. Roesler, Christian. (2022). *Development of a Reconceptualization of Archetype Theory.* Report to the IAAP. P. 49.

Fig. 16.22 C.G. Jung. "Phanes I". (1917). Kat.-Nr. 50. [Gouache and Goldbronze on cardboard]. Privat Collection. Digitized version of the original, kindly provided by Carl C. Jung, managing director of the Foundation of the Works of C.G. Jung. (© 2007 Stiftung der Werke von C.G. Jung, Zürich)

It is a coincidence that the musical events are congruent with the explained psychological process. Such a process of transformation is to be found in many myths. In C.G. Jung's description, when the "I" has achieved such a profound introverted state, an inner transformation takes place, whereupon a new hero is being created[150]. The child archetype points to an imminent transformation

[150] One example is Jung's analysis of the Hiawatha's myth. Cf. Jung, Carl Gustav. (2014). "Symbols of transformation". In: *The Collected Works of C.G. Jung. Vol. 5.* Part II. Chapter VII: "The Dual Mother". Similarly, Neumann describes: "[...] where the elementary character is dominant, all processes of change still take place within the unconscious [...]". Neumann, Erich. (2015). *The Great Mother.* (Trans. by Ralph Manheim). P.30.

process, i.e., points to the future[151]. Being in such a condition, the “I” has to emancipate itself from the Great Mother[152]. Consequently, the “I” has then to undergo a new (dragon) battle, that is played in the inner realm this time, since it is still in the introverted state[153]. If the dragon battle does not succeed, the “I” returns to a regressive state, i.e., undergoes a symbolic death anew. If the dragon battle is successful, then a rebirth comes about. Coincidentally, such an archetypal station can be detected in the music of the following fifth variation.

The beginning of the fifth variation reflects the imminent transformation that will occur. A cloudiness is to be initially perceived through the return to the minor tonality and the reappearance of the tremolando motifs, the octaviated and alternating tone repetitions. As an analogy with the aforementioned archetypal station, this would correspond to the shadow (*Thanatos*) that is reactivated and that needs to be fought and symbolically “killed”. A subsequent *catabasis* figure is to be noted in the cello (mm.129–131), which is then repeated in a slightly varied way in mm.133–134. From the point of view of the psychological process, these descents mark an important inner movement—the descent into the realm of Hades—which lead to a final wrangling of the “I” with the inner demons. Musically, it is striking that the cello part in mm.137–140 acts quite independently in relation to the other voices of the quartet, standing out due to the great diastematics featured. This self-sufficient or autonomous and spontaneous attitude might psychologically suggest the power of the shadow and the danger of a new inflation. This cello-inflation, pointing to the dragon battle itself, can have two ways out: either the “I” is definitely engulfed by it or the “I” raises ego-consciousness and succeeds. To briefly look at the end of this movement can be revealing in this regard.

The immediate appeasement occurring in the music after the cello-inflation suggests an imminent psychological turning point of a positive nature: the “I” seems to have been able to integrate and surpass the struggles[154]. Analysing the musical scores from mm.153 also speak in favour of this reading: while the tone repetitions are enclosed in the inner voice (viola), the fact that the alter-ego motif

---

[151] Roesler, Christian. Personal communication between Christian Roesler and the author. Freiburg im Breisgau: June 18, 2024.

[152] Ibid.

[153] Cf. Jung, Carl Gustav. (2014). “Symbols of transformation”. In: *The Collected Works of C.G. Jung. Vol. 5.* Part II. Chapter VII: “The Dual Mother”.

[154] Congruently, Massin speaks of a “conquered peace”, however she interprets this as a sign of the mortal peace or the sleep of the dead. Cf. Massin, Brigitte. (1977). *Franz Schubert.* P.1063. (Trans. by the author). French expression: “[…] une paix durement conquise”. This can however be differently interpreted, as it will be explained.

is featured in the violins (standing, as previously seen, for the light of consciousness), indicate how the "I" has gained the upper hand, i.e., ego-consciousness. Although Schubert retakes the main theme to end this variation, it is restated in the major tonality (mm.162–172). The major ending lends this passage a narrative undertone—reminiscent of an *illud tempus* quality. This analytical perspective thus differs significantly from traditional perspectives or interpretations. For instance, the tone repetitions in mm.153–158, conveying a special perception of time, are often interpreted as the fateful death condition[155]. However, taking into consideration the archetypal findings and the underlying psychic processes, the death semantics of the tone repetitions are more likely to be related here with the shadow itself that has been overcome (present in an inner voice) and not necessarily with the death of the "I". Ultimately, this will lead to an inner transformation of great psychological significance: after the inner transformation has taken place and the "I" has succeeded in integrating the inner demons, the birth of the new "I" is expected (Fig. 16.23).

If the second movement is to be described with the keywords of introversion and metamorphoses, the third movement can be termed the reinforcement and the birth of the new "I" (Fig. 16.24). A closer examination of the main theme can be helpful here to understand the reasons behind this conceptualization. The opening of the *Scherzo* is characterized by two musical elements: (i) the "new" theme featured as an upbeat and in the two upper voices, and (ii) a descending line of long held notes, marked by *fz* in the lower voices, beginning on a first beat. However, when examining the theme more carefully, it becomes clear how familiar it actually is. The alter-ego motif, as part of the main themes presented in the first and second movement, is presented here as part of a new theme, yet in its retrograde inversion form; it clearly illustrates the transformation of the alter-ego motif (Fig. 16.24). This fact substantiates the psychological analysis and archetypal stations that have been analysed previously. The *f* dynamics and the accent on the first anacrusis note only emphasize the powerful character of the newborn "I". Its dominance is such that it does not allow itself to become unsettled by the menacing descending line (shadow) of the viola and cello part. On the contrary, it seems to play with it: the grace notes in mm.13–18 lend a light dance-like character, which return time and again, e.g., mm.33–38. The Trio section is revealing, especially due the choice of tonality. D major, being the key

[155] Cf. Monsaingeon, Bruno. *The Alban Berg Documentary.* (1996). [Documentary/Masterclass].

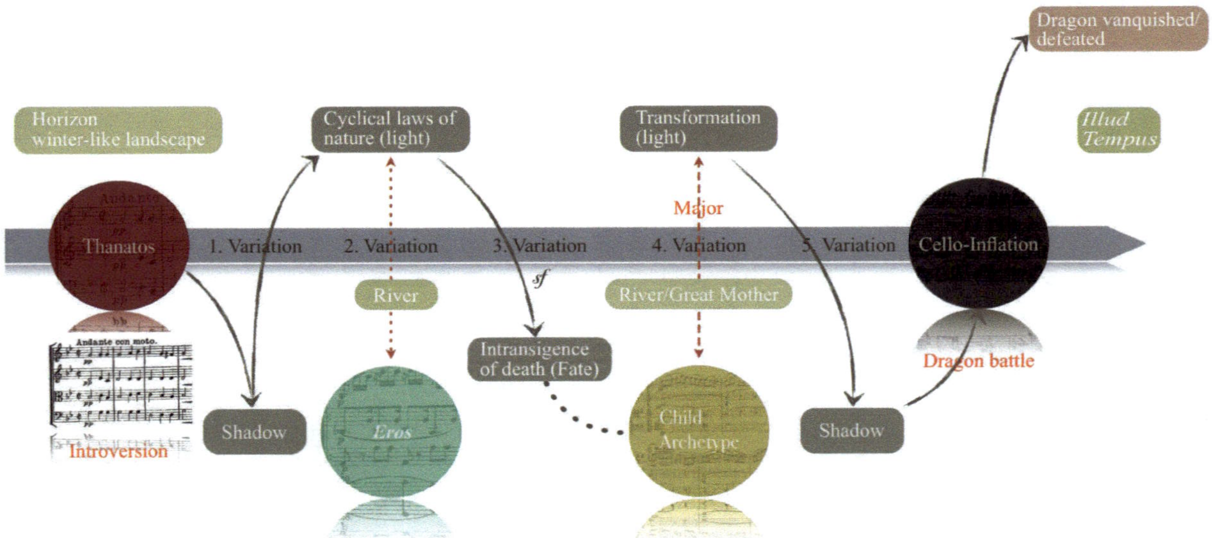

Fig. 16.23 Light-shadow play as a dialectic process in the second movement. The transformation process and the emerging of the child archetype. Dragon battle vanquished. (Sheet music excerpt taken and adapted from *IMSLP*)

of triumph and resurrection[156], can confirm the triumphal victory of the "I" and possibly foretell the moment of transcendence.

The last movement, being a tarantella, alludes to the folk traditional concept of the *danse macabre*. Written in the typical 6/8 measure, the rhythmic cell from which the movement lives is a quaver followed by a quarter note. Embedded in a *Presto* movement and beginning in anacrusis, this death dance motif (tarantella rhythm) is related to the heartbeat motif. This means that *Eros* and *Thanatos* are in fact united (Fig. 16.24); this fact speaks for a transcendental view of death in general, which is congruent with the folk traditional perspective of the death dance. If the focus is now turned to the secondary theme of this movement (m.88), a resemblance with the original alter-ego theme can be noted. However, by comparison, it is possible to confirm a major metamorphosis or even a transmutation of the same: the intervals between the notes of the theme become bigger (Fig. 16.24). Also, from the rhythmic perspective there is a further major variation to be noticed: the dactyl ductus has been inverted, transmuting itself into a baccheos. The latter is emphasized not only by the fact that all the voices are synchronized, declaiming this "new" theme in the *ff* dynamics, but also by the accents and the *con forza* marking. With regard to the psychological interpretation given, the motivic transmutation suggests a further form of the rebirth myth, namely resurrection:

> "3. Resurrection. This means a re-establishment of human existence after death. A new element enters here: that of the change, transmutation, or transformation of one's being. [...] the resurrection of the dead is the raising up of the *corpus glorificationis*, the 'subtle body' [...]"[157].

This suggests the importance of understanding these psychological phenomena from a broader perspective and not isolating the fourth movement, i.e., in respect to the psychological event of the end of the first movement, where a symbolic death has occurred. After having undergone an inner transformation (second movement), the "I" is reborn (third movement) and is now able to resurrect in the world of the living again (fourth movement), i.e., the "I" is a new hero.

---

[156] As previously explained through the key characteristics and further examples from the musical repertoire, D major might have been appealing for its the semantics of victory, triumph and resurrection. Cf. Böhm, Richard. (2006). *Symbolik und Rhetorik im Liedschaffen von Franz Schubert.*

[157] Jung, Carl Gustav. (2011). *Four Archetypes.* (Trans. by R.F.C. Hull). P.48.

Returning to a musical observation: the secondary theme will transform itself again some measures later. This new variation of the alter-ego theme reveals great similarities to one particular passage of the "Erlkönig" lied and which invokes the child's appeal and Erlking's verses of Goethe's ballad:

[Vater]:
"Mein Sohn, was birgst du so bang dein Gesicht? –
[Kind]
Siehst, Vater, du den Erlkönig nicht?
Den Erlenkönig, mit Kron und Schweif? –
[Vater]
Mein Sohn, es ist ein Nebelstreif. –
[Erlkönig]
‚Du liebes Kind, komm, geh mit mir!
Gar schöne Spiele spiel ich mit dir;
Manch bunte Blumen sind an dem Strand,
Meine Mutter hat manch gülden Gewand'."[158].

[Father]:
"My son, why hide thou thy face so dauntingly? –
[Child]
Father, do thou not see, the Alder King?
The Alder King, with court and crown?
[Father]
My son, it is a wisp of mist.
[Erlking]
Thou lovely child, come, come with me!
Then jolly plays will I play with thee;
Many colourful flowers, there, on the shore they are;
Many golden garments does my mother own."[159].

The interconnection with this musical reference is particularly perceptible in the B-flat pedal passage (mm.133–149)[160]. Psychologically, the intriguing point still lies in the fact that this quotation refers to the verses of "Erlkönig" itself: "Thou lovely child, come, come with me" ("Du liebes Kind, komm, geh mit mir"). This means that the alter-ego theme embodies the "Erlkönig" here. In view of the complexity of a psychological or hermeneutic interpretation of this passage, no definite answer can be given as to this specific passage and citation: the reason why Schubert recalls the Erlking at this point of the psychological transformation remains an enigma. Hypothetically, it could be that death is addressed here as an inner call—an inner call that the "I" might still hear as an inner resonance or simply as a reminiscence of something that has passed; it can also be that this cross-reference revived further associations with the child archetype, this time referring to the new child from the second variation. Possibly, the ending of the movement could shed some light on this open question.

158 Goethe, Wolfgang. (1782). „Der Erlkönig". The Project Gutenberg.

159 Ibid. (Trans. by the author).

160 This musical finding relating the B-flat pedal passage of the fourth movement with the "Erlkönig" song has already been previously acknowledged by musicologists, namely by Brigitte Massin. Cf. Massin, Brigitte. (1977). *Franz Schubert.* P. 1064.

Apart from recurring canonic imitations (e.g., mm.17–21 or mm.33–38), this rondo-sonata movement is especially marked by densifications in rhythm and strikingly increasing *unisono* passages throughout the movement. The latter gain importance especially in the coda section (*Prestissimo* m.707). The movement eventually ends with a final ascending line and *fff* chords (mm.748–754). The quartet ends with an apotheotic rising movement. This gesture suggests the resurrection of the soul, which would definitely confirm the successful transformation process and the consequent "enlargement of the personality"[161]. Thus, after experiencing a regression linked with an inflation in the first movement, the second movement represents the introversion state of the "I" in a moment of incubation, which presupposed an inner transformation. The full metamorphosis is then heard in the third movement with the birth of the new "I". Ultimately, the string quartet psychologically renders another aspect of the rebirth myth, namely the transcendence of the "I" in the fourth movement. Recalling the analogy between death and the negative aspect of the Anima, respectively of the Great Mother, this latter fact could suggest the complete integration of the Anima or the feminine principle *per se*, achieved in the last movement. A death dance incorporates both poles of the archetype, whereby the transcendent aspect symbolically predominates. Such an integration can be crucial for the individuation process and above all for the development of the creative process of Schubert. Congruently, in relation to the transformative character (positive pole) of the Anima, Neumann writes:

> "The anima is the vehicle par excellence of the transformative character. It is the mover, the instigator of change, whose fascination drives, lures, and encourages the male to all the adventures of the soul and spirit, of action and creation in the inner and the outward world."[162].

It can be advantageous to consider this quartet in comparison with past as well as future compositions to eventually discern better the validity of the novel interpretation presented here.

If these thoughts were now to be contextualized in the development of Schubert's musical language over the years, a revealing outcome arises. Schubert's desire to accomplish a great symphony may be a direct result of the experienced archetypal process that was found in the D minor string quartet D 810.

[161] Jung, Carl Gustav. (2011). *Four Archetypes*. (Trans. by R.F.C. Hull). P.54.

[162] Neumann, Erich. (2015). *The Great Mother.* (Trans. by Ralph Manheim). P. 33.

According to Jungian concepts, when the Anima is integrated it provides for a great creative power and source of inspiration. When related to previous works, such a liberation as achieved herein was marked by several previous attempts and accompanied by other processes of psychological transformations. A similar process was notably initiated in *Die Schöne Müllerin.* Like in *Die Schöne Müllerin,* a process of transformation is to be recognized in the D minor string quartet D 810. The specific phenomenon inherent in both compositions is called by Jung a "magical procedure" in which the "I" "[...] has to pass through a symbolic death [...]"[163]. While the mentioned song cycle ended with the "I" being in this state, the string quartet only closed its first movement in such a condition, allowing an expected development.

At the microlevel of the analysis, further connecting musical and symbolic elements that were found in both compositions were also revealing in this respect. These include the role of the G major tonality. As previously seen, G major in *Die Schöne Müllerin* is associated with the brooklet, accordingly, bearing the symbolic meaning of water as a healing agent and associated with the Great Mother archetype. In fact, Schubert precisely used the G major key in the string quartet as the tonality for the only major variation of the second movement—the variation that corresponds to an inner transformation of the "I". If death was previously attributed to the triplets, here the latter rather relates to the water motif, bringing about healing[164]. In this sense, a further connection with the Great Mother archetype was possible. Moreover, this variation musically transmitted a general innocence and a childlike ambiance, alluding archetypally to the child archetype. As already explained, this archetype emerges in moments of imminent transformations[165]. However, the fact that the "I" still was in an introverted condition, this archetype was conveyed in its more abstract form, i.e., in the form of an overall atmosphere. To describe this process in symbolic terms, the transformation was still occurring in the womb of the mother. After the inner transformation, it affirmed itself transformed in the third movement (retrograde inversion form) and ultimately, transmuted rhythmically and in terms of intervals in the fourth movement (secondary theme). Across these transformations and transmutations the child archetype is musically linked to the alter-ego theme, which underlines

163 Jung, Carl Gustav. (2011). *Four Archetypes.* (Trans. by R.F.C. Hull). P.63.

164 This reflection also explains, musically, the two antagonistic poles of a same archetype or archetypal principle, i.e., the one being destructive and the other bringing healing.

165 Cf. Roesler, Christian. (2022). *Development of a Reconceptualization of Archetype Theory.* Report to the IAAP. P. 49.

the need of understanding this theme in relation to the lyrical "I" of Schubert himself, i.e., reflecting the psychic processes underneath his creative act.

To return concludingly to the two Schubert letter excerpts cited at the beginning of the chapter, Schubert composed both quartets, the *Rosamunde* and the *Death and the Maiden*, with a larger aim in mind—the one to "pave [his] way to the grand symphony"[166]. In the second excerpt cited above, Schubert expressed how he attempted "to embellish as much as possible"[167] "the no longer […] happy time […] with [his] imagination."[168]. The latter suggests that he processed his struggles through working, i.e., through the act of creation, which means that the psychic processes identified in the analysis of the string quartet were possibly inner lived experiences of Schubert himself. These inner transformations of the (new born) "I" might possibly have allowed Schubert to undergo an important development of his musical language, ultimately marking the leap towards the *Great* C major symphony that he started to compose one year later.

There are naturally further compositions in between the D minor string quartet and the C major symphony, which have certainly contributed to the latter achievement as well or to a better maturation of the lived experiences reflected in the D minor string quartet. Elizabeth Norman McKay for instance drew parallels between the C major symphony and the C major *Reliquie* piano sonata D 840, especially with regard to the linear progressive form, responsible for the narrative ductus of both works[169]. McKay also pointed out that these traits are especially to be noted in compositions after 1825[170]. In contrast, Hinrichsen already observed a stylistic shift in "the works composed after the 'break' of 1824"[171]. These statements once again underline the importance of the psychological processes experienced in the D minor string quartet, which were certainly developed further in other works. These considerations are congruent with the majority of the

166 Schubert, Franz: Letter to Leopold Kupelwieser. (31.03.1824). In: Deutsch, Otto Erich. (1964). *Schubert—Die Dokumente seines Lebens.* P. 235. (Trans. by the author).

167 Schubert, Franz: Letter to his brother Ferdinand. (18.07.1824). In: Deutsch, Otto Erich. (1964). *Schubert—Die Dokumente seines Lebens.* P. 250.

168 Ibid. (Trans. by author).

169 Cf. McKay, Elizabeth Norman: "Franz Schubert: A Biography". (1996). Cited after: Gardner, Cameron. "(Re-)Theorising Schubert's 'Reliquie'. Precedents, the ‚Great' Symphony, and Narrative.". In: Bodley, Lorraine Byrne. Horton, Julia. (2016). *Rethinking Schubert".* P.147–172.

170 Cf. Ibid. P.147.

171 Cf. Hinrichsen, Hans-Joachim: „Is There a Late Style in Schubert's Œuvre?". In: Ibid. P.23.

analytical findings in this string quartet analysis: for an inner change of being can naturally generate a change of the musical language.

In this context, Robert Schumann's lines about the C major symphony are revealing. The "heavenly lengths"[172], acknowledged in the C major symphony, result from an idiosyncratic cyclic formal construction[173], which is related to Schubert's tendency to circle around (*circulatio*), and which also indicates how the themes are motivically interwoven throughout the entire symphony[174]. Such a unity has already been worked out *inter alia* in the *Forellenquintett, Wandererfantasie* and in the string quartet *Der Tod und das Mädchen.* It can be fruitful to reconsider another of Schumann's comments on this symphony, in order to point to a final psychological observation: the "[...] never straying too far from the center, always returning to it"[175]. Psychologically, these lines would be read as the turn and return towards the center as the Self (12). Finally, this trait marks Schubert's own language and reaches its apogee in this composition.

[172] Schumann, Robert. (1854). *Gesammelte Schriften über Musik und Musiker. Vol. 3.* P. 201. German expression: "himmlische Länge" (12.).

[173] Cf. Sourtzi, Maria. (2014). *Franz Schuberts Grosse C-Dur Symphonie D 944.*

[174] Cf. Ibid.

[175] Schumann, Robert. (1854). *Gesammelte Schriften über Musik und Musiker. Vol. 3.* P.202. (Trans. by the author). German expression: „[...] niergends zu weit vom Mittelpunkt wegführend, immer wieder zu ihm zurückkehrend.".

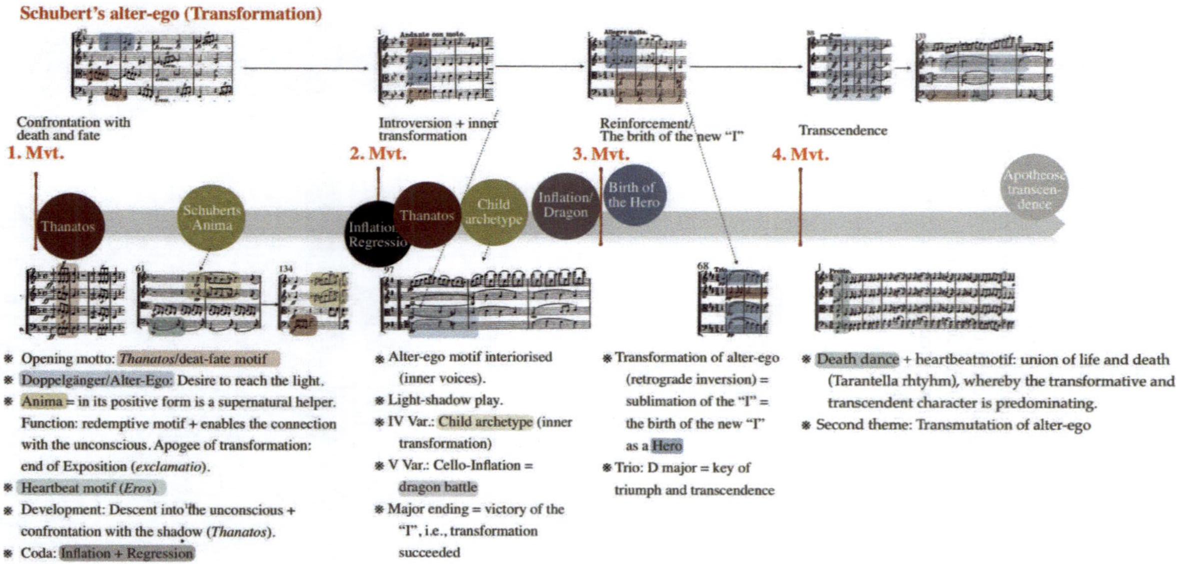

Fig. 16.24 Diachronic overview on the string quartet and the inner transformations. The rebirth myth: Going through a symbolic death, rebirth and transcendence. (Sheet music excerpt taken and adapted from *IMSLP*)

The "Cultural Unconscious" in Schubert's A Major Sonata D 959, II Movement: "The Sleep of Reason Produces Monsters"

17

"The purpose of individuation is now none other than to free the Self from the false shells of the Persona, on the one hand, and from the suggestive power of unconscious images, on the other."[1].

---

[1] Jung, Carl Gustav. (2023). *Die Beziehung zwischen dem Ich und dem Unbewussten.* P. 68. (Trans. by the author). German expression: "Der Zweck der Individuation ist nun kein anderer, als das Selbst aus den falschen Hüllen der Persona einerseits und der Suggestivgewalt unbewusster Bilder andererseits zu befreien.".

The music analytical and psychological findings developed in this chapter were presented by the author herself in public for the first time under the title "'(Wiener) Weltschmerz'—Schuberts A-Dur Klaviersonate D 959, 2. Satz. Eine formale und hermeneutische Analyse mit der Archetypenlehre von C.G. Jung" in the form of a one-and-a-half hour and slide-assisted lecture in the frame of a music analysis seminar at the University Mozarteum, Salzburg (Mai 4th, 2023), under the supervision of Barbara Dobretsberger. In addition, the topic was presented in: Dill, Leonor. (2024, February 22nd). "Dances as Masked Confessions—The Cultural Unconscious Reflected in Schubert's idiom, Exemplified by the A-major Piano Sonata D 959, 2nd Movement". [Conference Abstract and Presentation].

L. Dill, *Schubert's Metamorphoses*,
https://doi.org/10.1007/978-3-662-73476-6_17

The year of 1828 was particularly characterized as having been a time of great creative production. Schubert himself confessed his zealous urge to achieve artistic excellence[2]. The A major Sonata was composed as part of the piano trilogy D 958–960, which was originally dedicated to the pianist and composer Johann Nepomuk Hummel. That Schubert had the concept of a trilogy in mind is explicable due to the heading present in the manuscript of the B-flat major sonata, marked by the title "3. Sonata"[3]. While the exact date of origin remained for a long time questionable, the possibility that the entire trilogy was composed between the months of May until September 1828 is nowadays defended[4]; these sonatas are therefore considered as being the last compositions of Schubert, along with the String Quintet D 956. The first sonata, the C minor sonata D 958, is, according to source studies (including the sketches), dated back to the month of May (shortly after the composition of the E-flat minor piece of the *Drei Klavierstücke* D 946)[5], while both the A major and B-flat major sonata seem to have concurrent origins within the period of June to August (the fair copy is attributed to the month of September)[6]. This fact means that all three sonatas have been conceptualized as a unity and feature the symbolism of the number three, which had already fascinated other composers prior to Schubert[7]. As such, they present themes and motifs that are linked to each other and that undergo a transformation. This transformation of motifs was realized by the so-called motif-metamorphose technic, to which Arthur Godel[8] has already pointed out. From the interpreter's

---

[2] The author is specifically referring to the following words Schubert expressed: "I only mention these latter compositions so that you are familiar with my striving for the highest in art.". Schubert, Franz: Letter to B. Schotts Söhne. (21.02.1828). In: Deutsch, Otto Erich. (1964). *Schubert—Die Dokumente seines Lebens.* P. 495. (Trans. by the author). German expression: "Diese letztern Comp. zeige ich nur darum an, damit Sie mit meinem Streben nach dem Höchsten in der Kunst bekannt sind.".

[3] Cf. Godel, Arthur. (1985). *Schuberts letzte drei Klaviersonaten (D958—960).* P.40.

[4] Cf. Krause, Andreas: „Die Klaviermusik—'So frei und eigen, so keck und mitunter auch so sonderbar'". In: Dürr, Walther., Krause, Andreas. (2020). *Schubert Handbuch.* P.421.

[5] Cf. Godel, Arthur. (1985). *Schuberts letzte drei Klaviersonaten (D958—960).* P.39.

[6] Cf. Krause, Andreas: „Die Klaviermusik—'So frei und eigen, so keck und mitunter auch so sonderbar'". In: Dürr, Walther., Krause, Andreas. (2020). *Schubert Handbuch.* P.421.

[7] Already Schiff drew attention to this inherent symbolism: cf. Schiff, Andras. *Sir András Schiff—Schubert Lecture-Recital. Live at Wigmore Hall.* [Lecture-Recital]. It should be recalled that composers before Schubert conceived works as a trilogy, e.g., Mozart's last Symphonies E-flat major, G minor and C major; Beethoven piano sonatas op. 2, op. 10, op. 31 but also the last three sonatas Op. 109 to Op. 111, to name just a few examples. The symbolism of the number three has already been examined previously (III).

[8] Cf. Godel, Arthur. (1985). *Schuberts letzte drei Klaviersonaten (D958—960).*

side, the pianist Alfred Brendel[9] has made a significant contribution to the analysis of the last three piano sonatas by specifying the motivic interrelations and developments of all themes and motives. His idea of thinking of them in terms of the Hegelian dialectics can also be stimulating and noteworthy. In his interpretation, the C minor sonata represents the thesis, followed by the A major as antithesis and finally, the B-flat major as synthesis. Possibly, these sonatas bear a core which goes beyond the motivic interrelations, alluding to concerns of Schubert with a more philosophical or spiritual undertone, as it will be elaborated in this chapter. For this purpose, this analysis requires a short introduction with the aim of contextualizing the A major sonata in the trilogy.

17.1 Preliminary Considerations on the Sonatas Trilogy D 958–960

If Alfred Brendel's Hegelian concept of the trilogy is extended further in a Jungian manner, then Schubert's three last piano sonatas can be understood as containing an underlying important psychological development. Following this thought, the C minor sonata D 958, being the thesis, could be described in general terms as featuring a telluric character, as the expression of being caught up in earthly attachments.

From all three, the first sonata is most often compared with Beethoven's work—not only with the *Pathétique* op. 13, but especially with the *32 Variations* in C minor WoO 80. The resemblance with the latter is particularly recognizable from the first audible experience due to a similar ductus in the construction of the opening measures of Schubert's C minor sonata. However, when taking a closer look at the musical details, the conclusion is that Schubert conducts them in an idiosyncratic way[10]. This could indicate a personal subject that Schubert is trying to come to terms with or is trying to address at this point of his life: the desire for liberation from the father figure Beethoven remains a possible hypothesis, which has been discussed time and again in the Schubert research circles and among Schubert interpreters, as an explanation for this possible tribute[11]. The fact that

[9] Cf. Brendel, Alfred. (1996). *Musik beim Wort genommen.* P. 80–153.

[10] Cf. Brendel, Alfred. (1898). *Les trois dernières Sonates de Franz Schubert.* Akerman, Chantal (Director). [Programme].

[11] Several musicologists and musicians draw attention to the parallels between the works of these two composers, elaborating not only the affinities between Schubert's and Beethoven's works but also pointing to the existent divergences. Exemplarily named: Cf. Godel, Arthur. (1985). *Schuberts letzte drei Klaviersonaten (D958—960).*; Cf. Hinrichsen, Hans-Joachim.

Schubert refers to his own "Erlkönig" lied of 1815 in the fourth movement of the C minor sonata, as e.g., Brendel states in his analysis[12], which focuses on the father figure and the motif of death, can be an additional detail substantiating this hypothesis. Therefore, there are many similarities and dissimilarities between Schubert's D 958 and Beethoven's C minor Variations (*inter alia*), which may be pointing to Schubert's worship but also to his will to finally free himself from living in Beethoven's shadow[13]—ultimately, Schubert shows a distinctive way of conducting the musical narrative ductus[14]. To better illustrate the aforementioned hermeneutic statement of seeing the C minor sonata as the expression of earthly matters, it might be relevant to mention, in due brevity, some noteworthy passages of the C minor Sonata by directly ascribing the corresponding psychological reading of the musical score.

Beginning with the first movement of D 958: the entire passage from m.119 to m.152 is characterized by harmonic ambiguity, as a consequence of the chromatic instability of the melodic motif in the lower register of the piano. Shortly before the beginning of the recapitulation, from mm.142–152 the "I" seems to be conspicuously lost on unknown paths and trapped in dark, menacing murmurs of the piano left hand (based on repeated sequences). The right hand is characterized by almost endlessly chromatic descending and ascending lines, which points to the lost sense of orientation—this, speaking in Jungian terms, alludes to the archetype of the path, respectively, how the "I" is disoriented[15]. At the same time, the left hand quite independently whispers a mysterious spell-like motif in the dark register of the piano, also based on a chromatic series of notes. This latter motif begins already to develop from m.119 on and is based on the first theme's "second formula"[16], as Alfred Brendel indicated. A brief look into specific passages of the other movements might be valuable as well.

(1994). *Untersuchungen zur Entwicklung der Sonatenform in der Instrumentalmusik Franz Schuberts.*; Cf. Brendel, Alfred. (1996). *Musik beim Wort genommen.* P. 80–153. Schubert himself expressed his deep veneration towards Beethoven several times, aiming for the same artistic excellence. Cf. Chusid, Martin: "Schubert's chamber music: before and after Beethoven". In: Gibbs, Christopher H. (1997). *The Cambridge Companion to Schubert.* Chapter 9. Part II: "Schubert's music: style and genre". Herein, Martin Chusid particularly examines several of Schubert's chamber works in this regard.

[12] Cf. Brendel, Alfred. (1996). *Musik beim Wort genommen.* P. 80–153.

[13] Cf. Brendel, Alfred. (1898). *Les trois dernières Sonates de Franz Schubert.* Akerman, Chantal (Director). [Programme].

[14] Ibid.

[15] Cf. Neumann, Erich. (2021). *Die Große Mutter.* P.23.

[16] Brendel, Alfred. (1996). *Musik beim Wort genommen.* P.129–130.

The second movement of the same C minor sonata, for instance, features, sporadically, dark eruptive expressions, e.g., mm.82–92 (although not to the same extent as in the slow movement of the A major, as it will be examined later on). Another noteworthy fact is the character of the death dance of the last movement: from a comparative analysis perspective, this tarantella has a different character than the death dance from the last movement of the D minor quartet D 810 (16). In the latter, there is an apotheotic gesture and a rising movement towards heaven, which depicts a transcendental image, a change of spiritual state. In contrast, the last movement of the C minor sonata ends with a downward movement (down to the earth), as if the "I" would not yet be ready to transcend this time, as if it would need to (re)face and reconsider or rethink some (inner) questions again, that will finally be dealt with in the course of the trilogy.

In addition to the urge of liberation from the father figure—an important psychological step in the individuation process—other specific themes, of a more philosophical-spiritual nature, seem to come to light: the religious context (cf. 11.2), provided by the identifiable plagal harmonic twists present in several moments of all three sonatas[17], could be an indicator of an additional subject in Schubert's life that possibly still needed further processing. Of particular interest in this regard is the second movement of the C minor sonata: if plagal cadences would be linguistically reformulated as utterances of "Amen"[18], due to its associations with church music, then several "Amen" statements are repeated, followed successively by short rhetorical interruptions (fermatas/pauses), especially at the end of the movement. These can function as moments of introspection. Placing these in the context of the trilogy and crisscrossing the analytical observations can be revealing since further allusions to religious matters and questionings are created in the subsequent sonatas.

After the thesis of the C minor Sonata D 958 (to continue using Alfred Brendel's Hegelian analogy), in which the "I" seems to be desperately entrapped in earthly problems, the A major piano Sonata opens with a credo-like[19] theme in the bright A major tonality, as a contrast to the previous C minor tone colour. Yet, the choral ductus, evoking religious associations, is quickly interrupted by a rhetorical question mark—a suspension moment by lingering on a dominant chord, at the end of these opening measures (m.6). References of a religious

[17] The existence of the plagal harmonic twists in all three last piano sonatas have been identified, e.g., by Brendel. Cf. Ibid.

[18] *Grove Music Online.* (2001). "Plagal cadence [Amen cadence]".

[19] Also Alfred Brendel hints at this credo character, which is especially noticeable in the manuscript copy. Cf. Brendel, Alfred. (1996). *Musik beim Wort genommen.*

nature are to be found also in the B-flat major sonata, yet with another character, as it will be explained in the next chapter (18).

Based on these observations, it seems as if Schubert treated themes with biographical reference[20] in these sonatas, but also with a cultural, social, and religious orientation. This reading proves to be fruitful and conclusive when carefully examining the other movements of the A major sonata. The second movement of D 959 turns specifically to questions related with society, as it will be elaborated in this analysis chapter, due to the existence of a dance-like rhythmic reference. In the third movement of the same sonata the archetypal figure of the "Dümmling" emerges (a variant of the trickster figure), which, as it will be described later (17.7), will help to integrate the split elements stated until that point in the sonata's narration. This figure will trigger an important psychic and spiritual development. Yet, this development requires time both internally and musically: the positive psychic evolution can be heard in the rather heroic culmination at the end of the last movement of D 960, which expresses a fulfilled character.

17.2 Dances as Masked Confessions[21]: The Function of Dances Historically Observed—the Role of (Collective) Masks and Their Impact on the Individual "I"

The dance-like or at least dance-related second movement of the A major Piano Sonata D 959 is here analysed within the context of Schubert's cultural environment, where the expression of the impact of masks in a society strongly influenced by the censorship regime of Metternich comes to light. When contextualized in the Metternich censorship regime, dances can be understood as mirroring the image of an idyllic society[22] (10).

In this cultural context, it becomes clear how the symbolic meaning of dances has changed—it is detached from the primordial and transcended search for wholeness with nature and with the cosmos as a ritual (5). Literally, ritual dances

[20] For references to biographical themes in Schubert's life and work see 11. Motifs of biographical and archetypal nature are often interconnected. This is due to the fact that the archetype can only be active if it holds an emotional significance for the person.

[21] The title of this subchapter "Dances as masked confessions" stems from the Abstract and the presentation of the author at the *Second Workshop of the Schubert Research Center.* (2024, February 22–23).

[22] For the primal semantic meaning of dances see: Mollwo-Oesterreicher, Marianne. (1978). *Herder Lexikon Symbole*. P. 165–166.

were experienced as "a connection between heaven and earth"[23]. This fact already generates a split: living in a big city, as Vienna already was in Schubert's time, creates a certain distance from nature[24], which intensifies the longing for the aforementioned primordial feeling of unity with nature. It can be fruitful to explore the meaning of dances found in the fairy tales, myths and legends of Schubert's time (e.g., Brother Grimm's fairy tales), since these folk narrations contain elements of a collective nature. Herein, the symbolic meaning of being one with its counterpart is described, i.e., the junction of opposites is experienced in the "rhythmic and harmonious circle movement"[25] specific to circle dances.

Following these general reflections on the ritual meaning and symbolism of the dance, these are now to be considered in the context of Schubert's environment: from the moment there is a censorship regime, in which "peace and order" are the motivating motto, dances are part of social gatherings of a society marked by the "introverted" necessity[26] not to express oneself on certain matters (historical-political situation, etc.). In this context, dances are perceived as an ideal activity of society, fulfilling a specific function. In the context of a society grounded in a censorship regime, dances can be perceived as the expression of "mere appearance"[27], as serving the purpose of a mask. Reformulating this thought in terms of C.G. Jung's model of the psyche, dances mirror aspects of the collective Persona particular of that societal group. As the collective has an impact on the individual, it is now relevant to investigate, how these facts might have affected Schubert and subsequently, how these elements find their way in the second movement of the A major sonata D 959.

From the examination of available documents, Schubert's alertness in spirit towards political issues and the societal environment can be noted. This underlines the fact that Schubert certainly must have had periods in which he suffered

---

[23] Ibid. P. 166. (Trans. by the author). German expression: „Rituelle Tänze galten in vielen Kulturen als Mittel, eine Verbindung zw. Himmel u. Erde herzustellen, […]".

[24] Already Walther Dürr pointed to this fact. Cf. Dürr, Walther: „Schubert in seiner Welt". In: Dürr, Walther. Krause, Andreas. (2020). *Schubert Handbuch.* Chapter: „Schubert—das ‚Kind der Großstadt". P.2.

[25] Drewermann, Eugen. (2023). „3. Sommervorlesung 2023: Grimms Märchen tiefenpsychologisch gedeutet. Eugen Drewermann interpretiert Aschenputtel.". [Lecture]. Minutes 1:24:01.

[26] The term "introverted" is not used here in psychological terms, but in a Biedermeier sense, meaning that in times of a censorship regime, Austrian society was compelled to turn inwards to innocent occupations related to home and family. Cf. Erickson, Raymond. (1997). *Schubert's Vienna.* P. 25.

[27] Arendt, Hannah. (2016). *Vom Leben des Geistes.* Part I, Chap. 2: „(Wahres) Sein und (bloße) Erscheinung: die Zwei-Welten-Theorie".

more from the censorship regime and life in Vienna at the time. Several excerpts from letters that Schubert addressed to his friends can attest to this interpretation[28].

> "Above all, I must announce to you a lament about the state of our society as well as about all other circumstances; […] everything is miserable."[29].
>
> "[…] the idle, insignificant life that characterizes our time. […] it feels very painful."[30].
>
> "[…] how everything has now just petrified into bland prose, how most people quietly watch and even feel comfortable with, how they entirely and leisurely glide over the mud into the abyss."[31].

---

[28] The author is aware that these excerpts were written during a period of his life that was probably marked by a crisis, and that Schubert also expressed a more positive description of social gatherings at other times, particularly in regard to the gatherings with his close circle of friends. However, the fact that he did make these strong statements shows Schubert's suffering as genuine expressions at the time of writing them down. They can, for this reason, be taken as a legitimate source to be referred to in this context. C.G. Jung himself has explained at several passages time and again, that the inner experiences are perceived by the person in question as true occurrences. In one passage Jung writes: "Both realities are psychic experiences. […] we experience, however, different effects, through the sense from the outside and through the imagination from the inside.". Jung, Carl Gustav. (2023). *Die Beziehung zwischen dem Ich und dem Unbewussten.* P.121. (Trans. by the author). German expression: "[…] beide ‚Wirklichkeiten' [sind] psychisches Erlebnis […] Wir erleben aber verschiedene Wirkungen, durch die Sinne von ‚aussen', durch die Phantasie von ‚innen'.". Jolande Jacobi underlines this fact in her synopsis of Jung's theories: "[…] everything, that was once captured by the human being in image or in word, features an absolute psychic reality […]". Jacobi, Jolande. (2006). *Die Psychologie von C.G. Jung.* P.88. (Trans. by the author). German expression: "[…] alles, was einmal vom Menschen in Bild oder Wort gefaßt wurde, absolute psychische Realität besitzt, […]".

[29] Schubert, Franz. Letter to Schober. (1823). In: Deutsch, Otto Erich. (1964). *Schubert—Die Dokumente seines Lebens.* P. 207. (Trans. by the author). German expression: "Vor allem muß ich Dir ein Lamento über den Zustand unserer Gesellschaft wie über alle übrigen Verhältnisse ankündigen; […] geht alles miserabl.".

[30] Schubert, Franz. Letter to Schober. (1824). In: Ibid. P. 258. (Trans. by the author). German expression: "[…] wo mir besonders das Thatenlose unbedeutende Leben, welches unsere Zeit bezeichnet, sehr schmerzliche fühlte, […]". Subsequently Schubert wrote the well-known poem entitled "Klage an das Volk!", a complaint to the people. Cf. Ibid.

[31] Schubert, Franz. Letter to Spaun. (1825). In: Ibid. P. 296. (Trans. by the author). German expression: "[…] wie jetzt alles zur faden Prosa sich verknöchert, wie die meisten Leute dabey ruhig zusehen oder sich gar wohl dabey befinden, wie sie ganz gemächlich über den Schlam in den Abgrund glitschen.".

"[…] Vienna […] although a bit large, it is devoid of warmth, openness, of real thoughts, reasonable words and, in particular, of spirited deeds."[32].

17.3 The "I" Trapped in a World of "Mere Appearances"—the Conflict Between the Outer Reality and the Two Wills. The Expressive Role of the *Suspiratio* Motif

In the second movement of the A major piano sonata D 959, the (Viennese) Weltschmerz (8) comes poignantly to light, already through the tonality choice of F-sharp minor; the key characterized by the dark tone: "Resentment and displeasure is its language"[33]. In a similar way, Böhm's addendum links this key with the "ephemeral past and [with] tears"[34]. Being the home key, this tonality expresses, in general terms, the initial situation and the bare outer reality. The semantic level of the indicated key characteristic is additionally emphasized by the chosen dynamics and further musical elements, to be subsequently addressed.

Firstly, the ***p***-dynamic generates an amplification of the space dimension (7)[35]. Consequently, it assigns an epic quality to the A-section (12)[36], as if a past remembrance from afar and its impact on Schubert himself are being narrated. These tone characteristics are accentuated by several musical elements which constitute the first periodic theme construction (mm.1–18). The melodic line seems to be trapped within sighs: the opening falling second core motif, the musical

[32] Schubert, Franz. Letter to Mrs. Pachler. (1827). In: Ibid. P. 451. (Trans. by the author). German expression: "[…] Wien […],'s freylich ein wenig groß, dafür aber ist es leer an Herzlichkeit, Offenheit, an wirklichen Gedanken, an vernünftigen Worten, und besonders an geistreichen Thaten.".

[33] Schubart, Christian Friedrich Daniel. (1977). "Ideen zu einer Ästhetik der Tonkunst". Cited after: Böhm, Richard. (2006). *Symbolik und Rhetorik im Liedschaffen von Franz Schubert.* P. 80. (Trans. by the author). German expression: „Groll und Missvergnügen ist seine Sprache".

[34] Böhm, Richard. (2006). *Symbolik und Rhetorik im Liedschaffen von Franz Schubert.* P. 80. (Trans. by the author). German expression: "Vergänglichkeit und Tränen".

[35] Cf. Schlesinger, Max. (1967). *Symbolik in der Tonkunst.*

[36] Cf. Korstvedt, Benjamin M. "'The prerogative of the late style': thoughts on the expressive world of Schubert's late works".

rhetorical figure of *suspiratio*, expresses a sorrowful, painful sigh, which is elaborated in m.3 and additionally marked by suspensions in m. 7. In this manner, the melody turns obsessively around the central notes g-sharp and a. The deep melancholic quality of this sigh is emphasized by Schubert's accent on the second note. Yet, by inverting the movement of a falling second to a rising second in mm. 5–6, Schubert transforms this emotional gesture into a hopeful sigh, as if pleading for redemption in the world of *Elysium.* Reading this musical observation in a psychological or philosophical manner could lead to the possible interpretation of understanding the hopeful sigh gesture as being the expression of the will. However, the counter-will is immediately expressed in m. 6 with the accentuated E-sharp note in the inner voice of the right hand, as if there was a "negative" inner force willing to remain in the F-sharp melancholy (the E-sharp note is related to the F-sharp minor reality, as it is its leading-tone, seeking for resolution in the F-sharp minor sphere).

Resuming the inner occurrences of this beginning, the antecedent phrase (mm.1–8) juxtaposes, in this way, the miserable outer reality (descending sigh motif mm.1–2) with an inner expectation (rising sigh motif mm.5–6), that is immediately contradicted in the second beat of m.6 (E-sharp note). The rising sigh motif expresses the "longing for an ideal world"[37]—an inner posture of expectation that can be understood as the manifestation of the one will, which desires to believe in that, in fact utopic, reality. This is immediately followed by the negation of the counter will, to persist in that "miserable" reality. It can already be foretold that the attraction to the tonal centre of F-sharp minor alludes to a nihilistic "predisposition"[38], that will culminate at the end of the movement.

The consequent phrase (mm. 9–18) is extended to ten-bars by the two additional measures at its end. On the surface, this prolongation seemingly functions as a restatement of the inherent suffering caused by the confrontation with the outer reality. However, by repeating the same motif again from mm. 15–16 in mm.17–18, Schubert not only accentuates the asymmetry between the two phrases

[37] Dobretsberger, Barbara. Personal communication between Barbara Dobretsberger and the author. Salzburg/Lisbon: November 25, 2021.

[38] The term "nihilistic" is here understood less as senselessness/meaninglessness but more as an attitude of rejection and neglection of the norms and values existent in Schubert's historical and sociological environment.

but is also referring to the echo phenomenon that can be found in nature (4)[39]—the last two measures of the theme function as an inner *retour* (resonance) to what was previously said, as an externally audible projection of an inner voice. It can be recalled that in ancient philosophy, the echo was a musical phenomenon of nature tied with the outer projection of inner images in form of mythological beings (4)[40]. In Jungian terms: it is as if the "I" is trying to find a way to be connected and to merge with the outer reality, to resolve or dissolve the painful felt dialectic[41].

The rhythmical ostinato of the left hand, omnipresent during the whole A-section (mm. 1–68) and characterized by the harmonic oscillation between tonic and dominant, brings the rhythmical component of a "stylized Ländler"[42]. It is important to recall that, historically observed, there was a growing awareness typical of European countries in the 19th century to integrate folk music and national dances in art music[43]. The Ländler, a dance specific of the Austrian culture[44], is characterized by being a moderately slow circle dance ("Drehtanz")[45] which was performed both as a couple and as a group dance. The rupture is evident between the meaning of dances inherent in folk narrations (cultural unconscious[46]) and

---

[39] This reading is understood in the context of the aesthetics of Romanticism, where nature is a crucial element of the creative psyche.

[40] Cf. Sorgner, Stefan Lorenz. Schramm, Michael. (2010). *Musik in der antiken Philosophie.* P.222.

[41] The term dialectic is here understood in the sense of Schelling's *Naturphilosophie*, where the "Zerrissenheit" (the state of being torn) is transcended by the fusion with nature (4).

[42] Platinga, Leo. (2016). "Schubert, Social Music and Melancholy.". In: Bodley & Horton. *Rethinking Schubert.* P. 243. Definitely, the articulation of the left hand together with the characteristic jump between the first and second note, featuring the Ländler dance rhythm, is clearly more in the foreground here than the harmonic oscillation quality of a potential barcarolle, a description to be found *inter alia* in Riezler, Walther. (1967). *Schubert's Instrumentalmusik.* P. 149. Also, Guy Sacre shares Riezler's perspective. Cf. Sacre, Guy. (1998). *La Musique de Piano.* P. 2495. However, the fact that this movement is written in a ternary measure contradicts this hypothesis, since what characterizes a Barcarolle is the binary measures of 6/8 or 12/8. Moreover, examples of Barcarolles in Schubert's instrumental music seem to be scarce.

[43] Cf. Dobretsberger, Barbara. (2016). *Formen der Instrumentalmusik.* P. 193.

[44] For the characteristics of the Ländler in specific: Cf. Ibid. P. 197. See also: Flotzinger, Rudolf. (2004). *Oesterreichisches Musiklexikon. Band 3.* P.1219–1221.

[45] Cf. Michels, Ulrich. (2008). *Dtv-Atlas Musik.* P. 155. Turning or winding figures ("Dreh- und Wickelfiguren") are also described in this context by Flotzinger. Cf. Flotzinger, Rudolf. (2004). *Oesterreichisches Musiklexikon. Band 3.* P.1220.

[46] C.G. Jung already pointed out that cultural factors have an influence on the unconscious, i.e., on archetypal manifestations. Cf. Roesler, Christian. (2016). *Das Archetypenkonzept*

their different functions within the context of the censorship regime mentioned above (17.2). Therefore, the sigh motif of the right hand can be interpreted here as an implicit emotional expression of the concealed meaning inherent in dances, i.e., as the resulting impact of the masks of society on the psyche (Fig. 17.1). Under these circumstances, the entire A-section functions as a narration of the true occurrences (that might happen) when embedded in social gatherings, namely the identification with the Persona and the emotions that this can evoke[47].

When this "Zerrissenheit" (i.e., the state of being torn) is felt, it can be a natural reaction of the "I" to merge in an illusory utopic world. Musically, the moment of self-illusion comes especially to light in the A major section (mm.19–32) when Schubert repeats the same melodic and rhythmic pattern from the beginning in this tonality; the key of "the 'pretence' of positive moods"[48]. The A major section functions therefore as the expression of a wished (inner) reality, which stands in a split relationship to the outer reality. In this sense all dark emotions are contained under the mask, i.e., repressed in the unconscious, while the inner and outer realities are constantly being juxtaposed, by being alternately repeated (all through the A-section). For the time being, these repressed elements are only perceived through a general melancholic state that has established itself by the expression of the *suspiratio* motives. However, these shadow elements will take on other proportions, when embedded in a fantasy-like state of the "I", and which will follow in the middle section of this movement).

C.G. Jungs. Chapter 2.8.: "Zur Begriffsgeschichte". The concept of the cultural unconscious was first proposed by Joseph Henderson in 1991. Cf. Roesler, Christian. (2024). *Deconstructing Archetype Theory.* P.245.

47 Jung deals with this topic *inter alia* in: Jung, Carl Gustav. (2023). *Die Beziehung zwischen dem Ich und dem Unbewussten.*

48 Böhm, Richard. (2006). *Symbolik und Rhetorik im Liedschaffen von Franz Schubert.* P. 57. (Trans by the author). German expression: "die 'Vortäuschung' positiver Stimmungen (vor dem Hintergrund von z.B. Täuschung, Resignation, [...]".

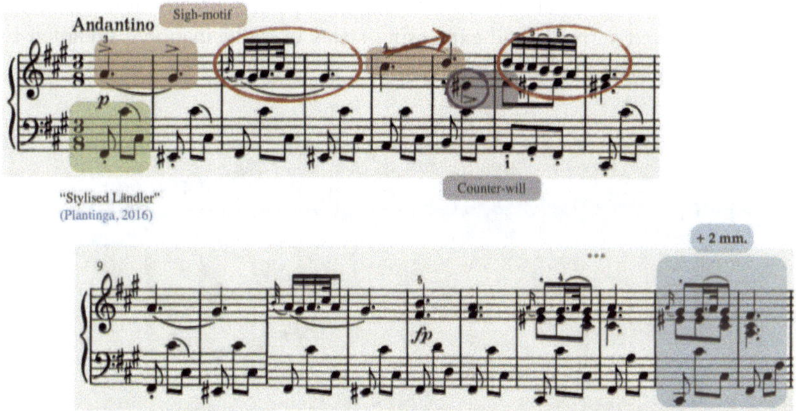

Fig. 17.1 Periodic theme construction: Antecedent phrase mm.1–8, consequent phrase mm.9–18. The Ländler rhythm in the left hand as a symbol for dances as masks (in society) with their effects on the individual "I" as a sigh of lament of the right-hand. In the following measures (mm.5–6), the inversion of the sigh motif is to be seen as the expression of the wished inner reality, immediately contradicted, however, by the counter will, manifested through the E-sharp note. (Sheet music excerpt taken and adapted from *Henle digital edition*) © 2016 G. Henle Verlag, Munich

17.4 Entering a State of Fantasy and the Consequent "Irrational Explosion"[49]: the Collective Shadow Taking the Upper Hand and Overflooding the "I"

> "[…] night falls, the light of consciousness fades and the dark sea of the unconscious breaks in."[50].

With the beginning of the middle section (B-section, mm.69–158), the "I" enters in the realm of the unconscious. Traits of the unconscious, such as abrupt shifts and the chaotic autonomous emergence of dark elements, disproportionate reactions, are immediately recognizable in Schubert's creative process. These are revealed not only through the music's audible perception but also in Schubert's handwriting, in the facsimile. In the latter for instance, the G natural, which

---

[49] Brendel, Alfred. (1996). *Musik beim Wort genommen.* P. 92.

[50] Jung, Carl Gustav. (2020). *Archetypen. Urbilder und Wirkkräfte des Kollektiven Unbewussten.* P.30. (Trans. by the author). German expression: „[…] es wird Nacht, das Licht des Bewusstseins erlischt, und das dunkle Meer des Unbewussten bricht herein.".

comes prepared in the printed version in m. 75, is placed already in m.73, creating an unexpected surprise, and expressing states of hallucination[51] common to dreams and fantasies (indicated in Fig. 17.2).

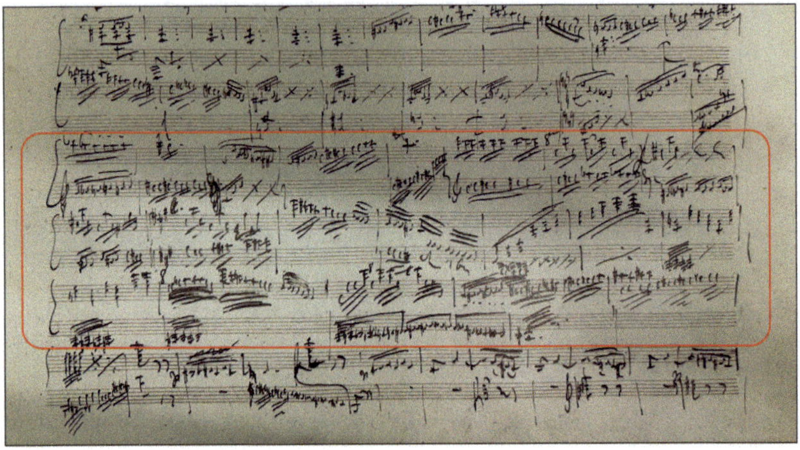

Fig. 17.2 The unconscious reflected in Schubert's handwriting. The unprepared and unexpected G natural in m. 73 as a spontaneous act of the creative unconscious. (Picture taken and adapted from: *Drei große Sonaten für das Pianoforte. D 958, D 959 und D 960. Facsimile published by Hans Schneider Tutzing after the autographs in the Vienna City and State Library*)

This sudden outburst on the part of the unconscious can be a natural result of being embedded in a historical context (Metternich censorship) that suppresses the individual and where the role of masks is predominant and even a necessity for survival. As a result, the singular and unique aspect of the "I" is annihilated in the collective world of appearances. C.G. Jung described this process and the reasons behind such a development as follows:

> "This overlooking of the individual naturally means a stifling of the individual, whereby the element of differentiation in a community is eradicated. The element of differentiation is the individual. […] The larger a community is, and the more the summation of collective factors, which is peculiar to every large community, is supported

[51] Cf. Brendel, Alfred. (1898). *Les trois dernières Sonates de Franz Schubert*. Akerman, Chantal (Director). [Programme].

> by conservative prejudices to the detriment of the individual, the more the individual is morally and spiritually destroyed, and thus the only source for the moral and spiritual progress of the society is also blocked. Thus, of course, only the society and everything collective about the individual can flourish. Everything singular about the individual, however, is doomed to destruction, that is, to repression. In this way, the individual becomes unconscious and transforms itself into the fundamentally bad, into the destructive [...]"[52].

The succession of diminished seventh chords, which are featured in the beginning of this middle section (e.g., mm.73–74 and mm.77–84), recall an affinity with the fantasy genre. The formal construction of a fantasy, as musical genre, is rather free, and chords successions, usually arpeggiated chords, are commonly used, like in a free improvisation[53]. Fantasies evoke the theme of the night, as a particular fascination of Romanticism (4.3). In this genre, chords with a particular tone colour were favoured, such as the diminished seventh chords. The tone quality of these chords captivated composers in Romanticism especially due to their "gloomy colouring and tonal shimmer"[54]. Interpreting this fact in psychological terms, this corresponds to the process when the "I" submerges itself in a fantasy, being subsequently confronted with unconscious elements. A fantasy, in this sense, refers to a psychological and, in fact, creative process of the mind, i.e., to the activity of the unconscious that is unleashed when the "I" enters a fantasy-like state, which can be described as an immersion in an imagination or (day)dream. This corresponds to a gradual process where ego consciousness is

---

[52] Jung, Carl Gustav. (2023). *Die Beziehung zwischen dem Ich und dem Unbewussten.* P. 41–42. (Trans. by the author). German expression: „Dieses Hinwegsehen über das Individuelle bedeutet natürlich eine Erstickung des Einzelwesens, wodurch das Element der Differenzierung in einer Gemeinschaft ausgerottet wird. Das Element der Differenzierung ist das Individuum. [...] Je größer eine Gemeinschaft ist, und je mehr die jeder großen Gemeinschaft eigentümliche Summierung der Kollektivfaktoren zuungunsten des Individuellen durch konservative Vorurteile unterstützt wird, desto mehr wird das Individuum moralisch und geistig vernichtet, und damit wird auch die einzige Quelle für den sittlichen und geistigen Fortschritt der Sozietät verstopft.
Damit gedeiht natürlich nur die Sozietät und alles Kollektive am Einzelnen. Alles Individuelle am Einzelnen aber ist zum Untergang, das heißt zur Verdrängung verurteilt. Damit gerät das Individuelle ins Unbewusste und verwandelt sich dort gesetzmäßig in das prinzipiell Schlechte, in das Destruktive [...]". P.42.

[53] Cf. Rosen, Charles. (1998). *The Romantic Generation.* P.47–48 and P.362.

[54] For the tonal qualities of the diminished seventh chords in romanticism see: Kühn, Clemens. (2005). *Analyse lernen.* P. 74. (Trans. by the author). German expression: „[...] die Romantik interessiert eher seine düstere Färbung und sein tonales Schillern.".

progressively dimmed into "oblivion", where a diminution, extinction or "dissolution of consciousness"[55] takes place. Reaching such a state brings the "I" closer to the origins of every myth[56]. C.G Jung used to denote this state as an "abaissement du niveau mental"[57]; such a process is understood in Analytical Psychology as a regressive movement (3.1 Fig. 3.4)[58].

Returning to the musical observations: diminished seventh chords have harmonically an ambivalent nature, since there are multiple possibilities of resolving them (each note of the chord can be a leading tone)—this "opacity", to speak in Ralf Vogel's[59] terms, represents another trait of the unconscious sphere. As the "expression of the dreadful, [...] of pain and death"[60] the diminished seventh chords are often used as a means to increase the drama[61]. Associations with the dark night (i.e., the unconscious) can naturally emerge. In this manner, bearing in mind the formal structure of this sonata movement, it can be noted that there is a contrast in the musical narrative ductus, going from an epic character in the A-section, to the drama of the soul in the B-section.

This process follows the natural unconscious urge, the necessity of the individual to undergo such a process:

> "With the dissolution of the persona, the involuntary imagination is unleashed, which is apparently nothing other than the specific activity of the collective psyche. This activity brings to consciousness contents of whose existence one previously had no idea. However, as the influence of the collective unconscious grows, consciousness loses its guiding power. It imperceptibly becomes the led, as an unconscious

---

55 Jung, Carl Gustav. (2014). "Psychology and Alchemy". In: *The Collected Works of C.G. Jung. Vol. 12.* (Trans. by Gerhard Adler and R.F.C. Hull). Chapter: "Initial dreams".

56 Cf. Jung, Carl Gustav. (2014). "Archetypes and the Collective Unconscious". In: Ibid. *Vol. 9*, Part I. Chapter: "The Psychology of the child archetype".

57 Ibid. *Vol. 12*: "Psychology and Alchemy". Chapter: "Initial dreams". This terminology that Jung used is in reference to Pierre Janet.

58 Roesler, Christian. Personal communication between Christian Roesler and the author. Freiburg im Breisgau: June 18, 2024.

59 Cf. Vogel, Ralf T. (2024). *Das Geheimnis der Seele.*

60 De la Motte, Diether. (1976). „Harmonielehre". Cited after: Böhm, Richard. (2006). *Symbolik und Rhetorik im Liedschaffen von Franz Schubert.* P. 165. (Trans. by the author). German expression: „[...] aus diesem Grunde wurde er [der verminderte Septimakkord] „schon sehr frühe in der dramatischen Musik als Ausdruck des Schreckens, der Überraschung, des Schmerzes, des Todes, usw. verwendet.".

61 Cf. Böhm, Richard. (2006). *Symbolik und Rhetorik im Liedschaffen von Franz Schubert.*

> and impersonal process gradually takes the lead. [...] The entry into this process is inevitable wherever there is a need to get beyond an insoluble difficulty.[62]

In the musical passage in question, the diminished seventh chords are lined up, unresolved, repeated one after the other, each time a half tone step lower than the previous one, on the basis of a sequence (mm.77–84). This process can psychologically reflect the state of clouding of the consciousness (Fig. 17.3), as if it were gradually entering/descending further and further into the unconscious; a gesture, which mimetically depicts the inner archaic movement that goes from light to darkness, from heaven to the underworld, towards a primordial reality (7.1)[63]. By adding the pedal point G throughout this passage, Schubert creates a tone-carpet, which harmonically provides for additional obfuscation effects. Furthermore, G is the dominant of C minor, the tonality which will be achieved in m. 85. Therefore, G seeks resolution in the C minor world and, by delaying it, Schubert increases the harmonic tension. This delaying of the C minor arrival is understandable from the psychological point of view, since C minor is the key of despair, pain and death[64]. In a nutshell, the tonal centre is veiled, constantly being shifted and the resolution delayed creating tension. Commenting on this musical observation in Jungian terms, it is as if the "I" were inactive, paralysed or as if it were letting itself sinking further and further down into the unconscious world (lacking a will of its own), while at the same time an inner force were gradually taking over the leading position. C. G. Jung acknowledged a "loss of initiative"[65] of the "I" when it enters the above-described state related to the "abaissement

[62] Jung, Carl Gustav. (2023). *Die Beziehung zwischen dem Ich und dem Unbewussten.* P.51–52. (Trans. by the author). German expression: „Mit der Auflösung der Persona erfolgt nämlich eine Entfesselung der unwillkürlichen Phantasie, welche anscheinend nichts anderes ist als die spezifische Tätigkeit der Kollektivpsyche. Diese Tätigkeit bringt Inhalte zum Bewusstsein, von deren Existenz man zuvor nichts ahnte. In dem Maße aber, in dem der Einfluss der kollektiven Unbewussten wächst, verliert das Bewusstsein seine führende Macht. Es wird unmerklich zum Geführten, indem ein unbewusster und unpersönlicher Prozess allmählich die Führung übernimmt. [...] Der Eintritt in diesen Prozess ist unvermeidlich, wo immer die Notwendigkeit vorhanden ist, über eine unlösbare Schwierigkeit hinauszugelangen.".

[63] This archetypal gesture has been mentioned previously (7), notably in reference to Karbusicky. Cf. Karbusicky, Vladimir. (1986). *Grundriß der musikalischen Semantik.*

[64] Cf. Böhm, Richard. (2006). *Symbolik und Rhetorik im Liedschaffen von Franz Schubert.* P. 86. (Trans. by the author).

[65] Jung, Carl Gustav. (2014). "The Practice of Psychotherapy". In: *The Collected Works of C.G. Jung. Vol. 16.* (Trans. by Gerhard Adler and R.F.C. Hull). Part Two: "Specific Problems of Psychotherapy", Chapter III: "The Psychology of transference".

du niveau mentale"[66]. Similarly, Jacobi describes: "The individual falls from an active-conscious state into a passive overwhelmed state"[67]. This psychological process would correspond to the musical successions of the ambivalent diminished seventh chords, since, when entering into such a state, new centres of the personality are created[68]. This movement towards the under-ground will set in motion a process of inner transformation to come. Symbolically formulated, these are the archetypal forces interacting with the "I" and imposing their will over the will of the "I". When in such a position, the "I" is subject to threats, which Jung termed as the "peril of the soul"[69]:

> "By descending into the unconscious, the conscious mind puts itself in a perilous position, for it is apparently extinguishing itself. It is in the situation of the primitive hero who is devoured by the dragon."[70].

---

[66] Jung, Carl Gustav. (2014). "Psychology and Alchemy". In: Ibid. *Vol. 12.* (Trans. by Gerhard Adler and R.F.C. Hull). Chapter: "Initial dreams". This terminology that Jung used is in reference to Pierre Janet.

[67] Jacobi, Jolande. (2006). *Die Psychologie von C.G. Jung.* P.45. (Trans. by the author). German expression: "Das Individuum fällt von einem aktiv-bewußten Zustand in einen passive, ‚ergriffenen'.".

[68] Cf. Jung, Carl Gustav. (2014). "The Practice of Psychotherapy". In: *The Collected Works of C.G. Jung. Vol. 16.* (Trans. by Gerhard Adler and R.F.C. Hull). Part Two: "Specific Problems of Psychotherapy", Chapter III: "The Psychology of transference". In order to avoid any misconception, this is to be understood as part of the process of a lowering of the mental level, that, as previously explained, basically consists of a regressive movement involving the psychic energy (*libido*). As such, this means that the "psychic energies flow towards the unconscious". Klaus-Uwe, Adam. (2000). *Therapeutisches Arbeiten mit Träumen.* Chapter 8.2. "Regression und Progression", p. 67. (Trans. by the author). German expression: "In der Regression fließt die psychische Energie zum Unbewussten hin, [...]". In this sense, the formulation above in the text is by no means to be understood as a pathological condition.

[69] Jung, Carl Gustav. (2014). "Psychology and Alchemy". In: *The Collected Works of C.G. Jung. Vol. 12.* (Trans. by Gerhard Adler and R.F.C. Hull). Chapter V: "The myth of the hero".

[70] Ibid. (Trans. by Gerhard Adler and R.F.C. Hull).

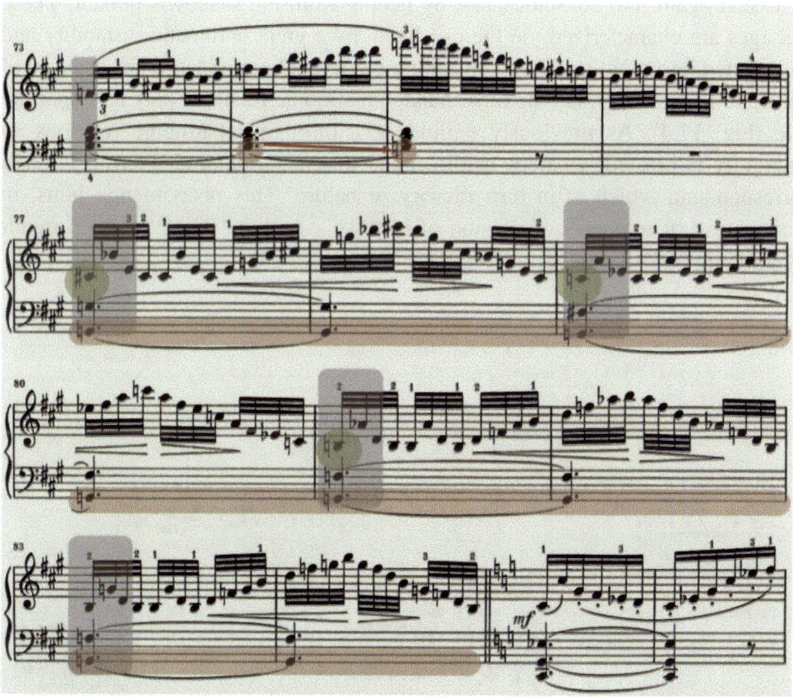

Fig. 17.3 The process of clouding of consciousness: the diminished seventh chords and the tonal carpet achieved by G pedal point which increases harmonic tension and provides for further obfuscation effects. (Sheet music excerpt taken and adapted from *Henle digital edition*) © 2016 G. Henle Verlag, Munich

Reaching C minor (m.85), the "I" enters, *de facto*, the state of an endangered being, since C minor stands in a tritone relationship with the initial tonality of F-sharp minor. It shall be recalled that in music the tritone interval has the symbolic connotation of the *diabolus in musica.* Precisely at this moment, Schubert makes use of the imitation technique—a technique, which has as its roots in the ancient tradition of the *caccia*[71]. Therefore, the image of a hunting shadow imposes itself musically: firstly, in the C minor section in mm.85–88; secondly, a new attempt is made a third higher, this time beginning in E minor in mm. 94–97, as if trying

[71] For further characteristics of the *caccia* see: von Fischer, Kurt. „Caccia". In: Sadie, Stanley. (1980). *The New Grove Dictionary of Music and Musicians. Vol. 3.* P.574–576.

to ascend again into consciousness, by fleeing from the shadow's pursuit. These passages are characterized, on the one hand, by a great chromatic instability and unexpected harmonic shifts, which can be interpreted as sudden inner changes of perception (Fig. 17.4). On the other hand, enharmonic relations play an important role (Fig. 17.4). As previously outlined (7), through enharmonic relations an ambiguity is created, whereby the intended tone is "confounded" with its akin correspondent, which is in turn illusory in nature. This phenomenon hints, in this context, at moments of illusion of identity, e.g., mm. 92–93 C-sharp minor enharmonic of D-flat minor.

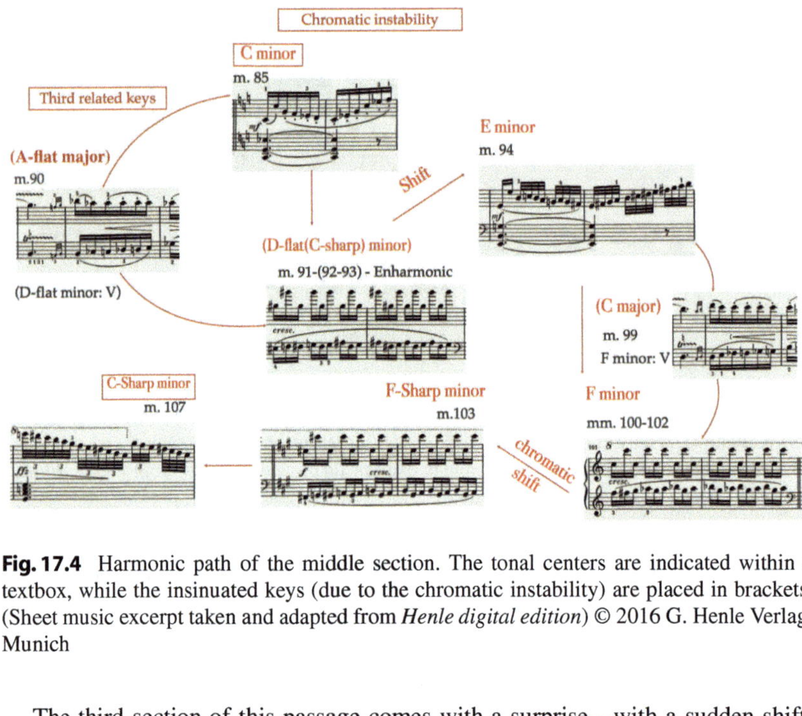

Fig. 17.4 Harmonic path of the middle section. The tonal centers are indicated within a textbox, while the insinuated keys (due to the chromatic instability) are placed in brackets. (Sheet music excerpt taken and adapted from *Henle digital edition*) © 2016 G. Henle Verlag, Munich

The third section of this passage comes with a surprise—with a sudden shift: Schubert changes the key signature to F-sharp minor in mm.103 (Fig. 17.4), as if an impulsive change of perception had autonomously occurred or as if the shadow element had definitely gained the upper hand. In fact, the following passage translates an inflated state of the "I", as if being engulfed by the obscure, chthonic structures of the unconscious.

The depth of the unconscious is subsequently reached in its most chaotic state in mm.107–116 (Fig. 17.2), where not only (i) hectic chord jumps through the entire keyboard, (ii) velociously (chromatic) scales, (iii) syncopes, but also (iv) the rhetorical figure of a *passus duriusculus*[72] can be identified in the tremolo-like bassline from mm. 109–116, beginning with the note G-sharp—A—A-sharp—B—C—C-sharp. The tremolo can be seen as a madrigalism, depicting a feverish affect (trembling), expressing the emotional and physical impact of the unconscious shadow elements on the "I". Extreme ranges also contribute to the characterization of the B-section and the chaotic shadow taking the leading position (engulfment):

> "A collapse of the conscious mind is no little event; it invariably marks the end of the world, when everything returns to its original chaos."[73].
>
> "[…] through the addition of the deeper layers of the unconscious, which I recommend calling the collective unconscious, an expansion of the personality takes place that leads to the state of inflation. [...] Inflation [comes about] as an unfortunate consequence of the process of making conscious"[74].

In m. 122 (Fig. 17.5) the confrontation with the shadow takes place; the "I" becomes conscious of its own shadow by recognizing its doppelgänger.

[72] The definition of *Passus duriusculus* is "hard step": *passus* = step, *duriusculus* = hard, cruel. In music this figure is related to passages featuring chromatic lines, dissonances and/or tones not belonging to the prevailing tonality. Cf. Bartel, Dietrich. (2010). *Handbuch der musikalischen Figurenlehre.* P. 222.

[73] Jung, Carl Gustav. (2023). *Die Beziehung zwischen dem Ich und dem Unbewussten.* P. 54. (Trans. by the author). German expression: „Ein Zusammenbruch der bewussten Einstellung ist keine kleine Sache. Es ist immer ein kleiner Weltuntergang, bei dem alles wieder zum anfänglichen Chaos zurückkehrt.".

[74] Ibid. P.46. (Trans. by the author). German expression: "[…] durch die Anfügung der tieferen Schichten des Unbewussten, die ich das kollektive Unbewusste zu benennen empfehle, eine Erweiterung der Persönlichkeit erfolgt, die zum Zustand der Inflation führt. […] jene bereits besprochenen Inflation [kommt zustande], die gewissermaßen als eine unerfreuliche Folge der Bewusstmachung anzusprechen wäre. […]". C.G. Jung subsequently explains that a state of inflation "occurs wherever people are overwhelmed by knowledge or realization.". Ibid.

17.5 The Confrontation of the "I" with the Shadow and the Dialogue with the Inner Furies—Entering the Elysium: a Propitious Place to Integrate the Split Elements of the Personality—The Moment of Integration of the Opposites

This moment of shock (Fig. 17.5)—musically rendered through the rhetorical figure of the *aposiopesis*[75]—initially creates a petrified state, which is emphasized by the musical *stasis* (pauses). A series of attempts at resolutions ensues which are the natural result of the *aposiopesis*, as if the "I" would be groping around in the dark. The tritone interval, symbolizing the shadow (*diabolus in musica*) at the transition from m. 125 to 126, will cause a descent into the realm of Hades, which can be perceived by the chromatic descending line, the musical rhetorical figure of the *catabasis*[76] in mm. 126–127 (Fig. 17.5). Congruently, Susan Wollenberg compares this passage with the descent to the underworld in Gluck's opera *Orpheus und Eurydike*[77]. Once arrived in the underworld, a dialogue with the inner demons takes place. This corresponds in the psychological process to the "attempt to liberate [the own] individuality from the collective psyche"[78], the stage following the liberation of the Persona.

[75] *Aposiopesis* is defined as a concealment ("Verschweigen") related to an interruption in the musical narrative ductus and to a change in affects. Cf. Bartel, Dietrich. (2010). *Handbuch der musikalischen Figurenlehre.* P. 103.

[76] *Catabasis* means the same as *descendit ad infernos,* i.e., is related to a descend both as a movement downwards and as a tone painting means to translate disparagement ("Niedrigkeit") or oppressive affects. Ibid. P.113. German expression: "Dies heißt, daß eine Anwendung der Figur in einem Text wie *descendit ad infernos* nicht nur das Absteigen, sondern den mit diesem Text verbundenen Affekt der Niedrigkeit ausdrücken soll.".

[77] Cf. Wollenberg, Susan. (2011): *Schubert's Fingerprints: Studies in the Instrumental Works.* P. 166.

[78] Jung, Carl Gustav. (2023). *Die Beziehung zwischen dem Ich und dem Unbewussten.* P. 54. (Trans by the author). German expression: "Die Versuche zur Befreiung der Individualität aus der Kollektivpsyche".

Fig. 17.5 *Aposiopesis* as the shock moment, the confrontation with the shadow, and the following measures of groping around, as an attempt to work out the shock moment. The tritone (*diabolus in musica*) bringing a *descendit ad infernos* mm.125–127 (*catabasis*). (Sheet music excerpt taken and adapted from *Henle digital edition*) © 2016 G. Henle Verlag, Munich

Symbolically speaking, the Furies are expressed by the sudden ***sf*** chords in the left hand. Unexpectedly, there is a turning point to C-sharp major, which occurs with the majorization of the third of the C-sharp major chord in 6/4 position. The Furies subsequently appear tamed in the ***p*** dynamic (m. 141, in m.144 in ***pp*** dynamic). Here, this dynamic change in the music—in contrast to the beginning of the second movement—could rather hint at an inner transformation in character of the chthonic elements that occurred after the dialogue. It could be an indication that the "I" has critically looked upon the shadow elements, eventually integrating them partially or entirely. This is understood by Jung as the ideal case of outcome[79] and usually results from a dialectic procedure of the "I" with the unconscious structures, in form of a dialogue[80].

The new major tonality is confirmed in m. 147, a passage which functions as a transition from the middle section to the A'-section. A new flowing motif

[79] Cf. Ibid. Jung also addressed this case as the "critical understanding". Ibid. P.55. (Trans. by the author). German expression: "[...] den Idealfall, das kritische Verstädnis, [...]".

[80] Cf. Ibid. In addition see Jacobi, Jolande. (2006). *Die Psychologie von C.G. Jung*. Chapter: „Das dialektische Verfahren". P.72–73.

is introduced here (Fig. 17.7). Foretelling promptly the psychological process inherent in this passage, this instant can be seen as functioning as a moment of redemption, when the "I" enters the *Elysium,* the paradise on earth, the moment much longed for in the past (Fig. 17.7). The just mentioned flowing motif can be termed as the lyre motif, due to the specific associations that it evokes. On the one hand, this reading is musically substantiated through the characteristic broken chords, on the other hand, it is symbolically validated through the allusion to the *Elysium.* The latter symbolic relation can be derived from the Orpheus myth analogy, since it is with this instrument that Orpheus enchanted the shadow elements and was subsequently given the right to enter the *Elysium*[81] (Fig. 17.6), a place where music is omnipresent. In Gluck's opera, this instrument functions as the connecting element that makes the reencounter with Eurydice in the *Elysium* possible.

Fig. 17.6 Orpheus singing and playing his lyre, enchanting all the animals and elements of nature around him. *Mosaic from Tarsos*, 3rd cent. b.c. Antakya Archeology Museum. (Image taken from Wikimedia Commons © D. Osseman)

[81] Cf. Grand, Michael. Hazel, John. (2008). *Lexikon der antiken Mythen und Gestalten.*

Continuing the interpretation of this passage in Jungian terms, this moment represents a crucial instant in one's own development: the paradise on earth creates the conditions necessary to the "I" to release all fears[82]. In this psychological state, an attempt can be made to reintegrate the repressed or split elements that have fallen into the shadow. The reintegration of repressed elements can be identified musically in the lyre motif since elements of the Ländler motif can be found camouflaged within the lyre motif (Fig. 17.7). The fact that Schubert himself indicates this motivic interrelation through his own articulation markings (*stacc.* + accent in the last beat) substantiates this interpretation. Such spontaneous occurrences during the creative process exemplify Jung's concept of synchronicity, in which an inner state is reflected as an outer event. The evidence presented here demonstrates that this phenomenon plays an essential role in the creative process.

Musically, the trill in the dark register of the bass in m.152—another connecting link with other works, e.g., the B-flat major Sonata D 960—functions here as a further turning point (Fig. 17.7). It generates the appearance of the four-note rhythmical motif of the mm. 153–154, which due to its closeness with Beethoven's fate motif might be termed accordingly. The new elements introduced in the transitional passage mm.147–158 are all carried over into the A'-section, where the theme with the sigh-motif and its elaborations are to be found in the middle line (Fig. 17.7). The phenomenon of fusion between the lyre motif and the fate motif is perceptible, whereby the theme remains in the inner voice—as if it were interiorized and accompanied by further elements of the own personality that developed through this musical narrative. The fate motif manifests itself in form of tone-repetitions (m. 159), before it develops into an almost independent countermelody (e.g., m.163). Since this is a motif that is usually semantically charged with the symbolism of death in Schubert's music[83], a biographical parallel can be drawn that is inherent to this musical motif. In other words, this passage might translate the experience of the "I" which lives the expression of the parallel worlds. In short, the experience of the simultaneity of opposites can be identified by the expression of, on the one side, the bliss as a reminiscence of the *Elysium* (left-hand), which carries in itself the integration of the Ländler (attempt to integrate the split elements from the opening of the movement). On the other side, and simultaneously, the sufferings resulting from the strokes of fate, which bear the undertone of death, are to be perceived in the

[82] Cf. Drewermann, Eugen. (2023). „2. Sommervorlesung 2023: Märchen als Therapie. Auslegung von Grimms ‚Das Mädchen ohne Hände'". [Lecture]. Minutes: 01:07:45.

[83] Cf. Dittrich, Marie-Agnes. "Die Lieder. 'Für Menschenohren sind es Harmonien'". In: Dürr, Walther. Krause, Andreas. (2020). *Schubert Handbuch.* P.165.

tone repetitions (right hand). It should be highlighted that the just described junction of opposites is a trait of archetypal nature, since archetypes carry a polarity in themselves (Fig. 17.7).

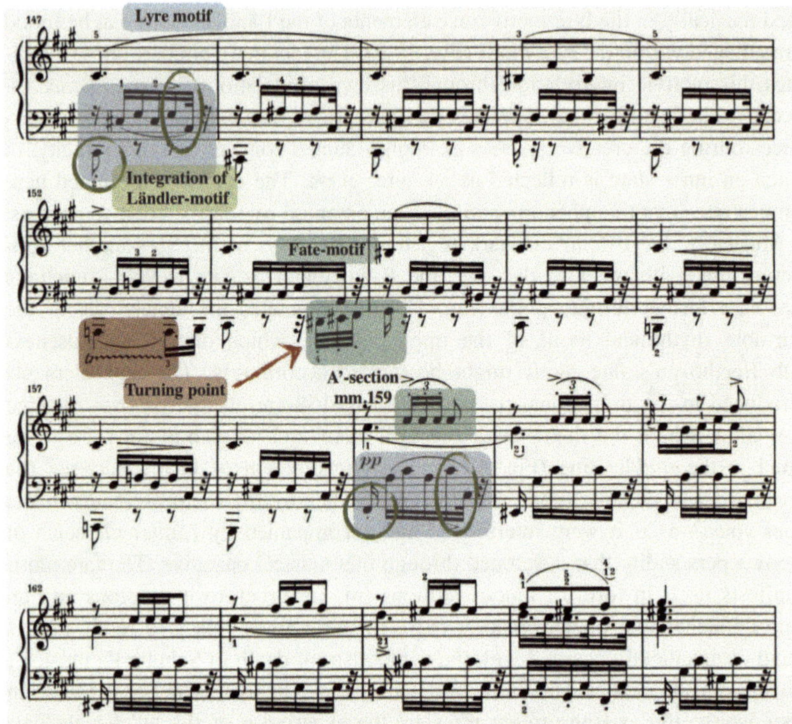

Fig. 17.7 The Elysium as the place allowing an integration attempt of the split elements: The Ländler motif integrated in the Lyre-motif. The apparition of the trill in the dark color range of the piano as a turning point and the subsequent emergence of the fate-motif, later in the beginning of the A'-section, tied with the death semantic (tone repetitions). (Sheet music excerpt taken and adapted from *Henle digital edition*) © 2016 G. Henle Verlag, Munich

17.6 An attempt of a "regressive recovery of the Persona"[84]—The refusal attitude of the "I"—A new attempt to resolve the dialectics and the resulting expression of "poetic nihilism"[85] in Schubert

Following the passage in the *Elysium* as an attempt to integrate the opposites, a psychological regression happens subsequently: the "I" shifts back into the realm of self-illusion, when the Ländler motif is restated in its initial form in m. 177, yet in A major (the tonality of the "pretence of positive moods"[86] as stated above). In Jungian terms, this might be an attempt that reflects a process of a "regressive recovery of the Persona"[87], but which may be doomed to failure due to the tonality into which the "I" has fallen. The fate motif is reduced to one note, repurposing its original meaning into the role of a death knell (the e natural of the right hand). Bearing the context of A major in mind, the death knell almost has the quality of the characteristic longing for death ("Todessehnsucht"). Death is perceived by the "I" as a luminous, positive atmosphere, congruently with the Romantic aesthetics (12). It expresses an infinite quality of time, characteristic of the unconscious realm, as if the return to the primordial state is unconsciously being foretold. Musically, the ***fp***-chords from the A-section are restated (e.g., for the A major passage mm.27–28). Yet, this time in mm.185–186, these chords remain in the ***f***-dynamics and are marked by accents. Additionally, the movement depicts a rising gesture—in opposition to the akin passage in the A-section

[84] Jung, Carl Gustav. (2023). *Die Beziehung zwischen dem Ich und dem Unbewussten.* P55. (Trans by the author). German expression: "Die regressive Wiederherstellung der Persona.".

[85] The term "poetic nihilism" refers to Jean Paul's "Vorschule der Ästhetik" of 1804. It has as its foundation the concepts of "arbitrariness" ("Willkür"), which is linked to the concept of fantasy. The latter is understood by Jean Paul as a "religious intuition" ("religiöse Intuition") and the reverse side of it represents poetic nihilism. As such, poetic nihilism means the "bottomless depth" ("bodenlosen Tiefe"). Arendt, Dieter. (1972). *Der 'poetische Nihilismus' in der Romantik. Band I.* Part II, Chap. 3: "Die Formel: 'Poetischer Nihilismus'". P.44–50. Gernot Gruber in particular has applied this concept to Schubert. Cf. Gruber, Gernot. (2010). *Schubert. Schubert?*

[86] Böhm, Richard. (2006). *Symbolik und Rhetorik im Liedschaffen von Franz Schubert.* P.57.

[87] Jung, Carl Gustav. (2023). *Die Beziehung zwischen dem Ich und dem Unbewussten.* P.55. (Trans by the author). German expression: "Die regressive Wiederherstellung der Persona.".

expressing a falling movement—and comprises the ambit of an octave, i.e., corresponds to the musical rhetorical figure of an *exclamatio.* After this *exclamatio,* a descending line in a *catabasis* manner follows, beginning with a painful *sforzando* on the first beat of m.187. Interpreting these facts, out of the musical analytical observations and in a Jungian manner can lead to a fruitful conclusion: when confronted again with the bare outer reality, a cry of despair and denial follows (mm. 185–188), inducing the inner will of total annihilation (mm.201–202). In this sense, when wholeness is always sought but, on the contrary, only fragments are perceived, the nihilistic attitude may present itself as an answer.

Yet, beforehand, a final attempt to solve this dilemma occurs in the Coda section, precisely in the mm.189–194 (Fig. 17.8). The transformation of the sigh motif, initially featuring the half-tone step, is evident through the whole tone step of the melody. This change brings an unexpected harmony in m. 191, which conveys a momentarily illumination in D major. This tonality is described by Schubart as the key of victory and triumph; Böhm, on the other hand, recognizes the closeness with the Beyond[88]. The ***p***-dynamic slightly contradicts the tone of triumph and victory, it rather points to this moment as a possible illusory triumphal instant or apparent victory of the "I"[89]. The harmony quickly shifts back, through the chromatic descending bassline in m.192, which will lead to the Neapolitan sixth chord in m. 193, the symbol of pain[90]. Simultaneously, the sigh motif returns to its initial form as a descending semitone, firstly present in the bass line (with the note sequence: natural C–H in mm. 192–193), secondly, echoing in the octaviated melodic gesture of the right hand, as part of the thematic melodic line (note sequence: natural G–F-sharp in mm.193–194). The painful element predominates in this harmonic statement.

[88] Böhm, Richard. (2006). *Symbolik und Rhetorik im Liedschaffen von Franz Schubert.* P.54.

[89] A similar occurrence can be found in the march section of the *Introduktion und Variationen* for flute and piano on the lied "Trockne Blumen" out of *Die Schöne Müllerin* song cycle (cf. 15).

[90] The Neapolitan sixth harmony is seen as a "lamentation chord" ("Klageakkord") until the romantic period inclusive. Cf. Kühn, Clemens. (2005). *Analyse lernen.* P. 76.

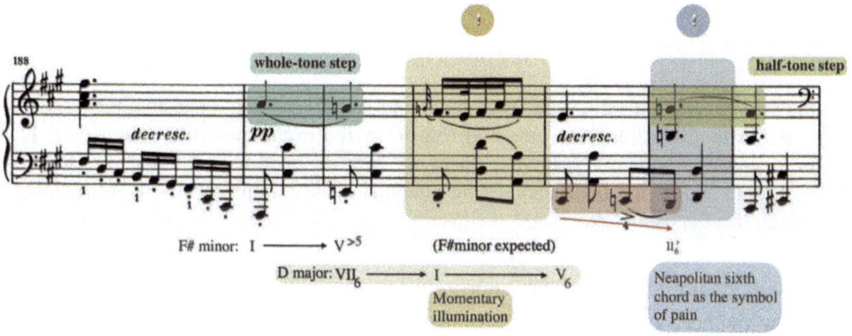

Fig. 17.8 Coda section mm. 189. A new attempt to solve the dilemma. The momentary illumination moment and the return to pain with the Neapolitan sixth chord. (Sheet music excerpt taken and adapted from *Henle digital edition*) © 2016 G. Henle Verlag, Munich

The second movement ends with the rhetorical figure of death, the bare octave, which must be interpreted from a philosophical point of view. As Weischedel explains in Heideggerian terms, the "nothingness is a process"[91] and "the being [" das Sein"] has […] the same ground structure of the nothingness; it is an occurrence, a 'basic process of happening', an 'event'"[92]—and this event is an inner one; the nothingness, in which the "I" now finds its existence, functions here as a turning point, from which new elements can emerge.

This ending may thus function as a psychological rebirth. Strikingly, Schubert will open the subsequent sonata movement with the arpeggiated chords that preceded the bare octaves (mm.196–200). The arpeggiated chords, in turn, recall the Furies of the middle section of the second movement. They are, in the third movement, presented transformed in spirit (*Scherzo*). The character quality change in the *Scherzo* movement indicates their integration in the new "I" as a "Dümmling"[93]—an archetypal personification characterized mainly by its open, naïve

91 Weischedel, Wilhelm. (1988). *Die philosophische Hintertreppe.* P.280. (Trans. by the author). German expression: "Das Nichts ist ein Vorgang".

92 Ibid. P.281. (Trans. by the author). German expression: "Das Sein nun hat für Heidegger dieselbe Grundstruktur wie das Nichts; es ist ein Geschehen, ein ‚Grundgeschehnis', ein ‚Ereignis'".

93 The "Dümmling", an archetypal figure, is related to the trickster, however, in its nature quite distinct from the trickster—the "Dümmling" figure is rather characteristic of European culture, and his personality traits can be comprehended through Brother Grimm's fairy tales, e.g., "Die Drei Federn" ("The Three feathers"). Cf. Grimm, Jacob. Grimm, Wilhelm. (2015). *Grimms Märchen.*

nature, moved by intuition and love, which permits a new perspective on the situation in a playful manner:

> "Jung illustrates in his discourse that this figure [the Dümmling"] has an almost religious meaning and plays an essential role in sacred events in many cultures. [...] These figures frequently point the finger on painful wounds or taboos in a society, openly addressing them and setting potential healing transformations in motion through this exposure"[94].

Analytical results allow for the interpretation that Schubert seems to find a resonance with the figure of the "Dümmling", who will help resolve all questions, as will be examined in the Epilogue (17.7). The fermata at the end of the second movement functions as a bridge and indicates the interconnectedness between the two movements and the subsequent psychological development. Within this fermata (nothingness), the decisive transformation happens, which will allow the above-mentioned integration of the Furies in the new, yet to be born "I" of the third movement.

17.7 Conclusions on the Second Movement of the A Major Sonata D 959. Epilogue: The Archetype of the "Dümmling" and Preliminary Considerations on the B-flat Major Sonata D 960

To summarize, the second movement of the A major sonata can be interpreted as the representation of the relationship between the shadow and the Persona, between the cultural, collective unconscious and the elements of a biographical nature (Figs. 17.10 and 17.11). Alfred Brendel's description of this movement as an "irrational explosion"[95], embedded in a sonata, which itself displays a positive, luminous activity[96], is confirmed by these analytical findings. Brendel's choice of words points to the spontaneity in the act of creation, which is musically perceptible (both audibly and visibly, especially in the facsimile). This spontaneity

[94] Roesler, Christian. (2022). *Development of a Reconceptualization of Archetype Theory.* Report to the IAAP. P. 51.

[95] Brendel, Alfred. (1996). *Musik beim Wort genommen.* P. 92.

[96] Ibid. P. 150. (Trans. by the author). German expression: „die Antithese leuchtender, ins Positive gewendeter Aktivität, [...]". Brendel's statement is contextualized in his understanding of the piano trilogy in a dialectic sense of thesis-antithesis-synthesis, being the A-major sonata the antithesis to the c-minor Sonata D 958.

reveals the participation of the archetypal shadow which clearly takes the upper hand. In this sense, the parallelism made by Brendel between Goya and Schubert, presented previously (10), can be understood here under the motto "The [Dance] of Reason Produces Monsters"—derived from Goya's title of the aquatint series of *Los caprichos,* "The Sleep of Reason Produces Monsters" (Fig. 17.9). For Goya, the title possibly points to the "Enlightened [who] had fallen into the dark"[97] and to the monsters that arise when reason is asleep[98]. For Schubert, "reason" may be understood more in connection with the censorship regime and to the good manners of behaviour of such a society; the monsters as the shadows, in turn, reveal the other façade behind this world of appearances. As explained previously, dances were a popular means of socialising at that time. The reference to the world of appearances is given by the dance element that Schubert incorporates into the sonata movement, the Ländler motif.

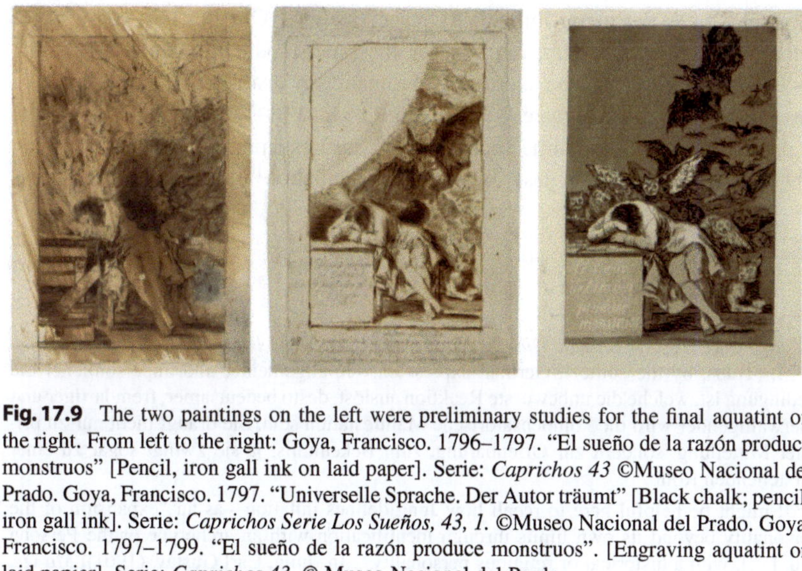

Fig. 17.9 The two paintings on the left were preliminary studies for the final aquatint on the right. From left to the right: Goya, Francisco. 1796–1797. "El sueño de la razón produce monstruos" [Pencil, iron gall ink on laid paper]. Serie: *Caprichos 43* ©Museo Nacional del Prado. Goya, Francisco. 1797. "Universelle Sprache. Der Autor träumt" [Black chalk; pencil; iron gall ink]. Serie: *Caprichos Serie Los Sueños, 43, 1.* ©Museo Nacional del Prado. Goya, Francisco. 1797–1799. "El sueño de la razón produce monstruos". [Engraving aquatint on laid papier]. Serie: *Caprichos 43.* © Museo Nacional del Prado

The Ländler motif, representing the mask element in this context, expresses an over-developed Persona. This conclusion arises from the extreme proportions

[97] López-Linares, José Luis. *Francisco de Goya—Der Schlaf der Vernunft.* [Documentary].
[98] Cf. Ibid.

that the shadow expression took in the middle section—an expression of the archetypal shadow, that culminates in annihilation, the destructive urge typical of the collective shadow. This shows the repressed and split-off elements that resulted from an over-developed Persona:

> "The more general and impersonal the condition that triggers the unconscious reaction, the more significant, strange and overwhelming the compensatory manifestation will be. It urges not only to private communication, but to revelation, to confession, indeed it even compels to a performing role"[99].

Out of this experience, there are elements of the personality which get split and are repressed, falling in this manner into the depths of the unconscious. There, they gain a life of their own, acting autonomously and chaotically, and eventually engulfing the "I". This emergence of the shadow structures is distinctly perceivable in the middle section through the uncertain harmonies (e.g., the suggested harmonies of A-flat major mm.89–90, respectively, of C-major mm. 98–99), the enharmonic ambiguity (e.g., mm.91–92), the rapid modulation shifts (e.g., mm. 93–94, mm. 102–103), the increased chromaticism characteristic of the whole passage, the use of accentuated syncopations (mm. 114–115), the extreme ranges in pitch within the short time span of five measures (mm. 105 top note to mm. 109 lowest note), etc. The described process of inflation[100], after a first conscious

---

[99] Jung, Carl Gustav. (2023). *Die Beziehung zwischen dem Ich und dem Unbewussten.* P. 74. (Trans. by the author). German expression: "Je allgemeiner und unpersönlicher die Bedingung ist, welche die unbewusste Reaktion auslöst, desto bedeutsamer, fremdartiger und überwältigender wird die kompensatorische Manifestation sein. Sie drängt nicht nur zu privater Mitteilung, sondern zur Offenbarung, zum Bekenntnis, ja sie zwingt sogar zu einer darstellenden Rolle.".

[100] It might be helpful here to recall how Jung defines inflation—as an "expansion of the personality beyond its own limits through identification with an archetype or the Persona and, […], with a historical or religious personality.". In: Jung, Carl Gustav. (1961). *Ma vie.* P.630. (Trans. by the author). French expression: "Inflation. Expansion de la personnalité au-delà de ses propres limites par identification avec un archétype ou avec la persona et, […] avec une personalité historique ou religieuse.". This phenomenon is understood as a process of "an overwhelming identification, or even a conflation with a particular archetype, or archetypal image flooding out of the collective unconscious into consciousness, so that consciousness drowns, metaphorically speaking, in the archetype". Roesler, Christian. (2022). *The Archetype Concept of C.G. Jung.* (Trans. by Alexander Ulyet and Christian Roesler). Chapter 5.2: "Clinical application—5.2.1. Character—identity—biography". P.123.

processing, will finally lead, through a process of regression, to a nihilistic experience[101], from the nothingness of which new things can generate again, what will subsequently happen in the third movement. Such outburst was the result of an "abaissement du niveau mental"[102] since the experience of such a condition reveals itself through "logical discontinuity, fragmentary character, […] irrational expressions […]"[103]—characteristics that were musically identifiable as such in the analysis of the middle section. With the diminished seventh chord passage, all possibilities of a tonal/personality centre were in fact multiplied. It is of importance to understand these musical and psychological processes in the context of the entire sonata, indeed of the entire trilogy, due to the intrinsic interrelationships of the motivic material[104]. This final step of contextualization will point to the importance of the "Dümmling" figure for the outcome of the creative psychic process of Schubert's piano trilogy.

Remarkably, the "Dümmling" archetype, with its capacity to integrate repressed elements in a playful manner (cf. its appearance in the piano trio in E-flat major D 929 of 1827, 19, 19.2), will accompany the "I" more closely from then on, and will reappear e.g., in the last movement of the B-flat major sonata. Brendel had already pointed to the "playful power" ("spielerische Kraft")[105] of this movement:

> "'Fatigue' and 'resignation'? No: graceful determination, playful power. Ironic wink; great cantabile flow; obstinate belligerence. Overcoming the C minor fixation on the ninth attempt: Moment of greatest self-forgetfulness. Emphatically cheerful expression at the end."[106].

---

[101] The author understands this particular movement as an example of what Gernot Gruber termed "poetic nihilism" in Schubert. Cf. Gruber, Gernot. (2010). *Schubert. Schubert?*

[102] Jung, Carl Gustav. (2014). "Psychology and Alchemy". In: *The Collected Works of C.G. Jung. Vol. 12.* (Trans. by Gerhard Adler and R.F.C. Hull). Chapter "Initial dreams".

[103] Jung, Carl Gustav. (2014). "The structure and dynamics of the Psyche". In: Ibid. *Vol. 8.* Chapter "The transcendent function".

[104] For the motivic interrelations between all three last piano sonatas see: Brendel, Alfred. (1996). *Musik beim Wort genommen.* P. 80–153.

[105] Brendel, Alfred. (1996). *Musik beim Wort genommen.* P.137.

[106] Ibid. (Trans. by the author). German expression: "'Ermüdung' und 'Resignation'? Nein: graziöse Entschlossenheit, spielerische Kraft. Ironisches Augenzwinkern; großer kantabler Fluß; obstinate Streitlust. Überwindung der c-Moll-Fixierung beim neunten Anlauf: Moment größter Selbstvergessenheit. Betont fröhliche Miene am Schluß.".

In the analytical context of D 960 the appearance of the "Dümmling" archetype shows a quite multifaceted musical manifestation: in the beginning of the last movement of D 960 sonata, it will embody the sigh motif (as the representation of suffering, e.g., m.3f.) in order to integrate it. Its function at this point seems to be to process the *suspiratio* sigh motif, which is here associated with the theme of death. In fact, the fourth movement of D 960 opens with the rhetorical figure of the "bare" octave, which, as previously seen, bears the death semantic. In addition to the terrifying octaviated G at the beginning, the theme begins with the B natural, suggesting the C minor tonality—the beginning is harmonically ambiguous. The melody abruptly engenders a harmonic shift to B-flat major, as if nothing were, i.e., in a quite playful manner, typical of the "Dümmling". The "I" as the "Dümmling" will help to process this biographic related motif along the movement and fulfill its archetypal function of self-regulation.

The artistic creative process of Schubert that was here examined musically exemplifies Jung's thoughts on the self-regulation tendency of the psyche[107]:

> "I therefore regard the loss of equilibrium as something expedient, because it replaces the failing consciousness with the automatic and instinctive activity of the unconscious, which aims to establish a new equilibrium and also achieves this goal—provided that the consciousness is able to assimilate, i.e., understand and process, the content produced by the unconscious."[108].

The "loss of equilibrium" mentioned by Jung in this citation can be pinpointed in the second movement of the A major Sonata D 959. In turn, the "assimilation of consciousness" is subsequently achieved through the autonomous emergence of the "Dümmling" figure, first in the *Scherzo* of the A major sonata (furies motif), then in the last movement of the B-flat major sonata (sigh motif).

---

[107] This will also be verified again later (20).

[108] Jung, Carl Gustav. (2023). *Die Beziehung zwischen dem Ich und dem Unbewussten.* P.53–54. (Trans. by the author). German expression: „Ich betrachte daher den Gleichgewichtsverlust als etwas Zweckmäßiges, denn er ersetzt das versagende Bewusstsein durch die automatische und instinktive Tätigkeit des Unbewussten, welche auf die Herstellung eines neuen Gleichgewichts abzielt und dieses Ziel auch erreicht—vorausgesetzt, dass das Bewusstsein imstande ist, die vom Unbewussten produzierten Inhalte zu assimilieren, das heißt, zu verstehen und zu verarbeiten.".

The observations presented in this chapter have shown that the "Dümmling" of the B-flat major sonata is no longer related to the semantic meaning of the arpeggiated chords of the recitative section of the slow movement of the A major sonata, where the Furies were representative of the collective shadow. This suggests that the split element of the Furies has meanwhile been integrated, and that the same is intended with the sigh motif. The "I" needed the appearance of the ludic "Dümmling" to finally integrate the aspect related to the *suspiratio.* This can also explain psychologically why the persona-shadow problematics is addressed so "late" in the individuation process, when it usually is described as the first station in the individuation process (3). Could this point to a rather spiral-like development, that Jung himself had already mentioned, especially in connection with dreams (7.2)[109]? This question will be verified and discussed again later (20) (Figs. 17.10 and 17.11).

[109] Cf. Jung, Carl Gustav. (2014). "Psychology and Alchemy". In: *The Collected Works of C.G. Jung. Vol.12.* (Trans. by Gerhard Adler and R.F.C. Hull). Chapter 3: "IV. The Symbols of the Self.".

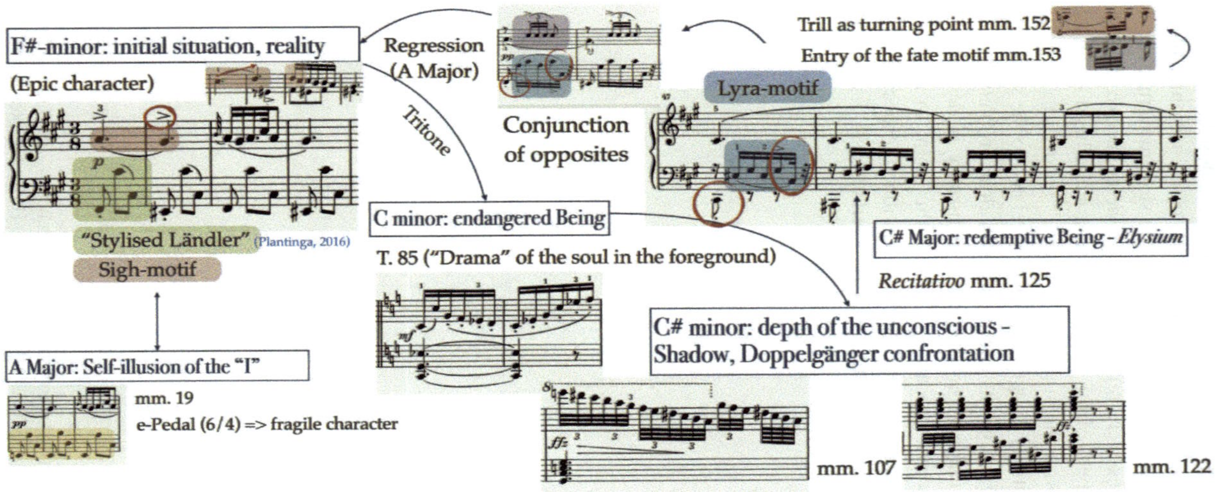

Fig. 17.10 The psychological stations and key relationships. (Sheet music excerpt taken and adapted from *Henle digital edition*) © 2016 G. Henle Verlag, Munich

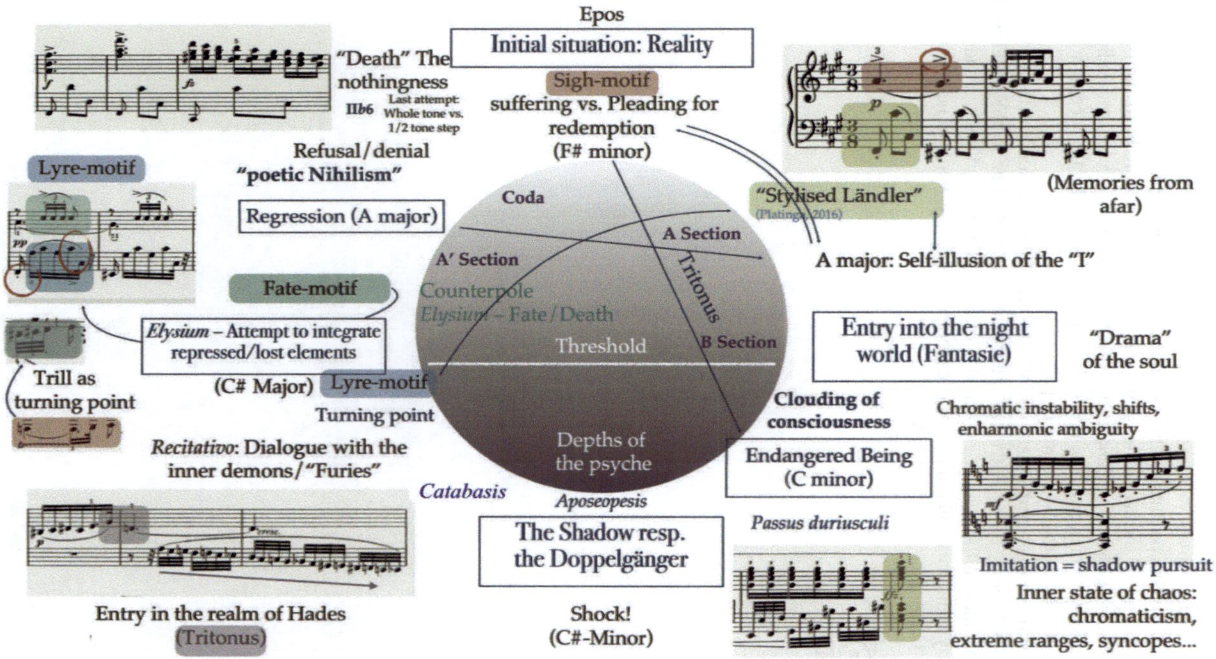

Fig. 17.11 The inner psychic process inherent in the second movement of the A major piano sonata D 959. (Sheet music excerpt taken from *Henle digital edition*) © 2016 G. Henle Verlag, Munich

B-Flat Major Piano Sonata D 960, II. Movement: The Phenomenon of Rapture and the Subsequent Spiritual Transformation

18

The *Andante con moto* of the B-flat major sonata inherits several archetypal and musical motifs from the *Andantino* of the A major sonata, as it was composed concurrently with the previously analysed sonata movement. These include, presented here in general terms: the sigh motif, the theme of the paradise on earth and the fate motif. However, these are worked out here from a different perspective.

The importance of the *suspiratio* figure was in the foreground of the *Andantino* of the A major sonata; there it represented the expression of the Persona-shadow dialectic, i.e., embedded in the context of the meaning of dances, respectively of masks, in a society marked by a censorship regime. As it will be demonstrated in the analysis, this sigh motif—in both forms, as an ascending and descending gesture—can be found again in the midpoint of the slow movement of the B-flat major sonata. Here, the *suspiratio* appears intertwined with a particular rhythmic motif that is linked to a specific archetypal manifestation, the Titan, Atlas. This reference is due to the recurrence of this motif in several of Schubert's works, notably in the lied "Der Atlas" D 957, from which the specific analogy presents itself. As already suggested by Arthur Godel, both motifs, the sigh, and the Atlas motif[1], play an important role throughout the entire trilogy D 958–960 (Fig. 18.2). Observed from a symbolic perspective, this mythological figure

The music analytical and psychological findings developed in this chapter were presented by the author herself in public for the first time under the title "Schuberts Klaviersonate B-Dur D 960, 2. Satz. Eine Formale und Hermeneutische Analyse mit der Archetypenlehre von C.G. Jung" in the form of a one-and-a-half hour and slide-assisted lecture in the frame of a music analysis seminar at the University Mozarteum, Salzburg (November 24th, 2022), under the supervision of Barbara Dobretsberger.

[1] Cf. Godel, Arthur. (1985). *Schuberts letzte drei Klaviersonaten (D958—960).*

L. Dill, *Schubert's Metamorphoses*,
https://doi.org/10.1007/978-3-662-73476-6_18

has fascinated humankind since the dawn of History, having been the subject of numerous artistic expressions throughout the centuries. To amplify the associated Christian symbolism seems pertinent, as this encompasses Schubert's religious environment. This is specifically true for this musical work since—as already suggested in the introduction of the previous chapter (17)—the theological content of Schubert's late sonatas seems substantial. In particular, the one aspect of the Atlas as the bearer of a painful world finds its parallel, on the one hand, in the Old Testament (the book of Job), and in the New Testament (Christ), on the other.

The related theme of the *Elysium* is featured in the contrasting B-section of the movement (unlike the *Andantino* of the A major sonata where it appeared in the A'-section). In connection with this archetypal subject, the musical semiquaver-triplets motif that arises in this passage of the B-flat major sonata is of symbolic significance. The archetypal superordinated component that emerges for the first time in this movement is the symbol of water. Due to the context of the Atlas myth, or of the Christian tradition, this motif can be named as the river motif[2], as it will be explained later in the chapter. The fate motif, in turn, will emerge in the A'-section, as in the Andantino D 959, manifesting itself in its original Beethovenian form as four successive notes (short-short-short-long).

It is of particular interest to ascertain the repercussion of these archetypes in the creative process, i.e., how Schubert dealt with these questions artistically, and the impact they have on the individuation process of the composer, who himself had a life full of peripeties and was approaching his own death at the time of composition. In order to work out the semantics of the symbolic and archetypal content inherent in Schubert's work, it is necessary to begin with an introduction to the myth of the Atlas and its Christian parallel[3], followed by a concise analysis of the Heine setting D 957. References to other works will be made, from which this musical motif derives. The Weltschmerz undertone (8),

---

[2] The justification for associating this musical motif with the water symbol lies on the examples to be found in other works by Schubert, where the accuracy of this semantic is obvious, e.g., the brooklet motif in *Die Schöne Müllerin* (15).

[3] This methodological approach, which focuses on the overarching principle and the interconnections between the different archetypal elements of various traditions, is characteristic of the Jungian amplification method. Jolande Jacobi stated: "For the method of amplification [...] when using analogies [...], the equality of the core of meaning is what is fundamentally decisive [...]". Jacobi, Jolande. (2006). *Die Psychologie von C.G. Jung*. P. 88. (Trans. by the author). German expression: "Für die Methode der Amplifikation sind [...] bei der Heranziehung von Analogien, [...] die Gleichheit des Bedeutungskernes das prinzipiell Maßgebende.".

which is already existent in the A major sonata, is elevated into another degree of expression in the *Andante sostenuto* of the B-flat major sonata.

18.1 Atlas: From the Mythological Figure to the Origins of the Atlas Motif in Schubert's Music and its Existence in the Sonata Trilogy D 958–960

The fate of the Titan Atlas, as it is known from the ancient Greek mythology, was to carry the entire world: the pillars that supported the vault of heaven above the earth, which were grounded in the seabed. Atlas is commonly thought to be situated near his daughters, the Hesperides (nymphs), in the vicinities of the garden of Hesperides, in a blissful spot on the horizon where heaven and earth, light and darkness, the origins and the abyss meet:

> "The usual location of Atlas is considered to be the uppermost west of the Hesperides, where heaven descends to earth, on the border of light and darkness, the regions of the origin and abyss of heaven and earth, where 'the regions of great dreamed bliss crowd together'."[4].

This helpful description is suitable for an in-depth psychological interpretation: it suggests that Atlas knew the light and the dark side of life, the celestial heights of heavens as well as the deep uncharted waters of the sea[5]—possibly even incorporating both aspects in himself, as the warrior that he was. Due to his participation in the war of the Titans against the Gods of Olympus Atlas was condemned to the destiny of carrying "the entire world of pain" ("die ganze Welt der Schmerzen"[6])

---

[4] Furtwängler, Adolf. (1889). „Atlas". In: *Ausführliches Lexikon der Griechischen und römische Mythologie. Band I.* Roscher, W.H. (Ed.). (Trans. by the author). P. 706. German expression: „Als der gewöhnliche Standort des Atlas gilt der äußerste Westen bei den Hesperien, wo der Himmel sich auf die Erde senkt, an der Grenze des Lichts und Dunkels, den Gegenden des Ursprungs und Abgrunds von Himmel und Erde, wo ‚die Gegenden der großen geträumten Glückseligkeiten sich zusammendrängen.".

[5] Eugen Drewermann explains the origins of Homer's description of Atlas as being aware of the depths of the ocean. Cf. Drewermann, Eugen. (2013). *Liebe, Leid und Tod.* „Anhang, Anmerkungen".

[6] Heine, Heinrich. (2002). *Buch der Lieder.* The Project Gutenberg. (Trans. by the author).

on his shoulders. The fact that his name has the etymological connotation of "carrier", "sufferer" or "endurer"[7] indicates his reality (Fig. 18.1).

Fig. 18.1 Left image: Singer Sargent, John. (1925). "Atlas and the Hesperides". [Oil on canvas]. Museum of Fine Arts Boston. On the right: Atlas carrying the vault of heaven. Roman statue of Atlas (2nd century AD). National Archeological Museum of Naples. (Taken from wikipedia.org © 2007 Lalupa)

This one aspect of Atlas' story finds its echo in the Christian tradition. The tragic component of Atlas' destiny, having to endure a world full of pain and suffering, can also be found analogously in the biblical book of Job in the Old Testament. Job, by contrast guiltless, had to prove his faith and trust in God by going through paths of darkness and incomprehensibility, bearing several painful challenges and, eventually, illness[8]. Redemption was accorded to him through his

[7] Grant, Michael. Hazel, John. (2009). *Lexikon der antiken Mythen und Gestalten.* P. 81. (Trans. by the author). German expression: „sein Name bedeutet wahrscheinlich 'Träger' oder ‚Dulder'".

[8] With this comparison, the author is only pointing out this specific aspect in common and is aware of the discrepancies and differences between the Atlas myth and the book of Job. Jung has provided his reading of the book of Job in *Antwort auf Hiob,* first published in Zurich 1952. Cf. Jung, Carl Gustav. (2014). "Psychology and Religion: West and East". In: *The Collected Works of C.G. Jung. Vol.11.* (Ed. and trans. by Gerhard Adler and R.F.C. Hull). Part one, Chapter VI: "Answer to Job".

questioning and indignation[9]. Similarly, in the New Testament Christ's death on the cross stands for the symbol of suffering but also of triumph[10]. Despite accepting the designs of his Father, Christ also expressed his doubts at the moment of crucifixion. For Jungians, the crucifixion of Christ points to the need of accepting to carry one's own cross—symbolically, this attitude sets a process in motion and represents an important moment in the individuation process[11].

The biblical equivalents are helpful to consider in the context of the music analysis of Schubert's musical setting and the last sonata, since the manifestation of pain and of inner questioning of fate is to be found in these last piano works (17). If these mythological or biblical stories are understood as bearing a common archetypal core, then a bridge can be built between the collective unconscious and the personal, biographical level, since motifs of these two spheres are often interconnected.

---

[9] Cf. Evangelisch-Reformierte Landeskirche des Kantons Zürich Kirchenrat. (2008). *Zürcher Bibel.*

[10] Cf. Mollwo-Oesterreicher, Marianne. (1978). *Herder Lexikon Symbole.* P. 93.

[11] As a sidenote: Jung himself had a copy of a glass-painting depicting Christ's crucifixion in his therapy room to remind his patients of this message. The glass-painting in question is from the Church in Königsfelden from the 14th century (Fig. 18.9). This image had been thoughtfully placed in the room. As Angelica Löwe explains, every object and its placement in Jung's therapy room had a symbolic reason behind it, with the aim of having an effect on the patient who enters it. In her article, Löwe points to the following main aspects, that she describes as a "dynamic Trias" ("dynamischen Trias"): (i) the three glass-painting windows (Tradition), depicting the Scouring of Christ, the Crucifixion and the Entombment of Christ, (ii) the Shroud of Turin (death of God), which was intended as a devotional image ("Andachtsbild")—a practice incorporating a dialogue with a picture—an image that was kept concealed from the eyes of the patient, and (iii) Jung's own illustrations in the *Red* Book as the element of "Vision" ("objective Psyche"); featuring the artistic result of his inner confrontations, fantasies and of his practice of active imagination. The latter was left open and often used for discussion with the patient. According to Löwe, Jung's idea was to allow the unconscious to be stirred, so to speak, by being seized by the image of the death of God, to be confronted and to deal with it, and thus to bring, through a rather unconscious manner, the missing fourth element (i.e., Resurrection) to life. Cf. Löwe, Angelica. "Diaphanie, Verhüllung, Vision in Jungs Arbeitszimmer—eine Raumerkundung". (2023). In: *Analytische Psychologie. Zeitschrift für Psychotherapie und Psychoanalyse. Heft 200. 2/2023. 54 Jg.* Bovensiepen, G., Kast, Verena., Wilke, H.-J. (Eds.) P. 310–317. In other words, Jung provokes a reaction on the part of the patient's unconscious that generates an inner movement upon which the fourth element, i.e., wholeness, is achieved. This is an important observation that will be referred to in the conclusions (20).

Schubert was deadly ill at the time he composed the piano trilogy. Besides, the fact that Schubert had a life full of personal and work-related challenges[12] is in this sense of relevance. It is highly probable that these archetypal narratives found an inner resonance in Schubert at that time:

> "[...] if some great idea takes hold of us from outside, we must understand that it takes hold of us only because something in us responds to it and goes out to meet it."[13].

The findings of Arthur Godel on the musical Atlas motif can support this thought. Following Godel's own words, this motif almost fulfilled a "programmatic"[14] function in his late works, as it will be elaborated with due brevity.

While working on the piano trilogy, Schubert also composed a series of musical settings on poems by Rellstab, Heine and Seidl, which date back to August of the same year. Later, these collections of songs were bound together and originated the song cycle known today as *Schwanengesang.* Amongst Heinrich Heine's *Buch der Lieder* ("Die Heimkehr"), one poem is dedicated to the myth of the Atlas (XXIV: "Ich unglückseliger Atlas"). Here, Heine emphasizes the suffering of Atlas, having to endure a world of pain. Heine's characteristic ironic element comes to expression in the second stanza:

„Ich unglücksel'ger Atlas!
Eine Welt, die ganze Welt der
Schmerzen muss ich tragen.
Ich trage Unerträgliches,
und brechen will mir das Herz im Leibe.

Du stolzes Herz, du hast es ja gewollt!
Du wolltest glücklich sein, unendlich
glücklich,
oder unendlich elend, stolzes Herz,
und jetzo bist du elend."[15].

"I wretched Atlas! a world, the entire
world of pain must I carry. I bear the
unbearable, and my heart will shatter
in my flesh.

Thou haughty heart, thou wanted it so!
Thou wanted to be joyous, endlessly
joyous, or endlessly miserable, [thou]
haughty heart,
and miserable are thou now."[16].

[12] Some of the personal or work-related challenges are mentioned in part III and others are contextualized and mentioned objectively in individual analysis chapters.

[13] Jung, Carl Gustav. (2011). *Four Archetypes.* P. 54. (Trans. by R.F.C. Hull).

[14] Godel, Arthur. (1985). *Schuberts letzte drei Klaviersonaten (D958—960).* P. 27.

[15] Heine, Heinrich. (2002). *Buch der Lieder.* The Project Gutenberg.

[16] Ibid. (Trans. by the author).

This poem inspired Schubert, who set these verses into music under the title of "Der Atlas"[17]. This song is featured in the autograph as the eighth of the entire *Schwanengesang* cycle. To musically incorporate the character of Atlas, Schubert drew on a powerful rhythmic cell, which is recognizable as a short note followed by two equal longer notes (Fig. 18.2). This rhythmic reference permits naming this motif accordingly as the Atlas motif[18], semantically tied to the Titan's sufferings. According to Godel, the same rhythmic cell seems to have fulfilled a significant function throughout Schubert's "late works", appearing simultaneously in different instrumental works (Fig. 18.2)[19]. Its first appearance within the late compositions has been identified in the *Klavierstück* in E-flat minor D 946, composed in May 1828[20]. As delineated in Godel's research, Schubert referred to a Beethovenian motif, existent in *Egmont*[21]. A further finding of Godel consisted of the observation that the meaning of the Atlas' motif changes across several works:

> "A variety of associations could be linked to this motif in 1828: Suffering under the burden of artistic responsibility that he had been encumbered with since Beethoven's death, fighting against isolation as expressed particularly clearly in the "Winterreise", rebelling against the unattainability of personal and social ideals, hoping for a future freedom like Egmont and, in all of this, an awareness of futility that takes the edge off the combative gesture, moves the emotional cipher into the distance of romantic irony and exposes it to constant change. The meaning of the small rhythmic formula, for example, changes from time to time, without much purpose of its own, therefore always in need of interpretation like a symbol, i.e. ideal process material"[22].

---

[17] The underlined verses or passages in the poem are the ones that Schubert repeats in his musical setting.

[18] Cf. Godel, Arthur. (1985). *Schuberts letzte drei Klaviersonaten (D958—960).*

[19] Cf. Ibid.

[20] Cf. Ibid. P. 27.

[21] Cf. Ibid. Whether this "takeover" is a conscious tribute to Beethoven or a rather unconscious act of association on Schubert's part cannot be determined with certainty.

[22] Ibid. P. 27. (Trans. by the author). German expression: "Vielfältige Assoziationen, konnten sich 1828 mit diesem Motiv verbinden: Leiden unter der Last, die ihm seit Beethovens Tod an künstlerischer Verantwortung aufgebürdet war, Ankämpfen gegen die Isolation wie sie in der "Winterreise" besonders deutlich zum Ausdruck kam, Aufbegehren gegen die Unerreichbarkeit der persönlichen und gesellschaftlichen Ideale, Hoffnung auf eine zukünftige Freiheit wie Egmont und bei all dem ein Bewusstsein von Vergeblichkeit, das dem kämpferischen Gestus seine Spitze nimmt, die Gefühls-Chiffre in die Distanz romantischer Ironie rückt, sie einem steten Wandel aussetzt. So ist auch die Bedeutung der kleinen rhythmischen Formel von Mal zu Mal wechselnd, ohne viel eigene Bestimmung, daher immer wieder wie ein Symbol interpretationsbedürftig, also ideale Prozessmaterie.".

In congruence with Godel's statement, the fact that this motif reappears time and again in different concurrent musical contexts could point to a broader network of meanings, i.e., to symbolic manifestations bearing an archetypal core. Spinning this thought a further—this specific process of creation could possibly delineate the rising of consciousness with regard to the symbolic content of this musical motif across the different compositions. Said differently: increasing awareness with regard to the different aspects inherent in this archetypal motif can be deduced by Schubert's final semantic attribution of the motif to the Atlas' character featured in Heine's poem. This could mean that by the time of composing the second movement of the B-flat major sonata, Schubert possibly had this conscious association in mind or at least was developing it within himself. For this reason, it is important to briefly analyse the general significance of the Atlas motif in Heine's musical setting and subsequently uncover its different meanings that are specifically inherent in this piano trilogy, before moving to the analysis of the second movement of the B-flat sonata.

Compared to the beginning of Beethoven's *Egmont* ouverture, the Atlas rhythmic cell appears in rhythmical diminution in Schubert's Heine setting (and was similarly employed in the *Klavierstück* in E-flat minor, e.g., Fig. 18.2). This diminution immediately recreates the indignation, the revolting, fierce and struggling character of Heine's Atlas, as well as the overpowering destiny over him. The motif is featured in the deep registers of the piano, expressing the dark undertone of the poem, and it includes a rhetorical figure of symbolic importance: the *passus duriusculus* (diminished fourth B-flat–F-sharp). This is already featured in the piano prelude bars (mm.1–2) and is subsequently mirrored in the vocal part (mm.5–6) under the words "wretched Atlas" ("unglücksel'ger Atlas"). The voice begins in the same obscure tone, although it is generally marked by a substantial diastematics, often featuring the diminished fourth, fifth and the sixth intervals[23].

[23] Cf. Dittrich, Marie-Agnes. "Die Lieder. 'Für Menschenohren sind es Harmonien'". In: Dürr, Walther. Krause, Andreas. (2020). *Schubert Handbuch*. P. 261.

Fig. 18.2 Atlas motif across Schubert's works of 1828. (Figure taken and adapted from: Godel, Arthur. (1985). *Schuberts letzte drei Klaviersonaten (D958–960)*. P. 28. © 1985 Verlag Valentin Koerner, Baden-Baden)

The heaviness of the giant's steps, who carries the world on his shoulders, is immediately perceivable through tone painting means, e.g.: (i) through the low octaviated sound in the piano accompaniment and (ii) through the sound density, achieved by the tremolando chords in the right hand, creating an ongoing harmonic support throughout the entire A-section (mm.1–21). As such, Schubert does justice to Heine's all-encompassing poetic expression "the entire world" ("die ganze Welt"). It is through harmonic means, that the emotional condition of the Atlas is musically underlined. Not only are tone repetitions to be identified, but also the use of chromaticism, e.g., mm.16–17, punctually allows for the intensification of the Atlas's burden. Striking is the way Schubert musically renders the process of heart break by explicitly transforming it into a long-lasting gesture with the modulation path from G minor towards B minor (mm.16–20). The fundamental tone of the G minor chord is first chromatised (m.17), creating a diminished chord under the word "unbearable" ("unerträgliches"), which is then extended. Finally, the dominant of B is attained in m.19 yet veiled with a suspension note (B–A-sharp). Once again, the resolution is delayed in time, before arriving at the B minor chord of m.20 under the word "flesh" ("Leibe"). To emphasize the actual moment of inner laceration, the high dissonant chord of m. 21 is placed, which emotionally takes the upper hand. Shortly after, a surprising effect is given with the shift to B major in m.22. Not only do harmonic means play a central role in Schubert's musical setting, but also music rhetorical figures fulfill an important function: several *exclamatio* figures can be noted. Occasionally they appear consecutively one after the other, e.g., mm.8–9, respectively, mm.9–10 coinciding with the words "a world, the entire world" ("eine Welt, die ganze Welt").

This character is then contrasted in the B-section (mm.22–39) by the lighter bouncing pulsation of a dancing nature. The Walz-like rhythm, marked by ***fp*** accents on the first beat of each measure, could be interpreted as the musical equivalent of the Heinesque irony: Marie-Agnes Dittrich points out that this trait is achieved by merging the Walz rhythm with the dark register of the piano, highlighting the undertone of "bitter mockery"[24]. Not only Dittrich but also Stefanie Steiner and Michael Kube explain the sarcastic trait with the melody's inability to free itself from the constraints of the dotted rhythm, which is linked to the Atlas's burden in the A-section[25]. Musically, the triplets can support this reading

[24] Cf. Dittrich, Marie-Agnes. "Die Lieder. 'Für Menschenohren sind es Harmonien'". In: Dürr, Walther. Krause, Andreas. (2020). *Schubert Handbuch.* P. 261.

[25] Cf. Ibid. For both after-mentioned authors see: Steiner, Stefanie. Kube, Michael: "Schwanengesang—13 Lieder nach Gedichten von Rellstab und Heine (D 957)". In: Dürr, Walther. Kube, Michael. [et al.]. (2013). *Schubert Liedlexikon.* P. 822.

as well since, when they occur against a binary rhythm, they are known as a conflict rhythm[26]. In this respect, the off-beat repeated chords of mm.22–37 are also noteworthy: if observing this musical notation with the purpose of a psychological interpretation, it could be said that they reveal the self-ironic tone linked to a phenomenon of dissociation present in the poem—a dissociation that is related to the romantic concept of "Zerrissenheit" (4, 12). A short return to an observation of the poetic level can be instructive in this regard: dissociation and self-irony are perceptible in the opening verses of the second stanza: "Thou haughty heart, thou wanted it so! Thou wanted to be joyous, endlessly joyous […]" ("Du stolzes Herz, du hast es ja gewollt! Du wolltest glücklich sein, unendlich glücklich […]"[27]. It is as if there is another voice within, that mocks the "I" in a condescending way for its burden[28].

When the tone of the poem switches back to the lyrical "I" expressing its despair, Schubert accentuates this change harmonically by shifting back to the minor key (modulating from E minor back to G minor in mm.31–39). It is significant to mention that the *suspiratio* motif appears precisely at the moment when his misery is addressed again, e.g., under the words "endlessly miserable" ("unendlich elend") mm.30–34, both in its rising (B–C) and descending gesture (C–B and B–A–G). Coincidentally, the singing voice merges with the triplet rhythm of the piano for the first time in mm.30–31, supporting the upcoming change of atmosphere. Schubert highlights the Titan's conflicted feelings and the torn emotions by repeating the initial two verses of the closing stanza (mm.40–52) as the final refrain (A'-section). This reiteration is characterized by harmonic expressive means and by a noticeable larger ambit of the singing voice in the final measures, e.g., mm.49–50. A G minor chord is decomposed as an ascending line, surpassing the octave ambit, and thereby expressing musically the laceration gesture. This is underlined once again with the arrival at the painful A-flat note, as

[26] Dobretsberger, Barbara. Personal communication between Barbara Dobretsberger and the author. Salzburg: March 22, 2024.

[27] Heine, Heinrich. (2002). *Buch der Lieder.* The Project Gutenberg. (Trans. by the author). German expression: "Du stolzes Herz, du hast es ja gewollt! Du wolltest glücklich sein, unendlich glücklich […]".

[28] A similar description is to be found in a case-description of C.G. Jung, where he addresses such a psychological phenomenon. Cf. Jung, Carl Gustav. (2014). "Psychogenesis of mental disease.". In: *The Collected Works of C.G. Jung. Vol. 3.* (Trans. by Gerhard Adler and R.F.C. Hull). Chap. 5: "Analysis of a Case of Paranoid Dementia as a Paradigm. Continuous Associations. Subchapter: E. "Supplement". Musically, from a different perspective than that of the author, David Ferris has come to a similar interpretative outcome. Cf. Ferris, David: "Dissociation and Declamation in Schubert's Heine songs". In: Bodley, Lorraine Byrne. Horton, Julia. (2016). *Rethinking Schubert.*

the highest note of the entire song (m.50). The octave range is thus extended to a minor ninth interval and with that, the breaking ("shattering") of the heart is put directly in connection with his painful burden. Harmonically, this represents a moment of great dissonance, which is marked by the *fff* dynamics and characterises the highest emotional point of the song (*climax*).

The ensuing lament, tinged with indignation, is conveyed by the subsequent chromatic steps of the vocal part (A-flat–G–F-sharp–G), which function as a *cambiata* (m.50). Considering the way in which the half-tone steps circle around the note G, it is possible to interpret this gesture as conveying the sensation of being trapped in fate (G minor), which is musically congruent with several transmissions of the Atlas myth itself[29]. The final octave jump, that is coupled with the downwards gesture semantically charged with the meaning of Atlas's affliction ("bear", i.e., "tragen", mm.51–52), functions as a rhetorical exclamation mark. This *exclamatio* simultaneously tone paints the degree of the burden that the Titan has to carry. In this sense—and to return to a final music analytical remark—it is of interest to relate the range of the two analogous passages.

By way of comparison, the interval ambit of the previous passage of m. 14 ("bear", i.e., "tragen") featured the ambit of a minor third, which has changed to an octave range. From an interpretative point of view, this musical fact shows how the focal point has meanwhile shifted: initially the "entire world" ("die ganze Welt") itself is emphasized as an exclamation, while at the end, the act of carrying, or as translated poetically, "bearing" the entire world is particularly stressed as painful. In this manner, the withal oppressive and crushing real burden has the last word.

With these brief analytical observations on the D 957 lied, it can be stated that Schubert is faithful to the message of Heine's text in all aspects[30], even the tone volume of the poem: the *fff*-dynamics are undeniably striking for a Schubert lied and definitely raise the exclamation marks of the poetic tone its corresponding

[29] In different transmissions of several myths linked to the Atlas, the return to his fateful duty of carrying the world is described. Either he is condemned to be petrified as such, e.g., in the story involving Perseus and the medusa head, or, in the context of the Heracles' eleventh (or twelfth) task, he has to carry the world again, after having tried to escape his duty. Cf. „Atlas" in: Grant, Michael. Hazel, John. (2009). *Lexikon der antiken Mythen und Gestalten.* P. 81–82. For the second example cited see the article concerning Heracles "XI. Die goldenen Äpfel der Hesperides", in: Ibid. P. 197.

[30] The only point in which Schubert slightly differs from Heine is the form, in that he restates the initial verses again at the end of the poem, which is not a contradiction in itself but rather an emphasis of the message.

expression in the musical sphere. The atlas rhythm is tied here with the burden semantic and the indignant undertone of the Atlas.

The same sharpness of rhythm that is found in Heine's setting can also be recognized in the opening of the piano trilogy, namely in the first movement of the C minor Sonata D 958. Combining Godel's aforementioned analytical findings with the interpretative indications of Alfred Brendel can be of particular interest for carrying out an analysis of the psychological processes. The opening character of the C minor sonata is congruently described by Brendel as being "at once heroic and fearful, nervous and determined, threatening and menacing."[31]. This character changes across the trilogy, as Godel had already noted (Fig. 18.3). The atlas motif opens the A major sonata D 959, in its augmented form[32]. Contrastingly, it features a credo-like ductus. This hymnal atmosphere has been described by Brendel, who specifically portrays this beginning as a "Credo ma con fuoco"[33]. This musically utters the declaration of "I believe" (17). The B-flat major sonata is different in that it does not begin with the recovering of the Atlas motif, as it was the case in the previous one. Instead, the reappearance and transformation of this motif is to be expected in the core of the entire sonata, in its second movement. Here, the Atlas motif conveys the expression of the *Weltschmerz* in a different light, where the fateful designs of life are to be found placed in the foregrounded.

The *Andante sostenuto* of the B-flat major sonata is constructed similarly to the previously analysed sonata movement, featuring a three-part song form (A-B-A'). The oppressive atmosphere of the A-section (mm.1–42) is perceptible through various musical elements. These will be first musically analysed by immediately attaching their importance for, and function in this movement. In a second step, the psychological and symbolic analogies to the Atlas myth and elements of the Christian tradition will be drawn.

[31] Brendel, Alfred. (1996). *Musik beim Wort genommen.* P. 136. (Trans. by the author). German expression: „Zugleich heroisch und angstvoll, nervös und entschlossen, bedrohlich und bedroht.".

[32] Cf. Godel, Arthur. (1985). *Schuberts letzte drei Klaviersonaten (D958—960).*

[33] Brendel, Alfred. (1996). *Musik beim Wort genommen.* P. 136.

Fig. 18.3 General observations on the Atlas motif and its transformations across piano trilogy D 958–960 based on Godel's and Brendel's analytical observations above mentioned. (Sheet music excerpt taken and adapted from *IMSLP*)

18.2 The Sigh of Atlas. The Epic Character of the A Section and the Fusion of two Levels of Expression

Some aspects of this second movement are particularly striking in both the first analytical examination of the musical score and the first listening experience (Fig. 18.4). This is the case of the organ point, which dominates the entire A-section, determining the musical and harmonic events. Even though the fundamental tone of the *ostinato* changes from time to time underlining the harmonic path—e.g., going to the dominant sphere (mm.9–13), then harmonically shifting to the tonic parallel (m.14–29)[34]—this *ostinato* aesthetically expresses the monotonous atmosphere characteristic of this section. On the other hand, the rhythmical element of the *ostinato* features the Atlas motif discussed above. It consists of a rising gesture, encompassing three octaves in total. This motif will be present throughout the A-section, except for mm.34–42, where the Atlas rhythm is omitted; the rising gesture of the ostinato is the only element retained. Coincidentally, measure 34, marks the moment in which an *abgesang* will close the A-section.

The left-hand motif, featuring the Titan's sufferings, appears here as a simultaneous occurrence with the elements that are to be found in the right hand. The main component that characterises the thematic material of the latter is the sigh motif or *suspiratio*. It is presented as a typical descending gesture mm.1–2, but also as a rising one mm.2–3 (Fig. 18.4). These movements of expression—to

[34] The modulation to the tonic parallel tonality occurred quite unexpectedly through a sudden chromatic shift between mm.13–14. To compare, Godel draws the harmonic path in: Cf. Godel, Arthur. (1985). *Schuberts letzte drei Klaviersonaten (D958—960)*. P. 173–174.

speak in terms of Hausegger[35] (7)—can be interpreted as conveying a lamenting tone, respectively, a hopeful, even pleading, questioning undertone, which is in line with Atlas's condition. Noteworthy is the splitting of the melody into two voicings. The doubling of the melodic line a third below exhibits a further characteristic: the secondary line will eventually flow, or develop itself into an independent voice, e.g., m.4 and m.5—brief moments, in which it will no longer follow the same path of the primal line.

Regarding the structure of these musical phrases, a periodic construction can be observed[36]. Although they present a four-bar unit (occasionally extended to a five-bar structure in, e.g., m.13), the musical thought behaves much more in a fragmentary style—as if it were an undeveloped main idea that needs further processing[37]. For this reason, it is justifiable to speak in terms of an "absent theme"[38] rather than to affirm the existence of a cohesive thematic structure. These fragmentary utterances are enlivened by an upbeat gesture and developed according to the principle of variations[39] (Fig. 18.4). The aforementioned moment, featuring an irregularity of the overall phrase structure, functions as a moment of suspension in time[40] or—to anticipate a psychological reformulation of this musical event—as an instant of inner stagnation. Further halting moments in the musical ductus can be identified, e.g., m. 17 or m.29, before the shattered melody retakes its habitual path. The same applies to mm.41–42 before the B-section begins. The melodic yet disjointed core idea turns around in a circling manner throughout the entire A-section. Still, there is a development, of rather emotional nature, to be recognized: a first dynamic high point is reached in m.12 creating a slight contrast with the previous musical statements, that in turn lingered in the ***p*** dynamic range (***pp*** dynamic). Nevertheless, these instants in the ***f*** dynamic will not last long. While drastically decreasing the tone level within one and a half measures to a ***pp*** again, the musical phrase is extended by one additional measure, again creating an irregular five-bar unit (mm.12–13). Similarly, the same dynamic gesture is retaken later, though emphasized by the higher range of the piano's right hand (m. 28). These dynamic regressions ultimately recreate the feeling of suspension, characteristic of the previously analogous passages. At this point in the analysis,

[35] Cf. Hausegger, Friedrich von. (2018). *Music as Expression.*

[36] Cf. Godel, Arthur. (1985). *Schuberts letzte drei Klaviersonaten (D958—960).*

[37] Cf. Dobretsberger, Barbara. Personal communication between Barbara Dobretsberger and the author. Salzburg/Lisbon: November 25, 2021.

[38] Ibid.

[39] Cf. Godel, Arthur. (1985). *Schuberts letzte drei Klaviersonaten (D958—960).*

[40] Cf. Ibid.

it can be enriching to observe how the two examined elements, the *ostinato* of the Atlas motif and the *suspiratio* figure, are linked and merged together, featuring one level of expression. There is a further indication that hints to this analytical conclusion.

The beginning of this movement strikingly opens with the marking *con pedale.* This rather unusual notation of Schubert causes the rhythmic ostinato of the Atlas motif to merge with the sigh motifs that dominate the thematic material of the right hand. The organ point and the additional marking *con pedale* permit these two levels of expression to fuse together, forming a unity. Godel speaks of this rather unique sound experiment of Schubert as a moment of "fusion of foreground and background"[41]—an observation that is particularly suitable for a depth psychological reading. For this purpose, the left-hand ostinato is taken as bearing the semantic of the Atlas motif, i.e., as a manifestation of the one archetype, whereas the right hand is understood in general terms as the utterance of the Titan's burden. The fact that the Atlas motif transitions and crosses the threshold that separates the left-hand area from the right-hand domain immediately suggests that an (emotional) identification of the "I" with the figure of Atlas and with his sufferings might be taking place.

As a result of this reflection—if the "I" were Atlas himself—, then the identified splitting of the melodic line can hint at a further archetypal manifestation inherent in this figure—an archetype that is to be found especially active in Romanticism (4.3). The doubled voice is not quite identical to the co-starred higher one. Due to the shadow character (featured a third step below) and the self-driven behaviour it presents, this inner voice could be attributed to the doppelgänger. As seen in the previous subchapter, the Titan contains a light and a shadow side. Consequently, it is possible to understand the split aspect of the musical thematic material as the archetypal shadow element of the Atlas.

[41] Ibid. P. 172. (Trans. by the author). German expression: „Die Begleitung ist komplementärrhythmisch so eng mit der Melodie verwoben, dass Vordergrund und Hintergrund ineinander übergehen.".

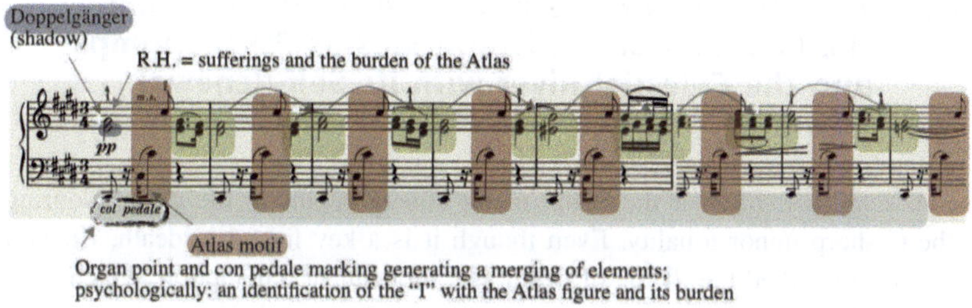

Fig. 18.4 Right hand: The absent theme and the upbeat variation principle of the sigh motif. Left hand: Organ point and the rhythmical ostinato featuring the Atlas motif. The merging of the two levels of expression and the identification of the "I" with figure of Atlas. The doppelgänger as the Atlas's shadow side inherent in the sigh motif. (Sheet music excerpt taken and adapted from *Henle digital edition*) © 2016 G. Henle Verlag, Munich

Interpreting these observations: the split "I" is submerged in the unconscious world and as such, the myth of Atlas and his sighs function as a mirror of the one level of reality (Fig. 18.10). With this particular technique, Schubert achieves to recreate an idiosyncratic time perception: a time of suspension, yet where all sufferings of the "I" are existent. Congruently, the spatial dimension is recreated with the soft dynamics[42]: it is as if these emotions are being expressed from afar, which contributes to the described feeling of a particular time dimension. These details unveil an epic undertone. The intensification of the dynamics to a *f* that were mentioned, are both times just short-lived—as if these elements were approaching, yet not being close enough to justify speaking of a dramatic undertone (as it was the case, e.g., in the B-section of the A major sonata's second movement, 17).

Even though the epic character remains rather unchangeable all through the second movement of the B-flat major sonata—differently as the previous analysed sonata movement (D 959), where it was a particular trait of A-sections only—the monotonous tone quality and the aforementioned space-time perception will change in the B-section (mm.43–89). With an activation of inner movement, the "I" will transcend into another sphere, in which celestial beings and angelic epitomes are to be identified.

[42] As worked out in previous chapters (7), the dynamic is an element pointing to the space dimension. Cf. Schlesinger, Max. (1912). *Symbolik in der Tonkunst*.

18.3 The Choir of Angels and Entering the *Elysium*: the Function of the Hesperides as Psychopomps and the Celestial River with its Self-Renewal Power

The *Andante sostenuto* of the B-flat major sonata begins in the dark colouring of the C-sharp minor tonality. Even though it is a key linked to death, Richard Böhm has identified the theme of death as a moment of redemption, which suits the musical expression of this movement, as will be unveiled at a later point in the analysis[43]. This choice of tonality can describe the overall character of the A-section[44]. Musically observed, a first major change of atmosphere is achieved through the tonality shift coinciding with the beginning of the B-section. The accentuated note G-sharp, announced on the last quaver of m. 42, functions harmonically as a leading note to what is subsequently coming. Schubert introduces the new tonality of A major for the B-section. This key functions here as an antithesis in relation to the C-sharp minor reality of the A-section, as it will be explained at a later point. There are further formal elements that shall be firstly addressed. Brief remarks adjacent to the musical observations from a psychological standpoint are intended to create a helpful Ariadne's thread, before unveiling the corresponding symbolic interpretations, presented at the end of this subchapter.

Taking into consideration the general unfolding of the B-section, a form related to a theme with variations can be considered (Fig. 18.5). The first section is characterized by a theme with a choral ductus (B-theme, mm.43–50). Representative of this theme is its hymnal quality that comes to light through the chordal compositional technique. In contrast to the circling around a main but not developed idea that characterized the "absent theme"[45] in the A-section, the melodic theme here is obviously much more concrete: a symmetrical eight bars periodic construction (made of 4 + 4 bars) is clearly definable (antecedent phrase going from mm.43–46 and consequent phrase from mm.47–50). The theme in itself

[43] For Böhms description of the C-sharp minor tonality see: Böhm, Richard. (2006). *Symbolik und Rhetorik im Liedschaffen von Franz Schubert*. P. 80–81.

[44] Even if the A-section presented episodes in the major tonality (E major key), C-sharp minor still dominates the overall character of this section. In addition, E major stands in a relationship to the fundamental tone, as it is the major parallel of C-sharp minor. In turn, the E major of the A'-section will be highlighted, having a different effect on the listener, that will be explained later.

[45] Dobretsberger, Barbara. Personal communication between Barbara Dobretsberger and the author. Salzburg/Lisbon: November 25, 2021.

relates to the undeveloped, absent theme of the A-section, both rhythmically and melodically (Fig. 18.5). The elements of the melodic shattered line presented in the previous section are finally developed into a real theme here. There is not only a thematic development to be noted, alongside with the aforementioned change in tone-colour, but also a modification of the ostinato level is perceptible. The introduction of the sixteenth notes in the left-hand in m.43 creates a new rhythmical ostinato for this section.

Even though this novel *ostinato* includes tone repetitions, it still transmits the impression of more (inner) movement. While the sixteenth notes convey a kind of stillness due to the inherent tone repetitions, the right hand's melody in turn suggests an ascending movement that is being set in motion through the hymnal tone and through the initial rising line towards the third note of the A major key (A–C-sharp). Noteworthy is the behaviour of the sixteenth notes of the left hand in the measures closing the antecedent, respectively, the consequent phrase. In the first case, there is a descending gesture from the fifth of the scale towards the tonic (E–D–C-sharp–H–A, mm.46–47). In the second, a rising gesture going from C-sharp to A (mm.50–51) marks the transition to the following subsection. With this movement, not only the first variation is introduced but it also brings new musical and archetypal elements with it—a thought which includes symbolic associations, and which will be developed more thoroughly later. The ascending gesture can be understood as an elevation of the spirit that occurs at the beginning of the B-section. To reformulate this in psychological terms, this melody acts as raising the "I" into another sphere or reality, which enables the "I" to detach itself from an earthy level (first/outer reality).

Following the announced hymnal theme, a first variation (mm.51–58) is introduced, which portrays the style of melody with accompaniment (b'). Such writing conveys the character of a song-without-words. The melodic material of this variation is retaken from the theme. A new flowing motif of great figurative significance is introduced in this variation, namely in the inner voice of the right-hand. This semiquaver-triplet motif, which is somehow also related to the *circulatio* figure, is responsible for bringing more movement in. Symbolically, it refers to the superordinate water motif, which can be analogously found in other works of Schubert[46]. Due to the underlying mythical semantics, which will be later explained, this musical motif shall be titled the river motif (Fig. 18.5).

In contrast, the second variation (b" mm.59–67) returns to the chordal writing[47] and includes the same *ostinato* figure presented in the B-theme. The

[46] This overarching motivic semantic is clear for instance from *Die Schöne Müllerin* (cf. 15).
[47] Cf. Godel, Arthur. (1985). *Schuberts letzte drei Klaviersonaten (D958—960).*

melodic line shows a first particularity in that it extends the ascending gesture of the theme, surpassing the third ambit mentioned above. Consequently, the melodic line firstly encompasses the interval range of a fifth (H–F-sharp mm.59–60), ascending further until subsequently reaching the note A (m.61). Harmonically observed, the B-theme and first variation (b') are both stable in the A major sphere, while the second variation (b") is modulatory in character, crossing the keys of D major (m.62) and B-flat major (m.63)[48]—it should be recalled that the first is the key of triumph and the latter, as the fundamental key of the entire sonata, has a similar semantics as the A major key, i.e., refers to an utopic or idyllic world[49]. Godel draws particular attention to the coincidence that the B-flat major tonality occurs precisely in the midpoint of this second movement[50]. This might explain the quite enigmatic ornamentation of m.64[51]. A prominent moment of sudden harmonic uncertainty is m.68: the presence of the ambivalent diminished chord gives this measure a particular colour and a sense of vagueness—which, psychologically describes an instant in which the "I" is confronted with a shadow element, yet simultaneously reflects a certain distance to it. Even though the sense of fear or terror is implicit in the coloration of the diminished seventh chord, the static nature of this measure, and the tone repetitions of the left hand, there is no emotional movement that could hint at a closer engagement or confrontation with it, e.g., no noticeable dynamic change nor particular accent. It is precisely due to the harmonic occurrence of this bar that the regularity of the phrases, characteristic of the B-section up to this point, is broken. The musical phrase in question thus features an asymmetry by being extended for one additional bar (mm.63–67).

[48] It should also be noted that this type of modulation refers to the modulation in thirds, typical of Schubert (12).

[49] Cf. Böhm, Richard. (2006). *Symbolik und Rhetorik im Liedschaffen von Franz Schubert*. Further keywords for the B-flat major tonality are hope, nature, longing and wandering. Ibid. The main semantic difference between both tonalities, A major and B-flat major, is that the latter does not bear an illusory undertone. Cf. A major and B-flat major in: Ibid.

[50] Cf. Godel, Arthur. (1985). *Schuberts letzte drei Klaviersonaten (D958—960)*. P. 175.

[51] Cf. Ibid.

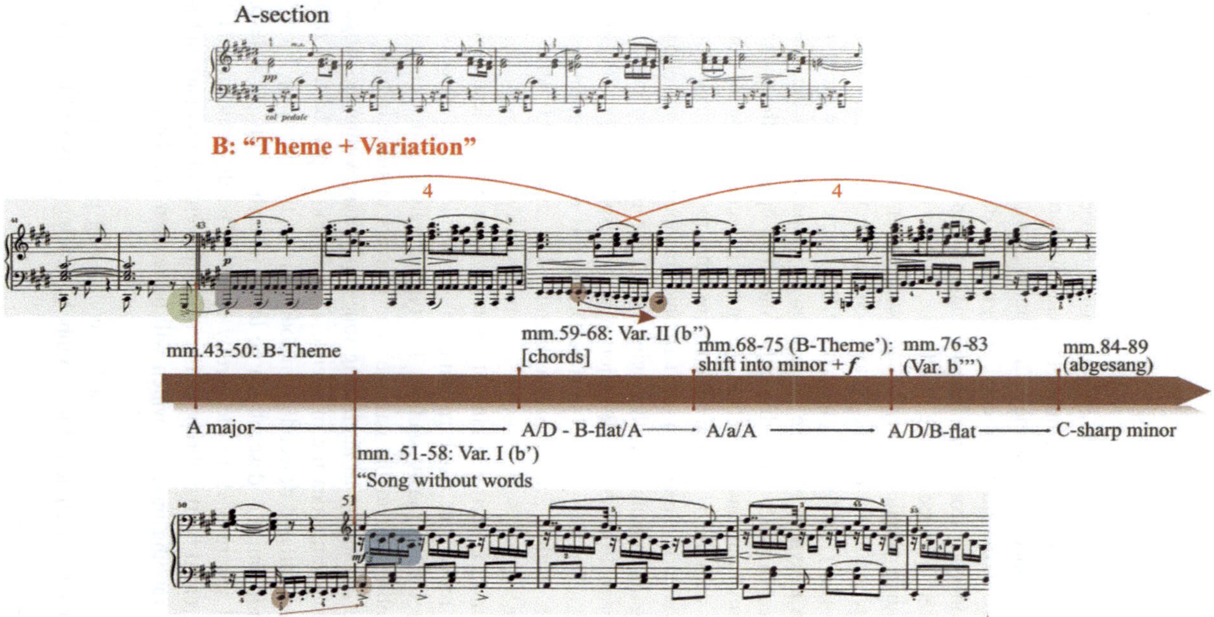

Fig. 18.5 Above: A-section for the comparison of the thematic material with the choral theme of the B-section, featuring a form of "Theme and variations". Periodic construction and the rough tonalities plan are delineated here. In blue: the river motif in the inner voice of the right hand. (Sheet music excerpt taken and adapted from *Henle digital edition*) © 2016 G. Henle Verlag, Munich

From mm.68–75, a new section can then be recognized that recalls the B-theme again, but with the main feature of a modulatory passage that goes through A minor and C major before returning to A major (mm.72–75). Even though this episode in the minor key is brief in time, the emotional expression is quite intense, as is the rather surprising turn and return to C major, respectively, to A major. For this harmonic reason and due to the major thematic similarities with the B-theme, this section will be named the B-theme'. The dynamic modifications that are to be noted here accompany the emotional condition given by the mentioned harmonic path. The evolution goes from a ***p*** range (A major, m.68) towards a ***f*** (m.72), whereby the crescendo happens quite rapidly, i.e., within the time of an upbeat. This dynamic change simultaneously occurs with the modulation to A minor (m.72). While crescending further, the phrase then unexpectedly shifts to C major, culminating then in a *fp* subito. Again, within that same measure the dynamic swiftly drops to a ***p*** dynamic. These latter changes coincide with the return to A major, confirmed in m.75. After this rather unsettled episode, the river motif returns in m.76, remaining until m.88 (i.e., the end of B-section). The melodic line is now acquainted with the b" section but contains other motivic elements that are ascribed to the b' section. Seen from the harmonic standpoint, this novel passage (mm.76–83) is again modulating, although passing through more familiarized keys, i.e., D major and the shift to B major in m.79, respectively, m.80. Such a harmonic path is known from the b" section. Due to this reasoning, this episode is a synthesis of b' with b", as Godel has identified[52], and should therefore be termed as b"' here.

To close the entire B-section a kind of *abgesang* (mm.84–88) leading to the home key of the movement (C-sharp minor) is to be identified, which slowly prepares for the return to the A'-section. The typical trait of a descending line gives a more sombre note to the passage. The quavers of the left hand begin gently to stagnate, persisting in alternating tone repetitions within the range of an octave. An astonishing measure of silence abruptly interrupts the flow of the river motif and the initiated descending melodic line of the *abgesang.* From an interpretative standpoint, this descent can be taken metaphorically, as a descent from the celestial sphere back to the earthly sphere. The disconnection of the musical ductus, created by the abrupt pause, marks the end of this part and is a special attention-grabbing moment, which will be retaken at a later point in the analysis.

Due to the several associations that this contrasting part evokes, the entire B-section is particularly well-suited to a symbolic reading. This will be done by

52 Cf. Ibid.

adducing the just-stated musical elements and linking them with the corresponding symbolic interpretation.

The choral writing, including the theme and introducing the B-section, is revealing since it refers to the characteristic liturgical writing, making the relation with church music evident. Further pictorial associations can emerge in this context, allowing speech about a choir of angels. This musical epitome is congruent with a Christian perspective. The pianist Andras Schiff[53] drew attention to the striking similarities with the E-flat major mass D 950 (*et incarnatus est*)[54]. As a consequence, the "I" is embedded in another reality in which the environment is characterized by a luminous atmosphere. It is due to the shining tonal quality of the A major that the sensory experience of being in a dreamlike or paradisiac world is primarily provided. As a tonality particularly favoured by Schubert[55], it often depicts an idyllic world, as Richard Böhm's survey has already confirmed: it is the key related to nature and God[56]. However, as already seen in formerly analysed works, A major can also be attributed to a "positive characterisation, in particular to the pretence of positive moods"[57]. In this sense and considering the specific symbolic/mythical context of this sonata, the A major section can depict another, rather inner reality level of spiritual nature.

Speaking in Jungian terms, most of the passages featured in this B-section can be understood as a luminous experience of the Self. Archetypally observed, the act of raising the "I" into another reality level is possible due to the emergence of the so-called psychopomps. Etymologically, psychopomp means "guide or conductor of spirits or souls to the other world"[58]. As Jung himself elucidated, they have a specific psychological function as mediators between this world and the Beyond, or between the consciousness and the unconscious realm[59]. Depending on the tradition, these spiritual guides correspond to angelic figures, nymphs, or

---

[53] Schiff, Andras. Sir András Schiff—Schubert Lecture-Recital. Live at Wigmore Hall. [Lecture-Recital].

[54] It shall be explained that such an interconnectedness of episodes is only a natural consequence of works that have been composed concurrently.

[55] Cf. Böhm, Richard. (2006). *Symbolik und Rhetorik im Liedschaffen von Franz Schubert*. P. 47.

[56] Cf. Ibid.

[57] Ibid. P. 57. (Trans. by the author). German expression: "positive Charakterisierung, insbesondere auch die 'Vortäuschung' positiver Stimmungen [...]".

[58] Online Etymology Dictionary. "Psychopomp". [Artikel].

[59] Cf. Jung, Carl Gustav. (2014). "Aion. Researches into the Phenomenology of the Self". In: *The Collected Works of C.G. Jung. Vol. 9. Part II.* (Ed. and trans. by Gerhard Adler and R.F.C. Hull). Part II: Subchapter III: "The Syzygy: Anima and Animus.".

other anthropomorphic creatures that fulfill this task[60]. The motif of the river frequently appears related with this notion.

The *Elysium* is the next closest connecting element in this network of symbolic associations. The ensuing symbol that is to be found in the *Elysium*, is water. Conforming with the musically identified flowing motif in the first variation (entitled the river motif), the river, as a symbol may allude to one of the four rivers surrounding the Edenic Garden. Both the water symbol in this musical passage and its inherent flowing element ensure a different perception of time and space—as if being in another, higher and imagined realm. From a Christian perspective, water is the symbol of purification, as Eugen Drewermann has explained[61]. Being an element of healing and renewal, water may imply a new creative force arising since it enables the flow of psychic energies: it brings along a transformation of the previous condition, renovating, healing and setting an inner movement in motion.

---

[60] There are several references to psychopomps in the *The Collected Works of C.G. Jung*. For example, an anthropomorphic manifestation is the horsewomen (Valkyries), whereas the horse is also viewed as a psychopomp, but as a theriomorphic manifestation: "The horse also plays the part of a psychopomp who leads the way to the other world—the soul of the dead are fetched by horsewomen, the Valkyries.". Cf. Jung, Carl Gustav. (2014). "Symbols of Transformation". In: *The Collected Works of C.G. Jung. Vol. 5.* (Trans. by Gerhard Adler and R.F.C. Hull). Part II, Chapter VI. "The Battle for Deliverance from the Mother". Furthermore, in Indian culture, Jung mentions "Indra, who in the form of a falcon has stolen the soma (the treasure hard to attain), is the psychopomp who delivers the souls to the wind, to the generating pneuma, the individual and universal prana (life-breath), to save them from 'repeated death'". Cf. Ibid. Chapter: "The sacrifice". One last example should be cited, namely the analogy with Sophia, the Goddess of wisdom, often being a projection of the archetype of the Great Mother. She was also considered by C.G. Jung as a psychopomp: "[…] she leads the way to God and assures immortality.". Cf. Ibid. *Vol. 11.* "Psychology and Religion: West and East". Chapter IV: "Answer to Job". Out of this reasoning, psychopomps can be understood here as the link between two possible readings: a more Christian based one, in which the B-section is associated with the Edenic garden, a choir of angels and one of the four rivers of paradise; or a second mythological interpretation. This is linked to the Atlas myth and the garden of the Hesperides, where the latter function as one psychological aspect of the Anima, as it will be developed in the analysis. The overarching principle is, however, the same: the beyond, immortality and transformation.

[61] Cf. Drewermann, Eugen. (2024). „Vortrag Grimms Märchen ‚Das Wasser des Lebens'. Konflikte überwinden.". [Presentation]. This reading has already been worked out in *Die Schöne Müllerin* analysis (15).

In the context of revisiting the elements of the Atlas myth, the association with the Hesperides can naturally emerge at this point[62]. Atlas was situated near his daughters, the Hesperides. The Titan's descendants were nymphs[63] and lived in an idyllic garden called the Garden of the Hesperides (Fig. 18.6), wherein they guarded the golden apples, together with a hundred-headed dragon or snake named Ladon[64]. Symbolically, the golden apples stand for immortality[65], which appeals to questions related to the Beyond. With this image in mind for this particular musical passage, the nymphs can stand for the inner feminine image, i.e., the Anima. They not only enchant but liberate the "I" from the earthly matters with their angelic singing and transport the"I" into another realm, the realm of the after-life. As such, they act as psychopomps in this specific context:

> "[…] the idea of liberty has been changed back to its original […] state – into the shining figure of the anima, freed from the weight of the earth and the tyranny of the sense, the psychopomp who leads the way to the Elysian fields."[66].

Jung also referred to the Anima as an angelical epitome fulfilling the function of a psychopomp:

> "[…] for the anima can appear also as an angel of light, a psychopomp who points the way to the highest meaning […]"[67].

These statements indicate how psychopomps can initiate a process of transformation by unveiling the path or guiding the "I" towards the ultimate (inner) truth. Emma Jung described the function of psychopomps as the following:

---

[62] Both viewpoints, the Christian or the mythological can be seen as concurrently valid. This again refers to the Jungian methodological approach of amplification, already above mentioned.

[63] Cf. „Hesperiden" in: Grant, Michael. Hazel, John. (2009). *Lexikon der antiken Mythen und Gestalten.* P. 207.

[64] Cf. Ibid.

[65] Cf. Mollwo-Oesterreicher, Marianne. (1978). *Herder Lexikon Symbole.* P. 16.

[66] Jung, Carl Gustav. (1970). *Aion.* (Trans. by R.F.C. Hull). P. 29–30.

[67] Cf. Jung, Carl Gustav. (2014). "Archetypes and the Collective Unconscious". In: *The Collected Works of C.G. Jung. Vol. 9. Part I.* (Ed. and trans. by Gerhard Adler and R.F.C. Hull). Chapter: "Archetypes of the Collective Unconscious".

"[...] as true psychopomps the Animus [or Anima] guide and accompanies a transformation and metamorphosis of the soul."[68].

Fig. 18.6 Leighton, Frederic. (1891–1892). "The Garden of Hesperides". Painting: [Oil on Canvas]. Lady Lever Art Gallery. (Image taken from: National museums Liverpool)

These angelic beings act as a spiritual guide. As such, and Jung himself pointed this out, they no longer interact with the "I" in the form of an inner dialogue, "[...] but instead the response appears as the action of the other, i.e., as an outward event"[69]. Curiously, this corresponds to the occurrences in the

[68] Jung, Emma. Cited after: Jacobi, Jolande. (2006). *Die Psychologie von C.G. Jung*. Chapter: „Animus und Anima". P. 119. (Trans. by the author). German expression: "[...] das er [der Animus] als wahrer Psychopompos Wandel und Verwandlung der Seele leite und begleite.".

[69] Cf. Jung, Carl Gustav. (2014). "Archetypes and the Collective Unconscious". In: *The Collected Works of C.G. Jung. Vol. 9. Part I.* (Trans. by Gerhard Adler and R.F.C. Hull). Section III, Chap. 2: "The Psychology of Rebirth" Subchapter II: "Subjective Transformation—h. Natural Transformation (Individuation). In this context, Jung also explained how Hermes was

analysed musical example. The choral ductus emerged autonomously and presented itself as another reality to the "I"—there is no conversation or dialectic procedure that takes place, it is a mere direct, inner spiritual experience of transformational nature. With this specific pictorial imagination evoked by this musical passage, Schubert created a parallel counter-world—a world that came into being by itself. This realm of light, or this numinous experience of the Self—to speak in Jungian terms—enables the "I" to endure the outer reality. Consequently, the B-section has more than just a comforting, redeeming and self-regulative effect on the psyche; it opens another dimension of being to the "I".

Given Schubert's biographical context, this may mirror the answer to the spiritual or religious questions that had been previously noted, i.e., raised in earlier sonata movements, e.g., of the C minor or A major sonatas, and which was here not only expressed artistically but experienced spiritually during the creative process. This occurrence is seen as an autonomous activity of the unconscious during the act of composing. The question that immediately arises at this point is how Schubert will transition from this state of mind or this inner reality back to the other, outer reality. A subsequent question of significance is how this imagination affected the "I" and changed his perspective on this reality. This is of particular interest here since this sonata is one of Schubert's last utterances. It is recommended now to analyse the means by which Schubert returns to the A'-section. The identified *abgesang* (mm.84–88) can musically point to the act of sinking to the earthly realm; however, an unforeseen silence, of great psychological power, interrupts this descent.

18.4 The Abyss and the Nothingness as a Psychological Turning Point. The Echo of the Hesperides and the Recreation of a New Reality Level. The Importance of Acceptance in the Individuation Process. Final Thoughts

The "I" is embedded in the flowing movement of the river, in a parallel world of light that recalls the Beyond, when it comes to an abrupt silence. This sudden and unattended stop in the musical ductus, which corresponds to the musical rhetorical figure of the *aposiopesis*, is extremely powerful and has a strong effect on the listener or interpreter. The same spontaneous reaction is conceivable during

considered to alchemists a psychopomp, and made subsequently the analogy with the figure of Christ. Cf. Ibid.

Schubert's creative process. There are several possible adjectives or formulations to describe this measure of silence: it can be felt as a moment of introspection, a standstill, or a freezing of the "I"; it can convey a feeling of suffocation, or it can be interpreted as an awakening to the outer reality, to what is, in opposition to what is wished, or what was imagined. Finally, it acts as a rift that has opened in the bottom and recreates, hence, the image of the wanderer at the abyss—a concept already suggested by the pianist Alfred Brendel[70] and also shared by musicologists[71] (8). Similar nihilistic phenomena in Schubert's music are to be found in other works but are especially characteristic of Schubert's later works, as discussed earlier[72]. Arthur Godel contextualized this with the theme of death: "The standstill of the inner pulse is also an allegory of death"[73]. Similarly in previously discussed works, the theme of death in Schubert's works is to be taken rather as a psychological transformation process (15). More precisely, such episodes conveying the void are to be understood as moments of a psychological turning point. In symbolic terms, this moment of halt could function as a water well, a transparent gate in the landscape (abyss), or as a bridge that brings the "I" back into the first level of reality[74].

In Jungian terms, such psychological events are addressed as *Enantiodromia* or as a "phenomenon of reversal" (3.2)[75]. To briefly recall these concepts: the "phenomenon of reversal" refers to the moment when the "I" approaches one of the archetypal poles, as they powerfully attract the "I", triggering subsequently a shift in perspective, i.e., acting as a turning point. In the musical context in question, the "I" finds itself in this utopian counter-world. Being in such a condition turns out to be crucial for its psychological development, because only through this state the "I" can have a new perspective on the situation. As already

[70] Cf. Brendel, Alfred. (1898). *Les trois dernières Sonates de Franz Schubert.* Akerman, Chantal (Director). [Programme].

[71] Cf. Gruber, Gernot. (2010). *Schubert. Schubert?*

[72] The survey of literature covering this debate and the respective findings have already been presented in 11.

[73] Godel, Arthur. (1985). *Schuberts letzte drei Klaviersonaten (D958—960).* P. 252. (Trans. by the author). German expression: „Der Stillstand des inneren Puls ist auch eine Allegorie des Todes.".

[74] The reader could think of the following fairy tales: "Frau Holle" or "Alice in Wonderland", where similar symbols function as a mediator to bring the "I" into another reality or fantasy plane. Cf. Grimm, Jacob. Grimm, Wilhelm. (2015). *Grimms Märchen,* respectively, cf. Carroll, Lewis. (2024). *Alice im Wunderland.*

[75] The first term of *Enantiodromia* is used by Jung. The second term is to be attributed to Erich Neumann. For the theoretical fundamentals concerning both terms and the corresponding bibliographic references presented in this dissertation see 3.2.

suggested above in the musical analysis, the identified diminished chord of the B-section (m.68) can be seen as a moment of threat that relates to one aspect of the shadow; however, this shadow element is observed from the outside, as if the "I" had a certain distance from it—or as if the "I" was protected by being embedded in this world of light. Since the "I" was embedded in a realm of light, it can better integrate its counterpart. In other words: through the journey into the shining world of the B-section and through the moment of nothingness that installed itself (the silence of m.89), the outer reality will undeniably be perceived differently by the "I" (in the subsequent A'-section). A transformation of the motifs as well as new musical elements can be identified when examining the A'-section more closely. These changed and novel structures can in turn substantiate the exposed interpretation of the B-section. To better understand this musical phenomenon, the A'-section will now be formally analysed.

With the return to the outer reality (A'-section), the melodic line retreats to the original shattered structure. The first element which is perceptible as having undergone a process of transformation through the stay in the counter-world, is the rhythmical *ostinato* that previously featured the Atlas motif: the Atlas rhythmic cell is no longer present, at least not in its original form; instead, the return of the *ostinato* resumes itself in its erstwhile rising gesture, encompassing the three-octaves range. The corresponding Atlas rhythm has changed, acting as regular quavers (Fig. 18.7) now. In addition to this change, a new motivic element emerges in the left hand that lends to this passage another undertone. It involves a further rhythmic motif that can also be traced back to Beethoven and that is known as the fate motif (Fig. 18.7). These metamorphoses are revealing with regard to the underlying psychological process that has been described.

The fate motif, being introduced as an upbeat gesture, consists of two successive tone repetitions, a descending half tone step and a return to the previous note. Its existence is here sinister and sounds in the obscure dark registers of the piano, acting as a fateful shadow presence. As Godel had already noted, the sixteenth notes that compose the fate motif are retaken from the B-section, and the descending half tone steps recall an important thematic moment that refers to the first movement[76]. The form of its appearance will change in pertinent musical[77] and psychological moments, as it will be elucidated in due brevity. Beforehand it should be recalled that tone repetitions in Schubert's music are often tied with the symbolism of death. Thus, the notion of destiny tied with the theme of death is once again present. Furthermore, from the fact that it appears in the dark register

[76] Cf. Godel, Arthur. (1985). *Schuberts letzte drei Klaviersonaten (D958—960)*. P. 175.

[77] Cf. Ibid.

of the piano, it can be determined—in archetypal terms—that it behaves like a shadow. The link to fate is also established on another level: the fact that the fate motif musically appertains to the sixteenth notes movement of the previous section, which have then developed into the semiquaver-triplets, directly relates them with the *circulatio* figure. The latter bears the connotation with the norns and fate, as already explained in previous chapters[78]. The fate motif is therefore existent in the background as a universal truth, surpassing any perception of time or space and mirroring the intransigence of death, imposing itself on the "I". As a result of the B-section and given the transformations and new elements that have arisen in the A'-section, it can be concluded that a new level of reality has been created (Fig. 18.10). There are two significant harmonic moments that require special attention, and which will confirm this analytical hypothesis since they underline the aforementioned transformative character leading to a transcendental experience (rebirth). Due to this reason, these harmonic statements, which also act as a reminiscence of the luminous atmosphere in the Garden of the Hesperides, can be taken as a conclusive message of this second movement.

The echoes of the B-section atmosphere can be heard in the A'-section, particularly in two important harmonic turning points of great psychological significance. These occur in a quite unexpected manner: being back in the realm of C-sharp minor (m.90), the turn to the tonic parallel key is awaited in m.103 (as in the equivalent passage of the A-section)[79]. Yet—to describe this moment of harmonic transformation, immediately by means of archetypal language—instead of going to the expected E major, the "I" shifts into the world of C major, as if moved by unknown inner forces. It is evident that C major is harmonically quite remote from the tonal centre of C-sharp minor, as Godel himself explains. However, the musical fact that the C major is enharmonically used here as B-sharp major[80] is of psychological significance. As explained in previous chapters (7.1), an enharmonic relation can point to a moment of illusion or of imagination[81]. This implies that this harmonic occurrence recalls the *Elysium*, beforehand created (B-section). It is as if the reality level of the "I" has now been moved to a higher level, as a consequence of the experience in the paradisiacal world of the B-section. There is a resultant evolution of the "I"—the elements stated in

78 As musical examples the *circulatio* of "Gretchen am Spinnrade" (8) or the brooklet motif of *Die Schöne Müllerin* can be cited (15).

79 Cf. Godel, Arthur. (1985). *Schuberts letzte drei Klaviersonaten (D958—960)*. P. 175.

80 Cf. Ibid.

81 Cf. Friedrich, Siegfried. (2015). *Zu Funktion und Wirkung gradueller Tonhöhenänderungen in Johann Sebastian Bachs ‚Das Wohltemperierte Klavier' I und II sowie in Franz Schuberts ‚Die schöne Müllerin'"*.

the A-section are being integrated in the A'-section due to the archetypal manifestations in the B-section. This change has such a major impact that the fate motif instantly emancipates itself from its former death semantics. This can be confirmed music-analytically due to the lack of tone repetitions—it now features a three-step tone sequence. This reflects a more dynamic behaviour, lasting for three consecutive measures (mm.103–105). In the first two manifestations of the changed fate motif, a seventh downwards jump is even noticeable. Applying Neumann's thoughts, the harmonic path mentioned above evokes the transformation circles depicting the higher evolution of the "I" when moving towards a spiritual transformation (this is additionally described with the following keywords: immortality, rebirth, wisdom, inspiration)[82].

Musically, before the second transformation takes place, Schubert still modulates to E major (m.111) in order to return to C-sharp minor once again (m.119). Due to the unexpected arrival of C major in m.103 and the resulting delay of the E major, the latter tonality gains another shade in meaning and is differently felt. As Godel also points out, this effect is emphasized by the anticipation of one measure of the E major[83]. This harmonic fact substantiates a transformation of the "I", since it sees or experiences E major differently now than in the A-section. In a similar way to the previous sudden modulation to C major, Schubert once more, shifts unexpectedly to C-sharp major in m.123. This harmonic alteration takes place in the softest possible dynamics (***ppp***). From a hermeneutical viewpoint, this shift, which is now linked to the softest dynamic, has nearly the effect of a divine secret that is being told. With the majorization of the fundamental key, Schubert initiates the *abgesang* section of the entire second movement. Here too, this harmonic illumination brings some important changes on the motivic level: the fate motif becomes more mobile and changes its shape to the equivalent three consecutive notes, hence,—as psychologically observed earlier—liberates the "I" from its fateful designs. This musical moment could psychologically also hint at a possible acceptance of fate or conciliation with it. Retaking the analogy with Erich Neumann's diagram—after the threshold of the first transformation has been crossed, the second is reached, leading subsequently to a psychic state of immortality, to a world of the Beyond (third circle of transformation).

The last modulation to C-sharp major was psychologically significant, since the "I" will remain in this luminous atmosphere until the end of the movement. Schubert musically approaches the end of the movement with three luminous

[82] For the reference and illustration of Neumann's helpful diagram for this analysis see: Fig. 3.9, or cf. Schema III, in: Neumann, Erich. (2021). *Die Große Mutter.*

[83] Cf. Godel, Arthur. (1985). *Schuberts letzte drei Klaviersonaten (D958—960).* P. 175.

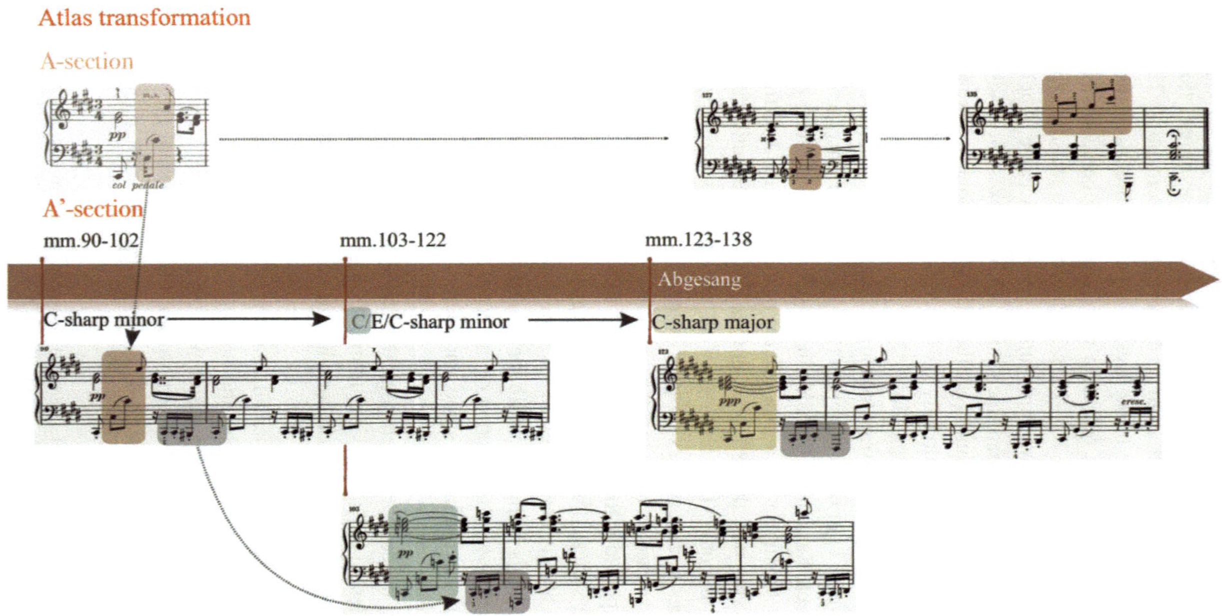

Fig. 18.7 A'-section with the introduction and transformation of the fate motif in harmonic expressive moments, in turn, relating to psychological turning points. The metamorphoses of the atlas motif (comparison with the beginning and A'-section). (Sheet music excerpt taken and adapted from *Henle digital edition*) © 2016 G. Henle Verlag, Munich

bell strokes on the C-sharp note (mm.134–136)[84], which corresponds to a further metamorphosis of the Atlas motif (this is the second major motivic change triggered by the modulation to the major tonality). Symbolically, the three bell strokes can point to the Christian concept of trinity. Up to that point in the musical ductus, the fate motif is still featured, however, it ceases to exist in the last two measures. The movement is subsequently closed with a rising gesture, possibly as an echo of the three bell strokes, which are to be heard in the penultimate measure. Finally, it comes to rest serenely on a prolonged C-sharp major chord, marked by a *fermata*, in the following ending measure. This ascending movement, which is a reminiscence of the initial rising gesture of the Atlas motif, is now stretched from the original three octave range to a four octave ambit. From a symbolic perspective, this musical observation hints at the moment of wholeness (I) that is hereby achieved—the "I" is no longer trapped in the earthly burdens (the original semantics of Atlas) but transcended to another sphere. Such a phenomenon is described by C.G. Jung as being part of the rebirth mysteries[85].

As a concluding thought, it can be said that the Anima had an important contribution here, when compared to its appearance in other works. By fulfilling the function of a psychopomp in the central section of this movement (B-section), the Anima guided the "I", that was trapped in earthly burdens, and helped to transcend into another sphere. As a result, not only was the "I" freed from the weight associated with the Atlas' figure, present in the music through the Atlas rhythmic motif (A-section), but it also made the "I" perceive the outer reality differently, creating another level of existence in the A'-section. The key moment of transition from the inner reality (B-section) back to the outer reality (A'-section) has musically occurred through a moment of silence (*aposiopesis*). This happened abruptly; its psychological purpose is a significant turning point ("phenomenon of reversal"[86]). It is important to restate that the abyss is a powerful archetypal image since it expresses a process and an inner primordial experience. With the positive reminiscences of the angelic realm, the "I" subsequently shifts perspectives (A'-section), musically moving from the return of C-sharp

[84] These have already been suggested from m.127 on, i.e., occurred after the C-sharp major shift of m. 123, which points once more to the importance of this harmonic change.

[85] Cf. Jung, Carl Gustav. (2011). *Four Archetypes.* Part II "Concerning Rebirth".

[86] Neumann, Erich. (2021). *Die Große Mutter.*

minor ultimately towards the C-sharp major tonality, the tonal realm in which the "I" finally remains—psychopomps led to an important inner transformation of spiritual nature.

To put these analytical findings in context with the entire trilogy, the answer Schubert was seeking, with his *Amen* statements that were erstwhile set in form of rhetorical questions[87], is not given here in the form of a dialogue but of a direct and numinous inner experience (B-section). In analogy with theological terms, this occurrence corresponds to the phenomenon of rapture. Such a phenomenon comprises the existence of two reality levels (Fig. 18.10). The theologian Christfried Böttrich explains that such a journey to heaven, or the crossing of one reality level into another, can only happen to a human being before or after death through supernatural help[88] (Fig. 18.8).

[87] This reading can also be understood analogically with the initially stated examples from the Biblical texts. For instance, Job too, turned to God in a spirit of questioning, yet in this sense he remained the faithful believer. Through this attitude he received an answer from God. Cf. Evangelisch-Reformierte Landeskirche des Kantons Zürich Kirchenrat. (2008). *Zürcher Bibel.* P. 42. For the Book of Job see: Ibid. P. 669–717. For the mentioned musical *Amen* statements in previous sonatas see 17.

[88] Cf. Böttrich, Christfried. (2013). "Entrückung" in: *Das wissenschaftliche Bibellexikon im Internet. Deutsche Bibel Gesellschaft.* [Article]. In this article Böttrich gives several biblical examples of the phenomenon of rapture and explains that it is inseparable from the Ascension, the rise into heaven. Examples given include Job, whose soul is brought to God on a heavenly carrier by the archangel Michael, and the Ascension of Christ. This kind of phenomenon was also a widespread religious conviction in popular piety ("Volksfrommigkeit"), in which, as explained in III, Schubert also believed. Thus, often angels are the mediators who take the souls to another realm. Cf. Ibid.

Fig. 18.8 The Phenomenon of Rapture of Elias depicted in the Speculum Humanae Salvationis around 1360. (Picture used to depict the phenomenon of rapture and taken from: Böttrich, Christfried. (2013). Article “Entrückung” in: *Das wissenschaftliche Bibellexikon im Internet*. P. 11)

This supernatural aid is archetypically present through the Anima as a psychopomp and can be musically perceived in the middle section of this sonata movement. It is advisable to understand these spiritual experiences in context with the biographical circumstances of Schubert in mind (20).

Metaphorically speaking, this sonata is usually considered as the swan song of Schubert. From a soteriological perspective, Schubert's resignation and acceptance of fate can be perceived here as the experience of being one with the universe (4). The analogies drawn in this chapter with the Christian tradition were also beneficial for a final conclusive thought: the cross symbolizes the fateful path of pain (Fig. 18.9), which is expressed in music, in the just analysed sonata movement, by the *suspiratio* motif—with the return of the sigh motif in the last section, alongside with the emergence of the fate motif and the major brightenings at the end, Schubert might be expressing here, how pain is always existent, yet also how it transforms itself upon acceptance. According to C.G. Jung's theory, such an attitude is an essential step in the individuation process[89]. In congruence with the musical findings, it can be said that Schubert psychologically achieved transcendence to a higher spiritual sphere through his creative activity.

> "[...] Numinosity, however, is whole outside conscious volition, for it transports the subject into the state of rapture, which is a state of will-less surrender."[90]).

[89] Cf. Roesler, Christian. Personal communication between Christian Roesler and the author. Basel: January 12, 2023.

[90] Jung, Carl Gustav. (2014). "The Structure and Dynamics of the Psyche". In: *The Collected Works of C.G. Jung. Vol. 8.* (Trans. by Gerhard Adler and R.F.C. Hull). Part III, chapter: "On the Nature of the Psyche". Subchapter 5: "Conscious and Unconscious".

Fig. 18.9 The crucifixion of Christ. Glass window Church Königsfelden (14th century). © Museum Aargau. (Picture taken from: Kloster Königsfelden, Museum Aargau)

This experience was only possible due to the phenomena of rapture, experienced in the middle section. In Jungian terms, and bearing the Christian analogy in mind, the B-section could thus function as the fourth element (ascension) that brings about wholeness (Chap. 18 Footnote 12).

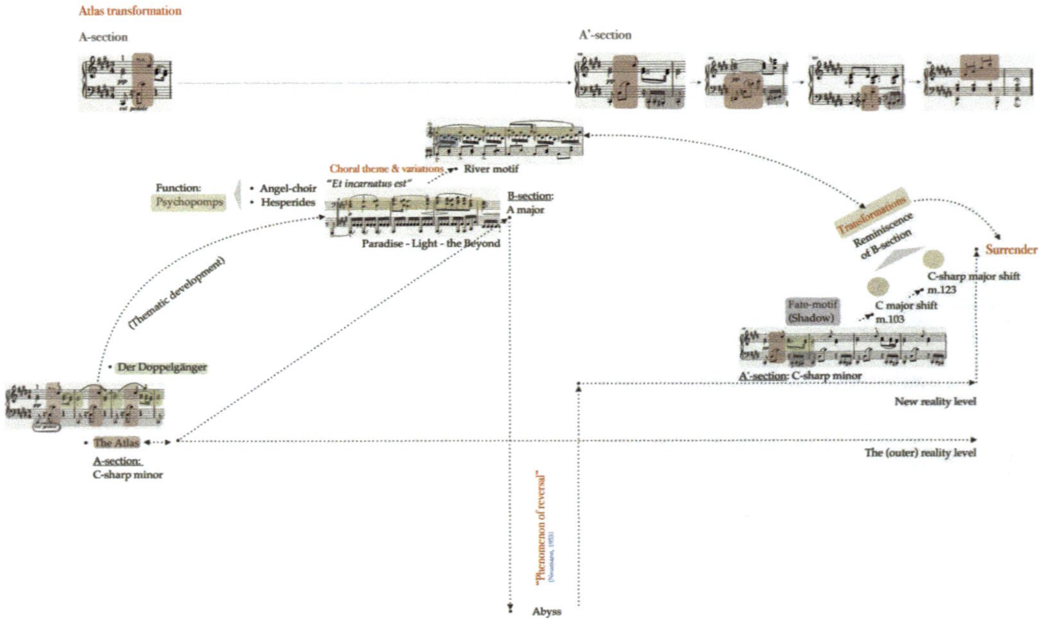

Fig. 18.10 The different reality levels. Above: The motif metamorphoses of the Atlas motif. Left: The sigh motif and the Atlas motif (doppelgänger). B-section: The choral theme and variations with the choral theme being the angelic expressions of the Hesperides (Anima) and the introduction of the river motif in its first variation as the symbol of purification, bringing inner movement. A'-section: The fate motif and the harmonic turning points of great significance for the individuation process. End of the movement figuring the transcendence gesture and the acceptance of fate. (Sheet music excerpt taken and adapted from *Henle digital edition*) © 2016 G. Henle Verlag, Munich

19 Post-Analytical Supplement: The Wanderer and the "Dümmling" Archetypes

For the final analytical overview in the concluding section of this dissertation (20), it is necessary to extend the analytical chapters with a supplement comprising two compositions that have been briefly presented or mentioned so far (III), namely the *Wandererfantasie* in C major D 760 and the Piano Trio in E-flat major D 920. The aim of this chapter is to cursorily address the main interrelated overarching archetypal motifs and principles inherent in these two works.

As a core motif of Romanticism, the wanderer archetype plays an essential role in Schubert's music (III). William Kinderman has already noted that in Schubert's songs the Wanderer "assumes the role of the lyrical subject"[1]. In reference to Schelling's *Naturphilosophie* (4), the Wanderer has a particular bond with nature and experiences a duality within himself—the duality that is the fruit of the dialectic tension between the inner and outer world. Kinderman has noted how this tension between the opposites is reflected in Schubert's music in general, namely by "a combination of heightened thematic contrast, juxtaposition of major and minor keys, and abrupt modulation"[2]. It is now the task of this chapter to address this archetype in more detail.

The wanderer archetype has been present in Schubert's music since early on, namely in the musical setting of Lübeck's poem "Der Wanderer" D 493, composed in 1816, and later, in the *Wandererfantasie* D 760 of 1822, also known as the Fantasy in C major D 760. The "Dümmling" archetype is frequently associated with the wandering principle., e.g., in fairy tales. In music, the Piano Trio in E-flat major D 920 is an example. Here, the "Dümmling" undergoes a

[1] Kinderman, William. "Schubert's piano music: probing the human condition". In: Gibbs, Christopher .H. (1997). *The Cambridge Companion to Schubert*.

[2] Ibid.

L. Dill, *Schubert's Metamorphoses*,
https://doi.org/10.1007/978-3-662-73476-6_19

wanderer's-journey, as will be elaborated later on. It does so with the final purpose to find the hidden treasures and integrate what is "missing" or repressed in a playful manner. Since the main topic in common is the wanderer's-journey, this topic is dealt with in more detail first (19.1) to establish the necessary foundation to understand the underlying processes in the Piano Trio (19.2). Finally, concluding and comparative observations on the dragon battles will be made (19.3). As this chapter functions as an addendum, the analytical observations are to be concise and described directly linking the musical phenomenon with the emotion, archetypal structure or psychological process underlying it. Such a procedure also allows for a better focus on the main archetypal themes and principles.

19.1 The Echoes of the „Der Wanderer" D 493 in the Wandererfantasie D 760: From an Introverted Wanderer to the Extraverted Hero Figure. The Dragon-Battles of the "I" as a Wanderer

The *Wandererfantasie* has always perplexed musicologists and interpreters for its rather unusual virtuosic writing, extravagant ductus and particular formal structure. It is therefore of interest to investigate the source of this new impulse. The C major Fantasy, composed in 1822, has its apparent origin in an assignment given to Schubert by a pupil of Johann Nepomuk Hummel, the amateur pianist Emmanuel von Liebenberg de Zsittin[3]. The main influential source from the thematic point of view is considered to be the previous lied, "Der Wanderer" D 493 from 1816. In addition, it is known that Schubert's involvement with Beethoven's works took on an increasing importance in his life (III). According to Martin Chusid, it was particularly the cyclical form and the variation form that most took hold of Schubert's attention[4]. This admiration for Beethoven might have given him an additional drive to pursue his quest towards the great form and to create something new (12).

In light of the previous analytical findings, it appears that the process of liberating himself from Beethoven as a father Figure, which represents also the breakthrough to the great symphonic form, may have spanned several years. The *Wandererfantasie* is included in this period. However, as noted earlier (16), the

[3] Cf. Massin, Brigitte. (1977). *Franz Schubert.* P. 975.

[4] Cf. Chusid, Martin. "Schubert's chamber music: before and after Beethoven". In: Gibbs, Christopher. (1997). *The Cambridge companion to Schubert.*

year of 1824 certainly marks an important moment in this development, with the birth of the new "I" in *Death and the maiden* D 810 and the integration of certain aspects of the Anima. Both the *Wandererfantasie* and the string quartet D 810, have the wanderer rhythm as their core cell—a motif that undergoes transformations in both works. Psychologically observed, such an emancipation can take years and includes several attempts at integrating certain elements, but also a critical attitude towards other elements, while developing an individual language; ultimately, it implies what in Jungian psychology is symbolically entitled as a dragon battle (3.1)[5]. In contrast to the lied, dragon battles can be identified in the *Wandererfantasie*, which features a progressive energy.

From a musical perspective, Schubert combined the cyclical form with the variation form in the C major Fantasy. The motif that provides unity lies in the thematic core idea from "Der Wanderer" D 489. Yet, the reminiscences of Lübeck's verses are differently processed in the Fantasy. The poem cited below, featuring Schubert's version, is intended to emphasize the main atmosphere of the poem that is existent in the musical setting. To juxtapose the core elements from the lied and the Fantasy is pertinent to understanding the transformation of the Wanderer.

„Ich komme vom Gebirge her, Es dampft das Thal, es braust das Meer, Ich wandle still, bin wenig froh, Und immer fragt der Seufzer wo? Immer wo?	"I come from the highlands, The valley steams, the sea roars, I wander quietly, I'm hardly joyous, and the sigh ever wonders where? forever where?
Die Sonne dünkt mich hier so kalt, Die Blüte welk, das Leben alt, Und was sie reden, leerer Schall, Ich bin ein Fremdling überall.	The sun hither methinks so cold, The blossom withers, the life's old, And what they say, a deaf sound, I am a stranger everywhere.

[5] Cf. Neumann, Erich. (1949). "Ursprungsgeschichte des Bewusstseins". Cited after: Vogel, Ralf T. (2017). *Individuation und Wandlung*. P. 65. See also: Campbell, Joseph. (2004). *The Hero with a thousand faces.*

Wo bist du, mein geliebtes Land, Gesucht, geahnt und nie gekannt? Das Land, das Land so hoffungsgrün, Das Land, wo meine Rosen blühn? Wo meine Freunde wandeln gehen, Wo meine Todten auferstehn, Das Land, das meine Sprache spricht, O, Land, wo bist du?	Where are thou, my beloved land Sought, sensed and never known? The land, the land so hopeful green, The land, where my roses bloom? Where my friends wander Where my dead ones revive, The land, that speaks my language, Oh, land, where are thou?
Ich wandle still und bin wenig froh, Und immer fragt der Seufzer wo? Immer wo? Im Geisterhauch tönt's mir zurück: Dort wo du nicht bist, dort ist das Glück!"[6].	I wander quietly, I'm hardly joyous, and the sigh ever wonders where? forever where? In the ghostly breeze it sounds back to me: thither where thou are not, thither is bliss"[7].

Lübeck's poem about the wanderer appeals to a concept characteristic of Romanticism (4.3)—the eternal search for utopian bliss and for the fatherland ("Sehnsucht"). The lyrical I tells of his origins and describes the surrounding landscape first, while his tone imminently turns to a lament. His rhetorical question "and the sigh ever wonders where?" ("und immer fragt der Seufzer wo?") leads to a moment of inner contemplation, in which the sun is cold, the blossom is withered, and life is old; his eternal condition of being "a stranger everywhere" is stated. This moment of introspection, triggered by the first question, leads to a daydream or fantasy about the desired fatherland. Later, another rhetorical question functions as a bridge, this time leading the lyrical I back to his tragic reality: "Oh land, where are thou?" ("O Land, wo bist du?"). The final verses narrate about the echo, that gives him the long awaited but painful answer, related to his *conditio humana*: "Thither where thou are not, thither is bliss" ("dort wo du nicht bist, dort ist das Glück").

The landscape descriptions in the poem are all metaphors of the inner state of the lyrical "I", towards which Schubert reacted musically. By using tone painting

[6] Lübeck, Georg Philipp Schmidt. (1808). "Des Fremdlings Abendlied". In: Schubert, Franz. (1816). "Der Wanderer" D 489. Petrucci Music Library (IMSLP).

[7] Ibid. (Trans. by the author).

means such as madrigalisms, Schubert conveys the inner landscapes and emotions of the wanderer. Amongst these, four main musical elements stand out, which will appear six years later in the *Wandererfantasie*. These include: (i) the dactyl rhythm, (ii) the triplets/tremolo, (iii) the rhetoric questions linked to the sigh motif (*suspiratio*) and, lastly, (iv) the dance-like rhythmical gesture of the "Etwas geschwinder" section (m.32f.), which conveys the fantasy of the "I" towards the beloved fatherland. The long pedal notes in the deep register at the opening of the lied are responsible for rendering the vastness of the landscape. The sense of an unattainable fatherland[8] is conveyed through the harmonic disposition of the lied's beginning: a "wrong tonality"[9], as Michael Raab describes it, opens the lied; it does not begin in the principal key (C-sharp minor), but in the dominant of F-sharp minor. By inference, as the secondary dominant bears a particular tension, it expresses a potentialization of a "centripetal force", a "leading" towards a certain direction[10] (7.1). It describes the torn feelings of the wanderer, the "Sehnsucht", for the beloved fatherland. Emotionally, the aforementioned harmony also conveys the sense of being lost or distant from one's homeland, ultimately, the impossibility of finding the (dreamt-of) fatherland[11]. This is accentuated by further harmonic peculiarities. E major is established as the tonality of the "beloved land" ("geliebte Land")[12]. As Raabe points out, this key is then "almost ironic[ally]"[13] linked to the words "a stranger everywhere" ("Ein Fremdling überall", m.30)[14] just before the fantasy of the dreamed land begins, which emphasizes the impossibility to find this utopic land. Furthermore, the dissonances already present in m.2 suggest the omnipresence of inner conflicts. It is thus through harmonic means that Schubert sheds light on the emotional state of the wanderer.

---

[8] Cf. Raab, Michael: "Der Wanderer op. 4, 1 (D 489)". In: Dürr, Walther. Kube, Michael. [et al.]. (2013). *Schubert Liedlexikon*. P.386.

[9] Ibid. (Trans. but he author). German expression: „ [...] der falschen Tonart [...]".

[10] Acker, Heinz. (2009). *Modulationslehre*. P.19.

[11] Cf. Raab, Michael: "Der Wanderer op. 4, 1 (D 489)". In: Dürr, Walther. Kube, Michael. [et al.]. (2013). *Schubert Liedlexikon*. P.386.

[12] Ibid.

[13] Ibid. (Trans. by the author). German expression: "beinahe schon ironisch".

[14] Ibid. P.386.

The tone repetitions of the slow triplets, which have a slight tremolando-like effect, alongside with the deep register, tone paint the steaming of the valley and the roaring of the sea, described by the lyrical I. The mentioned dactyl rhythm, known as the wanderer rhythm, is to be noted from m.1 in the piano left hand (Fig. 19.1). This rhythm conveys the fatigued condition of the wanderer, by having a long first beat as a resting step. It reappears later (m.23 f.) in diminution form, featuring a crochet and two quavers. This rhythm is semantically charged with the words corresponding to the second stanza of the poem "the sun methinks so cold [...]" ("Die Sonne dünkt mich hier so kalt [...]", Fig. 19.1)—Schubert will precisely refer to these verses in his later composed *Wandererfantasie* as a self-quotation. However, in the latter, "the melody has taken on a new, genuinely instrumental form: any connection with the declamation of the words ('Die Sonne dünkt mich hier so kalt'...) has disappeared"[15]. The figure below is intended to illustrate some of the interrelations between the motivic level of the lied and the Fantasy. Further interrelations will now be pointed out by turning the observations towards the *Wandererfantasie.*

Even though a similar general atmosphere is still conveyed in the quotation from the Fantasie's *Adagio* (Fig. 19.1), Schubert uses the wanderer motif to open the first movement with a contrasting and significant output of energy: it is marked by accents on the first beat and the *ff* dynamics (Fig. 19.1). This core motif of the Fantasy will, however, transform itself and acquire different expressions throughout the work, e.g., the second theme of the first movement (E major, m.47, Fig. 19.1) develops into the E-flat major melody of m.112, featuring the rhythm inverted (m.112, Fig. 19.1). The triplet tone repetitions of the lied, which were present alongside the dactyl rhythm, are to be reencountered in the Fantasy in form of a tremolando, or in form of tone repetitions conveying a similar effect, as e.g., m.23 of the *Presto,* or in several passages of the *Allegro,* notably in the coda section (Fig. 19.1).

[15] Cf. Riezler, Walther. (1967). *Schubert's Instrumentalmusik.* P. 44. (Trans. by the. Author). German expression: „Die Melodie hat dabei eine neue, echt instrumentale Gestalt angenommen: jeder Zusammenhang mit der Deklamation der Worte (‚Die Sonne dünkt mich hier so kalt... ‘) ist geschwunden.“.

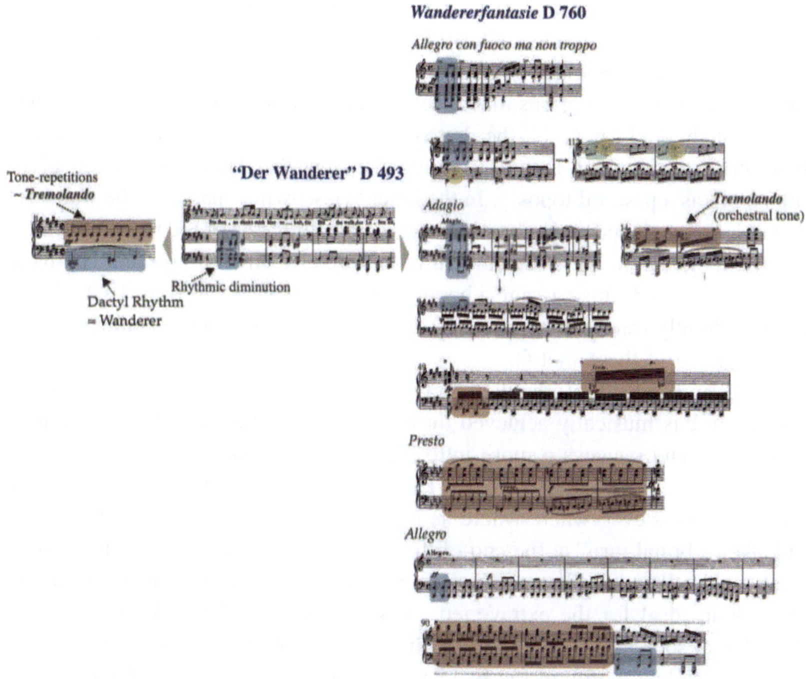

Fig. 19.1 Motivic interrelations between "Der Wanderer" and the *Wandererfantasie.* Motifs relating to tone repetitions/tremolo and the dactyl wanderer rhythm. (Sheet music excerpt taken and adapted from *IMSLP*)

The rhetorical question from the lied, "and the sigh ever wonders where, forever where?" ("und immer fragt der Seufzer wo, immer wo?"), can be perceived in form of an elaborated *suspiratio*[16] in the consequent phrase of the *Adagio's* melody from the Fantasy (right hand of m.12, Fig. 19.2)[17]. A cross-reference can additionally be found later, for instance, in the left hand of m.40f., (Fig. 19.2). Finally, the unexpected turn towards a dance-like character in the *Presto* of the

[16] In addition, the lied verse "oh, land where are thou?" (O Land, wo bist du?") also features this rhetorical figure (Figure 19.2).

[17] Riezler pointed particularly to the consequent phrase of the *Adagio*'s melody as being an echo of the lied. Cf. Riezler, Walther. (1967). *Schubert's Instrumentalmusik.* P. 44.

Wandererfantasie (m.79 f.)[18] can have its origins in the "Etwas geschwinder" (m. 32f.) and in the "Geschwind" (m.41f.) passages of the lied "Der Wanderer" (Fig. 19.2). As seen before, both passages in the song relate to the utopian fatherland and the hopeful emotions that arise when imagining it. In the first mentioned passage of the lied (m.32 f.), the dotted rhythm followed by a falling gesture is characteristic—the piano texture in thirds also appeals to imaginary associations with nature as a pastoral topos[19]. In the latter "Geschwind" passage, the wanderer rhythm is refunctioned and subdivided between both hands of the piano (m.46 f.). The first long beat in the left hand that is followed by off-beat repeated chords in the right hand lends this passage a hopping waltz-like character (Fig. 19.2). These are then slightly transformed in the *Wandererfantasie*, and can be understood as a development of these motifs.

The overall mood of the lied, referring to the lyrical "I" as a "stranger everywhere", is musically achieved through harmonic means and the word-tone relationship, and conveys a more introverted state of mind. As Andreas Krause has pointed out, the wanderer ends his lament uttering his own ontological tragedy that happiness is everywhere where he is not: the question of a hopeful "utopian land takes a brutal turn" at the end of the song[20]. In comparison, the choice of C major for the *Wandererfantasie* is a contrast that emphasizes an instantly bright tone colour, ideal for the extraverted energy of the "new" wanderer as a hero. The external sources of inspiration for this transformation have just been touched upon, and the key motifs of the lied and their connection with the *Wandererfantasie* have been comparatively shown with necessary brevity. It now remains to examine the possible inner impulse that led to such an important turning point in Schubert's creative process and to unfold further elements present in the C major Fantasy.

---

[18] Already Riezler pointed to both the Scherzo-like character of the Presto and the dance-like rhythm that appears quite surprisingly. Cf. Ibid.P.45.

[19] Joan Grimalt accounts parallel thirds in the major mode as a "pastoral musical topoi". Grimalt, Joan. (2021). *Mapping musical signification.* P.212.

[20] Cf. Krause, Andreas: „Die Klaviermusik—'So frei und eigen, so keck und mitunter auch so sonderbar'". In: Dürr, Walther., Krause, Andreas. (2020). *Schubert Handbuch.* P. 403. (Trans. by the author). German expression: "Nimmt die Frage nach dem Land der Utopie eine wenig hoffnungsvolle, wenn nicht sogar brutale Wendung [...]".

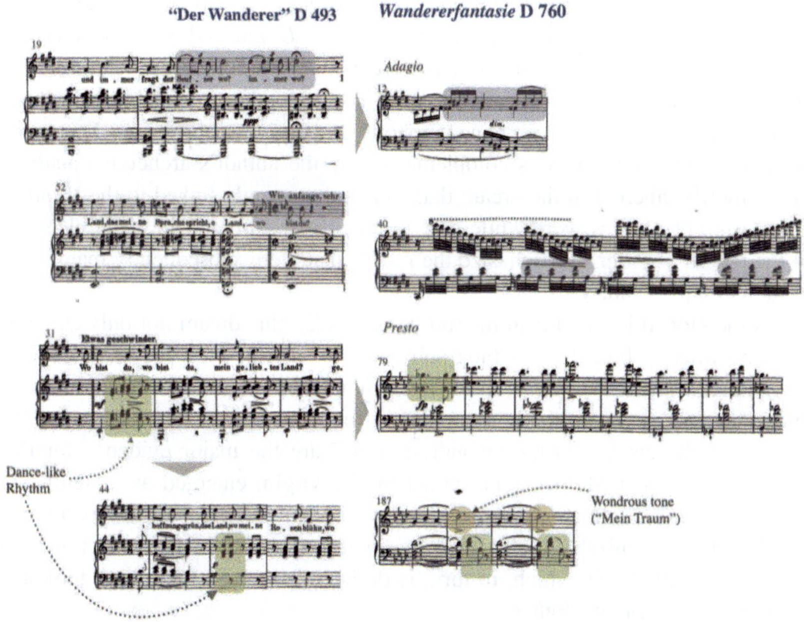

Fig. 19.2 Motivic interrelations between "Der Wanderer" and *Wandererfantasie.* Motifs related to the rhetoric questions and dance-like rhythm. (Sheet music excerpt taken and adapted from *IMSLP*)

An important source of inspiration that shaped the creation of this piano work, seems to have come from within. Although the above facts (Beethoven as a paragon, commissioned work, lied "Der Wanderer" D 489, etc.) may have acted as an important external impulse, they do not necessarily explain the reasons behind the change in musical language or virtuosic writing. The source may, in fact, lie in some parallels that can be drawn between the *Wandererfantasie* and Schubert's report on his dream from 1822. Apparently, this dream had an impact not only on the Fantasy but also on other compositions.

Since the C major Fantasy and the *Unfinished* Symphony have a concurrent genesis, a brief digression is pertinent to emphasize the effect of the dream on the composer: Arnold Schering has developed in his hermeneutic analysis a parallel that can be drawn between the dream and the symphonic work[21]. As previously noted (11.2), he interpreted Schubert's *Unfinished* Symphony D 759 (October 1822) by comparing its structure with the dream's twofold structure and interrelated motifs[22]. Thereby, he observed that there is an intrinsic interconnection between the B minor symphony and the C major piano Fantasy[23]. Schering's interpretation was complemented by the author's archetypal analysis of the motifs inherent in the dream that were subsequently linked to the *Wandererfantasie* (11.3). It is worthwhile now to reconsider some of the main elements of the dream in order to emphasize the motifs that were subsequently manifested in the C major Fantasy.

As mentioned in the dream interpretation (11.2), this dream not only contains elements directly linked to his biography but also reveals material of an archetypal nature (Tab. 11.1). Observed from a Jungian perspective, Schubert had a numinous encounter in this dream, pointing to a moment of Self-experience: the symbol of the circle and the "wondrous tone" are the major evidence for this reading. The Great Mother, represented by the virgin, emerged as a significant archetype that brought about reconciliation with the father figure. This "wondrous tone" is also recognizable in the *Wandererfantasie* and appears in connection with the Anima (Fig. 19.3), which, in turn, is derived from the overarching feminine principle of the Great Mother.

In this respect, the overarching wanderer motif shows different manifestations: the main theme of the wanderer evolves into the Anima theme—a musical observation that confirms psychologically that the Anima is the inner soul image of the wanderer. In the Anima theme, the "wondrous tone" can be identified as the long note, emphasized either by its syncopated nature or by a clear accent (Fig. 19.3). As previously seen (11.3), this note happens to be the perfect fifth of the harmony. Such observation allows for interpreting the character of this note as being of spiritual nature and symbolizing the pure tone, since it is considered a consonant interval. In the context of the *Wandererfantasie,* with the numerous dragon battles in mind (11.3), the function of the Anima is ultimately that of a supernatural helper in the confrontation with the unconscious elements.

The dragon battles are numerous and can be perceived in all movements, often juxtaposed with the Anima theme. Examples constitute:

---

[21] Cf. Schering, Arnold. (2012). *Franz Schuberts Symphonie in H-Moll („Unvollendete") und ihr Geheimnis.*

[22] Cf. Ibid.

[23] Cf. Ibid.

- 1st movement: mm.83–107 (dragon battle) vs. mm. 112–131 (Anima theme);
- 2nd movement: mm.22–26 (dragon battle, whereby the shadows start to emerge in m.18f.), mm.43–49 (including *trem.*) vs. mm.27–39, mm.50f. (Anima theme);
- 3rd movement: mm.59–78, mm.95–119 (dragon battles, or threatening descents, e.g., mm.214–234) vs. mm.179–277 (Anima related or Anima themes). Towards the end of the third movement dragon battles start to be increasingly present, leading to the fourth movement, e.g., m.309f., and are especially visible from m.327f.
- 4th movement: almost omnipresent.

With regard to the transformative and spiritual nature of the Anima (Figure 3. 9)[24], there is a compelling passage that effectively translates this spiritual quality into musical form—this can be perceived musically in mm.39–42, conveying the circle from the dream narration and the movement "from the periphery to the centre"[25]. Yet, even if a numinous experience has occurred in the second movement, the dragon battles persist.

Although there is an attempt at the fugue genre (last movement)—it should be recalled that Beethoven had already mastered this genre to perfection—Schubert quickly dropped this compositional technique and returned to the virtuosic writing of the dragon battles. Following Neumann's thesis of the creative process[26], the artist, or in this case the composer, does not follow the usual path of the hero, but needs constant connection to the source of creativity: the feminine principle of the Great Mother (11.3). Schubert himself pointed out the importance of fantasy[27] as the "spring from which both artists and scholars drink!"[28] (11.2).

[24] Cf. Neumann, Erich. (2015). *The Great Mother*.

[25] Ibid. P. 9. (Trans. by Ralph Manheim).

[26] Cf. Neumann, Erich. (1959). *Der schöpferische Mensch.* See also: Neumann, Erich. (2004). *Kunst und schöpferisches Unbewusstes.*

[27] Here, fantasy is used as a psychological term, as the creative power of the mind.

[28] Schubert, Franz. "Aus einem verlorenen Notizbuch Schuberts von 1824". In: Deutsch, Otto Erich. (1964). *Schubert—Die Dokumente seines Lebens.* P.233. (Trans. by the author). German expression: „[…] Quell, aus dem sowohl Künstler als Gelehrte trinken! […]".

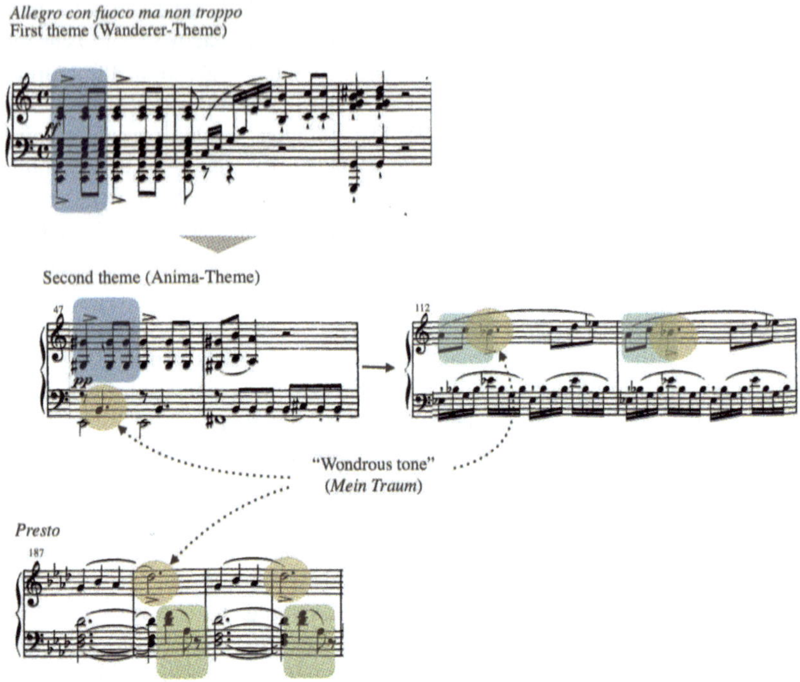

Fig. 19.3 *Wandererfantasie* D 760: Wanderer-Theme, Anima-Theme and the "wonderous tone" of Schubert's dream narration. (Sheet music excerpt taken and adapted from *IMSLP*)

19.2 Piano Trio in E-Flat Major D 920, 4th Movement: The Dragon-Battles of the "I" as a "Dümmling"

The chamber music work composed in 1827, which is the subject of this chapter, is considered by many musicians and musicologists to be a pivotal moment in Schubert's musical language, leading to his last instrumental compositions[29]: "It is a work that reveals, in exemplary fashion, the directions the composer was taking in his last years"[30]. In this context, Walther Dürr highlights three areas

[29] Cf. Dürr, Walther. (2016). "Compositional Strategies in Schubert's Late Music". In: Bodley, Lorraine Byrne. Horton, Julia. (Ed.). *Rethinking Schubert.* Dürr makes reference to Peter Gülke's point of view on this matter as well.

[30] Ibid. P.29.

in particular: an increased interest in contrapuntal techniques such as canonic constructions and free imitations, thematic and motivic interrelationships that provide a cyclical form, and a new conception of sonority[31]. However, as has been mentioned, such themes were already being processed in the *Wandererfantasie*. These are recurring themes in Schubert's musical language and creative process. In the Piano Trio, these subjects are tackled by another related archetype, the "Dümmling" (Simpleton).

Similar to the wanderer archetype, the "Dümmling" archetype also appears in Schubert's creative process. Its emergence is to be found at key moments (17) with the function of "point[ing] the finger on painful wounds or taboos [...], openly addressing them and setting potential healing transformations in motion [...]"[32]. This enables the integration of the topics that had fallen into the shadow realm. In fairy tales, the "Dümmling" character is often described in the context of a wandering journey, in which he deals with the tasks at hand in a rather naïve and open manner, e.g., "Die drei Federn" ("The three feathers")[33]. Yet precisely these characteristics, his goodwill as well as his deep connection with and intuitive understanding of nature, allow him to tackle his missions with success, i.e., to find the hidden treasures.

This character can be observed in the rondo-like opening theme of the fourth movement of the E-flat major piano trio D 929. Here, the "Dümmling" as a wanderer undergoes a wandering. Massin even emphasizes the connection of this movement with the wandering thematic as a "voyage intérieur"[34]. The movement begins with an *illud tempus* quality, in which the "Dümmling" theme (Theme A) is presented in the E-flat major tonality. A first important contrast, not only thematically but also in terms of harmonic colour, is given with the presentation of theme B in C minor (*L'istesso tempo*, m. 73 f.). This theme, which is first presented in the first violin (m.73 f.), then in the cello (m.89 f.) and later in broken octave repetitions in the piano from m.105, is based on broken chords combined with tone repetitions (Fig. 19.4). Emotionally, the fact that the melodic line is

---

[31] Ibid.

[32] Roesler, Christian. (2022). *Development of a Reconceptualization of Archetype Theory.* Report to the IAAP. P.51.

[33] Cf. Grimm, Jacob. Grimm, Wilhelm. (2015). *Grimms Märchen.* P.341–344.

[34] Massin, Brigitte. (1977). *Franz Schubert.* P.1204.

rendered in broken chords and by means of note repetitions conveys a contradictory emotional state: a courageous "approaching" of something, the unknown or the center, with a certain hesitation. There is movement (the melodic line inherent in this motif), but there is also a certain reluctance in this melody through the tone repetitions, i.e., there is a simultaneous stagnation, or willingness to remain on one note or in one place (Fig. 19.4 illustrated with a yellow stripe). In other words, this motif alone can be understood as an expression of the contrasting structure (polarity) of the archetype (the movement vs. the stagnation or the remaining in one place).

Due to the *movens* quality, this passage could be understood as an initiated wandering. In m.121f., for the first time in this movement, sixteen-note chains run up and down the piano keyboard. This gesture may depict a characteristic of the "Dümmling"—his cheerful bond with nature, ultimately his ontological condition of being one with nature in a childlike naivety. Soon, however, the romantic "Zerrissenheit" (i.e., the state of being torn) of the wanderer (4) comes to the fore. A significant rhythmic ambivalence can already be felt in m.137 with the off-beat accents in the violin and then, in m.139 f., with the syncopated motif in the piano (Fig. 19.4, blue stripe marking). The confrontation with these opposing aspects creates a rather obsessive inner movement—a circular search for the lost condition. This circular search can be perceived in the obsessive repetition of the two-measure cell, mm.157–158, and the return of the accentuated F note in the violin, repeated a total of three times. The result is a first moment of impasse, rendered by the musical rhetorical figure of *aposiopesis* (m.163). This moment of "holding in" or introspection is followed in the subsequent measures by an attempt at resolution—musically, this attempt is made with the material of the B-theme (m.167 f.). Such moments are recurrent throughout the movement.

During this journey, the "Dümmling" comes to moments of impasse several times, which are characterized by the musical rhetorical figure of the *aposiopesis*, e.g., m.163, m. 178, m.382, m.395, m.408, m.423, m.691, m.706. These can be understood as difficulties to be overcome and are particularly frequent in the development-like section, occurring here four times in total. From the more traditional perspective where the development section is considered the moment where the previously exposed material is developed, psychologically it can be analogously understood as the moment of the descent into the unconscious realm. The development-like section (mm.231–539) functions as the *peripeteia* and *climax* of the narrative. It begins with a bare octave as the rhetorical figure symbolizing death, on the note B—this could point to the fact that the "I" entered the shadow realm. It unfolds with a dialogue-like ductus or question-response prototype (e.g., mm.236–239 vs. mm.240–244), that may convey psychologically a dialogue with the inner protagonists—what Jung called a dialectic process[35]. It features the musical rhetorical figure of the *interrogatio* and includes the pleading or supplicatory undertone of *interrogatio* as well (e.g., mm.252–253 vs. mm.254–255). This ductus continues for several measures, until m.272, after two Neapolitan chords have underlined an inner suffering (m.265 or m.269). The pain expressed by this harmony is intensified by the *exclamatio* of the piano part in the same measures.

Then, a moment of introspection takes place (an "Er-innerung" passage), with the remembrance of the cello-theme from the second movement as a self-quotation. This return of the cello theme points to the cyclical form. There are some interpretations that link this theme semantically with a death march[36] (m.279 f.). Here, however, this theme is embedded in a different context—as if the semantic charge of this theme is about to undergo a transformation. Soon, the musical ductus changes and turns to dragon battles, e.g., passages beginning on m.337 f. and m.438 f. These dragon battles frame several moments of "holding in" (following the *aposiopesis* at m.382, m.395, m.408 and m.423) in this development-like section. The main musical theme of the dragon battle passage is related to the material of Theme B yet slightly altered, and featuring a more combative character, and the imitation technique. As already seen previously (e.g., 15, 16, 17), this technique is related to the ancient traditions of the *caccia* and can thus stand for a shadow pursuit. Attempts are made to resolve the moments of impasse (*aposiopesis*). These attempts also grasp the original material of Theme B, however, they draw on the atmosphere related to the characteristic naivety and openness of the "Dümmling"'s personality—ultimately, the characteristic that enables the "Dümmling" to tackle his missions. This analytical observation shows once more how a motif can have different characters or shades of semantics—as if it would reflect different facets of the same personage (e.g., light-shadow side).

---

[35] Cf. Jung, Carl Gustav. (2023). *Die Beziehung zwischen dem Ich und dem Unbewussten.*

[36] Cf. Massin, Brigitte. (1977). *Franz Schubert.* P.1204.

The second battle of the hero appears at m.438 f. This dragon battle (mm.438–473) involves and generates a third modulation path and shifts that indicate an imminent and important transformation: it reflects the path going from E-flat minor (m.438) to B minor (m.460). Following the Jungian tradition, chaotic moments or dragon battles precede the moment of the junction of opposites[37] (e.g., as in the hero journey). The fusion of simultaneous ambivalent and polyvalent aspects arrives in mm.473–512 (Fig. 19.4), which can be perceived as the actual process of transformation occurring, as a numinous experience: all motifs coalesce into the primordial wholeness. As such, the split elements are re-integrated. It is a striking passage (Fig. 19.4) exemplifying the spontaneity of the creative process, where the cello-theme of the second movement emerges as a reminiscence (or, as Jung would call it, as "Er-innerungen", I 2), and where a great intrinsic overlap in musical thoughts and motifs can be identified (Fig. 19.4). This compelling passage is only existent in the original version, which is rarely performed, and is missing in the final version—however, such moments in the creative process point to the veracity of the archetypal nature of music. It is the direct result of a spontaneous act. It is a great loss that this passage, symbolizing a moment of wholeness and transformation, was cut out, after revision, from the final version. The original version would merit being performed more often.

From an archetypal perspective, Jung understood the "Dümmling" archetype as bearing a "religious meaning"[38]. The final and unexpected turn to major at the end of the movement speaks in favour of a positive outcome moved by the numinous experience: a "transformation of pain towards love [...], the triumph of a heroic tenderness"[39], as described by Brigitte Massin.

---

[37] Roesler, Christian. Personal communication between Christian Roesler and the author. Freiburg im Breisgau: June 18, 2024.

[38] Roesler, Christian. (2022). *Development of a Reconceptualization of Archetype Theory.* Report to the IAAP. P.51.

[39] Massin, Brigitte. (1977). *Franz Schubert.* French expression: „une mutation de la douleur à l'amour [...] c'est le triomphe de la tendresse héroïque.".

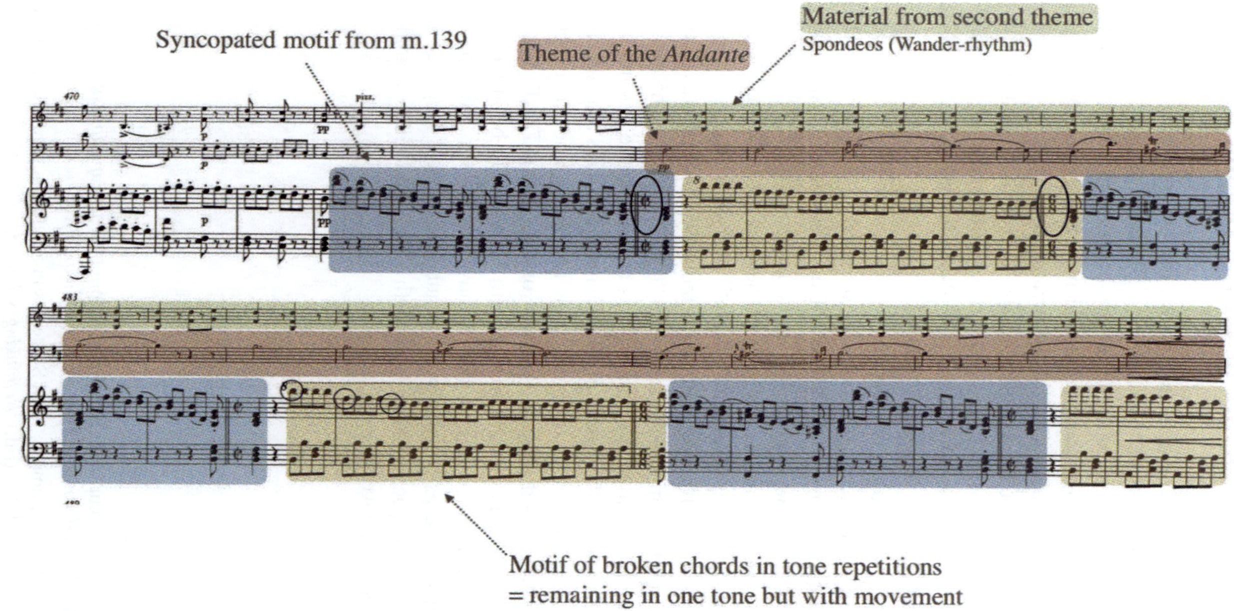

Fig. 19.4 Moment of simultaneity of musical-thoughts in the piano trio E-flat major D 929. (Sheet music excerpt taken and adapted from *Urtext of the New Schubert Edition*. Bärenreiter Verlag. (Digital Edition) © 1975 Bärenreiter-Verlag Karl Vötterle GmbH & Co. KG, Kassel)

19.3 Concluding Observations on the Dragon Battles

To conclude this chapter, a comparison between the two works, analyzed only cursorily, offers some insights. The distinctive "I"s, as a wanderer (1822) and as a "Dümmling" (1827), deal with the dragon-battles differently. Although a numinous moment of transformation has been identified in the second movement of the *Wandererfantasie* (reminiscence of the dream), the wanderer remains in a combative mode for most of the Fantasy. This is especially evident in the last movement—until, from a hermeneutic perspective, it succumbs at the end. This attitude during the compositional process was also reflected in Schubert's first performance of this work, as previously seen (11.3).

The "Dümmling", in contrast, resorted to numerous moments of introspection that were the result of moments of shock (*aposiopesis*). Even if similar rhetorical figures also interrupt the musical ductus of the *Wandererfantasie* (*abruptio* or punctually also *aposiopesis*, e.g., m.165 in the first movement, or m.70 in the fourth movement), in the piano trio there is another quality associated with *aposiopesis*, notably a significant change of affects[40] or even a change of roles: in this musical context, it is as if these "halting in" moments functioned as a connection to the deeper centre of his personality—the "real" "I" (Self). The manner in which the "Dümmling" resolves such impasses is revealed in the playful musical ductus that follows. Such is the nature of the "Dümmling". This attitude enabled him to integrate all aspects more easily—a transformative numinous experience visible in the aforementioned passage (junction of opposites). The final shift to the major tonality at the end of the movement (m 819f.) could be interpreted as a confirmation of the positive turn in the narrative, as a *lysis*. This archetypal *lysis* may have functioned as a gateway to Schubert's musical language in the last compositions, which goes hand in hand with Dürr's and Gülke's analytical observations mentioned above[41].

[40] This observation is congruent with Bartel's description of the *aposiopesis*. Cf. Bartel, Dietrich. (2010). *Handbuch der musikalischen Figurenlehre*. P.103.

[41] Cf. Dürr, Walther. (2016). "Compositional Strategies in Schubert's Late Music". In: Bodley, Lorraine Byrne. Horton, Julia. (Ed.). *Rethinking Schubert*.

20 Final Considerations

> "Whoever speaks in primordial images speaks with a thousand voices; he enthralls and overpowers, while at the same time he lifts the idea he is seeking to express out of the occasional and the transitory into the realm of the ever-enduring. He transmutes our personal destiny into the destiny of mankind, and evokes in us all those beneficent forces that ever and anon have enabled humanity to find refuge from every peril and to outlive the longest night. That is the secret of great art, and of its effect upon us. The creative process, so far as we are able to follow it at all, consists in the unconscious activation of an archetypal image, and in elaborating and shaping this image into the finished work. By giving it shape, the artist translates it into the language of the present, and so makes it possible for us to find our way back to the deepest springs of life."[1].

Numerous insights have been obtained from the individually performed in-depth examination of Schubert's selected works that allow gaining an overview of the development of the composer's creative process over several years (1814–1828). The musical analysis carried out with the inclusion of C.G. Jung's theory of the archetypes produced results that confirm the initial thesis of this project, namely the correlation between compositional creativity and the individuation process, and the fact that archetypes have a significant influence on the musical language of the composer.

This approach to the selected works comprised many building blocks or puzzle pieces: biographical facts, interrelationships of musical motifs, self-quotations, key characteristics, and archetypal manifestations were included in the considerations. The analysis of Schubert's creative process and musical language revealed

[1] Jung, Carl Gustav. (2014). "Spirit in Man, Art and Literature". In: *The Collected Works of C.G. Jung. Vol. 15.* (Trans. by Gerhard Adler and R.F.C. Hull). Chapter: "On the relation of analytical psychology to poetry". Paragraph 129–130.

L. Dill, *Schubert's Metamorphoses*,
https://doi.org/10.1007/978-3-662-73476-6_20

intrinsic interconnection between these aspects, from which an inner development of motifs could be recognized. To illustrate this, a concluding synopsis of the findings obtained from the previous analytical chapters (14–19) will be made. This will also include some of the analytical observations that have been made in part III. In this way, it will be possible to gain an analytical overview of the processes of transformation in Schubert's works and to close the circle on the research questions. The final section intends to present some reflections on the further application of this archetype-based method of music analysis and considerations to bear in mind.

20.1 The Inner Transformations in Schubert's Works: Analytical Overview[2] and Synopsis

Schubert's use of the "motif metamorphose technique"[3] allows for reflections on the interrelation between musical, archetypal and biographical motifs. Schubert's idiosyncratic path to achieve cyclical unity is equally instructive in this regard. As explained in part III, Schubert increasingly showed a special concern in combining the cyclical form with the variation form or a variation principle (9 or 11.1). This can be noted in works such as e.g., the *Forellenquintett*, the *Wandererfantasie* or the string quartet *Der Tod und das Mädchen.* On the one hand, the variation form, alike the "motif metamorphoses technique"[4], reflects the musical thought process, i.e., the inner developments and transformations of a motif (7.2). On the other hand, the cyclical form suggests a constant return or points of intersection of these musical or archetypal motifs (7.2). Lastly, when both are used interconnectedly, this conveys a spiral-like process, which, according to Jung, is

[2] The music analytical and psychological findings across Schubert works that are summarized in this chapter were presented by the author herself in public in the following conference: Dill, Leonor. (2024, October 4th). "Archetypes in Music and Individuation—An Integrated Approach". [Conference Abstract and Presentation]. In: *The Process of Transformation.* (2024, October 4–6).

[3] Godel, Arthur. (1985). *Schuberts letzte drei Klaviersonaten (D958—960).* P.19–20. As it was possible to see from the music analysis chapters, this technique is not only to be noted in his "late" works.

[4] Ibid. P.19–20.

equivalent to the characteristics of the individuation process[5]. In addition, it can be affirmed that the identified archetypes and symbolic content individually found in the analysed works had a direct impact on Schubert's musical language. This observation is in line with Jung's thesis that archetypes are autonomous structures and the basis of creativity (I).

This subchapter aims to give an overview of this development and the effects of the archetypal manifestations on Schubert's creative process in order to draw concluding thoughts. For this overview, it is important not to restrict the focus to one musical genre but to consider observations across the genres, since the creative psyche knows no boundaries but rather works in a serendipitous, associative way with reminiscences of motifs and their developments (the borrowing of motifs, quotations, the "motif metamorphosis technique"[6], etc. should be recalled). In addition to the works discussed in-depth in part IV (14–18) the following compositions that were partly and punctually highlighted in other chapters will also need to be considered, notably "Gretchen am Spinnrade" D 118 (1814, 8), *Wandererfantasie* D 760 (1822, 11.3 and 19), *Ellens Gesang III* ("Ave Maria") D 839 (1825, 11.2), the *Große Symphonie* in C major D 944 (1825, 16.3) and the piano trio in E-flat major D 929 (1827,19).

Figure. 20.1 and Fig. 20.2 were designed to illustrate the final considerations and better present the analytical results. As already explained in the introduction, both figures include the four categories that feature the Ariadne's thread for the construction of each of the following paragraphs: (i) archetypes and their metamorphosis, (ii) the psychological process, (iii) idiosyncrasies of Schubert's musical language, (iv) specific and important biographical events derived from the examination of correspondences, etc. At the same time, addressing each of these points will allow conclusions to be drawn about the research questions.

[5] Cf. Jung, Carl Gustav. (2014). "Psychology and Alchemy". In: *The Collected Works of C.G. Jung. Vol.12.* Chapter 3 "IV. The Symbols of the Self.". The same thought is described in *Traumsymbole des Individuationsprozesses.* See also: Jung, Carl Gustav. (2019). *Dream symbols of the Individuation process.* Gieser, Suzanne. (Ed.).

[6] Godel, Arthur. (1985). *Schuberts letzte drei Klaviersonaten (D958—960).* P.19–20.

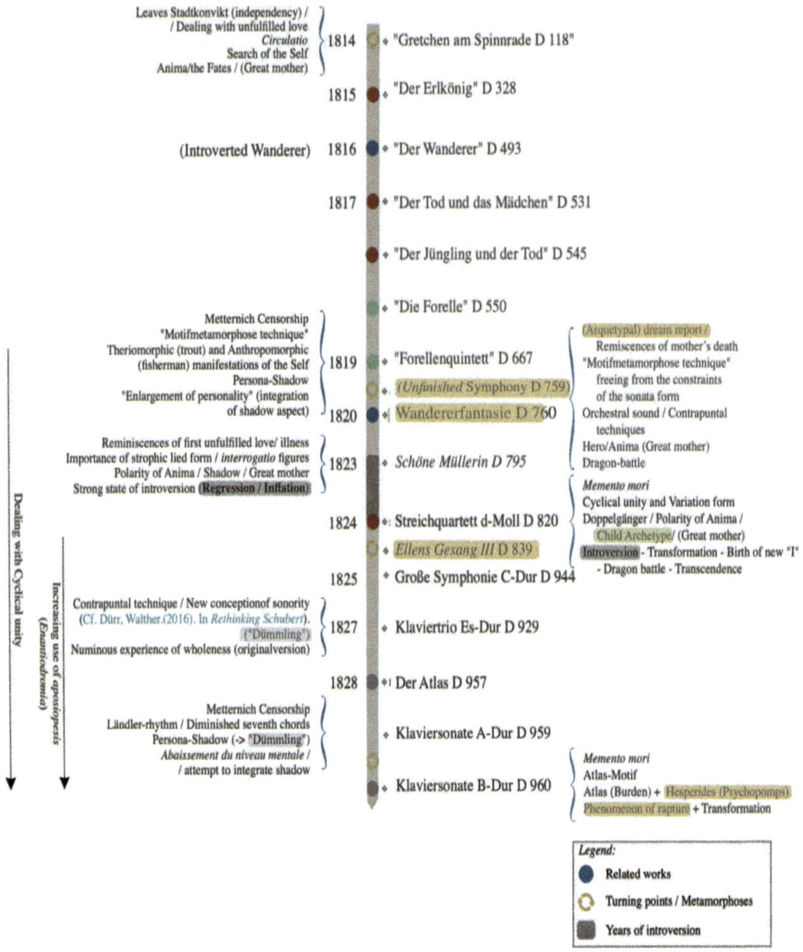

Fig. 20.1 Overview I on the analytical findings

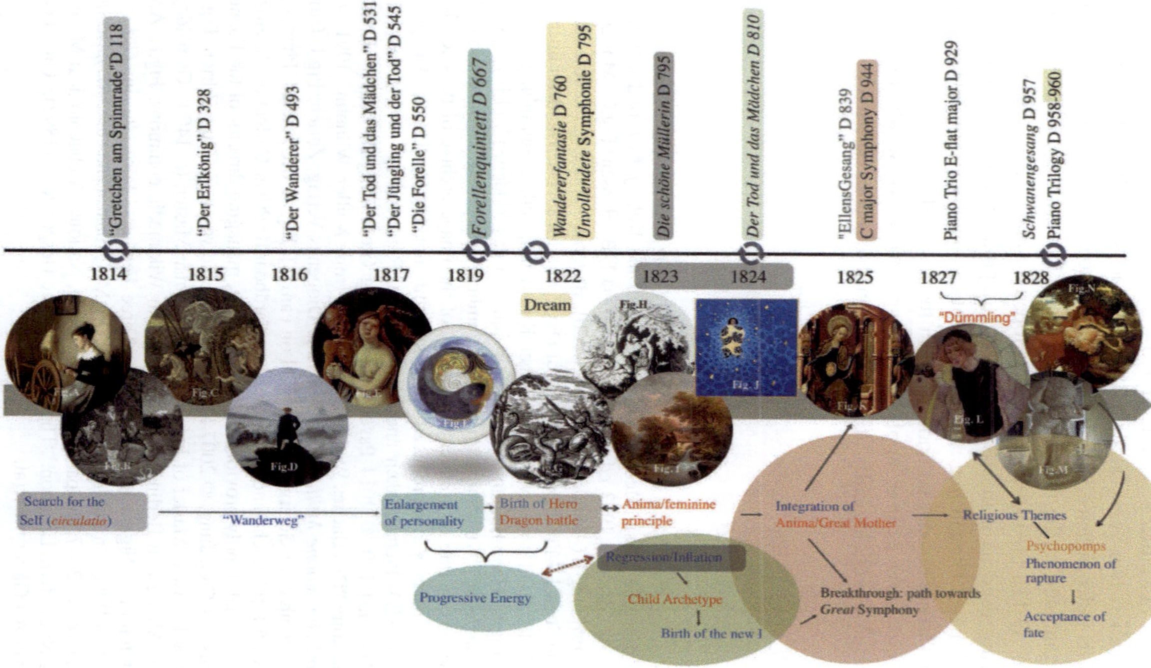

Fig. 20.2 Overview II on the archetypal manifestations across the creative/individuation process and the psychological turning points[7]

Schubert left the city college ("Stadtkonvikt") in 1813 and became independent, working at his father's school, in 1814. Even though he only ceased his lessons with Salieri two years later, in 1816, this act in itself already represents a move towards independence, which, from a psychological point of view, signifies an important step in the individuation process. Congruently, with "Gretchen am Spinnrade" D 118 (1814), Schubert developed an idiosyncratic language: the *circulatio* figure used as a means to depict the spinning wheel became Schubert's own hallmark. The circling around moment can be observed in many works throughout his life. This can be understood in the sense of the above-mentioned reflections, which serve as an example of the characteristics of Schubert's musical thought process[8]. Psychologically, it may represent the means he used to process

[7] Fig.A: Cover image from Mindock, Rebecca. (2018). *Franz Schubert—Gretchen am Spinnrade.* © 2018 Imagine Music Medina. Fig.B: *Norns at the Well of Urd.* (n.d.). [Engraving] From Fredrik Sander's 1983 ed. of *Poetic Edda.* © L.B. Hansen. Fig.C: Moritz von Schwind. "Der Erlkönig". (~1860). [Oil on oakwood]. Bayerische Staatsgemäldesammlungen—Sammlung Schack München. Fig.D: Caspar David Friedrich. "Der Wanderer über dem Nebelmeer". (1817). [Oil on canvas]. Hamburger Kunsthalle. Online Sammlung. © Foto: Elke Walford. Fig.E: Hans Baldung Grien. "Der Tod und das Mädchen". (1517). [Mixed Technique on limewood]. Kunstmuseum Basel. Sammlung online. Fig. F: Illustration "008 AHAF, Anonymous picture of a patient". Property of the image archive of the C.G. Jung Institut Zürich-Küsnacht and reproduced with its permission. Fig.G: "Drachenkampf aus Lambsprinck". (1677). Picture taken and adapted from: Rasche, Jörg. (2014). *Das Lied des Grünen Löwen.* P.130. © 2014 Psychosozial-Verlag Gießen. Fig.H: Ludwig Richter. [Drawing illustrating "Des Baches Wiegenlied"]. Taken from: Müller, Wilhelm. (1991). *Die Winterreise und Die schöne Müllerin.* P.83. ©1984 Diogenes Verlag, Zürich. Fig.I: Guido Hampe. "Wassermühle im Gebirge". (n.d.). [Oil on canvas]. Fig. J: C.G. Jung. "Phanes I". (1917). Kat.-Nr. 50. [Gouache and Goldbronze on cardboard]. Privat Collection. Digitized version of the original, kindly provided by Carl C. Jung, managing director of the Foundation of the Works of C.G. Jung. © 2007 Stiftung der Werke von C.G. Jung, Zürich. Fig.K: *The Virgin Mary Weaving.* Master of Erfurt. Upper Rhenish Master. (c. 1400). Gemäldegalerie, Staatliche Museen zu Berlin. Picture taken from Wikimedia commons. Fig.L: Anne Anderson. "Dümmling" Figure illustrating the "Three Feathers" fairy tale, in: *Old, Old Fair Tales.* © 1935 Whitman Publishing Company. Fig.M: "Atlas". (2nd cent. AD). [Roman statue]. Photograph: © 2007 Lalupa. Farnese Collection, National Archaeological Museum of Naples. Fig.N: Frederic Leighton. "The Garden of the Hesperides". (1892). [Oil on canvas]. Lady Lever Art Gallery, Wirral.

[8] Cf. Zacharias, Christian. (2019). *Why does Schubert sound like Schubert?* [Lecture-Recital]. Stagecast Ltd (Production).

specific themes; ultimately, according to Jung, it stands for the search for the Self[9] and the activation of "the light and dark forces"[10].

In addition, Brigitte Massin has pointed out a possible biographical parallel that lends itself to an archetypal reading and inspires a slight reformulation of one of her statements: the "maiden [motif], beautiful in […] [its] purity [of spirit] and innocence"[11], to take up Massin's characterisation of Marguerite, could have been associated by Schubert himself with his first love, Theresa Grob[12]. This emphasizes the Jungian reading that Gretchen functions archetypally as the Anima. Furthermore, this song alludes to the fate goddesses, the norns. In symbolic terms, they are connected with the spinning wheel (8). Featuring the round form, this can also allude to the archetype of the Great Mother as the "Great Round"[13]—the overarching feminine principle connecting both the Anima and the norns.

In contrast, the *Forellenquintett* D 667 (1819) refers less to biographical elements but rather to the historical and political circumstances. This is due to the reference of the song "Die Forelle" D 550, which was first composed in 1816/17. This work was analysed from the perspective of the impact that the Metternich censorship regime might have had on Schubert himself. From a comparative analysis between the earlier song and the piano quintet it was concluded that Schubert added a moment of *lysis* in the narration in the latter composition, which was absent in the song. This fact, alongside with further identified musical elements, pointed psychologically to the assimilation of split shadow elements.

---

[9] It can be helpful to recall that Jung speaks of *circulatio* and *circumambulatio* in similar terms. Cf. Jung, Carl Gustav. (2014). "Psychology and Alchemy". In: *The Collected Works of C.G. Jung. Vol.12.* Chapter 3 "The Symbolism of the Mandala—II. The Mandalas in the Dreams". Jung explains how the wheel, as an important symbol in alchemy, features a circulating process. Cf. Jung, Carl Gustav. (2014). "Alchemical studies". In: Ibid. *Vol. 13.* Chapter: "3. Fundamental concepts, B. The circular movement and the centre". C.G. Jung speaks of *circumambulatio* as the circular movement bringing an important inner movement: "Psychologically, this circulatio would be the 'movement in a circle around one-self', so that all sides of the personality become involved. 'The poles of light and darkness are made to rotate', that is, there is an alternation of day and night.".

[10] Ibid. "The circular movement thus has the moral significance of activating the light and dark forces of human nature, and together with them all psychological opposites of whatever kind they may be. It is nothing less than self-knowledge by means of self-brooding […].".

[11] Massin, Brigitte. (1977). *Franz Schubert.* P.554. (Trans. by the author). French expression: "[…] la jeune fille, belle dans sa pureté et son innocence, […]".

[12] Cf. Ibid.

[13] Cf. Neumann, Erich. (2015). *The Great Mother.* Part II, B: "The transformative Character", Chapter 12: "The Great Round". P.211–240.

This led to a process of transformation. This process of transformation, in view of its positive outcome, was here considered, according to C.G. Jung's theories, as an "enlargement of the personality"[14]. In terms of musical language, it was striking to note how Schubert achieved a motivic unity, based on small variations or metamorphoses of one specific motif: the sextuplet motif. Having been attributed to the environment of the trout or its lively condition in the brooklet, this element represented the overarching motif, from which diversions were identified. These variations were subsequently subdivided into epitomes of the light side, respectively the shadow side of the psyche. Congruently, the trout symbolically stood for the theriomorphic manifestation of the light side of the Self and the fisherman for the anthropomorphic manifestation of the shadow side of the same entity. A further important psychological turning point could be noted in the year 1822 with the *Wandererfantasie* D 760, composed in the month of November.

The *Wandererfantasie* was examined, on the one hand, in connection with its earlier song reference "Der Wanderer" D 493 (1816), and, on the other hand, in the context of a significant document by Schubert: his dream narration "Mein Traum"[15], dated July 3rd, 1822. This dream featured not only personal elements, but above all important archetypal motifs and a numinous Self experience (11.2). The description of the virgin/maiden pointed to the active feminine principle of the Anima/Great Mother. The description of the circle was, from a Jungian perspective, indicative of an experience of the Self, that habitually emerges in times of change[16], i.e., functions as an impulse or catalyst from the part of the unconscious towards an imminent transformation. That this represented a numinous experience is also evident in Schubert's description of crossing the threshold and moving towards the centre of the circle, where a "wondrous sound" was heard.

The dream created an important inner movement that impacted Schubert's psychic energy and brought about a change in his musical language. Ultimately, in a comparative analysis between the song "Der Wanderer" and the piano Fantasy it was possible to note that the archetypal content of the dream led to a transformation of the wanderer archetype: the main protagonist became less introverted; in fact, he gained a progressive energy and an extraverted attitude (11.3 and 19)—much alike the hero archetype that starts a journey into the wide outer, and at the same time, into the depths of the inner world (e.g., hero-journey,

[14] Jung, Carl Gustav. (2011). *Four Archetypes.* (Trans. by R.F.C. Hull). P.54.

[15] Schubert, Franz: „Allegorische Erzählung von Schubert—‚Mein Traum'". 1822. In: Deutsch, Otto Erich. (1964). *Schubert—Die Dokumente seines Lebens.* P. 158–159.

[16] Cf. Roesler, Christian. Personal communication between Christian Roesler and the author. Freiburg im Breisgau: June 18, 2024.

3.1). Thereby, he needed to fulfill the task of winning the so-called "dragon battle" (3.1). This dragon battle was understood here in relation to Schubert's engagement with Beethoven's works and his search for the great form (11.3/19). Schubert achieved an orchestral writing of the piano and to open the path to a new form[17]. The attempted fugato compositional technique was abandoned, and thus the aforementioned dragon battles remained the overarching feature underlying the psychological process of this work.

If, from a musical perspective, *Gretchen am Spinnrade* is to be taken as the composition that marks Schubert's independence (III 9)—both in the biographical sense and with regard to the development of an idiosyncratic musical language[18]—then, from a psychological point of view, the *Wandererfantasie* reveals a progressive energy that equally marks an important step in the individuation process. As such, the C major Fantasy could be taken as the beginning of a new creative period, in which Schubert musically searched for the great form and an orchestral tone (12)[19]. From an archetypal point of view, a comparison of the Anima motifs in Schubert's works could show how the Anima, in its function, was transformed from *Gretchen am Spinnrade* (1814) to the *Wandererfantasie* (1822), inheriting a more spiritual function in the latter composition. Considering Neumann's illustration (3.2 Fig. 3.9), this transformation went from the containing, "elementary character" to the inspirational "transformational character"[20]. This important metamorphosis brought about a great creative potential. However, it can happen that, after such a progressive energy output, the opposite is needed in order to integrate further elements—the "I", that was trapped in dragon battles in D 760, subsequently needed a return to the womb of the mother, i.e., to the source of creativity for the artist, as a regressive movement (11.3).

In the song cycle *Die Schöne Müllerin* D 795, the archetypal themes of the Anima, the Great Mother and the shadow returned. In the analysis of this song cycle, two traumatic events of Schubert's biography were recalled which might have been activated by reading the likewise biographically oriented poems of Wilhelm Müller. These included the death of Schubert's mother and his first

---

[17] Cf. Krause, Andreas: „Die Klaviermusik—'So frei und eigen, so keck und mitunter auch so sonderbar'". In: Dürr, Walther., Krause, Andreas. (2020). *Schubert Handbuch.* P.392.

[18] It shall be recalled that Schubert left the city college ("Stadtkonvikt") in 1813, and that this song features several idiosyncratic elements in the way Schubert treats the musical ductus; most particularly the *circulatio* figure as Schubert's life-long hallmark is here, apparently for the first time, processed in depth (9).

[19] Cf. Krause, Andreas: „Die Klaviermusik—'So frei und eigen, so keck und mitunter auch so sonderbar'". In: Dürr, Walther., Krause, Andreas. (2020). *Schubert Handbuch.* P.392.

[20] Neumann, Erich. (2015). *The Great Mother.* (Trans. by Ralph Manheim).

unfulfilled love towards Theresa Grob. It was also mentioned that 1823 was a year of great distress for Schubert, in which he was not only diagnosed with a potentially fatal illness but also suffered particular setbacks in relation to operatic compositions. From the point of view of the musical language, Schubert's music generally reflects the symbolic content and the emotional utterances of Wilhelm Müller's poems. In this lieder cycle, two songs were identified as important stepping-stones in the process of transformation: "Thränenregen", representing the midpoint of the cycle, and "Trockne Blumen". In both songs, the lyrical I embarked on a fantasy, respectively, an active imagination. In the first one, the miller had an epiphany, which led the "I" to confront its shadow side; in the second one, the "I" became active for the first time. The latter moment was crucial to the archetypal stages, since it enabled the encounter with the great Mana personality of the Great Mother. The "I" was eventually drawn towards the great power of the archetype and immersed in the Self, entering a profound state of introversion. This reflects the psychic process of regression linked to an inflation.

The same process was identified in the string quartet in D minor *Der Tod und das Mädchen* D 810, composed in 1824. This state was achieved not at the end of the entire composition but at the close of the first movement. This presupposed an imminent process of transformation. The second movement begins—unlike the song "Der Tod und das Mädchen"—with the verses of death in the foreground. Having been in this introverted state, the new "I" began to be generated. Congruently, the child archetype emerged in the only major variation of the second movement. The use of the G major tonality allowed parallels to be drawn with the symbolic semantic of this key from the previously composed work D 795. G major, as the tonality of the brooklet (IV 15), alluded to the archetype of the Great Mother. This substantiated the reading of the emergence of the child archetype and the generation of a new "I". The real transformation of the "I" (attributed to the alter-ego motif), could be acknowledged in the third movement: the motif is presented in the retrograde inversion form and is reinforced by the dynamics. The last movement, as a *danse macabre*, symbolizes the transcendence of the "I". The alter-ego motif is transmuted here, which confirmed the birth of the new "I". This composition features a powerful transformational process: first, an inflation linked to a regression, then a transformation of the "I", and ultimately a transmutation of the "I" (transcendence). From the standpoint of the musical language, the main motif, entitled the alter-ego motif, clearly showed these different stages. With regard to the debate on the categorization of work-phases (early-works vs. late-works, cf. III 12), from 1824 there was an increased use of *aposiopesis,* and, in regard to harmony, sudden shifts, and third relations. These and other aspects—to speak in Hinrichsen's terms, the "interactive harmonic and structural measures"[21]—led to an historical paradigm shift in relation to "the dramaturgical model of sonata form"[22].

With the string quartets, Schubert– as he himself expressed in the letter addressed to Leopold Kupelwieser dated from March 31st 1824—found the path towards the *Great* C major Symphony, composed in 1825. In the latter work, the cyclical form once again plays an important role. Schubert developed an idiosyncratic conception of the sonata form, which led Schumann to compare the C major symphony with Jean Paul's literary style, attributing to it the expression of the "heavenly lengths"[23]—a formal aspect which would find echoes later in music History, notably in Bruckner's symphonic works[24]. Overlapping and correlating the just-mentioned analytical findings of the works that coincided with the years that have been entitled as the "years of crisis" (1818–1823), brought more insight to this debate. In fact, taking into consideration the results of the musical and psychological analysis, the author proposes to refer to them simply as years of introversion, in agreement with musicologists who prefer to entitle these years as "years of [...] spiritual upheaval"[25]. Thereby, the process of transformation was not a straightforward process but rather mirrors a spiral like process, with a constant return to process similar questions.

A progression was attributed to the year of 1819 with the *Forellenquintett* (integration of a split aspect) and the *Wandererfantasie* (dragon battle). According to this analysis, the years to be considered as the years of introversions would rather correspond to 1823 and 1824, especially traceable to *Die Schöne Müllerin* (the highlighted dark strip drawn in the timeline of Fig. 20.1 and Fig. 20.2). Through the D minor quartet, i.e., by integrating the Anima aspect, Schubert achieved the transcendence of this state, which brought about a great personal development, and led to the achievement of writing the *Great* C major Symphony (1825). The child archetype that emerged in the second movement of D

[21] Hinrichsen, Hans-Joachim. "Is there a late style in Schubert's Œuvre?". In: Bodley, Lorraine Byrne. Horton, Julia. (2016). *Rethinking Schubert.* P.23.

[22] Ibid.

[23] Schumann, Robert. (1854). *Gesammelte Schriften über Musik und Musiker.* Vol. 3. P. 201.

[24] This Schubertian influence is in fact much discussed in scholarly literature. Not only Hinrichsen has pointed to this fact in the previously cited article, but this also reflects a subject of dialogue between interpreters. Cf. Brendel, Alfred. In: Brendel, Alfred. Gülke, Peter. (2020). *Die Kunst des Interpretierens.*

[25] "These were not so much 'years of crisis' as years of a significant spiritual upheaval.". Hilmar, Ernst. (1997). *Franz Schubert.* P. 31. (Trans. by the author). German expression: "Es waren weniger 'Jahre der Krise' [...] als vielmehr Jahre eines hochbedeutenden geistigen Umbruchs.".

810 fulfilled the function of an important transformation. Musically, the use of *aposiopesis* gained increasingly on significance from D 810 onwards, often functioning as psychological turning points, i.e., as "phenomenon of reversal"[26] or "enantiodromia"[27], as Jung himself designated this phenomenon. A great cumulation of this musical rhetorical figure was found in Schubert's E-flat major piano trio. However, in this chamber music work, this figure gained another semantic, linked with the emergence of a new archetype.

In 1827, the archetype of the "Dümmling" came forth. The main function of this archetype is to address hurtful topics in a playful manner[28]. The underlying psychological theme addressed here was the integration of unresolved subjects. In the E-flat major piano trio, the "Dümmling" was linked to the musical rhetorical figures of *interrogatio* and *aposiopesis* (19), as if through this archetype Schubert's inner "I" was processing and attempting to resolve pending quests. Here, however, the moments of *aposiopesis* in the musical ductus were less representative of an abyss as a turning point but rather of moments of a "holding in" (introspection) in order to be able to resolve the missions assigned to him during the wander journey. The archetype of the "Dümmling" reappeared in the last piano trilogy, especially in the A major and B-flat major sonatas (D 959–960, 1828). It first emerged in the third movement of the A major sonata. Prior to that, i.e., in the second movement, Schubert addressed a particularly painful subject to him (17). While some aspects were integrated in the piano trio (1827) through the emergence of the "Dümmling", there were other factors that still needed to be processed.

The moments of socialization were of great importance to Schubert. Friendships were also highly valued[29]. In the historical time in which Schubert lived, society was strongly shaped by the censorship regime of Metternich. According to Jung, the structure of a society strongly impacts the psyche[30]. For Schubert, these times of censorship sometimes led to friends being driven apart, as was the case

[26] Cf. Neumann, Erich. (2021). *Die Große Mutter.* P.84. German expression: "Der Pol ist nicht nur ein Endpunkt, sondern auch ein ,Wendepunkt'".

[27] Roesler, Christian. Personal communication between Christian Roesler and the author. Freiburg im Breisgau: June 18, 2024. The definition of Enantiodromia is to be found in: Cf. Jung, Carl Gustav. (2013). *Kleines Lexikon der Analytischen Psychologie.*

[28] Cf. Roesler, Christian. (2022). *Development of a Reconceptualization of Archetype Theory.* Report to the IAAP. P.51.

[29] Schubert's friends were like a second family to him. Cf. Dürr, Walther: „Schubert in seiner Welt". In: Dürr, Walther Krause, Andreas. (2020). *Schubert Handbuch.*

[30] Cf. Jung, Carl Gustav. (2023). *Die Beziehung zwischen dem Ich und dem Unbewussten.*

with his exiled friend Johann Chrysostomus Senn[31]. Schubert expressed several laments on the state of society and life in Vienna (8, and 17), which also referred to the close circle of friends (17)[32]. These correspondences were highlighted in the analytical context of the second movement of the A major piano sonata D 959 since this movement was interpreted as expressing in itself a lament about these questions. The psychological process addressed in the second movement of D 959 brought the Persona-shadow dialectic to the fore again[33]. Here, the dance functioned as the epitome of society (ländler motif), with the *suspiratio* revealing the state of the "I" in relation to this societal factor. Ultimately, the "I" entered a fantasy state from which the deepest structures of the unconscious (shadow) emerged, which gave origin to the chaos of the B-section. The confrontation with these shadow elements generated again a moment of shock (*aposiopesis*). The dialectic procedure subsequently identified, characterized by a dialogue with the inner furies, permitted the analogy with the Orpheus myth[34]. Once the furies tamed, the "I" entered the *Elysium*—a place prone to the integration of the split elements. Strikingly, at this moment, Schubert integrated the ländler motif in the new emerging lyre-motif. In the course of the composition, the "I" eventually refused to integrate the shadow aspect leading to an experience of nothingness of the "poetic nihilism" (17.6)[35]. It was precisely after this nothingness, which functioned as a turning point, that the "Dümmling" arose in the subsequent third movement, embodying the motif of the furies from the second movement. In a

---

[31] Cf. Gramit, David: "'The passion for friendship': music, cultivation, and identity in Schubert's circle". In: Gibbs, Christopher H. (1997). *The Cambridge Companion to Schubert.* Cambridge: Cambridge University Press. (E-book).

[32] Cf. Schubert, Franz: Letter to Schober. (30.11.1823). In: Deutsch, Otto Erich. (1964). *Schubert—Die Dokumente seines Lebens.* P. 207.

[33] Since this type of Persona-Shadow confrontation is typically described as a first stage of the individuation process, the question arises as to why this theme could be identified here, i.e., in one of the last's piano sonatas of Schubert's life. On the other hand, considering Jung's hypothesis that archetypal themes in dreams are arranged in spiral-like form was insightful: a similar topic may be retaken by the unconscious or processed again from another perspective while the individual is in another life stage. As a side note, it could be appended that Nietzsche's "eternal return" concept could be linked to this thought. For Jung's reference on the spiral-like process see: Cf. Jung, Carl Gustav. (2014). "Psychology and Alchemy". In: *The Collected Works of C.G. Jung. Vol.12.* Chapter 3 "IV. The Symbols of the Self.". The same thought is described in *Traumsymbole des Individuationsprozesses.* See also: Jung, Carl Gustav. (2019). *Dream symbols of the Individuation process.* Gieser, Suzanne. (Ed.).

[34] This analogy had already been drawn by Wollenberg, Susan. (2011): *Schubert's Fingerprints: Studies in the Instrumental Works.* P. 166.

[35] The concept of "poetic nihilism" in Schubert's oeuvre has been addressed by Gruber, Gernot. (2010). *Schubert. Schubert?*

playful manner, the "Dümmling" achieved the integration of this shadow element (furies motif). After such a chaotic moment as in the B-section of the second movement, the phenomenon of enantiodromia was expected to occur imminently. It is relevant to recall that, according to Jung's theory, the union of the opposites is often achieved after a phase of disorientation[36]. This was confirmed with the subsequent analysis.

The B-flat major sonata D 960 took up again the motif of the preceding sonata, the sigh motif. Here, however, it is embedded in the context of the Atlas myth. The analogy with the Atlas myth was drawn from the rhythmic core motif, which was entitled the Atlas rhythm[37] by Arthur Godel, in reference to the lied "Der Atlas" D 957. This mythological figure functioned here as the expression of the one level of reality. Eventually, this ontic plane was elevated into another, new reality level (A'-section) that emerged after a phenomenon of rapture (B-section). Such "existential" experience as the phenomenon of rapture enabled a crucial transformation in the personal development. Archetypally, this numinous event occurred due to the Hesperides—or to draw the parallel to Christian context, the angels—that functioned as psychopomps. The rhythmic motif of the Atlas transformed itself (A'-section) and left its burden behind. A new motif then emerged, the fate motif—a cross-reference in Schubert's works—which here, together with the tonal majorizations, that in turn functioned as reminiscences of the B-section, led to the interpretation of an ultimate transformation or acceptance of fate. This acceptance is crucial in the individuation process.

It is revealing that such a process occurred in the last work for piano solo, i.e., two months prior to Schubert's death. The piano trilogy is often referred to as Schubert's swansong by many musicologists and musicians; some others have contested this idea. From a Jungian perspective, however, it is possible that Schubert's unconscious was pointing to his imminent death, enabling an intuitive knowledge of what was about to befall him: in an oneiric plane the dream-"I" can be confronted with the *memento mori*, which has to deal with these questions, especially when death is approaching[38]. From a musical perspective, the fact that the "I" experienced here a phenomenon of rapture[39], underlines this thesis.

[36] Roesler, Christian. Personal communication between Christian Roesler and the author. Freiburg im Breisgau: June 16, 2024.

[37] Cf. Godel, Arthur. (1985). *Schuberts letzte drei Klaviersonaten (D958–960).*

[38] Marie-Louise von Franz has addressed such themes. Cf. Von Franz, Marie-Louise. (1984). *Traum und Tod.*

[39] As already explained (18.), this spiritual phenomenon of crossing the threshold to another world can happen before or after death. Cf. Böttrich, Christfried. (2013). "Entrückung" in: *Das wissenschaftliche Bibellexikon im Internet. Deutsche Bibel Gesellschaft*. [Article].

Ultimately, with this experience the "I" accepted to carry its own cross. It is only through this step (acceptance of fate) that the wheel of life can turn forwards and all earthly conditions of the"I" can be transcended.

Finally, bearing the whole trilogy in mind, the transcendence expressed in the middle section of the second movement of the B-flat major sonata D 960 can be read as a response to the darkness of the soul—or the depths of the unconscious—expressed in the middle section of the A major Sonata D 959, 2nd movement. In the light of Angelica Löwe's considerations outlined earlier (18), it could be observed that an important inner motion occurred between both second movements of the A-major and the B-flat major sonatas. This could be determined by the fact that the "I" was exposed to the shadow elements in D 959, and as a result, this confrontation led to the junction of the fourth element (*Quaternio*) in D 960. That means: wholeness was experienced and expressed by the phenomenon of rapture/ascension. These hermeneutical findings complement Brendel's conceptualization of the trilogy as thesis-antithesis-synthesis (17).

20.2 Conclusions

From the research on Schubert's creative process, which has been summarized and illustrated in this final overview, it became clear how specific archetypes emerged, embedded in a particular biographical or cultural context. These archetypes impacted the "I" and the creative process of Schubert, consequently shaping the musical language of the composer. In particular, it was possible to confirm that symbols of wholeness/of the Self, such as the circle, the theriomorphic manifestation of the Self (e.g., the fish), the divine child, appeared in times of disorientation or re-orientation[40], thereby generating crucial transformations. In broader terms, the examination of the creative process also demonstrated that "to be one with everything [...] in self-oblivion"[41], as Hölderlin poetically expressed in *Hyperion*, appears to be the ultimate urge or quest of the (Romantic) artist/composer—being the core of the creative process itself. Such longing reflects the artist's need for the archetypal *unio mystica*—the urge to experience the primordial state of being, *de facto* a spiritual experience of numinous nature, in which all opposites are unified in the uroboric state. To refer to the ideas inherent in Schelling's *Naturphilosophie* (4), such urge originates from the tension existent

[40] Cf. Jung, Carl Gustav. (1970). *Aion.* P.31–32.

[41] Hölderlin. Friedrich. (2019). *Hyperion or the Hermit in Greece.* (Trans. by Horward Gaskill). Cambridge: Open Book Publishers. P.8.

in the dialectic between the inner and outer world, with which the artist feels constantly confronted.

This interdisciplinary approach has enabled shedding light on several musical phenomena that would have remained undiscovered through the sole application of a more conventional music analytical methodology. Within musical analysis itself, various methods were applied that proved to be fruitful in association with a Jungian interpretation of the creative process. These methods, including (i) formal analysis, (ii) motivic-thematic, rhythmic and harmonic analysis, (iii) semantic analysis, (iv) key characteristics, theories of topoi, musical rhetorical figures, etc., permitted objective identification of the musical elements well-suited to symbolic reading. This step subsequently allowed finding the corresponding psychological processes underlying a musical passage. The unveiling of these processes through the archetypal theory of C.G. Jung has led to a deeper understanding of Schubert's creative process, offering a new perspective in the general understanding of music and the composer in question. In this sense, music is understood as a "storytelling" of the inner archetypal movements of the soul. However, while operating in the field of hermeneutics, it is important to modestly recognize that such findings represent possibilities for interpretation, which however, when observed altogether in context, prove to be significantly conclusive.

It is evident that the knowledge gained from this analysis is particularly meaningful for interpretative purposes, and that studies on the creative process from a Jungian perspective will have a considerable impact on artistic interpretation and performance practices. For the performer, it is of the utmost importance to gain an understanding of the composer's world in order to convey the essence of the composition. This world encompasses the archetypal content of the compositions and their polarity, which have hitherto rather remained in uncharted waters. In conclusion—since the Jungian approach permits to unveil, or at least approximate, these ambivalences and the "ineffable" aspect of music, it encourages the further application of Analytical Psychology in the musicological field. In this way, it is possible to come closer to the "soul" of a composition or composer.

20.3 Reflections on the Further Application of this Archetype-Based Analysis Approach

The analytical approach performed in this dissertation represents a fundamental research carried out with a specific focus on the creative process of Franz Schubert. The results of this new archetype-based music analytical approach not only confirmed the hypotheses stated at the beginning of this project but also yielded compelling insights into the archetypal nature of Schubert's music, the relationship between the archetypal material and biographical, historical and cultural elements, and the processes of transformations underlying Schubert's creative process. It is, nevertheless, a matter of fact that there is a paucity of research conducted on such subjects from this interdisciplinary field. This underlines the necessity of extending the individualized and integrative line of analysis, as performed here on Schubert, to other composers. This means undertaking further musical analysis based on the application of C.G. Jung's archetypal theory in order to gain a deeper understanding of the creative process of other composers, as there are still many questions to be researched in this field. This application requires certain aspects to be considered that will be cursorily pointed out in the following.

In the aforementioned statement, at the beginning of this chapter (20), Jung emphasized how archetypes, being psychic structures, are the acting inner forces that constitute the basis of creativity. In *Über das Phänomen des Geistes in Kunst und Wissenschaft,* Jung explained that an artistic work is the result of a psychological activity, and thus the creative process can be subject to be analysed accordingly (i.e., in psychological terms)[42]. The applicability of this archetype-based music analysis to works of other composers is evident. There are, however, several questions that remain unanswered. The following paragraphs delineate the essential elements or key questions that future research should consider as a foundation for their work.

Subsequent studies should focus on the symbolic elements that can be objectively researched in music[43], investigating the extent to which composers are influenced by archetypal material, and more particularly, their ability to access these unconscious structures. This raises the related question of how the composer responds to the impulses from the unconscious and actually approaches archetypal material.

---

[42] Jung, Carl Gustav. (2014). "Spirit in Man, Art and Literature". In: *The Collected Works of C.G. Jung. Vol. 15.* (Trans. by Gerhard Adler and R.F.C. Hull). Chapter: "On the relation of analytical psychology to poetry". Paragraph 97. The passage in question reads as follows: "[…]. These connections arise from the fact that the practice of art is a psychological activity and, as such, can be approached from a psychological angle.".

[43] By objectively researched elements are meant all of the musical structures that can be identified using music analytical tools and that are particularly well-suited to a symbolic reading, such as motifs, harmonies, rhetorical figures, key characteristics, topoi, etc. Basically, this is an approach to exploring and interpreting the archetypal content of music, as the author performed in this dissertation.

A further question that can be posed is as to which archetypes can be identified in the works of different composers—for example, would Schumann's music reveal the same archetypal patterns as Schubert's? It would be of interest to find out at what point in a composer's life these archetypes emerge and what processes of transformation they set in motion from the perspective of the creative and individuation process. As demonstrated by the findings presented in this dissertation, even archetypes can undergo transformations in the course of the creative and individuation process, which should also be investigated. Finally, how does the interplay between consciousness and the unconscious vary from composer to composer during the creative act, and what insights does this interaction reveal about the connection between archetypes and compositional language?

In order to approach such complex questions, it is important to bear in mind that an interplay of a variety of singular elements takes place during the compositional process. As illustrated in 13, there is a direct expression or processing and elaboration of unconscious elements that occur during creation. This indicates that the musical language can be understood as the consequence of an aesthetization process of unconscious elements, which implies the transformation and transmutation of unconscious material above mentioned. It would therefore be worth investigating how archetypes manifest and take shape in the music of specific composers, and to identify the characteristics of the musical language that reflect the underlying archetypes. The question thus arises as to the origin of this aesthetization process—how much of the spontaneous nature of the archetypes remains intact vs. how much conscious work is involved? As this dissertation focuses on the connection between archetypes, biographical elements and aspects linked to the respective zeitgeist, these questions should be researched in the context of biographical, cultural and historical experiences.

The results of these investigations will have a significant influence on artistic interpretation, as was previously highlighted.

Future research could also fruitfully employ the analytical findings on identified archetypal phenomena in music for psychotherapeutic purposes. This would entail departing from a solid foundation and knowledge of the patients' psychic conditions to confront them with a composition in which a pertinent archetypal process is inherent. Such approach in a therapeutic context could potentially bring about inner motion and activate the necessary archetypal principle, which ultimately should promote healing[44]. This idea leads to the question of whether there are common reactions from listeners to the archetypal material present in

[44] This thought is based on Jung's idea that there are inner instances capable for a self-regulatory process.

a composition. On the basis of self-observation[45], it was possible to notice, for example, that highly emotional reactions during the listening and analyzing process often coincided with passages in the music that expressed a simultaneity of opposites, namely the "ambivalent", "ineffable" aspects of music. These moments of junction of the opposites create such strong emotional tension in the listener that, in Jungian terms, they can generate a numinous archetypal experience. A similar phenomenon may well occur during musical practice and performance.

This observation gave rise to further questions, such as whether individuals with different typologies respond differently to the archetypal material in the music and whether these reactions differ depending on the momentary state of the individual. As explained in 7., the fact that an external element finds an inner resonance is directly related with emotional states and lived experiences. Such inquiries open the field of empirical research. To address these questions further meticulous research is required into depth psychological and empirical studies performed with test subjects. To conduct such a survey, it would be essential to consider a number of factors, including all aspects that characterize the heterogeneity of the test subject (e.g., psychological types and the operational capturing and processing mode of the subject[46], as well as the entire bandwidth of complex internal and external factors). This procedure would allow cross-checking and comparison of results, as well as the observation of whether a common mechanism of an archetypal nature exists that can trigger the above-mentioned emotional phenomena in listeners.

In conclusion, these reflections would not only prompt the consideration of diverse methodologies, encompassing historical musicology (e.g., music analysis), systematic musicology (e.g., music psychology), Analytical Psychology (e.g., archetypal theory), and the conduct of empirical studies, but would, in fact, encourage the concept of interdisciplinary collaboration between these fields.

---

[45] The self-observation approach is based on the Jungian method of active imagination (IV 13), which enabled the author to arrive at some reflections, and which cannot be generalized due to the subjective character of this specific observation.

[46] Cf. Jacobi, Jolande. (2006). *Die Psychologie von C.G. Jung*. Chapters on „Die Bewußtseinsfunktionen“ P.20–27 and „Die Einstellungstypen“ P.27–32. Strikingly Jacobi dedicated one entire chapter to the "typology problem in the creative human being". Ibid. Chapter "Das Typenproblem beim schöpferischen Menschen". P. 32–36.

Bibliography

Primary Sources

On C.G. Jung

Jung, Carl Gustav. (1938/1984). *Dream Analysis: Notes of the Seminar given in 1928–1930 by C.G. Jung*. McGuire, William (Ed.). New Jersey: Princeton University Press.
Jung, Carl Gustav. (1961). *Ma vie. Souvenirs, rêves et pensées*. Collected and published by Aniéla Jaffé. (Translation: Roland Cahen). Saint-Amand: Éditions Gallimard.
Jung, Carl Gustav. (1970). *Aion. Researches into the Phenomenology of the Self.* Second Edition. (Translation: R.F.C. Hull). London/New York: Routledge Edition.
Jung, Carl Gustav. (2001). *Traum und Traumdeutung*. München: dtv.
Jung, Carl Gustav. (2011). *Four Archetypes. Mother. Rebirth. Spirit. Trickster.* 2010 Edition with a foreword by Sonu Shamdasani. (Translation: R.F.C. Hull). Bollingen series XX. New Jersey: Princeton University Press.
Jung, Carl Gustav. (2011). *Über das Phänomen des Geistes in Kunst und Wissenschaft.* Sonderausgabe, 2. Auflage. Ostfildern: Patmos Verlag.
Jung, Carl Gustav. (2013). *Kleines Lexikon der Analytischen Psychologie. Definitionen.* Ostfildern: Patmos Verlag. (E-book).
Jung, Carl Gustav. (2014). *Nietzsche's Zarathustra. Notes of the Seminar given in 1934–39 by C.G. Jung*. Jarrett, James L. (Ed.). New York: Routledge Edition.
Jung, Carl Gustav. (2014). *The Collected Works of C.G. Jung: Complete Digital Edition. Vol.1–19.* Adler, Gerhard., Fordham, Michael., Read, Herbet., McGuire, William. (Eds.). Trans. by R.F.C. Hull. Bollingen Series XX. Princeton, NJ: Princeton University Press. (E-book).
Jung, Carl Gustav. (2019). *Dream symbols of the Individuation process: Notes of C.G. Jung's Seminars on Wolfgang Pauli's Dreams*. Gieser,Suzanne. (Editor). Princeton NJ: Princeton University Press.
Jung, Carl Gustav. (2020). *Archetypen. Urbilder und Wirkkräfte des Kollektiven Unbewussten.* 4. Auflage. Ostfildern: Patmos Verlag.

L. Dill, *Schubert's Metamorphoses*,
https://doi.org/10.1007/978-3-662-73476-6

Jung, Carl Gustav. (2023). *Die Beziehung zwischen dem Ich und dem Unbewussten*. 6. Auflage. Ostfildern: Patmos Verlag.

Media

Jung, Carl Gustav. (1957). *Great Minds of the 20th Century: Dr. Carl Jung*. Evans, Richard. [Interview]. Zurich, Switzerland. [DVD]. Pennsylvania State University. (2005). https://youtu.be/bs3HK3pxVAY.

Jung, Carl Gustav. (1959). *Face to Face*. Carl Jung. Freeman, John (Presenter). Burnett, Hugh (Producer). [Interview]. BBC Four Collection, 1988. https://youtu.be/ALrHYiO1S7k.

Jung, Carl Gustav. (1960). *Das Einzelne, das Religiöse und das Transzendente*. Gerster, Georg. [Interview]. Schweizer Radio. Available as: *Carl Jung—The Individual, the Religious and the Transcendent. Carl Gustav Jung interviewed by Georg Gerster. 1960. Swiss Radio*. In: https://youtu.be/ezsd4GuWQwU

On Franz Schubert

Deutsch, Otto Erich. (1964). *Schubert—Die Dokumente seines Lebens. Gesammelt und erläutert von Otto Erich Deutsch*. Wiesbaden: Breitkopf & Härtel.

Deutsch, Otto Erich. (1983). *Schubert. Die Erinnerungen seiner Freunde*. Leipzig: Breitkopf & Härtel.

Schubert, Franz. (1814). "Gretchen am Spinnrade" D 118. Poem by Johann Wolfgang von Goethe. [Musical scores]. Petrucci Music Library (IMSLP).

Schubert, Franz. (1815). "Erlkönig" D 327. Ballad by Johann Wolfgang von Goethe. [Musical scores]. Petrucci Music Library (IMSLP).

Schubert, Franz. (1816). "Daphne am Bach". Poem by Fr. L. Grafen zu Stolberg. [Musical scores]. Petrucci Music Library (IMSLP).

Schubert, Franz. (1816–1821). "Die Forelle" D 550. Poem by Christian Friedrich Daniel Schubart. [Musical scores]. Petrucci Music Library (IMSLP).

Schubert, Franz. (1816). "Der Wanderer" D 489. Poem by Georg Philipp Schmidt von Lübeck. [Musical scores]. Petrucci Music Library (IMSLP).

Schubert, Franz. (1817). "Der Tod und das Mädchen" D 531. Poem by Matthias Claudius. [Musical scores]. Petrucci Music Library (IMSLP).

Schubert, Franz. (1817). "Der Jüngling und der Tod" D 545. Poem by Josef von Spaun. [Musical scores]. Petrucci Music Library (IMSLP).

Schubert, Franz. (1819). *Quintet for piano, violin, viola, violoncello and double bass in A major op.post.114 D 667 (Forellenquintett)*. Haug-Freienstein, Willtrud. (Ed.). [Musical scores]. München: Henle Digital Edition.

Schubert, Franz. (1822). *Symphony in B minor nr. 8 (Unfinished)*. [Musical scores]. Petrucci Music Library (IMSLP).

Schubert, Franz. (1823). *Die Schöne Müllerin D 795. Ein Cyclus von Liedern von Wilhelm Müller*. [Musical scores]. Petrucci Music Library (IMSLP).

Schubert, Franz. (1924). *String quartet in A minor D 804 (Rosamunde).* [Musical scores]. Petrucci Music Library.

Schubert, Franz. (1824). *String Quartet in D minor D 810 (Death and the Maiden).* [Musical scores]. Haug-Freienstein, Willtrud. (Ed.). München: Henle Digital Edition.

Schubert, Franz. (1825). "Ellen's Gesang III. Hymne an die Jungfrau" (*Ave Maria*) D 839, Op.52, No.6. From Walter Scott's „The Lady of the Lake" (Trans. By Ad. Storck). [Musical scores]. Petrucci Music Library (IMSLP).

Schubert, Franz. (1825). *Symphony in C major (The Great) D 944.* [Musical scores]. Petrucci Music Library (IMSLP).

Schubert, Franz. (1827). *Trio for piano, violin and violoncello in E-flat major D 929, op.100.* Urtext of the New Schubert Edition. 10. Auflage (2015). Feil, Arnold (Ed.). [Musical scores]. Kassel: Bärenreiter Verlag (Digital Edition).

Schubert, Franz. (1828). *Schwanengesang. D 957.* Poems by Rellstab, Heine, Seidl. [Musical scores]. Petrucci Music Library (IMSLP).

Schubert, Franz. (1828). *Drei große Sonaten für das Pianoforte. D 958, D 959 und D 960. Facsimile after the autographs in the Vienna City and State Library.* With a text and Commentary by Ernst Hilmar. [Musical scores]. Tutzing: Hans Schneider Verlag.

Schubert, Franz. (1828). *Piano Sonata in A major D 959.* Mies, Paul. (Ed.). [Musical scores]. München: Henle Digital Edition.

Schubert, Franz. (1828). *Piano Sonata in B-flat major D 960.* Mies, Paul. (Ed.). [Musical scores]. München: Henle Digital Edition.

Schubert, Franz. (1973). *Piano Sonatas. Volume I–II.* Mies, Paul. (Ed.). [Musical scores]. München: Henle Verlag.

Schubert, Franz. (1974). *Fantasy (Wanderer Fantasie) in C major op.15* D 760. Herttrich, Ernst. (Ed.). [Musical scores]. Henle Edition.

Media

Schubert, Franz. (1962). *Schubert: Die Schöne Müllerin D 795 op.25.* [Album recorded by Dietrich Fischer-Dieskau. Gerald Moore]. Warner Classics.

Schubert, Franz. (1974). *Schubert Lieder. Ave Maria. Der König in Thule. Klärchens Lied. Gretchen am Spinnrade. Der Tod und das Mädchen.* [Album recorded by Christa Ludwig. Irwin Gage]. Deutsche Grammophon.

Schubert, Franz. (1978). *Schubert Forellenquintett Op.114.* [Album recorded by Alfred Brendel. Cleveland Quartet]. Universal International Music. Philips Classics.

Schubert, Franz. (1983). *Schubert: Quintet in C. Alban Berg Quartett. Heinrich Schiff.* [Album recorded by Alban Berg Quartett. Heinrich Schiff.]. Warner Classics.

Schubert, Franz. (1986). *Schubert: String Quartets.* [Album recorded by Alban Berg Quartett]. Warner Classics.

Schubert, Franz. (1989). *Schubert: Piano Works 1822–1828. Sonatas. Moments Musicaux. Impromptus. „Wanderer"; Fantasia.* [Album recorded by Alfred Brendel]. Decca.

Schubert, Franz. (1990). *Schubert: Lieder. Der Wanderer. Der Lindenbaum. Die Forelle. Heidenröslein. Erlkönig. Der Musensohn.* [Album recorded by Dietrich Fischer-Dieskau. Gerald Moore]. Deutsche Grammophon.

Schubert, Franz. (1990). *Schubert: Schwanengesang, D. 957.* [Album recorded by Peter Schreier. András Schiff]. Decca.

Schubert, Franz. (1992). *Schubert: Trout Quintet/Beethoven: Piano Trio No. 5 "Ghost".* [Album recorded by Samuel Rhodes. Georg Hörtnagel. Beaux Arts Trio]. Universal International Music. Philips Insignia label Classical.

Schubert, Franz. (1999). *Schubert: Lieder.* [Album recorded by Barbara Hendricks. Radu Lupu. Bruno Schneider. Sabine Meyer]. Warner Classics.

Schubert, Franz. (2000). *Schubert: Fantasie in C Major, Op.15, D. 760 "Wanderer-Fantasie".* [Album recorded by András Schiff. Yuuko Shiokawa]. ECM Records.

Schubert, Franz. (2000). *Schubert: Symphony No.9 „The Great" & Rosamunde Overture.* [Album recorded by Vienna Philharmoniker. Riccardo Muti]. Warner Classics.

Schubert, Franz. (2007). *András Schiff—Concertos & Chamber Music. Beethoven, Bartók, Veress, Mozart, Schubert, Dvořák.* [Album recorded by András Schiff. Budapest Festival Orchestra. Heinz Holliger. Iván Fischer. Stattskapelle Dresden. Erich Höbarth. Bernard Haitink. Yuuko Shiokawa. Dénes Vårjon. Miklós Perényi. Panocha Quartet. Dénas Vár-jon. Elmar Schimd]. Warner Classics International.

Schubert, Franz. (2011). *Schubert: Piano Sonatas. Impromptus.* [Album recorded by András Schiff]. Decca.

Schubert, Franz. (2013). *Schubert: The Complete Piano Sonatas Played on Period Instruments.* [Album recorded by Paul Badura-Skoda]. Arcana.

Schubert, Franz. (2015). *Franz Schubert Symphonien 1–8.* [Album recorded by Berliner Philharmoniker. Nikolaus Harnoncourt.]. Berlin Phil Media.

Schubert, Franz. (2015). *Schubert Edition. Mass No. 5 in A-Flat Major, D. 678.* [Album recorded by Berliner Philharmoniker. Nikolaus Harnoncourt. Rundfunkchor Berlin. Birgit Remmert. Luba Orgonasova. Kurt Streit. Christian Gerhaher]. Berlin Phil Media.

Schubert, Franz. (2015). *Schubert Edition. Mass No. 6 in E-Flat Major, D. 950.* [Album recorded by Berliner Philharmoniker. Nikolaus Harnoncourt. Rundfunkchor Berlin. Dorothea Röschmann. Bernarda Fink. Jonas Kaufmann. Christian Elsner. Christian Gerhaher]. Berlin Phil Media.

Schubert, Franz. (2017). *Schubert: Forellenquintett. Trout Quintet.* [Album recorded by Anne-Sophie Mutter. Daniil Trifonov. Hwayoon Lee. Maximilian Hornung. Roman Patkoló]. Deutsche Grammophon.

Secondary Sources/Further Literature

Acker, Heinz. (2009). *Modulationslehre. Übungen. Analysen. Literaturbeispiele. Ein Handbuch für Studium und Lehre.* Kassel: Bärenreiter-Verlag.

Allen, Philip S. (1899). "Wilhelm Müller and the German Volkslied. I.". In: *The Journal of Germanic Philology. Volume 2, Nr.3.* P. 283–322. http://www.jstor.org/stable/27699075

Almén, Byron. (2008). "Jung's function-attitudes in music composition and discourse.". In: Rowland, Susan (Ed.). *Psyche and the Arts. Jungian Approaches to Music, Architecture, Literature, Painting and Film.* Sussex/New York: Routledge.

Amon, Reinhard. (2005). *Lexikon der Harmonielehre.* Wien-München: Doblinger Musikverlag.

Arendt, Dieter. (1972). *Der 'poetische Nihilismus' in der Romantik. Studien zum Verhältnis von Dichtung und Wirklichkeit in der Frühromantik. Band I-II.* Tübingen: Max Niemeyer Verlag.

Arendt, Hannah. (2016). *Vom Leben des Geistes. Das Denken. Das Wollen.* 9. Auflage. München/Berlin: Piper Verlag.

Arlettaz, Vincent. "L'expression dans la musique ancienne (I)". In: *Revue musicale de Suisse Romande.* Vol. 65/3. Septembre 2012.

Arlettaz, Vincent. "L'expression dans la musique ancienne (III)". In: *Revue musicale de Suisse Romande.* Vol. 66/1. Mars 2013

Arlettaz, Vincent. "L'expression dans la musique ancienne (VI)". In: *Revue musicale de Suisse Romande.* Vol. 67/1. Mars 2014.

Arthur, John., Schachter, Carl. (1989). "Mozart's 'Das Veilchen'". In: *The Musical Times, Voume 130, No.*1753. P. 149–164. https://www.jstor.org/stable/1193823

Auhagen, Wolfgang. (1983). *Studien zur Tonartencharakteristik in theoretischen Schriften und Kompositionen vom späten 17. Bis zum Beginn des 20. Jahrhunderts.* Frankfurt am Main/Wien: Peter Lang Verlag.

Balint, Michael. (1987). *Regression: Therapeutische Aspekte und die Theorie der Grundstörung.* Ungekürzte Ausgabe. München/Stuttgart: dtv/Klett-Cotta.

Bartel, Dietrich. (1997). *Musica poetica—Musical-rhetorical Figures in German Baroque Music.* Lincoln/London: University of Nebraska Press.

Bartel, Dietrich. (2010). *Handbuch der musikalischen Figurenlehre.* 6. Auflage. Laaber: Laaber-Verlag.

Beach, David. (2017). *Schubert's mature instrumental music. A theorist's perspective.* Rochester: University of Rochester Press.

Berger, Ludwig. (1841). *3 Gesänge aus einem gesellschaftlichen Liederspiel "Die Schöne Müllerin" mit Begleitung des Pianoforte: op.11.* [Musical scores]. Leipzig: Hofmeister.

Bellman, Jonathan. (1991). "Toward a Lexicon for the Style hongrois". In: *The Journal of Musicology.* Vol.9 no.2. https://doi.org/10.2307/763553

Bernstein, Leonard. (1976). *The unanswered Question. Six talks at Harvard.* Cambridge: Harvard University Press.

Bianconi La Face, Giuseppina. (2013). *Das Haus des Müllers. Zu Interpretation von Franz Schuberts Liedzyklus 'Die schöne Müllerin'.*Translation: Markus Köller Wien: Praesens Verlag.

Bodley, Lorraine Byrne. Horton, Julian. (2016). *Rethinking Schubert.* Oxford: Oxford University Press.

Bodley, Lorraine Byrne. Horton, Julian. (2016). *Schubert's Late Music. History, Theory Style.* Cambridge: Cambridge University Press.

Boetticher, Wolfgang. (1983). *Einführung in die musikalische Romantik.* Wilhelmshaven: Heinrichshofen's Verlag.

Böhm, Richard. (2006). *Symbolik und Rhetorik im Liedschaffen von Franz Schubert.* Wien: Böhlau Verlag.

Braun, Christiane. Berke, Dietrich. "Die Schöne Müllerin op.25 (D 795)—Liederzyklus Wilhelm Müller". In: Dürr, Walther. Kube, Michael. [et al.]. (2013). *Schubert Liedlexikon.* 2. Auflage. Ed.: Dürr, Walther., Kube, Michael. [et al.].(2013). Kassel: Bärenreiter Verlag. P.633–661.

Brendel, Alfred. (1989). "Schubert's Last three piano sonatas". In: *RSA Journal*, Vol. 137, No. 5395, P.401–411. http://www.jstor.org/stable/41374923

Brendel, Alfred. (1996). *Musik beim Wort genommen. Über Musik, Musiker und das Metier des Pianisten.* 2. Auflage. München: Piper Verlag.

Brendel, Alfred. (2001). *Ausgerechnet Ich. Gespräche mit Martin Meyer.* München: Carl Hanser Verlag.

Brendel, Alfred. (2022). "Naivety and Irony: Goethe's Musical Needs". In: *Publications of the English Goethe Society.* Vol. 91 (no.1), P.75–87. Routledge Taylor & Francis Group.

Brendel, Alfred. Gülke, Peter. (2020). *Die Kunst des Interpretierens. Gespräche über Schubert und Beethoven.* Kassel/Berlin: Bärenreiter/Metzler Verlag.

Brown, Maurice J.E. "Franz Schubert". In: Sadie, Stanley. (1980). *The New Grove Dictionary of Music and Musicians. Vol.16.* London: Macmillan Publishers. P.752–778.

Budde, Elmar. (2003). *Schuberts Liederzyklen. Ein musikalischer Werkführer.* München: C.H. Beck Verlag.

Butzer, Günter. Jacob, Joachim (Ed.). (2012). *Metzler Lexikon literarischer Symbole.* 2. Auflage. Stuttgart: Springer Verlag.

Campbell, Joseph. (2004). *The Hero with a thousand faces.* Bollingen Series XVII. New Jersey: Princeton University Press.

Carrol, Lewis. (2024). *Alice im Wunderland: mit den Illustrationen von John Tenniel.* (Translation Dorothee Lehlbach). Hamburg: Nikol Verlag

Casement, Ann. (2001). *Carl Gustav Jung. Key Figures in Counselling and Psychotherapy series.* London: Sage Publications.

Chevalier, Jean., Gheerbrant, Alain. [et. al.]. (1982). *Dictionnaire des Symboles. Mythes, rêves, coutumes, gestes, forms, figures, couleurs, nombres.* Paris: Robert Laffont et Éditions Jupiter.

Chusid, Martin. "Schubert's chamber music: before and after Beethoven". In: Gibbs, Christopher H. (1997). *The Cambridge Companion to Schubert.* New York: Cambridge University Press. (E-book). Chapter 9.

Collins, Alfred. (1994). "The Dialectics of Individuation Sean M. Kelly. Individuation and the Absolute: Hegel, Jung and the Path toward Wholeness". In: *The San Francisco Jung Institute Library Journal 13 no. 3.* P.31–42. New York: Paulist Press.

Cooper, Jean C. (1978). *An illustrated Encyclopedia of Traditional Symbols.* London: Thames & Hudson. (E-book).

Cottrell, Alan. (1970). *Wilhelm Müller's Lyrical Song-cycles. Interpretations and Texts.* Chapel Hill: University of North Carolina Press.

Danuser, Hermann., Plebuch Tobias. (Ed.). (1998). *Musik als Text. Bericht über den Internationalen Kongreß der Gesellschaft für Musikforschung Freiburg im Breisgau 1993. Band I-II.* Kassel: Bärenreiter Verlag Karl-Vötterle

Davies, Joe. "Stylistic disjuncture as a source of drama in Schubert's late instrumental works". In: Davies, Joe. Sobaskie, James William. (2019). *Drama in the music of Franz Schubert.* Woodbridge: The Boydell Press.

Deutsch, Otto Erich. (1915). *Das Urbild der "Schönen Müllerin": Dichtung und Wahrheit; Vortrag gehalten in der 33. Schubertiade des Schubertbundes am 30. Jänner 1915.* Aus Jahresbericht des Schubertbundes; 52. Wien: Verlag des Schubertbundes.

Diergarten, Felix. (2014). *Musikalische Analyse. Begriffe, Geschichten, Methoden.* Laaber: Laaber-Verlag.

Dill, Leonor. (2022). "Die Natur (in) der Musik Schuberts—Das Quartett 'Der Tod und das Mädchen' im Lichte des Archetypenkonzepts von C.G. Jung". In: *Eros und Thanatos.* Hofbauer, Gerhard (Editor). Salzburg: International polyaesthetic society IGPE. Print in progress.

Dill, Leonor. (2024, February 22nd). "Dances as Masked Confessions—The Cultural Unconscious Reflected in Schubert's idiom, Exemplified by the A-major Piano Sonata D 959, 2nd Movement". [Conference Abstract and Presentation]. In: *Second Workshop of the Schubert Research Center.* (2024, February 22–23). Clubraum, Austrian Academy of Sciences (ÖAW): Vienna, Austria.

Dill, Leonor. (2024, October 4th). "Archetypes in Music and Individuation—An Integrated Approach". [Conference Abstract and Presentation]. In: *The Process of Transformation.* (2024, October 4–6). Joint conference IAAP/Catholic University Freiburg in cooperation with DGAP and INFAP3. Catholic University of Applied Sciences Freiburg: Freiburg im Breisgau.

Dittrich, Marie-Agnes. "Die Lieder. 'Für Menschenohren sind es Harmonien'". In: Dürr, Walther. Krause, Andreas. (2020). *Schubert Handbuch.* 6. Auflage. Ungekürzte Sonderausgabe. Kassel: Bärenreiter Verlag Karl Vötterle.

Dobretsberger, Barbara. (2016). *Formenlehre. Formen der Instrumentalmusik. Ein Weg zum Musikverstehen.* Wien: Doblinger Musikverlag.

Dobretsberger, Barbara. (2019). *Formenlehre. Formen der Vokalmusik. Ein Weg zum Musikverstehen.* Wien: Doblinger Musikverlag.

Domokos, Mária. (1993). "Über die ungarischen Charakteristiken des Divertissement à l'hongroise D. 818". In: *Schubert durch die Brille: Internationales Franz Schubert Institut—Mitteilungen / 11.* P. 53–62. © RILM Schneider, Hans.

Drewermann, Eugen. (1991). *Tiefenpsychologie und Exegese. Band I. Traum, Mythos, Märchen, Sage und Legende.* Olten: Walter Verlag.

Drewermann, Eugen. (1993). *Lieb Schwesterlein, lass mich herein. Grimms Märchen tiefenpsychologisch gedeutet.* 5. Auflage. München: dtv Verlag. (E-book).

Drewermann, Eugen. (2013). *Liebe, Leid und Tod. Daseinsdeutung in antiken Mythen.* Ostfildern: Patmos Verlag. (E-book).

Dürr, Walther. (2002). "'Die Allmacht' (D 852). Schubert, Schelling und der Pantheismus.". In: *Laudato Si, mi Signore, per sora nostra matra terra: Zur Ästhetik und Spiritualität des Sonnengesangs in Musik, Kunst, Religion, Naturwissenschaften, Literatur, Film und Fotografie.* 2. Interdisziplinäres Symposion der Hochschule für Musik und Darstellende Kunst in Frankfurt am Main 6.-8. Juni 2001. Bern: Peter Lang Verlag. P. 103–116.

Dürr, Walther. "Der Erlkönig op.1 (D 328). Johann Wofgang von Goethe". (2013). In: *Schubert Liedlexikon.* 2. Auflage. Ed.: Dürr, Walther. Kube, Michael. [et al.]. Kassel: Bärenreiter Verlag. P.269–272.

Dürr, Walther. "Compositional strategies in Schubert's late music". In: Bodley, Lorraine Byrne. Horton, Julian. (2016). *Rethinking Schubert.* Oxford: Oxford University Press. P.29–40.

Dürr, Walther. "Schubert in seiner Welt". In: Dürr, Walther. Krause, Andreas. (2020). *Schubert Handbuch.* 6. Auflage. Ungekürzte Sonderausgabe. Kassel: Bärenreiter Verlag Karl Vötterle. P.2–76.

Dürr, Walther. Kube, Michael. [et al.]. (2013). *Schubert Liedlexikon.* 2. Auflage. Kassel: Bärenreiter Verlag.

Dürr, Walther. Krause, Andreas. (2020). *Schubert Handbuch*. 6. Auflage. Ungekürzte Sonderausgabe. Kassel: Bärenreiter Verlag Karl Vötterle.

Edinger, Edward. (1972). *Ego and Archetype. Individuation and the religious function of the Psyche*. New York: G.P. Putnam's Sons.

Egermann, Hauke. Kreutz, Gunter. (2018). "Wirkung—Emotionen und ästhetische Gefühle". In: Lehmann, Andreas C. Kopiez, Reinhard. *Handbuch Musikpsychologie*. Bern: Hogrefe Verlag.

Eggebrecht, Hans Heinrich. (1970). "Prinzipien des Schubert-Liedes". In: *Archiv für Musikwissenschaft, Vol.* 27, No.2. P.89–109.

Einstein, Alfred. (1952). *Schubert: Ein musikalisches Porträt*. Zürich: Pan-Verlag.

Erickson, Raymond. (1997). *Schubert's Vienna*. New Haven: Yale University Press.

Evangelisch-Reformierte Landeskirche des Kantons Zürich Kirchenrat. (2008). *Zürcher Bibel*. 2. Auflage. Zürich: Verlag der Zürcher Bibel beim Theologischen Verlag.

Feil, Arnold. (1996). *Franz Schubert. Die Schöne Müllerin. Winterreise*. 2. Auflage. Stuttgart: Philipp Reclam jun.

Ferris, David. "Dissociation and Declamation in Schubert's Heine Songs". In: Bodley, Lorraine Byrne. Horton, Julia. (2016). *Rethinking Schubert*. New York: Oxford University Press. P.383–403.

Floros, Constantin. (1989). *Musik als Botschaft*. Wiesbaden: Breitkopf & Härtel,

Floros, Constantin. (2008). *Hören und verstehen. Die Sprache der Musik und ihre Deutung*. Mainz: Schott Verlag.

Floros, Constantin. (2016). *Gustav Mahler I: Die geistige Welt Gustav Mahlers in systematischer Darstellung*. 4. Auflage. Wiesbaden: Breitkopf & Härtel.

Flotzinger, Rudolf. (2004). *Oesterreichisches Musiklexikon*. Wien: Österreichischen Akademie der Wissenschaften.

Friedrich, Siegfried. (2015). *Zu Funktion und Wirkung gradueller Tonhöhenänderungen in Johann Sebastian Bachs 'Das Wohltemperierte Klavier' I und II sowie in Franz Schuberts 'Die schöne Müllerin'*. Wien: Böhlau Verlag.

Furtwängler, Adolf. (1889). "Atlas". In: *Ausführliches Lexikon der Griechischen und Römischen Mythologie*. Band I. Roscher, W.H. (Ed.). Leipzig: Teubner Verlag.

Gabriel, Markus. (2013). *Warum es die Welt nicht gibt*. Berlin: Ullstein Buchverlage.

Gabriel, Markus. (2016). *Sinn und Existenz: Eine realistische Ontologie*. Berlin: Suhrkamp.

Gardner, Cameron. "(Re-)Theorising Schubert's 'Reliquie': Precedents, the 'Great' Symphony, and Narrative". In: Bodley, Lorraine Byrne. Horton, Julia. (2016). *Rethinking Schubert*. New York: Oxford University Press. P.147–172.

Gebser, Jean. (1986). *Ursprung und Gegenwart—Zweiter Teil*. 2. Auflage. München: dtv.

Georgiades, Thrasybulos. (1967). *Schubert Musik und Lyrik*. Göttingen: Vandenhoeck & Ruprecht.

Gibbs, Christopher H. (1997). *The Cambridge Companion to Schubert*. New York: Cambridge University Press. (E-book).

Gibbs, Christopher H. Solvik, Morten. (2014). *Franz Schubert and his World*. Oxfordshire: Princeton University Press. (E-book).

Gieser, Suzanne. (2005). *The Innermost Kernel. Depth Psychology and Quantum Physics. Wolfgang Pauli's dialogue with C.G. Jung*. Berlin Heidelberg: Springer Verlag.

Godel, Arthur. (1985). *Schuberts letzte drei Klaviersonaten (D958–960): Entstehungsgeschichte, Entwurf und Reinschrift. Werkanalyse*. Baden-Baden: Koerner Verlag.

Goethe, Wolfgang. (1988). *Gedichte und Epen I. Band 1.* Hamburger Ausgabe. München: dtv.

Gramit, David. "'The passion for friendship': music, cultivation, and identity in Schubert's circle". In: Gibbs, Christopher H. (1997). *The Cambridge Companion to Schubert.* Cambridge: Cambridge University Press. (E-book). Chapter 3.

Grant, Michael. Hazel, John. (2008). *Lexikon der antiken Mythen und Gestalten.* 19. Auflage. München: dtv.

Grant, Michael. Hazel, John. (2009). *Lexikon der antiken Mythen und Gestalten.* 1. Auflage. Berlin: List Taschenbuch (Ullstein Verlag).

Greifenstein, Johannes. (2021) "'Affectus exprimere' und 'Ausdruck der Empfindung'. Musik, Gefühl und Sprache im 17. und 18. Jahrhundert.". In: Stolzenberg, Jürgen. (2021). *Ausdruck in der Musik. Theorien und Formationen.* München: Richard Boorberg Verlag. P.145–167.

Grimalt, Joan. (2021). *Mapping musical signification.* 1st ed. 2020. Vol. 15. Cham: Springer International Publishing https://doi.org/10.1007/978-3-030-52496-8

Grimm, Jacob., Grimm, Wilhelm. (2015). *Grimms Märchen. Vollständige Ausgabe. Illustriert von Otto Ubbelohde.* München: Anaconda Verlag.

Gruber, Gernot. (2010). *Schubert. Schubert? Leben und Musik.* Kassel: Bärenreiter Verlag.

Gülke, Peter. (2020). *Franz Schubert in seiner Zeit.* 6. Auflage. Laaber: Laaber Verlag.

Gunter, Pete A. Y. (1982). "Bergson and Jung". *Journal of the History of Ideas*, Vol. 43, Nr. 4. P. 635–652. https://doi.org/10.2307/2709347

Hagen, Marie-Rose and Rainer. (2012). *Francisco Goya. Am Aufbruch der Moderne.* Köln: Taschen Verlag.

Hascher, Xavier. "Narrative dislocations in the first movement of Schubert's 'Unfinished' Symphony". In: Bodley, Lorraine Byrne. Horton, Julian. (2016). *Rethinking Schubert.* Oxford: Oxford University Press. P.127–146.

Hatten, Robert. "Schubert's alchemy: transformative surfaces, transfiguring depths". In: Bodley, Lorraine Byrne. Horton, Julian. (2016). *Schubert's Late Music.* History, Theory Style. Cambridge: Cambridge University Press. P.91–110.

Hatten, Robert. (2004). *Interpreting Musical Gestures, Topics, and Tropes. Mozart, Beethoven, Schubert.* Bloomington: Indiana University Press.

Hausegger, Friedrich von. (2018). *Music as Expression.* (Trans. by Robert J. Crow). Vienna/London/New York: Universal Edition.

Heuchemer, Dane. (2008). "Gallus Dressler Praecepta musicae pöeticae (Percepts of Poetic Music)". Ed. and trans. by Robert Forgács. Studies in the History of Music Theory and Literature 3 Urbana: University of Illinois Press, 2007. *Renaissance Quarterly.* (2008). Vol.61, No.1, P.266–267. Web. https://doi.org/10.1353/ren.2008.0119

Hilmar, Ernst. (1997). *Franz Schubert. Rororo Bildmonographien.* Hamburg: Rowohlt Taschenbuch.

Hinrichsen, Hans-Joachim. (1994). *Untersuchungen zur Entwicklung der Sonatenform in der Instrumentalmusik Franz Schuberts.* Tutzing: Hans Schneider.

Hinrichsen, Hans-Joachim. "Is there a late style in Schubert's Œuvre?". In: Bodley, Lorraine Byrne., Horton, Julian. (2016). *Rethinking Schubert.* Oxford: Oxford University Press. P.17–28.

Hinrichsen, Hans-Joachim. (2019). *Franz Schubert.* 3. Auflage. München: C.H.Beck Verlag. (E-book).

Hinrichsen, Hans-Joachim. "Die Kammermusik: 'Bergendes Gehäuse' und 'Hang ins Unbewgrenzte'.". In: Dürr, Walther. Krause, Andreas. (2020). *Schubert Handbuch*. 6. Auflage. Ungekürzte Sonderausgabe. Kassel: Bärenreiter Verlag Karl Vötterle. P.452–511.

Hölderlin. Friedrich. (2019). *Hyperion or the Hermit in Greece*. Trans. by Horward Gaskill. Cambridge: Open Book Publishers. https://www.openbookpublishers.com/books/10.11647/obp.0160

Howatt, Roy. "Architecture as drama in late Schubert". In: Newbould, Brian. (2017). *Schubert Studies*. New York: Routledge. P.166–190.

Hrncirik, Peter. "Tendenzen der Kirchenmusik im Biedermeier. Historische und stilidiomatische Aspekte.". In: Harrandt, Andrea. Partsch, Erich Wolfgang. (2010). *Kirchenmusik im Biedermeier—Institutionen, Formen, Komponisten*. Tutzing: Hans Schneider Verlag. P.9–60.

Huovinen, Erkki. Kaila, Anna-Kaisa. (2015). "The Semantics of Musical Topoi: An Empirical Approach". In: *Music Perception: An Interdisciplinary Journal*, Vol. 33, No. 2, P.217–243 https://doi.org/10.1525/mp.2015.33.2.217

Jacobi, Jolande. (2006). *Die Psychologie von C.G. Jung. Eine Einführung in das Gesamtwerk. Mit einem Geleitwort von C.G. Jung*. 21. Auflage. Frankfurt am Main: Fischer Verlag.

Jahrmärker, Manuela. "Von der liturgischen Funktion zum persönlichen Bekenntnis—Die Kirchenmusik". In: Dürr, Walther. Krause, Andreas. (2020). *Schubert Handbuch*. 6. Auflage. Ungekürzte Sonderausgabe. Kassel: Bärenreiter Verlag Karl Vötterle. P.346–378.

Jung-Rauschenbach, Emma. (1988). *Animus und Anima*. 3. Auflage. Stuttgart: Bonz.

Jung-Rauschenbach, Emma. von Franz, Marie Louise. (1980). *Die Graalslegende in psychologischer Sicht*. Neuauflage. Solothurn: Walter.

Karbusicky, Vladimir. (1986). *Grundriß der musikalischen Semantik*. Darmstadt: Wissenschaftliche Buchgesellschaft.

Kast, Verena. (1974). *Kreativität in der Psychologie von C.G. Jung*. Philosophische Fakultät der Universität Zürich. [Dissertation]. Zurich: Juris Druck und Verlag Zürich.

Kast, Verena. (2014). *Die Tiefenpsychologie nach C.G. Jung. Eine praktische Orientierungshilfe*. Ostfildern: Patmos Verlag der Schwabenverlag. (E-book).

Kinderman, William. "Schubert's piano music: probing the human condition". In: Gibbs, Christopher H. (1997). *The Cambridge Companion to Schubert*. New York: Cambridge University Press. (E-book). Chapter 8.

Klassen, Janina. (2001). "Musica poetica und musikalische Figurenlehre—ein produktives Missverständnis.". In: Wagner, Günther. (2001). *Jahrbuch des Staatlichen Instituts für Musikforschung Preußischer Kulturbesitz*. P.73–83. Stuttgart: J.B. Metzler, https://doi.org/10.1007/978-3-476-02821-1_4

Klaus-Uwe, Adam. (2000). *Therapeutisches Arbeiten mit Träumen. Theorie und Praxis der Traumarbeit*. Berlin: Springer-Verlag.

Kohs, Ellis. (1976). *Musical Form. Studies in Analysis and Synthesis*. Boston: Houghton Mifflin Company.

Korstvedt, Benjamin M. "'The prerogative of the late style': thoughts on the expressive world of Schubert's late works". In: Bodley, Lorraine Byrne. Horton, Julian. (2016). *Schubert's Late Music*.

Krause, Andreas. "Die Klaviermusik—'So frei und eigen, so keck und mitunter auch so sonderbar'". In: Dürr, Walther. Krause, Andreas. (2020). *Schubert Handbuch.* 6. Auflage. Ungekürzte Sonderausgabe. Kassel: Bärenreiter Verlag Karl Vötterle. P. 380–434.

Krebs, Wolfgang. (2006). "Zwischen Schopenhauer und Freud. Ernst Kurths Musiktheorie als hermeneutisches Potenzial.". In: *Zeitschrift der Gesellschaft für Musiktheorie,* Vol. 3, No. 2, P.223–243 https://doi.org/10.31751/226

Kremer, Detlev. (2007). *Romantik. Lehrbuch Germanistik.* 3. Auflage. Stuttgart: Springer Verlag.

Kühn, Clemens. (2005). *Analyse lernen.* 5. Auflage. Kassel: Bärenreiter-Verlag.

Kurth, Ernst. (1920). *Romantische Harmonik und ihre Krise in Wagners „Tristan".* Berlin: Max Hesses Verlag.

Kurth, Ernst. (2022). *Music Psychology.* Tan, Daphne. (Ed.). Trans. by Daphne Tan and Christoph Neidhöfer. New York: Routledge.

Legler, Margit. (2023, Ocotber 13th). "Genre Conventions in the Early German Lied and the Declamatory Tradition". [Conference presentation]. *Combining the Arts. Multimedia Performances in the early 19th century Habsburg Empire.* Schubert Research Center. Vienna: University of music and performing arts (mdw).

Lévi-Strauss, Claude. (1990). *Mythologica 1 : Das Rohe und das Gekochte.* 4. Auflage. Frankfurt am Main: Suhrkamp.

Lindmayr-Brandl, Andrea. "Music and Culture in Schubert's Vienna". In: Hirsch, Marjorie W., Feurzeig, Lisa. (2021). *The Cambridge Companion to Schubert's Winterreise.* Cambridge: Cambridge University Press.

Linke, Cosima. (2023). "Arabella Pare, Franz Schubert. The fragmentary Piano Sonatas (= Schubert: Perspektiven—Studien, Bd.7). Stuttgart: Steiner 2022". In: *Zeitschrift der Gesellschaft für Musiktheorie.* Volume 20/1. P.111–115.

Litschauer, Walburga. "Tänze und Märsche für Klavier—'Halt's enk zsamm'". In: Dürr, Walther. Krau Andreas. (2020). *Schubert Handbuch.* 6. Auflage. Ungekürzte Sonderausgabe. Kassel: Bärenreiter Verlag Karl Vötterle. P.436–450.

Löwe, Angelica. "Diaphanie, Verhüllung, Vision in Jungs Arbeitszimmer—eine Raumerkundung". In: Deutsche Gesellschaft für Analytische Psychologie. (2023). Bovensiepen, G., Kast, Verena., Wilke, H.-J. (Hrsgg.). *Analytische Psychologie. Zeitschrift für Psychotherapie und Psychoanalyse. Heft 200. 2/2023. 54 Jg.* P.310–317. https://doi.org/10.30417/ap-54-199

Lück, Helmut E. (2009). *Geschichte der Psychologie. Strömungen, Schulen, Entwicklungen. Grundriss der Psychologie Band I.* 4. Überarbeitete und erweiterte Auflage. Stuttgart: Kohlhammer Verlag.

MacDonald, Hugh. (1978). "Schubert's volcanic temper". In: *Musical Times.* Vol. 119, No.1629. P.949–952. https://www.jstor.org/stable/960118

Mak, Su Yin. "Formal ambiguity and generic reinterpretation in the late instrumental music". In: Bodley, Lorraine Byrne. Horton, Julian. (2016). *Schubert's Late Music. History, Theory Style.* Cambridge: Cambridge University Press. P.282–306.

Massin, Brigitte. (1977). *Franz Schubert.* Paris: Fayard. P. 975.

Mattheson, Johann. (2020). *Der vollkommene Capellmeister. Neusatz des Textes und der Noten.* 5. Auflage. Kassel: Bärenreiter-Verlag Karl Vötterle.

McKay, Elizabeth Norman. (2001). *Franz Schubert: A Biography.* Reprinted Edition. Oxford: Oxford University Press.

McKay, Elizabeth Norman. "Schubert's string and piano duos in context". In: Newbould, Brian. (2017). *Schubert Studies.* New York: Routledge. P.62–111.

Menke, Johannes. (2014). "Mehr als 'Figurenlehre'. Giacomo Carissimi: Jonas und Jephte". In: Diergarten, Felix. (2014). *Musikalische Analyse. Begriffe, Geschichten, Methoden.* Laaber: Laaber Verlag.

Michels, Ulrich. (2008). *Dtv-Atlas Musik.* München: dtv. Kassel: Bärenreiter Verlag.

Mills, Jon. (2018). "The Essence of Archetypes". In: *International Journal of Jungian Studies.* Vol. 10, Nr. 3, P.1–22. https://doi.org/10/1080/19409052.2018.1503808

Mollwo-Oesterreicher, Marianne. (1978). *Herder Lexikon Symbole.* Freiburg im Breisgau: Herder Verlag.

Montgomery, David. "Franz Schubert's music in performance: a brief history of people, events, and issues.". In: Gibbs, Christopher H. (1997). *The Cambridge Companion to Schubert.* New York: Cambridge University Press. (E-book). Chapter 16.

Moßburger, Hubert. (2012). "'Res' oder 'Verba'? Zum historischen Ursprung der Kontroversen über das Wort-Ton-Verhältnis und ihren analytisch-hermeneutischen Konsequenzen.". In: *Zeitschrift der Gesellschaft für Musiktheorie*, Vol. 9, No.2, P.159–185 https://doi.org/10.31751/689

Müller, Ingo. (2020). *Maskenspiel und Seelensprache. Zur Ästhetik von Heinrich Heines Buch der Lieder und Robert Schumanns Heine-Vertonungen.* Band 1. *Heinrich Heines Dichtungsästhetik und Robert Schumanns Liedästhetik.* Band 2: *Heinrich Heines Buch der Lieder und Robert Schumanns Vertonungen.* Baden-Baden: Rombach Wissenschaft.

Müller, Jan. (2002). *Der Komponist als Prediger: Die deutsche evangelisch-lutherische Motette als Zeugnis von Verkündigung und Auslegung vom Reformationszeitalter bis in die Gegenwart.* [Dissertation]. Universität Oldenburg.

Müller, Wilhelm. (1991). *Die Winterreise und Die Schöne Müllerin. Mit Zeichnungen von Ludwig Richter.* Zürich: Diogenes Verlag.

Munch, Edvard., Langaard, J.H., Revol, R. (1963). *Edvard Munch: malerier og grafik.* Norwegen: Forlaget Norsk Kunstreproduksjon.

Nestler, Gerhard. (1997). *Geschichte der Musik. Die großen Zeiträume der Musik von den Anfängen bis zur elektronischen Komposition.* 5. Auflage. Mainz: Schott Music international.

Neumann, Erich. (1959). *Der schöpferische Mensch.* Zürich: Rhein-Verlag.

Neumann, Erich. (2002). *The origins and history of consciousness.* London: Routledge. E-book.

Neumann, Erich. (2004). *Kunst und schöpferisches Unbewusstes.* 4. Auflage. Einsiedeln: Daimon Verlag.

Neumann, Erich. (2015). *The Great Mother. An analysis of the Archetype.* (Trans. by Ralph Manheim). With a foreword by Martin Liebscher. Bollingen Series XLVII. Princeton: Princeton University Press.

Neumann, Erich. (2021). *Die Große Mutter. Bilder und Symbole des Weiblichen.* 2. Auflage. Ostfildern: Patmos Verlag.

Newbould, Brian. (2017). *Schubert Studies.* New York: Routledge.

Nietzsche, Friedrich. (2010). *Also sprach Zarathustra.* 9. Auflage. München: dtv C.H.Beck.

Nietzsche, Friedrich. (2020). *The birth of tragedy.* Trans. by WM.A. Haussmann. (E-book). Gialunca Publisher. (E-book).

Nünning, Ansgar (Editor). (2013). *Metzler Lexikon. Literatur- und Kulturtheorie. Ansätze—Personen—Grundbegriffe*. Stuttgart: J.B. Metzler Verlag.

Pare, Arabella. (2022). *Franz Schubert: the fragmentary Piano Sonatas*. Stuttgart: Franz Steiner Verlag.

Pethő, Csilla. (2000). "'Style Hongrois'. Hungarian Elements in the Works of Haydn, Beethoven, Weber and Schubert". In: *Studia Musicologica Academiae Scientiarum Hungaricae*, Vol. 41, No. 1/3. P. 199–284. http://www.jstor.org/stable/902575

Platinga, Leo. "Schubert, Social Music and Melancholy". In: Bodley, Lorraine Byrne. Horton, Julia. (2016). *Rethinking Schubert*. New York: Oxford University Press. P.237–250.

Polzonetti, Pierpaolo. "La Casa Del Mugnaio: Ascolto e Interpretazione Della Schone Mullerin: Com l'edizione Del Ciclo Liederistico Secondo la Neue Ausgabe Schubert-Ausgabe.". [Review]. In: *Music Library Association, Notes, vol.62, no.1*. (2005), pp. 130–33. https://doi.org/10.1353/not.2005.0114

Raab, Michael. "Der Wanderer op.4, 1 (D 489)". In: Dürr, Walther. Kube, Michael. [et al.]. (2013). *Schubert Liedlexikon*. 2. Auflage. Kassel: Bärenreiter Verlag. P.385–387.

Radcliffe, Philip. (1967). "Schubert Piano Sonatas". In: *BBC Music Guides*. London: British Broadcasting Corporation.

Rasche, Jörg. (2014). *Das Lied des Grünen Löwen. Musik als Spiegel der Seele*. Giessen: Psychosozial-Verlag.

Redmann, Bernd. (2002). *Entwurf einer Theorie und Methodologie der Musikanalyse*. Gruber, Gernot., Mauser, Siegfried (Eds). Laaber: Laaber Verlag.

Riedel, Ingrid. (1990). *Farben. In Religion, Gesellschaft, Kunst und Psychotherapie*. 8. Auflage. Hamburg: Kreuz-Verlag.

Riezler, Walther. (1967). *Schubert's Instrumentalmusik*. Zürich: Atlantis Verlag.

Ritter, Hans Martin. (2014). "Winterreise. Wilhelm Müller entdeckt das lyrische Monodram". In: *Musik und Text. Band 3*. Berlin: LIT Verlag.

Roesler, Christian. (2016). *Das Archetypenkonzept C.G. Jungs. Theorie, Forschung und Anwendung*. Stuttgart: Kohlhammer Verlag. (E-book).

Roesler, Christian. (2022). *Development of a Reconceptualization of Archetype Theory*. Report to the IAAP. Freiburg: Katholische Hochschule Freiburg (IAF).

Roesler, Christian. (2022). *The Archetype Concept of C.G. Jung. Theory, Research, and Applications*. (Trans. by Alexander Ulyet and Christian Roesler). Oxford: Routledge. (E-book).

Roesler, Christian. (2024, October 4th). "Introduction to the conference theme 'The process of transformation'". In: *The Process of Transformation*. [Conference Lecture and Abstract]. (2024, October 4–6). Joint conference IAAP/Catholic University Freiburg in cooperation with DGAP and INFAP3. Catholic University of Applied Sciences Freiburg: Freiburg im Breisgau.

Roesler, Christian. (2024). "Emotion Regulation, Relationship and Therapeutic Change in Analytical Psychology and Contemporary Psychodynamic Approaches". *Journal of Analytical Psychology*, 2024, 69, 4, 1–18. https://doi.org/10.1111/1468-5922.13031

Roesler, Christian. (2024). *Deconstructing Archetype Theory. A Critical Analysis of Jungian Ideas*. Oxford: Routledge.

Rosen, Charles. (1997). *The Classical style: Haydn, Mozart, Beethoven*. New York: W.W. Norton & Company. (E-book).

Rosen, Charles. (1998). *The romantic generation*. Cambridge: Harvard University Press

Rosen, Charles., Zerner, Henri. (1984). *Romanticism and Realism. The Mythology of the Nineteenth-Century Art.* New York: The Viking Press.
Sacre, Guy. (1998). *La musique de piano. Dictionnaire des compositeurs et des œuvres.* Paris: Éditions Robert Laffont.
Schanze, Helmut. (2018). *Erfindung der Romantik.* Stuttgart: J.B. Metzler Verlag.
Schering, Arnold. (2012). *Franz Schuberts Symphonie in H-Moll („Unvollendete") und ihr Geheimnis.* Bremen: Outlook Verlagsgesellschaft.
Schick, Hartmut. (2007). "Christian Friedrich Daniel Schubart: Der Dichter-Musiker, Nördlingen und Wallerstein". In: *Rosetti-Forum. Mitteilungen der Internationalen Rosetti-Gesellschaft.* Nr. 8. P15–26.
Schiff, Andras. "Schubert's piano sonatas: thoughts about interpretation and performance". In: Newbould, Brian. (2017). *Schubert Studies.* New York: Routledge. P.191–208.
Schilling, Gustav. (1974). *Encyclopädie der gesammten musikalischen Wissenschaften oder Universal—Lexikon der Tonkunst.* Hildesheim: Georg Olms Verlag. Nachdruck der Ausgabe Stuttgart 1835.
Schlesinger, Max. (1967). *Geschichte des Symbols. Symbolik in der Tonkunst.* Hildesheim: Georg Olms Verlagsbuchhandlung.
Schlüter, Christiane. (2014). *Die wichtigsten Psychologen im Porträt.* 4. Auflage. Wiesbaden: Marix Verlag.
Schmidt-Beste, Thomas. (2006). *Die Sonata. Geschichte—Formen—Ästhetik.* Kassel: Bärenreiter Verlag Karl Vötterle.
Schmidt, Hans Ulrich, Stegemann, Thomas, Spitzer, Carsten. (2019). *Musiktherapie bei psychischen und psychosomatischen Störungen.* München: Elsevier/Urban & Fischer.
Schmierer, Elisabeth. (2017). *Geschichte des Kunstliedes. Eine Einführung.* Laaber: Laaber Verlag.
Schönberg, Arnold. (1986). *Harmonielehre.* Wien: Universal Edition.
Schopenhauer, Arthur. (2024). *Die Welt als Wille und Vorstellung. Band I-II.* München: Boer Verlag.
Schumann, Robert. (1854). *Gesammelte Schriften über Musik und Musiker.* Leipzig: Breitkopf & Härtel. Reprinted Edition. (1985). Volume 1- 4.
Schumann, Robert. (2010). *Schriften über Musik und Musiker.* Häusler, Josef (Ed). Stuttgart: Philipp Reclam.
Senancour, Etienne Pivert. *Obermann* (1804). In: Liszt, Franz. (1976). *Les années de pèlerinages*: "Vallée d'Obermann". Budapest: Editio Musica Budapest.
Shamdasani, Sonu. (2012). *C.G. Jung. A Biography in Books.* New York: W.W. Norton & Company.
Sloterdijk, Peter. (2015). *Der ästhetische Imperativ. Schriften zur Kunst.* Berlin: Suhrkamp. [E-book].
Sorgner, Stefan Lorenz. Schramm, Michael. (2010). *Musik in der antiken Philosophie. Eine Einführung.* Würzburg: Königshausen & Neumann Verlag.
Sourtzi, Maria. (2014). *Franz Schuberts Grosse C-Dur Symphonie D 944: Analyse und Unterrichtsentwurf.* Hamburg: Diplomica Verlag.
Sproccati, Sandro. (2014). *Guia de História da Arte.* Trans. by de Figueiredo, Maria Jorge Vilar. 7° Edição. Barcarena: Presença.

Steblin, Rita. "Schubert: The nonsense society revisited". In: Gibbs, Christopher H. Solvik, Morten. (2014). *Franz Schubert and his World.* Oxfordshire: Princeton University Press. (E-book). Chapter 1.

Steblin, Rita. "Schubert's relationship with women: a historical account". In: Newbould, Brian. (2017). *Schubert Studies.* New York: Routledge. P.220–243.

Steiner, Stefanie. Kube, Michael. "Schwanengesang—13 Lieder nach Gedichten von Rellstab und Heine (D 957)". In: Dürr, Walther. Kube, Michael. [et al.]. (2013). *Schubert Liedlexikon.* Kassel: Bärenreiter Verlag. P.810–827.

Tilly, Margaret. "The Therapy of Music". (1956). In: *C.G. Jung Speaking.* McGuire, William. Hull, R.F.C. (Ed). (1977), New Jersey: Princeton University Press.

Tunbridge, Laura. "Singing against late style: the problem of performance history". In: Bodley, Lorraine Byrne. Horton, Julian. (2016). *Schubert's Late Music. History, Theory Style.* Cambridge: Cambridge University Press. P.426–442.

Vogel, Ralf T. (2017). *Individuation und Wandlung. Der 'Werdensprozess der Seele' in der Analytischen Psychologie C. G. Jungs.* Stuttgart: Kohlhammer Verlag.

Vogel, Ralf T. (2024). *Das Geheimnis der Seele. Grundlagen einer zeitgemäßen Psychotherapiewissenschaft.* Stuttgart: Kohlhammer. (E-book).

von Fischer, Kurt. "Caccia". In: Sadie, Stanley. (1980). *The New Grove Dictionary of Music and Musicians. Vol. 3.* London: Macmillan Publishers. P.574–576.

von Franz, Marie-Louise. (1984). *Traum und Tod. Was uns die Träume Sterbender sagen.* München: Kösel-Verlag.

von Franz, Marie-Louise. (1995). *L'interprétation des contes de fées suivi de L'ombre et le mal dans les contes de fées.* (Trans. Francine Saint René Taillandier avec la collaboration de Jacqueline Blumer). Paris: Albin Michel.

von Franz, Marie-Louise. (2014). *Dreams.* Boston: Shambhala Publications.

von Humboldt, Wilhelm. (2016). *Über die Verschiedenheiten des menschlichen Sprachbaues.* Berlin: Sammlung Hofenberg Digital.

Waidelich, Till Gerrit. "Der Jüngling und der Tod (D 545). Joseph von Spaun". (2013). In: *Schubert Liedlexikon.* 2. Auflage. Ed.: Dürr, Walther., Kube, Michael. [et al.]. Kassel: Bärenreiter Verlag. P.444–445.

Walach, Harald. (2013). *Psychologie. Wissenschaftstheorie, philosophische Grundlagen und Geschichte. Ein Lehrbuch.* 3. Überarbeitete und erweiterte Auflage. Stuttgart: Kohlhammer Verlag.

Wehr, Gerhard. (1969). *C.G. Jung. Rororo Bildmonographien.* Hamburg: Rowohlt Taschenbuch.

Wehr, Gerhard. (2014). *C.G. Jung Leben—Werk—Wirkung.* Neuauflage, Version 4,02. Stuttgart: Opus Magnum.

Weischedel, Wilhelm. (1988). *Die philosophische Hintertreppe. 34 große Philosophen in Alltag und Denken.* München: dtv.

Werner-Jensen, Arnold., Ratte, Franz-Joseph., Ernst, Manfred. (2001). *Das Reclambuch der Musik.* 2. Auflage. Stuttgart: Philipp Reclam jun.

Wilhelm, Richard., Jung, Carl Gustav. (1929). *Das Geheimnis der Goldenen Blüte. Ein chinesisches Lebensbuch.* München: Dornverlag Grete Ullmann.

Wollenberg, Susan. (2011). *Schubert's Fingerprints: Studies in the instrumental works.* Burlington: Ashgate Publishing Company.

Youens, Susan. (1991). “Behind the scenes: ‘Die schöne Müllerin’ before Schubert”. In: *19th Century Music, Vol. 15, Nr. 1,* P. 3–22. JSTOR, https://doi.org/10.2307/746295

Youens, Susan. (1991). *Retracing a Winter's Journey. Schubert's Winterreise.* New York: Cornell University Press.

Youens, Susan. (1997). *Schubert, Müller, and ‘Die Schöne Müllerin’.* Cambridge: Cambridge University Press.

Zilkens, Udo. (2000). *Franz Schubert. Vom Klavierlied zum Klavierquintett. Die Forelle im Spiegel ihrer Interpretationen durch Musiktheoretiker und Musiker.* 2. Auflage. Köln-Rodenkirchen: P.J. Tonger Musikverlag.

Zoltai, Dénes. (1970). *Ethos und Affekt. Geschichte der Philosophischen Musikästhetik von den Anfängen bis zu Hegel.* Translated by: Béla Weingarten. Budapest: Akadémiai Kiadó.

Zwinggi, Stefan. (2021). “Ausdruck in der Musik als Thema der analytischen Musikphilosophie”. In: Stolzenberg, Jürgen. *Ausdruck in der Musik. Theorien und Formationen.* München: Richard Boorberg Verlag.

Documentaries, Interviews, Broadcasted Lectures & Media

Ackroyd, Peter. (2011). *The romantics—Nature.* Sam Hobkinson (Director, Producer). [Documentary]. BBC/The Open University. https://youtu.be/liVQ21KZfOI. January 8, 2023.

Bernstein, Leonard. (1973). Norton Lectures 1973. *The ‘Unanswered Question’.* Harvard University. Smith, Douglas (Producer). Clark Santee (Director). Amerson Production in cooperation with WGBH Boston. [Lectures]. https://youtu.be/hwXO3I8ASSg. Last accessed: January 21, 2023.

Brendel, Alfred. (1989). *Les trois dernières Sonates de Franz Schubert.* Akerman, Chantal (Director). [Programme]. Guisard, Claude (Director of the Programme). Opus Série de Mildred Clary. © 1989 La Sept et l'I.N.A. En Association avec FR3.

Daniel, Renate. “Das Selbst—ein zentraler Begriff der Analytischen Psychologie”. [Lecture]. C.G. Jung Institut Stuttgart. Broadcasted on the 21.02.2019: https://youtu.be/EbLeI-oPDn4. Last accessed: January 20, 2022.

Drewermann, Eugen. (2023). “1. Sommervorlesung 2023: Märchen zeigen den Weg zur Liebe, wo Sehnsucht Realität wird”. [Lecture]. https://www.youtube.com/watch?v=sO_z9OofWVg Last accessed: June 25, 2024.

Drewermann, Eugen. (2023). “2. Sommervorlesung 2023: Märchen als Therapie. Auslegung von Grimms ‘Das Mädchen ohne Hände’”. [Lecture] https://www.youtube.com/watch?v=H6dsnbdmEV0 Last accessed: June 19, 2024.

Drewermann, Eugen. (2023). “3. Sommervorlesung 2023: Grimms Märchen tiefenpsychologisch gedeutet. Eugen Drewermann interpretiert Aschenputtel.”. [Lecture]. https://www.youtube.com/watch?v=n4zH_MzoETQ Last accessed: February 3, 2024.

Drewermann, Eugen. (2023). “5. Sommervorlesung 2023: Heilende Märchen. Drewermann deutet das Märchen Brüderchen und Schwesternchen”. [Lecture]. https://www.youtube.com/watch?v=UlN6dW3uOMM Last accessed: September 28, 2024.

Drewermann, Eugen. (2024). “Vortrag Grimms Märchen ‘Das Wasser des Lebens’. Konflikte überwinden”. [Presentation]. Offenburg: March 5, 2024. https://www.youtube.com/watch?v=Ub-oMh9VoTU Last accessed: March 26, 2024.

Goblot, Pascal. *(2020). Sapiens, et la musique fut.* Pérès, Guillaume (Producer). [Documentary]. Arte France—Grand Angle Productions.

Hillman, James. (2010, June 19th). In: *Carl Gustav Jung and the Red Book.* [Symposium]. Library of Congress. Washington D.C.: Library of Congress. Digital ID: https://www.youtube.com/watch?v=Oy-x7BLlBYg&feature=share Last acessed: June 26, 2022.

Kast, Verena. (2009). *Das sagenumwobene 'Rote Buch' von C.G. Jung—Die Psychologin Verena Kast im Gespräch mit Norbert Bischofberger.* [Interview]. Programme: Sternstunde Philosophie. SRF https://www.youtube.com/watch?v=w_o9CpIzX6Y. Last accessed: July 12, 2022.

López-Linares, José Luis. *Francisco de Goya—Der Schlaf der Vernunft.* [Documentary]. Written by: Cristina Otero Roth. Bernard de la Villadière—Ligne de Front., Stéphane Sorlat—Mondex et Cie (Prod.): ©2019 Arte France. Available at: https://www.arte.tv/de/videos/082769-000-A/francisco-de-goya-der-schlaf-der-vernunft/ Last accessed: November 10, 2024.

Monsaingeon, Bruno. *The Alban Berg Documentary.* (1996). [Documentary/Masterclass]. Der Bayerische Rundfunk. Schleswig Holstein Musik Festival. Lübeck Masterclass.

Moritz. Reiner, E. (2020). *Hans Zender—Mit den Sinnen denken.* [DVD]. Studio Arthaus Musik.

Pires, Maria João. (2012). "Maria João Pires". [Interview]. Kasica, Katarzyna (Direction). Mierzejewska, Agata (Interviewer). Produced by: Three Mirrors Poland for the Fryderyk Chopin Institute. Narodowy Instytut Fryderyka Chopina. https://youtu.be/aEVNwYl6ybs Last accessed: April 21, 2023.

Schiff, Andras (2019). *Sir András Schiff on The Music of Franz Schubert.* [Recording presentation]. ECM Records. https://www.youtube.com/watch?v=t3FQ1uDEFp8&feature=youtu.be. Last accessed: April 17, 2023.

Schiff, Andras. *Sir András Schiff—Schubert Lecture-Recital. Live at Wigmore Hall.* [Lecture-Recital]. Wigmore Hall. 2021/22 Season Broadcast Series. Parkin, Matt (Director). Stagecast Ldt (Production). ©2021 The Wigmore Hall Trust. Broadcasted on November 26th, 2021. https://www.youtube.com/watch?v=ViZu8ATTqc8. Last accessed: May 3, 2024.

Schiff, Andras. (n.d.). *Schiff András filmje Schubertről—András Schiff tells about Schubert.* [Documentary] Scorer Associates. A Production for BBC MCMXCVII https://youtu.be/G4R-qf6E7XI Last accessed: May 19, 2023.

Tilson Thomas, Michael. (2004). *Keeping score. Ludwig van Beethoven: Eroica.* (Documentary). Halvorson, Gary (Director). Bronson, Michael and Warner, Elaine (Producer). © 2006 SFS Media The San Francisco Symphony https://www.youtube.com/watch?v=J5zFitBASEw. Last accessed: August 12, 2022.

Van der Post, Laurens. (1972). *The Story of Carl Gustav Jung.* Stedall, Jonathan (Producer). Les Newman (Editor). [Documentary]. BBC Colour. https://www.youtube.com/watch?v=mJIc2w6PvRg. Last accessed: June 20, 2022.

von Franz, Marie Louise. (1982). *Marie-Louise von Franz.* De Rahm, Diana (Interviewer). Selhofer, Françoise (Director). Ammann, Peter (Producer). [Interview Bollingen September 1982]. Fotorotar AG. © 1982 Stiftung für Jung'sche Psychologie, Küsnacht.

von Franz, Marie Louise. (1987). *Die Visionen des Niklaus von Flüe.* Guido Ferrari (Director). [Documentary/Interview]. Fotorotar AG. © RTSI Televisione della Svizzera Italiana.

Zacharias, Christian. (2019). *Why does Schubert sound like Schubert?* [Lecture-Recital]. Wigmore Hall. Live-Broadcast. Kealey, Robert (Director). Stagecast Ltd (Production). © 2019 The Wigmore Hall Trust. RCM Studios. https://youtu.be/2dWlyLNEWPI?feature=shared Last accessed: May 13, 2023.

Online Consulted Sources

Altenburg, Detlef. (2016). "Programmusik". In: Laurenz Lütteken (Ed.), *MGG Online*. New York/Kassel/Stuttgart: RILM, Bärenreiter, Metzler. https://www.mgg-online.com/article?id=mgg15930&v=1.0&rs=mgg15930 Last accessed: September 2, 2024

Bellamy,Olivier. "Le quatuor 'La jeune Fille et la Mort' de Schubert: découvrez sa signification profonde". [Article]. https://www.radioclassique.fr/histoire/oeuvres/le-quatuor-la-jeune-fille-et-la-mort-de-schubert-decouvrez-sa-signification-profonde. Publié 20/07/2020 à 16:00 | Modifié le 06/11/2021. Last accessed: May 8, 2024.

Betz, Otto. (2016). "Der Lebensfaden. Des Motiv des Fadens aus Mythos und Märchen ist ein wichtiges Symbol für unser Leben, für den Verlauf unseres Schicksals". In: *herder.de*. [Article]. Freiburg: Verlag Herder. https://www.herder.de/cig/geistesleben/2016/01-06-2016/schicksal-der-lebensfaden/ Last accessed: March 17, 2024.

Böttrich, Christfried. (2013). "Entrückung". In: *Das wissenschaftliche Bibellexikon im Internet. Deutsche Bibel Gesellschaft*. [Article]. https://bibelwissenschaft.de/stichwort/56050/ Last accessed: May 5, 2024.

Claudius, Matthias. (1774/1775). "Der Tod und das Mädchen". Sämtliche Werke I/II. In: *Claudius-Gesellschaft*. https://www.claudius-gesellschaft.de/texte/gedichte/der-tod-und-das-mädchen/ Last accessed: May 21, 2024.

DWDS—Digitales Wörterbuch der deutschen Sprache. Berlin-Brandenburgische Akademie der Wissenschaften. https://www.dwds.de/wb/etymwb/Ethos Last accessed: September 29, 2023.

Goethe, Wolfgang. (1782). "Der Erlkönig". The Project Gutenberg. https://www.projekt-gutenberg.org/goethe/gediletz/chap109.html Last accessed: November 2, 2024.

Grove Music Online. (2001). "Plagal cadence [Amen cadence] (Fr. cadence plagale; Ger. plagale Kadenz, unvollkommene Kadenz; It. cadenza plagale)". In: *Grove Music Online*. https://www.oxfordmusiconline.com/grovemusic/view/10.1093/gmo/9781561592630.001.0001/omo-9781561592630-e-0000021888 Last accessed: October, 3, 2024.

Heine, Heinrich. (2002). *Buch der Lieder*. The Project Gutenberg. https://www.gutenberg.org/cache/epub/3498/pg3498-images.html Last accessed: May 6, 2024.

Krones, Hartmut. "Musik und Rhetorik". In: Laurenz Lütteken (Ed.). *MGG Online*. (2016). Article first published in 1997. https://www.mgg-online.com/mgg/stable/12553 Last accessed: April 1, 2023.

Küng, Hans. (2012). "Komponisten und ihr Glaube". In: *Neue Zürcher Zeitung*. [Article]. https://www.nzz.ch/komponisten-und-ihr-glaube-ld.789469 Last accessed: June 8, 2023.

Machart, Renaud. (2021, June 27th). "'Sapiens, et la musique fut', sur Arte: des orgues stalagmitiques pour symphonie préhistorique.". [Article]. https://www.lemonde.fr/culture/article/2021/06/27/sapiens-et-la-musique-fut-sur-arte-des-orgues-stalagmitiques-pour-symphonie-prehistorique_6085885_3246.html Last accessed: August 16, 2023.

Martínez Guzman, Fernando. (2021). "El legado religioso y sinfónico de Franz Schubert: Reflexiones de Nikolaus Harnoncourt". *Humanitas* 97, año XXVI, Septiembre 2021. P. 510–523. https://www.humanitas.cl/arte/el-legado-religioso-y-sinfonico-de-franz-schubert-reflexiones-de-nikolaus-harnoncourt. Last accessed: June 7, 2023.

McLellan, Joseph. (1988). "Alfred Brendel and the Schubert statement". *The Washington Post*. [Article]. http://www.washingtonpost.com/archive/lifestyle/1988/04/20/alfred-brendel-and-the-schubert-statement/cea44201-5082-44b0-bf78-2ed296da4f28/?tid=ss_mail Last accessed: May 19, 2023.

Meier-Seethaler, Carola. "Nixe". In: Symbolonline.de. [Article]. https://symbolonline.eu/index.php?title=Nixe. Last accessed: April 2, 2024.

Novalis. *Fragmente I—Individuelle Sprache*. Project Gutenberg. https://www.projekt-gutenberg.org/novalis/fragmen1/chap022. Last accessed: September 25, 2024.

Online Etymology Dictionary. "Psychopomp". [Artikel]. https://www.etymonline.com/word/psychopomp. Last accessed: May 2, 2024.

Peter, Mathias. "Schubert und sein Verhältnis zur Katholischen Kirche—Schubert, der Kirchenrevoluzzer?". *Domradio*. [Article]. https://www.domradio.de/artikel/schubert-und-sein-verhaeltnis-zur-katholischen-kirche Last accessed: April 25, 2023.

Schubart, Christian Friedrich Daniel. (1785). *Gedichte aus dem Kerker*. Zürich: Orell, Geßner, Füßli und Comp. https://archive.org/details/bub_gb_ULw7AAAAcAAJ Last accessed: June 6, 2024.

Seifert, Ang Lee. "Fünf". In: Symbolonline.eu. [Article]. https://symbolonline.eu/index.php?title=Fünf. Last accessed: April 18, 2024.

Spaun, Joseph von. (1827). "Der Jüngling und der Tod". In: The LiederNet Archive. https://www.lieder.net/lieder/get_text.html?TextId=15189 Last accessed: May 21, 2024.

Szabó-Knotik, Cornelia. Art. "Zigeunermusik". In: *Österreichisches Musiklexikon online*. Rudolf Flotzinger (Begr.), Barbara Boisits (Hg.) https://doi.org/10.1553/0x001bd07f Letzte inhaltliche Änderung: 9.11.2022. Last accessed: August 30, 2024.

Tobisch, Léopold. (2020). "Le pouvoir expressif et affectif des tonalités". [Article]. *France Musique*. https://www.francemusique.fr/culture-musicale/pouvoir-expressif-et- affectif-des-tonalites-86146 Last accessed: December 20, 2021.

Wehnert, Martin. (2016). "Romantik und romantisch". In: *MGG Online*. Laurenz Lütteken (Ed.). New York/Kassel/Stuttgart: RILM, Bärenreiter, Metzler. https://www.mgg-online.com/mgg/stable/45427. Last accessed: August 8, 2023.

Wiener Staatsoper. "Die Geschichte des Wiener Opernballs". [Article]. https://www.wiener-staatsoper.at/opernball/geschichte/ Last accessed: April 17, 2023.

Additional Sources consulted for the Illustrations

Mindock, Rebecca. (2018). *Franz Schubert—Gretchen am Spinnrade. Transcription for Clarinet Quartet*. New York: Imagine Music Medina. [Cover Photo].

Online Sources

"Anonymous, colored manuscript, around 1550". Universitätsbibliothek Basel, L IV, S. 293. Picture taken from: Historisches Lexikon der Schweiz HLS (online). https://hls-dhs-dss.ch/de/articles/008251/2001-06-05/ Last accessed: February 11, 2024.

"Atlas". (2nd cent. AD). [Roman statue]. © Photograph: Lalupa. Farnese Collection, National Archaeological Museum of Naples. Picture taken from Wikipedia.de. https://de.wikipedia.org/wiki/Atlas_(Mythologie)#/media/Datei:MAN_Atlante_fronte_1040572.JPG Last accessed: September 22, 2024.

Anne Anderson. "Dümmling" Figure illustrating the "Three Feathers" fairy tale. In: *Old, Old Fair Tales. Illustrated by Anne Anderson.* (1935). Wisconsin: Whitman Publishing Company. © 1935 Whitman Publishing Company. http://www.maerchenatlas.de/deutsche-maerchen/grimms-marchen/die-drei-federn/ Last accessed: September 22, 2024.

Atlas carrying the vault of heaven. Roman statue of Atlas (2nd century AD). National Archaeological Museum of Naples. Taken from: https://en.wikipedia.org/wiki/Atlas_(mythology) Last accessed: May 16, 2024.

Caspar David Friedrich. (1817). "Der Wanderer über dem Nebelmeer". [Oil on canvas]. Hamburger Kunsthalle. Online Sammlung. © Foto: Elke Walford. https://online-sammlung.hamburger-kunsthalle.de/de/objekt/HK-5161 Last accessed: September 22, 2024.

Feyerabend, Johann Rudolf. (1806). [Watercolour drawing]. Basel, Historical Museum. https://www.archaeologie.bs.ch/ausgraben/abgeschlossene-ausgrabungen/innerstadt/am-totentanz.html Last accessed: May 10, 2024.

Frederic Leighton. (1892). "The Garden of the Hesperides". [Oil on canvas]. Lady Lever Art Gallery, Wirral. https://www.liverpoolmuseums.org.uk/artifact/garden-of-hesperides Last accessed: September 22, 2024.

Goya, Francisco. (1796–1797). "El sueño de la razón produce monstruos". [Pencil, iron gall ink on laid paper]. Serie: Caprichos 43 © Museo Nacional del Prado. https://www.museodelprado.es/coleccion/obra-de-arte/el-sueo-de-la-razon-produce-monstruos/c3f5fb9f-983c-43b7-8784-74710bdc3544 Last accessed: October 21, 2024.

Goya, Francisco. (1797). "Universelle Sprache. Der Autor träumt" [Black chalk; pencil; iron gall ink]. Serie: Caprichos Serie Los Sueños, 43, 1. © Museo Nacional del Prado. https://www.museodelprado.es/coleccion/obra-de-arte/ydioma-universal-el-autor-soando/66035ec0-f635-4dc1-9bd9-ecce857e254c Last accessed: October 21, 2024.

Goya, Francisco. (1797–1799). "El sueño de la razón produce monstruos". [Engraving aquatint on laid papier]. Serie: Caprichos 43. © Museo Nacional del Prado. https://www.museodelprado.es/coleccion/obra-de-arte/el-sueo-de-la-razon-produce-monstruos/e4845219-9365-4b36-8c89-3146dc34f280 Last accessed: October 21, 2024.

Guido Hampe. (n.d.). "Wassermühle im Gebirge". [Oil on canvas]. https://www.artnet.de/künstler/guido-hampe/wassermühle-im-gebirge-WnngN2dRamwC2LFyUy9qGw2 Last accessed: September 22, 2024.

Hans Baldung Grien. (1517). "Der Tod und das Mädchen". [Mixed Technique on limewood]. Kunstmuseum Basel. Sammlung online. https://sammlungonline.kunstmuseumbasel.ch/eMP/eMuseumPlus?service=ExternalInterface&module=collection&objectId=1031&viewType=detailView Last accessed: September 22, 2024.

Leighton, Frederic. (1891–1892). "The Garden of Hesperides". Painting: Oil on Canvas. Lady Lever Art Gallery. Image taken from: National museums Liverpool. https://www.liverpoolmuseums.org.uk/artifact/garden-of-hesperides September 22, 2024.

Master of Erfurt. Upper Rhenish Master. (c. 1400). *The Virgin Mary Weaving*. Gemäldegalerie, Staatliche Museen zu Berlin. Taken from Wikipedia commons https://commons.wikimedia.org/wiki/File:Master_of_Erfurt,_The_Virgin_Weaving,_Upper_Rhine,_ca_1400_(Berlin).jpg Last accessed May 4, 2026.

Moritz von Schwind. (~1860). "Der Erlkönig". [Oil on oakwood]. Bayerische Staatsgemäldesammlungen—Sammlung Schack München. https://www.sammlung.pinakothek.de/de/artwork/5RGQ1baGz3 Last accessed: September 22, 2024.

Mosaic from Tarsos. (3rd cent. b.c.). Antakya Archeology Museum. Image taken from Wikimedia Commons. https://commons.wikimedia.org/wiki/File:Antakya_Archaeology_Museum_Orpheus_and_beasts_mosaic_sept_2019_6017.jpg Last accessed April 10, 2024.

Norns at the Well of Urd. (n.d.). [Engraving] From Fredrik Sander's 1983 ed. of Poetic Edda. © L.B. Hansen. https://de.wikipedia.org/wiki/Nornen#/media/Datei:Nornorna_spinner_ödets_trådar_vid_Yggdrasil.jpg Last accessed: September 22, 2024.

Singer Sargent, John. (1925). "Atlas and the Hesperides". [Oil on canvas]. Museum of Fine Arts Boston. https://collections.mfa.org/objects/32219 September 22, 2024.

The crucifixion of Christ. Glass window Church Königsfelden (14th century). © Museum Aargau. Picture taken from: Kloster Königsfelden, Museum Aargau. https://www.ag.ch/de/verwaltung/bks/kultur/kulturvermittlung/museum-aargau/kloster-koenigsfelden/glasfenster Last accessed: August 10, 2024.

MIX
Papier aus verantwortungsvollen Quellen
Paper from responsible sources
FSC® C105338

If you have any concerns about our products,
you can contact us on
ProductSafety@springernature.com

In case Publisher is established outside the EU,
the EU authorized representative is:
Springer Nature Customer Service Center GmbH
Europaplatz 3, 69115 Heidelberg, Germany

Printed by Libri Plureos GmbH
in Hamburg, Germany